Profiles of Northwest Fungi

Buck McAdoo

Profiles of Northwest Fungi
by Buck McAdoo
Third Edition

Published by GL Design
3345 Chisholm Trail #206
Boulder, CO 80301

ISBN # 978-0-9889669-2-5

Library of Congress Control Number: 2021911756

Photos
Buck McAdoo, except where noted

Cover Photo
Helvella vespertina at Squalicum Harbor

Cover Design
Alex McAdoo

Drawings
Dan Digerness

Graphic Design
Rose Alyea, Alex McAdoo

Layout and Production
Erin Moore

Written contributions to manuscript by Fred Rhoades, Richard
Morrison, Tillman Moore, Christine Roberts, Sam Leathers, and
Chas Gilmore.

Contents

This guide is dedicated to my parents, Francis and Cynthia McAdoo, who have waited since 1973 for my next publication.

A mushroom is a powerful force. Here, a white Amanita erupts through the tarmac in a graveyard in Vineyard Haven. While I crouched in front of it to take the photo, a pick-up truck pulled up alongside. In the back of the truck were four high school kids with rakes and shovels. At the wheel was a huge guy, the head groundskeeper. He stared balefully out the window at me. "Wanna know something, mister?" he advised, "the last person who took that mushroom home with him…why he's still here."

Preface

Profiles of Northwest Fungi is a compilation of "Mushroom of the Month" articles published by our nonprofit mushroom club, Northwest Mushroomers Association, in our official newsletter. If a club member found a mushroom and wanted to know about it, an article was written and in it went. What came first was extensive research to include as much information about that species as I could find. Close relatives and look-alikes were also described, and I have enhanced that feature in this guide with photos whenever possible.

Anyone in our club is free to write up a mushroom of the month, and some others did. Dr. Fred Rhoades authored an article on page 337; Dr. Richard Morrison coauthored three articles on pages 243, 255, and 463; Dr. Christine Roberts authored one on page 435 and coauthored another on page 440; and Dr. Tillman Moore authored a piece on page 496. Sam Leathers coauthored an article on page 468 and Chaz Gilmore wrote two April Fool stories, on pages 536 and 537. The April Fool mushrooms are in a special section near the back of this book. Although many of the places mentioned and some of the people are real in these pieces, the events are pure fiction. These special Mushrooms of the Month were introduced on April Fool's Day over the years and are presented in chronological order. The real mycologist is encouraged not to visit this section. It is primarily for the benefit of the spouses, to keep them entertained while they go about their taxonomy challenges.

Perhaps more significantly, between the fake mushrooms and the real deal are a few pages of extraordinary fungi found by club members that we either couldn't find names for or were of special interest to some, but didn't become mushrooms of the month. They are here in the hopes that professionals could be on the lookout for them and eventually bring them to publication or recognize them as already published.

If no one in the club came forward with a species of interest, the newsletter editor or I would choose one that we thought would interest the club members. Or at least interest us.

As you move through the species descriptions you will notice a lot of script devoted to edibility. This is no accident. Most people initially join a club to find out what mushrooms they can eat. Those into collecting for the table will always outnumber the dismal few wrapped up in taxonomy. Since the flavors of wild mushrooms are so varied and occasionally so unique, attention has been spent on the opinions of past experts. It's like shopping. If you prefer one expert to another, you might want to follow his taste buds as well.

The mushrooms in this guide are arranged alphabetically rather than chronologically. This makes them easier to find. At the back of the book there is an index to the fungi. Just prior to it is an index of the people. It includes club members who found mushrooms, photographed them, commented on them, or ate them without dying. It also includes professionals who helped me over the years with advice concerning a specific species. You can surmise who the professional mycologists are because doctor (Dr.) precedes their names. There is no particular key for this separation. But even from a professional viewpoint it is nice to have the name of the person who found something, in case the mushroom turns out to be extraordinary. Beyond this, it is just simple courtesy.

Northwest Mushroomers Association started up in Bellingham, Washington, in 1988 when the students of two primary forces collided in a coffee shop. One group consisted of the students of Dr. Fred Rhoades. Fred represented the academic side. He was teaching mycology at Western Washington University (WWU) and has a Ph.D. in Biology from the University of Oregon. Fred taught all levels. When WWU eventually dropped its mycology program, Fred continued teaching biology there. He also taught at the North Cascades Institute, led field trips deep into the Olympic Peninsula, and lectured extensively. He is such a popular instructor that when our club reached 50 members, 17 of us signed up for his course in microscopic features. It is now more than two decades later, and he is still teaching an identification course for the club.

The other group consisted of the students of Dave Jansen. Dave didn't even have a classroom. He took students on field trips out of the North-

west Freedom University. This was a university unlike any other. Its public face consisted of a brochure with a number of courses in it. You simply paid an upfront fee and phoned up the individual teaching the course to get enrolled. You paid the instructor $15 to $30 to join the class. Everything was taught, from yoga to languages to dance to wild mushroom identification. Enter Dave Jansen. He was totally self-taught from years of perusing mushroom field guides. Like Fred, he was one of the most likeable people you could ever hope to meet. There was also a certain bravado about him. He was known for sampling fungi associated with the term "edibility unknown," and this also seemed to endear him to students. He especially enjoyed dining on mushrooms in Clitocybe and Melanoleuca. This was a bit perturbing to Fred who openly wondered if Dave would serve up an Amanita to one of his classes. It never happened. Dave had done the essential homework. Although he once served up an unknown member of the Pleurotaceae instead.

Once that hurdle was surmounted, the club could officially begin. Dave Jansen became the first president; Dr. Fred Rhoades, the perennial scientific adviser; and Bob Mooers, the first editor of the club newsletter.

I came aboard about five months later. I still remember the occasion. I had just walked out of the front door of the Herald Building. It was raining, and as I waited for a light to change, two women with umbrellas accosted me at the corner. Assuming they were Jehovah's Witnesses, I started to turn away. Then I heard the word "mushrooms." They identified themselves as Kathi Marlowe and Lee Whitford, and both would eventually became presidents of our club.

Over the years, the club has thrived. Very talented people from all walks of life have joined up and contributed in different ways. We have had great editors, great cooks, great treasurers, great foray leaders, folks just born to organize things, and volunteers who step up for special events. They know who they are. This guide is for them as well.

—*Buck McAdoo*

Acknowledgments

Both Margaret Dilly and Dr. Fred Rhoades are about as natural to teaching as they are to breathing. On our Thursday night meetings, they have produced more lectures than anyone else. Fred specializes in Mycena while Margaret holds forth on Agaricus and the morels. Both have always been available for advice on the fungi whenever it is needed.

Margaret Dilly is a major force in our club. She arrived in our midst after the club had been going for about five years. It didn't take her long to be noticed. Forays and shows became more streamlined. Advice on how to collect the fungi and what to notice while in the act of collecting the fungi became annual events. It turned out that Margaret had been a past president of the giant Puget Sound Mycological Society down in Seattle, and now we were benefiting from her experience in that role. She is such a mushroom fanatic that she is still a member of that Society and also the Vancouver Mycological Society, besides our own club. If at all possible she makes the fall mushroom shows of all three mushroom clubs every year. She first joined the Puget Sound Mycological Society in 1964 and in 2014 was awarded the Golden Mushroom Award for her 50 years of membership that also honored her research on morels in the Pacific Northwest. Above all, Margaret has really gone to bat for the recreational picker. She has been to Olympia to crusade against indiscriminate practices of commercial pickers, and was most likely instrumental on the laws that have been passed since.

She and her husband Claude Dilly joined up after moving to Oak Harbor on Whidbey Island. Margaret hosts the Deception Pass Park foray every year. It is always our last foray of the year in mid-November and officially closes down our mushroom season. Appropriately, we now call this the Dilly Foray.

As our scientific adviser for life, Dr. Fred Rhoades is the person we all defer to on issues about fungal ecology and identification. Besides being one of the top authorities on lichens in the Pacific Northwest, Fred teaches classes on lichens and fungi every fall for the North Cascades Institute. He is a past president of the Pacific

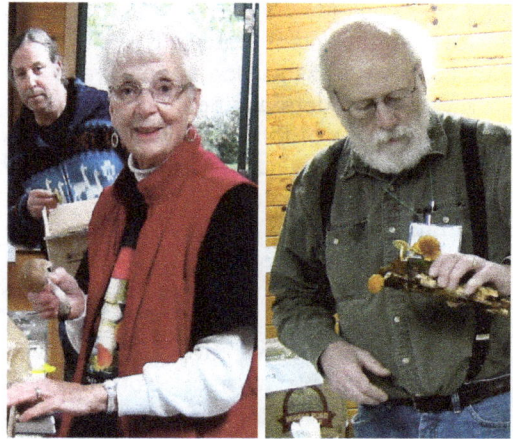

Margaret Dilly and Fred Rhoades

Northwest Key Council, a group of mushroom devotees from British Columbia, Montana, Idaho, Washington, and Oregon who convene twice yearly to hover over the fungi. His classes for our mushroom club are so fun that there are people in them who belong to the club but are seen nowhere else but in these classes. One of these aficionados told me, "It's better than Zen. The process of successfully keying out a mushroom to species is deeply satisfying. I've been able to drop yoga entirely."

Beyond these plaudits, Fred has never turned me down when I needed help. Some of the species in these pages might not have made it to this level if not for Fred's shrewd interpretation of the microscopic features. Northwest Mushroomers Association is incredibly blessed to have two such people amongst them.

This book's graphic design and concept was created by Rose Alyea and Alex McAdoo. These are young people just finishing BAs in graphic design. I wanted the book to include some youthful inspirations, and both have come through wonderfully.

All fungal drawings in this book are the work of local mushroom aficionado, Dan Digerness. To this day I haven't seen better renditions in ink. It is an honor to have them in these pages.

Except where noted, all photos are by Buck McAdoo; many are scanned from original prints.

Introduction

In the bylaws of the Northwest Mushroomer's Association, Article II states, "It shall be the purpose of this association to encourage and develop the understanding of mycology. In the furtherance of this goal the Association shall provide for the collection of data and the dissemination of information to the scientific community and the general public. The Association shall also promote an educated approach towards the collection and consumption of edible mushrooms."

With this in mind we have presented both poisonous and edible "mushrooms of the month" since November 1989. After each mushroom species description there is a list of look-alikes or close relatives. These are accompanied by photos whenever possible. Near relatives may bear no resemblance to look-alikes mentioned in the literature. The thing to keep in mind is that the list is not inclusive. It is likely there are more look-alikes out there that have been forgotten or have yet to be discovered.

Beyond its brief sojourn on earth, each species bears a nomenclatural history, and when seemingly appropriate, I trace some of the synonym changes through the ages and indicate where the type was from. The range of the species is also mentioned.

Following the look-alikes there may be a paragraph on microscopic features. This may be boring or intimidating to newcomers but they are a critical part of each mushroom's total identity. They have also been included for future reference. Very common and well known species may not be accompanied by the micro characters. Nonetheless, such features are at the heart of any description of the more cryptic species, such as those presented by Dr. Fred Rhoades, Dr. Morrison, and Dr. Roberts.

To counter-balance the heavy going with the microscopic terms, we finish with the issue of edibility. If myself or various club members have sampled the flavor, we render our opinions. Whether we have or not partaken of that particular species, I present the opinions of experts from the past. Every now and then there is a recipe.

At the end of each species presentation there is an extensive bibliography. The taxon specific bibliographies allow experts to check on the source material without having to pick through a massive general bibliography at the end.

Without a doubt the most sensitive issue in this guide are the opinions of experts sent to me via letters or emails over many years. I feel privileged to have received them. But rather than hoard this educational information for myself, I am taking a more populist approach by sharing them here whenever agreed upon. It must be taken into account that many of these opinions occurred prior to the DNA era. If asked again today, many of these opinions may have changed.

And we encourage feedback. If anyone has an issue with an identification I can either look into my own herbarium for the specimens under inquiry or refer them to Dr. Joe Ammirati. Specimens under my control can be forwarded under the right circumstances. A box holding close to 400 species collections was once bequeathed to the University of Washington herbarium. If a researcher has an inclination to visit with one of those, I can only refer them to Dr. Ammirati.

The goal, of course, is to get the species right. Ironically this is more problematic now than ever before.

Even as I embark on the next sentence, new DNA results are altering the nomenclatural landscape. From one species description to the next, you will now see an 'addendum' tacked on at the end. This is most likely a name change I had just become aware of. Whole genera can be sunk overnight. While presently disturbing, you need to realize that the goal is to stabilize generic concepts and the species within them.

DNA not only achieves this, it also illuminates how the genera are related to each other. It is an entire new discipline with its own terminology, but one that mycology can no longer live without. Stay tuned. Half the Latin names in this guide may be changed within ten years.

EXPLANATION OF AUTHOR CITATION

For the uninitiated many of the abbreviations around species names may be confusing. A brief explanation may prove helpful. Here are some of the more common ones in alphabetical order:

auct. means author
cf. means near
f. means form
nom. illeg. means illegitimate name
nom. prov. means provisional name
sp. nov. means new species
s.l. means sensu lato (in the broad sense)
s.s. means sensu stricto (in the narrow sense)
ss. means in the sense of
subsp. means subspecies
var. means variety

And as for author citations, here are the most common samples below:

Agaricus augustus Fries: Fries authored the species.

Stropharia ambigua (Peck) Zeller: Peck authored it and later Zeller moved it to another genus.

Psilocybe stuntzii Guzman & Ott: Both Guzman & Ott authored it together.

Amanita pachycolea Stuntz in Thiers and Ammirati: Stuntz introduced it in a publication by Thiers & Ammirati.

Amanita phalloides (Vaillant ex Fries) Link: Vaillant authored it but acknowledges Fries as having first discovered or described it, and then later, Link moved it to another genus.

Tricholoma odoratum Cool ss Pearson: In the sense of Pearson.

Hydnum impracticatum Lyle, Smithers, Gorth, Sampson, Jeaneau, Weideracker, Forthwith, Astorias, Trundle, Bragg, Heptone, and Girardi: This means all the DNA contributors got into it, too.

A WORD ON NOMENCLATURE

This is a turbulent time for mushroom names. Many of the names in this guide will be unfamiliar to the reader. While exciting and even exhilarating to the professionals, it can be frustrating to the amateurs who had reached a comfort zone with former Latin names. There are two main reasons for the proliferation of new names. First, the accepted starting point for fungal nomen-clature used to be with Fries and Persoon in the early nineteenth century. This time has now been pushed back to the era of Carl Linnaeus in the 1730s. It means that species authored by Bulliard and even earlier mycologists now have nomenclatural priority.

The other reason is the ripple effect from DNA profiling. Like some sort of erratic seesaw, DNA studies are solving long time mysteries and con-troversies in one genus while creating new dilem-mas in another. Some fungi that look exactly like each other to our senses turn out to have radi-cally different DNA. Others that don't look at all alike can end up in the same clade. There aren't enough mycologists out there to do all the work simultaneously, so some genera are way ahead of others in the processing. News of these name changes also trickles down unevenly.

It is becoming apparent that name changes due to new DNA sequencing results are becom-ing so prolific that aficionados like myself cannot keep up. The DNA effected changes are so per-vasive that quite a few species in these pages will have Latin name changes before this ever sees publication. Even as this guide goes to press, we learn that **Inocybe geophylla** does not appear on our West Coast. It is now either **Inocybe insinuata** or two other unnamed spe-cies. We also discover that the common deer mushroom, **Pluteus cervinus**, which fruits on hardwood logs is now **Pluteus exilis**. So if there is a major name change, the former name will follow it in parenthesis. These are examples of the cascade of name changes to come.

If you find a species name in parenthesis under a photo, it's an indication this species concept is under reconstruction in the Pacific Northwest or else more info is needed to verify its presence in our region.

The online *Index Fungorum* tries to keep up to date. If you are uncertain whether a mushroom name has been changed or not, visit *Index Fun-gorum*, click on "Search Index Fungorum," and enter the mushroom name you want to check out. The current name will come up in green. Click on that and you will see the list of syn-onyms. But remember, you don't have to always agree.

Northwest Mushroomers Association members in 2012 pull off a miracle mushroom show even during a drought.

Photo by Vince Biciunas

In this guide I am using Dr. Largent's nomenclatural system for the Entolomaceae.

ASSISTS FROM THE EXPERTS

Over many years, various professional and non-professional experts have sent advice or helped me with identifications. Some won't be listed here because they helped with fungi that don't appear in these pages. Perhaps to the relief of some and the chagrin of others, this book is evidence that their communications were not in vain. This knowledge doesn't just expire on my desk. I have always felt it was meant for a larger audience.

Fungal knowledge trickles down from a relatively small number of experts to a few interested amateurs who then pass it on to club members. From here it can dissipate out to the general public. It must be tempting for professionals who have reached the pinnacle to only communicate among themselves. So I would like to expressly thank the following who went beyond the brotherhood to share with me: Pablo Alvarado, Dr. Joe Ammirati, Dr. Robert Bandoni, Dr. Mike Beug, Philippe Clowez, Steve Czarnecki, Dr. Robert L. Gilbertson, Dr. Jim Ginns, Matt Gordon, Alick Henrici, Dr. Richard Kerrigan, Geoffrey Kibby, Paul Kroeger, Dr. Dave Largent,

Brian Luther, Dr. Juancho Mata, Dr. Brandon Matheny, Dr. Ireneia Melo, Danny Miller, Dr. Orson Miller, Dr. Richard Morrison, Dr. Machiel Noordeloos, Dr. Lorelei Norvell, Dr. Clark Ovrebo, Dr. Ron Petersen, Dr. Donald Pfister, Roger Phillips, Dr. Scott Redhead, Dr. Fred Rhoades, Dr. Christine Roberts, Judy Roger, Dr. Leif Ryvarden, Dr. Greg Thorne, Dr. James Trappe, Dr. Rod Tulloss, Dr. Else Vellinga, and Dr. Roy Watling.

THE GENERAL TERRAIN

Northwest Mushroomers' Association is centered in Bellingham, Washington, on the shore of Bellingham Bay and just half an hour south of the Canadian border. Immediately south are the Chuckanut Mountains, a short range with some madrone where they descend to the coastline. From the Chuckanuts there is a flat plain east stretching to the foothills of the western Cascades and north to the Fraser River and Vancouver, British Columbia. To the west lie the San Juan Islands, an archipelago drier than the coast, with mushroom species more similar to what occurs in northern California. And finally we have the western Cascades in the Mt. Baker-Snoqualmie National Forest. Yet another habitat is the alpine meadows above the tree line.

So there is no lack of variable habitat in the area. There are coastal cottonwood swamps, pastures and fields, lots of medium growth mixed woods, some old-growth coniferous forests, and plenty of scrub and choking understory from recent clear cuts. The clear cuts represent the greatest threat to recreational mushrooming. Both private companies and the state-run Department of Natural Resources are in the area. Both point out that the trees are a renewable resource. They will return, maybe not in our lifetime, but our grandchildren will have them again. No type of forest is immune. A forest of stunted trees and black birch will be clear cut for toilet paper. We can't really raise a fuss because we shouldn't have been on their property to begin with. Every couple of years we lose a fabulous mushroom habitat. There has been no dialogue between our club and the timber interests. We understand that it would be cost prohibitive to purchase any of the property because of the value of the timber within. A university would have to step up, and we know how strapped for cash they are.

Good mushroom woods are like local shrines. We live from season to season praying that our special spot doesn't get eradicated this year.

When it does fall, it puts a squeeze on someone else's spot. Every year we seem to get herded into diminishing mushroom niches. One thing in our favor is that mushrooms can expand. Chanterelles can reappear in 20-year-old clear cuts. It might take you an hour to walk 100 feet, but they are there, hidden beneath the brambles and the salal.

Finally, for those aficionados who enjoy wild mushrooming, you must realize you belong to a special group. You can go almost anywhere in the world and have something to do besides lie on a beach or go shopping. Every foray out the front door might bring in something new or different, even in your own backyard. The haphazard factor is one of the great charms of mushroom foraying. And if you get skunked, you appreciate the harvest even more the next time out. If you do collect noteworthy fungi, you should try to establish a connection with the local expert. These folks are national treasures. They are often teaching full time and don't get out as often as they would like. If you can take a digital photo of the specimens, note down where they were found and what trees were nearby, this could advance the local fungal knowledge immensely.

Chief Vendovi watches over all mushroom hunters in the San Juans. The author cannot follow suit: the author, GL Design, and Ingram Lightning Source cannot be responsible for misinterpretations.

The Key to Species

This key encompasses all the fungi in this guide from the Pacific Northwest. It does not represent all the rest of the Northwest fungi. If your specimen doesn't key out, it probably is not in this guide.

Key shortcuts:

1) All mushrooms with gills or veined reduced gills 2
1) All other non-gilled fungi 383
2) All mushrooms with veined or ridged or reduced gills 3
2) All mushrooms with normal thin gills 9
3) Mushrooms with blue or bluish caps . . . . Arrhenia chlorocyanea
3) Mushroom caps colored otherwise 5
4) Purple black to blue-black mushrooms . . . . Polyozellus marymargaretae
4) Mushrooms colored otherwise 5
5) Thin, delicate looking fungi with yellow to orange-yellow stipes . . . . Craterellus tubaeformis
5) Larger fleshy fungi 6
6) Stipes with purplish tints . . . . Gomphus clavatus
6) Stipes without purple tints 7
7) Carophores white to cream color . . . . Cantharellus subalbidus
7) Fruiting bodies with other colors 8
8) Mushrooms with orange to pale orange caps and paler gills . . . . Cantharellus formosus
8) Trumpet shaped mushrooms with flesh-tan gills and brighter orange caps . . . . Turbinellus floccosus
9) Fungi with white to cream colored spores 10
9) Fungi with spores of other colors 202
10) Fungi with decurrent to short decurrent gills 12
10) Fungi with free gills or gills attached in other ways 75
11) Mushrooms with funnel shaped or shoe horn shaped caps 12
11) Mushrooms with differently shaped caps 13
12) Mushrooms with brownish caps that fruit in tight clusters . . . . Hohenbuehelia petaloides
12) Caps whitish to pale gray, scattered or solitary . . . . Hohenbuehelia thornii
13) Gills grayish blue-green . . . . Hygrophorus caeruleus
13) Gills colored differently 14
14) Gills saffron orange and distinctly forked . . . . Hygrophoropsis aurantiaca
14) Gills not saffron orange 15
15) Gills lilac to lilac-gray or lilac-tan . . . . Panus conchatus
15) Gills colored differently 16
16) Gills greasy or waxy to the touch 17
16) Gills neither greasy nor waxy 27

Mushrooms of the Month

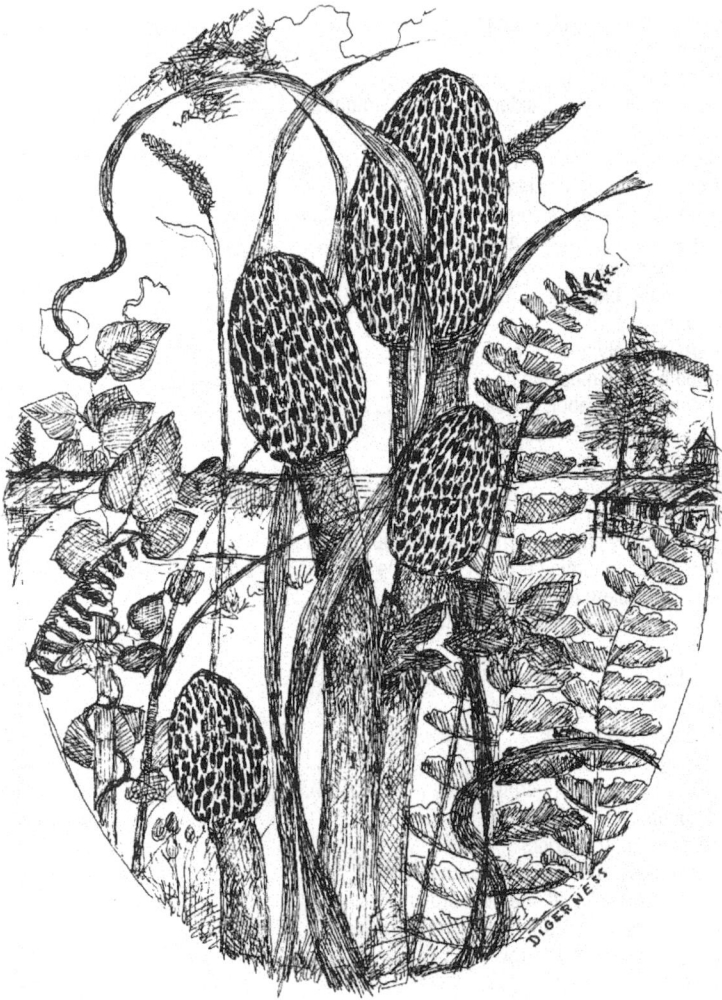

Agaricus augustus Fries

Dessicated Agaricus augustus in midsummer   Photo by T.J. Olney

The Prince can be truly enormous, attaining a cap width of 35 centimeters!

Off and on from 1997 to 2004 a very odd looking Agaricus appeared in urban lawns under blue spruce in Bellingham in the middle of summers. It was so cracked from the heat that it was hard to determine whether it had cap scales or was just areolate (fissured). It was surmised that early morning bands of fog had brought them up. This fog would dissipate so fast that the hapless fruiting bodies would dry up by midday, rendering them inedible. Even more problematic, they would no longer give off a color reaction when scratched.

What we did know is that the odor of almonds, the catenulate cheilocystidia, and the large spores pointed towards **Agaricus arvensis, Agaricus augustus, Agaricus coepiochraceus** nom.prov. (Isaacs), **Agaricus crocodilinus**, **Agaricus macrosporoides**, or **Agaricus fissuratus** as candidates. According to the literature, these are the yellowish bruising species of Agaricus that can have fissured caps in dry, hot climates. (**Agaricus bernardii** also has fissured caps in dry weather, but it bruises reddish instead.) This is a big list, but when considering the size of the genus, it becomes a select group.

Dan Digerness may have been the first to spot them around town in the mid 1990s. But T.J. Olney, our late professor of marketing at Western Washington University, was the first to bring them to my attention. He found them on the WWU campus under blue spruce back at around the same time. The introductory photo shows one of these findings.

T.J. finally alerted me to them on August 2, 1997. It took me a day to reach the site at the Bellingham Library. Here a colony had cropped up under a blue Atlas cedar. By then the heat had taken its toll. The bizarre, sculptured caps had partially shriveled up into contorted clumps sending various odors into the sky. The largest cap reached 14 cm in width, but the rings on all the caps had collapsed against the stems. I collected a few samples as an afterthought, and eventually obtained microscopic data from one of them.

A few years passed, and the sculptured monstrosity struck again. This time, it was found by Nadine Lihach in Fairhaven under blue spruce. Nadine is our wine connoisseur and greeter of the public at all our fall shows. Then T.J. found it again, but this time with Douglas fir. He theorized he had found a dried-up version of the Prince. We tended to agree. The Prince is the one large Agaricus that does fruit in the summer in the Pacific Northwest, and it can be found with Douglas fir.

When Dr. Richard Kerrigan, a specialist on Agaricus, informed us that **Agaricus augustus** can develop these extremely cracked caps in exposed sites in California during summers, we felt we finally had our solution.

Microscopic examination provided the following information. The spores were ellipsoid and thick-walled and measured 8–11 x 5–6.5 µm. The only basidium that I found was 4-spored and measured 34.3 x 7.9 µm. The pileipellis was a cutis of repent hyphae with clumps of exerted ends where the scales were. The cheilocystidia were catenulate (in chains), usually with elongated apices. The basidium seemed too long for the species, but perhaps it was heat stressed and overcompensated for the conditions.

Although we can't be 100% sure until it is found again and a DNA sequencing test can be made, it seems like Margaret Dilly's comment rings true: "It looks like a toad came along and sat on the Prince."

More typical Agaricus augustus   *Photo by Richard Morrison*

LOOK-ALIKES

Agaricus crocodilinus   Photo by Erin Moore

Agaricus subrufescens from Calif.   Photo by Fred Stevens

And what a Prince it is! I remember cooking up my favorite Prince recipe for a friend of mine who hadn't eaten wild mushrooms before. About halfway through the meal, tears welled up in his eyes. I couldn't tell whether these were tears of self-pity for having not experienced this flavor before or whether it was the flavor itself. He was almost beyond speech.

Agaricus augustus can show up as early as June. From then on it becomes the source of much conversation. Who saw it last? Where was it? Were any left behind? I remember once finding it at Whatcom Falls Park back in the late 1980s. I harvested the three mature caps and left about seven buttons behind. I carefully covered them with branches and leaves. When I returned three days later to harvest more mature caps, they were gone. They had probably outgrown their cover and been easy pickings for the next Prince aficionado who came along.

At a later date, I remember being out on the Olympic Peninsula when I spotted a giant Prince next to a biker's campground. Every couple of hours I would exit my tent and meander over to their campsite, only to find they were still up. The area around the Prince was littered with beer cans. At about 4:30 a.m. I finally nailed the specimen. Spilled beer had soaked the ground at its base, and to this day, this is the best **Agaricus augustus** I ever cooked up.

The same holds true out in the San Juan Islands. You are more likely to find the Prince by an outhouse that had just been installed or an older outhouse with lots of foot traffic than in the surrounding woods. The legend that it shows up year after year in the same place is only partially true. Eventually it uses up the local nutrients and moves on to somewhere else.

Out here on the West Coast it can show up in weird places like the edges of lawns under conifers, along roadsides and paths, or in woodland clearings near fir. It has been seen in flower gardens and trash heaps. It also seems to be partial to western red cedar. This would imply a saprophytic relationship since no macrofungi are known to be mycorrhizal with that conifer. In California it is often found with redwood. In Europe it prefers pine, spruce, and even oak, especially in calcareous soils.

The Prince can be truly enormous, attaining a cap width of 35 centimeters! The caps are usually convex with a flattened disc, and even when young have tawny-brown scales over a buff ground. It is perhaps called the Prince because it takes on a rich golden hue as it ages. The cap becomes yellowish when rubbed, the stem base orange-brown.

Sometimes the flesh turns slowly yellowish when cut, and sometimes there is no reaction at all. The gills are free from the stalk. They are at first whitish, then briefly pinkish before turning gray-brown to black-brown at the end. The stalk is long, thick, rather fibrous, and whitish. Older specimens have rusty discolorations at the base. It is smooth above the membranous ring and very white scaly below. The base can be equal or clavate and is usually buried in the ground. The thick, white ring has cottony patches on the underside, but these can disappear. The spore print is chocolate brown, and the odor is either of almonds or anise or a combination thereof.

Microscopically, Kerrigan gives us the spore sizes as 7.7-9.4 x 5.1-6 μm. They are long ellipsoid with a prominent hilar appendix. Cheilocystidia are catenate and subglobose in shape. The pileipellis is a cutis of periclinal hyphae with exerted ends where the scales are. No pleurocystidia and no clamps. The cap cuticle turns yellow with KOH.

Agaricus augustus has been reported from Europe, North America, North Africa and Asia. A solitary specimen has also showed up in a garden

Agaricus buckmacadooi

Agaricus perobscurus from Calif.

Agaricus sp. found by Sue Blethen

LOOK-ALIKE

Chlorophyllum rhacodes

in Nairobi, and a break was found along the shores of Lake Ngwazi in Tanzania. These were found with acacia.

In the Pacific Northwest, folks new to mushrooming often confuse the Prince with **Chlorophyllum rhacodes** and vice versa. Luckily they are both good edibles. **Chlorophyllum** (Lepiota) **rhacodes**, however, has white spores, no odor, flesh that bruises from pale orange to reddish, and large flaky cinnamon-brick colored scales on the caps.

Agaricus perrarus, for decades considered a close relative of smaller stature with ochre-yellow scales on the cap and underside of the ring, is now a synonym. Other possible look-alikes are listed as follows:

Agaricus smithii: Differs by having caps up to 13 cm wide, tawny-orange squamules on the cap surface, an abruptly bulbous stem base, and an association with Sitka spruce from Mendocino north along the Pacific Coast.

Agaricus perobscurus: A.k.a. the Princess, this has caps up to 17 cm wide, darker brown to almost black cap scales on a whitish ground that becomes more polished and orange in age, and a much thinner ring. According to Arora, it is only found in California.

Agaricus cuniculicola: Has ochre caps that become tawny in age. It is found with white spruce in the Rockies and has spores that are shorter than those of the Prince.

Agaricus subrufescens: Has a stockier stature, more tawny fibrils on a flattened cap disc, and a skirt-like ring. (There is also a white squamulose variant of **Agaricus augustus** that is rarely found in California.)

Agaricus sp.: Found by retired high school biology teacher Sue Blethen in grass under conifers in November 1991. Although caps were ochre-buff with uneven patches of rusty fibrils, the stature was much smaller than that of the Prince, the way the veil broke

from the cap was different, and the stems didn't change color when scratched at first. They did turn pale orange-straw color where handled in age.

Agaricus julius: This is the Prince of the Rockies and the Sangre de Cristos Mountains. Caps are more rounded and run up to 16 cm wide, and spores are broader. Same great flavor.

Agaricus nanaugustus: A smaller version of the Prince with a thinner stature and usually more appendiculate velar remnants. Found in the Midwest and once from Arizona.

Agaricus buckmacadooi: Differs by having dark brown flattened caps with a metallic luster and an odor of phenol instead of almonds. The tell tale 'golden look' of the Prince is missing. Common in yards in the Pacific Northwest. Poisonous to most people.

The Prince, in its prime, can be so rich in flavor that you can scarcely believe such a flavor exists. It is almost *de trop* for those with delicate mushroom sensitivities, and simply extracts raves from everyone else. Jack Czarnecki wrote that it was wonderful grilled. Other authors describe it as meaty and of fine flavor, edible and choice, excellent, savoureux, etc. After just one bite, one of our newer club members was heard to say, "Now I know why I joined this club." Roger Phillips, in *Wild Food*, has a fabulous recipe for an almond croustade featuring the Prince.

I only cook it one way. I sautée the Prince with chopped shallots in butter until the liquid evaporates. Then I add heavy cream, a good sherry, and a pinch of mace. This all cooks down to a golden glaze. It looks like the mushroom pieces have been shellacked. The whole pile is then dumped on a steak or grilled meatballs. Others prefer it with chicken and white wine. Either way, you can't lose unless you are cooking up a creosote species by mistake.

Although close, there is no paradise on earth. Joe Ammirati reminds us that **Agaricus augustus** is one of those species of Agaricus that contains dangerous levels of cadmium. A meal of half a pound of the Prince, the Field Mushroom, or the Horse Mushroom would contain nearly five times the amount of cadmium generally considered safe for consumption for an entire week. But nature, in its wisdom, has produced a counterbalance. There is a certain fly that awaits the arrival of the Prince from about mid-August onward. Collections found at this time and later are generally riddled with larvae, thereby discouraging humans from eating more than they should.

BIBLIOGRAPHY

David Arora, *Mushrooms Demystified*, 1986. Ten Speed Press, Berkeley, Calif.

Gabor Bohus, *Agaricus Studies, VI.* in *Annales Historico-Naturales Musei Nationalis Hungarici* 68 (45–49), 1976.

J. Breitenbach & F. Kranzlin, *Fungi of Switzerland, Vol.4*, 1995. Edition Mykologia, Lucerne, Switzerland.

Alberto Cappelli, *Fungi Europeae: Agaricus*, 1984. Libreria Editrice Bella Giovanna, Saronno, Italy.

Jack Czarnecki, *A Cook's Book of Mushrooms*, 1995. Artisan, New York, NY.

Margaret Dilly, *Trial Key to the Species of Agaricus in the Pacific Northwest*, 1981. Pacific Northwest Key Council, Seattle, Wash.

Ian Gibson, www.matchmakermushrooms.com

John Hotson & Daniel Stuntz, *The Genus Agaricus in Western Washington* in *Mycologia* 30 (204–234), 1938.

Bill Isaacs, *A Survey of Agaricus in Washington, Oregon, and California*, doctorate, 1963.

Richard Kerrigan, *Agaricaceae in The Agaricales of California*, 1986. Mad River Press, Eureka, Calif.

Richard Kerrigan, *A Key to Agaricus of North America*, 2009.

Richard Kerrigan, *Agaricus of North America* (Memoirs of The New York Botanical Garden, Vol. 114), 2016.

Geoffrey Kibby, *The Genus Agaricus in Britain*, 2011.

Peter McCoy, *Radical Mycology*, 2016. Chthaeus Press, Portland, Ore.

M. McKenny, D. Stuntz, & J. Ammirati, *The New Savory Wild Mushroom*, 1987. University of Washington Press, Seattle, Wash.

Meinhard Moser, *Keys to Agarics and Boleti*, 1983. Translated and published by Roger Phillips, London.

David Pegler, *A Preliminary Agaric Flora of East Africa*, 1977. Her Majesty's Stationary Office, London.

Roger Phillips, *Wild Food*, 1983. Pan Macmillan, London.

Albert Pilat, *The Bohemian Species of the Genus Agaricus* in *Acta Musei Nationalis Pragae*, Vol.VII, No.1, 1951.

Mirko Svrcek, *The Hamlyn Book of Mushrooms and Fungi,* 1983. Artia, Prague, Czechoslovakia.

Agaricus buckmacadooi Kerrigan

"The flavor is not all that great," he said.

Yes indeed. This is one of two large, fleshy, brown-capped species of Agaricus found in suburban lawns with conifers in the Pacific Northwest. It looks a bit like the Portobellos you find in the supermarket, but has more dark brown cap scales than the Portobello and a metallic luster in age. Perhaps because of this visual association, though, and the inviting meaty stature, a number of folks have tried eating it.

"Throw it out or throw it up!" exclaimed Eric Swisher, one of our former newsletter editors, "This mushroom won't leave you much to smile about."

Symptoms are of the gastrointestinal disorder and range from nausea to vomiting to diarrhea to stomach cramps. A few folks, such as Dan Digerness, can eat it with impunity. When asked about the flavor, he replied, "Not all that great."

Once upon a time, my cousin Rob Deford tried frying some up for breakfast when he lived in Palo Alto. The creosote odor was so overpowering it drove all the occupants out to the street. For those who eat one by mistake, expect the symptoms to arrive from 20 minutes to 4 hours after consumption. The unpleasant experience goes away when the mushroom is expelled, but at a severe price. You may never look at a Portobello quite the same way again.

Agaricus buckmacadooi has broadly convex and usually umbonate caps that measure 8–18 cm wide. They are dark brown at disc breaking up into squamules towards the margin on a dingy buff ground.

KOH on the cap produces a yellow reaction. The gills are free, changing from pale pink to dingy flesh color to finally dark brown. The stems measure 10–22 cm long and 1½–3½ cm thick. They are equal to clavate or rarely bulbous at the base. When handled they stain a pale yellowish-ochre that becomes browner in age. A few white rhizomorphs can often be found at the base. The veil is represented by a thick, rubbery, white ring with a grooved margin. Both the upper and lower surface of this ring are smooth. The spore deposit is dark brown. The spores themselves measure at an average of 5.6 x 3.9 μm. They are ellipsoid and smooth with a prominent hilar appendix. The basidia are mostly 4-spored, cylindro-clavate, and measure 14.5–21.5 x 6–8 μm. The cheilocystidia are clavate and measure 19.5–30 x 5–8.5 μm. Dr. Kerrigan mentions they aren't always easy to find. The odor is strongly phenolic and the range is from British Columbia on the West Coast down into California.

The challenge to identifying it comes with the name **Agaricus deardorffensis**, a near dead-ringer found from the Sierra Nevadas up into the Pacific Northwest. The caps of this species are generally smaller at 6–9 cm wide. They are more likely to be rimose, broke up in to shallow cracks, and the cap discs can have the same dark brown color as **A. buckmacadooi**. It differs in subtle ways. For instance it has the same thick, rubbery ring, but this ring is more easily detachable. Instead of a smooth upper surface, this ring has the grooved lines created by contact with the gills at an earlier time. The stem base usually stains a bright yellow. When handled, the mid-stipe bruises yellow-brown and then vinaceous brown over time. Stems run from 11–15 cm long and 1½–2 cm thick. They can be deeply rooted at the base. The caps are shallowly convex to flattened, not umbonate. They also have the strong

Agaricus deardorffensis

LOOK-ALIKES

Agaricus moelleri from Switzerland

Agaricus hondensis

Agaricus hondensis with pinkish tinge after absorbing much rain

phenol odor and are found along roads in compacted soil or on compacted forest litter. Microscopically they have different cheilocystidia, either subglobose or cylindrical with rounded apices.

Almost all the above information comes from Dr. Richard Kerrigan's massive new monograph on the genus Agaricus in North America. It's an honor to have this fungus named after me. Notice that he had to use my first name to separate me from all the other McAdoos in the fields. Nonetheless it is what it is and I find it a bit odd to be the first to describe it in a popular guide.

Agaricus buckmacadooi belongs in Section Xanthodermatei, a group David Arora once made infamous by calling them the "Lose Your Lunch Bunch." Also in the same section are **Agaricus kriegeri**, a more diminutive species from Pennsylvania, and probably **Agaricus pseudopratensis** from Europe. **Agaricus berryessae** also belongs here. It is a short, stout species with gray caps that instantly bruise bright yellow. Lake Berryessa in northern California is its home.

Prior to Kerrigan's reorganization of Section Xanthodermatei from DNA sequencing results, both **A. deardorffensis** and **A. buckmacadooi** were known collectively as **Agaricus moelleri** in the Pacific Northwest. Prior to this name, they were known as **Agaricus praeclaresquamosus**. And back in the hippy era, they were thought to be **Agaricus meleagris** or more rarely **Agaricus placomyces**. None of

Agaricus subrufescentoides

Agaricus phaeolepidotus from Sardinia   *Photo by Francesco Marotto*

these species are closely related to **Agaricus buckmacadooi**.

A few more lookalikes are as follows:

Agaricus moelleri: A European species with a much thinner stature. **A. praeclaresquamosus** is now considered a synonym.

Agaricus hondensis: Differs by its smaller stature, fawn to pale brown cap surface, much smaller spores, a thinner ring, no hint of a metallic luster, and a tendency for the caps to turn reddish in wet weather.

Agaricus subrufescentoides: Described by Murrill from Seattle, it differs by the dark cinnamon cap scales on a buff ground, thinner stature, and smaller spores. It yields a medicinal odor if left overnight in a waxed bag.

Agaricus phaeolepidotus: A European species that differs by its large skirt-like ring, stems that turn weakly yellowish when bruised, then reddish in age, and dull red-brown scales on a buff ground.

Agaricus meleagris: An epithet involving three concepts. **Agaricus meleagris** Withering of 1792. **Agaricus meleagris** Sowerby (white spores, now in Leucoagaricus). And **A. meleagris** (Schaeffer) Imbach, a synonym of **Agaricus moelleri**.

So much for the intricate nomenclature. The important facts to remember is that traditionally all species of Agaricus that bruise reddish are considered edible. All species that bruise yellowish and have an odor of almonds or anise are also considered edible. But those that bruise yellow and have an odor of phenol, creosote, or bad ink are considered inedible and even poisonous to most people. And those that don't change to any color at all? Toss them in the frying pan just to find out.

BIBLIOGRAPHY

David Arora, *All That the Rain Promises and More*, 1991. Ten Speed Press, Berkeley, Calif.

David Arora, *Mushrooms Demystified*, 1986. Ten Speed Press, Berkeley, Calif.

Denis Benjamin, *Mushrooms—Poisons and Panaceas*, 1985. W.H. Freeman, New York, NY.

Alan & Arleen Bessette & David Fischer, *Mushrooms of Northeastern North America*, 1997. Syracuse University Press, Syracuse, NY.

J. Breitenbach & F. Kranzlin, *Fungi of Switzerland, Vol.4*, 1995. Edition Mykologie, Lucerne, Switzerland

Margaret Dilly, *Trial Key to the Species of Agaricus in the Pacific Northwest*, 1981. Pacific Northwest Key Council, Seattle, Wash.

Alice Freeman, *Agaricus in the Southeastern United States* in *Mycotaxon* 8 (50–118), 1979.

Gerrit Keizer, *Encyclopaedia of Fungi*, 1997. Rebo Productions, Lisse, Holland.

Richard Kerrigan, *Agaricaceae* in *Agaricales of California*, 1986. Mad River Press, Eureka, Calif.

Richard Kerrigan, *Agaricus of North America* (Memoirs of The New York Botanical Garden, Vol. 114), 2016.

Gary Lincoff, *The Audubon Society Field Guide to North American Mushrooms*, 1981. Alfred A. Knopf, New York, NY.

Marijke Nauta, *Agaricus* in *Flora Agaracina Neerlandica* 5 (23–61), 2001.

—Digerness

Agrocybe dura (Bolton ex Fries) Singer

*Because of the violet tinge to
the brown gills, Agrocybe dura
resembles a number of pallid
Stropharias found in fields.*

Over the years, in fact ever since the beginnings of Northwest Mushroomers, Louie Byrd, a retired forester from Oregon, who has since passed away, had quietly deposited some noteworthy fungi on our identification tables. Many had been from the eastern Cascades where Louie foraged for morels and boletes. Others were from the Mount Baker area where Louie forayed for chanterelles. But this collection, found in grass alongside a freshly mulched flowerbed, came from his own property in the north part of Bellingham. Due to the purple-brown gills, most of us thought it belonged in Stropharia.

A look at the spores proved otherwise. They measured 10–14 x 7–8.5 µm, were truncate at one end, and had large germ pores. The spores alone indicated Agrocybe. The tough fruiting bodies, slender stature, and buff colored, areolate caps all pointed towards **Agrocybe dura**.

Agrocybe dura, literally meaning "the hard field cap," has caps 3–12 cm wide that are bell-shaped at first, then flatten out, retaining a low umbo. They are white to cream with a tinge of ochre at the disc, ageing to tan or pale brown. They are slightly viscid at first, but according to Glick, become powdery in age and then areolate, or as Rinaldi puts it, "cracking in dry weather into many polygonal scales." The cap margins of young specimens are often draped with velar material. Gills are rounded-adnexed to adnate, sometimes with a decurrent tooth (ask your dentist). They are pale gray to tan or vinaceous-buff at first, then dark brown to purple-brown in age. The gill edges are white floccose, a probable sign that cheilocystidia are there. Stems are 5–8 cm long and up to 1 ½ cm thick. They are ivory-white becoming slightly darker towards the base. According to A.H. Smith, they are pruinose at the apex and smooth to fibrillose below. The partial veil takes the form of a ring on the stem that soon collapses into one or more faint zones. Mycelial cords are usually present at the base.

LOOK-ALIKE

Protostropharia semiglobata

While most authorities agree on the above characteristics, they differ in their opinions over spore deposit color, odor, and flavor. While Barron, Lincoff, and Roody, along with most experts, describe a dark brown spore print, Watling describes a snuff-brown print, Hora found cigar-brown prints, Glick recorded yellow-brown, and McIlvaine, McDougall, Bandoni & Szczawinski saw rusty-brown. Spore colors may be changing according to the substrates. Odors are described as floury, mild, or mushroomy.

Agrocybe dura has been recorded all throughout Europe and North America, but is exceedingly rare in Whatcom County. The photo you see here represents the only collection I've seen. Just to show its range, Pegler has found it in the Rift Valley in Kenya and in shaded grass on the banks of the Matarawe River in Tanzania.

Like its larger cousin, **Agrocybe praecox**, it appears first in the spring, often in massive fruitings on wood chip beds, edges of woods, gardens, cultivated fields, or grasses over calcareous soils.

Microscopically, spores are among the largest in the genus. While Orson Miller and Bill Roody recorded spores measuring 11–14 x 6.5–8 µm, Clark T. Rogerson found a collection at Kansas State University in May of 1954 with spores measuring 13–15 x 9–10 µm. All spores have a prominent germ pore. Basidia are clavate, 4-spored, and measure 30–35 x 8–10 µm. There are no clamps. Cheilocystidia and pleurocystidia are utriform to broadly lageniform.

In many guides authors seem to use either **Agrocybe dura** or **A. molesta** indiscriminately for the species. **Agaricus durus** dates back to 1788, **Agaricus molestus** back to 1828. Most authors considered them to be synonymous, but *Index Fungorum* now separates them. **Agrocybe molesta** derives from **Pholiota dura var. xanthophylla**, a species with sulphur yellow gills. Dr. A.H. Smith used **Agrocybe dura** as the earlier name, but noted that it was a misnomer. He found the caps to be pliant and soft when fresh. Only in age did they turn hard.

In older guides you might find the species under the name **Pholiota dura**, a synonym. Because of the violet tinge to the brown gills, **Agrocybe dura** resembles a number of pallid Stropharias found in fields.

Thirteen look-alikes and varieties are as follows:

Stropharia albonitens: Differs by having viscid white caps with yellowish discs and floccose zone below the transient yellow-floccose ring. Spores 8–9 x 4–5 µm.

Stropharia melanosperma: Differs by having white gills at first that turn blackish-gray and a well-developed sulcate ring on the stem. Spores 10 x 6 µm.

Stropharia hardii: Differs by having slightly viscid, yellow-ochre caps and pale yellowish stems with white rhizomorphs. Found from Ohio eastward. Spores 5–9 x 3–4 µm.

Agrocybe temnophylla: Differs by having very broad gills and yellow-ochre caps. Phyllis

LOOK-ALIKES

Agrocybe praecox

Agrocybe pediades from California

Stropharia albonitens

Glick considers this conspecific with **Agrocybe praecox**.

Protostropharia semiglobata: Differs by its more slender stature, viscid cap and stem when fresh, and farinaceous taste.

Agrocybe pediades: Also appears in lawns and pastures but has creamy ochre to dark ochre caps and virtually no veil remnants.

Agrocybe praecox: Pallid forms of **Agrocybe praecox** could be confused with **Agrocybe dura**. Both have a liking for wood chips as a substrate, and both can have cracked caps in age. But **A. dura** lacks the enduring membranous ring of **A. praecox**, and never has spores shorter than 10 μm.

Agrocybe praecox var. cutefracta: Differs by having a strong farinaceous odor and different sized spores. It is now considered a synonym of **A. praecox**.

Agrocybe dura var. xanthophylla: Has traditionally differed from **A. dura** by having yellow gills. The *Index Fungorum* now lists it as a synonym of **A. molesta**.

Agrocybe dura var. obconipes: Differs by having a wrinkled and top-shaped stem.

Agrocybe dura var. squamulosipes: Differs by having dark scales on the stem, and a rooting base.

Agrocybe vermiflua: Differs by its floccose cap margins, and truncate spores. Gills become dark brown with white emarginate edges.

Inocybe geophylla: This dangerously poisonous small white Inocybe with brown gills differs by its smaller spores, 8–10 x 5–6 μm, and smaller stature. It can appear solitary or scat-

Inocybe pudica

Inocybe geophylla group

tered in grass near Douglas fir, pine, or oak. The caps are silky smooth and often bell shaped and umbonate simultaneously. The similarity to **Agrocybe dura** is close enough to warrant an outside opinion if eating **A. dura** for the first time.

Inocybe pudica: Another whitish Inocybe with brown spores, but this one develops salmon tints on cap or stem in age. It is equally poisonous.

As for edibility there are few raves. Most authors note "slightly bitter" or "mediocre at best."

Here are a few samples from the literature:

Roy Watling: "The taste and odor are insipid."

Orson Miller: "Edible but not choice."

A.H. Smith: "Edible, and in southern Michigan, frequently collected in good seasons."

Andrus Voikt: "Not a great edible, but welcome because it appears early in the year when other edibles aren't up."

Charles McIlvaine: "The caps are excellent."

Bill Russell: "Most authorities consider it edible, even excellent."

Furthermore, Russell suggested they were better as mulch decorations. You can transfer a few to your own mulch beds and watch them spread overnight. W.B. McDougall takes this concept a little farther by stating that **Agrocybe dura** is capable of geotropism. He wrote, "In very wet weather the caps become too heavy for the slender stems, and the caps bend over. As the fruiting bodies dry out, the stems endeavor to have the gill edges face the ground again, and they develop crooks. If it rains and dries out again, the stems develop more crooks."

Miron Hard, a former amateur mycologist from Ohio, may have found the Guiness record for the species. In a description of it from a finding on June 6, 1904, he wrote "I found Mr. Dillman's garden on Hickory Street in Chillicothe, white with this plant. Some were very large and beautiful, and I had an excellent opportunity to observe the irregularity in the form of the stem."

It must have been raining on and off for days.

Addendum: It has been discovered that true **I. geophylla** is found in Europe only. Our West Coast version is now **Inocybe insinuata** or a pair of ghost species not yet named. Also, **Inocybe pudica** is now listed as a synonym of **Inocybe whitei** in *Index Fungorum*.

BIBLIOGRAPHY

Robert Bandoni & Adam Szczawinski, *Guide to Common Mushrooms of British Columbia*, 1976. British Columbia Provincial Museum, Victoria, B.C.

George Barron, *Mushrooms of Northeast North America*, 1999. Lone Pine Publishing, Edmonton, Canada.

J. Breitenbach & F. Kranzlin, *Fungi of Switzerland, Vol. 4*, 1995. Edition Mykologie, Lucerne, Switzerland.

Dennis Desjardin, Mike Wood, & Fred Stevens, California Mushrooms, 2015. Timber Press, Portland, Ore.

Guillaume Eyssartier & Pierre Roux, *Le Guide des Champignons de France et Europe*, 2012. Editions Belin, Paris, France.

Phyllis Glick, *The Mushroom Trail Guide*, 1979. Holt, Rinehart, & Winston, New York, NY.

Miron Hard, *Mushrooms Edible & Otherwise*, 1908. Dover Publications, New York, NY.

Calvin Kauffman, *The Agaricaceae of Michigan*, 1918. Michigan Geological and Biological Survey, Lansing, Michigan.

Morten Lange & F. Bayard Hora, *A Guide to Mushrooms and Toadstools*, 1963. E.P. Dutton, New York, NY.

Gary Lincoff, *The Audubon Society Field Guide to North American Mushrooms*, 1981. Alfred A. Knopf, New York, NY.

W.B. McDougall, *Mushrooms*, 1925. Houghton Mifflin, Boston, Mass.

Charles McIlvaine & Robert Macadam, *1000 American Fungi,* 1902. Dover Publications, New York, NY.

Kent & Vera McKnight, *Peterson Field Guides—Mushrooms*, 1987. Houghton Mifflin, Boston, Mass.

Orson & Hope Miller, *North American Mushrooms*, 2006. Morris Book Publishing, Guilford, Conn.

David Pegler, *A Preliminary Agaric Flora of East Africa*, 1977. Her Majesty's Stationary Office, London.

Augusto Rinaldi & Vassili Tyndalo, *The Complete Book of Mushrooms*, 1972. Crown Publishers, New York, NY.

Clark T. Rogerson, *Kansas Mycological Notes: 1953–1954* in *Transactions of the Kansas Academy of Science* 59 (39–48), 1956.

William Roody, *Mushrooms of West Virginia and the Central Appalachians*, 2003. University Press of Kentucky, Lexington, Ky.

Bill Russell, *Field Guide to the Wild Mushrooms of Pennsylvania and the Mid-Atlantic*, 2006. Pennsylvania State University Press, University Park, Penn.

A.H. Smith & Nancy Weber, *The Mushroom Hunter's Field Guide*, 1980. University of Michigan Press, Ann Arbor, Mich.

A.H. Smith, Helen Smith, & Nancy Weber, *How to Know the Gilled Mushrooms*, 1979. William C. Brown, Dubuque, Iowa.

Christian Schwarz & Noah Siegel, *Mushrooms of the Redwood Coast*, 2016. Ten Speed Press, Berkeley, Calif.

Andrus Voitk, *A Little Illustrated Book of Common Mushrooms of Newfoundland and Labrador*, 2007. Gros Morne Co-operating Association, Rocky Harbour, Newfoundland.

Roy Watling, *British Fungus Flora III. Bolbitiaceae: Agrocybe, Bolbitius, and Conocybe*, 1982. Her Majesty's Stationary Office, Edinburgh, Scotland.

Aleuria aurantia (Fries) Fuckel

Photo by Dan Digerness

It is the only elf cup that is edible raw.

The cosmopolitan Orange Peel Fungus looks just like its popular epithet—an orange peel on the side of the road. How many times have you reached for one, hoping for a little extra vitamin C, only to be bummed by this fragile, colorful discomycete? Nonetheless it does brighten up the gravel at the end of your driveway, and if you take it a step further, the salad below your fork.

Aleuria aurantia has been reported from everywhere in the world except Greenland, Antarctica, and the Arabian Peninsula. It fruits solitary, gregarious, or cespitose on disturbed ground. It seems to prefer silicious and loamy soils. It is a saprophyte, probably feeding on nutrients brought up by a backhoe or plow. The fruiting bodies range in size from 2–10 cm wide and are at first globose before expanding until they are cup shaped or nearly flat in age with irregular margins. These are sometimes split, which simulates an Otidea. The interior hymenial surface is bright orange and smooth. The exterior is paler orange and slightly scurfy. The flesh is thin and brittle. It is found from June through October on the sides of logging roads, embankments, loose gravel, and newly graded terrain. Zoberi finds it on bare clay soil in the spring in East Africa. Other authors contend it can be found in mild winters in the Pacific Northwest.

Steve Trudell informs us that "it is one of several ascomycetes that will discharge many spores simultaneously when disturbed, producing a visible cloud." Yet the spores

LOOK-ALIKES

Sowerbyella rhenana from Calif.

Otidea onotica

Caloscypha fulgens from Calif.   *Photo by Richard Morrison*

themselves can come in different sizes. Abbott & Currah reported them as 13.5–16.5 x 7.5–9 µm in Alberta, while R.W.G. Dennis has them at 17–24 x 9–11 µm in England. It appears likely that the spores can increase in size as the fruiting bodies mature. The spores are rather unique in other ways. At first they are elliptical and smooth-walled with two oil drops in the contents. Then, as they mature, they become coarsely sculptured with strange, thorn-like projections (the apiculi) at both ends. The asci, which house the spores, are cylindrical and measure 175–250 x 12–15 µm. The paraphyses are abruptly enlarged at the apices into globose knobs that are filled with orange granules. It is these granules that give the orange color to the species. The spores and asci are inamyloid, which is why Fuckel transferred the species out of Peziza.

According to Mollen & Weber, sunlight is also needed to bring out the color, a similar situation to carotenoids in plants. Evidently, rare, all-white albino forms can be found in pure shade.

It is hard to confuse the Orange Peel Fungus with any other species. **Sowerbyella rhenana**, **Aleuria rutilans**, **Aleuria splendens**, and **Sowerbyella imperialis** all have stems. **Caloscypha fulgens** has an exterior surface that turns blue-green when touched. **Pseudoaleuria quinaultiana** has smooth, ellipsoid spores and matted hairs on the exterior surface. **Otidea onotica** has more of an orange-ochre color and a slit down one side, a trademark of Otideas. And all the orange species in Scutellinia are much smaller in stature and have hairs resembling eyelashes on their cup margins.

The orange color of the carpophores is due to carotenoids. We read that it was concocted in Europe in the past to give to cows "to cure them of colds and other ailments." As for food value, reports vary from inconsequential to pleasant tasting. Jean Marie Polese writes that it is the only elf cup that is edible raw. It adds color to salads and texture to ice creams. I found it to have a nice nutty flavor when sautéed in butter and the consistency of the better kind of taco chip.

BIBLIOGRAPHY

Sean Abbott & R.S. Currah, *The Larger Cup Fungi and Other Ascomycetes of Alberta*, 1989. University of Alberta Devonian Botanic Garden, Edmonton, Alberta, Canada.

David Arora, *Mushrooms Demystified*, 1986. Ten Speed Press, Berkeley, Calif.

J. Breitenbach & F. Kranzlin, *Fungi of Switzerland, Vol.1*, 1984. Verlag Mykologie, Lucerne, Switzerland.

Michael Castellano, Jane Smith, Thom O'Dell, Efren Cazares, & Susan Nugent, *Handbook to Strategy 1 Fungal Species in the Northwest Forest Plan*, 1999. U.S. Department of Agriculture, Forest Service, Portland, Ore.

R.W.G. Dennis, *British Ascomycetes*, 1978. J. Cramer, Vaduz.

Vera Evenson, *Mushrooms of Colorado*, 1997. Denver Botanic Gardens, Denver, Colo.

M. McKenny, D. Stuntz, & J. Ammirati, *The New Savory Wild Mushroom*, 1997. Univ. of Washington Press, Seattle, Wash.

Orson & Hope Miller, *North American Mushrooms*, 2006. Morris Book Publishing, Guilford, Conn.

Lawrence Millman, *Fascinating Fungi of New England*, 2011. Kollath+Stensaas Publishing, Duluth, Minn.

Cora Mollen & Larry Weber, *Fascinating Fungi of the North Woods*, 2007. Kollath+Stensaas, Duluth.

Roger Phillips, *Wild Food*, 1983.

Jean Marie Polese, *The Pocket Guide to Mushrooms*, 2005. Pan MacMillan, London. Tandem Verlag, Chamalieres, France.

Peter Roberts & Shelley Evans, *The Book of Fungi*, 2011. University of Chicago Press, Chicago, Ill.

Robert Rogers, *The Fungal Pharmacy, 2011*. North Atlantic Books, Berkeley, Calif.

Fred Seaver, *North American Species of Aleuria and Aleurina in Mycologia* 6 (273-278), 1914.

Fred Seaver, *North American Cup Fungi – Operculates*, 1928. Self-published, New York, NY.

Steve Trudell & Joe Ammirati, *Mushrooms of the Pacific Northwest*, 2009. Timber Press, Portland, Ore.

M.H. Zoberi, *Tropical Macrofungi – Some Common Species*, 1972. MacMillan Press, London.

Alpova diplophloeus (Zeller & Dodge) Trappe & Smith

After freezing, freshly
thawed specimens have a
pleasant fruity aroma.

The voles were robbed again when Dan Crape and Doug Stein unearthed a colony of this false truffle on September 17, 1996, in the Mt. Baker Snoqualmie National Forest. Dan and Doug found the little carpophores on a small island in the middle of Anderson Creek. I was in the weeds nearby closing in on a Tubaria when I heard the cries of discovery.

While generally considered a hypogeal, or underground fungus, most of these specimens were lying on the moss and humus like discarded jellybeans. According to my field notes, the nearest trees were alder and cottonwood. This was critical in later efforts to identify the species. **Alpova diplophloeus**, according to Trappe, Castellano, Maser & Maser, is an "obligate associate of alder."

First discovered near Friday Harbor on July 4, 1917 by Dr. Zeller, and given the name **Rhizopogon diplophloeus**, the species has since been found along the Pacific coast from California to Alaska, Colorado, Wyoming, the Northwest Territories, and Newfoundland. Arora reports it from the Sierra Nevada, and now Crape and Stein have located it in Whatcom County. **Alpova diplophloeus form europaeus** in the sense of Trappei is now considered to be **Melanogaster luteus**.

The term "diplophloeus means "double-barked" in Greek, perhaps referring to the unusually thick peridium.

The fruiting bodies, according to one of our finders, resembled bloated rat pellets. This might be a little unfair since we only found them in their mature brown phase. The literature tells us that the ovoid to subglobose blobs are at first pallid, then turn yellowish-pink, then ochre to pale reddish-brown, and finally to the dark brown to dark reddish-brown we see here. The peridium, or outer wall, is one millimeter thick. It stains dark reddish-orange when bruised. There is no stalk or columella, (the vestige of a stalk within the spore mass). When sliced in half, the interior gleba

LOOK-ALIKE

Gautieria monticola

changed color quickly from pale yellow to red-brown when exposed to air. The sticky, gelatinous surface consists of gel-filled chambers up to 3 mm broad. These chambers are separated by pale yellow veins. It is this gelatinous matrix that houses the spores. The spores are smooth, cylindrical, and measure 4–5.5 x 2.2–2.8 µm. While supposedly fruity in odor, we found the smell slightly spicy and unrecognizable.

The genus Alpova is closely related to Rhizopogon and Melanogaster, which all differ from each other by various combinations of microscopic characters. It was first introduced as a genus by Carroll Dodge from specimens found at Isle Royale, Michigan. He named them **Alpova cinnamomeus**. The genus was named in honor of Dr. Alfred H. Povah of the Isle Royale Superior Survey, who found the specimens at Siskowet Bay on September 4, 1930. Both men believed they were cinnamon colored at the time. It can now be told apart from other Alpovas by its easily separable peridium.

It was at first a puzzling species. According to Dodge, "it had the peridial characters of Hysterangium, the gleba of Leucogaster, the scattered basidia of Melanogaster, and the spores of Rhizopogon." It is today considered a basidiomycetous truffle in the order Hymenogastrales. Among the higher fungi, it is most closely related to the Boletaceae.

Spores in the genus Alpova are bacilliform (pencil shaped with erasers at both ends) with a slightly thickened wall, and hyaline under the microscope. The basidia are usually 8-spored and found on slender funiculi. The peridium is thick-walled and composed of large cells called "pseudoparenchyma." According to Dodge, "the spaces between the septa in the gleba are at first filled with large spherical cells which finally disintegrate."

Since Dodge introduced the Alpova concept in 1931, the genus has grown to have 14 known species from north temperate forests.

A few of the look-alikes are as follows:

Alpova trappei: Found in the Cascades and the Sierras with conifers, it differs by having a yellow gleba that becomes brown in age without the instant reddish reaction when cut.

Alpova concolor: An Oregon species with an outer layer of dark, appressed, innate fibrils. The gleba turns cinnamon-red when exposed to air. It also has dermatocystidia and a double-layered peridium, a combination of features not seen in other Alpovas.

Alpova nauseosa: Mimics **A. diplophloeus** in appearance but has a strong decaying fruity odor and is found on the east coast in deciduous woods.

Rhizopogon alexsmithii: Formerly placed in Alpova, this false truffle has a more irregularly lumpy appearance and large gel-filled chambers that exude a sticky fluid in wet weather. The yellow-brown to dark brown peridium turns black with KOH. It is associated with mountain conifers, mostly hemlock.

LOOK-ALIKE

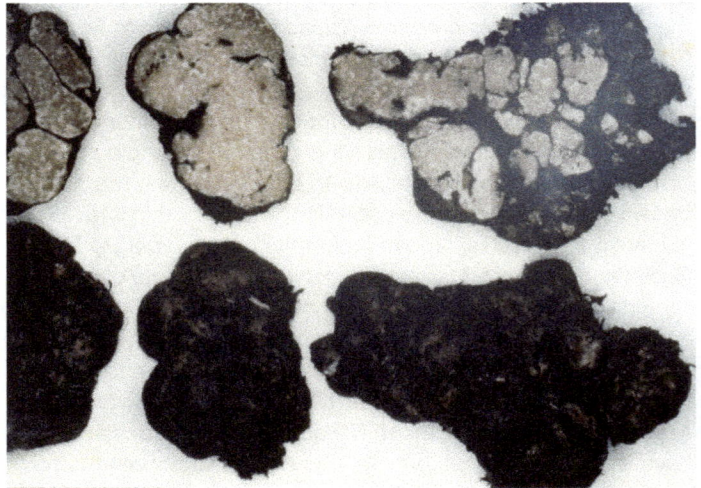

Rhizopogon alexsmithii from OR *Photo by Oregon Truffle Society*

Gautieria monticola: Another small, false truffle that appears locally, has much larger rusty spores with longitudinal grooves, and shows a branching columella when cut in half. This is a feature lacking in Alpova.

Of course, no truffle-like collection made in the Pacific Northwest can receive the attention it deserves unless sent to NATS, the North American Truffling Society based in Oregon. So I mailed a few fruiting bodies down to Dan Wheeler, truffle ambassador extraordinaire. Dan is one of those aficionados passionate about their subject. It didn't take long to get a reply.

Dan wrote back that **Alpova diplophloeus** appears to have an association only with red alder (*Alnus rubra*). It is considered edible, even tasty by some. He added, "While I find Alpova immediately after the first fall rains have denuded the red alder, most of what I collected was donated to the Forest Sciences Lab at Oregon State University where several flying squirrels were said to prefer it to fresh species of Tuber. After freezing, freshly thawed specimens have a pleasant, fruity aroma. These fungi have also been shown to have a relatively high fat content, unusual in truffles. Perhaps this is the reason squirrels esteem them so much."

Dan and the truffling society have added another dimension to the rewards of foraying. Besides enjoying the chanterelles and boletes that most of us go for in the fall, the less obvious world of truffles and false truffles, with all their exotic flavors, is also in their pantheon of fungal choices.

BIBLIOGRAPHY

David Arora, *Mushrooms Demystified*, 1986. Ten Speed Press, Berkeley, Calif.

Michael Castellano, James Trappe, Chris & Zane Maser, *Key to Spores of the Genera of Hypogeous Fungi of North Temperate Forests*, 1989. US Dept. of Agriculture, Forest Service, Corvallis, Ore.

Carroll Dodge, *Alpova, A New Genus of Rhizopogonaceae with Further Notes on Leucogaster and Arcangeliella* in *Annals of the Missouri Botanical Garden* 18 (457–464), 1931.

Jeremy Hayward, Samuel Tourtellot, & Thomas Horton, *A Revision of the Alpova diplophloeus Complex in North America* in *Mycologia* 106 (846–855), 2014.

Pierre-Arthur Moreau, Juliette Rochet, Franck Richard, Francois Chassagne, Sophie Manzi, & Monique Gardes, *Taxonomy of Alnus-Associated Hypogeous Species of Alpova and Melanogaster in Europe* in *Cryptogamie, Mycologie* 32 (33–62), 2011.

A.H. Smith, *Puffballs and Their Allies in Michigan*, 1951. University of Michigan Press, Ann Arbor, Mich.

A.H. Smith, Helen Smith, & Nancy Weber, *How to Know the Non-Gilled Mushrooms*, 1981. William C. Brown, Dubuque, Iowa.

James Trappe, *A Revision on the Genus Alpova with Notes on Rhizopogon and Melanogastraceae* in *Nova Hedwigia, Beihefte* 51 (279–310), 1975.

James & Matt Trappe, & Frank Evans, *NATS Field Guide to Selected North American Truffles and Truffle-like Fungi*, 2006. North American Truffling Society, Corvallis, Ore.

Samuel Zeller, *Some Miscellaneous Fungi of the Pacific Northwest* in *Mycologia* 27 (449–466), 1935.

Amanita muscaria (Linnaeus) Lamarck s.l.

Amanita muscaria buttons

*You can put one in
your fridge and it will
just keep growing.*

Just to the northeast of the Bellis Fair Mall in Bellingham, sits a mostly unused parking lot dotted with raised plots of shore pine. It was here that I spotted these pale yellow "puffballs"in the moss and the duff. They looked eminently edible, better than most puffballs that one usually finds in a decomposed state. A vertical slice through one of them revealed the embryonic outline of a cap and stem. What I had found were Amanita buttons instead.

As Nina Lane Faubion advises, it's always a good idea to vertically slice your puffball finds, just in case. It trumps the usual advise for puffballs, namely "if it is white inside, you can eat it." If you live anywhere in the Pacific Northwest and you have a toddler in your home, check your lawn daily. Ibotenic acid is not a good way to start their day.

If these had made it into your frying pan, the comforting cheesy flavor found in puffballs would have been lacking. Sadly, they would have been equally tasty. Muscimol, muscazone, and ibotenic acid, though bitter when extracted, combine to produce an attractive flavor. And during the cooking the odor arising from the frying pan is said to be close to parsley.

Amanita is a large and complex genus. Unless you know what microscopic features you can gather from buttons, it's hard to pinpoint which species you have. But we can try. The masses of tiny whitish studs on the cap surface will evolve into warts as the carpophores mature. Maybe they will darken into buff or pale tan. They don't look at all yellowish, which is important. The species almost certainly belongs in Section Amanita, which houses **Amanita muscaria**, **Amanita pantherina**, and **Amanita gemmata** among others. The only species of Amanita not in the muscaria complex with the same pinkish cap color in the Pacific Northwest would be **Amanita velosa**, but it seems to be restricted to California and Oregon, and has large, flattened volval patches on the cap, not warts. I have counted 14 different varieties for **Amanita muscaria** in temporate climates, some not listed by the *Index Fungorum*. Of these, only var. alba, var. flavivolvata, and var. formosa in the sense of Thiers are described in Janet Lindgren's *Key Council key for the Pacific Northwest*. The **var. alba** is out. The caps are white to pale tan. The **var. flavivolvata** has its own set of forms and can come in a bewildering variety of cap colors from red to almost white, but the velar material is always pale yellowish. This leaves the **var.**

Yellow-capped version of A. muscaria ss auct. northwest

formosa in the sense of Dr. Harry Thiers, who worked up a description for us in *The Agaricales of California* series. He simply writes, "in var. formosa the pileus is yellow to orange-yellow even when young." No mention of the velar color. David Jenkins in *Amanita of North America* describes an East Coast **var. formosa** as having yellowish to pale tannish volval remnants. He includes California in the states it has been recorded from, but not the Pacific Northwest.

The word *formosa* in Latin means "handsome." We in the Northwest have been calling all **Amanita muscaria** types with scarlet-orange to orange discs **Amanita muscaria var. formosa**. But there is a problem with this name. The **A. muscaria var. formosa** of Europe, described by Bertillon in 1866, has a different DNA profile. According to Courtecuisse & Duhem, it has fleecy yellow scales on cap, ring, and basal bulb.

According to Breitenbach & Kranzlin, it also has a yellow stem. Rolf Singer was evidently the first to realize that North American **var. formosa** was different. Now, decades later, thanks to DNA work, our Northwest **A. muscaria var. formosa** turns out to have the same DNA profile as what is considered typical **Amanita muscaria** of Europe.

Naoshi Nakamura, in an unpublished MSc thesis entitled *A Survey of Amanita in Western Washington*, thought there were three forms of the **var. formos**a in the Puget Sound area. Form A had caps from 9–20 cm wide and were

Amanita pantherinoides

entirely bright yellow to yellow, sometimes becoming orange to pale orange at disc. Form B had caps 8–15 cm wide, and light yellow or paler, rarely with a greenish tinge. The veil formed large, flat patches on the cap, and there was no pigmentation under the gelatinous cap pellicle. Form C had caps from 9.4–15 cm wide. They were yellow brown at disc becoming light yellow at the margins. The warts were floccose and white to pale orange white. Spores and basidia were a bit smaller than those of **Amanita muscaria**. Forms A & B were microscopically identical with **Amanita muscaria**. This unpublished thesis was produced in 1965. The buttons here might represent Form A, which Nakamura thought represented the **var. formosa** of the East Coast and Midwest.

This is an example of old school mycology at its best. Nakamura probably arrived at these form distinctions after several years of observations. The "new" mycology seems to kick off with the genetics. Once it has been established that several species are involved in a roundup of look-alikes, then the mycologist has to scramble to find the microscopic differences. No simple task. Sometimes there are no discernable differences and the resulting key becomes rather geographic in nature.

Recent DNA sequencing by Japanese researchers Oda, Tanaka, and Tsuda showed that the **Amanita muscaria** of North America and that of Eurasia were not the same species. Both occur in Alaska. Besides these, research has discovered that there are other types of **Amanita muscaria** in the southern United States, the Pacific Northwest and in the Channel Islands off southern California. In fact, these small islands harbor four different kinds of **Amanita muscaria**, only one of which occurs on the mainland.

LOOK-ALIKES

Amanita muscaria from Spain

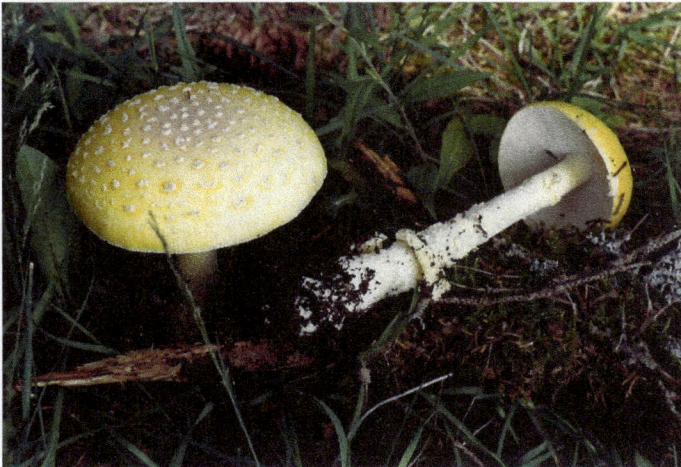

Amanita gussowii from Maine

One result from these DNA studies is that cap color differences scarcely matter. The **var. alba**, **var. formosa**, and **var. flavivolvata** are all simple color variants of **A. muscaria** in the broad sense, not even worth a "var." anymore. But there is an exception. Our local Northwest red-capped specimens of **Amanita muscaria** with yellow velar remnants should be called **Amanita muscaria var. flavivolvata** for now.

Amanita expert Rod Tulloss emailed me that you can tell the difference between Eurasian and North American **Amanita muscaria** microscopically. There are clear differences in spore size and shape, and also in the thickness of the gill trama.

Among the look-alikes are:

Amanita muscaria s.l.: Formerly **A. muscaria var. aureola**, it differed by the structure of the velar material at the stem base and the total lack of warts on the cap surface. Now considered as just **Amanita muscaria** via DNA sequencing.

Amanita velosa: A springtime Amanita of open fields in California that differs by its flesh-tan cap and volval sack. Said to be a great edible.

Amanita regalis: Differs by having a more brownish orange to liver-colored cap and yellow warts on the cap surface.

Amanita aprica: Differs by having a thinly stretched velar patch on the cap surface and practically no rolled velar collar on the stem base. Caps are yellow to yellow-orange beneath the pale gray veil.

Amanita breckonii: Has yellowish caps with prominent white warts and an abrupt basal bulb with white rhizomorphs hanging off the bottoms.

Amanita pantherinoides: As determined here by Rod Tulloss, has a dark flesh colored cap, a large superior ring, and a free margin of velar material at the stem base. Now considered a synonym of **Amanita pantherina** by *Index Fungorum*.

Amanta caesarea: A European species instantly told apart from **A. muscaria** by its yellow stem. A great edible Amanita named after Julius Caesar.

An Amanita button is a powerful force. You can put one in your fridge and it will just keep growing. The drastic drop in temperature only seems to inspire it more. Rod also emailed me that the microcharacters are constantly changing as a button develops. The form of the volva and the presence or absence of a pileipellis will show up eventually. The spores will be absent for some time. The pigmentation of the cap surface might or might not develop before the mushroom is beyond the button stage. Partly because of this uncertainty, Rod doesn't think buttons can be used to segregate species in the general case.

Perhaps one reason **Amanita muscaria** appears in so many continents is that it has a huge range of tree associates. Besides the typical fir, larch, and pine, it has been found with poplar, oak, birch, spruce, aspen, madrone, and hornbeam.

Medicinally it has been used for cancer, paralysis, eczema, epilepsy, chronic cough, ringworm, night sweats, and facial twitches. And as for use in remediation, it is highly tolerant of mercury and cadmium while able to degrade chrysene and phenanthrene.

Patrick Harding, in *Mushroom Miscellany*, writes that the principle chemical in **Amanita muscaria** is ibotenic acid. It breaks down, when the mushroom is dried, to a much more potent chemical called muscimol. "Muscimol is structurally similar to a chemical involved in our nervous system, helping to explain its likely mode of action. Most of the muscimol is not broken down by the kidneys and is rapidly passed into the urine, thus explaining the toxicity of mushroom eater's urine." Which variety of **A. muscaria** you decide to eat is going to be less important than a number of other factors. North American

TWO VERSIONS

Amanita muscaria ss auct. NW

Amanita muscaria (formerly var. formosa of Northwest authors)

Amanita caesarea from Spain

Amanita muscaria s.l. from Scotland (formerly Amanita muscaria var. aureola)   *Photo by Rod Tulloss*

specimens are reputed to be more toxic than their Eurasian counterparts. Fresh specimens are more likely to disturb your stomach than dried material. Harding notes that "some hallucinations may occur, but the main effect is an alternation between deep sleep and manic behavior, in total lasting for anything up to nine hours."

Even Charles McIlvaine, the "man who ate everything," made no bones about this one. "The **var. formosa**," he wrote, "is soft, fragile, poisonous to a high degree. Dizziness, nausea, exaggeration of vision, and pallor result from it. The pulse quickens and is full, and a dreaded pressure affects the breathing. Symptoms disappear in two hours, leaving a torturing, dull, skull pervading headache." He went on to add that vinegar does not extract the poison. It only amalgamates it.

Of course, this appraisal may have been prejudiced by the death of Count Achilles de Vecchi in 1897. This Italian diplomat, stationed in Washington, D.C., had purchased **Amanita muscaria** from a local market. He ate 24 of them, fell into a deep coma, and died the next day. He had thought them to be **Amanita caesarea**, a favorite in Italy.

European **Amanita muscaria** must not have the same toxicity. In certain areas of alpine Germany it is served raw with vinegar, oil, salt, and pepper for an appetizer. Others make a soup of it. The fly agaric is cut into thin slices and then boiled in water, garlic, bay leaf, and salt for about 15 minutes until soft. In Russia it is added to Vodka, and in the Shutul Valley in Afghanistan it is boiled with fresh jewelweed and goat cheese brine to make an enticing soup. They also brew a traditional ale with dried **A. muscaria**, fireweed, and cow parsnip.

Gary Lincoff has since made a deeper study. He noted that the whole **Amanita muscaria** complex has poisonous compounds. Besides ibotenic acid, muscimol, and muscazone, muscarine is also present in small amounts. Although the Siberian Amanita muscaria produces hallucinations, our version causes delirium, profuse sweating, nausea, vomiting, and occasionally violent muscle spasms. A friend of mine, who ate a small amount raw, still shudders at the memory.

Nonetheless, if we look back on earlier attempts at ingestion we can pick up clues on water solubility eliminating the toxins. As early as 1839 Dr. Felix Pouchet of France conducted wildly fluctuating experiments. He once boiled five **Amanita muscaria** caps in a liter of water for 15 minutes. He then removed the mushroom pieces and let his dogs drink the broth. They all died. Undaunted from this experience, he tried the reverse procedure. He dumped out the broth and fed the Amanita pieces to more dogs. Not only did they survive, over time they fattened on the **Amanita muscaria**.

Now flash forward to the early 20th century. African-American women throughout the south were selling them in regional markets. The method was to boil them in salted water, then steep them in vinegar. They could then be rinsed in cold water and added to stews. No deaths or ill effects were reported.

Another method of negating the toxins was discovered in Sanada, Japan. Pieces of **Amanita muscaria** were boiled and then preserved in salt.

Amanita muscaria enjoys the common name of Fly Agaric. This is not because you can fly after eating it. According to Robert Rogers, it has been used to kill flies for centuries. In French households entire fruiting bodies were hung from ceilings to attract them. The flies were attracted by the 1,3-diolein compound. After sucking up the juices, they died from the ibotenic acid.

There is also a report that Swedes in 1751 used **Amanita muscaria** to hamper bedbugs. They would mash the mushroom into a pulp and then apply it with a feather around the cracks in the walls where the bedbugs hid. No more bedbugs around.

According to R. Gordon Wasson, the native Koryaks of northern Siberia only ate dried **Amanita muscaria**. They would chew the specimens and get them down with water. This was much preferable to vodka because they could avoid hangovers. The Russians would go one step further and add the fly agaric to the vodka.

And there are other reports of successful dining and smoking. The Japanese mycologist, Imazeki, claimed fine results by roasting the **Amanita muscaria**. Rogers suggests smoking it with a small amount of pot for a "pleasant alteration." The physician Waldschmidt claimed that dosage was the most important thing to remember. A small tincture of the mushroom brings on a positive dream experience. After the trip, you will feel refreshed and more motivated. But if you consumed more than 10 grams, you would experience loss of

LOOK-ALIKES

Amanita aprica

Amanita breckonii

coordination, illusions, confusion, and manic attacks. One of the more prominent characteristics is that the slightest pressure causes pain. Rogers suggests that one should not eat anything for four to six hours before trying the mushroom. If it's not going well, it's helpful to remember that ibotenic acid is cleared from the body in 90 minutes.

Perhaps the strangest report I ever heard connected with the Fly Agaric was the association with reindeer and urine. According to Wasson, native Siberians prefer drinking their own urine after consumption of **Amanita muscaria** to get a smoother trip without nausea. The inebriation is increased. The resulting urine is even stronger and this goes on and on until ecstasy is reached. It was also noted that reindeer had a passion for both mushrooms and urine, especially the Fly Agaric and human urine. When the two were combined the result was reindeer nirvana.

After reading this piece of information, one of our Pacific

Northwest Key Council members had to check it out for himself. He was of Swiss origin and couldn't imagine anyone depraved enough to drink their own urine, much less offer it to reindeer. When the Iron Curtain was lifted he was among the first to travel to Russia. He landed in Vladivostok. By whatever means of travel available he made it into northern Siberia during the summer months. A family invited him to stay with them. The first morning was rough. Instead of orange juice he was offered a whole glass of vodka. He had to finish that before he could leave the home. Then they all headed for the reindeer pastures. Still reeling from the vodka, he realized he needed to take a leak. He had barely unzipped his pants when a sort of thunder assailed his ears. He looked up to see the entire herd running his way.

"This was unsettling," he told me, "They were running right over field mushrooms to get to me." He wasn't sure how much time he had. In the end, he stood about 15 feet away while the herd trampled itself to get to the urine. That's a lot of money spent to verify a report.

After reading several reports of edibility, I have to confess I had to try it myself. It was back in 1982 when I was living in San Francisco on Leavenworth Street near the Broadway tunnel. I had found a big break of the bright red **Amanita** muscaria out at Point Reyes. I chose three of the larger caps and peeled off the red pellicles. I then boiled them for about ten minutes until the water was bright yellow. I dumped this water and boiled them again. At this point the water was almost clear. I dumped this also. Then I sautéed them in butter. The flavor was surprisingly good after a double boil. And there were no ill effects.

There are those, of course, who aren't in it for the food. The best site I found for alternate preparations is www.shroomery.org. The author articulates many ways to prepare the mushroom for ingestion, but doesn't describe one method that guarantees no vomiting. Instead, if approached in just the right way, the experience can be so euphoric that the vomiting part can be looked at as a happy purge. Here are some of his suggestions: 1) Dry the caps in an oven or dehydrator. Then grind them into a very fine powder. You can then fill gel-caps with them and take them with water. 2) You can make a tea with the powder. Bring a cup of water to a simmer. Then decrease the heat until 190 degrees is reached. Pour the water into a cup and add 8 grams of the powder. Stir off and on for 30–45 minutes. Then drink the tea. A maximum dose might be 15–22 grams in one cup. That's if you want a totally preternatural experience. If you take the 8 grams you will begin to feel drowsy at

Amanita potpourri

first. Your vision may get blurry and you will start to relax. This is a good time to find a couch and go to sleep. You will have intense dreams. When you awake, "the experience will be like a caterpillar metamorphosing into a butterfly." You will soon vomit copiously. This will be followed by "endless euphoria, effortless movement, feelings of peace and superior pain relief." (It is helpful to have someone around to clean up the vomit.) At higher doses you will go through out-of-body experiences.

In general, mature, dry caps have the highest potency. Most of the alkaloids are in the cap cuticle. For best results some people just dry the pellicles and smoke that. Others get rid of the stem and gills before preparation. Drying and heating converts the ibotenic acid into powerful muscimol through decarboxylation. The author reported excellent results from roasting the caps over an open flame and eating them straight up. Another method that produced euphoric dancing and singing was to place the caps gill side up on an open grill. Liquid will soon fill the caps. About two tablespoons of this liquid will bring on the euphoria. But if you eat the mushrooms after taking the liquid, terrible retching will result.

You can see that one misstep produces the difference between heaven and hell. This is not just from a physical standpoint. You can also experience bliss or terror in the resulting trip. The author speculates that the mystery and awe surrounding **Amanita muscaria** derives from this unpredictability. You want to approach the mush-room with great care. If you find a big break you might want to lie down among the specimens to get better in tune. Only after this involvement should you hack off their caps.

Robert Rogers suggests that we need look no further than the chemical make-up to explain the unpredictability. Muscimol is a central nervous system hallucinogen. Muscarine is a highly toxic hallucinogen. Ironically they are physiological opposites. One is food for the spiritual body. The other is poison to the physical body. While the kidneys detoxify muscarine, muscimol passes through mostly intact. The muscimol then inhibits neurons while the ibotenic acid stimulates them. With this sort of action going on within the mushroom, small wonder there are varying reactions from people.

Of course we have to finish this piece with a health advisory. Whether you are in Asia, Europe, or North America, it is a safer practice to launch the double boil. Although I have heard through the rumor mill that the double boil also works for **Amanita gemmata** and **Amanita pantherina**, I wouldn't go there unless I learned more. One could mistake **Amanita phalloides** for the former, and the latter has a checkered past. The varied appearances of **Amanita muscaria** could lead to misidentification. If you are boiling up a deadly Amanita, no amount of boiling can fix it.

On behalf of our club, the Northwest Mushroomers Association, we would like to thank Rod Tulloss for contributing his insights on some of the technical aspects of this article.

BIBLIOGRAPHY

Joe Ammirati, J.A. Traquair, & Paul Horgen, *Poisonous Mushrooms of the Northern United States and Canada*, 1985. University of Minnesota Press, Minneapolis, Minn.

David Arora, *Mushrooms Demystified*, 1986. Ten Speed Press, Berkeley, Calif.

David Arora & William Rubel, *A Study of Cultural Bias in Field Guide Determinations of Mushroom Edibility using the iconic Mushroom, Amanita muscaria, as an Example* in *Ethnic Botany* 62 (223–243), 2008.

J. Breitenbach & F. Kranzlin, *Fungi of Switzerland, Vol.4*, 1995. Edition Mykologia, Lucerne, Switzerland.

Regis Courtecuisse & Bernard Duhem, *Mushrooms & Toadstools of Britain & Europe*, 1995. Harper-Collins, London.

Guillaume Eyssartier & Pierre Roux, *Le Guide des Champignons de France et Europe*, 2012. Editions Belin, Paris.

Nina Lane Faubion, *Some Edible Mushrooms and How to Cook Them*, 1972. Binfords & Mort, Portland, Ore.

David Fischer & Alan Bessette, *Edible Wild Mushrooms of North America*, 1992. University of Texas Press, Austin, Texas.

J. Geml, R.E. Tulloss, G.A. Laursen, N.A. Sazanova, & D.L. Taylor, *Evidence for Strong Inter- and Intracontinental Phylogeographic Structure in Amanita muscaria, a Wind-Dispersed Ectomycorrhizal Basidiomycete* in *Molecular Phylogenetics and Evolution* 48 (694-701), 2008.

Patrick Harding, *Mushroom Miscellany*, 2008. Harper-Collins, London.

David Jenkins, *Amanita of North America*, 1986. Mad River Press, Eureka, Calif.

Calvin Kauffman, *The Agaricaceae of Michigan*, 1918. Michigan Geological and Biological Survey, Lansing, Mich.

Gary Lincoff, *The Audubon Society Field Guide to North American Mushrooms*, 1981. Alfred A. Knopf, New York, NY.

Gary Lincoff & D.H. Mitchel, *Toxic and Hallucinogenic Mushroom Poisoning*, 1977. Van Nostrand Reinhold, New York, NY.

Janet Lindgren, *Trial Key to Amanita Species in the Pacific Northwest*, 1998. Pacific Northwest Key Council, Seattle, Wash.

Peter McCoy, *Radical Mycology*, 2016. Chthaeus Press, Portland, Ore.

Charles McIlvaine & Richard Macadam, *One Thousand American Fungi*, 1902. Revised and reprinted, 1973, Dover Publications, New York, NY.

Naoshi Nakamura, *A Survey of Amanita in Western Washington,* 1965. Unpublished MSc thesis, University of Washington.

Giovanni Pacioni & Gary Lincoff, *Simon & Schuster's Guide to Mushrooms*, 1981. Simon & Schuster, New York, NY.

Robert Rogers, *The Fungal Pharmacy,* 2011. North Atlantic Books, Berkeley, Calif.

David Rose, *The poisoning of Count Achilles de Vecchi and the Origins of American Amateur Mycology* in *McIlvainea* 16 (37-55), Spring, 2006.

Shroomery.org. *Amanita muscaria.*

Harry Thiers, *Amanitaceae in The Agaricales of California*, 1982. Mad River Press, Eureka, Calif.

Else Vellinga, *Toxic Amanitas* in *Fungi, Vol.2, No.2* (18-19), 2009.

R. Gordon Wasson, *Soma: Divine Mushroom of Immortality*, 1971. Harcourt Brace Jovanovich, New York, NY.

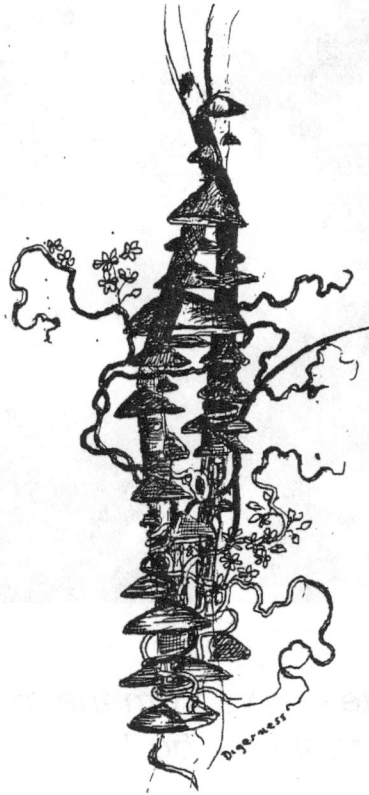

Amanita pachycolea Stuntz in Thiers & Ammirati

*The Western Grisette erupts from the forest
duff as a shiny dark umber "egg."*

This statuesque Amanita was found in the Stimpson Reserve near Lake Whatcom in the fall of 2003. About four of our ilk were thrashing around under the big leaf maple and Douglas fir when we heard a series of shrieks. Margot Evers, our excitable French octogenarian club member, had almost stubbed her toe on it. Also known as the Western Grisette, it looked like a small, shiny football emerging from the duff. This one, of course, was just beyond the button stage, but judging from the bulk alone, one can imagine it reaching a height of 30 cm and a cap width of 25 cm, the maximum width and height according to Arora.

The Western Grisette erupts from the forest duff as a shiny dark umber 'egg' encased in a thick, white, felty volva. The volva eventually sloughs away, sometimes leaving a white patch on the cap, but always ending up at the stem base as a thick, saccate cup attached only at the base. The caps become convex to plane, viscid when moist, varying in color from dark chestnut to the more common dark brown becoming paler at the margins. The margins are at first incurved, then uplifted and undulate in age. These cap margins are coarsely plicate-striate with striations up to 2 cm in length. One unique feature about **Amanita pachycolea** is that all the striations are the same length, which results in a darker band around the inner edge of the striations. The second photo shows this band, plus the relatively huge volva that encases the stem.

Cap widths are 7–25 cm wide. The context is white, rather soft, and up to 1 cm thick at disc. The gills are at first adnate to decurrent by a short, inconspicuous hook, but soon become free. They are broad, subdistant to crowded, often ventricose, and dry to a yellowish-buff. They often develop rusty stains in age. The gill edges are gray to gray-brown and fimbriate. This is another unique character of the species.

Amanita pachycolea—another view

The stems measure up to 3 cm thick and 30 cm long. They are equal or taper towards the apex, and are solid at first becoming hollow in age. The apex is white pruinose becoming more fibrillose below on a grayish-tan to pale brown ground. There is no ring and no basal bulb. The volva attached to the stem base develops rusty to yellowish colors in age. The odor can be unpleasant in mature specimens. The spores are white, subglobose, inamyloid, and measure 10–13.5 x 8.8–11.8 µm.

Amanita pachycolea is found along the Pacific coast from Monterey County, California northward into British Columbia, the center of its range being southern Oregon. It is found in mixed coniferous and hardwood forests in the fall.

Taxonomically it belongs in Subgenus Amanita, Section Vaginatae along with other Amanitas such as **Amanita fulva**, **Amanita constricta**, and **Amanita vaginata**. All of these have conspicuously striate cap margins, inamyloid spores, and no rings on their stems.

The literary history of **Amanita pachycolea** starts with Naoshi Nakamura, a graduate student at the University of Washington back in the 1960s. He first used the name "**Amanita pachycolea** nom. prov." in his unpublished thesis in 1965. Dr. Stuntz then officially described it, but didn't publish it in a scientific journal. This chore was left for Ammirati and Thiers who subsequently published the species in *Mycotaxon* 15 in 1982. Nakamura found it first at Priest Point Park in Thurston County in November, 1950. At the time, it was considered a rare species.

There are numerous brown capped Amanitas world-wide that could be considered look-alikes. Only a few are mentioned here. Among these are:

Amanita pachyvolvata: A French species that differs by having larger spores, caps that are more of an ochre-brown in color, no dark emarginate edges on the gills, and cap margin striations of uneven lengths.

Amanita battarae: A European species that differs by having smaller spores, pure white gills, and a paler brown cap.

Amanita lividopallescens— Another European species that has olive-gray to pale gray-brown caps, shaggy white floccose bands on the stipe, and sometimes a double volva at the stem base.

Amanita constricta: Locally common in some seasons, it differs by having a thin gray volva that hugs the stem base but easily disintegrates in age. It has a smaller, more slender stature than **A. pachycolea**.

Amanita Tulloss #NW04: Another local Amanita with strongly striate margins and brown caps. It differs by having rusty stains on its basal volva, and its smaller, more slender stature. Those pictured here were found on the Skyline Trail in the Mt. Baker-Snoqualmie National Forest at an elevation over 6,000 feet.

Amanita pantherina: Differs by having numerous white warts on its cap, lacks the marginal striations, and has rings of velar material at the stem base instead of a volva. We include it here because occasionally

LOOK-ALIKES

Amanita constricta

Amanita vaginata ss auct. northwest

Amanita porphyria

Amanita lividopallescens from Switzerland

Amanita Tulloss #NW04

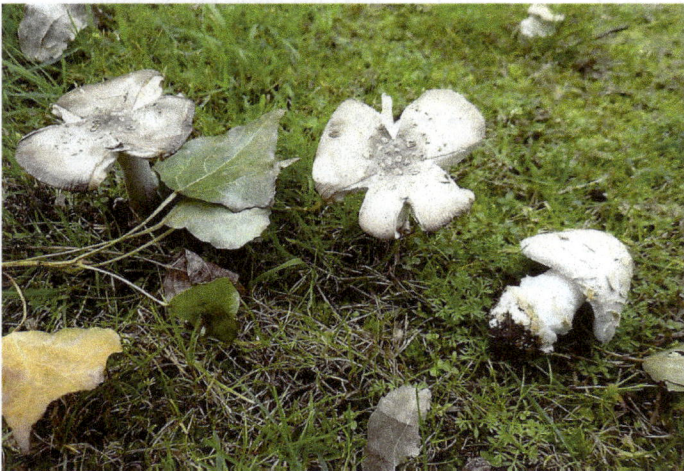

Amanita ceciliae from Spain

rains will wash the warts off. If this happens, check out the stem base. **Amanita pantherina** will have rings of volval material, never a volval sack. It is a dangerously poisonous mushroom that contributed to the death of a teenager in Nanaimo, B.C., who ingested it with Psilocybe mushrooms and copious amounts of alcohol.

Amanita porphyria: Another locally found grayish-brown Amanita, differs by having an abrupt basal bulb that is usually cleft on one side, and a stem with a chevron pattern.

Amanita brunnescens: Has brown to olive-brown caps, stems that stain reddish-brown, and a cleft volva at the stem base. Probably not a good idea to eat either of these.

Amanita vaginata: Differs from the Western Grisette by having a much smaller stature, more of a gray to gray-brown cap, and a thinner, loosely lobed volval sack. Seems to occur nationwide and is said to be a passable edible.

Amanita ceciliae: Differs by having a ring of loose grayish velar material around the stem base and a gray-brown cap with concolorous warts.

And finally, there are mixed reviews on the edibility of **Amanita pachycolea**. Arora wrote in *Mushrooms Demystified* that aged specimens had a fishy taste. Later, in *All That the Rain Promises and More*, he discovers that it is "more flavorful than any other grisette." David Biek claimed "it is better than **Amanita constricta**." Geoffrey Kibby concluded, "edible but best avoided." After all, culinary mistakes in the genus Amanita could prove deadly.

Eventually, realizing that it would be hard to make a mistake with this particular Amanita, I took the plunge. There was a perfect, young specimen at our 2011 Fall Show. At the end of the show I took it down to the galley on my boat and fried it up. It had a firm, encouraging texture and a slight smoky flavor that put it over the top. Although highly recommended for the table, I would urge all novices to seek a second opinion on the identity before cooking it up.

Addendum: Both **Amanita pantherina** and **Amanita vaginata** of North America have different DNA profiles from the original European species of the same names, so both will require new names eventually.

LOOK-ALIKE

Amanita pantherina ss auct. northwest

BIBLIOGRAPHY

David Arora, *All That the Rain Promises and More*, 1991. Ten Speed Press, Berkeley, Calif.

David Arora, *Mushrooms Demystified*, 1986. Ten Speed Press, Berkeley, Calif.

David Biek, *The Mushrooms of Northern California*, 1984. Spore Prints, Redding, Calif.

David Jenkins, *Amanita of North America,* 1986. Mad River Press, Eureka, Calif.

Geoffrey Kibby, *An Illustrated Guide to Mushrooms and Other Fungi of North America*, 1993. Dragon's World, Surrey, England.

Gary Lincoff, *The Audubon Society Field Guide to North American Mushrooms*, 1981. Alfred A. Knopf, New York, NY.

Jan Lindgren, *Trial Key to Amanita Species in the Pacific Northwest*, 1998. Pacific Northwest Key Council, Seattle, Wash.

Naoshi Nakamura, *A Survey of Amanita in Western Washington,* 1965. Unpublished MSc thesis, University of Washington.

Robert Rogers, *The Fungal Pharmacy, 2011. North Atlantic Books, Berkeley, Calif.*

A.H. Smith, Helen Smith, & Nancy Weber, *How to Know the Gilled Mushrooms*, 1979. William C. Brown, Dubuque, Iowa.

Harry Thiers, *The Agaricales of California: Amanitaceae*, 1982. Mad River Press, Eureka, Calif.

Harry Thiers & Joe Ammirati, *New Species of Amanita in Western North America* in *Mycotaxon* 15 (155–166), 1982.

Steve Trudell & Joe Ammirati, *Mushrooms of the Pacific Northwest*, 2009. Timber Press, Portland, Ore.

Rod Tulloss, *Type Studies in Amanita Section Vaginatae I: Some Taxa Described in this Century with Notes on Descriptions of Spores and Refractive Hyphae in Amanita* in *Mycotaxon* 52 (305–396), 1994.

Amanita phalloides (Vaillant ex Fries) Secretan

*The Death Cap
has arrived in
Bellingham.*

Traveling at an average of 5.13 kilometers a year, the Death Cap has arrived in Bellingham. It started out from the campus at UC Berkeley in 1945, or possibly from the grounds of the Del Monte Hotel in Monterey in 1938. These were the first authenticated reports of **Amanita phalloides** on the West Coast. Both the University of California at Berkeley and the Del Monte Hotel were known for importing exotic trees, and the Death Cap rode in with the root systems.

Although there have been far earlier reports of **Amanita phalloides** on both coasts, all were either misidentifications or poorly documented. The first genuine sighting of the Death Cap on the East Coast was at Laurel, Maryland, in 1967. After extensive DNA testing, it was ascertained that both East and West Coast specimens were invasive from Europe. The main difference in populations is that East Coast **A. phalloides** continues to fruit with imported trees in urban and suburban settings while West Coast Death Caps have jumped their boundaries and formed relationships with native trees, especially coastal live oak. They are now known as ectomycorrhizal symbionts, capable of associating with a number of trees including linden, pine, tanoak, Douglas fir, chestnut, beech, and hazelnut. (On the East Coast, according to Dr. Orson Miller, they associate mostly with eastern white pine, but also with Norway spruce, hemlock, oak, hornbeam, and Virginia pine.)

Once it formed a mycorrhizal relationship with Californian live oak, it spread like wildfire. (The lead photo shows it with oak in Olema, California.) It is now found from just north of Los Angeles up into Victoria on Vancouver Island. In the Pacific Northwest it has been seen in Seattle, Vancouver, Victoria, and now Bellingham, but only with trees not native to our area.

Paul Kroeger tells us that it started fruiting in Vancouver in 2008. It appeared in southern Washington 20 years before that. If one believes in the theory that prevailing southeasterly winds wafted the spores northward, these dates could make sense. On the other hand, the Kroeger theory is even more plausible. He speculates that hornbeam saplings imported from California carried the Death Cap mycelium with them. These trees must have come from nurseries where Death Caps had dropped their spores earlier. Since it takes 45 to 55 years for a fruiting body to appear once a root stock is infected, only mature hornbeams are found with **Amanita phalloides**.

Meanwhile, back in Bellingham, Northwest Mushroomers Association former president Pete Trenham first saw it on campus at Western Washington University on October 5, 2010. It was with pin oak. On October 12, 2011, he found it again on campus with the same oak. Jairul Rahaman, president of the Snohomish County Mycological Society, then found it a week later just inside the main gate of the Bayview Cemetery with oak and hazelnut. Hailing originally from British Guyana, she was on her way to check out Electric Avenue when she happened to glance to her left. The "grand salami" occurred in September of 2012 when a huge break was found just behind the

Young Amanita phalloides

Amanita phalloides at Western Washington University

Pizza Pipeline on Newell Street on a strip of lawn under filberts. This break was also discovered by Pete Trenham, who seems to have become a magnet for the taxon. All of these collections had the characteristic olive hue of European **Amanita phalloides**. Three years later Dr. Fred Rhoades and I revisited the site to discover that the proprietor had removed the entire line of hazelnut trees.

On about October 20, 2012, yet another fruiting was found under the pin oak on campus. This towering oak stands just to the right of the main door leading to the Viking Union information booth. Literally hundreds of students pass by it daily. On this occasion I found what looked like a gold bauble on the ground with a patch of white styrofoam on it. It looked like a Christmas ornament. I picked it up, careful to not break the stem base. The photos on the previous page shows this specimen. The firmness of texture, the golden cap, the pale yellow stem, and the white volva were all in their prime. The odor was a cross between new mown hay and crushed rose petals. It was the most gorgeous mushroom I'd ever seen.

I took it in to the information booth. The girl at the booth was talking to a friend. I felt I had to interrupt them. I needed to share this incredible specimen with someone. I told them that here was one of the world's most deadly mushrooms and that the student paper, *The Western Front*, should warn students about it.

They looked at me as if I was the problem.

"Well," she said, "You could go across to the Administration Building in Old Main and let them know there."

"I can't," I replied, "I'm illegally parked." And then I rolled out the door.

Once outside, I noticed another tree about 30 feet away from the pin oak. Realizing that this tree could also be associated with the Death Cap, I collected a small branch of it. Then I presented both branch and Death Cap to the Agricultural Center on Forest Street. Here is where tree identifications can be made. Within a day, the answer came back. The smaller tree was a Himalayan paper birch.

Point Reyes State Park on the Californian coast is the heartland. Here the Death Caps fruit all year round in the fog and get twice the size they do in Europe. One estimate is that they constitute 50% of the fungal biomass in that park. In many areas in California you can be fined $1,000 or more for taking mushrooms out of a park. So imagine getting fined that amount and then arriving home for a little research only to find out you had been fined for picking the Death Cap, an invasive species. Happens all the time.

In the Bay area surrounding San Francisco, **Amanita phalloides** had become so prolific that at the 2005 Mushroom Show hosted by the San Francisco Mycological Society, an entire table was devoted to it. Besides volumes of appropriate literature, there were photos of every aspect of it. A very lively lady named Anne Pringle was in charge of this display, and every time I brought up a potential foolproof characteristic for identifying **A. phalloides**, she countered with an exception. For instance, one could pick it from the ground and leave the basal volva behind, or banana slugs could devour the ring. This went on and on until she finally relented, allowing that if you checked off each key character one by one, you should stay out of trouble.

One of the biggest problems has been cap color variation. Early American descriptions allowed for white to olive to yellowish to brown caps. West Coast descriptions of white capped Death Caps turned out to be **Amanita ocreata**. Brown capped species from either coast turned out to be **Amanita porphyria** or **Amanita brunnescens**. A tan-capped version can be seen in Arora's *All That the Rain Promises and More*. The most sinister happenstance is the confusion of bronze tinged specimens with the edible and popular **Amanita calyptroderma**. Known as Coccora, this normally orange-brown capped species with a large white velar patch on the cap disc gets confused with the Death Cap every few years with disastrous results.

In 1985 four Mexicans died in San Diego County from eating **Amanita phalloides**. Maybe they confused them with Russulas. Laotians have succumbed to the Death Cap in the Napa Valley. In 1989, four out of five Koreans had liver transplants after dining on **Amanita phalloides** found under chestnut in the Columbia River Gorge. All survived. They thought they had eaten **Volva-**

Amanita calyptroderma from Calif.   Photo by Sonja Max

riella volvacea. Although true that the above groups were fooled by the Death Cap, blanket statements by the press that people from various ethnic groups more often confuse the Death Cap with edibles from their previous countries has no real foundation. Local Californians born and raised there have succumbed as well.

Deaths along the East Coast and westward to Michigan were not always accurately chronicled at the turn of the century. William Sturgis Thomas estimated about ten deaths a year in New York in the 1920s. Calvin Kauffman recorded sixteen deaths in southern Michigan over a ten-year period.

Dr. John Dearness described in detail the struggles and deaths of two families victimized by **Amanita verna** in London, Ontario in 1926. **A. verna**, an all white Amanita, was considered a variety of **Amanita phalloides** in that era. They had eaten a stew consisting of white Russulas, white Clitocybes, and **Amanita verna** steamed in milk and parsley. Can you imagine the horror of seeing your friends and family dying off one by one at different times and knowing you will not escape that fate either. You can read all about this grisly tale in *Mushrooms and Toadstools* by Gussow & Odell.

In Europe, perhaps the most infamous death recorded from **Amanita phalloides** is the poisoning of Emperor Claudius by Agrippina, the mother of Nero. To avoid detection it has been suggested that she merely squeezed the juices of the Death Cap onto the meal. That is one story. Another account has Agrippina substituting **Amanita phalloides** for **Amanita caesaria** and disguising the meal with a cream of colocynth soup. The colocynth is a bitter cucumber that was supposed to accelerate the poisoning. I have also heard that Lucretia Borgia used the Amanita to dispatch her enemies. But by far the most tragic occurrence were the deaths of 31 school

LOOK-ALIKES

Amanita vernicoccora from Oregon

Amanita gemmata

children in Poznan, Poland, in 1931 at a school lunch. The article did not suggest which mushroom the chef believed he was serving up, but confusion with **Tricholoma equestre** is a possibility. Since the gills of **Amanita phalloides** can sometimes have a pale yellow tinge and also be adnate or adnexed, this might have happened here. According to Lincoff & Mitchel, 40 more people died in Poznan from 1953 to 1962 from Death Cap consumption. This is hard to come to grips with, considering the local history.

When **A. phalloides** was first thought to be found along the East Coast of North America experts were confused about it. As a result, authors of early American mushroom guides offered a wide range of cap colors to consider. Examples:

Calvin Kauffman: "smoky olive to umber brown."
Miron Hard: "white, grayish-white, or smoky brown."
Verne Graham: "olive, smoky gray or light citron yellow."
Louis Krieger: "white to olive-gray to blackish-brown."
Charles McIlvaine: "shining white or lemon yellow."

Each one looks like a composite description of at least two Amanitas. Some of these have been tentatively identified as **Amanita pantherina**, **Amanita brunnescens**, **Amanita porphyria**, **Amanita mappa**, **Amanita ocreata**, and **Amanita virosa**. Therefore, be warned. Use a modern key when trying to key out your Death Cap.

Amanita phalloides first appears as an elongated egg totally covered by a whitish universal veil. At this stage it could be mistaken for a puffball. Take a knife and cut it in half vertically. If an outline of a cap and stem are visible, you have an Amanita. As the mushroom matures the universal veil will break apart to form the basal volva. The partial veil will also stretch and break. This is a thinner secondary veil that covers the gills. It can leave a fringe of white velar material on the cap margin (as seen in the lead photo), but more importantly a membranous and persistent grayish-green to white ring near the apex of the stem.

The caps of the Death Cap range from 4–16 cm wide. They are convex to almost plane, tacky to viscid when moist becoming shiny to metallic when dry. They are smooth except for occasional white velar patches, never with pointy warts. A critical character is the smooth cap margin in young specimens. The Coccora, on the other hand, has deep striations. However, older, water drenched specimens of the Death Cap can feature the cap pellicle collapsing against the gills and presenting the illusion of striations. One can imagine that mistakes have been made here.

The cap color is usually an attractive olive-gray, but according to Ammirati, Traquair, & Horgen, can also be nearly whitish or with a brownish or grayish cast. It can even have blackish streaks, usually darkest at disc. Bronze tinged specimens have been confused in the past with edible orange-ochre caps of **Amanita calyptroderma** with tragic results. The caps of **Amanita phalloides** are usually paler at the margins, radially streaked with innate fibrils, and have pellicles that are easily peeled. The context is thickish and white except for a yellow-green tinge just below the pellicle. The gills are free to adnate, setting up confusions with Tricholoma. They are crowded to subdistant, white with an occasional yellowish tinge, often slightly greenish in age. They do not stain when bruised. The lamellulae are numerous, and according to Jenkins, attenuate, gradually tapering at the ends. The stems range from 5–18 cm long and up to 3 ½ cm thick, equal or tapering at apex. They have a thick bulbous base enveloped by the prominent white volva. They are solid at first becoming hollow in age. The stem color is white to grayish-green with an overlay of minute fibrils or squamules concolorous with the cap. The partial veil forms a skirt-like ring on the upper stem. This ring is fragile, white to pale olive-yellow with fine striations on the upper part

LOOK-ALIKES

Amanita mappa ss auct. southeast from Florida

Amanita porphyria   *Photo by Richard Morrison*

Amanita gioiosa from Spain

LOOK-ALIKES

Amanita fulva from Mass.

Amanita brunnescens from Mass.

where it had pressed against the gills. The large saccate volva at the base of the stem has an irregularly lobed margin with an extended "limb" on one side. The interior can be olive tinged. It can be loosely attached to the substrate and left behind when picked.

The spores are white in deposit and amyloid in Melzer's solution. They are subglobose to ellipsoid and measure 7–12.8 x 5.5–10.2 μm. The odor is described as pleasant at first, but nauseous in age. It progresses from faded roses to raw potatoes to chlorine to ammonia. The taste described by victims was excellent.

Several tests have been developed with reagents to reveal the poisonous amatoxins in Amanitas. One of these is the Meixner Test. You start by squeezing a drop of uncooked Amanita juice onto a newspaper. Then circle the wet spot with a pen. Dry it with a hair dryer. When you add a drop of hydrochloric acid to the spot, the paper will turn blue. This indicates the presence of deadly amatoxins. The blue color derives from the interaction of the toxins with the lignin in the newspaper. No other kind of paper will work. This information comes from Jenkins, who further assures that dried specimens reconstituted in absolute methanol can also provide the bluing reaction.

A specific test for **Amanita phalloides** is the application of sulfuric acid to the gills. They turn lilac to purple, which separates paler forms of the species from the white **Amanita verna**, another deadly species.

Amanita phalloides was first described by Vaillant from the south of France in 1727. Across the Atlantic it now ranges from Morocco and Algeria north to the southern regions of Scandinavia. It has been found in Russia, Turkey, Iran, India, and Nepal, but whether it has been introduced to these countries via imported trees or not is not known to me. Dr. Else Vellinga and Anne Pringle performed DNA studies on three different populations of **Amanita phalloides** from Europe in an attempt to discover the origins of the California Death Caps. They studied specimens from lower Scandinavia, the south of France, and Corsica. One haplotype restricted to southern France and another restricted to Denmark and southern Norway were both found in California populations. Herb Saylor speculated that the first Amanita mycelium to arrive in California might have come over with cork oak imported for the wine industry. If cork oak grows in the south of France, this would make sense.

As one can imagine, there is no end to the list of look-alikes that have fooled people in the past. In the literature, species mentioned have been **Agaricus sylvicola**, **Agaricus campestris**, **Macrolepiota procera**, **Leucoagaricus leucothites**, **Melanoleuca cnista**, **Russula brevipes**, **Russula cyanoxantha**, **Tricholoma columbetta**, and **Volvariella volvacea**. A more sinister list is that of those who have succumbed to the Death Cap while believing they were eating the following: **Amanita calyptroderma**, **Amanita** fulva, **Amanita vernicoccora**, **Russula virescens**, **Tricholoma equestre**, **Tricholoma portentosum**, and **Volvariella volvacea**.

Following is a list of these look-alikes and how they differ from **Amanita phalloides**:

Agaricus campestris: Has pinkish gills and dark brown spores. The only possible confusion would be the whitish cap with **Amanita phalloides var. alba**, the white version of the Death Cap, now synonymized in Index Fungorum with the Death Cap.

Amanita brunnescens: Differs by having gray-brown caps with radially fibrillose striations, stems that bruise red-brown, and an emarginate basal bulb with a cleft on one side. Rumored to be edible, I know of no one who has tried it.

Amanita brunnescens var. pallida: Has whitish to pale olive-brown caps that resemble the Death Cap even more. Neither of these have the saccate volva at the stem base, a main feature of the Death Cap. Reported to have a strong odor of raw potatoes.

Amanita calyptroderma: A principle source of confusion, the popular Coccora has been responsible for deaths in California. Normally a bronze to orange-brown species, the caps can become tinged with olive, thereby leading to a misidentification with **A. phalloides**. It often appears at the same time and in the same places as the Death Cap.

Amanita vernicoccora: This is the springtime version of the Coccora. The caps are pale orange-tan color to olive-gray, and therefore even more

Amanita brunnescens var. pallida from Me.   *Photo by Richard Morrison*

Leucoagaricus leucothites

Volvariella volvacea from B.C.   *Photo by Fred Notzel*

Volvopluteus gloiocephalus; white form (from Calif.) on the right.

likely to confuse people. Known from California and Oregon. Differs from the Death Cap by its inamyloid spores.

Amanita mappa (formerly **A. citrina**): Has pale straw colored caps, often with a faint greenish tinge. They differ from the Death Cap by their emarginate basal bulb, a pale yellow ring, and lack of a saccate volva. (Rod Tulloss has informed me that our North American counterparts will need new names.)

Amanita fulva: Differs by its more slender stature, lack of a ring, orange-brown caps, and thin saccate volva that clings to the stem base.

Amanita gemmata: Perhaps the most widespread of all North American Amanitas, this ochre-capped Amanita is also reported as poisonous. It differs from the Death Cap by its ochre caps, white warts, and rings of velar material at the base of the stem instead of a saccate volva. It is eaten in southern France but causes gastrointestinal disturbances elsewhere.

Amanita porphyria: Differs by having dark gray-brown caps, a gray ring at mid-stem, and a collared rim at the top of the basal bulb. Manjon, Moreno, & Zugaza claim it is edible but mediocre.

Amanita gioiosa: A European species that differs by its brown caps and shallow, disappearing warts.

Floccularia pitkinensis: This southwestern Floccularia has tan to brown colored caps and cream colored gills that become pale yellow when mature. Differs from the Death Cap by the rolled up ring on the stem and the lack of a saccate volva.

Macrolepiota procera: An excellent edible that differs from the Death Cap by its brown papillate umbo, brownish cap scales, and slender stem with a chevron pattern of squamules, and no velar material at the base. The New England version of this taxon lacks the chevron pattern of scales on the stipe.

Leucoagaricus leucothites: Formerly known as **Lepiota naucina**, this all-white species of field and lawn could only be confused with white forms of the Death Cap. It has a ring and free gills, but no velar material at the stem base.

Melanoleuca subalpina: Formerly known in error as **Melanoleuca cnista**, this cream colored Melanoleuca with a pale ochre disc, attached gills, and bald stem looks nothing like **A. phalloides**, but is mentioned as a source of confusion in the literature.

Russula aeruginea: Differs by having pale yellow spores, a chalk-like stem, attached gills, and no velar material whatsoever. The greenish caps have caused confusions.

Russula cyanoxantha: Differs by its slate gray-blue to slate gray-green caps often tinged with lilac, the chalk-like stem, and no volval material.

Russula cyanoxantha var. cutefracta: Has

mottled olive colored caps. Nothing else about it is Amanitoid.

Russula cyanoxantha form peltereaui: A green-capped variety of the normally multicolored **Russula cyanoxantha**.

Russula graminea: A Northwest species with olive-green caps that differs by its ochreyellow spores.

Russula virescens: Reputed to be the best tasting of all Russulas, this one has gray-green caps with areolate cracks. All of these Russulas are brittle and will shatter when thrown against a tree. This won't happen with the Death cap.

Tricholoma equestre: Has a long history of being confused with the Death Cap in Europe. Also known as Man on Horseback, it has pale yellow gills and cap colors varying from pale olive-gray to dark brown to pale rusty-brown, but mainly differs by having attached and sinuate gills. Previously considered a good edible, it has recently caused deaths in Poland and France. DNA sequencing may point to an unforeseen variety to be the culprit.

Tricholoma auratum: A European species that looks like a larger, fleshier **Tricholoma equestre**. It also has recently been aligned with deaths in Europe, so confusion with the Death Cap is a moot point. It is now considered a synonym of **T. equestre**.

Tricholoma davisiae: Another Tricholoma with grayish-olive caps and questionable edibility. All of these Tricholomas differ from Amanitas by having attached gills.

Tricholoma intermedium: Another potential source of confu-

LOOK-ALIKES

Macrolepiota procera ss auct. northeast from Vermont

Agaricus campestris from Antelope Island, Utah

Tricholoma yatesii from Calif.

LOOK-ALIKES

Floccularia pitkinensis from Colo.

Russula 'aeruginea'

Russula graminea

sion because it looks just like Man on Horseback except with white gills, not yellow.

Tricholoma yatesii: A Californian Tricholoma with brighter yellow gills and greenish yellow caps found with live oak.

Tricholoma portentosum: A fine edible species that has been mentioned in the literature as having been confused with the Death Cap. Its viscid, purple-black streaked caps with yellowish margins, and lack of a ring or any velar material on the stem base make it difficult to believe it has been confused for the Death Cap.

Tricholoma subsejunctum: Has olive-yellow caps with blackish fibrillose streaks running radially from disc to margin. Thought to be poisonous. No velar material to cause confusions.

Some other North American Tricholomas with olive-ochre to yellowish-gray caps are **T. aestuans, T. arvernense, T. floridanum, T. olivaceobrunneum, T. quercophilus, T. palustre, T. subluteum**, and **T. tumidum**. None have velar material on cap or stem.

Volvopluteus gloiocephalus: This West Coast taxon can have white, gray, or tan colored caps. Although the free, white gills and sack-like volva mimic the Death Cap, the gills will eventually turn pink from the spores. This feature, along with the absence of a ring, separate it from the Death Cap.

Volvariella volvacea: Mostly known from the Gulf States and the Southeast, this mushroom has been confused with the Death Cap by foragers who think it is a relative of the edible Paddy Straw mushrooms of Southeast Asia. **V. volvacea** differs from the Death Cap by its dark-brown streaked caps, gray-brown volval sack, and pink spores.

Death from amatoxins will probably never evolve into a popular form of suicide. It is almost too gruesome to describe. Rather than try to amalgamate all the symptoms recorded from reading forty guides, I will reproduce the symptom descriptions from Duhem & Courtecuisse for the sake of simplicity.

"Symptoms appear from 6–12 hours after ingestion. The first symptoms consist of difficulty in breathing, dizziness, and vague discomfort. These are followed by a stage of acute gastroenteritis with violent and painful vomiting, severe cholera-like diarrhea, evil smelling and abundant, and signs of intense dehydration. If nothing is done, death by cardiovascular collapse may occur at this stage. This phase lasts for three or four days followed by a period of apparent but deceptive remission. The patient may resume his normal activities. The next stage is liver failure. This actually began in the first 24 hours and developed over several days. Signs of this attack, present very early and then weakening, can be detected by biochemical analysis. In severe cases the patient experiences severe pain, and a hepatomegaly may occur. Extremely severe liver poisoning leads to death."

But this is not all. Ammirati et al. point out that during acute liver necrosis, the white blood cell count can reach 25,000 or more. If the patient

LOOK-ALIKES

Russula virescens from Mass.

Russula cyanoxantha from Tibet

survives the liver ordeal, he must then deal with kidney failure. Amatoxin destroys cells in the kidney tubules. "Symptoms such as high blood urea, oliguria-anuria, high serum potassium, low serum sodium, acidosis, septicemia, internal bleeding, and pulmonary edema are seen." After 12 days secondary dysfunctions set in. These can be lesions in the pancreas and/or lesions in the heart muscle tissue.

Experts have disagreed on how long it takes victims to die. While Duhem & Courtecuisse claim no less than six days, I've read another account where the patient died after 57 hours from time of ingestion. (This is still far behind the length of time after eating **Galerina sulcipes** of Indonesia, which holds the world record at 7 hours.)

There is still no instant cure, just better knowledge on how to proceed. This knowledge was obtained through trial and error over centuries. To encapsulate the history we can start with the rabbit, the squirrel, and the slug. All of these creatures could eat the Death Cap with impunity. As E.A. Ellis put it in 1976, "Black and great spotted slugs feed avidly on the Death Cap, yet take no harm." Nonetheless, since rabbits were an already acceptable food source, early experiments involved ingesting ground up rabbit stomachs

LOOK-ALIKES

Tricholoma sejunctum

Tricholoma davisiae

Tricholoma portentosum   *Photo by Richard Morrison*

and brains in the raw. The author reported some success but no revealing percentages or other details. The next offering was a serum obtained from immunizing horses. The side effects were not pleasant. By the 1970s, however, more sophisticated "cures" arrived. A Dr. Bastien of France developed a "cocktail" consisting of ascorbic acid, nifuroazide, and abiocine. He advertised this product in 1981 by consuming 70 grams of the Death Cap in Geneva, and survived!

Meanwhile in Britain it was discovered that by filtering the blood through a device containing charcoal, liver failure was prevented. In China, lives were saved when victims were treated with standard penicillin and reduced glutathione combined with doses of **Ganoderma lucidum** pills.

Another breakthrough occurred in Europe when large doses of penicillin G were added to thioctic acid, glucose, vitamin K, and corticosteroids. According to Lincoff & Mitchel, the penicillin G prevented the amanitins from "hitching a ride onto other substances that are recycled through the bloodstream after passing through the kidneys. The amanitins then pass out of the body through the kidneys without causing damage."

Then seemingly out of the blue, a major breakthrough occurred from a most unlikely source: the milkweed thistle. It was discovered that silymarin and silibinin, both of them extracts from the milk thistle, interfered with the uptake of amanitin into the hepatic cells and thus interrupted the enterohepatic recirculation of the amatoxin.

By 1994 great strides had been made in treatments. Speed is of the essence. The best possible scenario is to treat the patient before the vomiting and diarrhea commence. One indication of the severity of the toxin is the rapidity of the onset of these symptoms. If they come on quickly it means a larger amount of the Death Cap was ingested which in turn implies more toxin. The first step is a gastric lavage immediately followed by doses of cathartics and activated charcoal. The charcoal interrupts the enterohepatic circulation. According to Spoerke & Rumack, hemodialysis and hemoperfusion are then advisable. If caught early enough, even victims who have hogged out on Death Caps can survive. The main aim of any treatment is to prevent the amatoxins from getting absorbed by the liver. This is what silibinin does. Penicillin G does the same thing, but Spoerke & Rumack caution against using the two together since cerebral convulsions could occur.

According to Jacqueline Seymour even the spores of **Amanita phalloides** are deadly. This must have been news to Dr. Harry Thiers. There was one afternoon at his field camp in the Sierra Nevadas when he convened a group of us paying guests in a forest glade near the camp. While a magical sunbeam enveloped Harry in light, the rest of us formed a half circle in front of him. He had something important to share with us. While we watched, he extracted a fresh Death Cap from a bag he carried with him.

LOOK-ALIKES

Tricholoma intermedium

Tricholoma equestre   *Photo by Richard Morrison*

He had brought it all the way from San Francisco. Then after holding it up so everyone could see it, he bit off a chunk. His lieutenant, Herb Saylor, beamed out at us. Then Harry carefully started to chew. Eyes bulged in disbelief. Women sagged against trees. Men winced. Herb just kept on smiling. Finally, Harry spat out the Death Cap. He pulled out his canteen and rinsed. He rinsed about three times before attempting speech.

"You see," he explained, "You can conduct the taste test on any poisonous mushroom as long as you spit it all out afterwards."

He had been careful to incline his head forward so no juices would flow down his throat. He was a natural showman. Mycology may never see another quite like him.

If he had swallowed, he would have had to go through the steps. The first move is to rid the body of the mushroom. The next is to drink a glass of salt water every half hour until you reach the hospital. Repetitive stomach rinses are called for to flush out any material clinging to the mucous membranes. The next step is to replenish the fluids and mineral substances lost in the vomiting process. In the 1980s you would receive infusions of sorbite solutions containing large doses of thioctic acid along with vitamins B and C. It was more effective if injected with glucose to combat the effects of low blood sugar. In the 1990s you would switch to silibinin and charcoal.

A cure could be on the horizon. It could be silipide, a relatively new complex of silymarin from milk thistle and lecithin. Both specifically target the liver. An IV of 20–50 mg daily would be an approximate dose. Sold under the name Siliphos, it is available over the counter and orally bioavailable. Clinical trials for humans are still being awaited.

Ironically, very low doses of **Amanita phalloides** have been useful in treating paralysis, jaundice, and acute yellow liver atrophy. Robert Rogers adds further that "it is also useful in paralysis or conditions with progressive physical deterioration."

Finally, Rogers writes that "Amanitin in a 2D solution has been helpful against leukemia." (I have no idea what a 2D solution is, but feel it worth reporting anyway.) This is because it stops the activity of the tumor cells, causing them to lyse and migrate. Similar results have occurred with colon, breast, and tongue root cancer.

I lost a good friend to a malignant tongue root tumor. Too bad we didn't know about this amanitin homeopathic solution at the time.

BIBLIOGRAPHY

Joe Ammirati, J.A. Traquair, & Paul Horgen, *Poisonous Mushrooms of the Northern US and Canada*, 1985. University of Minn. Press, Minneapolis, Minn.

David Arora, *Mushrooms Demystified*, 1986. Ten Speed press, Berkeley, Calif.

Anna Bazzicalupo, B. Buyck, I. Saar, J. Vauras, D. Carmean, & M. Berbee, *Troubles with Mycorrhizal Mushroom Identification where Morphological Differentiation Lags Behind Barcode Sequence Divergence* in *Taxon* 66 (791–810), 2017.

Denis Benjamin, *Mushrooms, Poisons, and Panaceas*, 1995. W.H. Freeman, New York, NY.

Alan & Arleen Bessette, William Roody, & Steve Trudel, *Tricholomas of North America*, 2013. University of Texas Press, Austin, Texas.

Michael Beug, *Amatoxin Poisoning in North America*, 2015-2016. www.namyco.org.

Michael Beug, *Worldwide Mushroom Poisoning, Diagnosis and Treatment: Comments on Some of the Recent Research* in *Fungi, Vol.2, No.3*, 2009.

Marcel Bon, *The Mushrooms and Toadstools of Britain and Northwestern Europe*, 1987. Hodder & Stoughton, London.

J. Breitenbach & F. Kranzlin, *Fungi of Switzerland, Vol.4*, 1995. Edition Mykologie, Lucerne, Switzerland.

Francisco de Diego Calonge, *Setas*, 1979. Ediciones Mundi-Prensa, Madrid.

Regis Courtecuisse & Bernard Duhem, *Collins' Field Guide to Mushrooms and Toadstools of Britain and Europe*, 1995. Harper-Collins, London.

E.A. Ellis, *British Fungi: Book 1*, 1976. Jarrold Colour Publications, Norwich, England.

J. Garcia, V. Costa, A. Carvalho, F. Carvalho, R. Silvestre, J. Duarte, D. Dourado, M. Arbo, T. Baltazar, R. Dinis-Oliveira, P. Baptista, & M. de Lourdes Bastos, *A Breakthrough on Amanita phalloides poisoning: An Effective Antidotal Effect by Polymyxin B* in *Archives of Toxicology* 89, Issue 12 (2305–2323), 2015.

Verne Ovid Graham, *Mushrooms of the Great Lakes Region*, 1944. Dover Publications, New York, NY.

J. Walton Groves, *Edible and Poisonous Mushrooms of Canada*, 1979. Research Branch, Agriculture, Ottawa, Canada.

Helmut & Renate Grünert, *Field Guide to Mushrooms of Britain and Europe*, 1991. Crowood Press, Wiltshire, England.

H.T. Gussow & W.S. Odell, *Mushrooms and Toadstools*, 1927. Dominion Experimental Farms, Division of Botany, Ottawa, Canada.

Karen & Richard Haard, *Poisonous and Hallucinogenic Mushrooms*, 1977. Cloudburst Press, Seattle, Wash.

Ian Hall, Steven Stephenson, Peter Buchanan, Wang Yun & Anthony Cole, *Edible and Poisonous Mushrooms of the World*, 2003. Timber Press, Portland, Ore.

Miron Hard, *Mushrooms, Edible and Otherwise*, 1908. Dover publications, New York, NY.

David Hawksworth, *Trouble Over Cap Colors and Species Concepts in Russula* in *Fungus* 8 (61-62), 2017.

David Jenkins, *Amanita of North America*, 1986. Mad River Press, Eureka, Calif.

Calvin Kauffman, *The Agaricaceae of Michigan*, 1918. Michigan Geological and Biological Survey, Lansing, Mich.

Henning Knudsen, Juhani Ruotsalainen, & Jukka Vauras, *Russula in Funga Nordica*, 2012. Nordsvamp, Copenhagen.

Louis C.C. Krieger, *The Mushroom Handbook*, 1967. Dover Publications, New York, NY.

Gary Lincoff, *The Audubon Field Guide to North American Mushrooms*, 1981. Alfred A. Knopf, New York, NY.

Gary Lincoff & D.H. Mitchel, *Toxic and Hallucinogenic Mushroom Poisoning*, 1977. Van Nostrand Reinhold, Co., New York, NY.

Janet Lindgren, *Trial Key to Amanita Species in the Pacific Northwest*, 1998. Pacific Northwest Key Council, Seattle, Wash.

Vincent Marteka, *Mushrooms: Wild and Edible*, 1980. W.W. Norton, New York, NY.

Charles McIlvaine & Richard Macadam, *One Thousand American Fungi*, 1902. Revised and reprinted, 1973, Dover Publications, New York, NY.

Margaret McKenny, Joe, Ammirati, & Daniel Stuntz, *The New Savory Wild Mushroom*, 1987. University of Washington Press, Seattle, Wash.

Kent & Vera McKnight, *Peterson Field Guides: Mushrooms*, 1987. Houghton Mifflin Co., Boston, Mass.

Orson & Hope Miller, *Mushrooms in Color*, 1980. E.P. Dutton, New York, NY.

Gabriel Moreno, Jose Luis Manjon, & Alvaro Zugaza, *La Guia de Incafo de Iso Hongos de la Peninsula Iberica, Tome II*, 1986. Incafo, S.A., Madrid.

Meinhard Moser, *Keys to Agarics and Boleti,* 1983. Translated and published by Roger Phillips, London.

Jean-Marie Polese, *The Pocket Guide to Mushrooms*, 2005. Tandem Verlag, Chamalieres, France.

Anne Pringle & Elsie Vellinga, *Last Chance to Know? Using Literature to Explore the Biogeography and Invasion Biology of the Death Cap Mushroom Amanita phalloides (Vaillant ex Fries ex Fries) Link in Biological Invasions* 8 (1131-1144), 2006.

Anne Pringle, Rachel Adams, Hugh Cross, & Thomas Bruns, *The ectomycorrhizal fungus Amanita phalloides was introduced and is expanding its range on the west coast of North America* in *Molecular Ecology* 18, Issue 5 (817-833), 2009.

John Ramsbottom, *Larger British Fungi*, 1965. Trustees of the British Museum, London.

Augusto Rinaldi & Vassili Tyndalo, *The Complete Book of Mushrooms*, 1974. Crown Publishers, New York, NY.

Robert Rogers, *The Fungal Pharmacy*, 2011. North Atlantic Books, Berkeley, Calif.

Jacqueline Seymour, *Mushrooms and Toadstools*, 1974. Crescent Books, New York, NY.

N. Siegel & C. Schwarz, *Mushrooms of the Redwood Coast*, 2017. Ten Speed Press, Berkeley, Cal.

A.H. Smith, *A Field Guide to Western Mushrooms*, 1975. University of Michigan Press, Ann Arbor, Mich.

A.H. Smith & Nancy Weber, *The Mushroom Hunters' Field Guide*, 1980. Univ. of Michigan Press, Ann Arbor, Mich.

David Spoerke & Barry Rumack, *Handbook of Mushroom Poisoning: Diagnosis and Treatment*, 1994. CRC Press, Boca Raton, Florida.

Mirko Svrcek, *The Hamlyn Book of Mushrooms and Fungi*, 1983. Artia, Prague, Czechoslovakia.

Harry Thiers, *The Agaricales of California: Amanitaceae*, 1982. Mad River Press, Eureka, Calif.

William Sturgis Thomas, *Field Book of Common Mushrooms*, 1928. G.P. Putnam's Sons, New York, NY.

Rod Tulloss, Steven Stephenson, R.P. Bhatt, & Ashok Kumar *Studies in Amanita in West Virginia and Adjacent Areas of the Mid-Appalachians* in *Mycotaxon* 56 (243-293), 1995.

Nancy Turner & Adam Szczawinski, *Common Poisonous Plants and Mushrooms of North America*, 1991. Timber Press, Portland, Ore.

Else Vellinga, *Toxic Amanitas* in *Fungi*, Vol.2, No.2 (18-19), 2009.

Elsie Wakefield, *The Observer's Book of Common Fungi*, 1964. Frederick Warne & Co., London.

Benjamin Wolfe & Anne Pringle, *Geographically Structured Host Specificity is Caused by the Range Expansions and Host Shifts of a Symbiotic Fungus* in *International Society for Microbial Ecology* 4 (745–755), 2011.

Benjamin Wolfe, F. Richard, Hugh Cross, & Anne Pringle, *Distribution and Abundance of the Introduced Ectomycorrhizal Fungus Amanita phalloides in North America* in *New Phytologist* 185 (803-816), 2010.

Amanita gioiosa: amanitaceae.org/?Amanita+gioiosa

Amanita smithiana Bas

The flavor of Amanita smithiana gives you no warning of the doom that lies ahead.

Amanita smithiana, one of our most beautiful autumn mushrooms, may arguably be the most dangerous native mushroom in Whatcom County, until **Amanita phalloides** arrived here in 2010. I saw only one at the Stimpson Family Nature Reserve in 1992, none for the two previous years, but two showed up in the fall of 1993 at the presentation to the local Audubon Society. According to Dutch Amanita expert, Cornelis Bas, who authored the species, Alexander Smith reported it first from Olympic Hot Springs on October 2, 1941. He then found it again in the Mt. Hood National Forest in 1947. Once Bas was able to separate it from **Amanita solitaria** of Europe and **Amanita chlorinosma** from the eastern United States, he was able to name it after Dr. Smith and introduce it to the world.

The problem with identifying **Amanita smithiana** is that it changes its appearance as it matures. The cap, which can get up to 17 cm wide, is at first whitish to ivory and tacky when moist but satiny when dry. As it ages it can acquire an overlay of pyramidal pale brown scales that soon become flattened. In moist weather the universal veil is usually whitish but can become tan to brownish in dry, warm weather, thus explaining the peculiar tan cap scales in some aged specimens. The cap margins are normally white appendiculate with hanging veil remnants.

The stipe, too, can change as the species ages. As you can see from the photo, young specimens have floccose to squamulose zones of white velar material adorning the length of the stem. In age, these squamulose bands can vanish, leaving a smooth white stem with a pruinose apex occasionally streaked with fibrils that can become brownish. And what is even more disconcerting, the gills can be free or adnate, setting up confusion with matsutakes and Tricholomas in general.

So how, then, can we be sure it's an Amanita? In the case of **Amanita smithiana** it is best to look at the base of the stem. Here you will find a more or less fusiform (spindle-shaped) bulb with broken rings of irregular warts from the universal veil at the top of the bulb. This bulb usually tapers into a long root, which is known as a radicating base. So if you are out in the mountains and hear a sharp snap as you pull up your matsutake, you've probably broken off the rooting base of **Amanita smithiana**. The West Coast matsutake, also known as **Tricholoma murrillianum**, does not have a turnip shaped rooting base. According to Steve Trudell, the matsutake also differs by its firmer flesh and more massive stature. Fortunately, there is an easier way to tell them apart. The matsutake has a spicy, fragrant odor whereas **Amanita smithiana** has no odor when fresh, and a sickening chlorine to rotten yeast odor when old. Besides the matsutake it can be confused with a number of look-alikes in both Amanita and Tricholoma. Here they are in no particular order:

Amanita silvicola: Differs from most other Amanitas by having adnate gills. It has a rounded basal bulb and usually a broad, flat patch of white velar material on the cap. If not for the velar patch and the basal bulb it would look like a large white Tricholoma, which one might be tempted to eat. It differs from **Amanita smithiana** also by the lack of a rooting stem base, a shorter, stockier stature,

LOOK-ALIKE

Tricholoma murrillianum — the West Coast matsutake

Amanita muscaria var. alba ss auct. northwest

Amanita silvicola

Amanita alba from Spain

and the adnate gill attachment. They both can have a white cottony cap surface.

Amanita muscaria var. alba: Differs by its volval rings at the stem base, the solitary ring that collapses against the stem, and the stem that turns yellowish when bruised.

Amanita subcokeri nom. prov.: East Coast aficionados have long urged Rod to publish this magnificent Amanita. The cap surface differs from that of **A. smithiana** by its raised white warts, and instead of cottony belts on the stipe, it has the remnants of the partial veil that became disengaged from the cap margin.

Amanita alba: Differs by its adnate gills, smooth caps with grooved margins, and saccate volva.

Amanita magniverrucata: Differs by its compacted pyramidal warts on the cap surface, and smoother stem decorated by a flimsy ring that easily shears off. Known from California, caps can reach 25 cm in width.

Amanita longipes: An East Coast look-alike that differs by its longer stem in relation to cap width and its densely granular cap surface. It prefers sandy soils under pine and oak.

Amanita subsolitaria: Another East Coast Amanita that has migrated north from Florida. It has a smoother cap than **A. smithiana**, with random warts or patches. Caps can be pinkish gray at disc.

Amanita cokeri: Has large, random pyramidal warts and a rooting stem base.

Amanita chlorinosma: Differs by its chloride of lime odor and a powdery white cap with volval patches on the disc.

Saproamanita thiersii: Another entirely shaggy, all-white Amanita, which only appears on lawns, is spreading northeastwards from Texas at an alarming rate.

Amanita strobiliformis: The closest European look-alike, caps of this taxon can reach 20 cm wide. It is an all-white species with equally shaggy caps, but the velar material on the caps does not turn brownish in age. It has a mildly pleasant odor and taste, and according to Peter Jordan, is edible. The name **Amanita solitaria** has been much confused with it in the past.

Tricholoma caligatum: Could only be confused with older specimens of **Amanita smithiana**, whose velar material turns brown in age. It also differs by its non-rooting stem base and dark cinnamon colored velar material on the stem.

Amanita smithiana has other features that might help identify it. The loose, floccose velar material on fresh caps separates it from other Amanitas. The cap margins are usually white appendiculate. The gills can be tinged pinkish buff and have fimbriate edges. According to Bas, the shorter lamellulae have truncate endings, the longer ones attenuate. The stems are equal or taper towards the apex. They can run from 6–18 cm long with a basal bulb up to 5 cm thick. Janet Lindgren mentions that the rooting end is rarely collected, which implies that it breaks off during the collecting of it. The floccose material on cap and stem can wash off in rain. This

LOOK-ALIKES

Amanita longipes from Mass.

Amanita subsolitaria from Mass.

is a big problem because then it more resembles the matsutake. The taste is mild and the spores are white and amyloid.

According to Rod Tulloss, it ranges from Idaho south to southern California and New Mexico. It has also been reported from British Columbia, Arizona, and the Mexican highlands. Besides coastal Douglas fir, hemlock, and spruce, it has been found with larch, oak, and manzanita. Here in Whatcom County it has showed up year after year at the Doran Road site close to Acme, but this fabulous mushroom area has long been clear cut by the Trillium Company, and it is having a hard time coming back.

Microscopically, the spores are thin-walled, broadly elliptic, and measure 8.7–12 x 5.8–7.8 µm. The pileipellis consists of interwoven hyphae, slightly gelatinized. Dr. Thiers calls this an ixotrichodermeum. The gill trama is of bilateral, inflated hyphae. The

LOOK-ALIKES

Amanita subcokeri nom. prov. from Mass.

Tricholoma caligatum from Virginia

subhymenium is ramose with occasional clamps. The basidia are 4-spored, measure 50–70 x 3–13 μm, and are clamped at the bases. The cheilocystidia are saccate to clavate and measure 20–40 x 12–35 μm. And the universal veil is composed of interwoven hyphae with numerous globose to clavate sphaerocysts 23–45 μm wide. We can acknowledge Dr. Thiers and Dr. Jenkins for this information.

Amanita smithiana attacks the tubes in the kidneys. According to Dr. Beug in his *Poisonous and Hallucinogenic Mushrooms* the toxins are thought to be 2-amino-3-cyclopropylbutanoic acid and/or 2-amino-4, 5-hexadienoic acid. In another report entitled *Thirty-Plus Years of Mushroom Poisoning: Summary of the Approximately 2,000 Reports in the NAMA Case Registry,* authors Beug, Shaw, & Cochran name allenic norleucine as the toxin involved. They speculate that it is probably bound to a sugar in the mushroom. "A second compound, chlorocrotylglycine, may also be toxic." The symptoms resemble those of orellanine poisoning, but they come on faster, sometimes only 4–11 hours after ingestion. Vomiting, diarrhea, abdominal pain, nausea, and inability to urinate comprise the syndrome. Chills, cramps, disorientation, malaise, weakness, sweating, thirst, warm feelings, polyurea, and oliguria have also been reported. Beug reports that it has caused at least one death and more than 14 kidney poisonings. One patient also lost liver function. Kidney failure occurs 5–6 days after ingestion. To add to the complications, Janet Lindgren reports that **Amanita smithiana** "gives a positive red-violet reaction with syringaldazine, indicating the presence of laccase, an enzyme that breaks down lignin." Whether this has any additional affect on the victims is not known.

Allenic norleucine is also present in **Amanita abrupta**. Other Amanitas that cause renal failure are **Amanita proxima** of Spain and **Amanita pseudoporphyria** of Japan.

Authors Lindgren, West, & Horowitz outline for us a case study. A 55 year-old male ate three raw specimens of **Amanita smithiana** in a salad. Within 6 hours he had severe nausea and vomiting. Treatment began with N-acetyl cysteine, penicillin, and milk thistle extract. The patient developed acute renal failure despite these medications. Dialysis started on the fourth day with a creatinine of 6.5 mg/dl, which increased on the seventh day to 10.2 mg/dl. This worked. The man was discharged on the tenth day for outpatient hemodialysis. This procedure continued for several weeks until creatinine returned to normal and urine output resumed.

The flavor of **Amanita smithiana** gives you no warning of the doom that lies ahead. A victim in 1976 described a young specimen fried in butter as having "a superb flavor which was somewhat raphanoid (like radish)." The older specimens were a bit bitter.

Many guides list it as "edibility unknown." Now, thanks to a few hapless souls who misidentified their matsutakes, we all know better.

BIBLIOGRAPHY

David Arora, *Mushrooms Demystified*, 1986. Ten Speed Press, Berkeley, Calif.

Cornelis Bas, *Morphology and Subdivision of Amanita and a Monograph on its Section Lepidella* in *Persoonia* 5 (285–579), 1969.

Denis Benjamin, *Mushrooms—Poisons and Panaceas*, 1985. W. H. Freeman, New York, NY.

Michael Beug, *Poisonous and Hallucinogenic Mushrooms*. http://academic.evergreen.edu/projects/mushrooms/phm/

Michael Beug, Marilyn Shaw, & Kenneth Cochran, *Thirty-Plus Years of Mushroom Poisoning: Summary of the Approximately 2,000 Reports in the NAMA Case Registry. McIlvainea 16 (2) Fall 2006.* https://namyco.org/docs/Poisonings30year.pdf

Britt Bunyard & Jay Justice, *Amanitas of North America,* 2020. Published by The Fungi Press, Batavia, Ill.

Vincent Danel & Philippe Saviuc, *New Syndromes in Mushroom Poisoning* in *Toxicological Reviews* 25, Issue 3 (119–209), 2006.

David Jenkins, *Amanita in North America*, 1986. Mad River Press, Eureka, Calif.

Peter Jordan, *The Encyclopedia of Fungi of Britain and Europe*, 1988. David & Charles, Newton Abbot, England.

Michael Kuo, *Amanita smithiana*. MushroomExpert.com

Gary Lincoff, *The Audubon Society Field Guide to North American Mushrooms*, 1981. Alfred A. Knopf, New York, NY.

Janet Lindgren, *Trial Key to Amanita Species in the Pacific Northwest*, 1998. Pacific Northwest Key Council, Seattle, Wash.

Mykoweb.com, *Amanita smithiana*.

Harry Thiers, *The Agaricales of California: Amanitaceae*, 1982. Mad River Press, Eureka, Calif.

Steve Trudell & Joe Ammirati, *Mushrooms of the Pacific Northwest*, 2009. Timber Press, Portland, Ore.

Rod Tulloss, *Keys to Amanita*, 2003–2009. http://amanitaceae.com/?Keys+and+Checklists

Rod Tulloss & Jan Lindgren, *Amanita Smithiana–Taxonomy, Distribution, and Poisonings* in *Mycotaxon* 45 (373–387), 1992.

P.L. West, Jan Lindgren, & B.Z. Horowitz, *Amanita Smithiana Ingestion: A Case of Delayed Renal Failure and Literature Review*, 2009. https://www.ncbi.nlm.nih.gov/pubmed/19191214

Wikipedia.com, *Amanita smithiana*

Ampulloclitocybe clavipes (Pers. ex Fr.) Redhead, Lutzoni, Moncalvo & Vilgalys

East and West Coast collections appear to differ in stature.

Ampulloclitocybe clavipes from Vermont

Do not be alarmed. This is just the latest genus for the cosmopolitan, attractive, club-footed species known in all your popular guides as **Clitocybe clavipes**. Almost every fall season here in the Pacific Northwest, we run into large fruitings of this brown-capped Clitocyboid species with a consistently clavate base. We have all seen it but have not tried to eat it due to possible confusion with other brown-capped Clitocybes in the area. I had always heard that it was a good edible species. When I spotted it for sale in a Maryland market in June 2009, for $43 a pound (the same price as fresh morels), I felt it was time to take a bite. They were being sold under the name of "Club Foot," and they looked like stout little brown hour glasses with white decurrent gills.

One of the problems has been the difference in stature between East Coast and West Coast specimens. Typical **Ampulloclitocybe clavipes** has been depicted as a large, fleshy mushroom with a thick, clavate stem base that can get up to 4 cm wide. The photo above depicts the normal version from Vermont. Our West Coast version is a lot slimmer. So much so that it won't key out in Bigelow's monograph entitled *North American Species of Clitocybe, Part I.* Because option number 10 gives us a choice between "Pileus and stipe large, fleshy" or "Basidiocarp not with combination of charac-

ters above,"one ends up on the rocks further in the key. It is difficult for any key to absorb all the idiosyncrasies of one species within a larger group. At the end of his description Bigelow takes care of the problem by writing, "Many collections made in the Pacific northwestern states have a slenderer stature and are more apt to have a fruity odor than the specimens found in the Midwest and Northeast. The other features of the basidiocarp are identical." One sentence can make a world of difference, and where it can be found in the key can be even more of a factor in tracking down the species.

Caps are usually described as 2–9 cm wide, gray-brown to ochre-brown, sometimes with an olive tinge. They are plane and broadly umbonate becoming shallowly depressed in age. Cap margins are incurved but not inrolled. There is often a whitish band at the margin. The caps are neither striate nor hygrophanous. They are smooth, greasy to subviscid in wet weather and felty in dry. The context is thicker and spongy at disc. The entire fruiting body can become saturated with water in rainy weather and be squeezed like a sponge. The gills are long decurrent, often forked and intervenose, white at first, then yellowish buff in age. Stems are 3 ½ to 6 ½ cm long and up to 1 cm thick at the apex and 4 cm wide at the clavate base. They are the same color as the cap but a

Ampulloclitocybe avellaneialba

bit paler and fibrillose streaked. The base is often covered with white tomentum. The odor is often fruity like grape bubblegum or cherry bark. Kuyper, Vellinga, & Noordeloos wrote that the odor is like iris. The taste is mild or slightly acidulous when saturated with water, and the spores white in deposit.

Ampulloclitocybe clavipes is a highly successful species. It shows up around the world in the temperate zone, preferring humid-rich acid soils, and can be found with conifers and deciduous trees. They seem to prefer Douglas fir and western hemlock in our area. In other parts of the world they have been reported with white pine, larch, and spruce. In southern Michigan, Kauffman found them with oak and maple. Hesler reported them with beech in the Smokies. Laessoe & Lincoff report it with birch. Roody called them saprobic, capable of living off of decaying matter. Miller pointed out that they were very long-lived and do not decay readily. Guzman has reported them from Mexico, and Hongo has found them in Japan.

The flavor is excellent, sort of like the Gypsy mushroom, but when fried in butter, our West Coast version has the consistency of a potato chip. I have hesitated for years to try them because there appeared to be two different versions in the local woods: one with a greasy ochre brown cap, the other with a matte gray-brown cap and stipe. Jack Waytz and I noticed the difference between several fruitings in the Stimpson Family Nature Reserve in the fall of 2010. I cooked up a few of the ochre brown-capped specimens with no ill effects. This was the cap texture most similar to descriptions in the popular guides. I then examined the darker capped specimens under the microscope. Spores were broadly ellipsoid, usually with one oil drop, and measured 7.2–8.5 x 4.3–5.5 µm. They were smooth-walled under 100x power, but are apparently endowed with roughened walls under the electron

microscope. Basidia were slenderly clavate, measuring 30–38.2 x 5–6.1 µm. Clamps were present in the pileipellis and stipitipellis. The gill trama were of intertwined hyphae 2.9–14.3 µm wide. The pileipellis was also of intertwined hyphae 2.9–5.4 µm thick. The only cystidia seen were filiform in shape and emerged from a squash mount of a cross section of a gill. All of this was in sync with other microscopic data accrued from the literature. It now appeared that the specimens with subviscid to greasy caps were the same as those with mat to subvelutinous caps.

Several authors point out that the species is very susceptible to humidity, subviscid in damp weather and matted velutinous in dry. In really wet conditions, the caps can have water spots.

All of this variation has raised a number of synonyms over time. Some of these have been **Clitocybe carnosior** (Peck) Sacc., **Clitocybe media** Peck, **Clitocybe squamulosoides** (Orton) Harmaja, and **Clitocybe comitialis** (Persoon) Kummer. According to Hard, **Clitocybe media** was so named because it was deemed halfway between **A. clavipes** and **Clitocybe nebularis**.

And of course, **Ampulloclitocybe clavipes** has a full retinue of look-alikes. Here are the ones gleaned from the literature in no particular order: **Clitocybe nebularis**: The Cloud Mushroom is generally a more robust species, often has an odor of skunk cabbage, has yellowish spores and pale gray-brown caps often with watery spots.

Ampulloclitocybe avellaneo-alba: A larger Clitocyboid fungus with darker brown caps and usually with lined or ridged cap margins. Spores are larger and subfusoid in shape. It also differs by fruiting on wood. This may be the easiest mushroom to confuse with **Ampulloclitocybe clavipes**. If you eat one by mistake you might survive. Dr. Stuntz wrote, "There have been reports of people eating it, but not a large enough number of them to establish its edibility beyond doubt."

Rhodocollybia butyracea var. asema: This taxon can have a similar stem base but the gills are notched instead of decurrent, and the spores are pale flesh color.

Clitocybe subclavipes: Also found in the Northwest, this species has paler caps and stems that are almost equal. Cap colors are alutaceous to pinkish-tan. The taste is slightly farinaceous.

Infundibulicybe costata: A European species with pip shaped, dacryoid spores and fluted, undulating cap margins. Stems differ by being coated with white longitudinal fibrils.

Pseudoclitocybe cyathiformis: Has smooth dark brown caps that quickly fade to a pale gray-brown (as seen here), white, amyloid spores, strongly fibrillose stems, and funnel-shaped caps when aged.

Infundibulicybe gibba: Has thinner grayish tan to ochre-brick caps that can develop flesh colored hues, and spores that are tear-shaped in profile.

Lepista subalpina: Another brown capped species found in Washington. It has lobed and lined margins and fruits

Clitocybe nebularis

Pseudoclitocybe cyathiformis

in dense clusters near conifers. For a photo of this species, see write-up for **Clitocybe albirhiza** later in the book.

Clitocybe leopardina: A species from southern California and Oregon with equal stems and watery spots on the vinaceous-brown cap surface. Gills described as pinkish-buff.

Clitocybe gibba var. occidentalis (now in Infundibulicybe): Reported from Alaska and California, this variety has gray-brown caps that become yellowish to pinkish-buff in age. Stems are equal or taper at the base and are found with copious white to yellowish mycelium.

Clitocybe subditopoda: Another brown Clitocybe from the Pacific Northwest with equal stems, strong farinaceous odor, and finely striate cap margins when young. In age, caps fade to whitish with discs remaining brown.

Clitopaxillus alexandri: A large species with pale brown caps

Infundibulicybe gibba from Spain

Clitocybe gibba var. occidentalis from Haida Gwaii, B.C.

that become dark brown in age, often areolate (with cracks) at the disc. Stems are white to sordid cream color, bases heavily tomentose. The odor is mild.

Clitocybe squamulosa: Caps are brown to tawny-ochre and minutely scaly (squamose) at the disc. Overall, they are matted fibrillose when young. It appears that western versions of this species have more ochre-tawny caps, implying that if you mixed these colors on a palette, you would see orange caps and stems.

Clitocybe virgata: Another large, fleshy, gray-brown Clitocybe with a clavate stem base, it differs by having an all-white stem with white mycelium at the base, gills that stain brown where eroded, and globose spores, 5–6.5 µm in size. Found in Michigan with oaks.

Clitocybe squamulosa var. sicca: Reported from Washington by Bigelow, caps vary from brown to cinnamon-buff with undulate or crenulate-ridged margins. Caps are dry and matted fibrillose, gills buff to pale pinkish-buff. Taste is disagreeable to slightly farinaceous.

Gen. Nov., Sp. Nov.: An unknown lookalike that fruited among **A. clavipes** at Cowichan Lake, B.C. It differs by having incredibly sticky caps, a flesh colored hue to the gills, and a densely interwoven pileipellis with polymorphic extended ends. DNA sequencing couldn't place it near any known genus. Every last specimen had an expanded stem base, further mimicking **A. clavipes**.

With so many look-alikes out there, why would anyone risk eating **Ampulloclitocybe clavipes** despite the appetizing sound of the name? If you peruse the literature, you can't help noticing that the warnings and accolades are about even. On the negative side, if you eat this species with alcohol, even if you drank some wine two days prior to ingestion, you get a reaction similar to coprine poisoning. This is the type of poisoning associated with mixing alcohol with **Coprinopsis atramentarius**. The effects might even be worse. Symptoms include chest pain, diarrhea, a metallic taste in the mouth, palpitation, vomiting, headaches, and upper body rash. Some victims have likened the experience to taking Antabuse, which is used to treat alcohol addiction. Andrus Voitk suggests that it only be served to teetotalers. Otherwise "consider the awful prospect of giving up wine for several days in a row."

Helene Schalkwijk-Barendsen sums up the experience as "miserable internal disturbances."

Clearly, this is not a mushroom for the beginner. There are many unknown Clitocybes in the Pacific Northwest, and according to Wikipedia, many small ones contain muscarine. **Clitocybe dealbata** and **Clitocybe rivulosa** have such high concentrations of muscarine that fatalities have occurred. Ingestion of **Paralepistopsis amoenolens** of France or **Paralepistopsis acromelalga** of Japan, both formerly in Clitocybe, has led to cases of erythromelalgia, which have lasted from 8 days to 5 months. According to Wikipedia, erythromelalgia is a rare neurovascular peripheral pain disorder in which blood vessels, usually in the feet or hands, are episodically blocked and then become inflamed. There are periodic attacks of severe burning pain and skin redness. According to Medscape, the coprine-like toxins found in **Ampulloclitocybe clavipes** "generate a metabolite that inhibits acetaldehyde dehydrogenase." This sort of terminology is way over my head, so I was relieved to read Dr. Beug's take on it. He feels that if alcohol is consumed along with it, you won't get sick from it. However, if you consume alcohol from 30 minutes to several days after you ingest the species, the symptoms will come on. The intensity of the headache depends on how much alcohol went down.

On the other side of the debate over edibility, we have McIlvaine, who extolled even the synonyms. For **Clitocybe**

LOOK-ALIKES

Gen. Nov., Sp. Nov. from Cowichan Lake, B.C.

Clitocybe squamulosa from Maine

Rhodocollybia butyracea var. asema

comitialis, he wrote "good texture and flavor. Like **C. clavipes**, but smaller, firmer, and inodorous."

For **Clitocybe media**, he asserted "I have known this fungus favorably since 1883 and regard it as one of the best."

For **Clitocybe clavipes**, he opined that the "substance is spongy and therefore does not stew well. Cooked in any other way, it is delicate and of excellent flavor."

William Sturgis Thomas claimed that "Fries says that this species is not edible on account of its spongy texture, but I find it pleasantly flavored and digestible, and see no reason why it may not be utilized if taken when dry. After heavy rains it is apt to be water soaked." Bill Russell, author of *Field Guide to Wild Mushrooms of Pennsylvania* writes that he has eaten it for years with no problems. Hesler commented that the flavor was "good to excellent."

If you decide to go for it, the main thing to consider is the stem base. It should be consistently clavate or gracefully expanded at the base. Stem bases should be white tomentose but not with copious mycelium. Gills should always be white to pale yellow and long decurrent in attachment. If you find collections that have some stems equal or tapered towards the base, bypass them completely. You don't want to eat an unknown and potentially poisonous species by mistake.

The only question remaining is why should the type species for the genus Clitocybe suddenly be switched to the new genus Ampulloclitocybe? This is, of course, a DNA related event. I will now quote the appropriate paragraph from Redhead, Lutzoni, Moncalvo, & Vilgalys without the accompanying citations for the sake of better clarity.

"**Clitocybe clavipes**, which occurs on a weakly supported clade with Rimbachia and Omphalina sensu lectotype, presents a dilemma because it seems to represent a distinct genus, phylogenetically more closely related to the type of Omphalina than the type of Clitocybe (which was **Clitocybe clavipes**). The sequence data are unlike other traditional clitocyboid taxa, most of which prove to be more closely related to the Lyophyllae. **Clitocybe clavipes** is uniquely characterized among clitocyboid taxa by the formation of coprine-like compounds and by ultrastructurally minutely roughened basidiospores compared to smooth-spored Clitocybe or echinate-spored Lepista. **Clitocybe clavipes** also produces a novel class of tyrosine kinase inhibitors, named the clavilactones. The combination of significantly different sequence data from other "Clitocybe," and ultrastructurally distinctive spores suggest that **C. clavipes** has been incorrectly classified as a Clitocybe. We therefore propose to recognize a distinct genus, Ampulloclitocybe, for the species." The authors then proceeded to elect **Clitocybe nebularis** as the new lectotype for Clitocybe.

As Dr. Ammirati has predicted, we will be seeing a lot more new genera as the sequencing data comes in.

Ampulloclitocybe clavipes demonstrates once again that nomenclature is always on the move, that each species has a unique relationship with humans, and no name can be taken for granted until a diagnostic trait stronger than DNA appears.

BIBLIOGRAPHY

Alan & Arleen Bessette & David Fischer, *Mushrooms of Northeastern North America*, 1997. Syracuse University Press, Syracuse, NY.

Michael Beug, *Poisonous and Hallucinogenic Mushrooms*, 2000. The Evergreen State College, Olympia, Wash.

Howard Bigelow, *The Genus Clitocybe in Michigan*, 1956. Doctorate.

Howard Bigelow, *North American Species of Clitocybe, Part I*, 1982. J.Cramer, Vazuz, Germany.

Howard Bigelow, *Ibid, Part II*, 1985. J.Cramer, Vazuz, Germany.

J. Breitenbach & F. Kranzlin, *Fungi of Switzerland, Vol.3*, 1991. Edition Mykologia, Lucerne, Switzerland.

Miron Hard, *Mushrooms Edible and Otherwise*, 1908. Dover Publications, New York, NY.

Patrick Harding, Tony Lyon, & Gill Tomblin, *How to Identify Edible Mushrooms*, 1996. Harper-Collins, London.

Lexemuel Hesler, *Mushrooms of the Great Smokies*, 1960. University of Tennessee Press, Knoxville, Tenn.

Rokuya Imazeki, Tsuguo Hongo, & Keisuke Tubaki, *Common Fungi of Japan in Color*, 1970. Hoikusha Publishing Co., Osaka, Japan.

Calvin Kauffman, *The Agaricaceae of Michigan*, 1918. Michigan Geological and Biological Survey, Lansing, Mich.

Geoffrey Kibby, *An Illustrated Guide to Mushrooms and Other Fungi of North America*, 1993. Dragon's World, Surrey, England.

Thomas Kuyper, Machiel Noordeloos, & Else Vellinga, *Flora Agaricina Neerlandica 3*, 1995. A.A. Balkema, Rotterdam, Holland.

Thomas Laessoe, Gary Lincoff, & Anna del Conte, *The Mushroom Book*, 1996. DK Publishing, New York, NY.

Medscape.com, *Disulfiramlike Mushroom Toxicity*.

Charles McIlvaine & Robert Macadam, *One Thousand American Fungi,* 1902. Dover Publications, New York, NY.

Margaret McKenny & Daniel Stuntz, *The Savory Wild Mushroom*, 1962. University of Washington Press, Seattle, Wash.

Kent & Vera McKnight , *Peterson Field Guides— Mushrooms*, 1987. Houghton Mifflin Co., Boston, Mass.

Orson & Hope Miller, *North American Mushrooms*, 2006. Morris Book Publishing, Guilford, Conn.

Orson Miller, *Mushrooms of North America*, 1972. E.P. Dutton & Co., New York, NY.

Umberto Nonis, *Mushrooms and Toadstools*, 1981.

Hippocrene Books, New York, NY.

Giovanni Pacioni & Gary Lincoff, *Simon & Schuster's Guide to Mushrooms*, 1981. Simon & Schuster, New York, NY.

Scott Redhead, Francois Lutzoni, Jean-Marc Moncalvo, & Rytas Vilgalys, *Phylogeny of Agarics: Partial Systematics Solutions for Core Omphalinoid Genera in the Agaricales* in *Mycotaxon* 83 (19–57), 2002.

Augusto Rinaldi & Vassili Tyndalo, *The Complete Book of Mushrooms*, 1972. Crown Publishers, New York, NY.

William C. Roody, *Mushrooms of West Virginia and the Central Appalachians*, 2003. University Press of Kentucky, Lexington, Kentucky.

Bill Russell, *Field Guide to Wild Mushrooms of Pennsylvania and the Mid-Atlantic*, 2006. Pennsylvania State University Press, University Park, Penn.

Helene Schalkwijk-Barendsen, *Mushrooms of Western Canada*, 1991. Lone Pine Publishing, Edmonton, Alberta.

Eric Soothill & Alan Fairhurst,*The New Field Guide to Fungi*, 1978. Michael Joseph, London.

Mirko Svrcek, *The Hamlyn Book of Mushrooms and Fungi*, 1983. Artia, Prague, Czechoslovakia.

William Sturgis Thomas, *Field Book of Common Mushrooms*, 1928. G.P. Putnam's Sons, New York, NY.

Steve Trudell & Joe Ammirati, *Mushrooms of the Pacific Northwest*, 2009. Timber Press, Portland, Ore.

Andrus Voitk, *A Little Illustrated Book of Common Mushrooms of Newfoundland and Labrador*, 2007. Gros Morne Co-operating Association, Rocky Harbour, Newfoundland.

Wikipedia.com, *Clitocybe clavipes*

Arrhenia chlorocyanea (Patouillard) Redhead, Vilgalys, Moncalvo, & Lutzoni

Rare in North America . . . it had been recorded only four times between 1939 and 1962.

It isn't often that I'll drive 25 miles out of town to check out a mushroom described to me over the phone. But when I got the call from long-time member Evan Sanford in the drizzly morning of April 14, 2007, it caught my attention. There was a blue mushroom on his lawn he hadn't seen before. As he began to describe the weird, thickish gills, I immediately thought he had **Polyozellus multiplex**, a large dark purple-blue Cantharelloid species. The largest of these, however, had a cap the size of his thumb nail.

Evan and wife Pam collect mushroom guides as a hobby. I realized that they would recognize an uncommon species when they saw one. I was at the site just beyond Kendall in half an hour.

I was greeted by Evan at his door. He pointed at a spot in is lawn. This seemed to be a signal for his dog, Nutmeg, a rambunctious female pug who began running routes over lawn and driveway, and had to be captured by Evan to save the specimens. Fortunately, he had already taken a photo, the one you see here, so whether my shot came out or not was no longer significant.

The species was indeed diminutive. The caps measured 6–10 mm. wide and were plane to shallowly depressed at first, then deeply funnel shaped in age. The cap color also changed from an inky, shiny blue-black at first to a slate blue-gray when mature. As the caps expanded they became deeply pleated with wrinkled margins. The gills were long decurrent, thick and ridge-like, intervenose, and pale gray-blue. The stems were smooth, measured up to 1 ¾ cm long, and were equal or tapered slightly towards the base. They were dark gray-blue. The taste was mild, the odor somewhat musty. The spores were white and inamyloid.

Examination by microscope revealed ellipsoid spores with a pointy end, almost lacrymoid in shape. They measured 7.2–10 x 4.6–7.2 μm. The gill trama was interwoven. There were no cystidia. The pileipellis was a cutis of repent hyphae with a few ends exerted. The hyphal walls were incrusted with pigmentation. Clamps were found in the pileipellis by both Dr. Fred Rhoades and Dr. Scott Redhead.

Just for fun, I decided to google the name **Arrhenia chlorocyanea**. A site came up that stated the species was to be found in the northern hemisphere in minimal lawns near bodies of water. Well, Evan's lawn isn't the best, and the bodies of water were represented by deep puddles in the driveway. So the habitat wasn't too far out of line. Other European sources claim that **A. chlorocyanea** can be found along paths in heaths, on lichens and mosses, and in the mountains. And finally a site informed me that the species was known as the Verdigris Navel by a select group of British aficionados. In England it is considered so rare that it made the Red List for Threatened British Fungi.

Arrhenia chlorocyanea also appears to be rare in North America. Under a former name, **Clitocybe smaragdina**, Bigelow and A.H. Smith reported that it had been recorded only four times between 1939 and 1962. Smith recorded three finds from Kalaloch,

LOOK-ALIKE

Clitocybe atroviridis

Washington, in a ten-day period in late April of 1939. The other find was made by M.C. Melburn in Uplands Park, Victoria, B.C., on February 6, 1959. (Now, many years later, it has been discovered that **Clitocybe smaragdina** really belongs in Omphalina and is restricted to Europe.)

The species has an interesting nomenclatural history. The only picture of it that I can find in any popular guide is a water color rendition in *Handbuch fur Pilzfreunde*, Vol. 3 by Michael, Hennig, & Kreisel. It was originally described as **Omphalia chlorocyanea** by the French mycologist, Patouillard. Clamp connections were not mentioned in the description of the type. Because of this omission, Dr. Howard Bigelow created a new species called **Clitocybe atroviridis** in 1982 that did have clamp connections.

Then, in volume II of his Clitocybe monograph, Bigelow stated that Dr. Gulden and Dr. Redhead found Norwegian collections of the original **Omphalia chlorocyanea**, and clamps were found in both. Unfortunately, the holotype representing the species concept in the Patouillard Herbarium has been lost. Perhaps for this reason, Dr. Redhead wanted to see Evan's specimens. He wanted to check for the presence of clamps one more time.

Satisfied that the issue over the clamps had been resolved, Dr. Redhead and associates created the new combination **Arrhenia chlorocyanea** in 2002. **Clitocybe atroviridis** was listed as a synonym, and along with it would belong **Clitocybe smaragdina** in the sense of Bigelow and Smith. But why Arrhenia? Until quite recently this was such a rare genus that Moser attached only one species to it in his *Agarics and Boleti,* orig-

inally published in 1978. He described the genus as "fruiting body young almost spherically closed and stiped, developing ridge-like and veined in the hollow inside; the hymenium, at first turned upwards, then opening and declining downwards, spatula or spoon shaped, more or less gray." This description pertained to **Arrhenia auriscalpium**. It was a species with reduced gills. On the very same page was described a **Leptoglossum acerosum**. This species had normal gills. It eventually became the type for the expanded genus Arrhenia, now with at least 24 members in temperate climates. DNA sequencing can often produce startling relatives.

However, the dark green **Clitocybe atroviridis** and the gray-blue **Arrhenia chlorocyanea** appear to differ in spore shape. Dr. Bigelow described the spores of **Clitocybe atroviridis** as "broadly ellipsoid, sometimes ovoid to obovoid." In Evan's collection of **Arrhenia chlorocyanea**, the spores were almost lacrymoid, pointy at one end. As of this writing, **Clitocybe atroviridis** has been resurrected.

Way back in 1966, mycologists Morten Lange and Ola Skifte conducted a fungal survey in northern Norway. Among their finds was a single specimen of **Omphalina chlorocyanea** in peaty soil near Tromsø. They noted the presence of clamp connections and the "slight narrowing of the spore towards the apiculus." There is no doubt that this is the same rare species found on Evan's lawn.

Thanks go out to Evan for reporting the species, to Dr. Fred Rhoades for verifying microscopic characters, and to Dr. Scott Redhead for verifying the identification.

BIBLIOGRAPHY

David Arora, *Mushrooms Demystified*, 1979. Ten Speed press, Berkeley, Calif.

Howard Bigelow, *North American Species of Clitocybe, Part II*, 1982. J. Cramer, Berlin.

Howard Bigelow & A.H. Smith, *Clitocybe Species from the Western United States* in *Mycologia* 54 (498–515), 1962.

Morten Lange, *Omphalina in Nordic Macromycetes, Vol.2*, 1992. Nordsvamp, Copenhagen.

Morten Lange & Ola Skifte, *Notes on the Macromycetes of Northern Norway* in *Acta Borealia A. Scientia* No. 23 (3–51), 1967.

Meinhard Moser, *Agarics and Boleti*, 1983. Translated and published by Roger Phillips, London.

Scott Redhead, Rytas Vilgalys, Francois Lutzoni, & Jean-Marc Moncalvo, *Phylogeny of Agarics: Partial Systematics Solutions for Core Omphalinoid Genera in the Agaricales* in *Mycotaxon* 83 (19–57), 2002.

Aureoboletus mirabilis (Murrill) Halling

Photo by Richard Morrison

*The Admirable Bolete
has had its shares of
taxonomic adventures.*

Picture yourself standing in deep moss in a dripping hemlock forest surrounded by devil's club when off to your right you spot a troop of maroon capped mushrooms as large as saucers marching down a rotten log. If you're in the Pacific Northwest you have undoubtedly found **Aureoboletus mirabilis**, a fine edible bolete, and a good one for beginners to learn.

As you sidle up to this extraordinary bolete that looks like an escapee from Alice in Wonderland you now realize why you have moved here from places like Chicago, Los Angeles, Houston, Germany, or even France. You just don't find this mushroom with any regularity anywhere in the world except the Pacific Coast from Alaska to north-central California, and in northern Idaho and parts of the Rockies. Unless, of course, you happen to live in China or Japan, where it is now showing up in popular guides.

Once you learn the characteristics, it's hard to mistake it for anything else. The caps are dry, convex to plane, and dark red-brown to maroon. In Alaska I've seen them the size of Frisbees. The cap texture is rather peculiar. As Trudell puts it, "they look like wine-red bath towels in texture." With the help of a magnifying glass you can pick up the tiny, erect maroon scales on a pallid yellowish ground. The pores are a light yellow at first, then a lurid greenish-yellow at maturity. They bruise a deeper mustard yellow when handled. The tubes have angular mouths. The stems are solid, thick, and clavate at the base. Specimens have been recorded with stems 8 cm wide and 22 cm long! They are covered with dark maroon fibrils on a pale yellow ground becoming broadly reticulate (netted) at the apex. The cap context is white to pale yellow with a vinaceous line under the cuticle. There is no sign of a veil and no particular odor. The taste is mild to slightly acidulous, and the spore deposit is olive-brown. The spores are exceptionally large for a bolete, measuring 19-24 x 7-9 μm, and according to A.H. Smith, some are weakly dextrinoid in Melzer's solution.

The fact that it fruits on wood or in deep humus next to a rotten stump is a major clue to its identification. Almost all boletes fruit on the ground. The one other possible look-alike that fruits on wood is **Boletellus chrysenteroides**, an East Coast species fond of oak and spruce.

Another close relative is **Aureoboletus projectellus**, which has a thinner stem and a dingy cinnamon colored cap with a subtomentose texture. It prefers sandy soils under pines and is common in Michigan and from Nova Scotia south to North Carolina.

But from the local standpoint **Xerocomellus zelleri** is one of three possible species you could confuse it with.
Xerocomellus zelleri: Differs by having a more irregularly wrinkled purple-brown cap that is often coated with a whitish powdery bloom when young. The cap margin usually has a pallid band and the yellow pores bruise weakly blue.
Xerocomellus 'atropurpureus': A semi-enigmatic species that mimics **X. zelleri** but has a very minimal pallid marginal band or none at all. A new species created by DNA sequencing.
Boletus fibrillosus: Has a more fibrillose brownish cap surface, smaller spores, and a much more reticulate stem.

Since all of these are also edible, you will still make the Survivors Banquet if you make a mistake.

The Admirable Bolete has had its shares of taxonomic

LOOK-ALIKE

Xerocomellus atropurpureus

adventures. Murrill placed it in his experimental genus, Cerio-myces. Singer had it placed in both Xerocomus and Boletellus. Thiers then removed it from Boletellus when he couldn't find the roughened spores associated with that genus.

Murrill first introduced **Boletellus mirabilis** from the Pacific Northwest in 1912. Since then a few mycologists have jumped at the chance to extend that range, most notably Kauffman, who claimed to have found it in the upper peninsula of Michigan. He had described a sort of cortina on young specimens, which prompted Thiers and Smith to issue the following statement: "We have never seen a veil of any sort on young basidiocarps though hundreds have been examined." Snell also identified a collection from Ross Run, Huntingdon County, Pennsylvania. The stems had long, narrow reticulations and were pinkish in color. Both sightings are indeed intriguing but seem a little bit off.

As for edibility, there is no lack of opinion on the subject. One general rule when eating large boletes is to peel off and discard the tubes before cooking. Young tubes are accepted by many, but old tubes tend to turn into a soggy, gelatinized mass in the frying pan. Notwithstanding such risks, we now turn to our surprise culinary expert, Dr. Alexander H. Smith, a mycologist who would far rather examine a mushroom

Xerocomellus zelleri   *Photo by Richard Morrison*

than eat one. In *Mushrooms in Their Natural Habitat*, he wrote "I have tried it, and in my estimation, it is the equal of **Boletus edulis** in flavor and consistency, and ranks as one of the best edible species in the Pacific Northwest. It does not discolor when cooked, and furthermore, it has certain advantages not possessed by any other bolete known to me. The flesh remains firm for a long time and also remains relatively free of insect larvae."

Other authors have found **Aureoboletus mirabilis** to have a lemony flavor. Bessette and Fischer also praise the species, suggesting it serves well in a wide variety of recipes, but is excellent simply sautéed in butter or served as a side dish with fish or meats. I have found the consistency to be a little slippery, something like **Suillus luteus** with a stronger lemony flavor than **Xerocomellus zelleri**. However, not all specimens are the same. Tylutki warns us that **Aureoboletus mirabilis** is susceptible to a white mold that most often attacks first from the base of the stem. This mold, according to Lincoff, is probably a stage in the life cycle of the Golden Hypomyces, a.k.a. **Hypomyces chrysospermus,** a species whose culinary value will probably never proceed beyond "edibility unknown." Besides avoiding any Boletes attacked by molds, it is a good idea never to eat any boletes with red or orange pores. Locally found blue-staining boletes are edible if not too bitter, but this may not be the case in other parts of the country.

BIBLIOGRAPHY

Robert Bandoni & Adam Szczawinski, *Guide to Common Mushrooms of British Columbia*, 1976. British Columbia Provincial Museum, Victoria, B.C.

Alan & Arleen Bessette & William Roody, *North American Boletes*, 2000. University of Syracuse Press, Syracuse, NY.

Alan Bessette & David Fischer, *Edible Wild Mushrooms of North America*, 1992. University of Texas Press, Austin, Texas.

Ernst Both, *The Boletes of North America*, 1993. Buffalo Museum of Science, Buffalo, NY.

Gary Lincoff, *The Audubon Society Field Guide to North American Mushrooms*, 1981. Alfred A. Knopf, New York, NY.

Margaret Mckenny, Daniel Stuntz, & Joe Ammirati, *The New Savory Wild Mushroom*, 1987. University of Washington Press, Seattle, Wash.

Orson & Hope Miller, *North American Mushrooms*, 2006. Morris Book Publishing, Guilford, Conn.

Robert & Dorothy Orr, *Mushrooms of Western North America*, 1979. University of California Press, Berkeley, Calif.

Lee Overholts, *Mycological Notes for 1936–1938* in *Mycologia* 32 (251–263), 1940.

Noah Siegel & Christian Schwarz, *Mushrooms of the Redwood Coast*, 2016. Ten Speed Press, Berkeley, Calif.

Rolf Singer, *Keys for the Identification of the Species of Agaricales, I* in *Sydowia* 30 (192–279), 1977.

A.H. Smith, *Mushrooms in Their Natural Habitats*, 1949. Sawyer's Inc., Portland, Ore.

A.H. Smith & Nancy Weber, *The Mushroom Hunter's Field Guide*, 1980. University of Michigan Press, Ann Arbor, Mich.

A.H. & Helen Smith & Nancy Weber, *How to Know the Gilled Mushrooms*, 1979. William C. Brown, Dubuque, Iowa.

Harry Thiers, *California Mushrooms: A Field Guide to the Boletes*, 1975. Mad River Press, Eureka, Calif.

Steve Trudell & Joe Ammirati, *Mushrooms of the Pacific Northwest*, 2009. Timber Press, Portland, Ore.

Edmund Tylutki, *Mushrooms of Idaho and the Pacific Northwest, Vol.2*, 1987. University of Idaho Press, Moscow, Idaho.

J.E. Underhill, *Guide to Western Mushrooms*, 1992. Hancock House Publishers, Surrey, B.C., Canada.

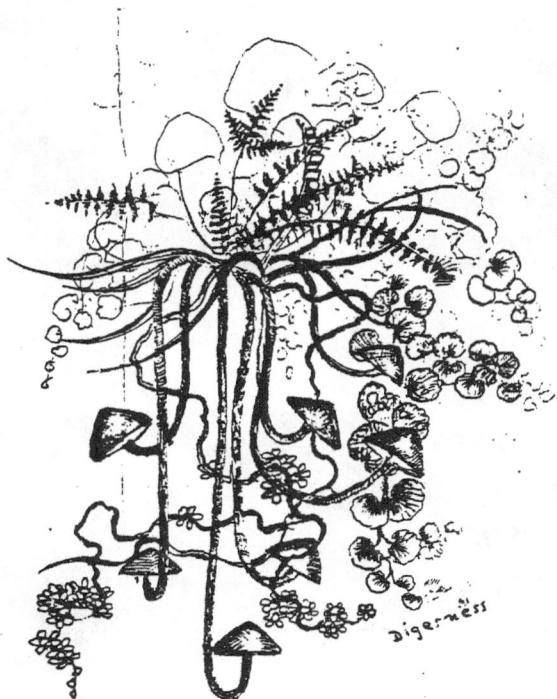

Digerness

Boletus fibrillosus (Thiers)

This gorgeous bolete rarely appears in quantity but definitely deserves culinary attention.

I got the call in my tiny, cluttered office on the morning of October 15th, 2002. "Hey, you oughtta drive over and check this out. I might have edulis on a lawn out here."

The caller was Jack Waytz, our ever-attentive newsletter editor. Sudden Valley was where he lived. Finding **Boletus edulis** on a lawn was unlikely but still possible. One had even showed up years ago in the lawn at Fairhaven Park during a fall show. Just in case, Jack urged me to bring out my new bolete book to key it out. For Jack, almost any kind of bolete was cause for celebration.

So I drove out there, and sure enough, there were four or five of these chunky boletes in a lawn in a knoll next to a thin strand of trees. As if offering an appetizer, the lawn featured **Clitopilus prunulus** scattered around the boletes. Ignoring the latter, we trotted off to Jack's with the boletes and discovered we had found **Boletus fibrillosus** instead. We then went on a hike up a trail leading to Galbraith Mountain and found more of the same on a mossy bank. These are the specimens in the previous photo.

LOOK-ALIKES

Aged specimens of Boletus fibrillosus from Baker Lake

Boletus edulis from Alaska

Boletus fibrillosus has caps 6–17 cm wide, convex to plane with an incurved margin when young becoming decurved in age. The surface is dry, fibrillose to velvety or tomentose, or sometimes wrinkled. The color is cinnamon-brown to dark brown, often with buff colored spots. The thick context is white to buff, unchanging when bruised. The cap stains red to pink with KOH. The pore surface is pale yellow at first becoming dark yellow in age. They turn a little darker on bruising, but no change to blue. The pore mouths are angular, about 1–2 per mm. The stem runs from 10–16 cm long and 2–4 cm thick. The above specimens were reticulated over most of the stem. They are yellowish at the apex becoming pale brown to cinnamon-brown below before ending in a whitish base that is often pinched. Odor and taste are mild. The spore deposit is dark olive-brown, and there is no sign of velar material. It can be found in dense, mixed coastal forests from May through December. The type (the original collection) was found in Jackson State Forest in Mendocino County, California, in 1961. Dr. Harry Thiers described it in 1975.

And now for the look-alikes:
Boletus edulis: Has a generally bulkier stature, a smooth cap surface, and a less yellowish pore surface.
Boletus regineus: Differs by its white stem that becomes brown in age, a whitish bloom on the smooth cap surfaces of young specimens, and generally thicker stature.
Xerocomus illudens: An eastern bolete that differs by its velvety cap surface and yellow

stipes with more of a longitudinal ribbing and a tendency to taper at the bases.

Boletus ferrugineus: Differs by its deeper yellow pores that usually bruise blue-green and pale yellow stems with raised longitudinal rust colored lines.

Imleria badia: Differs by viscid caps when young, and stems without coarse reticulations.

As for the edibility, Kit Scates wrote "probably edible." Dr. Steve Trudell noted that it was edible but inferior to **B. edulis**. Arora wrote that it was fairly good but not as good as **Boletus regineus**. Jack Waytz thinks otherwise. Having benefited from breaks just outside his backyard on October 15th and May 10th, he had the luxury of sampling them twice. Both times he sautéed them with shallots and finely chopped garlic in butter and found the flavor to be subtly reminiscent of **Boletus edulis**. Fien Hulscher, our gourmet foray cook from Anacortes, has also found **B. fibrillosus** in the vicinity of birch. She dehydrated them, then rehydrated them, cooking them with beef, rice, and soy sauce, plus her secret

LOOK-ALIKES

Boletus ferrugineus from Spain

Imleria badia from Spain

spices and herbs. The result, Jack reports, was superb. This gorgeous bolete rarely appears in quantity but definitely deserves culinary attention.

BIBLIOGRAPHY

David Arora, *Mushrooms Demystified*, 1986. Ten Speed Press, Berkeley, Calif.

Alan & Arleen Bessette & William Roody, *North American Boletes*, 2000. Syracuse University Press, Syracuse, NY.

Alan & Arleen Bessette & William Roody, *Boletes of Eastern North America*, 2016. Syracuse University Press, Syracuse, NY.

Ernst Both, *The Boletes of North America, A Compendium*, 1993. Buffalo Museum of Science, Buffalo, NY.

Dennis Desjardin, Michael Wood, & Fred Stevens, *California Mushrooms*, 2015. Timber Press, Portland, Ore.

Kit Scates, *Trial Field Key to the Boletes of the Pacific Northwest*, 1982. Pacific Northwest Key Council, Seattle, Wash.

Harry Thiers, *California Mushrooms—A Field Guide to the Boletes*, 1975. Mad River Press, Eureka, Calif.

Steve Trudell & Joe Ammirati, *Mushrooms of the Pacific Northwest*, 2009. Timber Press, Portland, Ore.

Edmund Tylutki, *Mushrooms of Idaho and the Pacific Northwest, Vol. 2*, 1987. University of Idaho Press, Moscow, Idaho.

Boletus rex-veris Arora & Simonini

Today, the Spring King is an important commercial species.

For several decades our club has been crossing the Cascades to the eastern side every spring to search for the elusive morel. If we happen to go in late spring we usually reap the benefit of running into a large, brick-capped bolete with mustard yellow pores. Many of our club members find it just as tasty as our local **Boletus edulis**, and therefore it helps us diminish the pain of finding no morels. The odd thing is that until now, this very showy bolete that stretches from British Columbia down to the Sierra Nevadas never had a correct name.

Roger Phillips probably came closer than most. We collected it together in the Cle Ellum area back in 1989. He photographed a collection, then took the specimens back to Kew Gardens for identification. They must have had the devil of a time finding a name for it. I can picture the research team becoming more incredulous by the minute. They finally settled on the name **Boletus edulis var. aurantioruber** and published the photo on page 232 of his *Mushrooms of North America*. Despite the lyrical flow of the specific epithet, this name never really caught on. We kept referring to it as "that eastern Cascade edulis," or eventually, trying to appear a little more erudite, **Boletus pinophilus**. Neither, it turns out, was correct.

The idea that it might be **Boletus pinophilus** may have originated with Dr. Ernst Both, an esteemed boletologist from the Buffalo, New York area. In his book, The Boletes of North America, he wrote under his

description of **Boletus edulis var. aurantioruber**, "this taxon appears to be very close to, if not identical with, the European **Boletus pinophilus**. The overall color scheme and the dimensions of spores and cytstidia are nearly identical." Notice that he didn't come right out and say they were the same. But he did make the suggestion. It was just enough. My hunch is that professionals who shied away from the name "aurantioruber" latched onto **B. pinophilus** with a sense of relief.

Frankly, I've always had problems with that concept. I had collected **Boletus pinophilus** with Dr. Roy Watling in Scotland years before. The caps were dark maroon-brown and the stems were tan to brown. I decided to send Roy specimens and photos from our foray last spring. I received an immediate email stating that "one thing it is not is **B. pinophilus**." A couple days later I received a second email declaring that our species did not occur in Europe, but that it was definitely part of the edulis group. **Boletus aurantioruber**, on the other hand, has been reported from Europe. Henning Knudsen listed it as **Boletus edulis form aurantioruber** in *Nordic Macromycetes*, Vol.2

Meanwhile, not everyone was shying away from aurantioruber. In Mushrooms of Cape Cod and the National Seashore, authors Bessette, Both, and Neill raised it to species status. Here at last was the first full macroscopic description of **Boletus aurantioruber**, by far the closest look-alike to our **Boletus rex-veris**. Photos of the two species look the same. Although Arora did not compare species in his introductory publication, the differences appear to be as follows: 1) **Boletus rex-veris** occurs in most mountain

Close-up of B. rex-veris showing beginning of radicating stem base.

Erin Moore with trophy Boletus rex-veris
Photo by Vince Biciunas

The signature photo with this article depicts specimens found by the Kuhn brothers near Fish Lake in the Lake Wenatchee area. The GPS is not provided here. Suffice it to say that they can be found with lodgepole pine and ponderosa pine mostly from June to July in the eastern Cascades. We have also found them near creek banks among vine maple.

Caps run from 5 ½ -30 cm wide and are broadly convex to plane. At first they are rusty brick to a sort of rosy cinnamon color eventually becoming more ochre-olive in age where exposed to sunlight. In dry conditions, the cap surface becomes cracked or areolate, showing the buff context beneath. They are viscid only when wet, glabrous except for an irregular whitish bloom when young. The pore surface is white at first, soon becoming lemon yellow, and then a sordid mustard color in age. The pores are more rounded than angular, about two per mm. They darken slightly when bruised or turn an olive-brown. The tubes are olive-ochre in maturity and run up to 2 ½ cm long. Stems range from 2 ½-10 cm thick and 5-20 cm long. They are equal to slightly clavate, almost always with a short radicating root at the base. The photo on the previous page demonstrates the dirt encrusted root lying atop a stone for contrast. The end has been chopped off by mistake. Stems are a pale brick color at the apex fading to cream towards the base. Five out of every six specimens last spring had no surface reticulation. Those with reticulation had a pallid buff network on a brick ground at the apex, the reticulations becoming brick color over a pallid ground further down the stem. The form of these reticulations varies from rounded to angular. The context of cap and stem is white and does not change when bruised.

Spores are olive-brown in deposit. They are ellipsoid to subfusiform with a prominent suprahilar depression, and measure 15-17 x 4.5-5 μm. Odor and taste are mild. **Boletus rex-veris** is usually associated with conifers, and as Arora emphasizes, it is a semi-hypogeous species, often revealing itself by just a hump in the duff.

Arora wrote that caps run up to 30 cm wide, and occasionally larger. In the spring of 2006 Erin Moore lugged one into camp that measured 35 cm wide. Whether this is a regional record or a world record, we may never know. The range is just too far. This incredible find might only be

ranges west of the Rockies while **Boletus aurantioruber** can be found from Michigan east to Cape Cod. 2) **Boletus aurantioruber** has a smaller stature. Caps run up to 12 cm wide with stems up to 2 ½ cm thick and 12 cm long. **Boletus rex-veris** has massive caps up to 35 cm wide and stems up to 10 cm thick! 3) **Boletus aurantioruber** fruits above ground while **B. rex-veris** is almost hypogeous, fruiting often below ground with only the top of the cap poking through the duff. 4) **Boletus rex-veris** often does not have reticulations on the stem, but if it does, the reticulations do not change color when bruised. **Boletus aurantioruber** has reticulations that bruise dark brown to black when handled. 5) Rolf Singer discovered that hynenophoral tissue dabbed with Melzer's had a fleeting amyloid reaction with **Boletus edulis var. aurantioruber**. This remains to be seen with **Boletus rex-veris**. 6) The stem base of **Boletus aurantioruber** can be either bulbous or narrowed to a point while the stem base of **Boletus rex-veris** usually has a distinct root-like extension. Arora writes that a more detailed treatment of the **Boletus rex-veris** is in preparation. Perhaps even more differences will emerge.

surpassed by one found by Jack Waytz. It was a quadruple headed specimen that weighed 9 ¾ pounds! **Boletus aurantio-ruber**, other look-alikes include the following:

Boletus fibrillosus: Differs by having a distinctly wrinkled or nodulose cap surface in age.

Boletus subcaerulescens: An east coast bolete that differs by its olive-yellow pore surface that bruises gray-blue, and more vinaceous colors on the caps and stems.

Boletus chippawaensis: A bolete from Michigan and New York having caps with a lemon yellow ground color and pores that bruise pinkish-cinnamon.

Boletus pinophilus: Differs by its dark red-brown caps and stem reticulation that darkens when handled.

Aureoboletus gentilis: Has intensely yellow pores and further differs by its pinkish tan to dull red brown caps.

Xerocomus illudens: An eastern species with a velutinous cinnamon colored cap, yellow stem, and much more slender stature.

Boletus rex-veris is an excellent edible. The type specimen is from the former mill town of McCloud in northern California. Italian immigrants who settled there were the first to discover the bounty. For over 65 years they would collect it for family consumption. Then in 1985, a commercial market for it sprang up. The first commercial buyer on the scene was horrified to discover the locals raking up the duff to find specimens.

"But we've been doing it this way for 60 years," one of

Front and back of Boletus pinophilus from Scotland

Xerocomus illudens from Mass.

them explained. The buyer figured they must have survived the raking because the locals only raked gently along the surface, not disturbing the mycelium below. Today, the Spring King is an important commercial species. According to Arora, 25,000-60,000 pounds are harvested each spring from the Mount Shasta area alone. Besides the commercial center in McCloud, others can be found in La Grande, Keno, and Sisters in Oregon, and at Trout Lake in southern Washington.

Almost every year that I can remember, Fien Hulscher has been our foray chef at Morel Madness. She probably brings her own butter and olive oil, but besides from that, pretty much relies on whatever herbs and spices others might bring. She graciously sautées whatever edibles we might find, and life might not be complete until you have sampled her sautéed squares of **Boletus rex-veris**.

Fien carefully removes the tubes from the older specimens

LOOK-ALIKE

Aureoboletus gentilis from Spain

before cooking. But she does not throw them away, as I have always done. Instead she will take them home, dehydrate them, and then grind them up to use as a stew thickener or even a spice with other meals.

The authors of the Wild Mushroom Cookbook out of Mendocino offer another concept for cooking this massive bolete. They turn the stems into mock scallops. Their recipe starts here:

3–4 large **B. rex-veris** or **B. edulis** stems
1 cup bread crumbs
1 egg
2–3 tblsp. crumbled dried seaweed
1 tsp. sea salt
2 tblsp. peanut oil

Preparation: Slice stems into rounds about 3/4 inch thick. Dredge stems in beaten egg. Let sit for 5 minutes, then dip into mixture of seaweed, sea salt, and breadcrumbs. Fry both sides in oil until done.

BIBLIOGRAPHY

David Arora, *California Porcini: Three New Taxa, Observations on Their Harvest, and the Tragedy of No Commons* in *Economic Botany* 62 (356–375), 2008.
Alan & Arleen Bessette & William Neill, *Mushrooms of Cape Cod and the National Seashore*, 2001. Syracuse University Press, Syracuse, NY.
Alan & Arleen Bessette, & William Roody, *North American Boletes*, 2000. Syracuse Univ. Press, Syracuse, NY.
Ernst Both, *The Boletes of North America, (100)*, 1993. Buffalo Museum of Science, Buffalo, NY.
Aurelio Garcia Blanco & Juan Antonio Sanchez Rodriguez, *Setas de la Peninsula Iberica y de Europa*, 2011. Editorial Everest, Leon, Spain.

Alison Gardner & Merry Winslow, *The Wild Mushroom Cookbook*, 2014. Barefoot Naturalist Press, Mendocino, Calif.
Henning Knudsen, *Boletus* in *Nordic Macromycetes, Vol.2* (58), 1992. Nordsvamp, Copenhagen.
Roger Phillips, *Mushrooms of North America*, 1991. Little, Brown & Co., Boston, Mass.
Rolf Singer, *Keys for the Identification of the Species of Agaricales, I.* in *Sydowia* 30 (192–279), 1977.
A.H. & Helen Smith, *How to Know the Non-Gilled Fleshy Fungi*, 1973. (First Edition). William C. Brown, Dubuque, Iowa.

Boletus smithii Thiers

Known in esoteric circles as the chameleon of Northwest boletes . . .

This well may be the Red Zinger of the Boletus world. A typical comment that one might overhear when in the presence of **Boletus smithii** might go like this: "Why I'd never eat that one. It has too much red on it. Aren't all red boletes bad?"

It depends, of course, on where the red is. The classical poisonous bolete has brilliant red or orange pores and stains a deep, nasty blue. Other potentially poisonous boletes are too bitter to eat. A reddish cap and a reddish stem, on the other hand, are not to be unequivocally disdained. Let's put it this way: If you were cooking up a batch of what you thought was **Xerocomellus chrysenteron** and it tasted like **Boletus edulis var. grandedulis**, you probably ate **Boletus smithii**. It's just that good.

Although our local variant of **Boletus smithii** is far more slender than the King Bolete, I notice in photos that it tends to gain bulk in Idaho and California. Caps measure 10–16 cm wide, are plane to convex, and velvety at first, ageing to matted fibrillose or smooth. As the cap texture changes, so do the cap colors.

Known in esoteric circles as the chameleon of Northwest boletes, the caps are first pale olive to olive-brown. As they mature, the olive

Juvenile Boletus smithii caps

LOOK-ALIKE

Caloboletus frustosus

pigments are replaced by reddish colors, often patchy in arrangement. In the end they can become completely dull red. The cap context is pale greenish yellow often with a pale red line beneath the cuticle. The caps can become rimose to areolate in dry weather. The tubes are straw yellow becoming olive yellow in age. They turn instantly dark blue when touched. The pores are 1–2 per mm, and yellowish becoming obscurely reddish in places in age. The stems are 1–3 cm thick and up to 15 cm long. They are slightly appressed-fibrillose, equal or tapered towards base or apex.

The context is yellow but turns blue where exposed. Thiers first described the stems as "usually red at apex and yellow below, but this pattern can be reversed or stems can be entirely red or yellow." In a later publication he wrote "the red band at the stem apex is distinctive." The spore deposit is olive-brown and the odor and taste is mild. Perhaps partly because of the red line under the cap cuticle, **Boletus smithii** has been placed in Subsection Subtomentosi along with **Xerocomellus chrysenteron** and **Xerocomellus zellerii**, two of its closest relatives. But **Boletus smithii** lacks the cracked and fissured cap of the former and the plum colored rugose or lumpy cap of the latter.

Other look-alikes are as follows:
Xerocomellus diffractus: Since it is now believed that **X. chrysenteron** does not exist on the west coast, this is the most likely replacement name. It differs by having a brownish

cap with pale yellow cracks that turn pinkish in age.

Aureoboletus mirabilis: This differs by always fruiting on wood, not having pores that stain blue when bruised, and a purple-brown cap surface roughened by tiny erect scales.

Caloboletus rubripes: The closest look-alike, it differs by a cap surface that never turns reddish, a red zone that is always at the stem base, and, unlike **B. smithii**, the taste of **C. rubripes** is instantly bitter.

Caloboletus calopus: A European species differing by its bitter taste, red band at the stem base, and concolorous reticulation.

Baorangia pseudocalopus: A far eastern bolete with a strong red band at the stipe apex and an association with oak and other hardwoods.

Caloboletus conifericola: Also has an instantly bitter taste and no red on the stem, but is now considered in North America to be a synonym of **C. frustosus**.

Caloboletus frustosus: Now elevated to species status, this former variety of **Caloboletus calopus** differs by its cracked cap surface in age plus the instantly bitter taste. It is our Pacific Northwest equivalent of the European **Caloboletus calopus**.

Boletus coccyginus: A smaller species with the same stipe colors, but the yellow-green pores do not turn dark blue when bruised.

Baorangia bicolor: A species found in Michigan eastward with reddish, granular surfaced caps and red at the base of the stem.

Xerocomellus chrysenteron: Differs by having fissured caps

Baorangia bicolor from Massachusetts

Aureoboletus mirabilis from Alaska

Xerocomellus diffractus

LOOK-ALIKES

Xerocomellus chrysenteron from Spain

Caloboletus rubripes from B.C.   *Photo by Daniel Winkler*

Boletus smithii was first collected in the Oregon Cascades. It fruits in late fall and early winter in dense mixed coastal forests, often found solitary on the banks of road cuts. Widespread but not really common, Dr. Thiers at first found it only near Mendocino in California. The type is from Jackson State Forest and dates to November, 1960.

As for culinary aspects, **B. smithii** was first considered "edibility unknown." Dr. A.H. Smith, for whom the bolete was named, wrote "I have no accurate data on its edibility and do not recommend amateur collectors experimenting with it. There are just enough poisonous species in Boletus that stain blue to indicate caution." The great bard has a point if one is considering Boletus nationwide. But **Boletus smithii** is confined to the western states where the closest look-alikes are so bitter only a slug could enjoy them. In our area it enjoys a long fruiting season from late August through early November depending on the frost arrival. In the opinions of a few local aficionados its culinary value has been vastly overlooked to the advantage of a few and the loss of many.

that are yellowish at first and then pinkish in age. The flavor is quickly forgettable.

BIBLIOGRAPHY

Noah Siegel & Christian Schwarz, *Mushrooms of the Redwood Coast*, 2016. Ten Speed Press, Berkeley, Calif.

Alexander Smith, *A Field Guide to Western Mushrooms*, 1975. Univ. Michigan Press, Ann Arbor, Mich.

Alexander & Helen Smith & Nancy Weber, *How to Know the Non-Gilled Mushrooms*, 1981. William C. Brown, Dubuque, Iowa.

Harry Thiers, *California Boletes I* in *Mycologia* 57 (524–534), 1965.

Harry Thiers, *California Mushrooms: A Field Guide to the Boletes*, 1975. Mad River Press, Eureka, Calif.

Edmund Tylutki, *Mushrooms of Idaho and the Pacific Northwest, Vol.2*, 1987. University of Idaho Press, Moscow, Idaho.

Butyriboletus abieticola (Thiers) Arora & Frank

The flesh of the cap looked exactly like a stick of butter.

The big, chunky bolete was lying on the side of the trail with its stem cut off at the base. We were at altitude, maybe around 4,000 feet, in a coniferous forest to the northwest of Baker Lake. Jack Waytz, our newsletter editor, gave it a nudge with his toe. A few maggots crawled out. Maybe this explained its presence on the trail. Jen Green, who had spotted it first, then found another more attractive specimen a few feet away. This one was in perfect condition.

We stood in a mini-circle, silently staring down at it. It was a huge bolete none of us had seen before.

Butyriboletus abieticola, the Fir Dwelling Bolete, is not normally seen this far north. The original find by British mycologist William Bridge Cooke was from the Mount Shasta, California area on August 8, 1967. Dr. Thiers eventually published it as a new species in 1975. Since then, it has been reported from the Montana Rockies, the Lassen National Volcanic Park in northeastern California, the high Sierras, southern Oregon, and Rainier National Park in Washington. Jen's discovery might be the most northerly report from Washington state yet.Small wonder we hadn't seen it before.

Our unusual find belongs to a select group known as the "Butter Boletes." This is because the stems are generally the color of butter. In this case, it was the context. Jack, on a whim, sliced the better specimen in half lengthwise. The flesh of the cap looked exactly like a stick of butter. Since the taste was mild and there were no obvious red flags, it was decided that Jack should take it home and give it the traditional culinary test.

Back at the car, we took a longer look at the specimens. The key characteristics were a fleshy cap with nacreous tan to pale pink flattened scales on a pale yellow ground, a yellow pore surface that bruised instantly dull blue-green, and a pale yellowish stem almost completely covered with a darker yellow reticulum, a raised net-like feature that is shared by many boletes.

Caps of **Butyriboletus abieticola** run from 9–13 cm wide. They are convex to plane with margins that remain inrolled for most of their lives. The ground color is straw yellow covered by flattened scales of a pallid tan to pinkish hue, and so nacreous as to be almost white. The flesh of the cap is whitish to yellow, and either does not change color when bruised or else goes pale blue very slowly and erratically. The pore surface is citron yellow at first, becoming a sordid olive-yellow in age. It instantly stains blue-green when touched. The tubes are 1–2 cm long, adnate at first, then shallowly depressed in age. The stems are 9-12 cm long and 4–6 cm thick, usually en-

LOOK-ALIKE

Caloboletus rubripes

larged at the base. They are pale yellow with a reddish flush on the lower half. The stem does not stain blue. The context is whitish becoming pale brick towards the base. A yellow reticulum covers nearly all the stipe. There was no velar material on the fruiting body. When KOH is applied to the cap surface, a pale violet reaction occurs. The spore deposit is olive-brown.

Microscopically, the spores are subcylindrical in profile and measure 14–17.5 x 4.5–6 µm. The cheilocystidia are rather varied in shape, and the hyphae of the pileipellis have spiral encrustations, a unique feature of the species. There are no clamps present.

Butyriboletus abieticola is a high altitude species that is found with Douglas fir and silver fir. David Biek has also found it with red fir in the fall.

The Fir Dwelling Bolete happens to have a bunch of look-alikes, and we thought we had found **Butyriboletus appendiculatus** until David Arora set us straight.

And now, without more ado, the look-alikes:

Butyriboletus appendiculatus: The original Butter Bolete. It differs by having pale brown to rusty-brown caps that do not have imbricate scales, an association that is nearly 90% with hardwoods, and smaller spores that measure 12–15 x 4–5 µm. Neither does it have reddish hues on the stem. In Europe, it is mostly a southern species that has been found as far south as Morocco.

Butyriboletus fechtneri: A related European bolete that differs by having silky gray-

LOOK-ALIKES

Suillus pseudobrevipes

Boletus regineus from Calif.

brown caps that stain rusty-brown when touched.

Boletus subappendiculatus: Another European bolete whose caps turn blood red when KOH is applied, and no part of the fruiting body turns blue when bruised.

Baorangia pseudocalopus: Differs by its areolate brownish caps tinged grayish-red and narrow stems with red at the apices.

Caloboletus conifericola: Another bitter bolete that has no red on it at all. Very abundant in the northwest.

Caloboletus radicans: Differs by its rooting stem and bitter taste. There are some who believe that true **Caloboletus radicans** does

Caloboletus conifericola

Baorangia pseudocalopus from Tibet

Caloboletus radicans

not occur in America.

Caloboletus frustosus: Common in the Pacific Northwest, differs primarily by its bitter taste, red zone at the stem apices, and cracked ochre-brown caps.

Caloboletus rubripes: Differs by its consistently reddish stem base, sour to bitter taste, and bluing of the pore surface when bruised that fades to grayish-tan over time. (You can see this in the photo, previous page.) Thanks to Carl Franz for bringing this specimen in from the Mosquitoe Lake area. When cut in half lengthwise, the cap context turned gray-blue at the disc, then yellow as it neared the stem apex. Below that area it turned dark blue and finally dark red at the stem base. Since the color changes were going off at different times, the entire surface appeared speckled. It was like looking at a mini aurora borealis in a mushroom.

Butyriboletus regius: Differs by its rose-pink caps that are tomentose at first, then smooth in age.

Boletus fibrillosus: Has a more fibrillose cap and stem, and no part of it bruises blue when touched.

Boletus regineus: Although the pore surface can vary from white to olive-yellowish, no part of the fruiting body turns blue when bruised.

Suillus pseudobrevipes: Also has a yellow cap context in age but differs by its viscid caps that often have a streaked appressed fibrillose appearance.

And now for the question everyone wants to ask...the edibility factor. Oddly, no one has even commented on it in the literature. But if you go online, a Herman Brown from

California asserts they are delicious. For those of you looking for a little more beef than this appraisal, here is what Jack Waytz had to say: "The flavor was excellent and reminded me of the taste of **Imleria badia** back in Germany in the old days. It also had a deep, buttery, rich texture. One noteworthy fact is that the flesh turned a deeper canary yellow in the frying pan."

So if you are looking for that perfect yellow to contrast with your beets and green beans on the dinner plate, look no further than here.

LOOK-ALIKE

Butyriboletus regius from Spain

BIBLIOGRAPHY

David Arora, *All That the Rain Promises and More*, 1991. Ten Speed Press, Berkeley, Calif.

Alan & Arleen Bessette & William Roody, *North American Boletes*, 2000. Syracuse University Press, Syracuse, NY.

David Biek, *The Mushrooms of Northern California*, 1982. Spore Prints, Redding, Calif.

Ian Gibson & Dick Bishop, *updated version of Trial Key to the Boletes in the Pacific Northwest by Kit Scates*, 2004. Pacific Northwest Key Council, Seattle, Wash.

Henning Knudsen & Andy Taylor, *Boletus L.:Fr. in Funga Nordica*, 2012. Nordsvamp, Copenhagen.

Umberto Nonis, *Guide des Champignons Gastronomiques*, 1984. Hippocrene Books, New York, NY.

Mirko Svrcek & Jiri Kubicka, *Champignons d'Europe*, 1979. Artia, Prague, Czechoslovakia.

Harry Thiers, *California Mushrooms: A Field Guide to the Boletes*, 1975. Mad River Press, Eureka, Calif.

Edmund Tylutki, *Mushrooms of Idaho and the Pacific Northwest, Vol.2: Non-Gilled Hymenomycetes*, 1987. University of Idaho Press, Moscow, Idaho.

Roy Watling & A.E. Hills, *Boletes and Their Allies in British Fungus Flora 1*, 2005. (Revised edition) Royal Botanic Garden Edinburgh, Edinburgh, Scotland.

Gang Wu, Kuan Zhao, Yan-Chun Li, Nian-Kai Zeng, Bang Feng, Roy Halling, & Zhu Yang, *Four New Genera of the Fungal Family Boletaceae* in *Fungal Diversity* 81 (1–24), 2016.

Caloscypha fulgens (Persoon) Boudier

It is the most common snowmelt cup fungus of the eastern Cascades.

Caloscypha fulgens, that other "Orange Peel," sometimes fruits in such numbers in moss and conifer duff that from a distance you think you have stumbled upon a field of yellow crocuses. It appears around the world in the northern hemisphere. It is mostly found with high altitude fir near snowmelt. It has also succeeded in merging with other hosts such as spruce in Norway, broadleaf trees in Switzerland, and cedar in Michigan. It is the most common snowmelt cup fungus of the eastern Cascades. Though much less common in the western Cascades, I have found it at Twin Lakes in North Cascades National Park in June.

"Caloscypha" means beautiful cup. "Fulgens" is from the Latin *fulgeo*, meaning shiny. Perhaps the name lacks specificity, but to this day I haven't heard forayers shouting, "Hey, over here! I've just found the Shiny Beautiful Cup!" If you are on the East Coast you may want to follow Lincoff and call it the Blue Staining Cup. After all, **Peziza cyanoderma** is one of its eleven synonyms. If you are on the west coast and follow Arora, you would call it the Snowmelt Orange Peel Fungus.

Our professionals weren't sure where to place it either. Persoon introduced it as **Peziza fulgens** in 1822. The type was from Neuchatel, Switzerland. Boudier created the genus Caloscypha for it in 1885. Since then it has spent time in Detonia, Aleuria, Lamprospora, Pseudoplectania, Cochlearia, Otidella, Barlaea, Plicariella, and Geniculodendron. Seaver has it described under Pseu-

Sowerbyella imperialis from Switzerland

doplectania, but Smith, Snyder, and others felt it was out of place there since the other two species were all black. Snyder argued for Lamprospora. He wrote, "the very poorly developed hairs on the exterior do not exclude it from Lamprospora since the outer cell walls of many species of Lamprospora run out into clavate growths." Few bought into it. Hairs are hairs, clavate growths are clavate growths, and Caloscypha remains the genus today.

The cups of **Caloscypha fulgens** measure 1–5 cm wide. They are very brittle and are sometimes split like an Otidea with a slit on one side. The interior hymenial surface (which bears the spores) is bright orange to yellow-orange, smooth to slightly wrinkled. The exterior is a darker orange and more likely to be stained olive-green to blue-green, especially near the cup margin. The texture is minutely pubescent. The context is thin, white. The stem is nonexistent or very short and white. It is found solitary or in dense clusters in which cases the deep cups become irregular in outline due to compression. It usually fruits from a dense mycelial mat. Arora mentions that "the mycelium apparently parasitizes the seeds of conifers." Dense clusters arise where the squirrels have stashed the cones.

Vera Evenson finds **Caloscypha fulgens**, normally a spring species, as late as August at 10,000 feet near Aspen, Colorado. She believes that the energy from the sun glistening off the snow banks provides the localized warmth for fungi. When combined with humidity, a few hardy species will fruit.

There is a little bit of opinion variation on the bluing of **Caloscypha fulgens**. Almost all authors note that the bluing appears with age. It is such a predominant feature that "Moldy Orange Peel" could be the best name for it. But Dr. A.H. Smith disagrees. In the spring of 1939 he studied the species intensely in the Olympic National Park. He came to the conclusion that the color of

LOOK-ALIKE

Aleuria aurantia   *Photo by Erin Moore*

truly fresh caps was blue-green over the exterior surface, but rapidly faded to yellow-orange. Evenson writes that the degree of bluing is affected by age, habitat, and light. But apparently they don't always fade to yellow-orange. Near Laird Park in northern Idaho in 1978, Dr. Jack Rogers found an albino form…blue-green stains on a white cup.

Microscopically, the spores are globose and measure 5–7 μm. They are smooth, 1–2 seriate, hyaline, without oil drops. The asci hold eight spores and measure roughly 150 x 10 μm. They are cylindric, tapering into a long stem-like base. They also have a lid at the apex, which opens when the spores mature. The paraphyses are slender and tapered at the tips. They are often branched near the bases and filled with yellow-orange granules. It is these granules that give the carpophores their orange coloration. Finn-Egil Eckblad discovered that recently discharged spores had a thin, mucilaginous sheath that soon disappeared in water.

According to A.H. Smith, the three characters that distinguish Caloscypha from other genera are the globose spores, the bright colored pigmentation, and the poorly developed hairs over the exterior surface. **Caloscypha fulgens** is the type species for the genus. The only other taxon in the genus was **Caloscypha incarnata**, a species so rare that it has only been recorded twice, once in Algeria and once in Morocco. And even this has taken a hit. According to *Index Fungorum*, it is now **Kallistoskypha incarnata**.

Look-alikes of **Caloscypha fulgens** are **Aleuria aurantia** and **Sowerbyella imperialis**; but neither of them develop blue-green stains, and **Sowerbyella imperialis** differs by having a stem and is more yellow in color. Botanical artist Mr. Jackson has an outstanding watercolor depiction of **C. fulgens**, and in *Mushrooms of North America*, Roger Phillips has photos of **Aleuria aurantia** and **Caloscypha fulgens** side by side for comparison.

And now for the part we've all been waiting for, the edibility issue. The vast majority of authors jot down "edibility unknown." Arora wrote, "there is no information on it." Only Dr. Ammirati gives us any kind of warning. In the *New Savory Wild Mushroom*, he wrote, "it is known that **Caloscypha fulgens** in the Pacific Northwest is poisonous, at least to some individuals."

That "some individuals" would have to include Bob Mooers. Bob is one of the pioneering spirits in our club. He served as our first newsletter editor. Perhaps of more significance, he and wife June would often go on long hikes at altitude, bringing back high mountain fungi few of us had seen before. Well, Bob did get poisoned by **Caloscypha fulgens** collected at Washington Pass, and here is the story behind it:

"At first, six of us tried it," Bob related, "We only ate a cup each. No, no, not a whole cup. Just a cup. Nobody had any ill effects. On the next day June and I found a big break. Since the flavor the day before had been good, nutty like **Aleuria aurantia**, we decided to fry up a big batch. June wouldn't eat any. I ended up eating every last one."

I asked him if he experienced any gastrointestinal symptoms.

"No. The thing that I remember most is near total loss of motor control. I felt rubbery. I had to sit down. It was rubbery without any accompanying hallucinations. When I tried to record the symptoms as they were happening I could hardly hold the pen."

June drove him to a hospital where Bob induced vomiting. He feels this saved him from a far worse fate in retrospect.

"At the hospital they couldn't come up with an antidote. There was no history, no information on it. At about the time they were going to pump the stomach, I started to improve, so they skipped that step."

Now contrast that experience with that of Kern's, a forayer who recorded his viewpoint in Schweizerische Zeitschrift fur Pilzkunde 17 (133).

"The species appears in the mountain forests of southern Germany and Switzerland so plentifully that you can collect it in masses. It is a very tasty, edible mushroom, but only worth collecting when found in masses. Since it is hard to clean the dirt and moss from the specimens, we only eat them when we find over a hundred." (Thank you, Anita Waytz, for the translation.)

A few other European authors comment on edibility. R.W.G. Dennis reported that a fellow named Rahm ate it in the Alps. But he would only partake of **C. fulgens** if no other edibles were around. Neuner wrote that it was edible but rarely collected. André Marchand contributed, "comestible mais peu charnu" ("edible but not very fleshy"). Perhaps it is one of those species that is edible in one part of the world but not in another.

So on behalf of all our club members in Northwest Mushroomers, I would like to thank Bob Mooers for taking the culinary plunge. Whether others can eat our Pacific Northwest **Caloscypha fulgens** with impunity is still on the table. At least we now know it must be approached with caution.

BIBLIOGRAPHY

Sean Abbott & R.S. Currah, *The Larger Cup Fungi and Other Ascomycetes of Alberta*, 1989. University of Alberta Devonian Botanic Garden, Edmonton, Alberta.

David Arora, *Mushrooms Demystified*, 1986. en Speed Press, Berkeley, Calif.

J. Breitenbach & F. Kranzlin, *Fungi of Switzerland, Vol.1*, 1984. Verlag Mykologia, Lucerne, Switzerland.

R.W.G. Dennis, *Two New British Discomycetes with Smooth Spherical Ascospores* in *Kew Bulletin* 23 (479–481), 1969.

Finn-Egil Eckblad, *The Genera of the Operculate Discomycetes* in *Nytt Magasin for Botanikk* 15, (1–191), 1968.

Vera Evenson, *Mushrooms of Colorado*, 1997. Denver Botanic Gardens, Denver, Colo.

James Ginns, *Fungi Canadensis 66*. Available from Agriculture Canada, Biosystematics Research Centre, William Saunders Bldg., C.E.F. Ottawa, Ontario KIA 0C6, Canada.

H.A.C. Jackson, *Mr. Jackson's Mushrooms*, 1979. National Gallery of Canada, Ottawa.

F. Kern, *Erlauschtes und Erlebtes* in *Schweizerische Zeitschrift fur Pilzkunde* 17 (130–133), 1939.

Paul Kirk (ed.), *Index Fungorum*, http://www.indexfungorum.org/names/Names.asp

Gary Lincoff, *The Audubon Society Field Guide to North American Mushrooms*, 1981. Alfred A. Knopf, New York, NY.

André Marchand, *Champignons du Nord et du Midi, Vol.4*, 1976. Societe Mycologique des Pyrenees Mediterraneennes, Perpignan, France.

Margaret McKenny, Daniel Stuntz, & Joe Ammirati, *The New Savory Wild Mushroom*, 1987. University of Washington Press, Seattle, Wash.

Andreas Neuner, *Chatto Nature Guides Mushrooms and Fungi*, 1978. Chatto & Windus, London.

Roger Phillips, *Mushrooms of North America*, 1991. Little, Brown & Co., Boston, Mass.

Schweizerische Zeitschrift fur Pilzkunde 17 (133), 1940.

Fred Jay Seaver, *The North American Cup Fungi (Operculates)*, 1928. Self-published, New York, NY.

A.H. Smith, *Mushrooms in Their Natural Habitats*, 1949. Sawyer's, Lancaster, Penn.

A.H. Smith & Nancy Weber, *The Mushroom Hunter's Field Guide*, 1980. University of Michigan Press, Ann Arbor, Mich.

Leon Snyder, *The Operculate Discomycetes of Western Washington*, doctorate, 1938.

Edmund Tylutki, *Mushrooms of Idaho and the Pacific Northwest: Discomycetes*, 1979. University Press of Idaho, Moscow, Idaho.

Cantharellus subalbidus Morse & A.H. Smith

If primitive tastes this good, we're all for it.

Cantharellus subalbidus is that "other" chanterelle that we forage for in the Pacific Northwest. Considerably less common than **Cantharellus formosus**, our yellow-orange chanterelle, it is generally larger and meatier while maintaining the same great flavor. There are those who believe the flavor superior to that of **Cantharellus formosus**, and for those folks in particular, this is one of the great treasures of the forests.

It is a secretive species. It is often obscured by duff or cleverly disguised among groups of **Russula brevipes**. I only know of one spot in the county where I could count on it year after year. This is no longer a sure thing since the Ukrainians have found the location. These people are superb mushroom hunters and to their credit they leave the forest in as pristine a state as they found it. Not a leaf is disturbed. Not a chanterelle is left behind. It just means heading back to the mountains to find a back-up spot in case they beat me to it again.

Common belief was that the White Chanterelle could only be found from the coast of Washington south to northern California. Now they have been reported from Vancouver Island south to San Mateo County in California, and eastward into Idaho. Very rarely they show up in the Sierra Nevadas. They are found under conifers in mixed woods and appear to be mycorrhizal with Douglas fir and maybe hemlock. Biek reports them from northern California in yellow pine forests or with madrone

and oak on the coast. Lincoff reports it with lodgepole pine, and indeed it is common in some years in the eastern Cascades. Olle Persson, author of *The Chanterelle Book*, believes the white chanterelles that fruit under evergreen oak in northern California belong to an undescribed species.

The caps of **Cantharellus subalbidus** run from 6–14 cm wide. They are convex at first but soon become depressed at the disc to funnel shaped with irregular, undulating margins. In age, the margins tend to become eroded. There are those who believe the caps start off smooth and end up roughly scaly. And there are those who believe the reverse is true. Caps and gills are dead white in color but bruise slowly yellowish when handled. Tylutki reports specimens with pastel pink gills in Idaho. We don't have that version in Whatcom County. (It may represent a new species.) The cap context is thick and white, also turning slowly yellow when exposed. The gills are blunt, decurrent ridges often branched and intervenose with cross-hatching shallower gills. The stems are up to 2 cm thick and 3–6 cm long. They are equal or taper towards the base. They, too, are white, but stain ochre to rusty, eventually becoming brown at the base. The texture is smooth to appressed fibrillose. The odor and taste are mild. The spores are white and inamyloid.

As for the microscopic characters, the spores measure 7–9 x 5–6 µm. They are smooth-walled and ellipsoid to subovoid in shape. The pileipellis consists of an interwoven cutis. Clamps are present, but there are no cystidia.

In the woods you will find them partially covered with humus. They will greatly resemble the large, whitish **Russula brevipes**, which fruits in the same places at the same time. This species has true gills instead of blunt ridges, and if you happen to cook it by mistake, it is so bland that you will wonder what the accolades

LOOK-ALIKE

Russula brevipes

Leucopaxillus albissimus from Colorado   *Photo by Daniel Winkler*

Leucopaxillus paradoxus

are about. Other look-alikes are as follows:

Hygrophorus subalpinus: Found in the eastern Cascades in the spring, this impressively stout fungus differs by its waxy gills and its faint bitter aftertaste when sautéed in olive oil.

Aspropaxillus giganteus: A large white species with decurrent, "true" gills that is often found under the name **Clitocybe gigantea** in popular mushroom guides.

Leucopaxillus albissimus: A large, very firm, white species that always has a white mycelial mat at the stem base. The taste can be bitter or mild.

Leucopaxillus paradoxus: A slightly smaller version of the above, it has a strong, unidentifiable odor, and tends to darken to dingy buff or pallid tan when old.

Russula brevipes: The Earth Movers are more funnel-shaped

than the white chanterelles and thus collect more earth on their cap surfaces. They are also a brittle species. They will shatter if thrown against a tree. **Cantharellus subalbidus** differs by not shattering.

And finally, Dr. Lorelei Norvell points out that old yellowing fruiting bodies of **Cantharellus subalbidus** can be confused with older carpophores of **Cantharellus formosus** because they become more pallid in age. In fact, much to our dismay, European buyers generally shun **Cantharellus subalbidus** because they mistrust the yellow staining reaction of cap, stem, and gills.

This seems a bit odd since two other European chanterelles with whitish caps that stain instantly yellow when touched are deemed edible. These are **Cantharellus pallens** and **Cantharellus alborufescens**. The caps of **C. pallens** are covered with a fine, white powder when young. **Cantharellus alborufescens**, a species found under Mediterranean oaks, has pure white caps at first with contrasting yellow-ochre or creamy yellow ridges. The *Index Fungorum* lists it as a synonym of **Cantharellus cibarius**, an orange-capped species.

It may be important to note that our white chanterelle is not the only one out there. For those who thrive in taxonomic mumbo-jumbo, have at it:

Cantharellus pallens: A fleshy, white-capped Swedish chanterelle with contrasting pale yellow ridges. It fruits under hazel and oak. Some authors believe it is a form of **Cantharellus cibarius.** Others contend it is a valid species due to DNA sequencing. The Index Fungorum now considers it to be a synonym of **Cantharellus cibarius**.

Cantharellus pallidus Velenovsky: This is a synonym of **C. pallens**.

Gloeocantharellus pallidus (Yasuda) Giachini: This Japanese chanterelle differs from all these other pallid chanterelles by having ornamented, ellipsoid spores that measure 8–12 x 4–4.5 μm. The photo of **Gloeocantharellus pallidus** Yasuda shows a clustered off-white carpophore that seems less fleshy than **C. subalbidus**. It would be interesting to compare that taxon with our oak associated version of **Cantharellus subalbidus** in northern California.

All of these are presumed edible. The good news is that none of these species and potential varieties are often attacked by maggots. While slugs are known to dine on **Amanita phalloides**, for some reason, the flesh of the chanterelles is only accepted by the most desperate of the mushroom flies.

As Phyllis Glick writes in *The Mushroom Trail Guide*, "**C. subalbidus** is a very fleshy, delicious mushroom, one of the choicest edibles around." No one seems to disagree with that assessment, not even A.H. Smith, who nonetheless couldn't help but take a parting shot at it. He wrote of **Cantharellus subalbidus**, "the fruit body of this species is a mod-

LOOK-ALIKES

Aspropaxillus giganteus

Hygrophorus subalpinus

el of nature's inefficiency in using raw materials for spore production. The amount of supporting structure relative to the amount of spore producing tissue is the reverse of that for most mushroom fruiting bodies and one reason for regarding this species as primitive in the scale of evolution."

If primitive is this tasty, we're all for it. No mushroom cookbook that I could find had a specific recipe for the white chanterelle. One treats it the same way as the orange chanterelle. Terrific photos of the taxon can be found in *The New Savory Wild Mushroom* and in Arora's *All That the Rain Promises and More*.

BIBLIOGRAPHY

David Arora, *All That the Rain Promises and More*, 1991. Ten Speed Press, Berkeley, Calif.

Robert Bandoni & Adam Szczawinski, *Guide to Common Mushrooms of British Columbia*, 1976. British Columbia Provincial Museum, Victoria, B.C., Canada.

David Biek, *The Mushrooms of Northern California*, 1984. Spore Prints, Redding, Calif.

Guillaume Eyssartier & Pierre Roux, *Le Guide des Champignons de France et Europe*, 2012. Editions Belin, Paris.

Phyllis Glick, *The Mushroom Trail Guide*, 1979. Holt, Rinehart, & Winston, New York, NY.

Rokuya Imazeki, Tsuguo Hongo, & Keisuke Tubaki, *Common Fungi of Japan in Color*, 1970. Hoikusha Publishing, Osaka, Japan.

Gary Lincoff, *The Audubon Society Field Guide to North American Mushrooms*, 1981. Alfred A. Knopf, New York, NY.

Teresa Marrone & Drew Parker, *Mushrooms of the Northwest*, 2019. Adventure Publications, Cambridge, Minn.

Margaret McKenny, Daniel Stuntz, Joe Ammirati, *The New Savory Wild Mushroom*, 1987. University of Washington Press, Seattle, Wash.

Lorelei Norvell, *Preparation for a Key to the Cantharelloid Fungi of British Columbia, Washington, Oregon, and Idaho*. Pacific Northwest Key Council, Seattle, Wash.

Olle Persson, *The Chanterelle Book*, 1997. Ten Speed Press, Berkeley, Calif.

Alexander H. Smith, *A Field Guide to Western Mushrooms*, 1975. University of Michigan Press, Ann Arbor, Mich.

Harry Thiers, *Agaricales of California: 2. Cantharellaceae*, 1985. Mad River Press, Eureka, Calif.

Edmund Tylutki, *Mushrooms of Idaho and the Pacific Northwest, Vol. 2*, 1987. University of Idaho Press, Moscow, Idaho.

Chlorophyllum molybdites (Meyer) Massee

. . . the only large, fleshy, North American agaric known to have a green spore print.

According to Dr. Beug, **Chlorophyllum molybdites** has now been reported from Washington state in the Tri Cities area. Global warming has brought it northward at last. It is also in these pages because it is the mushroom most likely to poison our club members on their vacations south of here. Although club members Jeremy Ferrera and Daniel Viney claim to have seen this around Bellingham; they most likely saw unusual fruitings of **Chlorophyllum brunneum**. As authors Siegel and Schwarz put it "Occasionally **C. brunneum** will be encountered with light teal green hues on its gills or near the stipe apex, and this may cause confusion with **Chlorophyllum molybdites**." Because it bears a strong resemblance to edible **Macrolepiota procera** in the button stage and edible **Chlorophyllum rhacodes** at any stage, experts speculate that it accounts for more mushroom poisonings in the United States than any other fungus. Yet some can eat it with impunity. It is a mushroom imbued with enigma from almost any angle you look at it. Whenever someone comes up with a theory, someone else finds a fact to contradict it.

The Green Sickener thrives in suburban lawns and cemeteries from southern California to Florida, all through the Midwest, and north to Denver, Ottawa, and New York. It is also common in the tropics where it can be found by roadsides, gardens, and banana plantations. It is so cleverly disguised as a giant Lepiota that it once poisoned a graduate class in mycology because the gills refused to turn green at maturity.

The good news is that 99% of the time it's easy to identify if you do one thing. Take The Spore Print. **Chlorophyllum molybdites** is the only large, fleshy, North American agaric known to have a green spore print. The big edible Lepiotas have white spore prints while the large, scaly capped members of Agaricus have chocolate spore prints. So, ironically, **C. molybdites** is one of the few species that I could safely identify over the phone once a spore print is taken. If you can't get a spore print, don't experiment with eating it.

The caps can get huge, up to 40 cm wide. When young they are covered with a tough cinnamon-brown cuticle, which breaks up into prominent scales as the caps expand. Patches on the cap are fragments of the cuticle on a snow-white ground. The gills are free from the stem and white until they turn olive green from the spores. The stems can run up to a foot in length. They are whitish to flesh color tinged with brown. They turn reddish and then yellowish when bruised. The cap context also turns pinkish or reddish when bruised, a characteristic that mimics the edible species of Agaricus. The large double ring is soft and subcoriaceous with ragged edges. It is movable up and down the stem. The taste is mild and the odor mild to very agreeable, reminding one of perfume or fruit, even when dried.

Chlorophyllum molybdites is a pan-tropical species that appears in civilized lawns especially after tropical downpours. It was first called **Agaricus molybdites** by Meyer in 1818. Unaware that it had already been described, Massee called it **Chlorophyllum esculentum** from a collection he made in Guyana in 1898. One can speculate that it was not only edible, but choice! The epithet "chlorophyllum" refers to the green of the gills as they mature. "Molybdites" comes from the Greek "molybdos," the word for lead, evidently the color of the gills when they are beyond mature. Molybdenum

LOOK-ALIKE

Chlorophyllum brunneum

might be a more modern inter-pretation. Besides Guyana, **Chlorophyllum molybdites** has been recorded from the South Pacific islands, South Africa, Tanzania, Kenya, Uganda, the Philippines, Belize, Martinique, Guadalupe, Argentina, and Brazil. It has even been introduced to Edinburgh from a tree imported from Florida.

Rolf Singer made a study of **Chlorophyllum molybdites**, and in 1946 concluded, "there exists variation in the reddening of the cap context, exact tone of the spore print, and amount of toxins in the fruiting bodies." There is even variation in the microscopic characters. Pegler discovered "considerable variety in spore sizes, even by those produced by the same fruiting body." Sundberg found clamps in the pileal context, which allied the species closer to Lepiota. Earlier, Smith and Singer had not found clamps.

Microscopically, the pileipellis is a trichodermial palisade of erect and septate hyphae 3–7 µm wide with slightly thickened pale brown walls. As the caps expand and scales are formed, these hyphae are aggregated into small tufts. The spores measure 10.2–13 x 6.8–8.8 µm. They are ellipsoid, smooth, triple-walled, and dextrinoid in Melzer's. They have a distinct germ pore. (I once found a Chlorophyllum in Palm Springs with huge truncated spores. It was sent to Jack States who kindly affirmed the genus for me.) Singer noted that in many spores the exosporium was separated from the endosporium by an intermembranal

Chlorophyllum rhacodes from Vermont

Leucocoprinus cepistipes from Virginia

layer that often turned pink in KOH-phloxine. The entire spore turned bright, deep blue in cresyl blue.

In the early days in the United States, **Chlorophyllum molybdites** was called **Lepiota morganii** and regarded as a mixed blessing. Some could eat it while others became violently ill. In general it was thought to be edible in parts of South America but poisonous in North America and the Philippines. Here then is a sampling of opinions from the experts:

Nina Faubion: "Personally, I find this a most delicious mushroom. The meat is fine and usually free from worms. But the amateur better not take a chance because the poisoning can be acute."

Gary Lincoff: "A drastic sickener causing one to two or more days of violent purging."

Miron Hard: "I have known several families to eat of it, making about half the children in each family sick."

Ansel Stubbs: "Headache, nausea, dysentery, sweating, and

Lepiota fuliginescens

Leucoagaricus erythrophaeus

skin irritation have been experienced by the author from a small piece eaten raw. But larger amounts, well cooked, caused no inconvenience."

Ammirati, Traquair, & Horgen: "Symptoms of poisoning begin 1–2 hours after eating it. Queasiness and thirst develop first, followed by mental haziness, nausea, and cold sweats alternating with chills, then intervals of vomiting for 4–5 hours. The victim finally has an attack of copious, watery, or sometimes bloody diarrhea which persists from several hours to a few days. Abdominal pain can be mild or intense. Most victims recover within two days."

Denis Benjamin: "With some people the abdominal pain can be very severe. Symptoms can persist for up to six hours. The diarrhea can be explosive in nature and can become bloody. A risk of dehydration and subsequent death exists for children." (In 1900, a two-year old girl died after eating an undetermined amount.)

Charles McIlvaine: "The meat is fine and usually more free from worms than other mushrooms. Six families here have eaten heartily of them. The experience is that one or two members of each family are made sick, though in two families, who have several times eaten them, no one was made sick. I enjoy them immensely. I doubt if we have a finer flavored fungus. The meat is simply delicious. One fairy ring yields a bushel."

One tends to doubt if the retching few are really dreaming of bushels. There are many theories out there. Zoberi believes that toxicity could depend on climactic and habitat factors. Lincoff and Mitchel concluded that if the mushrooms were cooked in water heated to 158 degrees Fahrenheit for thirty minutes, the toxin was inactivated. The inference is that sickness might be avoided if the mushrooms were well cooked. Another theory is that different levels of toxicity could exist in each specimen. Add to this the probability that some individuals are more allergic to it than others and you have the full spectrum of possibilities.

Some progress has been made in identifying the toxins. In 1977 Pegler noted that Floche, Labarbe, & Roffi found a toxic substance, possibly an alkaloid, which was water soluble and labile with respect to time and temperature. In the same year, Lincoff & Mitchel wrote that a protein responsible for the poisonings had been isolated. It was thermolabile and could be inactivated with prolonged cooking. Then in 1985, Dr. Benjamin wrote that "one toxin may be a heat-labile protein that has a mass of 400,000 daltons composed of subunits, each with a mass of 40,000–60,000 daltons. This compound only had an effect on experimental animals when given by intraperitoneal injection. Some of the compounds responsible for the stomach distress were oxolans, anthraquinones, nitrogen heterocyclics, amides, peptides, terpenoid compounds, hydrazines, polysaccharides, lipids, and sterols. The presence and amount of these compounds varies with each mushroom."

According to Dr. Benjamin, the procedure to follow in case you are poisoned by **Chlorophyllum molybdites** is to first remove all mushroom particles from the stomach as fast as possible. He mentions syrup of ipecac as the most effective emetic. Activated charcoal should then be used to bind any leftover toxins. Intravenous fluids might be needed if there has been excessive vomiting. Recovery accelerates after these steps are taken.

The Green Sickener has closer relatives than previously thought. Besides **Chlorophyllum molybdites var. marginata**, a variety with blackish gill edges, five species formerly in Lepiota have now been placed in Chlorophyllum by Dr. Else Vellinga due to DNA profiling and "similarities in morphology." Several of these plus a smattering of more look-alikes follow:

Chlorophyllum rhacodes: A popular edible that turns salmon-pink in the frying pan, it differs by having white spores but otherwise is a dead-ringer for **Chlorophyllum molybdites**

Macrolepiota procera from Austria   *Photo by Daniel Winkler*

Macrolepiota procera ss auct. northeast from Mass.

with its brick colored cap scales. The stems of **C. rhacodes** stain orange and then red when bruised.

Chlorophyllum brunneum: Looks just like **C. rhacodes**, but with brown cap scales. Some specimens will have a ridged basal bulb, and the stems also turn orange when bruised.

Macrolepiota procera: The Parasol Mushroom is another choice edible. It has white spores, a thinner, taller stature, and a dark nipple umbo at the cap centers. It also differs by having a chevron pattern of brownish squamules on the stem and an abruptly bulbous stem base instead of the more clavate base of **C. molybdites**.

Macrolepiota konradii from England

Macrolepiota sp. from Tibet

Macrolepiota procera ss auct. northeast: This differs from the European **M. procera** by the non-chevron pattern of the squamules on the stem and the paler tan colored cap scales and disc. It will probably need a new name. Spores of this collection in the photo measured 15–19 x 10–12.5 µm.

Macrolepiota procera var. pseudoolivascens: Similar to the above but has flesh that turns greenish when bruised.

Lepiota fuliginescens: A rarely seen species authored by Murrill that shows up occasionally at Deception Pass Park in the fall. It has white spores, a long, slender stem, a membranous ring, and smoother, paler caps than **Chlorophyllum molybdites**.

Macrolepiota excoriata: A European species that has ochre-brown cap scales and a double-layered ring on the stem.

Macrolepiota konradii: Another European species with lumpy cap margins and hazel brown scales on a white floccose ground.

Macrolepiota sp.: This Tibetan species was found near the Tsod-zong Gonpa Temple on Lake Draksun. Next to the temple grew a grafted tree that was half conifer and half willow. This tree was well over 100 years old. It was yet another symbol found at the temple representing the universality of life. It was probably not planted in order to confuse mycologists who now had to decide whether nearby mushrooms were mycorrhizal with the willow or the conifer. Maybe it was just saprophytic and none of this matters.

Leucoagaricus erythrophaeus: Differs by its smaller stature, vinaceous-brown cap scales, dark violet-brown ring margin, white spores, and stems that age vinaceous-brown.

Leucocoprinus cepistipes: Differs by its smaller size, more fragile fruiting bodies, onion shaped stem base, and mealy whitish caps with striate margins.

Chlorophyllum molybdites is a beautiful mushroom. It often fruits in spectacular fairy rings in hot, humid weather. I have seen it in Belize near a grade school in Forest Home. The caps were the size of frisbees and made an 80 foot circle around a mango tree. But we may have to wait for more climate change and the "greenhouse effect" before such rings become common in Washington State.

However, if you find a collection of large Lepiota-like specimens out on a lawn, it might be a good idea to take the spore print. If the species won't yield a spore deposit, try laying the gills face down on a mirror or a piece of glass. Wait a couple of hours and then scrape the surface with a razor blade. Check out the edge with a magnifying glass. If you still can't observe a spore color, don't take the risk. We won't know when or if **Chlorophyllum molybdites** decides to invade the Northwest on a regular basis. If you get a green spore print, that will give it away.

Addendum: This is pure hearsay, but one last Hail Mary attempt at a spore deposit may be to place the mushroom in the fridge for an hour. It may be fooled into thinking it is about to freeze and thereby produce its spores in a hurry.

BIBLIOGRAPHY

Joe Ammirati, J.A. Traquair, Paul Horgen, *Poisonous Mushrooms of the Northern United States and Canada*, 1985. University of Minnesota Press, Minneapolis, Minn.

David Arora, *Mushrooms Demystified,* 1986. Ten Speed Press, Berkeley, Calif.

Denis Benjamin, *Mushrooms—Poisons and Panaceas*, 1985. W.H. Freeman, New York, NY.

Colin Dickinson & John Lucas, *VNR Color Dictionary of Mushrooms*, 1979. Van Nostrand Reinhold, New York, NY.

Guillaume Eyssartier & Pierre Roux, *Le Guide des Champignons de France et Europe,* 2012. Editions Belin, Paris.

Nina Lane Faubion, *Some Edible Mushrooms and How to Cook Them*, 1938. Binfords & Mort, Portland, Ore.

J. Walton Groves, *Edible and Poisonous Mushrooms of Canada*, 1979. Research Branch, Agriculture Canada, Ottawa, Canada.

Miron Hard, *Mushrooms, Edible & Otherwise*, 1908. Dover Publications, New York, NY.

Gary Lincoff, *The Audubon Society Field Guide to North American Mushrooms*, 1981. Alfred A. Knopf, New York, NY.

Gary Lincoff & D.H. Mitchel, *Toxic and Hallucinogenic Mushroom Poisoning*, 1977. Van Nostrand Reinhold, New York, NY.

Charles McIlvaine & Robert Macadam, *One Thousand American Fungi*, 1902. Dover Publications, New York, NY.

Meinhard Moser, *Keys to Agarics and Boleti*, 1983. Translated and published by Roger Phillips, London.

William Murrill, *The Agaricaceae of the Pacific Coast.II* in *Mycologia* 4 (231–262), 1912.

William Murrill, *Agaricaceae, Parts 1–3* in *North American Flora* 10 (1–226), 1914–1917.

William Murrill, *Florida Lepiotas in Lloydia* 12, (56–61), 1949.

Alan Muskat, *How Not to Confuse a Green-Gilled Parasol with its Edible Cousin* in *Fungi*, Vol.8, No.5, 2016.

David Pegler, *A Preliminary Agaric Flora of East Africa*, 1977. Her Majesty's Stationary Office, London.

David Pegler, *Agaric Flora of the Lesser Antilles*, 1983. Stationery Office Books, UK.

Rolf Singer, *Agaricales in Modern Taxonomy* in *Lilloa* 22 (1–832), 1949.

Noah Siegel & Christian Schwarz, *Mushrooms of the Redwood Coast*, 2016. Ten Speed Press, Berkeley, Calif.

Rolf Singer, *New and Interesting Species of Basidiomycetes II* in *The Papers of the Michigan Academy of Science, Arts, and Letters* 32 (103–150), 1946.

A.H. Smith & Nancy Weber, *A Field Guide to Southern Mushrooms*, 1985. University of Michigan Press, Ann Arbor, Mich.

Ansel Stubbs, *Wild Mushrooms of the Central Midwest*, 1971. University Press of Kansas.

Walter Sundberg, *The Genus Chlorophyllum in California* in *Madrono* 21 (15–20), 1971.

Else Vellinga, *Type Studies in the Agaricaceae—The Complex of Chlorophyllum Rachodes* in *Mycotaxon* 85 (259–270), 2003.

Mary Wells & D.H. Mitchel, *Mushrooms of Colorado and Adjacent Areas*, 1970. Denver Museum of Natural History, Denver, Colo.

M.H. Zoberi, *Tropical Macrofungi—Some Common Species*, 1972. MacMillan Press, London.

Michael Beug, Mushrooms of Cascadia, 2021. The Fungi Press, Batavia, Illinois.

Chroogomphus tomentosus (Murrill) O.K. Miller

Accused of being chanterelle imposters . . .
Chroogomphus are the least likely to cause
damage if you make a mistake.

One of several mushrooms that have been accused of being chanterelle imposters, **Chroogomphus tomentosus**, or Wooly Chroogs, as they are cheerfully referred to by local fans, are the least likely to cause damage if you make a mistake. This is not only because all species of Chroogomphus are edible, but also because the Wooly Chroogs make themselves known in a frying pan by turning bright magenta when cooked.

I will never forget an evening when I was enjoying a quiet beer at the bar of the Fairhaven Restaurant. The restaurant in front of the bar was slowly filling up with clients. Suddenly there was an uproar originating from the kitchen. Quite a bit of hoarse shouting indicated accusations were flying about. A couple of us at the bar trotted back there to discover an apoplectic chef holding a frying pan of chanterelles with a few bright pink ones interspersed. My buddy, Dan Digerness, had sold the chanterelles to the restaurant that morning, but had forgotten to remove the Wooly Chroogs. Seeing nothing but lawsuits in the lane ahead, the head chef deep-sixed the whole batch.

Actually, no harm would have been done. The species is a little chewy when fried in its fresh condition…not all of the stem is digestible…and it has a rather sweetish, acidic taste that neither attracts nor repels. But it is also aciduous enough to pucker your mouth into a somewhat different shape. You don't go back for seconds. However, if dried and then reconstituted by soaking in water, the Wooly Chroogs are magically transformed. Arora notes that "they acquire a pleasant, chewy texture that is perfect with tomato sauce if they are finely chopped up and dried."

I keep a few jars of dried **Chroogomphus tomentosus** along with my jars of dried boletes and morels. Every couple years I will serve them at our mid-March Survivor's Banquet, a club event that celebrates those of us who survived eating wild mushrooms during the past year. The Wooly Chroogs never seem to win the culinary prize, but by the end of the evening, there's not one left on the plate. They go well in a poultry stuffing. Since reconstituted specimens turn an attractive plum-brown when cooked, they also contrast well with Spanish yellow rice.

In most guides the common name for **Chroogomphus tomentosus** is the Wooly Pine Spike. This name is totally inappropriate for our area where our two native pines are far outnumbered by fir, spruce, and hemlock; and **C. tomentosus** is found with all these conifers in abundance. The generally curved stems separate them immediately from a railroad spike. Following a more liberal policy towards common names, at one point championed by Gary Lincoff, we should be allowed to adjust a common name to suit the local ecology.

Wooly Chroogs differ from chanterelles by having true gills, smoky black spores, and a dry, matted-tomentose cap surface. Add to these characteristics a totally ochre-orange fruiting body and a growth habit with conifers, and you can't confuse them with any other species. The caps run from 3 ½–8 cm wide and are dome shaped at first becoming convex to plane. Purple stains can sometimes be found on older caps. The gills are the same pale

LOOK-ALIKE

Hygrophoropsis aurantiaca

Cantharellus formosus   *Photo by Richard Morrison*

Cantharellus subpruinosus from Spain

Microscopically, the spores are huge, narrowly elliptic to spindle shaped and measure 15-25 x 6-9 μm. The pleurocystidia are also huge. They are thick-walled and measure 118-225 x 20-21 μm. The terminal cells are cylindric and the hyphae of the pileal context are strongly amyloid in Melzer's.

Look-alikes and close relatives include the following:

Cantharellus formosus: Our Northwest chanterelles are often found in the company of **Chroogomphus tomentosus**. They can be told apart by their smoother caps and blunt ridges in lieu of true gills. They never have black spores.

Cantharellus subpruinosus: Differs by its strongly pruinose caps when young, lobed and inrolled margins, and yellow-cream colored spores.

Hygrophoropsis aurantiaca: This usually orange-capped species has a more slender stature than **Chroogomphus tomentosus**, white spores, and more brilliantly orange decurrent gills that fork more profusely. It is edible for some, allergic for others.

Chroogomphus leptocystis: Differs by having a grayer cap and thin-walled pleurocystidia.

Chroogomphus ochraceus: Found with pines in New England and the West Coast, it has the same orange-ochre coloration, but has smooth, viscid caps and slightly smaller spores.

Chroogomphus tomentosus has been reported from Hokkaido, Japan, and from the Rockies to the West Coast. Arora reports them from San Francisco northward along the coast. They are especially

ochre orange of the cap becoming grayish orange in age. They are deeply decurrent, distant, and often fork near the cap margin. According to Bessette & Fischer, "gills of very young specimens are covered by a fibrous and pale yellow-orange partial veil that only sometimes leaves a ring of fibers near the stem apex." This fibrillose annular zone on the stem often disappears in age. The gills blacken as the spores mature. Stems can run up to 17 cm long and are 1-2 cm thick. Often curved, they are equal or taper towards the base. They are appressed-fibrillose and solid. If you find pin holes, it means the maggots got there first.

Dr. Orson Miller, who moved the taxon from Gomphidius to Chroogomphus, noted that the cap tissue had an amyloid reaction with Melzer's solution.

abundant in the Priest Lake area of Idaho, the Olympic National Forest, and the western Cascades. They are also very common in Whatcom County, fruiting right alongside the chanterelles from early September through late November.

Instead of using the traditional chestnuts, try using reconstituted Wooly Chroogs for your Thanksgiving stuffing. The sautéed Chroogs have a fine mushroomy flavor with a tinge of sweetness. Later, whether wine has been included or not, your urine may also turn reddish. Either way, your guests will never forget you.

BIBLIOGRAPHY

David Arora, *Mushrooms Demystified*, 1986. Ten Speed Press, Berkeley, Calif.

Alan Bessette & David Fischer, *Edible Wild Mushrooms of North America*, 1992. University of Texas Press, Austin, Texas.

Aurelio Garcia Blanco & Juan Antonio Sanchez Rodriguez, 2011, *Setas de la Peninsula Iberica y de Europa*, Editorial Everest, Leon, Spain.

Margaret Mckenny, Daniel Stuntz, & Joe Ammirati, *The New Savory Wild Mushroom*, 1987. University of Washington Press, Seattle, Wash.

Kent & Vera McKnight, *Peterson Field Guides: Mushrooms*, 1987. Houghton Mifflin Co., Boston, Mass.

Orson Miller, *Mushrooms of North America*. E.P. Dutton & Co., New York, NY.

Orson Miller, *Monograph of Chroogomphus* in *Mycologia* 56 (526–549), 1964.

Orson Miller & James Trappe, *A New Chroogomphus with a Loculate Hymenium and a Revised Key to Section Floccigomphus* in *Mycologia* 62 (831–836), 1970.

Kit Scates, *Field Key to the Gomphidiaceae of the Pacific Northwest*, 1980. Pacific Northwest Key Council, Seattle, Wash.

A.H. Smith, *A Field Guide to Western Mushrooms*, 1975. University of Michigan Press, Ann Arbor, Mich.

A.H. & Helen Smith & Nancy Weber, *How to Know the Gilled Mushrooms*, 1979. William C. Brown, Dubuque, Iowa.

Harry Thiers, *Gomphidiaceae in Agaricales of California*, 1985. Mad River Press, Eureka, Calif.

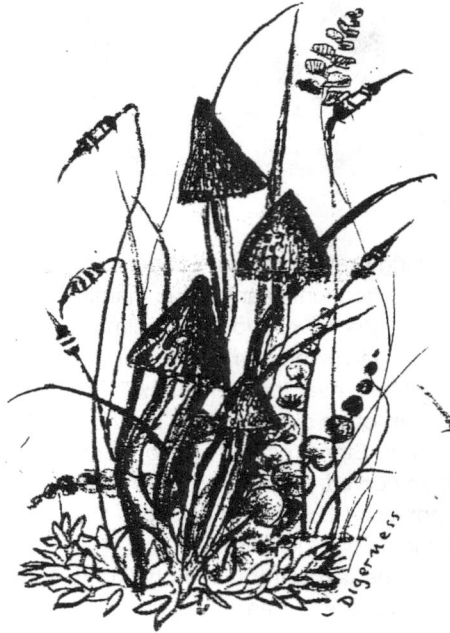

Ciboria rufofusca (Weberbauer) Saccardo

*It's somehow impressive
that such an innocuous cup
fungus can stand out . . .*

An increasingly common West Coast discomycete, the diminutive **Ciboria rufofusca** fruits on both Douglas fir cones and silver fir scales. It is the only brown Ciboria that fruits on these substrates, and so is identifiable by this fact alone. I first saw it at Cispus near Mount Adams years ago, and had no idea what it was. On April 8, 2001, I found it again at Deception Pass Park on a Doug fir cone. The photo here is of a Berthusen Park find near Lynden in the spring of 2009.

For years it was thought that **Ciboria rufofusca** only fruited on individual silver fir scales. But now that it has made the jump to Douglass fir cones, it seems to be found more often over a larger range. It is a saprophyte that decomposes fir scales and cones, returning the nutrients to the forest floor. The fruiting bodies are 1/3–1 1/2 cm wide, bladder shaped at first, and then goblet shaped with a stem or saucer shaped with very little stem. Colors vary from grayish tan to orange-brown to Prout's brown or even chestnut brown. The discs are always smooth and often dusted with a white powder. The cup margins can be wavy and split in age. Stems are 1/3–1 1/2 cm long and up to 2 mm thick. They are brownish becoming darker brown towards the base. Bessie Kanouse wrote there is no sign of a stroma or a sclerotia, which the original concept of Ciboria called for, but Breitenbach & Kranzlin found the cone scales to be stromatized.

Microscopically, the spores are uniseriate inside an ascus. There are 8 spores per ascus. The asci measure 45–90 x 4–6.5 µm. The spores are smooth, ovoid, and measure 4–7.5 x 2–3.5 µm. Many are imbued with two oil drops. The paraphyses are slender, non-septate, and faintly thickened at the apices.

Its closest look-alike may be **Sclerotinia veratri**, which fruits on rotten corn lily stems in the spring and further differs by arising from a black sclerotium the size of a rice kernel. **Dumontinia tuberosa** has much longer stems up to 10 cm long and fruits on old tubers of the garden flowers Ranunculus and Anenome. **Ciboria batschiana** is a dead ringer that fruits on old acorns in the fall. Another potential look-alike, **Donadinia nigrella**, also fruits near

LOOK-ALIKES

Dumontinia tuberosa (formerly Sclerotinia tuberosa)

Donadinia nigrella (formerly Plectania nannfeldtii)

spring snowmelt, but the cups have a slightly roughened grayish-black outer surface, and the stems are black with black mycelium arising from woody debris.

Otto Weberbauer first published the species as a Peziza in 1873. Saccardo moved it to Ciboria in 1889. In the 1930s, both Kauffman and A.H. Smith made several trips to the Olympic Peninsula, mainly to look for agarics and boletes. But between them they made over 400 collections of ascomycetes. Perhaps overloaded with these, plus collections from elsewhere, they relegated the ascomycetes to Bessie Kanouse to figure out. She was a fellow professor at the University of Michigan who had published on water molds prior to this assignment. She found two collections of **Ciboria rufofusca**, both collected by Smith. One was found at Boulder Lake at 4,500 feet on May 28, 1939, the other at Deer Lake on June 13, 1939. She surmised that these were the first records of this species in the United States.

Ciboria rufofusca is a spring to early summer species, appearing solitary or in scattered groups on fir cones and scales. It probably has no culinary value, but Gueho & Pesando found that it had strong anti-fungal properties. It's somehow impressive that such an innocuous cup fungus can stand out in that way.

BIBLIOGRAPHY

J. Breitenbach & F. Kranzlin, *Fungi of Switzerland, Vol.1*, 1984. Verlag Mykologia, Lucerne, Switzerland.
Dennis Desjardin, Michael Wood, & Fred Stevens, *California Mushrooms*, 2015. Timber Press, Portland, Ore.
Vera Evenson, *Mushrooms of Colorado*, 1997. Denver Botanic Gardens, Denver, Colo.
Ian Gibson, *Cup Fungi of the Pacific Northwest*, 2007. Pacific Northwest Key Council, Seattle, Wash.
E. Gueho & D. Pesando, *Antifungal Activity of Some Discomycetes. I. Biological Spectrum of Ciboria rufofusca (Weberb.) Sacc.* in *Mycopathologia* 77 (2), (123–128), 1982.

Bessie Kanouse, *A Survey of the Discomycete Flora of the Olympic National Park and Adjacent Areas* in *Mycologia* 39 (635–689), 1947.
Paul Kirk (ed.), *Index Fungorum*, http://www.indexfungorum.org/names/Names.asp
Roger Phillips, *Mushrooms and Other Fungi of Great Britain and Europe*, 1981. Pan Books, London.
Trond Schumacher, *Sclerotiniaceae in Nordic Macromycetes, Vol.1*, 2000. Nordsvamp, Copenhagen.
Steve Trudell & Joe Ammirati, *Mushrooms of the Pacific Northwest*, 2009. Timber Press, Portland, Ore.

Clavariadelphus caespitosus Methven

*Unfortunately we haven't seen
this species since 1993 . . .*

For our October foray of 1993, our club president at the time, Kathi Marlowe, had selected Darrington as the collecting site. This is a good two hours drive south from Bellingham, and I heard later that only two or three people attended. A few chanterelles were found, but not enough to warrant the drive. I thought the foray must have been a complete bust until a few days later Kathi dropped these on my desk. They looked like **Clavariadelphus pistillaris** but had more of a pale brick color and they bruised russet brown when touched. Kathi told me there were masses of them in caespitose clusters in moss under conifers. She only brought back these three fruiting bodies because she wanted the rest to spore and reproduce. It's the usual quandary . . . scientific identification versus the environment. I felt privileged to see these.

So camera in hand, I trudged out to a lawn for yet another

LOOK-ALIKE

Clavariadelphus occidentalis from Calif.

out-of-habitat photo.

We noticed that the core of the larger specimen had been devoured by worms and leaping fungus fleas, but hoped the context wouldn't be a major diagnostic zone. The specimens found by Kathi and husband Dave were narrowly clavate and longitudinally rugulose (wrinkled). They were a pale ochre-brick color becoming buff at the base. Andy Methven describes the colors as dull red to grayish red. The largest specimen measured 10.5 cm tall and 2.5 cm thick. The thinner specimens, on the right in the photo, were caespitose. Apices were subacute to obtuse. The taste was mild, and there was no staining reaction with KOH. The spores were broadly ellipsoid to almond shaped. They measured 8.4–10.3 x 5.7–7 µm. The basidia measured 41–50 x 7.5–8.2 µm.

When we herded it through Dr. Methven's key in Bibliotheca Mycologica 138, there were three other possibilities initially. **Clavariadelphus subfastigiatus** was eliminated because it has a strong green staining reaction with KOH. **Clavariadelphus occidentalis** differs by preferring tanoak and madrone on the West Coast, having longer spores at 9–13.5 x 5–6.5 µm, a more ochre-brown color, and according to Arora, a flavor of stale rope. **Clavariadelphus pistillaris**, an East Coast species, differs by its more orange-red clubs, bitter taste, and much larger spores at 10–16 x 5–10 µm. Carpophores can be close to the same color in age, but young fruiting bodies of **Clavariadelphus occidentalis** start off cream color to pale pink, which is partly diagnostic in Methven's key.

The holotype for **Clavariadelphus caespitosus** was found on the Upper Priest River in Idaho on September 21, 1968. Since then it has been recorded from California, Oregon, and Washington in mixed forests, usually in caespitose clusters. Clavariadelphus has thicker fruiting bodies than other genera in the Clavariaceae. They often arise from deep in the duff with scant mycelial hyphae at their bases.

We are grateful for Andy Methven's key. This is the sort of work that is so much needed to sort out poorly understood taxa in the Pacific Northwest. It's not that present mycologists are doing bad work. There just aren't enough of them to cover all the genera simultaneously.

As for edibility, it's anyone's guess. People who have eaten these but thought they were

LOOK-ALIKE

Clavariadelphus truncatus

eating **Clavariadelphus pistillaris** have either had the "stale rope" tasting experience of David Arora or that of McIlvaine's, who claimed that they (**C. pistillaris**) were delightful, that all the bitterness disappeared in the cooking. An even better culinary experience may be indulging in **Clavariadelphus truncatus**, an orange Clavariadelphus with a flattened apex. The flavor is reported as so sweet they can be sautéed in butter and served for dessert.

Unfortunately we haven't seen **Clavariadelphus caespitosus** since 1993, and all culinary adventures will have to wait.

BIBLIOGRAPHY

David Arora, *Mushrooms Demystified*, 1986. Ten Speed Press, Berkeley, Calif.

Dennis Desjardin, Michael Wood, & Fred Stevens, *California Mushrooms*, 2015. Timber Press, Portland, Ore.

Ian Gibson, *Trial Field Key to Club Fungi in the Pacific Northwest*, 2007. Pacific Northwest Key Council, Seattle, Wash.

Charles McIlvaine & Robert Macadam, *One Thousand American Fungi*, 1902. Dover Publications, New York, NY.

Andrew Methven, *The Genus Clavariadelphus in North America* in *Bibliotheca Mycologica* 138 (3–192), 1990.

Andrew Methven, *Notes on Clavariadelphus. III. New and Noteworthy Species from North Amerioca* in *Mycotaxon* 34 (153–179), 1989.

Orson Miller, *Mushrooms of North America*, 1972. E.P. Dutton & Co., New York, NY.

Clitocybe albirhiza Bigelow & A.H. Smith

The stem base is always
covered with a dense mat of
white mycelium.

Less-zonate specimens of Clitocybe albirhiza

Known by the cunning epithet of White Strings by the McKnights or as Snowmelt Clitocybe by Arora, **Clitocybe albirhiza** may well be our most common agaric in the eastern Cascades in the spring. It often fruits in big rings or arcs under larch and lodgepole pine. The copious white rhizomorphs, for which it is named in Latin, cling tenaciously to the needle duff. According to the McKnights, it fruits under snow banks in winter or early spring. But the spores won't develop until the snow melts. Those fruiting bodies that have formed under snow have a characteristically curved lower stem.

Clitocybe albirhiza appears to be a highly successful fungus. At first known only from Idaho and Wyoming (the type was found at Payette Lake in Idaho on June 27, 1954), the species now ranges from high altitudes in the Rockies westward to the eastern Cascades. I have found dead ringers at Deception Pass Park and at Lummi Island under conifers. Since these were at sea level they most likely represented different species.

Cap sizes for **Clitocybe albirhiza** are 2 ½–10 cm wide. They are convex to plane at first, with incurved margins, then more funnel-shaped in age with lobed or wavy margins. They are smooth and thick fleshed only at the disc. Young specimens are canescent with a whitish bloom in wet conditions. As the canescence wears off, the caps can appear concentrically zonate. Cap colors vary from dingy buff to flesh color or pale ochre tan to brown. Gills are adnate to short decurrent, buff to tan or a pallid flesh color. They are crowded, thin, usually forked and intervenose. Stipes are 3–8 cm long and ½ to 2 cm thick. They are concolorous with the cap color, solid at first becoming hollow in age. Young stems are canescent when wet and fibrillose-striate in dry weather. The base is always covered with a dense mat of white mycelium. (See specimen on left in second photo.) The spores are white and inamyloid. The odor is reported as disagreeable, the taste both disagreeable and bitter. In the high altitudes of the Rockies it is found with Engelmann spruce.

Microscopically, spores are ellipsoid, smooth, and measure 4.5–6 x 2.5–3.5 µm. The basidia are 2 to 4-spored with sterigmata sometimes germinated. The pileipellis is a cutis of radially parallel hyphae. The cap context has more inflated hyphae. The gill trama consists of undulat-

Clitocybe glacialis (formerly Lyophyllum montanum)

Clitocybe squamulosa var. montana

Lepista subalpina

ing subparallel hyphae, and clamps are present. The species was placed by Dr. Bigelow in Section Candicantes because of its canescent cap surface.

For a novice, **Clitocybe albirhiza** would be hard to identify. There are countless drab Clitocybes in the western states to confuse it with, but **Clitocybe albirhiza** is the only one that fruits in the spring in the eastern Cascades, can reach a cap size of 6–10 cm wide, and has a massive clump of white mycelium at the stem base. If you peruse Bigelow's Clitocybe monograph, you can't help noticing a fair number of other species with white mycelium at their stem bases. Most are found at lower altitudes, but they are too numerous to list them all here. A few of the more common look-alikes follow:

Clitocybe glacialis: This is another snowmelt mushroom appearing right along with **Clitocybe albirhiza,** but it has a glabrous grayish cap that appears hoary when young, and no rhizomorphs at the stem base.

Clitocybe squamulosa var. montana: This also has white rhizomorphs, but much less copious. It differs by having a minutely scaly cap of a pallid cinnamon color. Also found in needle duff or moss.

Infundibulicybe trulliformis: A grayish species with a wide geographic range, it differs by its farinaceous odor and minutely velvety cap surface. It can have both white mycelium and rhizoids.

Lepista subalpina: The photo here depicts a collection from

153

the gravelly roadside on Hannegan Pass Road. (I have no idea why I propped it on a log for the photo. This is a terrestrial species.) Cap colors vary from vinaceous brown to brown depending on what hygrophanous stage it is in. It can also have white rhizoids but differs in its often ribbed and wavy cap margins. Thanks go to Dr. Scott Redhead for the identification.

Every spring, usually in late May, our mushroom club migrates over to the eastern Washington Cascades for a special morel weekend. We call it Morel Madness. Often we don't hit it right weather-wise, and then it's just Morel Mad. What else could we eat if neither the morels nor **Boletus rex-veris** were out there? Dave Jansen, our first club president, fixed that for us.

I was new to the club back in the spring of 1989. Thus, I was mystified when I returned to the lodge kitchen on a late Saturday afternoon to find Dave sautéing a large batch of the White Strings on the camp stove. Culinary adventures in the genus Clitocybe were new to me. This is the genus that presents us with the poisonous species **Clitocybe dealbata** and **Clitocybe rivulosa**, the former actually sort of resembling **Clitocybe albirhiza**. Dave smiled happily and told me not to worry. He and other club members had been eating it for years!

It was an interesting case history. Dave had been told by Key Council member Charlie Volz that it was an edible but unnamed Melanoleuca! Charlie Volz is someone I had never met. He had a bit of a reputation as a maverick in the club. For instance, one of his favorite mushrooms to eat was **Gyromitra esculenta**, a species we are advised to parboil before eating, and then to consume only limited quantity at that. I had to admit that **Clitocybe albirhiza** did have some Melanoleucoid features. The white spores, gill attachment that was often adnate, and tough, fibrous stem that became fibrillose striate in dry weather are all features that are reminiscent of that genus. Although there is no modern monograph on North American Melanoleuca, no species of that genus had hitherto been reported as poisonous (if you discount Murrill who deemed all Tricholomas to be Melanoleucas at one point). It must have seemed to Charlie Volz a relatively safe genus to munch in. One has to admit that believing you are eating a species in a safe genus is a roundabout way to discover an edible in a dangerous genus.

So I took the plunge. With my inner alarm system on ready alert, I took my first tentative bite, then another . . . then another. They soon vanished from the frying pan. There was the faintest suggestion of bitterness, but it was attractive, like bitters in a Manhattan. Everyone agreed that as a back up to the morel in times of dearth that not even **Agrocybe praecox** could approach it in flavor. No one had ever reported being made ill by it, and suddenly we had another good edible from the eastern Cascades.

For the public at large, those who aren't skilled at wild mushroom identification, the words of Dr. Joe Ammirati still ring true. In *The New Savory Wild Mushroom* he cautioned, "It is one of a large group of species, some of which are poisonous, so it should not be experimented with." Good point. Make sure you are in good company before embarking on this adventure.

BIBLIOGRAPHY

David Arora, *Mushrooms Demystified*, 1986. Ten Speed Press, Berkeley, Calif.

Howard Bigelow, *The Genus Clitocybe in North America: Section Clitocybe* in *Lloydia* 28 (139–180), 1965. J. Cramer, Germany.

Howard Bigelow, *North American Species of Clitocybe. Part I* in *Nova Hedwigia* 72 (91), 1982.

Howard Bigelow & A.H. Smith, *Clitocybe Species from the Western United States* in *Mycologia* 54 (498–515), 1962.

Vera Evenson, *Mushrooms of Colorado*, 1997. Denver Botanic Gardens, Denver, Colo.

Margaret McKenny, Daniel Stuntz, & Joe Ammirati, *The New Savory Wild Mushroom*, 1987. University of Washington Press, Seattle, Wash.

Kent & Vera McKnight, *Peterson Field Guides—Mushrooms*, 1987. Houghton Mifflin Co., Boston, Mass.

Clitopilus cystidiatus Hausknecht & Noordeloos

An alien arrives at Oak Harbor.

Over the years Margaret Dilly has brought some unusual fungi to our shows and forays. After awhile you get an inkling which ones they are, namely those upon the identification table that don't seem quite right for the current foray site. You might even say something like, "where did these come from?" Margaret will fess up immediately. Almost invariably they come from the woods near her home on Whidbey Island. There, the climate is a little drier, a little more like northern California than the mainland. Margaret sometimes brings the poisonous **Clitocybe dealbata** to our shows. She makes a big point over how to distinguish it from the edible **Marasmius oreades** since both can be found in fairy rings in lawns. However, on the November 20th foray at Deception Pass Park in 1998, she arrived loaded with two Clitocyboid fungi that immediately caught my attention. Neither was **Clitocybe dealbata**.

The first one I examined turned out to be a potentially new species in Subsection Cinnamomeophyllae in the genus Clitocybe. It had grayish caps and cinnamon colored gills. It just didn't fit the descriptions of the smattering of others in that group in Bigelow.

The second species arrived in the form of a caespitose clump. Imagine my surprise the next day when the spores turned out to be flesh colored. Under the microscope they looked like elongated footballs with longitudinal ridges—the hallmark for Clitopilus. Although they looked like gray-capped versions of the edible **Clitopi-**

Clitopilus prunulus

lus prunulus, the spore sizes didn't match up, and the structure of the pileipellis was a cutis with clavate ends protruding, not the entangled hyphae of **C. prunulus**. The spores measured 9–12.5 x 5–6 µm. They had a flattened hilar depression and a pronounced apiculus. There were no clamps seen.

Then I worked on the macro-characters. Caps measured 6–6 ½ cm wide and were convex to plane with wavy, irregular margins. The surface was dry, mat, and a grayish-tan color becoming pale buff at the margins. The gills were decurrent, crowded, cream colored at first becoming flesh colored from spores in age. The stems were up to 1½ cm thick and only 2 cm long. They were slightly flattened, white pruinose over a grayish ground. The taste was mealy, the odor strongly farinaceous. Margaret had told me they were found in mixed woods on Whidbey Island.

Problem was, they didn't appear in North American literature. All the remaining Clitopilus species in North America not named **Clitopilus prunulus** had much smaller statures. I turned to my homemade index and discovered that Dr. Machiel Noordeloos of Holland seemed to have worked on this genus in Europe more than anyone else. I turned my photo into a postcard and mailed it off.

The response was immediate. He was keen on seeing the specimens. Perhaps to show goodwill, he sent me a copy of Fungi Non Delineati, Part 4, as a gift. It was a princely gift. Along with it was a key to the European species of Clitopilus translated from the German. A couple of months passed. Then, in late May of 1999, the main response:

"I finally got the time to look at the material. My conclusions are that it must be the first known North American record of **Clitopilus cystidiatus**. It is not rare in the coniferous and mixed forests of central and southern Europe. It is separated from other species of Clitopilus by the presence of filamentous and septate cheilocystidia."

It is always an uplifting experience to get a name for a species you never saw before. I went out on the street and bought a bottle of champagne. It doesn't happen very often that it all comes together like this.

Ian Gibson, author of the online fungus identification site, *Matchmaker*, was able to procure the original Latin description from Europe. I further learned that the caps had inrolled margins when young and were a mottled slate gray with a micaceous texture. They were only slightly hygrophanous. The gills became flesh colored from the spores, not pink. The stems were short and relatively thick, smooth at the apex and appressed fibrillose towards the base. The spores measured 9.5–13.5 x 5–6.5 µm. The cheilocystidia were filiform to lageniform (long necked) or slightly clavate. The species preferred acidic to calcareous soils. It was first described from the oak forests of Sardinia where it was plentiful. It had lingered for years in Dr. Marco Contu's herbarium under the name **Clitopilus prunulus var. sardoa**. It has been reported from Italy, Portugal, and the warmer areas of Austria.

Clitopilus cystidiatus differs visually from **C. prunulus** by its grayer cap and stem, and gills that don't turn pink in age. A closer look-alike is the European **Clitopilus paxilloides**. Caps of this taxon are more of a gray brown, and they also differ by having clamps and no cheilocystidia. And finally, from Costa Rica, there is a **Clitopilus griseobrunneus** with gray-brown caps fading to pale brown at the margins. It is only mentioned here because severe global warming may bring it north.

Subsequent DNA sequencing of species of **Clitopilus** throughout the Pacific Northwest are also indicating **Clitopilus cystidiatus**. This is an unforeseen result. Could our normal **Clitopilus prunulus** be morphing in this direction? Has anyone checked to see if it also has cheilocystidia? This is like throwing a large stone into a pond of goldfish.

On behalf of our club, we thank Dr. Noordeloos for pursuing this identification.

BIBLIOGRAPHY

Marco Contu, *Funghi della Sardegna: Note e Descrizione, III* in *Bolletino Amer.* 48, Anno XV (3–15), 1999.

Roy Halling & Greg Mueller, *Common Mushrooms of the Talamanca Mountains, Costa Rica*, 2005. New York Botanical Garden, Bronx, NY.

Anton Hausknecht & Machiel Noordeloos, *Neue Oder Seltene Arten der Entolomataceae aus Mittel-und Südeuropa* in *Österrische Zeitschrift fur Pilzkunde* 8 (199–202), 1999.

Clitopilus prunulus (Scopoli ex Fries) Kummer

The fabulous flavor and fine texture should place this mushroom in everyone's top five.

The Miller is one of those mushrooms that seem to appear at every other foray. Usually only one or two are found. It gets named by our experts and randomly placed on the table. It's an innocuous grayish-white species, easily overlooked in the midst of brighter companions. At the end of the day, no one bothers with it. It gets dumped with all the other undesirables.

This happens to be a mistake. The Miller doesn't taste anything like the odor of flour, for which it is popularly named. Nor does it taste like sweetbreads, another name one encounters in popular guides. It happens to be so rich in flavor that it makes you pause and take notice. Your next thought is why hadn't someone told you about this before. The fabulous flavor and fine texture should place this mushroom in everyone's Top Five.

British authors Lyon, Harding, and Tomblin can back me up. At least one of them attended a foray in England where the edibles

---

LOOK-ALIKES

Clitocybe suaveolens ss Fries, 1821

Clitocybe phyllophila

---

were sautéed in a taste competition at the end of the day. **Clitopilus prunulus** won the vote hands down, defeating both **Boletus edulis** and the chanterelle. As Count Cetto attests, the flavor is 'molto delicato'.

There are several reasons why it hasn't caught on. First, it very rarely appears in quantity. Secondly, it appears at around the same time as the chanterelle and **Boletus edulis**, which do appear in quantity. And thirdly, it does have its share of dangerous look-alikes in both Clitocybe and Entoloma. Once these are learned, however, a singular culinary experience awaits.

So what ensues when a gourmet mushroom chef runs into a big break of them? In Jack Czarnecki's own writing, here is how it went down: "It looked like the last remnants of fallen snow—white patches here and there in a random pattern as far as the eye could see in that dark August forest. I remember it as if it were yesterday, kneeling and plucking this strange and delicate mushroom and placing cluster after cluster in my basket. I didn't even want to separate the clusters or clean the dirt off, as if that would banish the magic and make them all disappear as if it was a dream. I had never seen any **Clitopilus prunulus** before—much less in this quantity—but in that year in that forest they were spread out before me like manna. I have returned to that forest every year since and been graced with an occasional single specimen here and there, as if I were being shown mercy by a higher power, who would nonetheless never allow me more than one vision of this mushroom in all its glory."

Imagine the mental agony in selecting a wine to go with it.

In an earlier time, the American mycologist George Atkinson found a mother lode around an old stump in the woods outside of Ithaca, New York, in 1898. The exceptionally large specimens all made it into his basket. Later he termed them "an excellent mushroom for food."

The fact that such collections are even brought up shows you how rare it is to find them in quantity.

Prunulus means little plum in Latin. Although it doesn't look or taste like one, we can surmise that the white pruina on cap and stem mimics the white bloom on a plum. But there may be another reason. The Grünerts maintain that an Italian named A. Cesalpino found it under a plum tree in the late sixteenth century. Later, much later, it was formally published as **Agaricus prunulus** by Scopoli in 1772. The place of origin was noted as Slovenia.

The caps of **Clitopilus prunulus** run from 3–13 cm wide. They are quite fleshy at the disc but thin at the margin. They are somewhat fragile and tend to crumble if not handled carefully. Convex and slightly umbonate at first, they become plane or centrally depressed in age. The cap texture is described as "kid glove," rather felty or pruinate in dry weather, but sticky in moist conditions. The color is white to cream to pale gray. The margins are at

LOOK-ALIKES

Clitocybe dilatata

Clitocybe dealbata

first inrolled, then become irregularly lobed and wavy. (Specimens with more viscid caps have been called **Clitopilus orcella** in the past. They have the same great flavor and are now considered a synonym by *Index Fungorum*.)

Stems are short in comparison to the caps. They usually run from 2–6 cm long and up to 1 ½ cm thick. They are white, firm, often curved, and taper towards the base, which itself can be cottony enlarged. Some authors describe the stem as longitudinally striated, others as pruinose. They are often eccentric. Gills are always decurrent, white to beige at first, then pinkish flesh-colored from the spores in age. They are subdistant and narrow with entire edges. An odd thing about the gills is that they can be readily peeled from the cap context, a trait they share with Paxillus. Fries gave this tendency a lot of clout and placed it in Paxillus before Kummer put it in Clitopilus in 1871.

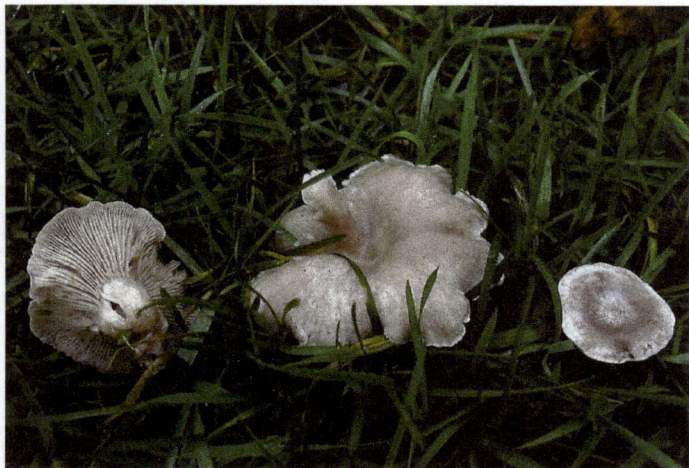

Clitocybe rivulosa from Silver Lake area, Wash.

Lepista irina from New Jersey

The odor of **Clitopilus prunulus** is strongly but pleasantly farinaceous. Some authors feel it smells like cucumber. The taste is mild, but bitter forms exist under the name "form amarus Foss." Such forms should be separated from the rest. The flesh of cap and stem is white. It turns dark purple with the application of sulfovainillina.

The spores are pinkish salmon in deposit. Under the microscope they look like elongated footballs with six longitudinal ridges. They measure 10–14 x 5–6 μm. The radially oriented hyphae of the pileipellis are sometimes in a gelatinous matrix, sometimes not. There are no clamps and no cystidia.

This exquisite edible can be found in forest glades and grassy areas near trees; it is equally at home with conifers or hardwoods. It is a saprobe. Various authors have reported it with heather and blueberry patches, woodland leaf litter, juniper bushes, and even on rotting boards at the bases of old buildings. Dr. Svrcek found it in Czechoslovakia in the wheel ruts of old logging roads in spruce forests. Jack Waytz finds it...Well, we won't go there.

The Miller is found in temperate zones around the globe. Imazeki & Hongo have reported it from Japan. Roberts & Evans have it shaded in for Central America, North Africa, Asia, North America, and Europe. It has been surmised that **C. prunulus** in a prolonged spectacular fruiting might have been the manna in the Holy Land.

But the road to Eldorado is not always straight or even simple. As I waded into the research, more and more look-alikes cropped up, some benign and others poisonous, until the whole prospect of identification became rather daunting. But don't give up the ship. None of the following species share all the characteristics of the Miller—the pinkish fusiform spores, the decurrent gills, the felt-like cap texture, the whitish caps and stems, the strong odor of flour, the relatively wide caps compared to short stems.

Here, then, is a long and prodigious list of look-alikes:
Clitocybe dealbata: Perhaps the most dangerous look-alike, and the one most often mentioned. This grayish-tan mushroom of lawns, pastures, and gardens does not smell like flour and the spores are white. It is generally smaller in stature, has glossier caps that are often radially zoned, and cream-colored gills. It often grows in fairy rings and is more likely to

be confused with **Marasmius oreades**.

Leucocybe candicans: Another small whitish Clitocyboid fungus with canescent caps, and gills that tend to turn yellowish when dried. It is also poisonous but easily separated by its white spores.

Neoclitocybe alnetorum: A small white European Clitocybe that fruits under green alder. It has satiny white caps, but the gills turn dark cream color in age and the spores are white.

Clitocybe phyllophila: Differs by its satiny white polished caps and cream-colored spores. It tends to fruit in clusters and is also deemed poisonous.

Clitocybe rivulosa: Right up there with **Clitocybe dealbata** for the reputation of poisonings. It has pale brown caps with a canescent covering that makes them look frosted. Dark circular zones are formed on the caps as they age. They also smell of flour and are found in meadows and footpaths, but spores are always white.

Clitocybe suaveolens ss Fries (1821): Sent to Dr. Bigelow on 1/29/87, this collection from the Kickerville Road area outside of Ferndale, Washington, had pale flesh-colored spores in deposit and a strong odor of hyacinth. The spores were narrowly elliptic with cyanophyllic contents. This could represent a different taxon, but in no way a Clitopilus.

Clitocybe dilatata: Differs by its glossy white caps with a mother-of-pearl luster and preference for fruiting on gravel roadsides in the Pacific Northwest. It has white spores and a checkered reputation for edibility. The flavor was superb

LOOK-ALIKES

Rhodocybe caelata from B.C.

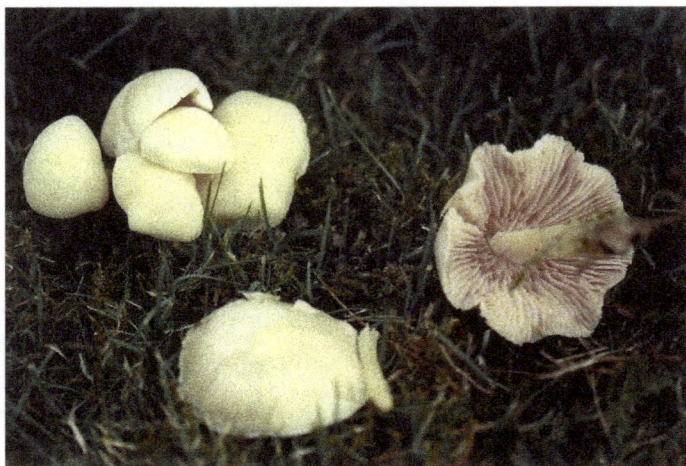

Alboleptonia sericella var. lutescens

the first time I sampled it, then slightly bitter and fairly unpleasant the second time. Maybe there is a complex involved. There are strong rumors of allergic reactions, and if you venture online, you pick up warnings of neurotoxins and the muscarine syndrome.

Cantharellula umbonata: A more slender species with umbonate to umbilicate smoky gray caps and forked, decurrent gills that bruise tawny reddish when touched.

Calocybe gambosa: A popular edible in Europe, this large, white Tricoloma-like species has sinuate gills and white spores. Literature tells us there have been confusions with the Miller before.

Almost all of the above are white-spored species. If you can't get a spore print, just refuse to eat. The main thing to remember is that since **Clitopilus prunulus** begins life with white gills, it is advisable to wait a day to make sure the spores turn pink before

Lepista subconnexa from New Jersey

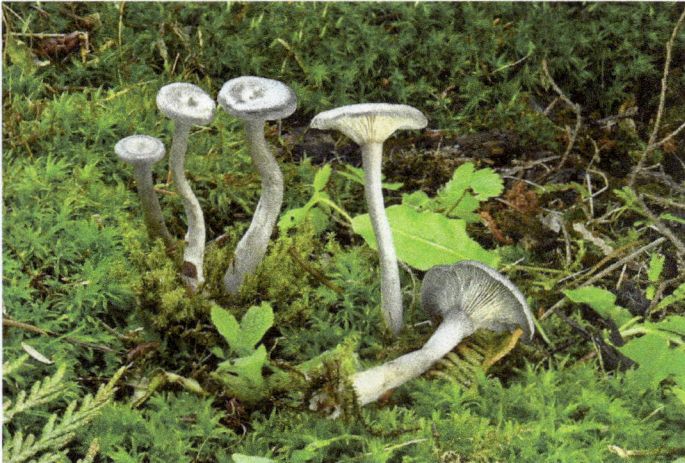

Cantharellula umbonata   *Photo by Richard Morrison*

trying to eat it.

And now we turn to the pink-spored look-alikes not in Entoloma:

Clitopilus amarus: A relatively large whitish Clitopilus from Europe with arcuate, deeply decurrent gills and a bitter taste. It also differs by lacking the floury odor.

Clitopilus blancii: Also differing by its bitter taste, it has whitish tomentose caps and occurs under Mediterranean pines.

Lepista subconnexa: Has a pinkish-cinnamon spore print, but differs by having a mild to fragrant odor, short decurrent gills that form a collar on the stipe, and opaque white caps.

Lepista caespitosa: Mimics **Clitocybe dilatata** by fruiting in big clusters on roadside gravel, and differs from the Miller by its lilac-gray spores, rancid farinaceous odor, disagreeable taste, and

elliptical, verrucose spores. Because of the pink spore print, care must be taken not to confuse **Clitopilus prunulus** with poisonous Entolomas. Luckily for us, none of these have decurrent gills and felt-like cap surfaces simultaneously.

Entoloma abortivum: Has also been suggested as a look-alike. It differs by fruiting in big clusters next to stumps, its smooth gray-brown caps, and the presence of aborted fruiting bodies (as seen on the right side of photo, next page). Considered a good edible on the East Coast.

Entoloma prunuloides: Appropriately named for its similarity to the Miller, it is a large, white Entoloma with pink spores and a farinaceous odor. Dr. Orson Miller has found it in Montana, and Dr. Largent reports it from Santa Cruz, California, northward along the coast up into Mendocino County. It differs from **Clitopilus prunulus** by having notched gills, and smooth, hygrophanous, sharply umbonate caps that fade from dark buff to a translucent white.

Entoloma sinuatum: A dangerously poisonous Entoloma (gastrointestinal issues), the large fleshy caps can be leather-ochre or paler as seen here. They differ by having yellowish gills when young and a much stouter stature when mature.

Alboleptonia sericella: An extremely fragile, wimpy white species with adnate to uncinate gills and pinkish spores. The **var. lutescens** with yellow tinges on cap and stem is sometimes found at Larabee Park, south of Bellingham, WA.

Other random pink-spored

look-alikes brought up by the literature are **Clitocella popinalis**, **Rhodocybe caelata** and **Lepista irina**.

Rhodocybe caelata: Differs by having dark gray-brown caps up to 3 cm wide, dingy beige gills, and finely verrucose spores.

Clitocella popinalis: Has pink spores but differs by its bitter taste and concentrically cracked cap surface.

Lepista irina: A large, fleshy species with adnate to notched gills, flesh to pale straw colored caps, and stem bases with copious mycelium.

The term "friable," when applied to the Miller, doesn't mean it fries up well in butter. It is actually what happens to fruiting bodies of **Clitopilus prunulus** if they are tossed haphazardly with other mushrooms in a collecting basket. They tend to crumble. The flavor is so good that grown men have been reported crouching over an upturned basket with forks and toothpicks, salvaging whatever they can. In the literature, there are no dissenting votes. Michael Kuo adds that the flavor increases after drying.

Fabulous recipes can be found in both Czarnecki cookbooks and also in Roger Phillips' *Mushrooms and Other Fungi of Great Britain and Europe*. It is excellent in a béchamel sauce. Hurst & Rutherford suggest sautéeing it in butter with chopped onions and marjoram or thyme. After the juices evaporate, add sour cream and garlic. This can then be tossed with spaghetti. Another way to go is with tomatoes, basil, olive oil, shallots, and black pepper.

LOOK-ALIKES

Entoloma abortivum from New Jersey

Entoloma sinuatum from Spain

The flavor is so rich it can handle stronger herbs and spices that would overwhelm milder mushroom flavors.

Dickinson & Lucas write that "it is good in stews, patties, and croquettes, and in Victorian times was popular cooked with minced beef." Joe Czarnecki advises that blanching takes care of the fragile cap dilemma. After that, braising is the best method of preparation. And finally, William Sturgis Thomas informs us that Dr. Badham had a special recipe for it. He would grind up almonds, lemon juice, salt, pepper, and water in a mortar until the mixture achieved the texture of table mustard. Then he would stew the Miller in that concoction.

It must have been a popular dish. A Leucocoprinus was eventually named for him.

Addendum: According to Dr. Beug, **Clitocybe dilatata** has proven lethal to dogs.

BIBLIOGRAPHY

David Arora, *Mushrooms Demystified*, 1986. Ten Speed Press, Berkeley, Calif.

George Atkinson, *Studies of American Fungi*, 1903. Hafner Publishing Co., New York, NY.

Cornelis Bas, Thomas Kuyper, Machiel Noordeloos, & Else Vellinga, *Flora Agaracina Neerlandica, Vol.1*, 1988. A.A. Balkema, Rotterdam, Holland.

Howard Bigelow, *North American Species of Clitocybe, Part I*, 1982. J. Cramer, Germany.

J. Breitenbach & F. Kranzlin, *Fungi of Switzerland, Vol.4*, 1995. Edition Mykologia, Lucerne, Switzerland.

Stefan Buczacki, Chris Shields, & Denys Ovende, *Collins Fungi Guide*, 2012. Harper-Collins, London.

Francisco de Diego Calonge, *Setas*, 1979. Ediciones Mundi-Prensa, Madrid.

Jack Czarnecki, *A Cook's Book of Mushrooms*, 1995. Artisan, New York, NY.

Colin Dickinson & John Lucas, *The Encyclopedia of Mushrooms*, 1983. Van Nostrand Reinhold Co., New York, NY.

Phyllis Glick, *The Mushroom Trail Guide*, 1979. Holt, Rinehart, & Winston, New York, NY.

Helmut & Renate Grünert, *Field Guide to Mushrooms of Britain and Europe*, 1991. Crowood Press, Wiltshire, England.

Miron Hard, *Mushrooms, Edible and Otherwise*, 1908. Dover Publications, New York, NY.

Patrick Harding, Tony Lyon, & Gill Tomblin, *How to Identify Edible Mushrooms*, 1996. Harper-Collins, London.

Jacqui Hurst & Lyn Rutherford, *The Mushroom & Truffle Book*, 1991. Salamander Books, Ltd., London.

Michael Jordan, *The Encyclopedia of Fungi of Britain and Europe*, 1995. David & Charles, Newton Abbot, England.

Calvin Kauffman, *The Agaricaceae of Michigan*, 1908. Michigan Geological and Biological Survey, Lansing, Mich.

Michael Kuo, *100 Edible Mushrooms*, 2007. University of Michigan Press, Ann Arbor, Mich.

Jean-Louis Lamaison & Jean-Marie Polese, *The Great Encyclopedia of Mushrooms*, 2011. Konemann, Cologne, Germany.

David Largent, *Entolomoid Fungi of the Western United States and Alaska*, 1994. Mad River Press, Eureka, Calif.

Charles McIlvaine & Robert Macadam, *1000 American Fungi*, 1902. Dover Publications, New York, NY.

Orson Miller, *Mushrooms of North America*, 1964. E.P. Dutton & Co., New York, NY.

Hope & Orson Miller, *North American Mushrooms*, 2006. Morris Book Publishing, Guilford, Conn.

Cora Mollen & Larry Weber, *Fascinating Fungi of the North Woods*, 2007. Kollath+Stensaas Publishing, Duluth, Minn.

Gabriel Moreno, Jose Luis Manjon, & Alvaro Zugaza, *La Guia de Incafo de los Hon gos de la Peninsula Iberica, Tome II*, 1986. Incafo, S.A., Madrid.

Meinhard Moser, *Keys to Agarics and Boleti*, 1983. Translated and published by Roger Phillips, London.

Roger Phillips, *Mushrooms and Other Fungi of Great Britain and Europe*, 1981. Pan Books, London.

Peter Roberts & Shelley Evans, *The Book of Fungi*, 2011. University of Chicago Press, Chicago, Ill.

William Roody, *Mushrooms of West Virginia and the Central Appalachians*, 2003. University Press of Kentucky, Lexington, Ky.

A.H. Smith, *A Field Guide to Western Mushrooms*, 1975. University of Michigan Press, Ann Arbor, Mich.

A.H. Smith & Nancy Weber, *The Mushroom Hunter's Field Guide*, 1958. University of Michigan Press, Ann Arbor, Mich.

Mirko Svrcek, *The Hamlyn Book of Mushrooms and Fungi*, 1983. Artia, Prague, Czechoslovakia.

William S. Thomas, *Field Book of Common Mushrooms*, 1928. G.P. Putnam's Sons, New York, NY.

Connopus acervatus (Fries) Hughes, Mather, & Petersen

The fragrance was so inviting
I couldn't imagine not eating it.

Connopus acervatus—another view

Photo by Richard Morrison

From time to time when sailing around the San Juan Islands, I will row ashore in some cove and check out the local mushrooms. Imagine climbing the hill above Inati Bay on Lummi Island on October 20, 1996, and finding an enormous clump of pleasantly fragrant fungi fruiting at the base of a rotten conifer stump. The featured photo on the previous page represents this collection. My first impulse was to rush the clump into the frying pan. The fragrance was so inviting I couldn't imagine not eating it. But caution prevailed. I sailed back to Bellingham to key it out in Mushrooms Demystified.

In those days it was known as **Collybia acervata**. It subsequently became **Gymnopus acervatus** before Petersen et al. transferred it to Connopus. Dr. Ron Petersen and associates discovered via DNA sequencing that **Connopus acervatus** landed in the Omphalotaceae somewhere near Rhodocollybia. It was all by itself between Gymnopus and Rhodocollybia. They also found two clades within Connopus acervatus. Clade #1 encompassed specimens from Idaho, Washington, and Alaska. Clade #2 included specimens from northern Europe, Newfoundland, the Great Smokies, and the East Coast. The two groups look alike. They only differ microscopically in the structure of the pi-

leipellis and the shapes of the cheilocystidia. Perhaps one day, another name will emerge....

Known as the Clustered Collybia or the "Clustered Coincap" (the McKnights), **Connopus acervatus** is an impressive sight in the forest. Jack Waytz and Phil Spanel once found it up the Canyon Creek Road in the Mt. Baker–Snoqualmie National Forest, fruiting like a giant bouquet of flowers from the forest floor. Only later did we discover that it could also fruit on buried wood or sawdust. Fischer and the Bessettes have also found it in clusters in sphagnum bogs.

Caps of **Connopus acervatus** run from 1 ½–5 cm wide. They are convex at first becoming irregularly wavy in age with upturned margins. They can also be slightly umbonate and have faintly striate margins when moist. They are red brown to vinaceous brown with paler margins fading hygrophanously to flesh buff or pale ochre brown when drying. The context is thin, firm, pliable, and white to dull pink. The gills are adnexed to almost free, sometimes with decurrent teeth. They are crowded to narrow, white to pinkish with entire, concolorous edges. The stems run from 3–10 cm long and 2–5 mm thick. They are the same red brown as the caps, only a little darker. They are smooth or finely grooved lengthwise, hollow, and paler at the apex. The base is decorated with whitish hairs below which the white to ochre-buff mycelium binds the stems in a cespitose habit. The stems are long in relation to cap width, another aid in identification. Spores are white, inamyloid, and measure 5–6.5 x 2.5–3.5 μm. They are elliptical to lacrymoid in shape. The odor has been described as mild by most authors, agreeable by a few, and of cumarin or bitter almonds by Antonin and Noordeloos. Breitenbach & Kranzlin described a "somewhat unpleasant odor," while Meinhard Moser chipped in with "an odor of rotten cabbages and garlic." The odors do seem to vary more in Europe than they do here. I would like to add "semi-euphoric" for our Pacific Northwest collections in their prime. The habitat is always on some kind of wood. They are known to produce a white rot of spruce.

As for taste, welcome to even more variety. Here are a few samples to digest:

A.H. Smith in 1949: "Edible, but all the collections I have tried were slightly bitter after cooking. The consistency is excellent, however, and if the bitterness could be removed or a mild form found, it would be a very fine esculent."

A.H. Smith in 1980: "Poisonous, at least to some people. We have a report from the Pacific Northwest of students made ill by it. Because of the bitter taste, it is not a desirable species."

Stuntz, McKenny, & Ammirati: "Generally considered edible. Some individuals have suffered gastrointestinal upset after eating it."

LOOK-ALIKES

Gymnopus confluens   *Photo by Richard Morrison*

Gymnopus erythropus from Lummi Island

Clitocybula familia

Gymnopus dryophilus

Mycena laevigata ss auct. N. America   *Photo by Richard Morrison*

Dick Graham: "The cap has a good flavor, but stems should be discarded because of tough texture."
Charles Fergus: "Taste strong and disagreeable."
Andrus Voitk: "Too bitter to be edible."
Ben Guild: "The taste is reported to be bitter even after cooking."
Soothill & Fairhurst: "Edible."
Charles McIlvaine: "The entire plant is tender, delicate, and of fine flavor."

My own inclination would be to try a small amount at first, keeping in mind that in *Edible and Poisonous Mushrooms of the World*, the authors have **C. acervata** listed among the mushrooms that cause gastrointestinal upsets. Of course, if you emerge from the woods with a load of **Boletus edulis**, why bother with it at all?

And there are look-alikes. A few of these follow:

Marasmius cohaerens: Another species growing in clusters with fused stems. It differs by fruiting on leaves and humus. It also has a velvety yellow-brown to dark brown cap and a light yellowish stem that darkens towards the base.

Clitocybula familia: Grows in cespitose clusters on wood, but they have buff to gray-brown stems and amyloid spores. The caps are also more of a uniform cardboard color.

Gymnopus erythropus: Most likely the closest look-alike. It also fruits in tight clusters, but only on hardwoods or buried wood. Other differences are the more orange-brown cap color and bicolorous stems: pale orange at the apex, then dark red-brown at the base.

Rhodocollybia prolixa: Differs by having a thicker stature, dark chestnut caps, and crenulate gill edges.

Gymnopus confluens: Has much longer stems in relation to cap width. The stems are covered from base to apex with white, downy hairs.

Gymnopus dryophilus: Differs by its terete pale yellow stems and solitary to densely gregarious growth habit.

Mycena laevigata: While also fruiting on wood in clusters, this differs by having amyloid spores, much paler caps with striate margins, and grayish tubular stems.

All in all, **Connopus acervatus** is a stunning sight in the autumn woods. Too bad we can't capture the odor in a canister and spray it around our kitchen prior to eating . . . preferably something else.

Addendum: Recent DNA sequencing has revealed that many collections of **Gymnopus confluens** in the Pacific Northwest differ from the **G. confluens** of Europe. It is in the act of becoming a new species, so the name **Gymnopus confluens subsp. campanulatus** has been launched.

BIBLIOGRAPHY

Vladimir Antonin & Machiel Noordeloos, *A Monograph of Marasmioid and Collybioid Fungi in Europe*, 2010. IHW Verlag, Eching, Germany.

Charles Fergus, *Illustrated Genera of Wood Decay Fungi*, 1960. Burgess Publishing Co., Minneapolis, Minn.

Alan & Arleen Bessette & David Fischer, *Mushrooms of Northeastern North America*, 1997. Syracuse University Press, Syracuse, NY.

Robert Gilbertson & K.J. Martin, *Synopsis of Wood Rotting Fungi on Spruce in North America, Part 3* in *Mycotaxon* 10 (479–501), 1980.

Dick Graham, *The Meandering Mushroomer*, 1978. Hancock House Publishers, Seattle, Wash.

Ben Guild, *The Alaskan Mushroom Hunter's Guide*, 1979. Alaska Northwest Publishing Co., Anchorage, Alaska.

Ian Hall, Steven Stephenson, Peter Buchanan, Wang Yun, & Anthony Cole, *Edible and Poisonous Mushrooms of the World*, 2003. Timber Press, Portland, Ore.

Lexemuel Hesler, *Mushrooms of the Great Smokies*, 1960. University of Tennessee Press, Knoxville, Tenn.

Karen Hughes, David Mather, & Ronald Petersen, *A New Genus to Accommodate Gymnopus Acervatus* in *Mycologia* 102 (1463–1478), 2010.

Karen Hughes & Ron Petersen, *Transatlantic Disjunction in Fleshy Fungi III: Gymnopus confluens* in MycoKeys 9, (37–63), 2015.

Gary Lincoff, *The Audubon Society Field Guide to North American Mushrooms*, 1981. Alfred A. Knopf, New York, NY.

Charles McIlvaine & Robert Macadam, *One Thousand American Fungi*, 1902. Dover Publications, New York, NY.

Margaret McKenny, Dan Stuntz, & Joe Ammirati, *The New Savory Wild Mushroom*, 1987. University of Washington Press, Seattle, Wash.

Kent & Vera McKnight, *Peterson Field Guides: Mushrooms*, 1987. Houghton Mifflin Co., Boston, Mass.

Hope & Orson Miller, *North American Mushrooms*, 2006. Morris Book Publishing, Guilford, Conn.

Meinhard Moser, *Keys to Agarics and Boleti*, 1983. Translated and published by Roger Phillips, London.

Machiel Noordeloos, *Collybia in Flora Agaracina Neerlandica, Vol. 3*, 1995. A.A. Balkema, Rotterdam, Holland.

Machiel Noordeloos, *Gymnopus in Funga Nordica*, 2008. Nordsvamp, Copenhagen.

Alexander H. Smith, 1947, *North American Species of Mycena*, University of Michigan Press, Ann Arbor, Mich.

A.H. Smith, *Mushrooms in Their Natural Habitat*, 1949. Sawyer's Inc., Portland, Ore.

Alexander & Helen Smith & Nancy Weber, *The Mushroom Hunter's Field Guide*, 1980. University of Michigan Press, Ann Arbor, Mich.

Eric Soothill & Alan Fairhurst, *The New Field Guide to Fungi*, 1978. Michael Joseph Ltd., London.

Steve Trudell & Joe Ammirati, *Mushrooms of the Pacific Northwest*, 2009. Timber press, Portland, Ore.

Andrus Voitk, *A Little Illustrated Book of Common Mushrooms of Newfoundland and Labrador*, 2007. Gros Morne Co-operating Association, Rocky Harbour, Newfoundland.

Cortinarius armillatus (Fries) Fries

A noble species, the chief of all Corts.

Somewhere out near the foothills of the western Cascades between Everson and Sumas sat a patch of flat forest we called Cortinarius Heaven. I know it sounds trite, but how else could we explain it? We don't know how old the patch was. It had reached a point in its tree succession where the vine maples had all died off recently, leaving only scattered black birch and a few alders as the only hardwoods left in a forest of western hemlock. And every couple of years among the few surviving birches you could find the majestic **Cortinarius armillatus** with its brick colored caps erupting through the moss. Elias Fries called it "a noble species, the chief of all Corts." Nowhere else in the county ha**s** this species been found.

Cortinarius armillatus, a.k.a. the Bracelet Cort, was first found in Sweden by Fries. It has since been found around the world in temperate zones from Japan across northern Asia, all of Europe and North America. They are found in mixed coniferous-deciduous forests, often in acid, nutrient poor soils. (The trees at Cortinarius Heaven did seem somewhat stunted.) Different authors have made sundry observations. Pace notes that they like to be in peat moss with bilberries. Jean-Marie Polese claims they like wet, boggy places, including sphagnum bogs. In the northeast and in northern Europe, they are associated with birch. Kauffman found them in Michigan on very rotten wood or in thick humus under conifers. David Biek found them in northern California in

high mountains under aspen. Ours were found not much above sea level.

On this particular day in mid-October, 2010, there were so many Corts in the woods that I feared we wouldn't even reach the area where the black birches were. It took fifteen minutes for Dr. Joe Ammirati to get from where the car was parked to the trailhead. That's a distance of 60 feet. It was a happy day. The only thing missing from the scene was Tuula, Joe's counterpart in Finland. Meanwhile, Jack Waytz, Richard Morrison, David Arora, and myself tried to make up for the absence of Tuula as best we could.

The caps of **Cortinarius armillatus** run from 5–13 cm wide and start off bell shaped before broadening out to convex with a low umbo. The surface is dry but not hygrophanous (does not fade when drying out). The colors are yellow-brown to rusty-brown with tiny brick-red squamules becoming more fibrillose towards the margins when young. The margins are often hung with veil remnants. The flesh is thin, pallid tan, and a bit spongy. In age it becomes gray brown. The gills are widely spaced, pale cinnamon at first, then dark rusty from the spores. The gill attachment is adnate to notched. The edges are sometimes crenulate and pallid, indicating the possibility of cheilocystidia. The stems are 7–15 cm long and 1–2 ½ cm thick. They are dry and generally dingy white to pale tan becoming more gray brown towards the clavate to bulbous base, often bruising darker where handled. According to McIlvaine the species is remarkable in having two well-defined veils, one a fibrillose white cortina that leaves white strands on the upper stem that soon turn rusty, and the other a universal veil that leaves brick-red bands near midstem. The spore deposit is rusty and the spores themselves elliptical to almond shaped and roughened with tiny warts. The basal mycelium is white. The odor is mild to strong of radish and the taste mild to slightly bitter. Moreno, Man-

LOOK-ALIKE

Cortinarius paragaudis from Alaska

172

Cortinarius sp. from South Pass Road near Sumas

jon, and Zugaza found that potassium hydroxide turns the flesh dark red, and iron sulfate brings a pale green reaction.

Microscopically, the spores measure 10–12 x 6–7 μm. They are thick-walled and dextrinoid in Melzer's solution. The basidia are 4-spored, slenderly clavate, and clamped at the bases. The cheilocystidia are clavate to cylindrical and found in clusters. They, too, are clamped at the bases. The pileipellis is of periclinal hyphae lightly encrusted in places.

The one place you will not find **Cortinarius armillatus** is on a lawn, at least a lawn without birch. There are many reasons a photographer may not be able to shoot on site, but here in the Northwest the main reason is sudden rain. It is just possible that this event took place here.

Reports differ on edibility. A British contingent consisting of Roger Phillips, Buczacki, Kibby, Pegler, and Spooner list the Bracelet Cort as either inedible, probably poisonous, or best avoided because of confusion with other Corts. Reports from North America vary from "edible and choice" to "usually of poor quality because often riddled with larvae." McIlvaine gave it the highest accolades, writing "the flesh is excellent, closely resembling **Pholiota subsquarrosa**." That sounded like the kiss of death to me, so I decided to look up the flavor of this enigmatic Pholiota. I didn't get far. **Pholiota subsquarrosa** in the sense of European authors is **Pholiota squarroso-adiposa**, a rather bland species at best, while in the sense of Kauffman and A.H. Smith it is something called **Pholiota subvelutipes,** not in anyone's popular mushroom guide. So by dropping the name of **Pholiota subsquarrosa**, McIlvaine has led us into a confusing area of Pholiota without describing the flavor.

At this point I have to confess that I cooked up the first batch I found at Cortinarius Heaven years earlier. They turned black in the frying pan when sautéed in butter and had a pleasant flavor that conjured up spinach. I was rather pleased with the memory of this flavor so when I ran into a giant break of them in Haines, Alaska, several years later, I tried them again. At the very first bite, I realized something was wrong. They had a distinct flavor of garbage. I proceeded to strike **Cortinarius armillatus** off my list of edibles until I got home and reexamined my notes on the collection. Nowhere was there any mention of the brick-red squamules on the cap surface. Although brick colored bands on the stem had been present, I came to realize I had eaten its close relative, **Cortinarius paragaudis** instead. I had partaken of the wrong species, never a great idea in Cortinarius. I had been so sure of the brick bands that I hadn't considered the rest of the carpophore. **Cortinarius paragaudis** differs by having a smooth ochre-brown to chestnut-brown cap with no scales on it. The spores are smaller and nearly spherical, and it is found under conifers.

After this experience, I can only support the advice of Bill Russell. He wrote that **Cortinarius armillatus** is "widely recognized as a good, even fine, edible mushroom, but many authorities now agree that beginners should not eat it because of possible misidentification." The species they most likely have in mind is **Cortinarius orellanus**, a kidney or liver-destroying mushroom that can have roughly the same cap and gill colors. It has a smaller stature than the Bracelet Cort. Most other look-alikes are in the "edibility unknown" category.

Almost all popular guides give no hint of the army of look-alikes out there, especially in

Europe, where if the mushroom blinks, it's a new species. Here, then, is a list of them and how they appear to be different:

Cortinarius orellanus: This life threatening Cortinarius has tawny brown caps and yellowish stems. It belongs in a different group, the Orellani. It's a European species that prefers beech and oak. Instead of reddish bands on the stem, the velar material consists of scant yellowish fibrillose shards.

Cortinarius veregregius: A French species with a brick-red cap and dull pink bands on a pallid stem.

Cortinarius oenochelis: A Cortinarius of pine and spruce forests in Scandinavia. It has pale pink mycelium at the stem bases and spores measuring 8.5–10 x 6–7.5 µm. Some experts consider it a subspecies of **Cortinarius paragaudis**.

Cortinarius luteo-ornatus: Similar to **C. armillatus** except the bands on the stem are yellow-brown instead of brick colored. This European species should never be eaten because of possible confusion with **Cortinarius rubellus**, another deadly species found in the Northwest, which has yellowish bands on its stem.

Cortinarius boulderensis: Found from Colorado to the Pacific Northwest under conifers. It has brick-brown bands on its stems, violet-brown caps, and violet at the stem apices.

Cortinarius subtestaceus: A smaller species from the eastern United States with a brown universal veil and vinaceous-brown cap flesh. It also has brick-brown bands on its stems.

Cortinarius haematochelis: Probably the closest look-alike. It has chestnut colored cap discs that fade to tan at the margins, and a minutely squamulose surface with radially cracked margins in age. The Index Fungorum deems it to be a separate species from **Cortinarius paragaudis.**

The look-alike photograph of **Cortinarius sp.** represents a species in the **C. armillatus** group that Dr. Ammirati would not put a name to. It was found two years earlier in the same location off the South Pass Road.

In recent years a group of authors working with the Féderation Mycologique et Botanique de Dauphiné-Savoie in the French Alps have produced a series of volumes entitled *Atlas des Cortinaires*. There are probably over 20 volumes by now of air-brushed renderings of the Corts. There are those who contend that a painting depicts the spirit of the mushroom better than a photograph can, but some of the differences between the painted versions of some species are so miniscule that you would need to count the hairs to separate them. Nonetheless, after thumbing through the volumes I found seven more species and varieties with velar bands on the stems that could be thought of as more look-alikes:

Cortinarius armillatus var. miniatus: Has more squamose caps, more slender stems, and the caps are a brighter red orange.

Cortinarius armillatus var. picetorum: Has scaly cap centers and is all-around paler than typical **Cortinarius armillatus**.

Cortinarius armillatus var. subcroceofulvus: A smaller species with fibrillose caps and short stems.

Cortinarius bresadolanus: Has rusty fibrillose caps and very shaggy stems.

Cortinarius craticius: A smaller species with stems that taper towards the base and small, tawny caps with abrupt papillate umbos.

Cortinarius salmonetomentosus: A species authored by Robert Henry that has umbonate tawny-brown caps and paler bands on the stem.

Cortinarius salmonicolor: Differs by having yellow stem bases.

What used to be a simple call is now a more disconcerting task. DNA sequencing has now shown many of the above species to be synonymous with each other.

Even the edibility is taking another hit. Andrus Voitk notes that **Cortinarius armillatus** contains anthraquinones, a favorite pigment of wool dyers. Since some of these compounds are thought to be toxic, he suggests the species is better suited for dyeing. For that select group who would rather dye than eat, it is supposed to produce a strong pink.

Unfortunately, we have to end on an even sadder note. The very next year after this momentous foray, the Bloedel-Donovan Corporation clear cut two-thirds of the site. Gone perhaps forever are a new species of Lactarius, potential break-throughs in Pholiota, and countless fruitings of Cortinarius we may never see the like of again. On the other hand, we had been trespassing on their property and had never given them any indication of the fungal treasures it harbored.

BIBLIOGRAPHY

David Arora, *Mushrooms Demystified*, 1986. Ten Speed Press, Berkeley, Calif.

Alan & Arleen Bessette & David Fischer, *The Mushrooms of Northeastern North America*, 1998. Syracuse University Press, Syracuse, NY.

David Biek, *The Mushrooms of Northern California*, 1984. Spore Prints, Redding, Calif.

Marcel Bon, *Mushrooms and Toadstools of Britain and Northwestern Europe*, 1987. Hodder & Stoughton, London.

Erik Brandrud, Hakan Lindstrom, Hans Marklund, Jacques Melot, & Siw Musko, *Cortinarius Flora Photographica, Vol. 2*, 1992. Cortinarius HB, Matflors, Sweden.

Erik Brandrud, Klaus Hoiland, Tuula Niskanen, Ilkka Kytovuori, Egil & Katriina Bendiksen, Tobias Froslev, Thomas Jeppesen, Hakan Lindstrom, & Kare Liimatainen, *Cortinarius in Funga Nordica*, 2008. Nordsvamp, Copenhagen.

J. Breitenbach & F. Kranzlin, *Fungi of Switzerland, Vol. 5*, 2000. Edition Mykologia, Lucerne, Switzerland.

Stefan Buczacki, *Fungi of Britain and Europe*, 1989. University of Texas Press, Austin, Texas.

Robert Henry, Andre Bidaud, Patrick Reumaux, & Pierre Moenne-Loccoz, *Atlas des Cortinaires, Pars 7*, 1995. Editions Federation Mycologique Dauphine-Savoie, France.

Rokuya Imazeki, Tsuguo Hongo, & Keisuke Tubaki, *Common Mushrooms of Japan in Color*, 1970. Hoikusha Publishing Co., Osaka, Japan.

Calvin Kauffman, *Cortinarius* in *North American Flora* 10, Part 5 (282–348), 1932.

Calvin Kauffman, *The Agaricaceae of Michigan*, 1918. Michigan Geological and Biological Survey, Lansing, Mich.

Geoffrey Kibby, *An Illustrated Guide to Mushrooms and Other Fungi of North America*, 1993. Dragon's World, Surrey, England.

Charles McIlvaine & Robert Macadam, *One Thousand American Fungi*, 1902. Dover Publishing, New York, NY.

Gabriel Moreno, Jose Luis Manjon, & Alvaro Zugaza, *La Guia de Incafo de los Hongos de la Peninsula Iberica, Tomo II*, 1986. Mundi-Prensa, Madrid.

Meinhard Moser, *Keys to Agarics and Boleti*, 1983. Translated and published by Roger Phillips, London.

Tuula Niskanen, Kare Liimatainen, & Ilkka Kytovuori, *Cortinarius Section Armillati in Northern Europe* in *Mycologia* 103 (1080–1101), 2011.

Giuseppe Pace, *Mushrooms of the World*, 1998. Firefly Books, Willowdale, Ontario.

David Pegler, *The Mitchell Beazley Pocket Guide to Mushrooms and Toadstools*, 1981. Mitchell Beazley Publishers, London.

David Pegler & Brian Spooner, *The Mushroom Identifier*, 1992. Smithmark Publishers, New York, NY.

Roger Phillips, *A Provisional Multi-Access Key to American Species of Cortinarius, Inoloma & Telamonia*, 1986. Self-published.

Roger Phillips, *Mushrooms of North America*, 1991.

Jean-Marie Polese, *The Pocket Guide to Mushrooms*, 2005. Tandem Verlag, Chamalieres, France.

Bill Russell, *Field Guide to Wild Mushrooms of Pennsylvania and the Mid-Atlantic*, 2006. Pennsylvania State University Press, University Park, Penn.

A.H. Smith, *A Field Guide to Western Mushrooms*, 1975. University of Michigan Press, Ann Arbor, Mich.

Andrus Voitk, *A Little Illustrated Book of Common Mushrooms of Newfoundland and Labrador*, 2007. Gros Morne Co-operating Association, Rocky Harbour, Newfoundland.

Cortinarius caperatus (Persoon) Fries

A solid Gypsy is indeed a prized find.

Cortinarius caperatus, perhaps better known as the Gypsy mushroom, is the best edible of all the Cortinariaceae, according to Arora. It is one of those feast or famine mushrooms, al least locally. It is a rare occasion when you run across it, but if you do find it, it often fruits in great quantities. It shows up on several steep hikes in the Mount Baker National Forest in the coniferous zones. They arrive in late August or early September with the first seasonal rains. Just a little rain can produce great colonies. Unfortunately, since it is among the first mushrooms to fruit after a long, dry summer, it is eagerly and perhaps desperately embraced by the larvae of the sciarid flies, miniscule critters who eat the mycelium first and then move upwards. They can turn a Gypsy mushroom into cheesecloth in a matter of hours. A solid Gypsy is indeed a prized find. Here now is a sampling of culinary opinions:

David Arora: "The best of the Cortinariaceae. It is especially good with rice after a long, hard day of backpacking. The tough stems should be discarded."

Charles McIlvaine: "The flavor is slightly acrid raw, but fine when cooked."

Jack Czarnecki: "Recommends cooking them with beef or veal. The only way to preserve them is to can them."

Helene Schalkwijk-Barendsen: "Good, mint-like flavor."

Giovanni Pacioni: Discovered they turned the water yellow when boiled. He liked the flavor.

My own feeling is that they are at best mediocre when aged, but excellent when fresh.

The caps of the Gypsy mushroom measure 5–15 cm wide. They are ovoid to campanulate at first, then expand to plane or with uplifted margins in age. They usually have a blunt umbo at the disc. They can be ochraceous in dry weather and a rich orange brown in humid conditions. Buttons are entirely coated with tiny, white, furfuraceous fibrils that remain only at the disc in age. It gives them a hoary aspect that helps separate them from other Corts. A better character for identification is the wrinkled cap. In dry weather, older specimens can have areolate caps or scalloped margins, or even have the margins deeply cracked. Another oddity is the fragility of the caps. You have to be careful when transporting them, if entire caps are important to you. The gills are adnexed becoming adnate to uncinate. They are unevenly serrate or toothed like a saw, with edges slightly paler than the faces. Whitish at first, they are soon pale rusty from the spores. The stems can get up to 12 cm long and 2 ½ cm thick. There is a membranous ring at around midstipe. Above the ring, the stem is white floccose. Below, it is smooth, silky-striate, and dingy buff to pale ochre tan. Unlike other species of Cortinarius, which have cortinas, **Cortinarius caperatus** has a partial veil and a universal veil. The partial veil is the buff to pale ochre membranous ring. The universal veil is represented by the cap hoariness, an evanescent and barely discernible "membrane" thinly attached to the area just below the ring, and some white floccose material at the stem base. The spore print is rusty brown. Odor and taste are mild. They are mycorrhizal with hardwoods and conifers, but are more successful with adaptation to different conifers around the world. They like sandy or

LOOK-ALIKE

Phaeolepiota aurea   *Photo by Gary McWilliams*

acidic soils, and are often found in the company of bilberry and huckleberry.

Microscopically, the rusty brown spores are almond shaped or slightly inequilateral in profile. They are verrucose and measure 11–15 x 7–10 μm. The gill trama is parallel, clamps are present, and the scattered cheilocystidia are subcylindrical to fusoid ventricose with pointy apices. The cap cuticle consists of a thick zone of subgelatinous, radially parallel hyphae above a subpellis of more or less globose cells. It is the presence of these globose cells that probably accounts for the fragility of the caps.

Gypsy mushrooms circle the globe. In Europe and Japan they are sold in farmers markets. In Alaska they are found with Sitka spruce near berry patches. They are also found in tundra with dwarf willow, and have even been reported north of the Arctic Circle. They can be locally abundant in the Scottish highlands, and have been collected in Lapland and Greenland. On the West Coast, they extend southward into northern California and the Sierra Nevadas where they associate with red fir and yellow pine. On the East Coast they extend south as far as the mountains take them. A website has reported them from Chile, and China has them in Jilin, Jiangsu, Qinghai, and Heilongjiang, among other places. They claim that the Gypsy contains anti-carcinogenic substances.

Confusion with other species is unlikely once you learn the combination of characters.

LOOK-ALIKES

Psathyrella annulata

Stropharia coronilla from Colorado

The total package of rusty, verrucose spores, wrinkled caps, hoary cap discs, membranous ring, and buff to pale rusty gills are unique to the taxon. Nonetheless, a few are mentioned in the literature:

Cortinarius corrugatus: Probably the closest look-alike, it has a radially corrugated cap surface but lacks the membranous ring and further differs by its violaceous gills when young. Listed as edible by Rinaldi & Tyndalo in Europe, we list it as edibility unknown in North America.

Psathyrella rugocephala: Has radiately rugulose caps, subannulate veil remnants, dark chocolate spores in KOH, and a habit of fruiting on wood.

Phaeolepiota aurea: a.k.a. Alaskan Gold, it differs by its stronger orange cap color and powdery granulose cap and stem.

Agrocybe praecox: A generally cardboard colored species found

Agrocybe praecox

Cystoderma fallax

in grasses, wood chip mulch, compost heaps, and roadsides. It usually develops cracked caps in dry weather.

Psathyrella annulata: Differs by its purple-black spores, skirt-like ring, and honey-brown caps covered with powdery white squamules when young.

Cortinarius talus: Has the same colored cap but lacks the ring, and has a bulbous, emarginate bulb at the stem base. Another source of danger could be the large fleshy Hebelomas with velar shards on their stems. They usually have brown spores and lack an entire ring at midstipe.

Stropharia coronilla: Has roughly the same cap color as the Gypsy and a white ring on the stem, but differs by its dark purple-brown spores and habit of fruiting in grassy areas and fields.

Cystoderma fallax: Differs by its white spores, thinner stature, granulose cap and stem, and granulose covering of the under part of the ring.

Long known as **Pholiota caperata** or **Rozites caperata**, the Gypsy mushroom was long thought to be the only member of the genus Rozites in the northern hemisphere. Then two others were found. These were **Rozites emodensis** from Tibet and **Rozites colombiana** from Costa Rica. Both have lilac to violaceous gills. And both have followed **Rozites caperata** back into Cortinarius along with 23 others from South America, Australia, and New Zealand. There are none left in Rozites. It is the death of a genus, nomenclaturally.

The sinking was announced by Peintner, Moser, Horak, & Vilgalys. It took a whole team of them to break the news. DNA sequencing studies had shown that Rozites belonged in Cortinarius. To perhaps soften the blow, they wrote, "molecular studies suggest that membranaceous veils have independently evolved several times in Cortinarius." A.H. Smith would not have been overly surprised. Way back in 1949 he commented that "Fries was not far wrong when he placed **Rozites caperata** in Cortinarius."

Here is a brief history of the nomenclature. Persoon first described it as **Agaricus caperatus** in 1796. Fries then transferred it to Cortinarius in 1838. Gillet moved it to Pholiota in 1878. Realizing Gillet had made a gross mistake, Karstens created the new genus Rozites for it in 1879. It was named for Ernst Roze, a French mycologist of the times. It was subsequently transferred to Dryophila in 1886 and Togaria in 1908, but neither of these genera changes was widely accepted.

If you are not comfortable with the return to Cortinarius you can always apply a popular name. The name Gypsy was bestowed on us by the Germans, who called it *Zigeuner*. No one really knows why. Perhaps the Gypsies were the first to eat it. Caperatus means wrinkled. So a few intrepid souls have called it the Wrinkled Roze, but never of course in France. The name for it in Sweden is Granny's Nightcap, not a bad image if you imagine the bell-shaped cap when it first appears, the frosted look on the surface, and the membranous ring plastered below the cap margin. So here again we have choices. And as for Cortinarius, there are now more choices than ever before.

BIBLIOGRAPHY

David Arora, *All That the Rain Promises and More*, 1991. Ten Speed Press, Berkeley, Calif.

David Arora, *Mushrooms Demystified*, 1986. Ten Speed Press, Berkeley, Calif.

David Biek, *The Mushrooms of Northern California*, 1984. Spore Prints, Redding, Calif.

Jack Czarnecki, *A Cook's Book of Mushrooms*, 1995. Artisan, New York, NY.

Eyssartier & Roux, *Le Guide des Champignons de France et Europe*, 2011. Editions Belin, Paris.

Michael Jordan, *The Encyclopedia of Fungi of Britain and Europe*, 1995. David & Charles, Newton Abbot, England.

Ying Jianzhe, Mao Xiaolan, Ma Qiming, Zong Yichen, & Wen Huaan, *Icons of Medicinal Fungi from China*, 1987. Science Press, Beijing, China.

McIlvaine & Robert Macadam, *One Thousand American Fungi*, 1902. Dover Publications, New York, NY.

Kent & Vera McKnight, *Peterson Field Guides: Mushrooms*, 1987. Houghton Mifflin, Boston, Mass.

Giovanni Pacioni & Gary Lincof, *Simon & Schuster's Guide to Mushrooms*, 1981. Simon & Schuster, New York, NY.

Harriette Parker, *Alaska's Mushrooms*, 1994. Alaska Northwest Books, Anchorage, Alaska.

Ursula Peintner, Meinhard Moser, Egon Horak, & Rytas Vilgaly, *Rozites, Cuphocybe, Rapacea are Taxonomic Synonyms of Cortinarius: New Combinations and New Names* in *Mycotaxon* 83 (447–451), 2002.

Helene Schalkwijk-Barendsen, *Mushrooms of Western Canada*, 1991. Lone Pine Publishing, Edmonton, Alberta.

Jakob Schlittler, *Champignons, Tome 1*, 1972.

A.H. Smith, *Mushrooms in Their Natural Habitats*, 1949. Editions Silva, Zurich, Switzerland. Sawyer's Inc., Portland, Ore.

A.H. Smith, *A Field Guide to Western Mushrooms*, 1975. University of Michigan Press, Ann Arbor, Mich.

Mirko Svrcek & Jiri Kubicka, *Les Champignons d'Europe*, 1979. Artia, Prague, Czechoslovakia.

Jan Vesterholt & Henning Knudsen, *Psathyrella in Nordic Macromycetes, Vol. 2*, 1992. Nordsvamp, Copenhagen.

Lucius Von Frieden, *Mushrooms of the World*, 1969. Bobbs-Merrill, Indianapolis.

Roy Watling, *Observations on the Bolbitiacea, II. A Conspectus of the Family* in *Notes from the Royal Botanic Garden, Edinburgh* 26 (289–323), 1965.

Nancy Weber & A.H. Smith, *A Field Guide to Southern Mushrooms*, 1985. University of Michigan Press, Ann Arbor, Mich.

Cortinarius gentilis (Fries) Fries

. . . eating Cortinarius gentilis and closely related species typically involves life threatening kidney failure.

One of the least known poisonous mushrooms of Whatcom County has got to be **Cortinarius gentilis**, a name usually neglected in our discussions of locally dangerous mushrooms. In fact, until the fall of 2010, I had never seen it in the county. When Jack Waytz and I found it off the South Pass Road, we had no idea what it was. We took it to our fall show where it was labeled "Cortinarius species." Within just a few hours this extremely hygrophanous fungus had gone from red brown to a golden ochre. A week later Dr. Joe Ammirati told us what we had found. He seemed surprised we didn't know it. After all, Dr. A.H. Smith had once written "gregarious in large numbers in the fall in the Pacific Northwest."

Even in its faded golden stage, this is a visually attractive mushroom as it protrudes out of deep moss under conifers. The stipes are long compared to cap widths and adorned with bright yellow veil remnants on the lower part. Caps range from 2–5 cm wide and are at first bell shaped before broadening to convex with a sharp papillate umbo. The color is tawny cinnamon when moist, fading quickly to ochre yellow when dry, often with a silky, appressed-fibrillose texture. Cap margins are incurved and sometimes silky-cortinate with yellow velar remnants. They can become incised in age. Stems are the same color, about 3–5 mm wide and 3–11 cm long. They are stiff or curved, hollow in age, fibrillose and dry, with one or more belt-like zones created by the yellow veil. The base is usually tapered and occasionally subradicating. Gills are adnate, thick, and very distant. They are ochre to olivaceous at first, then rusty from spores. Edges are fimbriate to flocculose becoming eroded in age. The spore deposit is rusty. The taste is mild and the odor is of raw potatoes or faintly of radish.

Microscopically, the spores are subglobose and verrucose, measuring 7.5–9 x 6–7 µm. They are weakly dextrinoid in Melzer's. Cheilocystidia are present as narrow cylindrical end cells, according to Ammirati, Traquaire, & Horgen. One test for identification is to apply KOH. The stem will have a blackish-red reaction and the gills will turn reddish lilac.

The Deadly Cort, as Lincoff calls it, can be found with conifers at any elevation. It thrives in moss and needle beds, and has even been found on rotten wood. The type was described by Fries from Sweden. Since then it has been found in the Pacific Northwest, Colorado, Michigan, and Newfoundland where it is called "The Moss Murderer" by Maria Voitk. Hesler reported it from Indian Gap in the Great Smokies. There it was found under red spruce on August 16, 1946.

Care should be taken not to confuse the distant but true gills of **Cortinarius gentilis** with the ridges of chanterelles. Other look-alikes might include the false chanterelles, **Hygrophoropsis aurantiaca** or **Chroogomphus tomentosus** with the faded specimens. But its closest look-alikes are also in Cortinarius. Some of these, mentioned in the literature or picked out at random are as follows:

Cortinarius malicorius: Can also have tawny-brown caps that fade in age, but differs by its more crowded gills and cap flesh that turns olive green when wet.

Cortinarius scandens: Differs by having more bluntly umbonate caps, more crowded gills, and whitish velar remnants.

Phaeomarasmius distans: Named for its distant gills, it lacks the

Cortinarius gentilis faded after a day

Cortinarius scandens

Cortinarius malicorius

Cortinarius sp. nov. in the Hinnulei

yellow velar hairs of **C. gentilis**.

Cortinarius rubellus: This species, also very poisonous, has dry, orange-red caps with erect squamules that become innately fibrillose in wet weather. The gills are scarlet-ochre, the stems dark tawny with yellow velar belts, a radish odor, and larger spores measuring 9–11 x 6.5–8 µm. **Cortinarius rainierensis** and **C. speciosissimus** are now considered synonyms.

Cortinarius gentilissimus: A Californian species that has a pale blue stem apex.

Cortinarius nothosaniosus: A European Cort with very distant gills and red-brown caps that dry to a bright yellow. It has a smaller but stouter stature than **C. gentilis**.

Cortinarius sp. nov.: Found locally with Norway spruce, this brick colored Cort with distant gills differs by its strong, sweetish geranium odor and the copious white velar material on the stems.

Cortinarius orellanus: This liver destroying Cort also bears a resemblance. It differs by having more ellipsoid spores, a broad rather than a sharp umbo, and an association with hardwoods instead of conifers. It has caused fatalities in Poland in the 1950s. This marked the first time anyone suspected any Cortinarius of being poisonous.

Cortinarius gentilis has deadly cousins. Because of its close resemblance to these unsavories, according to Ramsbottom, it was named *gentilis*, meaning "of the same race." In a tragic incident, a couple that was honeymooning in France mistook **Cortinarius rubellus** for the chanterelle.

They had collected the mushrooms in the fading light of dusk and cooked them for dinner. By dawn they knew they were in serious trouble. They were too far from any health clinic and both perished eventually.

Gary Lincoff wrote that "eating **Cortinarius gentilis** and closely related species typically involves life threatening kidney failure. Symptoms do not usually appear until 3 days to 2 weeks after ingestion. The long delay can make it difficult to pinpoint the culprit."

Arora, on the other hand, thinks that **C. gentilis** has toxins that destroy the liver. The confusion is understandable since the toxin in **Cortinarius gentilis** has not yet been identified. For years it was thought to be orellanin, a cyclic peptide that targeted the kidneys. Symptoms were insatiable thirst, lethargy, nausea, frequent urination, vomiting, shivering without a fever, headaches, and liver damage. Other species thought to be in this group are **Cortinarius rubellus** and **Cortinarius meinhardii**. Perhaps because orellanin has not been found in **Cortinarius gentilis**, it has been taken out of Subgenus Leprocybe and put into Subgenus Telamonia close to the **Cortinarius brunneus** group. The taxonomic transfer doesn't make it any less poisonous.

If you find yourself poisoned by The Moss Murderer, induce vomiting immediately.

LOOK-ALIKES

Hygrophoropsis aurantiaca group

Chroogomphus tomentosus

Follow this up with activated charcoal. For advanced cases, Turner & Szczawinski suggest taking corticosteroids and undergo peritoneal dialysis and hemodialysis to prevent kidney failure. They claim one of these toxic Corts has killed a sheep; it probably grazed more than one fruiting body.

It is probably not a good idea to eat any species of Cortinarius with distant gills until the taxonomies can be worked out and the toxins assigned accordingly.

BIBLIOGRAPHY

Joe Ammirati, J.A. Traquair, & Paul Horgen, *Poisonous Mushrooms of the Northern United States and Canada*, 1985. University of Minnesota Press, Minneapolis, Minn.

David Arora, *Mushrooms Demystified*, 1986. Ten Speed Press, Berkeley, Calif.

Erik Brandrud, Hakan Lindstrom, Hans Marklund, Jacques Melot, & Siw Muskos, *Cortinarius, Flora Photographica Vol.2*, 1990. Cortinarius HB, Matflors, Sweden.

Erik Brandrud, Hakan Lindstrom, Tuula Niskanen, Ilkka Kytovuori, Egil & Katriina Bendiksen, Tobias Froslev, Klaus Hoiland, Thomas Jeppesen, & Kare Liimatainen, *Cortinarius in Funga Nordica*, 2008. Nordsvamp, Copenhagen.

Stefan Buczacki, *Fungi of Britain and Europe*, 1989. University of Texas Press, Austin, Texas.

Michael Castellano, Jane Smith, Thomas Odell, Efren Cazares, & Susan Nugent, *Handbook to Strategy 1 Fungal Species in the Northwest Forest Plan*, 1999. U.S. Department of Agriculture, Forest Service, Portland, Ore.

Ian Hall, Steven Stephenson, Petyer Buchanan, Wang Yun, & Anthony Cole, *Edible and Poisonous Mushrooms of the World*, 2003. Timber Press, Portland, Ore.

Lexemuel Hesler, *Notes on Southern Appalachian Fungi—IX* in *Journal of the Tennessee Academy of Science* 26, No.1 (4–14), 1951.

Calvin Kauffman, *Cortinarius* in *North American Flora* 10, Part 5 (282–348), 1932.

Calvin Kauffman, *The Mycological Flora of the Higher Rockies of Colorado* in *Papers of the Michigan Academy of Science, Arts, & Letters* 1 (101–150), 1921.

Gary Lincoff, *The Audubon Field Guide to North American Mushrooms*, 1981. Alfred A. Knopf, New York, NY.

André Marchand, *Champignons du Nord et du Midi, Tome 7*, 1982. Societe Mycologique des Pyrenees Mediterraneennes, Perpignan, France.

Orson & Hope Miller, *North American Mushrooms*, 2006. Morris Book Publishing, Guilford, Conn.

Roger Phillips, *Mushrooms of North America*, 1991. Little, Brown & Co., Boston, Mass.

Roger Phillips, *A Provisional Multi-Access Key to American Species of Cortinarius, Inoloma, and Telemonia*, 1986. Self-published.

John Ramsbottom, *Larger British Fungi*, 1965. Trustees of the British Museum, London.

Alexander & Helen Smith & Nancy Weber, *How to Know the Gilled Mushrooms*, 1979. William C. Brown, Dubuque, Iowa.

Daniel Stuntz, *Macroscopic Field Key to Some of the More Common Species of Cortinarius Found in Washington*, 1981. Pacific Northwest Key Council, Seattle, Wash.

Steve Trudell & Joe Ammirati, *Mushrooms of the Pacific Northwest*, 2009. Timber Press, Portland, Ore.

Nancy Turner & Adam Szczawinski, *Common Poisonous Plants and Mushrooms of North America*, 1991. Timber Press, Portland, Ore.

Andrus Voitk, *A Little Illustrated Book of Common Mushrooms of Newfoundland and Labrador*, 2008. Gros Morne Co-operating Association, Rocky Harbour, Newfoundland.

Cortinarius lucorum (Fries) Karsten

*By 1978 Moser had brought
the purple back to the gills.*

This flamboyant Cortinarius was found by Stas Bronisz on September 22, 1996, at a Lake Padden foray. It was found in a mossy lawn between the jogging path and the ball field. The nearest trees were red alders with cottonwoods just behind them. Over the years, Stas has brought numerous Cortinarius specimens to our fall show, but none as stunning as this one.

The caps measured 3 ½–6 cm wide. They were convex to domed, dry, and appressed fibrillose. The cap color was pale grayish-violet becoming chestnut color at the disc. The context was buff and thickish. The gills were adnate and gray violet before turning rusty from the spores. There were two tiers of lamellulae. The stems were 7 ½–8 cm long and 1–1 ½ cm thick until the clavate base which measured 2 ½–3 cm thick. The stems were also dry. They were violet at the apex becoming gray violet below and then dingy ochre brown on the bulbous-clavate, partially rooting base. The stipe context was violet at the apex and buff below. It stained brown in KOH. The cortina was white and copious. There also appeared to be a mottled band of whitish, cottony velar material just above where the base widened out. This represented the remains of the universal veil, which can form a peronate sheath around buttons. The taste was soapy, the odor faintly musty raphanoid. Spores were rusty in deposit. They were ellipsoid, distinctly verrucose, and measured 9.3–10.4 x 6.1–6.3 µm. The quotient was 1.54.

Even in Europe, this is deemed a rare mushroom. According to Ammirati & Matheny, Washington State records have come from Redmond, Issaquah, and the Hazel Wolf Wetland. And now, thanks to Stas, Lake Padden. Unfortunately, when it was found, I hadn't noted whether it was hygrophanous or not. This feature alone is enough to send you dozens of pages away in a Cortinarius key.

Dr. Joe Ammirati came to the rescue. He took one look at the photo I emailed him and realized I was not considering the whole mushroom. I drove back out to Lake Padden and reaffirmed the trees. Tree associations can have great importance in helping to identify a species in Cortinarius. It is a genus with so many members and so many relationships and look-alikes that during Key Council forays, 90% are simply ignored. **Cortinarius lucorum** has a mycorrhizal relationship

LOOK-ALIKES

Cortinarius evernius from Haida Gwaii

Cortinarius saturninus

with cottonwoods. The red alders had simply grown there to throw me off course.

There's not too much to add to flesh out the above description. Various authors note that caps can be dark purple brown at first, fading quickly to pinkish buff. Margins are incurved. The surface and context turned brownish with KOH. The gills have even edges, are distant and thick, and turn darker when touched. The stems are fibrillose-streaked, and the base is sometimes found with rhizomorphs. The taste is mild to fungoid or slightly bitter. And finally the spores are dextrinoid in Melzer's solution.

One of the problems with **Cortinarius lucorum** is that both Jakob Lange of Denmark and Petter Karsten of Finland transferred the species to Cortinarius at different times. Both concepts seem to be a bit off from the modern interpretation we see here. In *Flora Agaracina Danica*, Vol. 3, Lange upgraded **Cortinarius impennis var. lucorum** to species status in 1937. In both his description and illustration there is no hint of any purple or lilac color. This same illustration is then used by his brother Morten Lange in 1963 in the first British Collins' guide, *A Guide to Mushrooms and Toadstools*. The entire fruiting body is a cinnamon-flesh color. Jakob Lange also noted that Karsten's version, which dated back to 1879 when he transferred it from Agaricus, had subglobose spores. This led Jakob Lange to conclude that Karsten had found a different species. Either two well-regarded experts interpreted

LOOK-ALIKES

Cortinarius biformis

Cortinarius cf subpurpureus

Fries differently, or there were two versions floating around with different origins.

And this had repercussions on this side of the Atlantic. Calvin Kauffman sunk his own **Cortinarius umidicola**, turning it into a synonym of **Cortinarius lucorum** (Fr.) J.Lge. His concept included subserrulate gill edges, a violet-white partial veil, and smaller spores at 7–9 x 5–6 µm. His concept differs from both Lange's and Karsten's, and Ammirati was able to equate it with **Cortinarius canabarba** in the sense of Moser.

Meanwhile Dr. A.H. Smith reported finding **Cortinarius lucorum** under spruce in 1935 at Lake Takhenitch in Oregon. **Cortinarius lucorum** is not a conifer associate. It is likely he found another look-alike.

By 1978, at least, Meinhard Moser put the purple back in the gills.

There are a number of look-alikes, some of which are not even in the same section. A partial list of these follows here:

Cortinarius saturninus: The most frequently noted look-alike, it differs from **C. lucorum** by its smaller spores at 7–9 x 4–5 μm, pallid gray to pale ochre stems, and white appendiculate velar patches on the cap margins.

Cortinarius canabarba: Differs by its girdles of dark brown velar material on the stem, grayish-white caps, and habitat in montane spruce forests.

Cortinarius adustus: Differs by its more crowded gills, little to no velar material, and association with conifers.

Cortinarius evernius: Has dark brown caps, fruits with spruce, and always has stems that taper at the bases. These were found on Haida Gwaii in July.

Cortinarius impennis: Differs by having gills with serrated edges, a non-bulbous stem base, a more pallid stem, and habitat among conifers.

Cortinarius 'cf' subpurpureus: Differs by having lubricous, mauve-brown caps with distinctly paler margins, and much larger spores at 10.7–15.7 x 5.3–7.6 μm.

Cortinarius biformis: Differs by its pale ochre-orange gills and association with conifers. These were found at the Alger Bog with western hemlock.

Cortinarius agathosmus: Looks like a slender version of **Cortinarius lucorum**, but differs by its association with mountain spruces and its strong perfume-like odor.

Cortinarius subtorvus: A subalpine species often found with dwarf willow, it further differs from **C. lucorum** by its dark purple-brown caps that fade to pale chestnut brown and slightly shorter spores.

Every Cortinarius, even **C. violaceus**, has a look-alike. They are very difficult to pin down taxonomically. When you add to this the problems in communication at the turn of the nineteenth century, it is not surprising there were different opinions and concepts. So it is especially gratifying to find a modern concept accepted by both the Scandinavian authors of Cortinarius in *Funga Nordica* and Dr. Ammirati of the Pacific Northwest. And if Stas hadn't happened to find it, we may never have known of this major advance with **Cortinarius lucorum.**

Cortinarius lucorum ss J. Lange: Caps a flesh tan color, gills a bit darker, and base of stem with a girdle of whitish velar material.

LOOK-ALIKE

Cortinarius lucorum ss J. Lange

Photo by Richard Morrison

BIBLIOGRAPHY

Joe Ammirati & Brandon Matheny, *Cortinarius lucorum (Fries) Karsten, a Populus Associate from North America* in *Pacific Northwest Fungi* 1 (1–10), 2006.

David Arora, *Mushrooms Demystified*, 1986. Ten Speed Press, Berkeley, Calif.

Erik Brandrud, Hakan Lindstrom, Hans Marklund, Jacques Melot, & Siw Muskos, *Cortinarius Flora Photographica, Vol. 3*, 1998. Cortinarius HB, Matflors, Sweden.

Erik Brandrud, Hakan Lindstrom, Tuula Niskanen, Ilkka Kytovuori, Egil & Katriina Bendiksen, Tobias Froslev, Klaus Hoiland, Thomas Jeppesen, & Kare Liimatainen, *Cortinarius (Pers.) Gray* in *Funga Nordica* (847), 2012. Nordsvamp, Copenhagen.

Calvin Kauffman, *The Agaricaceae of Michigan*, 1918. Michigan Geological and Biological Survey, Lansing, Mich.

Jakob Lange, *Flora Agaracina Danica, Vol. 3*, 1937. Society for the Advancement of Mycology, Copenhagen.

Morten Lange & F. Bayard Hora, *A Guide to Mushrooms and Toadstools*, 1963. E.P. Dutton Co., New York, NY.

Meinhard Moser, *Keys to Agarics and Boleti*, 1983. Translated and published by Roger Phillips, London.

A.H. Smith, *Studies in the Genus Cortinarius* in *Contributions to the University of Michigan Herbarium* 2 (5–42), 1939.

- Den Digerness

Craterellus tubaeformis ss auct. PNW

They fruit in the same location several years running, so you can mark your spot, and come back for more.

Sometimes called the Winter Chanterelle, this essentially edible, thin-fleshed member of the Cantharellaceae can often be found a month after our regular chanterelle has ceased to fruit. Unassuming and often mistaken from the aerial view for just another fiber-head, **Craterellus tubaeformis** ss auct. PNW may possibly be the most controversial mushroom we have yet handled in a newsletter. Not only is there a full range of opinions on the edibility, but the name of the species itself has jumped back and forth like a football on a rugby field.

For those of our readers who don't enjoy the Latin names, Craterellus is Latin for crater. Tubaeformis is Latin for trumpet formed. Thus, the Trumpet Formed Crater is your best bet for linguistic accuracy. The problem is... the Trumpet Formed Crater has long been confused with the Funnel Shaped Vase, or **Cantharellus infundibuliformis**, the Latin name we are most accustomed to associating with this species in our area. For years it has been debated up and down and across two continents whether they are the same species or not. Dr. A.H. Smith separated them by spore print color. The late Dr. Harry Thiers listed the main differences. **Cantharellus tubaeformis** had white to pale yellow spores, yellow to orange-yellow stems, and yellow-gray to yellow-brown caps. **Cantharellus infundibuliformis**, on the other hand, had yellow to ochraceous spores, lemon yellow stems, and gray-brown to black-brown caps. Others have described these cap colors as dull orange to orange brown to tan. There were, in fact, so many different combinations of cap colors to stem colors and eventually even spore colors that Dr. Bigelow and Dr. Ron Petersen came to believe we were all looking at variations of the same species. Dr. Thiers finally agreed, and in his *Cantharellaceae of California*, which has the most complete description of the species, he listed **C. infundibuliformis** as a synonym of **C. tubaeformis**. This is good news for us. It means that we no longer have to tell people at our forays that we can't put a name to it until we go home and get a spore print.

Caps of **Craterellus tubaeformis** ss auct. PNW are 1½–6 cm wide, thin-fleshed, at first convex with incurved margins, and then umbilicate to funnel shaped with wavy, irregular margins in age. The surface can be smooth or fibrillose-scaly, the fibrils slightly darker than the base color. The colors vary from tan to orange brown to dark brown with all sorts of variations in between. To complicate the picture, Von Frieden suggests that caps are hazel yellow in dry weather becoming dark brown in damp weather. The center of the cap is often perforated, leading directly to the hollow stem. The gills are blunt to ridgelike, yellowish to buff or pale cinnamon at first and then grayish to lilac gray in age. They are deeply decurrent, usually forked and somewhat intervenose. They have also been described as waxy in appearance, which suggests an affinity with Hygrophorus. The stems are 4–8 cm long and ½–1 cm thick. They are smooth, tough, often flattened or grooved, and generally hollow. (Kauffman believed that stems of **Cantharellus infundibuliformis** were hollow from the beginning while those of **C. tubaeformis** were solid at first, becoming hollow in age.) The stem colors range from pale yellow to yellow orange to even grayish yellow in age. The odor is pleasantly aromatic and the taste bitter to mild. The spore print can be white to yellow or ochre or

LOOK-ALIKE

Craterellus lutescens from France

Cantharellus lewisii from Va.

Chrysomphalina chrysophylla from Wash.

Craterellus ignicolor from Colombia

even pale pinkish buff in the Appalachians. What causes this variation in spore color, I have no idea. The spores, according to Thomas, measure .00035 to .00045 inches long. **Craterellus tubaeformis** ss auct. PNW prefers cool, wet forests with acid soils and is usually found next to rotting stumps or logs or its favorite habitat—decomposed logs that have just turned back into soil. It has also been found in sphagnum bogs. Its growth habit is gregarious to clustered, and more rarely cespitose. Although not particularly common, it can be found all across the northern hemisphere, down through Appalachia in the eastern U.S., and from Alaska to San Francisco on the Pacific Coast.

Craterellus tubaeformis ss auct. PNW, that innocuous little mushroom being tossed around in your pasta, has had a tumultuous nomenclatural history from the very beginning. According to Watling & Turnbull, Elias Fries himself was confused. What he originally called **Cantharellus tubaeformis** in 1821, he later changed to **Cantharellus infundibuliformis** in 1838. The former name became a different species. Fries had initially inherited the name "tubaeformis" from the Dutch mycologist, Persoon. The mistake was made in 1838 when he accepted the Scopoli name of **C. infundibuliformis**, not realizing it was identical with the earlier **C. tubaeformis**. Since **C. tubaeformis** was the earlier name used, **C. infundibuliformis** became an illegitimate name. The good news is that we no longer have to intimidate novitiates to Latin names with 'in-fun-di-bully-formis' at our forays anymore.

After it was discovered that leathery, thin-fleshed members of Cantharellus belonged in Craterellus, DNA sequencing further revealed that our West Coast **Craterellus tubaeformis** was different from the European counterpart. The European name, being over a century earlier, has precedence. This means a new name will have to be found for ours, which is temporarily being called **Craterellus tubaeformis** ss auct. PNW until that new name emerges. Furthermore, according to the authors of *The New Savory Wild Mushroom*, European mycologists believe that our former West Coast **C. infundibuliformis** probably represents a group of species differing slightly from one another. If so, these species would need to be clarified before the new Craterellus name could emerge.

Fortunately there aren't too many look-alikes if you discount the variations in the species itself. And just for the record, here they are:

Craterellus tubaeformis var. pallidus: Probably the closest relative, it is an all-yellow variety.

Craterellus lutescens: Has a yellower stem and darker brown caps.

Craterellus ignicolor: This pantropical species, also found in the southeastern U.S., has caps that are generally more orange. In age they become more orange-brown and thus become difficult to separate visually from **C. tubaeformis** in the field. They may only be

Gerronema strombodes from Maryland

separated geographically and microscopically with any certainty.

Chrysomphalina chrysophylla: Can mimic the colors and cap texture, but it has a flaccid cap, true gills, and belongs in the Omphalina group.

Cantharellus lewisii: This is a pale straw-colored southern species with appressed lilac squamules in their cap centers. Dr. Bart Buyck brought it to light along with several other diminutive ochre chanterelles from the Appalachians.

Gliophorus laetus: Common in our area, it can have a similar cap color when hygrophanously faded, but the waxy true gills and strongly striated cap margins separate it.

Gerronema strombodes: Differs by its true pale yellow gills and caps that can be obtusely lined at the margins. Stems are longitudinally hairy. Found in the Appalachians.

Gomphus clavatus: Differs by its much stockier stature, lavender ridges for a hymenial surface, and tendency to fruit in clusters.

If you focus on the ridgelike gills, small tan to brownish caps, yellowish hollow stems, and the tendency to fruit near rotten logs, you can generally nail **Craterellus tubaeformis.**

Unfortunately, you still have to decide whether to eat it or not. There are indeed conflicting reports on the edibility of the **C. tubaeformis** complex. While most authors agree that it is edible but not nearly as good as our fleshier chanterelles, there are a few who urge caution. Orson Miller, Kent McKnight, and Dr. Edmund Tylutki all report mild gastrointestinal disturbances from eating the species. My guess is that these reports are out of Idaho since all three of these mycologists are either from there or have spent time there repeatedly. My personal experience is even stranger. A friend's girlfriend became violently ill from eating it in San Francisco back in 1982. While Peter Robinson and I felt no ill effects, she had to be taken to emergency to have her stomach pumped out. The collection was probably from Mendocino County. Since then, I have heard of no cases remotely similar. In fact, Mike Beug, recent past president of the Pacific Northwest Key Council, and a member of the committee that reports on mushroom poisonings in our region, tells me there are no negative reports concerning **C. tubaeformis** ss auct. PNW.

And as you can imagine there are varying opinions on the flavor:

Dickinson & Lucas: "Experts disagree about the food value of this fungus. It is very tough, often dry and fibrous, and has a bitter taste.'

Smith, Smith, & Weber, 1973: "Not edible."

A.H. Smith, 1977: "Not recommended. The reports on C. infundibuliformis are that it is edible but not very good.'

David Pegler: "The flavor is excellent and ideal in stews."

Lorelei Norvell: "The species is commercially harvested and considered a choice edible."

David Arora, 1986: "Edible but small and thin-fleshed. Some people relish it nevertheless, and in Finland it is harvested commercially."

David Arora, 1991: "Edible. Not as meaty as the other chanterelles, but with a good flavor, especially when dry-sautéed."

Olle Persson: "It is only in the past fifty years that **Cantharellus tubaeformis** has become popular in the kitchen, and now it is being served in soups in restaurants. Because of its long shelf life, it is one of the few wild mushrooms served in Sweden today."

The Chinese have found a different use for **C. tubaeformis.** They found that extracts of sporophores have inhibitory action on certain species of bacteria.

Now that we have sampled the opinions of the mycologists, it is time we turned to the chefs. In *The Ultimate Mushroom Book* by Jordan & Wheeler, the authors note in their culinary section that the species dries well and can be preserved in virgin olive oil or wine vinegar. They also note, "they are very versatile in cooking,

LOOK-ALIKE

Gliophorus laetus

with an extremely nice, sweet flavor that goes especially well with fish."

Jack Czarnecki calls **C. tubaeformis** ss auct. PNW and other small chanterelles the "chop suey" chanterelles because that is what they look like in the pan when most of the liquid evaporates. He thinks the flavor is not bad, but not particularly distinct. He also writes that drying is the only method of preservation.

While cautioning that a few people have reported mild digestive discomfort after eating **Craterellus tubaeformis,** Bessette & Fischer claim that most people enjoy it. They note that "it is highly regarded by many mycophagists, not only for the aromatic flavor and delicate texture, but for their almost flower-like appearance." They suggest that dried specimens can be pulverized and added to various dishes as a flavoring.

To back up their claim to fine dining, they even have a special recipe for **Craterellus tubaeformis**. Jack Waytz, Northwest Mushroomers Association newsletter editor, tried this recipe: "In past years I had never found this mushroom in enough quantity to really consider trying to prepare a recipe in which it was featured. However, at precisely the end of the regular chanterelle season, upon checking on one of my favorite spots near home for the last gasp of chanterelles, I discovered that although I was late for them, there was an unbelievably thick crop of **Craterellus tubaeformis** ss auct. PNW in their place. I harvested them, and upon arriving home, promptly called Buck, who suggested this recipe. Whatever criticism of the flavor of this mushroom you have read should be utterly disregarded. I was very pleasantly surprised at its quality, a very unique and distinctive flavor."

Nonetheless, because of random reports of discomfort from eating the Trumpet Chanterelle, I would suggest trying a small amount at first to determine whether you are negatively affected by it or not. Then, if you are good to go, there is more good news on the horizon. Peter Jordan informs us that they fruit in the same location several years running, so you can mark your spot, and come back for more.

Finally we would like to thank Dr. Mike Beug for looking up the northwest poisoning report on **C. tubaeformis** for us.

As for the nomenclatural ambiguities associated with **C. tubaeformis**, never forget the words from one of our mycological sages: "The mushrooms never change. Only our opinions of them do."

The Trumpet Chanterelle Omelet

½ cup chopped green pepper
½ cup minced onion
3 tblsp. butter
2 cups trumpet chanterelles, beheaded
¼ tsp. mace
½ tsp. salt

¼ tsp. black pepper
dash of hot sauce
1 tblsp. minced parsley
4 eggs
¼ cup light cream
½ cup grated cheddar cheese

First sautée the onions and green peppers in 2 tblsp. of the butter. When tender, add the mushrooms and cook down until liquid is evaporated. Add spices and seasonings. In another pan, melt the remaining tblsp. of butter and pour in the whisked eggs and cream. When nearly set, sprinkle in the cheese and top with the mushroom mixture. Cook another minute, fold, and serve.

BIBLIOGRAPHY

David Arora, *All That the Rain Promises and More*, 1991. Ten Speed Press, Berkeley, Calif.

David Arora, *Mushrooms Demystified*, 1986. Ten Speed Press, Berkeley, Calif.

Alan & Arleen Bessette, Dail Dunaway, & William Roody, *Mushrooms of the Southeastern United States*, 2007. Syracuse University Press, Syracuse, NY.

Alan Bessette & David Fischer, *Edible Wild Mushrooms of North America*, 1992. University of Texas Press, Austin, Texas.

Stefan Buczacki, *Fungi of Britain and Europe*, 1989. University of Texas Press, Austin, Texas.

Bart Buyck & Valerie Hofstetter, *The Contribution of tef-1 Sequences to Species Delimitation in the Cantharellus cibarius Complex in the Southeastern U.S.A.* in *Fungal Diversity* 49 (35–46), 2011.

Jack Czarnecki, *A Cook's Book of Mushrooms*, 1995. Artisan, New York, NY.

Colin Dickinson & John Lucas, *The Encyclopedia of Mushrooms*, 1983. Von Nostrand Reinhold Co., New York, NY.

Karen & Richard Haard, *Foraging for Edible Wild Mushrooms*, 1978. Cloudburst Press, Seattle, Wash.

Miron Hard, *Mushrooms, Edible and Otherwise*, 1976. Dover Publications, New York, NY.

Ying Jianzhe, Mao Xiaolan, Ma Qiming, Zong Yichen, & Wen Huaa, *Icons of Medicinal Fungi from China*, 1987. Science Press, Beijing, China.

Peter Jordan & Steven Wheeler, *The Ultimate Mushroom Book*, 1995. Smithmark Publishers, New York, NY.

Calvin Kauffman, *The Agaricaceae of Michigan*, 1918. Michigan Geological and Biological Survey, Lansing, Mich.

Margaret McKenny, Daniel Stuntz, & Joe Ammirati, *The New Savory Wild Mushroom*, 1987. University of Washington Press, Seattle, Wash.

Kent & Vera McKnight, *Peterson Field Guides— Mushrooms*, 1987. Houghton Mifflin Co., Boston, Mass.

Orson Miller, *Mushrooms of North America*, 1977. E.P. Dutton & Co., New York, NY.

Lorelei Norvell, *Preparation for a Key to the Cantharelloid Fungi of British Columbia, Washington, Oregon, and Idaho*. Pacific Northwest Key Council, Seattle, Wash.

Giovanni Pacioni & Gary Lincoff, *Simon & Schusters' Guide to Mushrooms*, 1981. Simon & Schuster, New York, NY.

David Pegler, *The Mitchell Beazley Pocket Guide to Mushrooms and Toadstools*, 1981. Mitchell Beazley Publishers, London.

Olle Persson, *The Chanterelle Book*, 1997. Ten Speed Press, Berkeley, Calif.

Ronald Rayner, *Hamlyn Nature Guides-Mushroom & Toadstools*, 1979. Hamlyn Publishing Group, London.

William Roody, *Mushrooms of West Virginia and the Central Appalachians*, 2003. University Press of Kentucky, Lexington, Ky.

A.H. Smith, *The Mushroom Hunter's Field Guide*, 1977. University of Michigan Press, Ann Arbor, Mich.

Smith, Smith, & Weber, How to Know the Non-Gilled Mushrooms, 1981. William Brown & Co., Dubuque, Iowa.

Harry Thiers, *The Agaricales of California: Cantharellaceae*, 1985. Mad River Press, Eureka, Calif.

William Sturgis Thomas, *Field Book of Common Mushrooms*, 1928. G.P. Putnam's Sons, New York, NY.

Edmund Tylutki, *Mushrooms of Idaho and the Pacific Northwest, Vol. 2*, 1987. University of Idaho Press, Moscow, Idaho.

Lucius Von Frieden, *Mushrooms of the World*, 1969. Bobbs-Merrill, Indianapolis, Indiana.

Roy Watling & Evelyn Turnbull, *British Fungus Flora 8. Cantharellaceae & Gomphaceae*, 1998. Royal Botanic Garden, Edinburgh, Scotland.

DIGERNESS

Entocybe nitida (Quelet) Largent, Baroni, Hofstetter, & Vilgalys

Whatever genus you want to use, no authors consider it edible.

Sometimes if you aren't at the right place at the right time, someone else is. In this case it was Paula Mechel, a guest of former club member Ron Sawyer. She happened across these striking Entolomoid fungi at the base of an ancient Douglas fir at Milepost 44 on the Mount Baker Highway on October 1, 1998. Milepost 44 is a tiny patch of ancient growth forest that has never been clearcut. If the finding of **Entocybe nitida** at the site can help keep it that way, the more power to it. Thanks to Veronica Wisniewski, who had the foresight to save the two specimens, I was able to drive to her place to photograph, measure, and describe these fine specimens just after the foray.

LOOK-ALIKES

Leptonia subeuchroa

Leptonia serrulata

At the time, we figured **Entocybe nitida** must be one of the rarest mushrooms in North America. Not only had Dr. Dave Largent not included it in his key to northwestern Entomaceae, but Laessoe and Lincoff wrote in 1996 that it had never been recorded on the North American continent. They must not have paid attention to Arora who included it in his Entoloma key in 1986. Since then, the *Handbook to the Strategy 1 Fungal Species in the Northwest Forest Plan* reports it from three places in the Pacific Northwest where the spotted owl lives. It has been found in the Hoh River area, the Quinault Research area in the Olympics, and also at Barlow Pass in the Snoqualmie National Forest. So we felt a little deflated when a decade later Steve Trudell reported it as "widespread and sometimes abundant locally in conifer forests."

Nonetheless, it remains rare in most of Europe. The type was evidently from Jura up in the French Alps. The holotype, the original specimen chosen by the author to represent the species concept, no longer exists. Although common in the Scandinavian countries in the fall, and in southern Germany, it is considered rare elsewhere. It has also been reported from Chile.

The caps of these specimens measured 4–4 ½ cm wide. They were broadly convex with obtuse umbos. The color was blue-black fibrillose on a grayish ground. Margins were incurved and then rimose in age. The context was rather thin. The gills were adnexed, subdistant, and subventricose (they bellied out a bit). They were buff at first with an ochre hue, then flesh colored from the spores. They bruised slowly grayish when rubbed. The edges were entire, and there were four tiers of ascending lamellulae with some shallowly intervenose gills between them. The stems were 7–8 mm thick at the apex and up to 9 cm long. The apices were white pruinose, the rest of the stems a fibrillose, dark slate blue until the whitish tomentum at the base. They were hollow and slightly expanded at base and apex. Stems are consistently much longer than cap widths. The taste was mild and the odor mildly peculiar, perhaps a cross between radish and farinaceous. The spore deposit was flesh colored.

Microscopically, our specimens had roundly angular spores with mostly six sides and an oil drop in the center. They measured 7.2–8.6 x 7–7.2 µm. They had a low quotient of 1.09 (length to width ratio), and because of this quotient, they are termed isodiametric. The gill trama consisted of parallel hyphae 4–14 µm wide. The basidia were clamped at the bases, 4-spored, and clavate. The pileipellis was an ixocutis of repent hyphae 3–6 µm thick in a gelatinous matrix. At the cap disc, some of these hyphal ends were exerted. The subpellis had more inflated hyphae up to 17 µm wide. Clamps were abundant and most of the septa were wavy. The pigmentation of the pileipellis dissolved in a mauve cloud in KOH.

Differences between this collection and European de-

LOOK-ALIKES

Leptonia chalybaea from Calif.

Leptonia scabrosa from Calif.

scriptions were the gray bruising of the gills and the white powder at the stem apices, both features not described for European material.

Entocybe nitida could be confused with dark blue Leptonias, which generally differ by having more entangled hyphae in the pileipellis. Several of these potential look-alikes (among an ocean of others) in the Entolomaceae follow:

Leptonia scabrosa: Differs by its dark brown to ochre-brown caps with scaly-tomentose texture. Part of a complex, our West Coast version might acquire a new name.

Leptonia chalybaea: Differs by its blue-gray gills and slightly smaller spores.

Entoloma medianox from Calif. (formerly Entoloma madidum)

Entocybe trachyospora var. vinacea

Entoloma bloxamii from Switzerland

Leptonia carnea: Differs by having bluish-gray gills with blue-black emarginate edges at first, and much larger spores at 8.8–13.3 x 6–10.4 µm. Known mostly from California.

Leptonia euchroa: Differs by its blue-gray gills with flocculose blue-violet edges and lignicolous habit.

Leptonia subeuchroa: Differs by having squamulose caps less than 2 cm wide. It is also lignicolous.

Leptonia serrulata: Differs by having tomentulose caps (dark blue-black dots on the surface).

Entoloma bloxamii: A European species, is a much fleshier species with a broader umbo found in heaths and grasslands.

Entoloma atrocoeruleum: Has the same cap and stipe colors, but with larger spores and umbilicate caps.

Entocybe trachyospora var. vinacea: A rather fleshy species variety with appressed fibrillose purple-brown caps.

Entoloma medianox: Differs by its lubricous to viscid caps, and much thicker stature. Arora writes that it is a good edible.

Largent discovered that **Entocybe trachyospora** and **Entocybe nitida** had barely noticeable bumps on their spores. This ornamentation sent them to Rhodocybe before the transfer to Entocybe. It is interesting to note that the bumps are so subtle that they cannot be seen in an ordinary 100x lens. You need an electron microscope to discern them. Needless to say, if you can't afford having one of these in your home, and you aren't attached to a university lab, you are at a distinct disadvantage here.

Dr. Largent was glad to receive one of these specimens. The transfer to Rhodocybe was delayed for some years, perhaps because of DNA sequencing results. Now, Baroni, Largent, Hofstetter, & Vilgalys have transferred these Entolomoid species with ornamented spores to their own genus, Entocybe. This genus is typified by angular spores with 6–10 sides, pustulate ornamentation, and spore colors varying from flesh to vinaceous brown. The caps are mostly smooth and hygrophanous, the stems fragile and fibrillose striate. No spores are longer than 9 μm, and clamps are present in all tissues.

Whatever genus you want to use, no author considers them edible. An excellent photo of **E. nitida** can be seen on page 12 of Paul Starosta's *Fungi.*

BIBLIOGRAPHY

David Arora, *Mushrooms Demystified*, 1986. Ten Speed Press, Berkeley, Calif.

Timothy Baroni, Valerie Hofstetter, Dave Largent, & Rytas Vilgalys, *Entocybe is proposed as a New Genus in the Entolomataceae* in *North American Fungi* 6, No.12 (1–19), 2011. A.A. Balkema, Rotterdam, Holland.

Cornelis Bas, Thomas Kuyper, Machiel Noordeloos, & Else Vellinga, *Flora Agaracina Neerlandica 1*, 1988.

J. Breitenbach & F. Kranzlin, *Fungi of Switzerland, Vol. 4*, 1995. Edition Mykologia, Lucerne, Switzerland.

Stefan Buczacki, *Fungi of Britain and Europe*, 1989. University of Texas Press, Austin, Texas.

Michael Castellano, Jane Smith, Thomas Odell, Efren Cazares, & Susan Nugent, *Handbook to Strategy 1 Fungal Species in the Northwest Forest Plan*, 1999. U.S. Department of Agriculture, Forest Service, Portland, Ore.

Regis Courtecuisse & Bernard Duhem, *Mushrooms and Toadstools of Britain and Europe*, 1995. Harper-Collins, London.

Helmut & Renate Grünert, *Field Guide to Mushrooms of Britain and Europe*, 1991. Crowood Press, Wiltshire, England.

Thomas Laessoe, Gary Lincoff, & Anna del Conte, *The Mushroom Book*, 1996. DK Publishing, New York, NY.

Dave Largent, *The Genus Leptonia*, 1977. J. Cramer, Hirschberg, Germany.

David Largent, *Entolomoid Fungi of the Western United States and Aklaska*, 1994. Mad River Press, Eureka, Calif.

Machiel Noordeloos, *Entolomataceae in Nordic Macromycetes, Vol. 2*, 1992. Nordsvamp, Copenhagen.

Machiel Noordeloos, *Entoloma in Europe* in *Nova Hedwigia, Beihefte* 91 (1–419), 1987.

Machiel Noordeloos, *Entoloma Subgenera Entoloma and Allocybe in the Netherlands and Adjacent Regions with a Reconnaisance of their Remaining Taxa in Europe* in *Persoonia* 11 (153–256), 1981.

Paul Starosta & Christian Epinat, *Fungi*, 1999. Benedikt Taschen Verlag, Hohenzollernring, Germany.

Steve Trudell & Joe Ammirati, *Mushrooms of the Pacific Northwest*, 2009. Timber Press, Portland, Ore.

Else Vellinga, *A Mycolegium of Literature, the New North America Mushroom Species of 2015* in *Fungi*, Vol.9, No.2 (20), 2016.

Floccularia albolanaripes (Atkinson) Redhead

Edible and excellent. A greatly under-appreciated mushroom.

One of the most colorful surprises of the October 2011 Wild Mushroom Show was the enigmatic appearance of **Floccularia albolanaripes**. The fleshy yellow fruiting bodies dominated the Armillaria section, the genus where it had been before. Also known as the "Shaggy Stalk Mushroom" if you follow Mary Wells, or the "Scaly Bracelet" according to the McKnights, this was the first time it had arrived at our fall show. Since there are only seven Floccularias in the world, its presence was even more special. The problem with the species at the fall shows is that so many people bring in mushrooms that we often can't match the mushroom with the finder. So, whoever you are, congratulations on landing this "mushroom of the month."

But why Floccularia? George Atkinson placed it in Armillaria in 1908 from a collection found by E.R. Lake from Corvalis, Oregon, on November 6, 1906. There it lived for 81 years. Then in 1957, Pouzar erected the genus Floccularia. This was created for those species of Armillaria with no black rhizomorphs, fleshy fruiting bodies with some yellow in them, cap margins with appendiculate velar shards, and smooth, amyloid spores. Dr. Redhead herded **F. albolanaripes** into Floccularia in 1987.

As for identification, I had seen this species only once before. This was back at the Baker Lake foray in October of 2000. The caps had been brilliant yellow, glabrous, and viscid. This is how they often start out. The specimens in the top photo were merely sticky and

had flattened scales and fibrils of a cinnamon-brown color. The literature tells us that this is how the species changes in appearance as it ages. Older caps can turn from yellowish to brownish. Its closest relative, **Floccularia luteovirens**, differs by having crowded, erect scales on both cap and stem. A good comparison of the two species can be seen on adjacent pages in Alexander Smith's *A Field Guide to Western Mushrooms*.

Caps of **Floccularia albolanaripes** are 5–15 cm wide, broadly convex and usually umbonate. They are viscid at first, then sticky as they dry. The color is bright yellow becoming pallid at the margins, and usually decorated with flattened darker scales and fibrils. Cap margins are at first inrolled and covered with the white, appendiculate veil remnants. The context is white, but yellow beneath the cuticle. According to Wells and Mitchel, the caps are sensitive to light. In Colorado they can bleach to a cream color in sunlight or be cinnamon-brown in the shade. The gills are adnexed to notched, close to subdistant, and can have straight or serrated edges. They are white at first, then yellowish in age. The stems are 3–8 cm long and 1–2 ½ cm thick. The apex is smooth and white to pale yellow. Then there is an abrupt change. The rest of the stem is sheathed in a belt of dense white to yellowish cottony scales with brownish tips. The top of this sheath is a ring of the white cottony velar remnants that separated from the cap margin. A gorgeous photo of this can be viewed at www.mykoweb.com. Atkinson reported the stems to be hollow. The odor and taste are reported as mild by all authors except for Wells & Mitchel, who found the taste to be sour and acrid when raw.

Along the West Coast, **F. albolanaripes** is found mostly with alder and oak from fall through winter down into California. David Biek found it with yellow pine and oak through spring in Northern California. Wells & Mitchel reported it as common in high aspen meadows in Colorado in the summers. Barrows found it in New Mexico under mountain conifers. Dr. Dennis Thurber found it at Aspen, Colorado, with Engelmann spruce. Calvin Kauffman found

Young Floccularia albolanaripes—note viscid caps

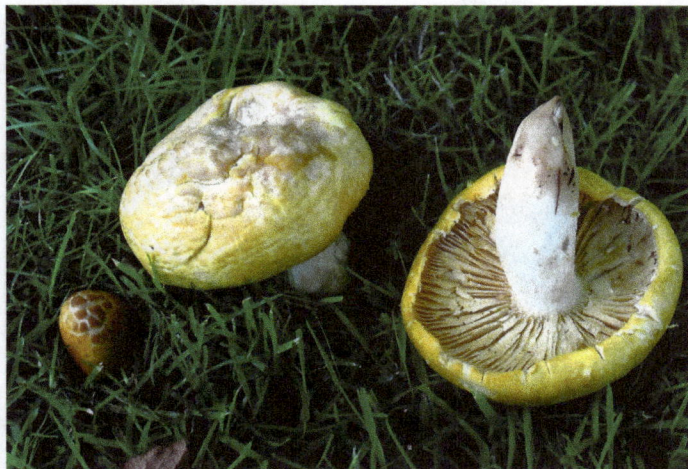

Floccularia luteovirens ss auct. Chinese from Tibet

Russula postiana

Tricholomopsis decora

it in the Olympics in 1922, but disagreed with Atkinson's spore sizes. (Just for the record, we looked at the spores and came up with 3.9–5.2 x 5.4–7.4 µm, which were closer to Atkinson's.) And Jack States thought so much of it that he put it on the cover of his popular guide, *Mushrooms and Truffles of the Southwest.*

In 1976, Smith & Mitchel found an albino form, which they introduced as **Armillaria albolanaripes form alba**. It is reputed to be one of the world's most beautiful mushrooms. As for the typical form, you can't confuse it with much. But just for the record, here are some possible look-alikes:

Floccularia pitkinensis: Has fleshy grayish caps with tinges of yellow in age, and cream colored gills that turn pale yellow in age.

Floccularia luteovirens ss auct. Chinese: Appears to lack the upright and curved cap scales of the original **F. luteovirens** from Europe. [Specimens were placed in grass for the photo; the stem had been pared down by collectors to make it more attractive in the Lhasa marketplace.]

Hygrocybe flavescens: Differs by having waxy gills, a tacky to viscid cap, and a smooth, yellow stem.

Russula postiana: Differs by being more fragile and having a smooth stipe, ochre gills, and ochre-yellow spores.

Tricholomopsis decora: Differs by its thinner stature, yellow gills, and habit of fruiting on wood.

Pholiota curvipes: Differs by its rusty spores, canary yellow stem and gills, and curvature of the stem arching out from the log.

Pholiota flammans: Differs by its shaggy yellow stems, yellow to pale rusty caps with recurved yellow scales, and rusty spores.

Jack States felt that **Floccularia albolanaripes** resembled large yellow Pholiotas, differing mainly by the white spores and the habit of fruiting on the ground.

And this brings up edibility. The Shaggy Bracelet has long been considered inferior to its floccose cousin, **Floccularia luteovirens**, highly esteemed in Europe, Tibet, and the Rockies. Here now is a sampling of the opinions from popular guides:

Wells & Mitchel: "Edibilty unknown."

David Biek: "Of little value as an edible."

Jack States: "Edible but lacks the quality of **Armillaria straminea**" (an earlier name for **F. luteovirens**).

David Arora: "Edible but insipid."

Helene Schalkwijk-Barendsen: "The taste is bland."

McKenny, Stuntz, & Ammirati: "Of uncertain edibility."

Mike Woods of Mykoweb: "Edible and excellent, a greatly under-appreciated mushroom."

Well, as far as I'm concerned, Woods has got it right. I took three of the specimens from the show down to my boat galley. Simply sautéed in butter, they were among the ten best mushrooms I've ever tasted. Besides having just the right ratio of crunchy exterior and juicy interior, the flavor had a gourmet aftertaste that brought

LOOK-ALIKES

Pholiota curvipes

Hygrocybe flavescens   *Photo by Richard Morrison*

Pholiota flammans   *Photo by Richard Morrison*

up visions of manna. I can only attribute its lukewarm reception to circumstance. Perhaps more so than other wild edibles, it should be consumed in prime condition. Older specimens may indeed become bland.

For those increasing members in our club who enjoy microscopic characters, we discovered that **Floccularia albolanaripes** had no cystidia whatsoever. It had parallel gill trama with hyphae 5–11.4 μm wide. The clavate basidia were 4-spored and measured 34–36 x 6.8–7.8 μm. Spores were smooth and ellipsoid. The pileipellis consisted of radially repent hyphae measuring 6–12 μm wide. A.H. Smith noted occasional clamps and a particularly narrow subhymenium in the gill trama. He and Mitchel also noted that the central strand in the gill trama tended to be more inflated than the surrounding hyphae. Meanwhile, keep your eyes open. Although possibly a first for Whatcom County, more could follow. If you don't want to risk eating them, bring them to one of our experts. They could exact a tax or consume the whole collection, if you prefer.

BIBLIOGRAPHY

David Arora, *Mushrooms Demystified*, 1986. Ten Speed Press, Berkeley, Calif.

George Atkinson, *Notes on Some New Species of Fungi* in *Annales Mycologici* 6 (54–62), 1908.

David Biek, *The Mushrooms of Northern California*, 1984. Spore Prints, Redding, Calif.

Vera Evenson, *Mushrooms of Colorado*, 1997. Denver Botanic Gardens, Denver, Colo.

Calvin Kauffman, *The Genus Armillaria* in *Papers of the Michigan Academy of Science, Arts, and Letters* 2 (53–66), 1922.

Gary Lincoff, *The Audubon Society Field Guide to North American Mushrooms*, 1981. Alfred A. Knopf, New York, NY.

André Marchand, *Champignons du Nord et du Midi, Tome 9*, 1986. Societe Mycologique des Pyrenees Mediterraneennes, Perpignan, France.

Margaret McKenny, Daniel Stuntz, & Joe Ammirati, *The New Savory Wild Mushroom*, 1987. University of Washington Press, Seattle, Wash.

Kent & Vera McKnight, *Peterson Field Guides—Mushrooms*, 1987. Houghton Mifflin, Boston, Mass.

Orson & Hope Miller, *North American Mushrooms*, 2006. Morris Book Publishing, Guilford, Conn.

D.H. Mitchel & A.H. Smith, *Notes on Colorado Fungi, II* in *Mycotaxon* 4 (513–533), 1976.

D.H. Mitchel & A.H. Smith, *Notes on Colorado Fungi, III* in *Mycologia* 70 (1040–1063), 1978.

Meinhard Moser, *Keys to Agarics and Boleti*, 1983. Translated and published by Roger Phillips, London.

Helene Schalkwijk-Barendsen, *Mushrooms of Western Canada*, 1971. Lone Pine Publishing, Edmonton, Alberta.

A.H. Smith, *A Field Guide to Western Mushrooms*, 1975. University of Michigan Press, Ann Arbor, Mich.

A.H. Smith & Lexemuel Hesler, *North American Species of Pholiota*, 1968. Lubrecht & Cramer, Monticello, NY.

Jack States, *Mushrooms and Truffles of the Southwest*, 1990. University of Arizona Press, Tucson, Ariz.

Mary Wells & D.H. Mitchel, *Mushrooms of Colorado and Adjacent Areas*, 1970. Denver Museum of Natural History, Denver, Colo.

MushroomExpert.com, *Floccularia albolanaripes*.

Mykoweb.com, *Floccularia albolanaripes*.

Suillus ochraceoroseus (Snell) Singer

*. . . an attractive species due
to the contrast of bright pinkish
caps with yellowish tubes.*

It's always exiting to meet a new bolete, and even more so when a pinkish, shaggy-capped specimen suddenly appears at a club meeting. It turns out there was a reason we hadn't seen it before. **Suillus ochraceoroseus** appears east of the Cascades, and club member Jeremy Ferrera had brought it to us from a campsite in the Okanogan.

Suillus ochraceoroseus is only known from the northern Rockies and the drier parts of the Pacific Northwest. It is particularly common in Idaho around McCall and the Payette Lakes, and was first recorded by Snell from Smith Creek in 1941. Jeremy's find in the Okanogan may have placed the species further westward.

Dr. A.H. Smith deemed it an attractive species due to the contrast of bright pinkish caps with yellowish tubes. But only when found in shade. It turns out that the Rosy Larch Bolete is sensitive to light. If they are found out in the open along roadsides the caps fade to a basic straw color with pinkish fibrils. Both the Orrs and Helene Schalkwijk-Barendsen noticed this peculiarity, paraphrasing the original observations by Snell and Smith.

The Rosy Larch Bolete is sort of like a typical Suillus and sort of not like one. Like Suillus, it has velar material in the form of appendiculate shards hanging from the cap margins and a slight fibrillose ring zone on the stem. Unlike Suillus, there are no glandular dots on the stipe, the spore print is purple-brown instead of ochre-brown, and there is reticulation above the ring zone. Pomerleau and Smith noted in 1962 that the caps were viscid while Thiers and Smith deemed them dry in 1971. Above all, **Suillus ochraceoroseus** is uniquely associated with larch. Its closest look-alike, **Suillus spraguei**, is found with white pine and has pale ochre-brown spores.

According to descriptions the caps can run from 8–25 cm wide. Whether you find them viscid or dry, they are matted fibrillose with pallid veil shards at the margins. Cap colors vary from light rose with buff colored fibrils to deep rose with yellow margins. You can also find straw colored caps with rosy fibrils. A strong character is a bright pink layer just under the cuticle. The rest of the cap flesh is pale yellow sometimes becoming pale blue green when bruised. The tubes are radially arranged and have large angular mouths that don't turn blue when bruised. They measure 5 mm long, are at first bright straw yellow, then ochre brown in age. The attachment is adnate to subdecurrent. The stems are

LOOK-ALIKES

Suillus ampliporus (formerly S. cavipes)

Suillus lakei

1–3 cm thick and only 3–5 cm long, absurdly short compared to cap widths. They are usually expanded at the apex and the base, the better to support the relatively large caps. Orson Miller reported reticulation at the apex. The stems are straw yellow becoming whitish towards the base. The submembranous veil is pallid to yellowish, leaving a slight zone of velar material instead of a ring. The spore deposit is dark vinaceous. The odor has been described as acidulous and the taste bitter to acrid. According to all sources, this bitterness does not disappear in cooking.

Suillus spraguei, on the other hand, is such an esteemed edible that it was once on the menu with bear paws at the Czarnecki wild mushroom restaurant in Reading, Pennsylvania. This was before they relocated to Dayton, Oregon.

A list of look-alikes includes:

Suillus pictus: Found in the northeast, it differs from the Rosy Larch Bolete by having a much narrower stem, and tubes that bruise pinkish brown when rubbed.

Suillus albivelatus: Also pink under the cap cuticle, it differs by having large white velar patches on the cap margins, and flesh that turns wine colored when bruised.

Boletus speciosus: Also has rose-pink caps that become matted fibrillose in age, but differs by having bright yellow tubes that instantly go blue when bruised. The spore deposit is olive brown.

In the summer of 2014, my cousin Rob Deford and nephew Ben and I had an opportu-

LOOK-ALIKES

Boletus speciosus from Mass.

Butyriboletus primiregius from Oregon

Butyriboletus regius from Spain

nity to taste this species just sauteed in butter. It had a delicious yet complicated flavor of roasted walnuts and soy sauce with a smoky, sweet contingent. These flavors would overlap with each new piece consumed.

Butyriboletus primiregius: Another large, fleshy bolete with rose pink to dark reddish caps, and yellow pores that bruise weakly bluish when touched. It differs by its massive stem up to 6 cm thick, olive-brown spores, and mild taste. Also found in the Cascades.

Butyriboletus regius: Differs by its olive-brown spore print and tomentose pinkish-red caps that become smooth and pitted in age.

Boletus pseudopeckii: A Michigan species with rose to brick-red caps that develop grayish overtones in age. It further differs by its olive-brown spores and a red zone at the stipe apex.

Suillus lakei: Possibly the closest local look-alike, it differs by having a much smaller stature, an association with Douglas fir, a tendency to bruise blue at the stem base, and dull cinnamon spores.

Suillus lakei var. pseudopictus: Differs by having dry caps with reddish fibrils and bright yellow tubes that bruise pinkish brown when handled.

Suillus ampliporus: Differs by its densely squamulose cap, hollow stem, and dark olive-brown spores.

Pulveroboletus ravenelii: Has the same lovely pinkish to reddish-brown cap but differs in the bright yellow stipe apex, a yellow universal veil that entirely covers a button, and yellow pores that instantly stain blue when bruised.

The Rosy Larch Bolete seems to be in a revolving door, going back and forth between Suillus, Fuscoboletinus, and Boletinus. In Jeremy's collection, we noticed one variation from the norm. Some authors have noted a reddening at the base of the stem. In Jeremy's collection, the reddening was at the stem apex. Would it be important enough to warrant a species amendment? Perhaps not. Migrating zones of red have also been noted for **Boletus smithii**. Meanwhile, recent DNA sequencing results have shown that Suillus is the correct genus for this taxon, not Boletinus or Fuscoboletinus.

BIBLIOGRAPHY

David Arora, *Mushrooms Demystified*, 1986. Ten Speed Press, Berkeley, Calif.

David Arora & Jonathan Frank, *Clarifying the Butter Boletes: A New Genus*, Butyriboletus in *Mycologia* 106 (464–480), 2014.

Ernst Both, *The Boletes of North America*, 1993. Buffalo Museum of Science, Buffalo, NY.

Margarert McKenny, Daniel Stuntz, & Joe Ammirati, *The New Savory Wild Mushroom*, 1987. University of Washington Press, Seattle, Wash.

Orson & Hope Miller, *North American Mushrooms*, 2006. Morris Book Publishing, Guilford, Conn.

Rene Pomerleau & A.H. Smith, *Fuscoboletinus, A New Genus of the Boletales* in *Brittonia* 14 (156–172), 1962.

Kit Scates, *Trial Field Key to the Boletales of the Pacific Northwest*, 1982. Pacific Northwest Key Council, Seattle, Wash.

Helene Schalkwijk-Barendsen, *Mushrooms of Western Canada*, 1991. Lone Pine Publishing, Edmonton, Alberta.

A.H. Smith, *Mushrooms in Their Natural Habitat*, 1949. Sawyer's Publishing, Lancaster, Penn.

A.H. Smith, *The Mushroom Hunter's Field Guide*, 1977. University of Michigan Press, Ann Arbor, Mich.

Alexander & Helen Smith & Nancy Weber, *How to Know the Non-Gilled Mushrooms*, 1981. William C. Brown, Dubuque, Iowa.

A.H. Smith & Harry Thiers, *The Boletes of Michigan*, 1971. University of Michigan Press, Ann Arbor, Mich.

Edmund Tylutki, *Mushrooms of Idaho and the Pacific Northwest, Vol. 2*, 1987. University of Idaho Press, Moscow, Idaho.

Ganoderma applanatum (Persoon) Patouillard

. . . these conks can live for fifty years. It is a highly successful polypore . . . long considered an immune stimulant.

Louie Byrd had been a member of Northwest Mushroomers Association about as far back as anyone could remember. He came from a third generation of loggers and grew up on the Oregon coast surrounded by old-growth forests and clear cuts. So it is not surprising that Louie knew his trees and the fungi that fruit on them. Nonetheless, for about a five-year period, a very odd polypore had been fruiting on the ground in his wife's garden that even eluded his understanding. His wife Lois also deserved plaudits for allowing it to dwell there year after year. In the main photo for this "mushroom of the month," you can see the immature version of the first carpophore breaking through her iris bed and engulfing stems as it expanded. This must have been hard to take. When asked about it, their daughter Laura replied, "Yes, we have sat here year after year and watched it grow and grow and grow."

The odyssey of this anomaly began back in 1986 when Louie buried a cottonwood stump under a foot of earth and mulch. In 1996 the polypore appeared as a hard, whitish lump that bruised brown when handled. Rounded brownish areas had begun to emerge from the cream colored pileal surface, which was extremely lumpy (tuberculose). The brown areas were glabrous but not lacquered in appearance. The carpophore was 23 cm wide, and the texture of the cream colored portion of the cap was subvelutinous, almost velvety. The whole thing weighed 5 ½ pounds. We conferred with Dr. Robert Gilbertson, the senior author of *North American Polypores*, who kindly agreed to have a go at it. Word soon came back that we had a species of Ganoderma because of the truncated spores.

At around this time Dr. Joe Ammirati arrived in our midst for a Thursday night presentation. He suggested we had **Ganoderma**

A second fruiting of G. applanatum from a buried stump

applanatum because it could fruit on both hardwoods and conifers. Above all, it had a history of fruiting on the ground from buried wood. The main thing was to decide whether the cap had a lacquered appearance or not. This was confusing because part of the cap looked shellacked and part didn't.

The second photo, below left, represents a second Ganoderma that had emerged from a spot next to the first one we had harvested and sent to Dr. Gilbertson. Louie had let it grow for five years. When harvested it reached a size of 40 ½ x 47 centimeters. The whitish, velvety, immature cap had evolved into an umber-black, tuberculose cap. Again, the whitish pore surface bruised instantly brown when touched.

There are two main subgroups of Ganoderma in North America—the Ganoderma group and the Elfvingia group. The Ganoderma group is comprised of those species with lacquered caps. In this group the cap cuticle is composed of a palisade of clavate cells. The Elfvingia group is comprised of species without lacquered caps. The cuticle of this group consists of entangled hyphae with the erect endings of both generative and skeletal hyphae breaking through it. Our Ganoderma belonged to the Elfvingia group. The spore sizes will then lead you to **Ganoderma applanatum** in any Ganoderma key. Dr. Joe Ammirati's suggestion had been right on the mark.

The photo of **Ganoderma applanatum** on the next page shows its typical form when fruiting on a trunk. We learned that these conks can live for 50 years. If it took 10 years for Louie's conk to reach the surface from the buried cottonwood stump, and another 5 years to reach 47 cm in width, it would reach 157 cm at the same growth rate in 50 years. The largest ever found was on Kuiu Island in southeast Alaska. It weighed just over 52 kilograms and had a circumference of 311 centimeters. It is thought to be the third largest fungus in the world.

According to Arora, a large Ganoderma can produce 30 billion spores a day over a six-month period. This works out to 21 million spores per minute.

Robert Rogers mentions that "**Ganoderma applanatum** is found only on dead, dying, or severely stressed trees. Its presence on a tree is an almost sure sign that the tree will not live. It doesn't kill the tree. It just colonizes it once the tree's doom has been sealed." Arora writes that it can also be parasitic on neighboring trees, decaying both sapwood and heartwood. "Infected trees can blow over easily, so if one appears on a tree near your house, watch out!" I forgot to ask Louie whether he noticed other Ganodermas popping up on his property.

The Artist's Conk, for that is its nickname, fruiting normally above ground, is impressive enough. It is a perennial polypore, expanding year after year from its cap margin, interspersed with dormant periods. As the margin expands, the tubes elongate. The tube layers become stratified with a layer of brownish-gray context between them. There is also a thin, darker reddish-brown zone just above the pore layer. The pores are circular to angular and average 4–6 per millimeter.

Microscopically, the Artist's Conk is trimitic, meaning it has three kinds of contextual hyphae. There is branched, binding hyphae that is not found at the growing margin. And there is generative and skeletal hyphae that both appear at the margin. A full-grown fruiting body will have four layers in the cap crust, including an intermediary layer of generative hyphae that can repair the crust if it gets damaged.

With so many billions of spores released, it is small wonder the caps get covered with a cinnamon powder of spores. André Marchand speculated on how the spores defeated gravity to get there, and came up with the theory that subtle differences in air temperature between pore surface and surrounding airs produced the subtle wind currents that wafted the spores aloft.

The Artist's Conk has been found from Alaska to Panama, Australia, Europe, and Asia. It produces a white mottled root and butt rot that weakens a tree from the base of the trunk, rendering it susceptible to high winds. Yet conks have been found as high as 30 feet above the ground. Trees that it favors have included red spruce, hemlock, Fraser fir, yellow birch, alder, cottonwood, aspen, beech, bay laurel, ash, maple, and bamboo. It is a highly successful polypore. Robert Dale Rogers speculates that it has been found on nearly every hardwood tree in North America.

Look-alikes mentioned have included the following:

Ganoderma australe: Differs by having slightly larger spores and a darker brown context without crustaceous lines within it.

Ganoderma adspersum: Has a much lumpier cap surface and is much thicker than **G. applanatum**. It also has much larger spores and a dark red-brown pileal context.

Ganoderma pfeifferi: Has a slightly varnished cap and breaks easily under pressure.

Hapalopilus nidulans: Differs by being soft and watery when fresh, brittle when dry. The pore surface is ochre to cinnamon brown, and all parts of the fruiting body turn purple with KOH.

As for the nomenclatural history, **G. applanatum** was first named **Boletus lipsiensis** by Batsch in 1786. Persoon, soon becoming aware that the fungus did not only exist in Lipsi, an island in the Greek archipelago, renamed it **Boletus applanatus** in 1799. It was then moved to Polyporus in 1833. Patouillard transferred it to Ganoderma in 1889, and here it has remained ever since.

Although not as powerful as **Ganoderma lucidum**, it does have medicinal usages. According to Christopher Hobbs it has antibiotic properties. According to David Spahr it contains polysaccharides and triterpenoids. Among the triterpenoids are ergosta, ergosterol, alnusenone, friedelin, and fungisterol. This is what you get when it is ground up and served as a tea. In China, **Ganoderma applanatum** is sold in bulk through herb dealers. The dosage is 30 grams a day in tea. It is used for tumor inhibition, stomach

Normal appearing Ganoderma applanatum, dark caps dusted with paler brown spores

cancer, rheumatic tuberculosis, and hemostasis. In a general sense, it reduces phlegm, resolves indigestion, removes heat, and stops pain. The more bitter the Ganoderma, the more effective it is. In China they call it the Red Mother Fungus, long considered an immune stimulant.

Dr. Rogers uses the Artist's Conk whenever **Ganoderma lucidum** is not available. In his article in *The Mycophile* he notes that, besides the health benefits mentioned, **G. applanatum** particularly targets rheumatoid arthritis, systemic lupus erythematosus, Guillain-Barré syndrome, and erythema etiologies. It is an analgesic, anti-viral, anti-bacterial, anti-inflammatory, blood sugar modulator, respiratory tonic, immune tonic, and agent for eye health. Peter McCoy adds that it is both an antioxidant and anti-diabetic. In China it has also been used for altitude sickness in combination with safflower seed and chrysanthemum. A footbath with chopped up Artist's Conk quickly relieves pain from gout. And when taken internally with lemon balm, it serves as an anti-viral combination for herpes simplex.

To make an effective Ganoderma tea, Rogers offers the following steps:

1. To one part by weight of finely chopped Ganoderma, add 5 parts by volume of 198 proof Everclear, available in duty free shops on the U.S. side of the Canadian border.
2. Seal tightly in a big jar and let marinate for two weeks. Shake the mixture daily.
3. Strain and press out the residue, reserving the liquid also.
4. Weigh the residue, place in a pot, and add 20 parts by volume of water.
5. At a low simmer, reduce by half.
6. Strain and press. Throw out the residue.
7. Combine this liquid with the alcoholic extraction of liquid from step 4.
8. Bottle for use. The therapeutic dosage is 3–5 milligrams daily in divided doses.

If you do plan on harvesting your own Artist's Conks for medicinal purposes, be sure to check for galls on the pore surfaces. These are excreted by the fly, *Agathomya wankowiczi*, as housing for their eggs until the weather gets warm enough for the larvae to hatch. The flies are bright orange with huge red-brown eyes. The presence of the galls alone can identify the Ganoderma. They do nothing for the medicinal quality.

Finally, I had no idea how intricate the technique for etching and drawing of the pore surface has become. Thanks to the McKnights, we learn the many ways one can approach the art. They advise, "Use a large needle or a sharp engraving tool to etch the pore surface when it's fresh. The sooner the better. If etched lightly, pale brown will appear. If etched strongly, you will get a dark brown. Soft shading can be made by lightly pressing with fingertips or a Q-tip. When it hardens it can be handled without more discoloration. When completely dry, white highlights can be scratched on the surface. If it gets too white, brown water color paint can be used for re-darkening."

Seldom have I come across a fungus with so many attributes.

Artist's Conk: Miscellaneous Facts and Hearsays

1 | The Athabaskans of Alaska burn it for a mosquito repellent.
2 | When fruiting on bay laurel, the normally mild taste becomes bitter and acrid.
3 | When ammonia is used as a mordant, a rust color is produced in wool.
4 | Dried pore surfaces can be used for oil paintings.
5 | It reduces sarcoma in mice.
6 | Paper hats and waistcoats have been made from it.
7 | Cats are attracted by the woodsy odor of fresh specimens.
8 | If the pore surface does not produce spores over the summer it means the Ganoderma is dead.
9 | David Arora has seen them used as stools.
10 | It was formerly used in Sweden for bottle corks.
11 | In India, a paste made from it is applied to the gums to stop excessive salivation.
12 | Lawrence Millman has seen it used as a bed by two raccoons.

BIBLIOGRAPHY

David Arora, *Mushrooms Demystified*, 1986. Ten Speed Press, Berkeley, Calif.

E.J.H. Corner, *Ad Polyporaceas I.* in *Nova Hedwigia, Beihefte* 75 (5–182), 1983.

Emilie Dressaire & Marcus Roper, *The Mushrooms, My Friend, are Blowing in the Wind* in *The Mycophile* 54, No.1, 2014.

Guillaume Eyssartier & Pierre Roux, *Le Guide des Champignons de France et Europe*, 2011. Editions Belin, Paris.

Robert Gilbertson, *The Polyporaceae of the Flathead Region of Western Montana*, doctorate,1951.

Robert Gilbertson & J. Page Lindsey, *Basidiomycetes That Decay Aspen in North America* in *Bibliotheca Mycologica* 63, 1978.

Robert Gilbertson & Leif Ryvarden, *North American Polypores, Vol.1*, 1986. Fungiflora, Blindern, Norway.

Lise Hansen, *On the Anatomy of the Danish Species of Ganoderma* in *Botanisk Tidsskrift* 54 (333–352), 1958.

Christopher Hobbs, *Medicinal Mushrooms*, 1995. Botanica Press, Santa Cruz, Calif.

Ying Jianzhe, Mao Xiaolan, Ma Qiming, Zong Yichen, & Wen Huaan, *Icons of Medicinal Fungi from China*, 1987. Science Press, Beijing, China.

Hack Sung Jung, *Wood-Rotting Aphyllophorales of the Southern Appalachian Spruce-Fir Forest* in *Bibliotheca Mycologica* 119 (1–260), 1987.

André Marchand, *Champignons du Nord et du Midi, Tome 4*, 1976. Societe Mycologique des Pyrenees Mediterraneennes, Perpignan, France.

Peter McCoy, *Radical Mycology*, 2016. Chthaeus Press, Portland, Ore.

Vera & Kent McKnight, *Peterson Field Guides—Mushrooms*, 1987. Houghton Mifflin Co., Boston, Mass.

Ireneia Melo, *Studies on the Aphyllophorales of Portugal. The Genus Ganoderma P Karst.* in *International Journal of Mycology and Lichenology* 2 (183–204), 1986.

Lawrence Millman, *Fascinating Fungi of New England*, 2011. Kollath + Stensaas Publishers, Duluth, Minn.

Lee Overholts, *The Polyporaceae of the United States, Alaska, and Canada*, 1953. University of Michigan Press, Ann Arbor, Mich.

David Pegler & Tony Young, *Basidiospore Form in the British Species of Ganoderma Karst.* in *Kew Bulletin* 28 (351–363), 1973.

John Roberts, *The Polyporaceae of Western Washington*, doctorate, 1936.

Peter Roberts & Shelley Evans, *The Book of Fungi*, 2011. University of Chicago Press, Chicago, Illinois.

Robert Rogers, *The Fungal Pharmacy*, 2011. North Atlantic Books, Berkeley, Calif.

Robert Rogers, *Lesser Lights of the Fungal World: A Bioregional Approach to Medicinal Mushrooms* in *The Mycophile* 53, No.5, 2013.

Paul Shope, *The Polyporaceae of Colorado* in *Annals of the Missouri Botanical Garden* 18 (287–456), 1931.

David Spahr, *Edible and Medicinal Mushrooms of New England and Eastern Canada*, 2009. North Atlantic Books, Berkeley, Calif.

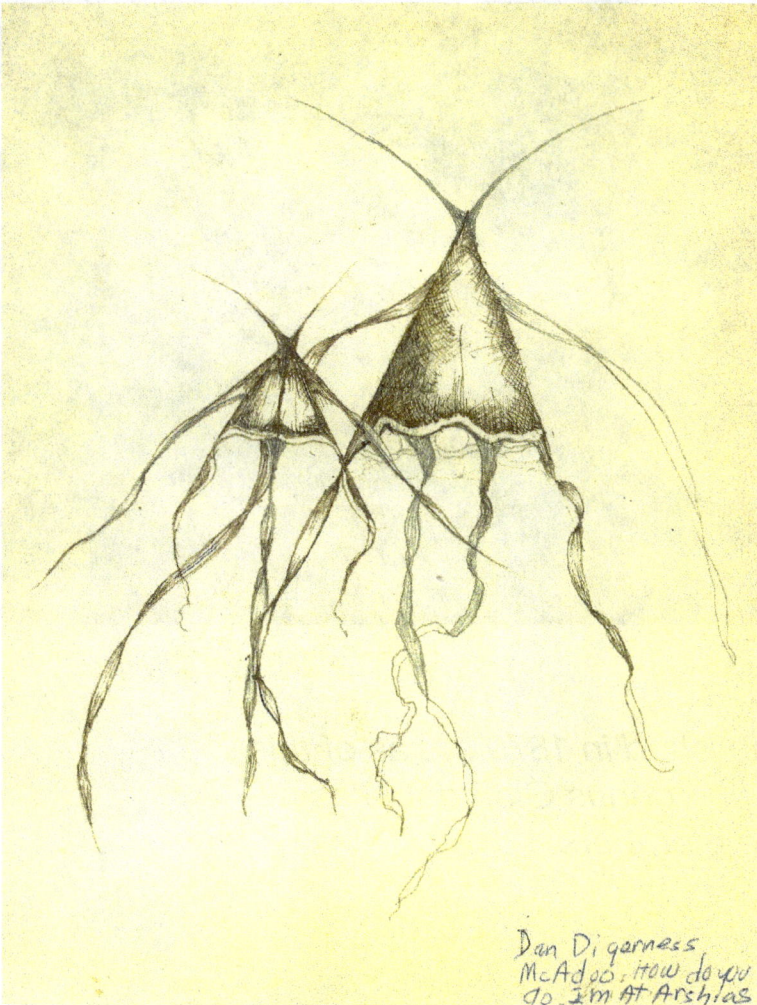

Gloiodon occidentale Ginns

*First established in 1879 . . . as of this
writing it [the genus Gloiodon] has
only three members.*

This very odd looking piece of nature, resembling more a voodoo fetish of teeth and feathers than anything we encounter on a mushroom foray, was found by Fien Hulscher off a trail at Schreiber Meadows near Mount Baker on September 20, 2003. As most of us know, Fien is our chef sans pareil who can be identified at all forays as the lady next to the stove. By foray's end there will be a beaten track between the specimen table and the frying pan. Without Fien I shudder to think what we might be eating, so it was with some dismay when we saw her abandon her table for her own brief trek into the woods. She emerged half an hour later with a fungus so strange that I couldn't tell whether it belonged to the Polyporaceae or the Hydnaceae. Nothing in Arora's Mushrooms Demystified came close. I had actually gone to this foray to load up on **Boletus edulis** (there were none), and now this…..a total enigma with half a dozen brand new members waiting for me to identify it.

The fruiting body was found shelving off the base of a cedar stump. The cap was dimidiate and more or less fan shaped, measuring 9 cm long by 3 ½ cm wide and 4 cm thick. The surface was covered with tan colored feathery projections up to 7 mm long. The context was tough, dark brown becoming beige towards the margin. Below the cap hung the cream to pale ochre spines. These were 2–4 cm long, tapered at the apices, and turned brown when bruised. The odor was similar to that of **Postia fragilis**, a strong resinous smell that is hard to describe. The spores were white and amyloid in Melzer's solution. It looked like a Thelephora with spines.

Back at my all-purpose lab-office, the search among the Hydellums and Sarcodons proved fruitless. No popular guide had anything close. The question now became who to send the "fetish" to. The presence of spines suggested Dr. Kenneth Harrison, the world expert on the teeth fungi, now retired in Nova Scotia. But the growth habit suggested some sort of Polypore, indicating that Dr. Jim Ginns, now retired in Penticton, British Columbia, might also be a source.

A coin toss decided the issue. Dr. Ginns, a member of our Pacific Northwest Key Council, won the toss. He agreed to look at the specimen after reading the field description in an email. This turned out to be a fortuitous coin toss. Dr. Harrison had passed away several years back while Dr. Ginns had authored the species. It was soon identified as **Gloiodon occidentale**. Jim had found it first in the Deep Creek area near Terrace, B.C., and authored it in 1988. Of course, his professional description differed from mine above. No more feathers and teeth! Instead he described the caps as "dimidiate with a dense strigose surface, undulating and lumpy, yellow-brown near the margin, tending to divide into fan shaped sectors with an extreme margin of black, fimbriate, horny split tongues 1–2 mm broad."

Fien Hulscher, chef for the Northwest Mushroomers Association, in her natural habitat: checking specimens for the cooking pot. Here she examines an endangered Ramaria.

He described the acicular spines as "white becoming lead gray in age." He also described it as laterally substipitate when I found no sign of a stem at all. This is an important distinction because it makes Gloiodon a closer relative to **Auriscalpium vulgare** than to other spined species without stems. And finally, the microscopic features, including gloeocystidia and different kinds of hyphae for every texture change in the carpophore, were extremely complicated.

The genus Gloiodon was first established by the Finnish mycologist Karsten in 1879. (It is now considered a member of the Bondarzewiaceae.) As of this writing it has only three members. One of these is **Gloiodon nigrescens** from Sri Lanka. The third is **Gloiodon strigosus**, a species found in the northern regions of Europe and in Ontario. A good photo of this species can be seen in *Svampar* by Ryman and Holmasen. According to Jim, **Gloiodon strigosus** differs from **Gloiodon occidentale** by fruiting on deciduous wood, having dark brown caps that are smaller in stature, spines up to 6 mm long, smaller verrucose spores with elongated warts, and no gloeocystidia extending into the cap structure. The expert Åke Strid adds that the spines

A SECOND LOOK

Gloiodon occidentale from Marblemount, Wash.   Photo by Erin Moore

of **Gloiodon strigosus** are at first dark brown and become grayish to bluish white in age.

It appears that Fien's unusual find may be the fourth collection ever made of **Gloiodon occidentale.** Since the first discovery it has been found in Revelstoke, B.C., and once down in Oregon. At Dr. Ginns' suggestion the specimen was mailed to the National USDA Systematic Botany and Mycology Laboratory in Beltsville, Maryland. It represents the second specimen ever recorded from the United States.

As a club we want to thank Jim Ginns for coming to our rescue and identifying the species. But what can we say about Fien? Just imagine what this sharp-eyed woman might find if she spent an entire day away from the food table. Fortunately for us mycophagists it is unlikely to happen. Fien may still live in angst that at any moment she may be called upon to give a speech on **Gloiodon occidentale** for the National Systematic Mycology Lab in Beltsville, Maryland.

Addendum: The second photo shows another collection of **G. occidentale** found by Jack Waytz and Caleb Brown at a Marblemount campground in October, 2015. Minutes after finding it Jack found a pile of semi-fresh bear scat but missed the Coprinellus fruiting on top of it.

BIBLIOGRAPHY

Jim Ginns, *New Genera and Species of Lignicolous Aphyllophorales* in *Mycologia* 80 (63–71), 1988.
Svengunnar Ryman & Ingmar Holmasen, *Svampar*, 1984. Interpublishing AB, Stockholm, Sweden.

Åke Strid, *Gloiodon* in *Nordic Macromycetes*, Vol. 3, 1997. Nordsvamp, Copenhagen.
Wikipedia.com, *Gloiodon occidentale*

Gomphus clavatus (Persoon) S.F. Gray

This is an impressive mushroom when found in massive lavender clusters in deep moss under hemlock or fir.

Gomphus clavatus, when found in full glory deep in a coniferous forest, is one of those, "My God! What is that?" kind of species. It turns out to be a good technical question besides. It started out as **Clavaria elveloides** Wulfen in 1781. For reasons only known to various experts, that name was skipped over in favor of **Merulius clavatus** Persoon in 1796. Gray then moved it to Gomphus in 1821. **Gomphus clavatus** has also spent time in Cantharellus and Craterellus, under which names you can find it in early North American guides.

Unfortunately, the common name of Pig's Ears, is no less puzzling. **Discina ancilis** (formerly **Discina perlata**), a fleshy brownish cup fungus, is also called Pig's Ears. Although Latin names these days can be as evanescent as a hanging veil shard, they can at least separate one common name from another. Whatever you prefer to call it (*clavatus* means club shaped), this is an impressive mushroom when found in massive lavender clusters in deep moss under hemlock or fir. It must be quite rare in Whatcom County. The top photo represents the only fruiting I found in the county, up the Hannegan Trail at the turn of the century. The relatively thin and flared out cap margins denote older carpophores, and as one might suspect, they were riddled with larvae holes (see photo this page). The photo below it shows a younger specimen found near Dead Horse Meadows in southern Washington in the fall of 2012.

The genus Gomphus can be defined as roughly thickish, vase shaped fungi with veined or wrinkled hymenial surfaces and warty to wrinkled spores. In an even stricter sense, they are the purplish ones with no scales on the cap surface; but that's another story only touched upon here. The fruiting bodies of **Gomphus clavatus** arise trunk-like from the base to flatten out at the top with lobed and undulate margins. The cap surface is felty to smooth, ochre to olive-brown, often with one side thicker than the other. They can run up to 15 cm wide and are club shaped at first becoming more irregularly lobed in age, with depressed discs. Instead of gills, **G. clavatus** has thick, decurrent ridges descending almost to the stem base. These are accompanied by myriads of cross-veins, sometimes so crowded as to appear poroid. This might explain why Persoon placed it in Merulius, a polypore, to begin with. The ridges are some shade of violet, purple gray, or lilac-flesh color, often dusted ochraceous from the spores. The cap context is whitish to pale rosy, usually

Larvae-riddled topside of Gomphus clavatus

Younger G. clavatus from Dead Horse Meadows

Panus conchatus from N.J.

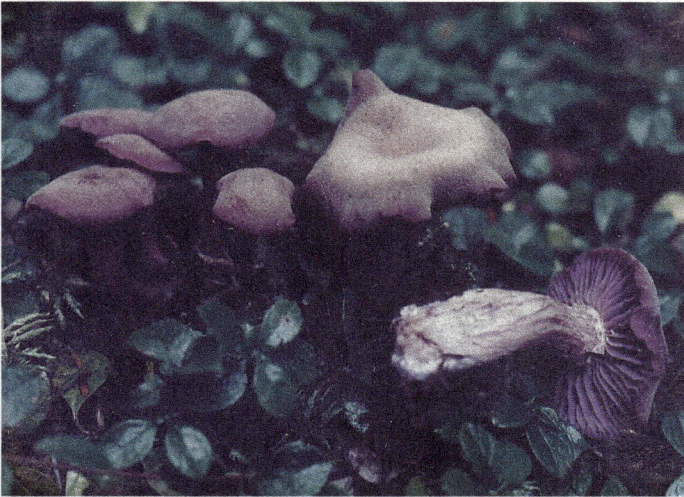

Laccaria amethysteo-occidentalis

sporting a marbled appearance due to watery spots. Stems can be 2–5 cm long and 1–2 cm thick. They are dull white, appressed fibrillose, central or eccentric, and sometimes bruise weakly brown when handled. Von Frieden described the stalk as "nothing more than a base connecting the fungus to the ground." They are truncate in solitary specimens but are often found fused in compound clusters.

The British mycologist E.J.H. Corner was so impressed with these clusters that he created the **var. parvisporus** for them. He noted that "the fruit bodies develop typically in caespitose masses from a common and possibly underground stem, making the caps appear to be pleuropodal." This is now considered a synonym by some.

The spore deposit of **Gomphus clavatus** is usually noted as ochre to tan, except by Svrcek in Eastern Europe, who terms them rusty ochre. The odor is mildly earthy or of almonds in the opinion of Von Frieden. The taste is mild and pleasant in young specimens, bitter in old. The cap surface turns peachy-salmon in KOH. They are found solitary or in caespitose masses, often in arcs or circles under mountain conifers in northern climes. Besides North America, **Gomphus clavatus** has been found in Europe, Russia, Turkey, Pakistan, China, Korea, Japan, and Mexico. It is particularly common in the lake districts of Bavaria. This is perhaps of interest because it is on the endangered species list in Hungary and legally protected in Slovenia.

Microscopically, the spores are ellipsoid, verrucose, and measure 10-14.5 x 5-7 µm. The warts are cyanophilous. The pileipellis is a cutis of repent hyphae with pileocystidia that produce a minutely crystalline exudate, a brownish agglutinating substance. Clamps are everywhere. Basidia are 4-spored and slenderly clavate.

Older specimens of **Gomphus clavatus** tend to be bitter and riddled with pinholes, evidence that larvae found them first. In the autumn of 2013 I finally had the opportunity to sample fresh specimens from the Quilcene. Two frying pans were going side by side in the Port Townsend kitchen of Lee Whitford. The **Gomphus clavatus** had an even firmer texture than the chanterelles, but half the flavor. It is said, however, to be very good pickled. A smattering of other opinions follows here:

David Arora: "Edible and considered choice by some, but I am not particularly fond of it."

A.H. Smith: "G. clavatus is a choice edible species in spite of its appearance."

Ammirati, McKenny, & Stuntz: "Considered by some to be the best of the chanterelles. Delicious when sliced and fried with meat."

Charles McIlvaine: "An excellent species. Its scarcity is regrettable."

Jack Czarnecki: "It has a firmness that many mushrooms lack. It generally retains this texture during cooking, and is a welcome addition to any casserole, even though the flavor is not distinct."

Roger Phillips: "Some people get severe gastric upsets from it. Others find it excellent."

Dave Tamblin of the Vancouver Mycological Society can back this up. He thought they tasted like chanterelles but weren't for everyone. Some individuals get a purgative result. The modus operandi would be to eat a small amount at first, wait a day to see what happens, then dive in with gusto.

Gomphus clavatus, Gomphus crassipes, and **Gomphus brunneus** are probably the only members of Gomphus sensu stricto. They differ from other species of Gomphus sensu lato by having smooth caps instead of scaly ones. There may be microscopic differences as well. Recent DNA studies have shown that these scaly-capped taxa are headed for other genera such as Turbinellus, Gloeocantharellus, or Phaeoclavulina.

TRADITIONAL RELATIVES

Polyozellus marymargaretae   Photo by Daniel Winkler

Turbinellus floccosus

Of the three possibly left in Gomphus, **Gomphus crassipes** has been rarely reported from Spain and North Africa. It has purple flesh and is associated with cedar. **Gomphus brunneus** is from the Congo, Cameroon, and Uganda. But **Pseudocraterellus pseudoclavatus** is a dead look-alike of **G. clavatus**. It was described from a single collection made by A.H. Smith from the Smith River in northern California. It differs from **Gomphus clavatus** by having inflated cells in the gill trama, smooth-walled spores, no clamps, and secondary septations in the gill hyphae. According to the McKnights, it was found with hardwoods.

Two other species with which it has been confused in the literature are **Gomphus brevipes** and **Gomphus canadensis**. The former is now considered a synonym of **Gomphus clavatus**, the latter a synonym of **Turbinellus floccosus**.

A short list of improbable look-alikes follows here:

Panus conchatus: Can have the same grayish-lavender caps, but differs by fruiting on wood, and has true, whitish gills instead of ridges.

Cantharellus amethysteus: A thinner European species with yellowish caps adorned with small lilac scales.

Polyozellus marymargaretae: The Pacific Northwest version of **Polyozellus multiplex**.

Polyozellus multiplex: Has a much darker purple-blue coloring and caps that stain blackish green with KOH.

Laccaria amethysteo-occidentalis: Faded specimens can have pale ochre-lavender caps, but the true purple gills and obvious stipe clearly separate them.

Turbinellus floccosus: Clearly differs by its orange cap surface with overlapping scales.

Gomphus clavatus is also thought to have medicinal properties. McCoy writes that it is an antioxidant, antifungal, and anti-cancer.

Otherwise we can follow the opinion of Zeitlmayr, "this is an excellent edible fungus that can hardly be confused with any other type."

For those who would rather not take the culinary risk, you can use it for dyeing wool. It yields a lavender color when used with an iron mordant.

BIBLIOGRAPHY

David Arora, *All That the Rain Promises and More*, 1991. Ten Speed Press, Berkeley, Calif.

David Arora, *Mushrooms Demystified*, 1986. Ten Speed Press, Berkeley, Calif.

David Biek, *The Mushrooms of Northern California*, 1984. Spore Prints, Redding, Calif.

J. Breitenbach & F. Kranzlin, *Fungi of Switzerland, Vol. 2*, 1986. Edition Mykologia, Lucerne, Switzerland.

E.J.H. Corner, *A Monograph of Cantharelloid Fungi* in *Annals of Botany Memoirs* 2 (1–255), 1966.

Jack Czarnecki, *A Cook's Book of Mushrooms*, 1995. Artisan, New York, NY.

Guillaume Eyssartier & Pierre Roux, *Le Guide des Champignons de France et Europe*, 2011. Editions Belin, Paris.

Admir Giachini & James Trappe, *Systematics, Phylogeny, and Ecology of Gomphus Sensu Lato*, 2004.

Miron Hard, *Mushrooms, Edible and Otherwise*, 1908. Dover Publications, New York, NY.

Peter McCoy, *Radical Mycology*, 2016. Chthaeus Press, Portland, Ore.

Charles McIlvaine & Robert Macadam, *One Thousand American Fungi*, 1902. Dover Publications, New York, NY.

Margaret McKenny, Daniel Stuntz, & Joe Ammirati, *The New Savory Wild Mushroom*, 1987. University of Washington Press, Seattle, Wash.

Vera & Kent McKnight, *The Peterson Field Guides: Mushrooms*, 1987. Houghton Mifflin, Boston, Mass.

Umberto Nonis, *Mushrooms and Toadstools: A Color Field Guide*, 1981. (Italian edition 1981, English edition 1982.) Hippocrene Books, New York, NY.

Ronald Petersen, *The Genera Gomphus and Gloeocantharellus in North America* in *Nova Hedwigia* 21 (1–112), 1971.

Robert Rogers, *The Fungal Pharmacy*, 2011. North Atlantic Books, Berkeley, Calif.

Roger Phillips, *Mushrooms of North America*, 1991. Little, Brown Inc., Boston, Mass.

A.H. Smith, *Mushrooms in Their Natural Habitats*, 1949. Sawyer's, Lancaster, Penn.

A.H. Smith, *The Cantharellaceae of Michigan* in *The Michigan Botanist* 7 (143–183), 1968.

Mirko Svrcek, *The Hamlyn Book of Mushrooms and Fungi*, 1983. Artia, Prague, Czechoslovakia.

Andrus Voitk, Irja Saar, Steven Trudell, Viacheslav Spirin, Michael Beug, & Urma Koljalg, *Polyozellus multiplex is a Species Complex Containing Four New Species* in *Mycologia* 109 (975–992), 2017.

Lucius Von Frieden, *Mushrooms of the World*, 1969. Bobbs-Merrill, Indianapolis, Indiana.

Linus Zeitlmayr, *Wild Mushrooms—An Illustrated Handbook*, 1955. Th. Knaur Nachf. Verlag, Munich, Germany.

Guepiniopsis buccina (Persoon ex Fries) Kennedy

This rare little plant has had quite
an enjoyable time being named.

Although unprepossessing in appearance, this odd little species with semi-spathulate cap and eccentric stem was brought to me by Fred Rhoades from Hoypus Point on Whidbey Island. It is an old-growth forest with a smattering of hardwoods that produces really unusual fungi. This collection of **Guepiniopsis buccina** was found in an alder bog on October 18, 1992.

Fred brought the log to the fall show. It didn't generate a lot of interest. After the show I gathered up the log just in time before the sweep-up, and then they sat on my desk for eight years waiting to be looked at. By this time the fruiting bodies had dried up and become as hard as bone.

It was hard to decipher what sort of fungus it was. The general shape of a half-flattened cup on a stalk suggested some sort of ascomycete. But it didn't key out in any of my guides among the cup fungi. Thinking it must only appear in monographs, I mailed specimens to Dr. John Haines in Albany, New York. Seven months passed, and no reply. I decided to look at it under the microscope. To my amazement I saw long basidia shaped like tuning forks. I had done the unthinkable. I'd sent a basidiomycete to an ascomycete expert.

At this point I realized I was looking at a jelly fungus. I mailed a photo of it to Dr. Robert Bandoni in Delta, B.C., who agreed to look at it. The answer was soon forthcoming. Fred Rhoades had found "a very distinctive fungus." Dr. Bandoni had made only one collection of it a few years earlier in the Capillano watershed. As far as he knew, this was the second recorded collection of it in the Pacific Northwest.

The caps of **Guepiniopsis buccina** are cupulate and externally ribbed, running from 3–9 mm in diameter. The stems are normally central and also ribbed longitudinally. The cups are ochre-yellow to ochre-orange, the stems slightly darker and swelling at the apices. The consistency is firm and gelatinous, drying very hard. They fruit in dense groups or cespitose clusters on hardwood sticks and coniferous wood, but prefer angiosperms such as willow, oak, beech, and alder. Dr. Bandoni mentioned that they seemed to prefer habitats near water.

The Dacrymycetales are generally considered hard to look at under the microscope. Throughout history, the genera seemed to have intergraded in the eyes of different experts. According to Bandoni, it is more of a challenge getting them to genus than to species. Dr. Derek Reid of England and Dr. R.F.R. McNabb of New Zealand had both worked with **Guepiniopsis buccina**. Dr. Reid separates **G. buccina** from other species of Guepiniopsis by its clampless hyphae, its capitate and sometimes catenulate cortical hairs, and by spore size. The spores, measuring 11–16 x 4–6 μm, are cylindrical to curved cylindrical with three septa at maturity. The oldest spores can sprout germ tubes that look like little feet. Germination is also achieved by hyaline, globose conidia formed on the exterior of the cups. The cortical hairs found on the exterior surfaces of the cups are described by McNabb as "thin-walled on the cup becoming thick-walled and roughened on the stem." Electron microscope images of the spores and a cross section of a hypha can be seen in Jean Keller's *Atlas des Basidiomycetes*.

Potential look-alikes and close relatives of **G. buccina** are:

LOOK-ALIKE

Chlorencoelia versiformis from B.C.   Photo by Poesh Binner

Guepiniopsis alpina: By far the most common in our area, this spring snowmelt species has a turbinate shape with a central depression in age, but differs by its yellow color and smooth carpophore with no external ribbing.

Dacrymyces chrysocomus: This one starts out cushion shaped becoming more cupular in age. It is yellow-orange, minute in size, but with much larger spores at 16–24 x 7.5–9 μm.

Ditiola radicata: Differs by having white hairs on its exterior surface and a tendency to root into the substrate.

Chlorencoelia versiformis: This is an ascomycete that bears only a superficial resemblance. It differs visually by having a powdery olive-brown exterior that becomes furrowed in age.

Hymenoscyphus peruni: Another ascomycete of about the same size, but having a more orange cap on a pale yellow stem. Found at Rockport State Park by Bruce Armstrong. Identified by Hans Otto Baral.

Dr. Reid lists 19 synonyms for **Guepiniopsis buccina.** Persoon first called it **Peziza buccina** in 1801. Not recognizing his own earlier discovery, he called a subsequent collection **Phialea merulina** in 1822. In 1853, it was moved to **Guepinia peziza** by Tulasne. Kennedy transferred it to Guepiniopsis in 1958. The infamous Curtis Lloyd also spent time mulling over it. Under the name **Guepinia peziza**, he wrote "Ever since we have been working on this subject, we have known **Guepinia peziza** scantily. We have an old

Ditiola radicata

Guepiniopsis alpina   *Photo by Richard Morrison*

Hymenoscyphus peruni

scanty collection from E.B. Sterling in New Jersey, and we made one collection in Florida of two little cups. That is as far as we know it in America. In Europe it is equally rare in the museums."

Further in the same article he relapsed into his usual lament over the state of mycology, writing "Every time the continental mycologists found this rare plant, they usually discovered it was a new species. Patouillard called it **Guepinia tostus**, and in addition found that it was a new species. Then Saccardo misreferred it evidently to **Peziza buccina** of Persoon, and called it **Guepinia peziza.** (Here he confuses Saccardo with Tulasne.) Quelet first referred it to **Tremella lutescens**, and gave a poor figure in an inverse position, and recorded that the hymenium exterior is formed of fine nerves. Leveille is said to have left a figure of it as a Cantharellus, which with other précieuses collections iconographiques,

was destroyed by the naughty Germans during the siege of Paris."

"Taking it altogether," Lloyd concluded, "This rare little plant has had quite an enjoyable time being named."

Although exceedingly rare, **Guepiniopsis buccina** can be found in a tremendous range of climates. Besides Europe, from Estonia to Italy, it has been found in the Blue Mountains of Jamaica, Secretary Island off New Zealand, in Japan, China, eastern Russia, Ecuador, Argentina, Mexico, South Carolina, Massachusetts, British Columbia, and Florida. And now, thanks to the discovery by Dr. Fred Rhoades and the analysis by Dr. Robert Bandoni, we now have it from Washington state at Hoypus Point.

A photo of this species in its normal configuration can be seen in Cetto's *I Funghi dal Vero*, Vol. 4.

BIBLIOGRAPHY

Stefan Buczacki, *Fungi of Britain and Europe*, 1989. University of Texas Press, Austin, Texas.

Bruno Cetto, *I Funghi dal Vero, Vol. 4*, 1984. BLV BVerlagsgesellschaft, Munich, Germany.

Henry Dissing, *Chlorencoelia in Nordic Macromycetes*, Vol.1, 2000. Nordsvamp, Copenhagen.

Jean Keller, *Atlas des Basidiomycetes*, 1997. Union des Societes Suisses de Mycologie.

Curtis G. Lloyd, *Mycological Writings of C.G. Lloyd, Vol.6*, 1920–1921. Self-published, Cincinnati, Ohio.

Bernard Lowy, *Tremellales* in *Flora Neotropica* 6 (1–143), 1971.

R.F.R. McNabb, *Taxonomic Studies in the Dacrymycetaceae, IV* in *New Zealand Journal of Botany* 3 (159–169), 1965.

Carleton Rea, *British Basidiomycetaceae*, 1922. Strauss & Cramer, Hirschberg, Germany.

Derek Reid, *A Monograph of the British Dacrymycetales* in *Transactions of the British Mycological Society* 6 (433–494), 1974.

Anna-Elise Torkelsen, *Dacrymycetales* in *Nordic Macromycetes, Vol. 3*, 1997. Nordsvamp, Copenhagen.

Gymnopilus aeruginosus (Peck) Singer

*. . . most species of Gymnopilus are
incredibly bitter, and Gymnopilus
aeruginosus is no exception.*

Referred to as the Magic Blue Gym by Paul Stamets, **Gymnopilus aeruginosus** is a widespread but not particularly common species in our neck of the woods. Therefore the arrival of the species at one of our meetings in the hands of Dave Jansen, our club cofounder, produced a ripple of excitement.

Dave reported that it fruits year after year on his farm near Acme in the foothills of the western Cascades. It fruits on a log so rotten that whether it is a hardwood or a coniferous log can no longer be determined by sight. (No matter. **G. aeruginosus** can fruit on either.) The log has long formed the border of his potato patch, which is fertilized by horse dung. "No clue left behind" is our motto, and with this taxon, you need every clue you can get.

As many of us know, most species of Gymnopilus are incredibly bitter, and **Gymnopilus aeruginosus** is no exception. However, since it is related to **Gymnopilus junonius**, the Big Laughing Gym, that didn't prevent one of Dave's students from trying. You can actually see the chomped cap in the left of the lead photo, an endeavor that produced no hallucinations, but at least showed us a yellow cap context, a character that mercifully (helping us along in the identification process) separates it from its nearest relative, **Gymnopilus braendlei**, known from Washington, D.C.

Gymnopilus aeruginosus, **Gymnopilus braendlei**, **Gymnopilus pulchrifolius**, and **Gymnopilus viridans** all belong to a group that changes cap colors and cap context colors as the fruiting bodies mature. With **G. aeruginosus**, the buttons are gray green to dull blue green becoming variegated yellow and green before their mature stage of salmon to pinkish brick or even vinaceous with darker tawny or brown squamules and greenish stains. The

LOOK-ALIKE

Gymnopilus aurantiophyllus

flesh of the caps also change color from whitish with blue to green tinges to a mature yellow or vinaceous. The result is a strikingly beautiful fungus at all stages.

The caps of **Gymnopilus aeruginosus** range from 5–15 cm wide with one specimen recorded at a whopping 23 centimeters (see Arora). They are dry, convex to almost plane, and hygrophanous, fading in age to buff or pinkish buff. The young gills are buff to ochre becoming yellow orange in age. They are adnexed to short decurrent, often seceding from the stem when fully mature. The stipes are colored like the caps but appressed fibrillose and usually striated longitudinally. They can run up to 12 cm in length and 4 cm in width, and are solid at first becoming hollow in age. Rolf Singer, who transferred the species from Pholiota to Gymnopilus in 1951, wrote that it had a distinct annulus when young. Ammirati, Horgen, and Traquaire contended in 1985 that it had no distinctive annulus. Stamets concluded that it had a cortinate partial veil, fragile and yellowish that soon disappeared, "leaving a fibrillose, annular zone on the upper stem." This is close to what we see here. The odor, according to Stuntz and Isaacs, is "oily farinaceous with a component of anise." The spores are rusty in deposit and dextrinoid in Melzer's.

Gymnopilus aeruginosus fruits from May to November in cespitose clusters on wood chips, sawdust, rotting logs and stumps, and even old railroad ties. It has been reported from China, Japan, Korea, all across Canada, and in the U.S. from Georgia to Pennsylvania, Michigan, Tennessee, California, Idaho, and the Pacific Northwest. The only published photos I could find of it were in Stamet's *Psilocybin Mushrooms of the World* and in Roger Phillips' *Mushrooms of North America*.

Lexemuel R. Hesler, in his monograph on Gymnopilus, listed four look-alikes to **G. aeruginosus**. To tell them apart, he stressed a careful noting of the cap color changes from button stage up, any change in cap context, the color of the young gills, whether the stem is hollow or solid, whether the spores are dextrinoid or inamyloid, and the presence or absence of caulocystidia and pleurocystidia.

Gymnopilus punctifolius: Differs by having bald caps and no velar material.

Gymnopilus viridans: Differs by having inamyloid spores and no pleurocystidia. It has an ochre cap that bruises green when handled, and was found on a burnt log near Seattle in 1911.

Gymnopilus braendlei: This is a smaller species with caps up to 5 cm wide and no caulocystidia. The young gills are white, and so is the cap context.

Gymnopilus auantiophyllus: Differs by its white cortina when young and its smooth rusty orange caps with yellowish margins. You can see a bit of white velar material on the stem apex of the button.

Gymnopilus junonius: Probably the correct name for **G. spectabilis**, it differs by having no vinaceous or greenish tinges on the cap surface, and

LOOK-ALIKES

Gymnopilus junonius (formerly G. spectabilis)

Gymnopilus punctifolius

gills with fimbriate edges. (This name is used because the original **G. spectabilis** turned out to be **Phaeolepiota aurea**.)

Gymnopilus luteofolius: That other Gymnopilus that changes colors drastically as it matures. It also differs by its maroon cap scales and more membranous velar material on its stem.

Paul Stamets describes **G. aeruginosus** as moderately active. It contains psilocybin and maybe other closely related compounds. There are not many reports on its hallucinogenic properties, probably due to the bitter taste. And finally the authors of *Icons of*

LOOK-ALIKE

Gymnopilus luteofolius from Blaine, Wash.

Medicinal Fungi from China write that its inhibition rate against sarcoma and Ehrlich carcinoma is 60 percent. What's not to like? With **Gymnopilus aeruginosus** you can help cure your cancer and enjoy an extrasensory experience at the same time.

Dave Jansen moved back to his family's farm in Ohio about 25 years ago, and the Magic Blue Gym has not been found by us since.

BIBLIOGRAPHY

Joe Ammirati, J.A. Traquair, & Paul Horgen, *Poisonous Mushrooms of the Northern United States and Canada*, 1985. University of Minnesota Press, Minneapolis, Minn.

David Arora, *Mushrooms Demystified*, 1986. Ten Speed Press, Berkeley, Calif.

Lexemuel R. Hesler, *North American Species of Gymnopilus*, 1969. Hafner Publishing Co., New York, NY.

Rokuya Imazeki, Tsuguo Hongo, & Keisuke Tubaki, *Common Fungi of Japan in Color,* 1970. Hoi-kusha Publishing Co., Osaka, Japan.

Bill F. Isaacs & Daniel Stuntz, *Pacific Northwestern Fungi* in *Mycologia* 54 (272–298), 1962.

Ying Jianzhe, Mao Xiaolan, Ma Qiming, Zong Yichen, & Wen Huaan, *Icons of Medicinal Fungi from China*, 1987. Science Press, Beijing.

Noah Siegel & Christian Schwarz, *Mushrooms of the Redwood Coast*, 2016. Ten Speed Press, Berkeley, Calif.

Rolf Singer, *Agaricales in Modern Taxonomy* in *Lilloa* 22 (1–832), 1949.

Stamets, Paul. *Psilocybin Mushrooms of the World*, 1996. Ten Speed Press, Berkeley, Calif.

Gymnopilus luteofolius (Peck) Singer

This yellow gilled Gymnopilus exhibits multiple cap color changes as it matures.

It was a Thursday night meeting like no other for the Northwest Mushroomers Association. People were still milling around in front of the cookie table when Margot Evers walked in. Margot was the octogenarian French lady who lived in Blaine near the Canadian border. She was carrying a whole bag of mushrooms. These were dumped on the identification table, some rolling a foot or more before stopping. It looked like she had found four of five species, all wildly colorful in their own ways.

Quite the buzz emanated from the table viewers.

She soon assured us they all came from the same woodchip pile in a roadside ditch from the Birch Bay area. They were found on April 16th, 1992. Margot allowed that the woodchip mulch consisted of vine maple and cottonwood.

LOOK-ALIKES

Cortinarius renidens ss auct. was Gymnopilus terrestris

Tricholomopsis rutilans

On most of the stems, wispy yellow shards and the torn remnants of a ring hinted at the presence of a partial veil. Many were thinking **'Cortinarius'.** This was understandable considering these velar shards were reminiscent of a vanishing cortina. However, the bright orange rusty spores, spiky dark red scales on some of the caps, and the very bitter taste, had a few folks leaning towards **Gymnopilus,** and if you were in that select group, treat yourself to a sloe gin fizz.

It was a taxonomic smorgasbord for the ages. The largest specimens with caps up to 12 cm wide had maroon scales on an ochre-yellow ground. Another group had pinkish-red scales. A third group had orange to yellowish scales, while two specimens had no scales at all. After discovering that each color variation had the same bitter taste (that was fun), we came to the conclusion that we were observing four phases of the same mushroom.

According to Lexemuel Hesler, who authored the monograph on **North American Gymnopilus,** the color of the cap context also changes as the carpophore matures. The cap context is at first red, then becomes lavender to purple before ending up yellow in age. Since there is no guarantee that the colors of the scales change in perfect sync with the color changes in the cap flesh, you have a varying cornucopia of colors.

But let's get on with the main description. Caps run from 3-12 centimeters wide and are plano-convex with strongly inrolled margins at first. The margins are fibrillose to appressed scaly, and according to Harley Barnhart, "may appear to stain light gray green where bruised." The gills are bright golden yellow with serrate edges. The gill attachment is adnate to sinuate or even short decurrent. They turn rusty in age from the spores. The velar remains are described as yellowish by Hesler, but white by Arora, Barnhart, and Gibson, and Schwarz and Siegel. The stems are 3–10 centimeters long and 1½–2 centimeters thick. They are pale yellow and threaded with purple brown fibrillose streaks, mostly enlarged at the base. They instantly stain reddish pink where bruised. The taste is bitter and the odor mild to most. Desjardin, Wood, & Stevens thought the odor faintly farinaceous, while Roux and Eyssartier thought the odor agreeable or of rubber. The caps stain orange with KOH. The spore deposit is bright rusty and dextrinoid in Melzer's solution.

Microscopically, the spores are ellipsoid and slightly roughened. They measured 5.9–7.3 x 3.2–4.1 microns. The pileipellis was a cutis of radially parallel hyphae with tufts of erect brown encrusted pileocystidia where the scales were. Caulocystidia, cheilocystidia, and pleurocystidia were all present, mostly lageniform to fusoid ventricose in shape.

There are, of course, both look-alikes and close relatives. Among the former, consider **Tricholomopsis rutilans,** which differs by its white spores and lack of velar material on the stem. The closest relative may be **Gymnopilus aeruginosus,** which differ by having a variegated cap color of pink, yellow, and green. Another close relative is **Gymnopilus brandlei** from the Washington D.C. area. This differs by its white gills when young and purplish cap that ages pink at the disc. Other look-alikes include **Gymnopilus fulvosquamulosus** which has a mild taste and tawny brown scales on a yellow ground, and **Gymnopilus pulchrifolius,** which has white gills, pink caps, and lacks both caulocystidia and pleurocystidia. A final look-alike could be **Cortinarius renidens,** which differs by fruiting on soil and having no velar material on the stipe.

Gymnopilus luteofolius seems attracted by a variety of woods. David Biek found it on digger pine logs in the winter in northern California. Both David Arora and Lexemuel Hesler feel it prefers coniferous wood. Calvin Kauffman found it on white oak. Helene Schwalkwijk-Barendsen found her collection on birch logs. Paul Stamets noted that it appears all across the U.S. on alder, eucalyptus, and pine. And the Bessettes report that Michael Kuo has even found it on treated lumber. It is a rare but widespread saprophytic fungus.

It has appeared all across north America from Florida to New Mexico and northwest to British Columbia. And eventually appearances were logged in Europe in Switzerland and France.

Due to the strongly bitter taste, there was little culinary interest until Stamets noted it could turn bluish in cold weather. A bunch of folks weighed in. Here are a few assorted opinions:
George Barron: "Poisonous."
Fischer and the Bessettes: "Hallucinogenic."
Schwarz and Siegel: "Mildly hallucinogenic."
Desjardin, Wood, & Stevens: "Toxic, mildly hallucinogenic."
David Biek: "The taste is not encouraging."
Charles Mcilvaine: "The caps are delicious."
Courtenay and Burdsall: "Poisonous."
Paul Stamets: "Probably weakly or moderately active."

Although unlikely to land a recipe soon, **Gymnopilus luteofolius** is a gorgeous sight to behold on any decaying log. The photographic possibilities are extensive.

BIBLIOGRAPHY

David Arora, *Mushrooms Demystified,* 1986. Ten Speed Press, Berkeley, Calif.
Harley Barnhart & Ian Gibson, *A Trial Key to Gymnopilus in the Pacific Northwest,* 2005. Pacific Northwest Key Council, Seattle, Wash.
Alan & Arleen Bessette & Michael Hopping, *A Field Guide to Mushrooms of the Carolinas,* 2018.

University of North Carolina Press, Chapel Hill, N.C.
Alan & Arleen Bessette, William Roody, & Dail Dunaway, *Mushrooms of the Southeastern United States,* 2007. Syracuse University Press, Syracuse, NY.
Alan & Arleen Bessette & David Fischer, *Mushrooms of Northeastern North America,* 1997. Syra-

cuse University Press, Syracuse, NY.

David Biek, *The Mushrooms of Northern California,* 1984. Spore Prints, Redding, Calif.

Booth Courtenay & Harold Burdsall, *A Field Guide to Mushrooms and Their Relatives,* 1982. Van Nostrand Reinhold Co., New York, NY.

Dennis Desjardin, Michael Wood, & Fred Stevens, *California Mushrooms,* 2015. Timber Press, Portland, Oregon.

Guillaume Eyssartier & Pierre Roux, *Le Guide des Champignons, France et Europe,* 2011. Editions Belin.

Lexemuel Hesler, *North American Species of Gymnopilus,* 1969. Hafner Publishing Co., New York, NY.

Calvin Kauffman, *The Agaricaceae of Michigan,* 1918. Michigan Biological Survey, Lansing, Mich.

Charles McIlvaine, *One Thousand American Fungi,* 1902. Dover Publications, New York, NY.

Helene Schalkwijk-Barendsen, *Mushrooms of Western Canada,* 1991. Lone Pine Publishing, Edmonton, Alberta.

Noah Siegel & Christian Schwarz, *Mushrooms of the Redwood Coast,* 2016. Ten Speed Press, Berkeley, Calif.

Paul Stamets, *Psilocybin Mushrooms of the World,* 1996. Ten Speed Press, Berkeley, Calif.

Gymnopus dryophilus (Bulliard ex Fries) Murrill sensu lato

. . . now an amalgamation of numerous previous concepts, many of its characters can change.

I was on the verge of heading into the Bellingham Public Library for our June meeting in 2005 when I felt a tap on my shoulder. It was Doug Hooks, a past president of our mushroom club. He had something to show me. In the dim light of a fading dusk I came face to face with the most beautiful mushroom in the **Gymnopus dryophilus** group. I knew instantly I had never seen it before. Doug kindly leant his camera for a flash photo just before the meeting began. The hurried shot can only hint at the strong contrast of lemon yellow gills and burgundy caps.

Doug reported that the collection was found by Rosa Tai at Lake Padden on June 9, 2005. Rosa, originally from Hong Kong, has often been praised by Jack Waytz as one of our club's premium mushroom finders. And she didn't disappoint here. This particular member of the **G. dryophilus** group was not in the

CLOSE RELATIVES

Gymnopus dryophilus sensu stricto

Gymnopus ocior from Serbia   *Photo by Dejan Zmaj*

Pacific Northwest Key Council key, implying that no one else had seen it either.

The caps of this collection measured 1¼—3½ cm wide. They were convex to plane with wavy, irregular margins. The margins can be faintly striate when wet, but these had dried to where they had now disappeared. They were smooth and sublubricous. The color was a shiny vinaceous-brown with some specimens already beginning to fade from the margins first. The cap context was thin and whitish. The gills were adnexed to adnate-emarginate, shallow, very crowded, and sometimes forked. They were pale lemon yellow with whitish pruinose edges becoming more ochre-yellow when dried. The gill edges were subentire to barely serrulate with a hand lens.

The stems were 3–7 mm thick and 2¼–4½ cm long. They were glabrous and terete or singularly grooved near the base. They were solid at first becoming hollow in age, and always tapered at the apex. The bases were orange becoming pale yellow at midstipe, and then cream at the top.

The taste was mild and the odor pleasantly mushroomy. The spores were white, inamyloid. Copious tan to buff mycelium had attached the stems to the substrate. They had fruited in cespitose clusters on conifer debris.

In the not so distant past this outstanding mushroom was known as **Collybia luteifolia**, the Golden Leaf Collybia, the 'folia' representing the gills. Then Dr. Halling discovered an earlier name for it, namely **Col-**

lybia dryophila var. funicularis Fries. The 'funicularis' was never raised to species level. But the yellow gills were not unnoticed. In 1987, Dr. Orson Miller and Dr. Rytas Vilgalys launched an investigation of the yellow gilled members of the **Collybia dryophila** complex in Europe. They soon discovered that "neither a type nor an authentic collection existed for **Collybia dryophila** or any other species in this group." Confusion in the group dated back to Bulliard's original plate in 1789 depicting several species when describing **Agaricus dryophilus**. By "applying expanded species concepts" they were able to find four distinct species emerging from this group. Most of the yellow-gilled species ended up being **Collybia ocior**. In its strictest sense, today's **Gymnopus ocior** is a striking fungus with a chestnut brown cap and a distinctive pallid band at the margin. It is a European species. If you were to herd our West Coast find described here through the keys in Antonin and Noordeloos' monograph on Marasmioid and Collybioid fungi in Europe, you would arrive at **Gymnopus ocior**. At this point, I felt DNA sequencing was called for. The Gen Bank number is JX536154. The ITS result was 99% **Gymnopus dryophilus**. Another interpretation could be called for, but at least we know it is in the **G. dryophilus** group. For those who have been tracking this group, it is yet one more example of the taxonomic engulfing of **Gymnopus dryophilus**. Like a column of army ants, it swallows everything in its path.

LOOK-ALIKES

Calocybe naucoria (formerly C. fallax)

Callistosporium luteo-olivaceum   *Photo by Daniel Winkler*

One more thing to remember is that the whole group is saprophytic, equally at home with conifers and hardwoods, flower beds and bark heaps, with wood chips and among mosses and rotten wood. A list of close relatives and look-alikes follows.

Gymnopus alpinus: Differs by its larger spores and the shape of the cheilocystidia. A beautiful species with dark purple-brown caps that is found in boreal regions of northern Europe and Greenland.

Gymnopus agricola: A Murrill species that does not have the dryophila type structure of the pileipellis, has non-coralloid chei-

LOOK-ALIKES

Calocybe carnea

Rhodophana nitellina

Calocybe onychina

locystidia, and darker stems.

Gymnopus dryophilus: Is pictured here because it is a sister species differing mainly in its white gills.

Calocybe onychina: Once found by Bob Mooers on a high altitude hike in the Mount Baker National Forest, it has golden yellow gills and a purplish to chestnut colored cap, but differs by its violet stipe.

Calocybe carnea: Differs by its crowded white gills, pinkish cap, and habit of fruiting on lawns.

Calocybe naucoria: Is another subalpine species that differs by having a cellular pileipellis. The stem is also a more uniform orange, not changing color from base to apex.

Callistosporium luteo-olivaceum: Has white spores that turn rusty with KOH.

Rhodophana nitellina: Differs by having flesh colored spores and a translucent striate cap margin when moist.

Clitocybe leucodiatreta—Differs by its adnate to subdecurrent gills, white stems that don't darken to orange-yellow in age, shorter spores, and different structure of the pileipellis.

As for edibility **Gymnopus dryophilus** has received mixed reviews. I have eaten it once and found it quite good. Others have experienced allergic reactions. Following are a few opinions from traditional mycophagists:

Charles McIlvaine: "I have eaten **Collybia dryophila** in all its forms and eccentricities since 1881 and never had an adverse reaction."

Michael Jordan: Called it inedible.

Konrad & Maublanc: Wrote that **Collybia dryophila subsp. funicularis**, yet another synonym, was edible.

Bruno Cetto: Named it edible, but of little value.

Not long after publishing this yellow-gilled Gymnopus as a Mushroom of the Month, I ran into Rosa Tai at Lowe's Hardware. She was delighted she had found something interesting.

"The mushrooming in Hong Kong...not so good as here," she smiled.

Clitocybe leucodiatreta from Spain

BIBLIOGRAPHY

David Arora, *Mushrooms Demystified*, 1986. Ten Speed Press, Berkeley, Calif.

Vladimir Antonin & Machiel Noordeloos, *A Monograph of Marasmius, Collybia, and Related Genera in Europe* in *Libri Botanici* 17, 1997.

Vladimir Antonin & Machiel Noordeloos, *A Monograph of Marasmioid and Collybioid Fungi in Euriope*, 2010. IHW Verlag, Eching, Germany.

V. Antonin, P. Sedlak, & M. Tomsovsky, *Taxonomy and Phylogeny of European Gymnopus Subsection Levipedes* in *Persoonia* 31 (179–187), 2013.

Timothy Baroni, Sarah Bergemann, & Kerri Kluting, *Toward a Stable Classification of Genera within the Entolomataceae: A Phylogenetic Re-evaluation of the Rhodocybe-Clitopilus Clade* in *Mycologia* 106 (1127–1142), 2014.

Bruno Cetto, *I Funghi dal Vero, Vol. 2*, 1976. Arti Grafiche Saturnia, Trento, Italy.

Dennis Desjardin, Michael Wood, & Fred Stevens, *California Mushrooms*, 2015. Timber Press, Portland, Ore.

Guillaume Eyssartier & Pierre Roux, *Le Guide des Champignons*, Editions Belin, Paris, 2011.

Roy Halling, *The Genus Collybia in Mycologia Memoir 8*, 1983.

Michael Jordan, *The Encyclopedia of Fungi of Britain and Europe*, 2004. David & Charles, Newton Abbot, England.

Paul Konrad & Andre Maublanc, *Icones Selectae Fungorum, Tome III*, 1927. Lechevalier, Paris.

Joanne Lennox, *Collybioid Genera in the Pacific Northwest* in *Mycotaxon* 9 (117–231), 1979.

George Massee, *British Fungi and Lichens*, 1900. George Routledge & Sons, London.

Juan Luis Mata, Karen Hughes, & Ronald Petersen, *An Investigation of Omphalotaceae with Emphasis on the Genus Gymnopus* in *Sydowia* 68, Series 2 (191–289), 2007.

Charles McIlvaine & Robert Macadam, *One Thousand American Fungi*, 1902. Dover Publishing Co., New York, NY.

Meinhard Moser, *Keys to Agarics and Boleti*, 1983. Translated and published by Roger Phillips, London.

Machiel Noordeloos, *Collybia in Flora Agaracina Neerlandica 3*, 1995. A.A. Balkema, Rotterdam, Holland.

Machiel Noordeloos, *Gymnopus in Funga Nordica*, 2012. Nordsvamp, Copenhagen.

Carleton Rea, *British Basidiomycetaceae*, 1922. Strauss & Cramer, Hirschberg, Germany.

Rytas Vilgalys & Orson Miller, *Biological Species in the Collybia Dryophila Group in North America* in *Mycologia* 75 (707–722), 1983.

Rytas Vilgalys & Orson Miller, *Morphological Studies on the Collybia Dryophila Group in Europe* in *Transactions of the British Mycological Society* 88 (461–472), 1987.

Hebeloma praeolidum (A.H. Smith, Evenson, & Mitchel)

By Dr. Richard Morrison with a contribution by Buck McAdoo

*. . . all Hebelomas should
be regarded as poisonous.*

While fishing with a friend on Heart Lake near Anacortes last October, we stopped for a break in the woods. It was then that I came across a group of brownish mushrooms with a strongly sweet odor and a thin cobwebby veil in the moss on the side of the trail. Not being certain of the genus and unable to pass up a potentially interesting mushroom, I took some photos, collected the group, and made a visit to Buck McAdoo, who thought they were most likely in the genus Hebeloma.

Using the monograph by A.H. Smith et al., entitled *The Veiled Species of Hebeloma in the Western United States*, the mushrooms keyed out to **Hebeloma praeolidum**, an intensely sweet smelling species found in the Pacific Northwest. It also keyed out to **H. praeolidum** in Ian Gibson's 2008 Key Council key. **Hebeloma praeolidum** is not included in David Arora's *Mushrooms Demystified*, but it lands in the **H. mesophaeum** group of veiled Hebelomas.

Dr. Morrison, closing in on a concept

The following description of **Hebeloma praeolidum** is based on the original one by Smith et al. combined with observations of specimens collected near Anacortes and Bellingham in the fall of 2010:

Caps—1 ½–6 cm wide, convex to expanded umbonate in age, bicolorous, the dingy brown to tan discs contrasting with a buff to grayish-buff band at the margin. Surface viscid and glabrous except for scattered fibrillose patches from the remains of the pallid buff cortina. Context buff-flesh.

Gills—Adnate to slightly notched, broad (up to 3 mm deep), moderately close, edges entire, pallid with a tawny-olive cast when mature. Not spotted or beaded.

Stipe—4–8 mm thick and 4–7 cm long. Equal to slightly enlarged at base. Pale pinkish buff at apex darkening to brown below in age. Fibrillose remnants of veil tissue sometimes evident on upper stipe.

Veil—A whitish to buff, evanescent cortina most evident in young specimens.

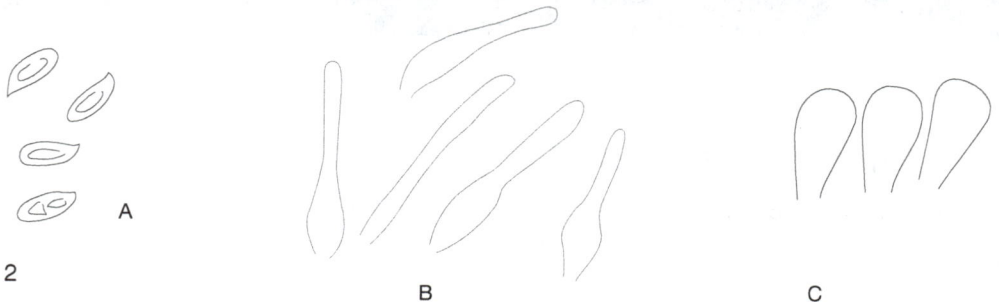

FIG 2
A Basidiopores
B Filamentous and fusoid-ventricose cheilocystidia
C Small thin-walled clavate cells found in hymenium

Hebeloma praeolidum—another look

Odor—Sweetly aromatic, often intense, somewhat unpleasant.
Taste—Disagreeable to mildly unpleasant, milder in some specimens.
Spores—Cigar brown, inequilateral in profile, ellipsoid to subfusoid, apiculate, faintly marbled, often with one large oil drop. 11.5–14 x 5.8–6.7 μm. Not dextrinoid in Melzer's. Our 2010 Washington collections averaged 12.3 x 6.4 μm for a quotient of 1.92.
Cheilocystidia—Polymorphous, some fusoid-ventricose with long necks and obtuse apices, others filamentous with slightly inflated bases. These being hyaline, smooth-walled, and measuring 36–50 x 5–8 μm. Also present in the hymenium were small, thin-walled, clavate cystidia 9–12 μm wide.
Habitat—Scattered to gregarious in moss or soil under mixed conifers.

The important field characteristics are 1) The mostly bicolorous caps with dingy tan to darker brown discs and pale buff margins, and the fragments of velar tissue sometimes hanging from the margins. 2) The pallid to buff, thin cobwebby veil present in young specimens, which may disappear in older ones. 3) Gills adnate to slightly notched, up to 3 mm broad, not beaded or spotted in age, tawny olive when mature. 4) Stems 4–7 cm long and 4–8 mm thick, equal or slightly enlarged towards base. Tawny buff above becoming brownish towards base, scanty buff colored fibrils from the veil sometimes present near apex. 5) Odor heavy, sweetly aromatic, and 6) taste disagreeable to mildly unpleasant.

Hebeloma praeolidum was described by Smith, Evenson, & Mitchel from a collection made in the Olympic National Park in 1941. The Heart Lake specimens and the other Whatcom County collections matched this description with these slight differences: The odor was not always as intensely sweet and the taste not as disagreeable, ranging from oddly unpleasant to somewhat mild in some fruiting bodies. The spores were also slightly larger, measuring 11.5–14 x 5.8–6.9 μm compared with 9–12 x 5–6.5 for the earlier Olympic National Park collections.

According to David Arora, about 200 Hebeloma species occur in North America. A.H.Smith et al. listed almost 100 species of veiled Hebelomas in the western United States. Many species are similar in overall appearance with colors that range from white to tan to varying shades of brown. Because of the many look-alikes and somewhat drab colors, Arora places them in his category of BUMS or "Boring Ubiquitous Mushrooms."

Species are difficult to identify and can often only be told apart by microscopic characters such as spores and cheilocystidia, or whether or not there is a veil, a character transient in itself. Most Pacific Northwest Hebelomas have a radish-like or unpleasant odor, but a few have a sweet or fragrant odor. Many species are poorly known, and some are undoubtedly undescribed. As noted by Trudell & Ammirati, Hebeloma in North America needs a thorough study using modern taxonomic techniques such as DNA analysis.

Hebeloma praeolidum may be fairly common in our area in the fall since I came across it while on mushroom forays in different locations in woods near Anacortes as well as in Sudden Valley just east of Bellingham. It has also been reported from Idaho.

Here are some of the look-alikes:

Hebeloma pinetorum: Another fragrant, veiled species described by Smith et al. from the Pacific Northwest. It was found with salal and lodgepole pine in Oregon and differs from **H. preaolidum** by having a cinnamon-buff to pinkish cap with narrow gills, spores with a blunt apex, and fusoid to subcylindrical cheilocystidia, which differ from the filamentous to elongated fusoid-ventricose cheilocystidia of **H. praeolidum**.

Hebeloma sacchariolens: A sweet or strongly fragrant species found in the Pacific Northwest that lacks a cobwebby veil and is in Subgenus Denudata. It has a larger cap, which is white to pale cream with a brown disc. The spores are distinctly larger at 12-17 x 7-9 μm, and the cheilocystidia are cylindric-clavate to capitate.

Mushroomers who collect for the table should certainly learn to recognize the genus Hebeloma since several species are known to be poisonous. For instance, the name "Poison Pie" is given to **Hebeloma crustuliniforme,** a fairly common, meaty species in Europe. The edibility of most species is not known, but as a practical matter, all Hebelomas should be regarded as poisonous.

However, according to Dr. Mike Beug, some intrepid souls claim that **H. crustuliniforme** or a look-alike is edible. The toxins found in species of Hebeloma affect the gastrointestinal tract causing mild to severe discomfort such as vomiting, diarrhea, and related symptoms of gastric distress.

Hebeloma sacchariolens

Hebeloma velutipes

Symptoms usually occur within 30 minutes to a few hours after eating the mushroom, and can last for a few hours to several days of very unpleasant feelings.

Based on the current literature, Hebeloma species are not considered to be deadly poisonous by themselves. However, any mushroom with toxic potential can have dire consequences for the very young, the very old, or those in poor health. The toxic compounds involved are apparently quite varied and not well known. Several triterpene glycoside compounds known as hebevinosides have been isolated from some species, such as **Hebeloma versipelle**. Certain of these and related compounds have been shown to have potential medicinal benefits, and there is active interest in pursuing them further for their beneficial bioactivity.

Note: If you decide to test a Hebeloma for the table, don't forget to have the species identified by an expert. If for some reason you decide to go ahead with it, do it at your own risk. If this warning still won't deter you, a report on your experience would be much appreciated as a valuable contribution to mushroom science!

BIBLIOGRAPHY

David Arora, *Mushrooms Demystified*, 1986. Ten Speed Press, Berkeley, Calif.

Michael Beug, *Poisonous and Hallucinogenic Mushrooms*, 2000. Evergreen State College Press, Olympia, Wash.

Ian Gibson, *Notes on Hebeloma in the Pacific Northwest*, 2008. Pacific Northwest Key Council, Seattle, Wash.

Orson & Hope Miller, *North American Mushrooms*, 2006. Morris Books Publishing, Guilford, Conn.

H.J. Shao, et al., *A New Cytotoxic Triterpinoid from the Basidiomycete Hebeloma Versipelle* in *Journal of Antibiotics* 58 (828–831), 2005.

A.H. Smith, Vera Evenson, & D.H. Mitchel, *The Veiled Species of Hebeloma in the Western United States*, 1983. University of Michigan Press, Ann Arbor, Mich.

Steve Trudell & Joe Ammirati, *Mushrooms of the Pacific Northwest*, 2009. Timber Press, Portland, Ore.

Hygrophorus bakerensis A.H. Smith & Hesler

H. bakerensis has a powerful smell of almond extract or maraschino cherries, or even crushed peach pits.

Hygrophorus bakerensis, also known as the Tawny Almond Waxy Cap, was first discovered in the Mt. Baker-Snoqualmie National Forest and described in Lloydia 5 (88), 1942. It seems to be a species intent on expanding its range. Besides being found in the Cascades, the Olympics, northern coastal California, the northern Sierras, British Columbia, and the Idaho Rockies, George Barron has recorded it from Ontario and adjacent New England. It is a common feature of our autumn fungi and makes it to our show every year. According to A.H. Smith, it is found under conifers at elevations of 1,000 to 4,000 feet. Here in Whatcom County we don't need much elevation to find it.

It's an instant halt when you find a cluster of these beauties erupting out of the moss or rotten conifer logs. The shining, viscid caps attract fir needles and bits of twigs until each one looks like a miniature dinner plate with spices sprinkled on top.

The caps of **Hygrophorus bakerensis** can run up to 15 cm wide and are convex to plane with incurved and often cottony margins. The cap color is a rich rusty to tawny-brown fading to buff at the margins. They are glutinous when wet, sticky when dry. Fine streaks of fibrils can be seen under the layer of slime, and the flesh is thick and white. The gills are adnate to short decurrent, crowded to distant, thick and waxy. Gill colors are white to buff or pale pinkish buff when viewed from an angle, and according to Largent, they dry reddish brown. The stems range from 4-15 cm long and 1-2 ½ cm thick. They are dry, white to pinkish buff, and smooth to slightly scabrous with a pruinose apex. The tops of the stems and the gill edges are often beaded with hyaline drops. Some basal mycelium is often present. The spores are white in deposit, and the taste is mild. The strongest character is the odor. **H. bakerensis** has a powerful smell of almond extract or maraschino cherries, or even crushed peach pits, in the opinion of Dr. Smith.

Microscopically, the spores are smooth, elliptical, and measure 7.5-10 x 4.5-6 µm. They turn yellowish in Melzer's solution. According to Hesler, clamps are present, gill trama is divergent, and the structure of the pileus is an ixotrichoderm. There are no cystidia. A decent photo of the divergent gill trama can be seen in *How to Identify Mushrooms to Genus III: Microscopic Features* by Largent, Johnson, & Watling.

Taste is another story. In the world of mushroom flavors perhaps only the coconut smelling **Lactarius glyciosmus** leads to greater expectations. Ironically, the most optimistic report

LOOK-ALIKES

Hygrophorus olivaceoalbus from Serbia   Photo by Marjan Kustera

Hygrophorus secretanii

came from Dr. Smith, who wrote "Edible, Mr. Gruber reports it as very good." This was in *Mushrooms in Their Natural Habitat*. Every other author thought the flavor to be bland, bitter, or of low quality. To get a more local opinion, we asked our club founders, Dave Jansen and Fred Rhoades, for their assessments. Fred replied that the Hygrophoraceae in general had little or no flavor. Dave had a one-word appraisal, "disappointing." George Barron, although admitting edibility, couldn't recommend them because a few other members of the genus were considered poisonous. And finally, Dr. A.H. Smith, in a later work, reversed his opinion, claiming there could be potential confusion with dangerous Clitocybes and Tricholomas.

There are a number of relatives and close look-alikes:

Hygrophorus laurae: Found from Tennessee to Ontario, the caps are whitish with a cinnamon-tan disc. It differs by having no odor, viscid stems, and flocculose white squamules at the stipe apex when young

Hygrophorus discoideus: Also found in the Pacific Northwest, it differs by its viscid stem, whitish gills tinged pinkish tan, and the lack of any odor.

Hygrophorus olivaceoalbus: Has glutinous caps, the slime layer covering blackish hairs on a brown ground. It differs further by having no odor and viscid stems.

Hygrophorus variicolor: Has a strong odor of almond extract, the lower half of its stem glutinous, and a radicating stem

WITH SIMILAR ODORS

Hygrophorus agathosmus

Hygrophorus variicolor

Rhodocollybia oregonensis

base. It is so named because both the cap and gills change color dramatically when dried.

Hygrophorus pacificus: This is a smaller species with russet to tawny caps with flesh colored margins, and a strong aromatic odor, but with "marguerite yellow" to cream-colored gills.

Hygrophorus secretanii: Similar to **H. pacificus** microscopically, but with pale ochre-tan caps with dull brown discs.

Hygrophorus tennesseensis: Has a more ochre-brown cap center, a bitter taste, and an odor of raw potatoes.

Hygrophorus monticola: Also has an odor of cherry pits, but differs by its caps becoming flushed vinaceous in age. Reported from Idaho and British Columbia.

Hygrophorus agathosmus: Shares the same odor of almond extract, but differs by its ashy-gray caps and paler gray stems.

Hygrophorus odoratus: Found in Oregon and Idaho, it looks like a thinner **H. agathosmus**, even sharing the same almond odor, but differs by the stems turning pale ochre when dried.

Rhodocollybia oregonensis: Shares the same almond extract odor but has a flesh colored spore print and maroon-brown caps.

Hygrophorus bakerensis is just one of those species that looks a lot better gleaming up at you from a bed of deep moss than it does drooling over your chanterelles in a crowded collecting basket. A great place to find it was off of the South Pass Road before the area was clearcut.

BIBLIOGRAPHY

David Arora, *Mushrooms Demystified*, 1986. Ten Speed Press, Berkeley, Calif.

George Barron, *Mushrooms of Northeast North America*, 1999. Lone Pine Publishing, Edmonton, Alberta.

Alan & Arleen Bessette & David Fischer, *Mushrooms of Northeastern North America*, 1997. Syracuse University Press, Syracuse, NY.

Alan & Arleen Bessette, Orson & Hope Miller, *Mushrooms of North America in Color*, 1995. Syracuse University Press, Syracuse, NY.

Anders Gjervan & Sigmund Sivertsen, *Hygrophorus secretanii E. Henn., a Long Forgotten Species in Europe* in Agarica 4, No.8 (330–336), 1983.

David Largent, *Hygrophoraceae in Agaricales of California*, 1985. Mad River Press, Eureka, Calif.

David Largent, David Johnson, & Roy Watling, *How to Identify Mushrooms to Genus III. Microscopic Features. Mad River Press, Eureka, Calif.*

Gary Lincoff, *Audubon Society Field Guide to North American Mushrooms*, 1981. Alfred A. Knopf, New York, NY.

Margaret McKenny, Daniel Stuntz, & Joe Ammirati, *The New Savory Wild Mushroom*, 1987. University of Washington Press, Seattle, Wash.

A.H. Smith, *Mushrooms in Their Natural Habitats*, 1949. Sawyer's, Lancaster, Penn.

A.H. Smith, *A Field Guide to Western Mushrooms*, 1975. University of Michigan Press, Ann Arbor, Mich.

A.H. Smith & Lexemuel Hesler, *North American Species of Hy.grophorus*, 1963. University of Tennessee Press, Knoxville, Tenn.

Alexander & Helen Smith, & Nancy Weber, *How to Know the Gilled Mushrooms*, 1979. William C. Brown, Dubuque, Iowa.

Steve Trudell & Joe Ammirati, *Mushrooms of the Pacific Northwest*, 2009. Timber Press, Portland, Ore.

Hygrophorus caeruleus O.K. Miller

*The odor has been described
as strongly fungoid or of a
rancid meal that can permeate
an entire room.*

The gray-green ghost of the Hygrophoraceae is on the move. This rare montane species was found by club member Lee Whitford near the Deer Creek Campground above Lake Wenatchee in May, 1995. The club was on its annual morel hunt in the eastern Cascades when she spotted it under pine. According to Dr. Orson Miller, this find represented a substantial distribution to the west from the original find in the Payette National Forest in central Idaho. Since then, it has showed up in eastern Oregon and down into the Sierra Nevada in California. It generally shows up near melting snow in the spring. Dr. Miller noted that in Idaho it has been found with Douglas fir, grand fir, and Engelmann spruce.

Caps run from 4–9.5 cm wide with a felty but moist texture. They are broadly convex with incurved margins at first. Older specimens are coarsely rimose with frequent areolations and small, appressed whitish fibrils over a pallid, gray green to dingy buff ground. Aged specimens can become pale brown at disc.

Hygrophorus caeruleus is a thick, chunky species. The context is buff with streaks of pale bluish green, and can be 2 cm thick at disc. The gills are adnate to short decurrent and grayish blue green in color. They are subdistant, thick, and waxy when crushed. The stems are 3–5 cm long and 1–2 ½ cm thick at the apex, tapering towards the base. They are lightly pruinose at the apex changing to appressed fibrillose below. The stem colors are pale gray green to pale brown and bruise darker when handled. The base is adorned with white rhizomorphs. The spores are white and inamyloid. They are smooth, elliptical, and measure 6.5–9 x 4–5 µm. The gill trama is of parallel hyphae.

Dr. Miller found that **Hygrophorus caeruleus** did not fit neatly into any one section in Hygrophorus. It had characteristics of both Section Hygrocybe and Section Camarophyllopsis. At one point several Key Council members were arguing whether it even belonged in Hygrophorus. DNA sequencing would let us know one way or the other.

And forget edibility. The odor has been described as strongly fungoid or of a rancid meal that can permeate an entire room. As it ages, the rancid meal odor turns into pure garbage. The taste is mild at first but soon astringent and disagreeable.

Hygrophorus caeruleus is fairly easily separated from its look-alikes. Nonetheless, if you stretch your credulity to the limit, here they are:

Clitocybe odora var. pacifica: Differs by having a much thinner stature, a strong odor of anise that does not disappear with cooking, more of a grayish blue-green color, and non-waxy gills.

LOOK-ALIKES

Clitocybe odora var. pacifica   Photo by Richard Morrison

Clitocybe odora from Spain

LOOK-ALIKES

Stropharia caerulea   *Photo by Richard Morrison*

Gliophorus psittacinus

Clitocybe odora: Shares the same anise odor as the **var. pacifica**, but differs by its white gills and stems.

Stropharia pseudocyanea: Another West Coast species that differs by its non-waxy, fawn to purple-brown gills, purple-brown spores, pale ochre caps with blue-green tinges, and a membranous ring on its stem.

Stropharia caerulea: Also can have gray-green caps, but they are viscid when moist, and the spores are umber brown in deposit.

Stropharia aeruginosa: Known from northern Europe and the Pacific Northwest, it differs by its purple-brown spores, appendiculate veil remnants on the cap margin, shaggy ring on the stipe, and lack of an anise odor. (See photo on page 447.)

Gliophorus psittacinus: Known as the Parrot for its variable cap colors, it has a much smaller stature than that of **H. caeruleus**, viscid caps, and no odor.

BIBLIOGRAPHY

Michael Castellano, Jane Smith, Thomas Odell, Efren Cazares, & Susan Nugent, *Handbook to Staregy 1 Fungal Species in the Northwest Forest Plan*, 1999. U.S. Dept. of Agriculture, Forest Service, Portland, Ore.

Dennis Desjardin, Michael Wood, & Fred Stevens, *California Mushrooms*, 2015. Timber Press, Portland, Ore.

Orson Miller, *A New Species of Hygrophorus from North America* in *Mycologia* 76 (816–819), 1984.

Alan & Arleen Bessette, Orson & Hope Miller, *Mushrooms of North America in Color*, 1995. Syracuse University Press, Syracuse, NY.

Mykoweb.com, *Hygrophorus caeruleus*

Roger Phillips, *Mushrooms of North America*, 1991. Little, Brown & Co., Boston, Mass.

Inocybe praecox Kropp, Matheny, & Nanagyulyan

By Dr. Richard Morrison with a contribution by Buck McAdoo

Photo by Richard Morrison

The species name praecox means "early," an apt name for this spring fruiting Inocybe.

Inocybe mushrooms most often fruit in the late summer and fall, so it was a bit surprising to come across an attractive, medium sized, brownish-yellow capped Inocybe in late March, 2010, in Sudden Valley just east of Bellingham, Washington. Several keys were used in an attempt to identify the specimens. A possible match was found in a 2008 key to Inocybe in the Pacific Northwest by Dr. Brandon Matheny. The best match was a species provisionally named **Inocybe praecox**. It was provisional because it had not as yet been described in a peer-reviewed scientific journal. I subsequently contacted Dr. Matheny, who had been a student of Dr. Ammirati's at the University of Washington, and he was kind enough to send me a very recent publication in the journal, Mycologia by Matheny, Kropp, & Nanagyulyan in which **Inocybe praecox** was officially described and discussed. This publication included a key to the **Inocybe splendens** complex of which **Inocybe praecox** is a member. From looking at photos of the Sudden Valley collection, Dr. Matheny felt that **I. praecox** was a likely candidate. After studying morphological and microscopic characteristics it was concluded that the Sudden Valley collection was indeed this newly described species.

The following descriptions of **Inocybe praecox** are based on the samples from Sudden Valley and the description by Kropp, Matheny, & Nanagyulyan in *Mycologia*.

A thumbnail sketch of the most important field characters includes: 1) Fruiting in spring under western red cedar, hemlock, alder or madrone. 2) A somewhat robust but medium sized Inocybe. 3) Caps brownish yellow, convex to plane, sometimes with broad umbo, surface matted fibrillose, but not scaly. 4) Gills attached, pallid becoming light brownish in age. 5) Odor lacking. 6) Stem pruinose (powdery) to at least halfway down the stem, equal, pallid to light tan. 7) Stem with a marginate bulbous base.

The following is a more complete description of **Inocybe praecox**:

Caps—2–6 cm wide, margins incurved when young, convex to plane at maturity, often with a broad umbo. Surface slightly greasy, with appressed fibrils or squamulose areas in age, not rimose. Color medium yellow brown to dark yellow brown, sometimes darkening to brown in age.

Gills—Close, narrowly attached, 2 ½–6 mm deep. Whitish at first becoming light grayish-brown in age. Edges pallid and indistinctly fimbriate.

Stems—2–7 cm long by 5–13 mm thick, solid, equal, terminating in a distinctly marginate basal bulb. Color pallid to light tan, pruinose down to the basal bulb when young, but possibly visible only part way down the stem in older specimens.

Odor—None.

Veil—Absent.

Spore print—Medium brown.

Spores—(7.5-) 8.6 (-13) x (4.5) 4.9 (-6) μm. Smooth, elliptical to almond shaped without a germ pore. Yellowish-brown in KOH. Apices subconical to obtuse.

Pleurocystidia—44–70 x 12–18 μm. Numerous thick-walled, clavate to fusiform-ventricose cystidia with obtuse apices often covered with crystals.

Cheilocystidia—32–65 x 12–17 μm. Numerous, thick-walled, clavate to fusiform ventricose to rarely ovate cystidia with obtuise apices often covered with crystals.

Caulocystidia—Clavate to subfusoid, typically thin-walled cystidia, some with apical crystals.

Clamp connections—Present.

Habitat—Solitary or in small groups on the ground in forests or in parks, mostly with conifers such as western red cedar, Douglas fir, and western hemlock, but also with deciduous trees such as red alder and madrone at lower elevations in Washington state.

The species name *praecox* means early, an apt name for this

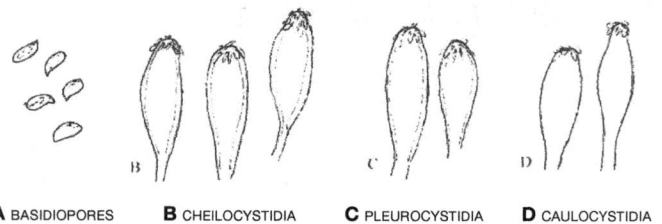

A BASIDIOPORES   **B** CHEILOCYSTIDIA   **C** PLEUROCYSTIDIA   **D** CAULOCYSTIDIA

LOOK-ALIKES

Inocybe ceskae from Calif.

Inocybe 'cf' nitidiuscula   *Photo by Richard Morrison*

sized terrestrial, brown-spored, often dull colored mushrooms, many of which fall into the LBM ("Little Brown Mushroom") category. Although members of the genus are fairly easy to recognize, species are another story. There are so many look-alikes as well as those that are poorly characterized or even undescribed. So, identifying species can be a chore, and currently available keys are often inadequate.

An example of another Inocybe found in the spring at Deception Pass Park is pictured here as a look-alike. **Inocybe nitidiuscula** differs from **I. praecox** by having a smaller stature, a pinkish stem, and white pruina only at the stem apex. The 'cf' here indicates that this is the North American version of true **I. nitidiuscula** of Europe.

Based on recent work with DNA analysis and microscopic traits, some researchers have suggested splitting Inocybe into several new genera. This work will be going forward as new information is revealed by the professional Inocybe-ologists.

Many Inocybe species are known to be poisonous. They contain dangerous amounts of muscarine and possibly other toxins. David Arora estimates that Inocybe contains a higher percentage of poisonous species than any other major mushroom group, including Amanita. Every mushroom enthusiast who collects mushrooms for food should learn to recognize the Inocybe characteristics and follow Arora's recommendation to avoid eating them.

spring fruiting Inocybe. There is no information on whether **Inocybe praecox** is poisonous or not, but as with other species of Inocybe, it most likely is, and should not be eaten. To date, **Inocybe praecox** has only been reported to occur at lower elevations in western Washington. However, it may be found to have a wider range now that it has been described, and mushroomers become aware of it.

Most, if not all species of Inocybe are mycorrhizal with various conifer and broadleaf trees. **Inocybe praecox** is probably no exception. The Sudden Valley fruiting was with Doug fir and hemlock. It has no distinctive odor, which is a contrast with many other Inocybes that have distinctive odors such as fishy, spermatic, of green corn or fragrant. It is also robust for an Inocybe.

The genus Inocybe contains a large group of small to medium

Addendum: In late November of 2012 two pugs tragically died near Lake Whatcom after eating Inocybes. The species suspected in the case was **Inocybe ceskae**, pictured on previous page. It was common in lawns all over Bellingham at the time but erroneously known as **Inocybe mixtilis**. This species has killed pets before. However, this particular case was complicated by the simultaneous presence of legions of a hitherto unidentifiable Galerina on the same lawn. This Galerina had no velar material so was not a part of the deadly **Galerina marginata** complex. It may or may not have played a part in the poisoning. So if you have pets and toddlers it's a good idea to periodically go over your lawn and rid it of all the little brown fiberheads you can find.

BIBLIOGRAPHY

David Arora, *Mushrooms Demystified*, 1986. Ten Speed Press, Berkeley, Calif.

F. Esteve-Raventos, D. Bandini, B. Oertel, V. Gonzalez, G. Moreno, & I. Olariaga, *Advances in the Knowledge of the Inocybe mixtilis Group through Molecular and Morphological Studies* in Persoonia 41 (213–236), 2018.

Bradley Kropp, P.Brandon Matheny, & Siranush Nanagyulyan, *Phylogenetic Taxonomy of the Inocybe Splendens Group and Evolution of Supersection 'Marginatae'* in Mycologia 102 (560), 2010.

Brandon Matheny, *Preface to Artificial Key to Common and Noteworthy Species of Inocybe from the Pacific Northwest*, 2008. http://mykoweb.com/CAF/keys/index.html

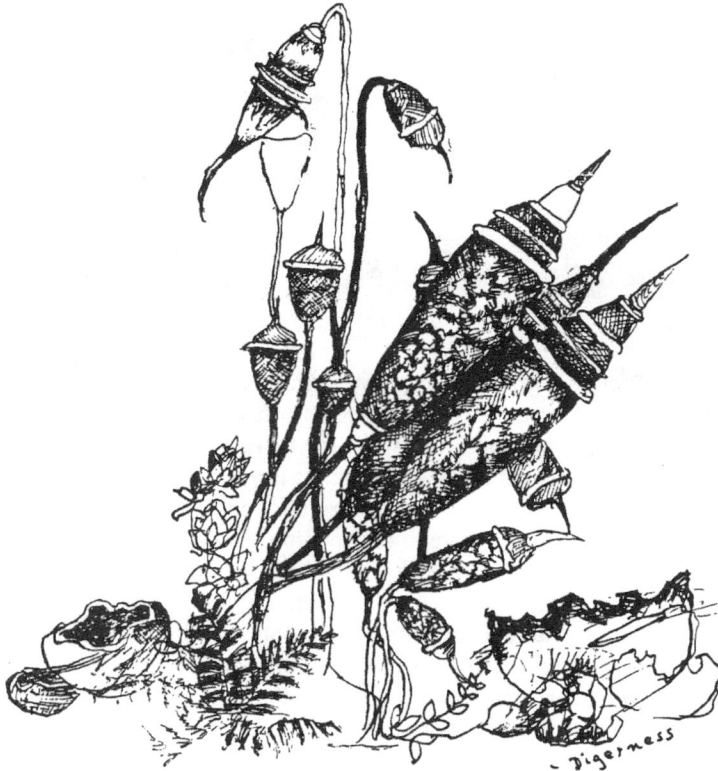

- Digermess

Kuehneromyces mutabilis (Schaeffer) Singer & A.H. Smith

The payoff is high if you get it right, but possible death if you make a mistake.

This is an interesting case. **Kuehneromyces mutabilis** is yet another of those Russian roulette mushrooms where the payoff is high if you get it right, but possible death if you make a mistake. Eaten widely in Europe, not one mushroom guide of North American fungi suggests that we eat it despite acknowledging the edibility. As Neuner informs us, "it is difficult to identify because it is so hygrophanous."

This is brought out by the name itself. *Mutabilis* means changeable. The cap color changes from a cinnamon brown to a straw color as the species dries out. Despite this chameleon act, the species is so popular in parts of Europe that the spawn is commercially available for home cultivation on hardwood or conifer logs. Schalk-wijk-Barendsen reports that it is as easy to cultivate as the Oyster mushroom.

The main photo here is of **Kuehneromyces mutabilis** from Haida Gwaii, B.C. in its full glory, before the cap discs have started to fade. Note the stem carefully. (A magnifying glass helps.) Tiny scales march up to the ring line. Above the ring line the stem is smooth and paler in color. The photo below is of younger fruiting bodies with the veil still covering the gills. There is less

humidity in the air because the cap discs have already faded.

A look-alike on the next page is of a close cousin, **Kuehneromyces lignicola**. Formerly known as **K. vernalis**, it bears such a close resemblance to the deadly **Galerina marginata** that one doubts that a report on flavor is imminent. Another close look-alike is **G. marginata**. In the photo next page, note the thinner and darker stem with a membranous ring. If this ring gets blown off or simply falls off in age, you could be in trouble here.

Known in most guides as **Pholiota mutabilis**, even the nomenclatural history houses controversies. The German mycologist Schaeffer introduced it to the world as **Agaricus mutabilis** in 1774. Kummer moved it to Pholiota in 1871. Singer and A. H. Smith moved it to Kuehneromyces in 1946, naming the genus after Robert Kuehner, a French mycologist from Lyons, who was the first to contend that it didn't belong in Pholiota. Orton subsequently moved it to Galerina in 1960. He may have been onto something because studies by Pegler & Young published in 1972 claimed the spores were ornamented with "exosporial verruculae that extended into the

Young Kuehneromyces mutabilis

LOOK-ALIKES

Kuehneromyces lignicola

Galerina marginata (potentially deadly)

germ pore." Since most other mycologists have described the spores as smooth-walled, I'm assuming the ornamentation can only be seen with an electron microscope. Good enough for a change of genus? Good question. DNA studies will trump either viewpoint, and it will be of interest to see whether they back up the findings from the compound microscope or the electron microscope.

Out of curiosity I looked up Moser to try and find out what distinguishes Kuehneromyces from Pholiota. It turned out to be a combination of features. Kuehneromyces species are those Pholiota-like species that have bald caps that fade in color as they dry, small cheilocystidia less than 29 μm in length, smooth-walled, ellipsoidal spores with truncated germ pores, and a membranous ring on the stem. I suppose if any of these features are missing, it's just a good old Pholiota.

The Changeable Kuehneromyces is a relatively common species in the Pacific Northwest with a long fruiting season from May through December. A. H. Smith suspects they stick around for a long time because the walls of the gill trama hyphae slowly thicken as they age. It usually fruits in dense, cespitose clusters on both hardwood and conifer logs and stumps, sometimes so prolific as to completely hide the stump from view. It has been found on beech, birch, oak, linden, poplar, alder, aspen, and various conifers. It has even been reported in the hollows of trunks of living hardwoods in Europe in cool weather.

The caps are 1 ½–6 cm wide, domed to campanulate at first becoming convex with an obtuse umbo in age. They are smooth, sticky in wet weather, and lubricous in dry. Sometimes called the Two-Toned Pholiota, the cinnamon colored caps dry out from the centers first, often leaving a darker band at the margin. They are a pallid orange-straw color when dried, sometimes with cracked or areolate surfaces. Gills are adnate to short decurrent, pale buff at first, then rusty from spores. They are crowded with several tiers of lamellulae (shorter gills that don't reach the stem). Stems run up to 10 cm long and 5–8 mm thick. They are tough, dry, slender, and often curved. They are whitish and smooth or finely lined above the flaring ring, and a darker rusty brown below the ring with recurved scales when young. The stem bases are dark brown becoming progressively paler towards the apex. The cap context is a pale straw color, the stem context a rusty brown. Spores are rusty and weakly dextrinoid in Melzer's. The taste is mild and the odor variously reported as vaguely fruity, of freshly sawed wood, or faintly of medicine. It causes a white rot of both hardwood and conifer stumps.

Kuehneromyces mutabilis is a cosmopolitan species. It has been found in North America from Alaska to Tennessee, all throughout Europe, Russia, the Umyrka River Valley in the Caucasus, the Altai Mountains in central Asia, Japan, and even in Java in the cooler zone of Mt. Gedeh. Even for a mushroom, it's a success story.

It also harbors medicinal values. According to Robert Rogers, it contains the active compound kuehnero-mycine B, which helps reduce blood platelet binding. Mycelium extracts showed activity against influenza viruses A and B.

They are also good to eat, much to the dismay of many. This ironic statement derives from its potential resemblance to **Galerina marginata**, now considered an earlier and more correct name for poisonous **Galerina autumnalis**. They both are little brown mushrooms that fruit on wood, have rings on their stems, hygrophanous caps that fade as they age, and stems that darken towards the base.

Kuehneromyces mutabilis differs mainly by the recurved scales below the stem. When in their prime, these scales are so thick as to produce a sheath-like appearance

Psathyrella piluliformis

Faded specimens of Psathyrella piluliformis

Pholiota malicola   *Photo by Richard Morrison*

Flammulina velutipes

Hypholoma fasciculare

up to the ring. Heavy rains or aged specimens may flatten out the scales until they appear fibrillose. If that happens, give them a wide berth for **Galerina marginata** has the same deadly amanitin toxins as **Amanita phalloides**, the Death Cap.

On July 24, 2012, Chuck Herbert, an arborist from Burnaby, my son Alex, and I ran into a huge fruiting of **K. mutabilis** on a pile of stacked alder logs on Graham Island on Haida Gwaii, British Columbia. We sautéed them in butter with a bit of chopped garlic and a fistful of fresh oregano. This was on a two-burner stove in Chuck's 1980-era Boler Camper. We ate them for three days running. They had a fine flavor but a slightly slippery texture. On the next day, we spotted a solitary specimen of **Galerina marginata**. It had the same hygrophanous cap, but a thinner stem that was all brown and the

evanescent shards of a ring about halfway up.

In the early 1960s there was a report of mushroom poisoning from Russia. There may be a traditional belief in Russia that if you parboil or pickle a poisonous mushroom it then becomes edible. In any case, the victims thought they were eating **Kuehneromyces mutabilis**, not **Galerina marginata**. The Marginate Galerina is smaller, has a farinaceous taste and odor, a stem that is fibrillose instead of scaly, ornamented spores, and fruits in groups on logs, not in dense, cespitose clusters. Nonetheless, the victims may have been following Rinaldi & Tyndalo who wrote mistakenly that **Galerina marginata** is harmless.

Kuehneromyces mutabilis has a number of look-alikes across several genera, two of them as poisonous as **Galerina marginata**. Let's line them up and proceed:

Galerina unicolor: Reported by Smith & Singer from Mount Rainier is another potentially deadly species to worry about. It has lubricous orange-brown caps, a white funnel-shaped ring on the stem, and appressed patches of grayish fibrils below the ring. It differs from **Kuehneromyces mutabilis** by lacking the recurved scales on the stem, the presence of pleurocystidia, and larger, ornamented spores. (It is now considered a synonym of **Galerina marginata**.)

Hypholoma fasciculare: Common in the Northwest, this is another extremely poisonous species that never gets eaten in North America because of its bitterness. The Sulphur Tuft also fruits in huge clusters on stumps, but it has yellow-green gills that turn purple black in age from the spores. It further differs by not having recurved scales on the stem.

Armillaria mellea group: This group has larger fruiting bodies, fruits in shelving tiers on logs, and has white spores, usually visible on the caps of the lower specimens on the log. It is edible to most, but caution is urged.

Flammulina velutipes: Usually has a dark brown, velvety stem that contrasts with the smooth, lubricous caps. Their spores are also white. It is also a good edible.

Psathyrella piluliformis: Formerly known as **Psathyrella hydrophila**, this brick-brown species also fruits on logs in the Pacific Northwest. It differs by having dark brown spores, a whitish, fragile, hollow stem, and veil remnants on the cap margin instead of a ring.

Pholiota malicola: Also fruits in clusters on logs and stumps. Bears a strong resemblance to **K. mutabilis**, differing mainly by having a fibrillose zone of fibrils near the stem apex, not an obvious ring with scales below. According to Arora, edibility is unknown.

Kuehneromyces marginellus: Reported by Overholts on conifer debris in the western mountains, this species has rusty, striatulate caps when young, and a whitish stem with an evanescent ring. Again, no recurved scales are reported.

Armillaria nabsnona: Differs by its striate cap margin and black stem, usually with veil remnants on it. Heavy rains

LOOK-ALIKES

Armillaria mellea from Calif.

Galerina unicolor from Minn.   Photo by Richard Morrison

Armillaria nabsnona

must have washed them off, in this photo. Only fruits on alder.

Kuehneromyces lignicola: Long known as **Kuehneromyces vernalis**, the Spring Time Kuehneromyces, is by far our most common Kuehneromyces. It has a thinner stature than **K. mutabilis**, an evanescent annular zone on the stipe, and bears such a strong resemblance to **Galerina marginata** that I can't recommend it for the table even though I know what it is. Moser describes this ring as "inconstant," noting that it is fibrous below the ring, not scaly. Edibility? "Non accertata" according to Bruno Cetto in I Funghi dal Vero, Vol.6.

    Kuehneromyces mutabilis gets good culinary grades in Europe. Here is a sampling of opinions:

Aurel Dermek: "This good edible mushroom is suitable for soups, sauces, and meat dishes. Only the caps are eaten because the stems are tough."

Mirko Svrcek: "One of the most popular edible lignicolous fungi."

Lucius Von Frieden: "It has a good flavor and can be dried."

Harding, Lyon, & Tomblin: "The caps have a strong mushroom flavor and impart a rich brown color to soups, sauces, and stews. They improve the flavor of less tasty mushrooms."

    Let's face it. If you are just starting out in this arena, it's a heart breaker. However, as you stand there in the woods staring at this great buttery looking clump of mushrooms adorning an alder stump, you are time and again saved from making any decision by the timely presence of the chanterelles all around it.

BIBLIOGRAPHY

David Arora, *Mushrooms Demystified,* 1986. Ten Speed Press, Berkeley, Calif.

J. Breitenbach & F. Kranzlin, *Fungi of Switzerland, Vol.4*, 1995. Edition Mykologia, Lucerne, Switzerland.

Bruno Cetto, *I Funghi dal Vero, Vol. 6*, 1989. Arti Grafiche Saturnia, Trento, Italy.

Aurel Dermek, *The Spotter's Guide to Mushrooms and Other Fungi*, 1984. Slovart Publishers, Bratislava, Slovakia.

Robert Gilbertson & J. Page Lindsey, *Basidiomycetes That Decay Aspen in North America* in *Bibliotheca Mycologica 63*, 1978.

Patrick Harding, Tony Lyon, & Gill Tomblin, *How to Identify Edible Mushrooms*, 1996. Harper-Collins, London.

Lexemuel Hesler & A.H. Smith, *The North American Species of Pholiota*, 1968. Lubrecht & Cramer, Monticello, NY.

Paul Kirk (ed.), *Index Fungorum*, http://www.indexfungorum.org/names/Names.asp

Meinhard Moser, *Keys to Agarics and Boleti*, 1983. Translated and published by Roger Phillips, London.

Andreas Neuner, *Chatto Nature Guides' Mushrooms and Fungi*, 1978. Chatto & Windus, London.

Lee Overholts, *A Monograph of the Genus Pholiota* in *Annals of the Missouri Botanical Garden 14* (87–210), 1927.

David Pegler & Tony Young, *Basidiospore Form in the British Species of Galerina and Kuehneromyces* in *Kew Bulletin 27* (483–500), 1972.

Scott Redhead, *Mycological Observations 4–12: On Kuehneromyces, Stropharia, Marasmius, Mycena, Geopetalum, Omphalopsis, Phaeomarasmius, Naucoria, and Prunulus* in *Sydowia Annales Mycologici 37* (246–270), 1984.

Augusto Rinaldi & Vassili Tyndalo, *The Complete Book of Mushrooms*, 1974. Crown Publishers, NY.

Robert Rogers, *The Fungal Pharmacy*, 2011. North Atlantic Books, Berkeley, Calif.

Helene Schalkwijk-Barendsen, *Mushrooms of Western Canada*, 1991. Lone Pine Publishing, Edmonton, Alberta.

Rolf Singer & A.H. Smith, *The Taxonomic Position of Pholiota Mutabilis and Related Species* in *Mycologia 38* (500–523), 1946.

A.H. Smith & Rolf Singer, *A Monograph of the Genus Galerina Earle*, 1964. Hafner Publishing Co., New York, NY.

Mirko Svrcek, *The Hamlyn Book of Mushrooms and Fungi*, 1983. Artia, Prague, Czechoslovakia.

Lucius Von Freiden, *Mushrooms of the World*, 1969. Bobbs-Merrill, Indianapolis, Indiana.

Laetiporus gilbertsonii Burdsall

Species can attack a living tree through a surface wound and expand inside for years before a fruiting body appears.

Back in 1949 in Mushrooms in Their Natural Habitats, Dr. A.H. Smith wrote of this species, "in the vicinity of Mt. Baker, it was found in great quantity on hemlock." As summer advances into autumn, 2009 looks to be another one of those years. Doug Morrison found those pictured here on August 2nd on an alder log. About two weeks later Jack Waytz found a break up at Schreiber's Meadow on an ancient but still living hemlock trunk. Jack has the ability to spot a mushroom from a speeding car, so he capped off the Laetiporus bonanza by finding another clump on a plum tree off Woburn Avenue in downtown Bellingham. According to the literature, this collection must also be **Laetiporus gilbertsonii.** I boiled it for 8 minutes in chicken stock and green peppers, then sautéed it with shallots and onions in butter. This is a simple recipe with no spices offered by Jack Czarnecki in Joe's Book of Mushroom Cookery. Jack Waytz and I both thought it had a pronounced citrus flavor and an excellent texture.

Laetiporus gilbertsonii has long been known as **Laetiporus sulphureus** or **Polyporus sulphureus** in older guides. Recent DNA profiling and mating compatibility tests have shown that **Laetiporus sulphureus** consists of six different species. The resulting key by Banik & Burdsall is the first key I've seen that features geographical location as a vital characteristic. True **Laetiporus sulphureus** is found on the East Coast on hardwoods. **Laetiporus conifericola** fruits on fir, spruce, and hemlock from Alaska down into California, and also in the Rockies. The Laetiporus formerly known as **L. sulphureus var. semialbinus** is now known as **Laetiporus cincinnatus**, since the type specimen was found in the vicinity of Cincinnati. It has a white pore surface instead of brilliant yellow. If you find the yellow-pored species fruiting on conifer wood in the Midwest and on the East Coast, you have **Laetiporus huronensis**. It mates with **L. conifericola** 15% of the time, about the same as dogs and wolves. **Laetiporus gilbertsonii** fruits on oak and eucalyptus in Arizona, New Mexico, California, and up into Washington, where it was found in 1998 on Prunus. It is probably less common than **L. conifericola** in our area. A paler

CLOSE RELATIVE

Laetiporus gilbertsonii var. pallida from Florida

version of this is **L. gilbertsonii var. pallida**, found in the Gulf States. Both **L. sulphureus** and **L. gilbertsonii** can fruit on beech, poplar, willow, oak, and plum, causing a red-brown heart-rot. **Laetiporus sulphureus** has even been found on telephone poles.

Although accused of being parasitic as well as saprobic, there are medicinal benefits. **L. sulphureus** is supposed to help with cuts and burns, inhibit staph, and help with cystic fibrosus.

The interesting thing about the Doug Morrison collection pictured on the previous page is that Doug had to return to the site to collect the wood from the log it was fruiting on. Only then could Dr. Fred Rhoades determine that it was a hardwood log and thus name the species correctly.

Whether you want to call them Chicken of the Woods or Sulfur Shelf, they can be absent from our woods for decades. Species of Laetiporus can attack a living tree through a surface wound and expand inside for years before a fruiting body appears. They produce a red-brown heart rot that hollows out the tree. Once they emerge from the host stump they can be found for several years at the same location. This may be why Doug was so elated with his find. A much appreciated past president of Northwest Mushroomers Association, Doug grew up in Moose Jaw, Saskatchewan, where a festival called Hobnobin with the Hobglobins takes place every August, about the time when the Sulfur Shelf might be expected to appear.

Doug and wife Noreen reminisce with some Argentinian red.

Must be a warm up for Halloween. Any one of these brilliant orange species of Laetiporus makes an astounding statement in its somber surroundings, and for a brief moment, Doug must have thought he was back in Moose Jaw. More to the point, Doug is no stranger to the higher fungi. He spent 22 years teaching chemistry at the University of Michigan, and during that time became acquainted with morels and boletes in the local woods. He found this collection somewhere north of Bellingham. When pressed for details, he replied "where Jack Waytz finds his matsutakes." End of story.

Laetiporus gilbertsonii has caps up to 20 cm wide, 15 cm deep, and 3 cm thick. Each one of these larger caps can weigh a pound by itself. A cluster might weigh 50–60 pounds. They are fan shaped, dry, and rugose to appressed fibrillose, or radially wrinkled. The color is pale pinkish orange to salmon-orange, often a little paler at the margin. The caps can become tan or light brown in age. There is no stem or a short, lateral one. The pore surface is a brilliant lemon yellow. The pores are 2–4 per mm, rounded at first, then angular in age. They weep in wet weather, producing colored water droplets. The tubes are pale yellow and 1–5 mm long. The cap context is pale yellow. The spores are buff to white. The odor is reported as musky or like eggs. The taste is mild becoming sour in age. Fruiting bodies are usually found shelving off stumps or logs, but near the ground they are often in a rosette pattern. In age, they fade in color, and are no longer edible.

At least that's the conventional wisdom. What I have noticed over the years is that our local species of Laetiporus are much of the time inedible even when fresh. Doug's specimens fit into this category. The caps were only 2 mm thick at the margins thickening to 7 mm at the basal point of attachment. They seemed perfectly fresh but were too woody to be digestible. The specimens found by Jack on conifer wood measured 5–6 mm thick at the cap margin and increased to 2 cm thick at the point of attachment. They were edible, of good flavor, but had a mealy, unattractive

Laetiporus cincinnatus from Maryland

Laetiporus conifericola   *Photo by Daniel Winkler*

eaten raw, while Lincoff reports that some allergic reactions have resulted in swollen lips.

Undeterred by the swollen lip syndrome or perhaps attracted by it, Fungi Perfecti, a company in Olympia, Washington, sells growing kits of **L. conifericola**. If you don't have a conifer stump to inoculate on your property, they suggest burying a conifer log vertically in sawdust, gravel, or sand. The fruiting bodies will appear in 6–12 months. The resulting fruiting bodies may be so heavy you will need sticks to prop them up.

The look-alike photo shows a plumper form of **Laetiporus conifericola**. Whatever species of Laetiporus you find, this is what you want to see. The thick yellow margin in its prime and the pale orange zone just beyond it should be cut off with a paring knife. The darker orange zone closer to the stump will probably be too tough to eat.

Michael Kuo, on his website www.mushroomexpert.com, states that **Laetiporus gilbertsonii** can fruit on dead or living hardwoods. They are morphologically indistinguishable from other species of Laetiporus except for slightly smaller spores, 5–6.5 x 3.5–4.5 μm for **L. gilbertsonii** compared to 6.5–8 x 4–5 for **L. conifericola**. Only three spores were found when Jack's **Laetiporus gilbertsonii** was subjected to the microscope. Not enough for government work.

Unfortunately, spores are not always visible in the microscope. They can only be found when sporulation is going on. Polypores sporulate depending

texture. The ones that are superb edibles are 1–1½ cm thick at the margins. They usually have a bright yellow band at the margin, concolorous with the pore surface. About a decade ago I found a break of the thicker form out on Matia Island in the San Juans. It was the high point of our cruise. We sautéed them in butter and onions, added cream and sherry, and ended up with an approximation of Lobster Newburg.

The white pored **L. cincinnatus** tastes nothing like this. It tastes like white chicken with a faintly aromatic herbal component.

Sadly, some people are allergic to Laetiporus. **Laetiporus conifericola** and **Laetiporus gilbertsonii** fruiting on eucalyptus are the usual culprits. Arora warns that they should never be on atmospheric conditions. Humidity and substrate are both factors in sporulation. **Laetiporus gilbertsonii** can appear in hot, dry weather, but it won't produce spores if the humidity falls below 50–60 percent. Perennial polypores have a continuous development of basidia over time periods that vary from several days to many years.

All of this may explain why, after three hours of agonizing suspense over the microscope, I was unable to find even one spore when examining one of Doug's specimens. Instead I found little piles of crystals scattered here and there in the hymenium, many of them resembling rectangular glass shards. It's the same problem with the basidia. They are often even harder to spot than the spores. So know that when you find drawings of the basidia accompanying a polypore description, that mycologist might have gone to hell and back in order to find them.

The variation in relative thickness and edibility of the fruiting bodies of our western Laetiporus species remains a mystery to me. Are they more edible when fruiting on fir as opposed to hemlock? Does the relative moisture inside the host stump play a part? Or does the degree of heart rot decay? Jack Czarnecki theorizes that either an arid environment or an ageing process that moves along faster than we think is responsible for the inedibility of most finds of Laetiporus. Almost all of the thinner fruiting bodies are too woody and fibrous to properly digest. What will be interesting to discover is if Doug returns to the same log next summer and finds **Laetiporus gilbertsonii** with much thicker fruiting bodies.

Dr. Orson Miller wrote that **Laetiporus gilbertsonii** can often be bitter and inedible on eucalyptus. It's just a matter of luck if you find it at the right time on the right host with the right thickness.

Finally, on behalf of the club, we would like to thank Doug Morrison for bringing this species to our attention, and Jack Waytz for gathering other specimens for comparisons.

BIBLIOGRAPHY

David Arora, *All That the Rain Promises and More*, 1991. Ten Speed Press, Berkeley, Calif.

David Arora, *Mushrooms Demystified,* 1986. Ten Speed Press, Berkeley, Calif.

Harold Burdsall & Mark Banik, *The Genus Laetiporus* in *North America in Harvard Papers in Botany* 6 (43-55), 2001.

Jack Czarnecki, *A Cook's Book of Mushrooms,* 1995. Artisan, New York, NY.

Stanislaw Domanski, Henryk Orlos, & Alina Skirgiello, *Fungi*, 1967. National Center for Scientific, Technical, & Economic Information, Warsaw, Poland.

Robert Gilbertson & Leif Ryvarden, *North American Polypores*, 1986. Fungiflora, Blindern, Norway.

James Ginns, *Annotated Key to Pacific Northwest Polypores*, 2007. Pacific Northwest Key Council, Seattle, Wash.

Michael Kuo, *Laetiporus sulphureus. MushroomExpert.com*, 2005.

Gary Lincoff, *The Audubon Society Field Guide to North American Mushrooms*, 1981. Alfred A. Knopf, New York, NY.

Peter McCoy, *Radical Mycology*, 2016. Chthaeus Press, Portland, Ore.

Margaret McKenny, Daniel Stuntz, & Joe Ammirati, *The New Savory Wild Mushroom*, 1987. University of Washington Press, Seattle, Wash.

Orson & Hope Miller, *North American Mushrooms*, 2006. Morris Book Co., Guilford, Conn.

Robert Rogers, *The Fungal Pharmacy*, 2011. North Atlantic Books, Berkeley, Calif.

Helene Schalkwijk-Barendsen, *Mushrooms of Western Canada*, 1991. Lone Pine Publishing, Edmonton, Alberta.

A.H. Smith, *Mushrooms in Their Natural Habitats*, 1949. Sawyer's, Lancaster, Penn.

Edmund Tylutki, *Mushrooms of Idaho and the Pacific Northwest, Vol. 2*, 1987. University of Idaho Press, Moscow, Idaho.

Lepiota magnispora Murrill

The only foolproof way of identifying it is to look at the spores.

Whoever thinks that mushrooms are devoid of personality need only look here. These veiled beauties discovered on North Pender Island, British Columbia, in November 2001 look ready to dance in a casbah. They were found on November 8, 1992, in a mossy glen under conifers. Sadly, this particular patch of old-growth forest was subsequently clear cut to make way for a vineyard. I feel privileged I got to visit it before it went down.

Introduced by William Murrill in *Mycologia* 4, 1912, **Lepiota magnispora** turns out to be an earlier name for **Lepiota ventriosospora** Reid, which was described in England in 1958. Dr. Else Vellinga, working on a monograph on North American Lepiotaceae, made the discovery. Having lost the literature reference, we have been calling it **Lepiota clypeolaria** for years. Else believes it is far more common on the West Coast than true **Lepiota clypeolaria**.

Lepiota magnispora is characterized by caps 4–8 cm wide, sharply conical at first, becoming convex to plane in age. The cinnamon-brown to ochre-brown discs break up into scales on a whitish to pale brown ground. The gills are free from the stem, whitish, and crowded. The stem is solid at first but hollow in age. The smooth, white stipe apex becomes abruptly wooly shaggy below. The ring, if seen at all, is yellowish to pinkish brown. It soon disappears. Most European authors stress the presence of yellow cap margins and yellowish scales on the stem, but the yellow can be missing

LOOK-ALIKES

Lepiota cristata from Deception Pass State Park, Wash.

Lepiota clypeolaria   Photo by Richard Morrison

entirely, as it is here. The odor and taste are pleasantly fungoid, the spore deposit is white becoming dextrinoid in Melzer's, and the species is found throughout the autumn season under conifers and birch.

Dr. Else Vellinga, who kindly verified this collection for us, separates this from **Lepiota clypeolaria** by its brighter, more intense coloration. Since this can be a rather arbitrary point of argument, the only foolproof way of identifying it is to look at the spores. Those of **L. clypeolaria** are 11–16 µm long and shaped like sections of an orange while those of **L. magnispora** have spores measuring 17–22 µm long with hilar appendages resembling short, hooked beaks. Dr. Vellinga refers to these as "penguin shaped." Dick Sieger, on the other hand, noted "they bulge out on one side like fat Egyptian mummies." Both Dr. Vellinga and Dr. Reid agreed that

LOOK-ALIKES

Leucocoprinus ianthinus

Leucoagaricus meleagris

Lepiota rubrotincta

the yellow coloration on cap and stem is not a reliable character, but it sure helps when observable. According to Reid, the surface of the cap is formed by long cylindrical and unicellular hairs with rounded apices. They arise from brown, septate hyphae to which they are joined by clamp connections.

Back in 1924, Calvin Kauffman described a **Lepiota fusispora** from decayed wood in Wyoming. This collection had huge spores measuring 21–26 x 5–6 µm. These spores had needle-like appendages. The species had plicate striate veils that soon disappeared. The caps were cinnamon brown breaking up into concentrically arranged scales near the margins. This species is now considered a synonym of **Lepiota magnispora** or belonging to the **L. ventriosospora var. fulva** group.

Oddly enough there are very few reports in the North American literature on **L. magnispora** since the original Murrill description. Dr. Helen Smith reported on it in 1966. Dick Sieger wrote up a thorough description of it for the Pacific Northwest Key Council Keys in 2000. Steve Trudell included it in his *Mushrooms of the Pacific Northwest*, and Else Vellinga touches upon it in recent monographs, but that's about it.

Look-alikes include the following:

Lepiota ventriosospora var. fulva: A Lepiota with a dark tawny-brown disc and paler yellow stipe scales. It is found in China and Europe. (The Index Fungorum now considers it to be a synonym of **Lepiota magnispora**.)

Lepiota spheniscispora: A species found under oak and eucalyptus in the San Francisco area that has yellow-brown caps and the odor of **Lepiota cristata**.

Lepiota cristata: A locally common smooth-stemmed species with tawny cap discs that break up into concentric scales towards the margin. It can be odorless or have a pungent odor so unique that it is referred to as the "Lepiota cristata" odor. It has a membranous ring that can fall off.

Lepiota clypeolarioides: Historically considered a potentially deadly species with amanitin toxins and a shaggy stem surface, the concept is now under revision in Europe, from where it derived.

Lepiota cortinarius: A Lepiota that differs by its pinkish orange-brown caps and short, narrow, cylindrical spores.

Lepiota xanthophylla: A European species with lemon yellow gills and a strong odor of rubber.

Lepiota castaneidisca: A lookalike of **L. cristata** that fruits under redwoods, Monterrey cypress, and oaks in mixed forests on the California coast. It has a sweet spicy-fruity odor rather than the **L. cristata** odor.

Leucocoprinus ianthinus: A species that differs by having a smoother stem with a distinct membranous ring and the habit of fruiting in greenhouses and cactus pots indoors.

Lepiota clypeolaria: Very similar to **L. magnispora**, but with paler cap scales and much smaller and elongated almond shaped spores at 11–18 x 4.5–6 μm.

Leucoagaricus meleagris: This differs by fruiting in huge clusters on wood chip mulch, and has a smoother white stem with an evanescent white ring. This collection, found by Dan Digerness near the Fairhaven tennis courts, had pinkish spores.

Lepiota rubrotinctoides: This very common northwest Lepiota differs by its smooth white stipe and very obvious white membranous ring.

Stefan Buczacki termed **L. ventriosospora** to be edible. Frankly I wouldn't put it anywhere near a dinner plate. Lepiota clypeolaria has now been proven to be poisonous.

BIBLIOGRAPHY

Marcel Bon, *The Mushrooms and Toadstools of Britain and Northwestern Europe,* 1987. Hodder & Stoughton, London.

J. Breitenbach & F. Kranzlin, *The Fungi of Switzerland, Vol. 4,* 1995. Edition Mykologia, Lucerne, Switzerland.

Stefan Buczacki, *Fungi of Britain and Europe*, 1995. University of Texas Press, Austin, Texas.

Dennis Desjardin, Mike Wood, & Fred Stevens, *California Mushrooms*, 2015. Timber Press, Portland, Ore.

Guillaume Eyssartier & Pierre Roux, *Le Guide des Champignons de France et Europe,* 2012. Editions Belin, Paris.

Calvin Kauffman, *The Genus Lepiota in the United States* in *Papers of the Michigan Academy of Science, Arts, and Letters* 4 (311-344), 1924.

Christian Lange, *Leucoagaricus in Funga Nordica*, 2012. Nordsvamp, Copenhagen.

Meinhard Moser, *Keys to Agarics and Boleti,* 1983. Translated and published by Roger Phillips, London.

William Murrill, *The Agaricaceae of the Pacific Coast, II* in *Mycologia* 4 (231–262), 1912.

Derek Reid, *New or Interesting Records of British Hymenomycetes, II* in *Transactions of the British Mycological Society* 41 (419–445), 1958.

Noah Siegel & Christian Schwarz, *Mushrooms of the Redwood Coast*, 2016. Ten Speed Press, Berkeley, Calif.

Dick Sieger, *Trial Key to the Pacific Northwest Lepiotaceae and Melanophyllum*, 1997. Pacific Northwest Key Council, Seattle, Wash.

Helen Smith, *Contributions Towards a Monograph on the Genus Lepiota I. Type Studies in the Genus Lepiota* in *Mycopathologia and Mycologia Applicata* 29 (97–117), 1966.

Steve Trudell & Joe Ammirati, *Mushrooms of the Pacific Northwest*, 2009. Timber Press, Portland, Ore.

Else Vellinga, *Studies in Lepiota, III. Some Species from California* in *Mycotaxon* 80 (285–305), 2001.

Lepiota sequoiarum Murrill

Now known to be poisonous. the one person who took the culinary plunge, had to be hospitalized.

The key words are "small, thin, and white." When William A. Murrill first spotted this diminutive species under the giant sequoias he must have felt it was uniquely associated with those trees. It must have attracted him like a magnet with its snowy cap contrasting with the dark debris of the forest floor. He found it in the Muir Woods north of the Golden Gate Bridge on November 22, 1911. He would be possibly shocked today to discover it has spread north along the coast up into British Columbia far beyond the sequoia belt.

David Arora called it "The Boring Lepiota." Upon closer examination it becomes almost alarming as it mimics the deadly white **Amanita bisporigera** in miniature with its free white gills and persistent white ring at mid-stem. At this point, **Lepiota sequoiarum** becomes less boring. The lack of basal volval material combined with other features, however, places it in Lepiota.

Although not considered exceedingly rare, I've only found it twice in Whatcom County. Once at Berthusen Park near Linden on October 19, 1986, and again at Birch Bay Park near the Canadian border in mid-September, 1999. This photo is of the Berthusen Park collection. The caps were 1–3 cm wide, campanulate becoming convex in age with a blunt umbo. They were pure white except for a yellowish-buff tinge at the disc. The discs were bald. The rest of the caps had scattered appressed white scales all the way to the lacerate margins. The gills were free, crowded,

and white. The stems were 2–3 mm thick and up to 4 ½ cm long. They were smooth, white, and equal with a superior collapsed ring at mid-stem. Odor and taste were mild. The spores were white and dextrinoid in Melzer's. They were found scattered in moss and dirt under alder, cedar, and vine maple in a low, wet area off a path.

Murrill's original description differed in two ways. The stems were larger, running up to 10 cm long and 5 mm thick. Also, the cap discs were densely fibrillose-scaly. There is a possibility that the **Lepiota sequoiarum** seen here may turn out to be part of a species complex and eventually receive another name.

Dr. Helen Smith examined the type microscopically. She found smooth, thin-walled ovoid-ellipsoid spores, flexuous, and narrowly clavate cheilocystidia in clusters, and tightly interwoven gill trama. There were no clamps and no pleurocystidia. Calvin Kauffman measured spores at 7–9 x 5–6 µm.

After finding it, I wondered if I had **L. sequoiarum** since there were no sequoias at the park. It turns out that most if not all of

LOOK-ALIKES

Amanita bisporigera from Maryland

Leucoagaricus serenus, Vermont version

Cystolepiota seminuda sensu lato

Alboleptonia sericella var. lutescens

Lepiota subalba from England

these diminutive Lepiotas are saprophytic and don't require a specific host tree. This explains the range expansion far from the original location with sequoia in the Muir Woods.

Microscopically, **L. sequoiarum** belongs in a group with no sphaerocysts in the cap surface. Instead the pileipellis is composed of two layers of interwoven hyphae. According to Sundberg, spores are ellipsoid and measure 6.7–9.5 x 3.5–4.7 µm. It is suspected that **L. sequoiarum** belongs to a group. Cheilocystidial shapes are reported as cylindrical to lageniform in some specimens and clavate to capitate to rostrate to ventricose in others. In some collections the flesh stains slowly olive brown when bruised. In others there is no color change.

Other look-alikes are listed here:

Leucoagaricus serenus: A close look-alike differing very minimally by having a cutis of narrow hyphae for a pileipellis instead of interwoven, and having a more sulcate cap margin. Spores are metachromatic in cresyl blue.

Cystolepiota seminuda sensu lato: Differs by its white powdery caps and dark flesh-colored stems. This photo encompasses the former **Cystolepiota sistrata**.

Cystolepiota pusillomyces: Another diminutive, all-white species with a granular floccose cap surface, more floccules draped from the margin, and a stem that turns reddish below the vanishing annulus.

Amanita bisporigera: Smaller than normal specimens can resemble **L. sequoiarum**, but the globose bulb at the stem base easily separates them.

Alboleptonia sericella var. lutescens: Differs by its pinkish spores and lack of any sort of ring on the stem.

Lepiota subalba: Differs by having a floccose ring with more floccose girdles on the stem below. It has an odor of rubber with a slight component of herring.

Lepiota subnivosa: Differs by its delicate, evanescent ring, a pruinose coating when young, and stems from 5–9 cm long that taper at the apices.

Lepiota pulcherrima: Differs by its bitter taste and viscid cap surface.

Fortunately, all the rest of these look-alikes are European species:

Leucoagaricus cygneoaffinis: Has silky to hairy white caps with ochre scales at the disc in age. Gills are white to a rosy-cream color.

Leucoagaricus sericatellus: Has 2-spored basidia, an upturned ring on the stem, and a swollen, fusoid stem base. Otherwise, it looks just like **Lepiota sequoiarum**.

Leucoagaricus crystallifer: Has cream-colored caps and cheilocystidia with crystals at their apices.

Leucoagaricus sericifer: Has white caps with pale brown discs in age, and lageniform cheilocystidia.

Leucocoprinus cygneus: This is another diminutive all-white species with sphaerocysts in the cap discs of young specimens.

Lepiota cristatella: Differs by its glabrous stem and pinkish tinge on the cap disc.

Lepiota boudieri var. alba: Has a velvety white cap surface, and a stem covered with a cottony veil.

Finally, it is important to stress that none of these small Lepiotas should be eaten. **Lepiota helveola**, **Lepiota subincarnata**, and others have proven to be deadly poisonous.

BIBLIOGRAPHY

David Arora, *Mushrooms Demystified*, 1986. Ten Speed Press, Berkeley, Calif.

Leif Døssing, *Sericeomyces* in *Nordic Macromycetes*, Vol. 2, 1992. Nordsvamp, Copenhagen.

Guillaume Eyssartier & Pierre Roux, *Le Guide des Champignons de France et Europe*, 2012. Editions Belin, Paris.

Calvin Kauffman, *The Genus Lepiota in the United States* in *Papers of the Michigan Academy of Science, Arts, and Letters* 4 (311–344), 1924.

Calvin Kauffman, *The Agaricaceae of Michigan*, 1918. Michigan Geological and Biological Survey, Lansing, Mich.

Geoffrey Kibby, *Fungal Portrait, No.57* in *Field Mycology* 15, No.1, 2014.

William Murrill, *The Agaricaceae of the Pacific Coast II* in *Mycologia* 4, (231–262), 1912.

William Murrill, *Agaricaceae, Parts 1–3* in *North American Flora* 10 (1–226), 1914–1917.

Robert & Dorothy Orr, *Mushrooms of Western North America*, 1979. University of California Press, Berkeley, Calif.

Noah Siegel & Christian Schwarz, *Mushrooms of the Redwood Coast*, 2016. Ten Speed Press, Berkeley, Calif.

Dick Sieger, *Trial Field Key to Pacific Northwest Lepiotaceae and Melanophyllum*, 2000. Pacific Northwest Key Council, Seattle, Wash.

Helen V. Smith, *Contributions Towards a Monograph on the Genus Lepiota .I. Type Studies in the Genus Lepiota* in *Mycopathologia and Mycologia Applicata* 29 (97–117), 1966.

Walter Sundberg, *The Family Lepiotaceae in California*, doctorate, 1967.

Elsie Vellinga, *Leucoagaricus* in *Flora Agaracina Neerlandica, Vol. 5*, 2001. A.A. Balkema Publishers, Lisse.

Michael Beug, *Mushrooms of Cascadia*, 2021. The Fungi Press, Batavia, Illinois.

Lepiota subincarnata J. Lange

. . . a number of small Lepiotas have the same amatoxins and phallotoxins as the deadly Amanitas.

This lovely coral hued Lepiota is not a household word among West Coast fungi afficionados, but it should be on everyone's radar by now. These yummy looking specimens were found on a crab grass lawn on the north shore of Port Browning on North Pender Island, B.C., on November 7, 1991. We had been invited by friends Kris Jensen and Poesh Binner to a Thanksgiving dinner midway between the Canadian date and our U.S. Thanksgiving. If we brought the turkey and the vodka, they would do the rest.

We arrived in the midst of a giant storm. The turkey was loaded into the oven. A mere ten minutes later a power outage struck the whole island. Nothing daunted, Poesh proceeded to fire up an ancient wood stove in their shed. Then we uncorked the vodka. This was no ordinary vodka. It came from the hold of a Russian freighter that had docked in Bellingham a week earlier. The crewman who sold it to me said it was from Vladivostok. It was tinted a pale red-brown color and had the scent of pine needles. It was so good, that once opened, you couldn't stop drinking it down. Then we staggered back to the kitchen to make the stuffing.

"Why not add these?" Poesh suggested.

He was pointing at the mushrooms halfway between cabin and shed. They indeed looked good. I noticed they had white, free gills, but so did some species of Agaricus when very young. It might be a cousin of the edible **Agaricus semotus** or the scrumptious **Agaricus diminutivus**, which has pallid gills when young. The delicate pinkish-brick colored caps stared invitingly out of the scruffy lawn. I told Poesh we ought to get a spore print just to make sure.

In fifteen minutes we could discern the vestiges of a white spore deposit, and I knew we had a potentially dangerous Lepiota instead.

A little over three years earlier on October 16, 1988, a 56 year-old landscaper in New Westminster, B.C., confused them with Fairy Ring mushrooms, also known as **Marasmius oreades**. Paul Kroeger reported the incident in the January 1989 issue of *Mycofile*, the newsletter of the Vancouver Mycological Society. Later, in the Winter, 1999-2000 issue of *Mushroom: The Journal of Wild Mushrooming*, Dr. Scott Redhead wrote up his own report. The following story is an amalgamation of both their reports.

LOOK-ALIKES

Marasmius oreades   Photo by Richard Morrison

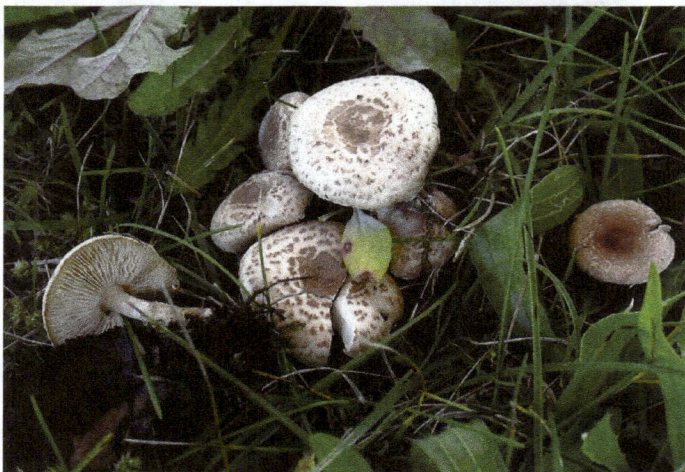

Formerly Lepiota josserandii from Concrete, Wash.

Lepiota castanea

Echinoderma echinacea from England

The landscaper found the mushrooms on his own lawn. He ate them in an omelet at 10 a.m. None of his other family members would eat of it. By 11 p.m. on October 16th, thirteen hours later, the landscaper began to experience abdominal pain, severe vomiting, and leg cramps. It appears that nothing was done until the next day.

By 10 a.m. on October 17th, 24 hours after ingestion, the B.C. Drug and Poison Information Centre was contacted. The landscaper was then taken to the Royal Columbian Hospital. By this time he had lost 20 pounds, according to his wife. He was severely dehydrated from vomiting, still had leg cramps, and could not hold down liquids. He was then transferred to another hospital since cyclopeptide poisoning was now suspected. There was some evidence of renal impairment, but initial liver function tests were within normal levels. Blood tests indicated low blood pressure with high urea and creatin levels, implying the possibilities for both liver and kidney failure.

At this time samples of the mushrooms were sent to an expert at the Department of Botany at University of British Colombia for identification. Unfortunately, these specimens were so deteriorated that identification was not possible. At this point, all mushrooms from the landscaper's lawn were gathered up and mailed to Dr. Redhead, the official mycologist for Agriculture Canada, based in Ottawa.

By October 18th, the patient appeared to improve, but still had stomach pains and diarrhea. The renal function was improved, but bilirubin levels had risen alarmingly, indicating liver damage. By October 19th, the patient was experiencing nausea, abdominal pain, more vomiting, and occasional diarrhea, but remained alert and oriented.

The patient's condition began to deteriorate again on October 20th, four days after ingestion. Besides the ever-present nausea and diarrhea, he became lethargic. On October 21st his diarrhea stopped, but he developed tiny hemorrhages on his abdomen. On October 22nd, he became unconscious. He was clinically diagnosed with jaundice, and tests showed he had liver failure. He was given eomycin and other medications. By October 23rd he was on a respirator. He showed no response to pain stimuli, had dilated pupils, and a flow of rectal fluids. He was given fresh frozen plasma and clotting factors. On October 24th, tests indicated both kidney and liver failure. He was placed on life support.

Meanwhile, the mushroom specimens mailed to Dr. Redhead in Ottawa didn't reach him until October 25th.

They had been misdirected to Montreal first! Scott described them as being in a condition of "late term decay."

With a pile of putrid mush on a slide in front of him, Scott learned that the patient just died. The pressure must have been intense. All of western Canada must have been waiting to find out what strange mushroom had killed a man in their midst. Somehow, and I don't know how Dr. Redhead succeeded, he managed to extract microscopic features from the mess in front of him. He identified the species as **Lepiota subincarnata,** a species of Danish origin, hitherto not reported from Canada. As Scott wrote, "what a terrible way to discover a new record."

Even with an identification made, the good ship Redhead was headed for a different kind of shoal... the varying opinions in Europe over the boundaries between **Lepiota subincarnata** and another closely related species, **Lepiota josserandii**. This latter species had been introduced by Bon & Boiffard in 1974. In a paper in *Flore Mycologique d'Europe, Serie 3*, Marcel Bon noted that **Lepiota josserandii** differed from **Lepiota subincarnata** by having a very clear ring zone of velar material and a strong fruity odor, much like that of **Russula fragilis**. While French mycologists believed these were two separate species, the German mycologist Gmelin created the combination **Lepiota subincarnata var. josse-**

Agaricus diminutivus

Lepiota helveola

randii. Meanwhile, Dutch mycologist Else Vellinga suspected they were the same species. How could Dr. Redhead possibly have decided between these opinions? By the time the specimens arrived, the fruity odor must have been replaced by an odor of rot, and the velar material rendered unrecognizable.

Nonetheless, history has proved him right. Subsequent DNA sequencing has shown that **L. subincarnata** and **L. josserandii** are conspecific. The name **Lepiota subincarnata** has priority because it was published earlier. Now, of course, came the fun part, the amalgamated concept of the two formerly separate species. According to Dr. Vellinga, who wrote it up, the odor can now vary from fruity to fungoid or even farinaceous. The velar material

LOOK-ALIKE

Agaricus kerriganii

at mid-stipe can be copious or very thin. The colors of the cap scales can be pinkish brown, red brown, vinaceous pink, or even gray brown.

For the North Pender Island collection pictured on the lead image for this article, the caps were 2–3 ½ cm wide, convex to plane, and sometimes umbonate. The surface was dry with pinkish-brick colored scales on a white to buff ground. Cap margins were often fringed with white velar remnants, and the caps did not stain when bruised. Neither did the free, white gills. The stems were a pale flesh color beneath the white, evanescent velar zone. There was no obvious ring, no color change when bruised. Odor and taste were unremarkable despite the opinion of Roux & Eyssartier that the odor is pleasantly fruity, like mandarine. The spores were white and dextrinoid, measuring 6–7.5 x 3.5–4.3 µm. The long, flexuous pileocystidia in this material had rather uniform lengths of 124–130 µm, whereas Helen Smith had measured some at 300 µm long in 1954.

It turns out that a number of small Lepiotas have the same amatoxins and phallotoxins as the deadly Amanitas. Else Vellinga sent me a letter stating that two Frenchmen, Gérault & Girre, screened 32 species of Lepiota for amanitins in 1975. They found that nine of them contained deadly toxins. These were **Lepiota subincarnata, L. josserandii, L. helveola, L. elaiophylla, L. brunneoincarnata, L. ochraceofulva, Lepiota brunneolilacea, L. pseudolilacea,** and **Cystolepiota hetieri**. Since the time of this discovery it has been ascertained that all species of Lepiota sensu stricto with ellipsoid spores and only long elements in the cap surface seem to have amatoxins. According to Dr. Vellinga these can be recognized by their tomentose caps and bands of the same material on their stipes. To avoid severe amatoxin poisoning, no small members of the Lepiotaceae should be eaten.

There are a number of look-alikes. In no particular order, they are:

Lepiota castanea: A small species with chestnut colored scales on the cap, a membranous ring on the rusty colored stems, and spores with short spurs. Also reported as toxic.

Lepiota scobinella: A larger species with a more darkly squamose cap surface.

Lepiota brunneoincarnata: Another dangerously poisonous species that differs by its purple-brown cap scales and longer spores.

Lepiota subgracilis (Kuehner): Differs by its much longer spores and gray-brown cap colors with just a tinge of pink.

Lepiota helveola: Another deadly species with orange-brown cap scales and a fringed cap margin. Found at Hoypus Point.

Lepiota kuehneri: Looks like **L. subincarnata** but has an all-white stem that narrows at the base and no odor.

Lepiota lilacea: Has an ample but fragile ring with a brick-colored underside and pale rose-brown scales on the cap surface.

Lepiota severiana: Another close look-alike that differs by having a strong odor of parsley as it dries, and cap margins adorned with raggedy bits of the rose-brown scales. Often found with locust trees.

Lepiota lepida: A Mediterranean species with concentric red-brown cap scales and a bright pinkish-orange tinge at the stem base.

Agaricus diminutivus & **Agaricus kerriganii**: Both of these good edibles have pallid gills at first that quickly become pinkish to grayish-flesh color. Leave them in the fridge overnight to make sure. The spores of both will be chocolate brown.

Echinoderma echinacea: Differs by its pointy dark red-brown scales on the cap and the pale chestnut-brown stem with warts below the ring.

Common in Europe, **Lepiota subincarnata** has been reported from Uganda on rotting wood, Kenya under conifers, China, Turkey, Israel, and Pakistan. It is often found in small groups in city parks, gardens, mixed woods, and even in mine waste heaps. A year after the discovery on North Pender Island, a few specimens showed up in my own yard in Bellingham under Norway spruce.

Even though they are considered saprotrophic, they seem to have an affinity for Norway spruce since they appear almost every fall in the Bow Cemetery, which is ringed by these conifers.

Finally, on behalf of our club, we would like to thank Else Vellinga for verifying the identification of the **Lepiota subincarnata** we found. She wrote, "as far as I can tell, it really is **Lepiota subincarnata** J. Lange. Spore sizes, cheilocystidia, and pileus covering all fit."

For anyone wanting to become better acquainted with this killer, check out the Bow Cemetery after a heavy rain in late October.

BIBLIOGRAPHY

Margit Babos, *Studies on Hungarian Lepiota Species IV* in *Annales Historico-Naturales Musei Nationalis Hungarici* 66 (67–75), 1974.

Marcel Bon, *Les Lepiotes* in *Flore Mycologique d'Europe* 3, 1993.

Alain Gerault & L. Girre, *Recherches Toxicologiques sur le Genre Lepiota Fries* in *Comptes Rendus Hebdomadaires des Séances de l'Academie des Sciences, Paris*, 1975.

Mustafa Isiloglu & Roy Watling, *Poisonings by Lepiota helveola Bres. in Southern Turkey* in *Edinburgh Journal of Botany* 48 (91–100), 1991.

Paul Kroeger, *Mycofile*, January 1989. Mycofile is the newsletter of the North American Mycological Assoc (NAMA).

Meinhard Moser, *Keys to Agarics and Boleti*, 1983. Translated and published by Roger Phillips, London.

M.E. Noordeloos, T.W. Kuyper, E.C. Vellinga (eds), *Flora Agaricina Neerlandica 5*, 2001. A.A. Balkema Publishers, Lisse.

David Pegler, A Preliminary Agaric Flora of East Africa, 1977. Her Majesty's Stationary Office, London.

Scott Redhead, *Letters to Mushroom* in *Mushroom the Journal*, Winter 1999–2000.

Helen Smith, *A Revision of the Michigan Species of Lepiota* in *Lloydia* 17 (307–328), 1954.

Else Vellinga, A. Razaq, A.N. Khalid, & S. Ilyas, *Lepiota brunneoincarnata and L. subincarnata: Distribution and Phylogeny* in *Mycotaxon* 126 (133–141), 2013.

Lepista nuda (Bulliard) Cooke

Blewits usually grow in arcs or rings, so if you find one, keep poking around.

From mid-October through November we can expect to find Blewits provided the weather is wet and mild. At about this time the last of the chanterelles are getting old and moldy, so it's nice to know an alternative lurks in the thickets. And "thickets" is no exaggeration. Whereas most woodland fungi prefer not to compete with brambles, sallal, and vine maple, the blewits seem to prefer these choked locations. Since whole colonies of **Lepista nuda** can hide under the fallen, broadleaf maple leaves, it can be a challenge to find them.

According to Arora, Blewits can thrive on almost any kind of organic debris from compost to shredded newspaper to elephant seal dung. Larry Stickney, the great mycophagist from San Francisco, has witnessed massive fruitings on piles of discarded coffee grinds near Manteca. And I've seen enormous specimens around 20 cm wide under eucalyptus, an acidic tree that most other North American fungi avoid like the plague. Blewits usually grow in arcs or rings, so if you find one, keep poking around.

Blewits are successfully cultivated in France. In their natural habitat they have an affinity for conifer duff, old sawdust piles, compost piles, hardwood leaf mulch, and humus rich earth. Commercially, they do well on 10% horse manure and straw compost after receiving a cold shock first.

Lepista nuda was the second wild mushroom I ever ate. They came up in the orchard of my uncle's farm in rural Maryland. He called them Purple Riders and expected to see them every year around Halloween. He always made time for them, even if it was peak harvest time at the farm.

The caps of **Lepista nuda** measure 4–20 cm wide and are convex to plane and broadly umbonate. The margins are inrolled at first, then uplifted in age. The surface is smooth and lubricous (buttery) when fresh, then shiny when dry. Cap colors vary from purple to purple gray, purple brown, or dark brown, fading to cinnamon buff in age. Margins usually remain purplish at maturity. They appear to be sensitive to light since specimens out in the open change colors dramatically. Gills are adnate to adnexed, sometimes short decurrent. They are purple to grayish purple fading to pinkish buff or brownish in age. Stems can run up to 10 cm long and 1–3 cm thick. They are equal or enlarged at the base, dry, fibrillose, and some shade of purple. The odor is fragrant, a bit like anise, or according to Arora, like frozen orange juice. The taste is mild to slightly bitter. The base of the stem is imbued with violet mycelium, and the spore deposit is pinkish buff.

Microscopically, the spores are elliptical and finely verrucose (spiny). They measure 5.5–8 x 3.5–5 µm. There are clamps at the bases of the basidia and also in the irregularly branched hyphae of the pileipellis.

In Europe, **Lepista nuda** favors beech thickets. They can be grown on sweepings of deciduous woods, and are now sold commercially in Europe and North America. A close relative, **Lepista personata**, was being sold in a Towson, Maryland, market for $39.95 a pound in June of 2009! They were marketed as "Blue Legs."

The blewit or Purple Rider is a highly successful species. It is found around the globe in temperate climates, and has been introduced to Australia and Tanzania in pine plantations.

In 1969, Dr. A.H. Smith and Dr. Howard Bigelow came out with a paper that transferred Lepista to Clitocybe. In essence they found so many characteristics that intergraded between the concepts of Clitocybe and Lepista that they simply made Lepista into

LOOK-ALIKE

Lepista nuda var. tridentina from Switzerland

LOOK-ALIKES

Lepista personata

Lepista tarda

Lepista glaucocana

a section of Clitocybe. In other words, they sank the genus Lepista.

The outcry in Europe could be heard in Japan. Tracts defending Lepista broke out in several languages. Even twenty years after this crime had been committed I heard more about the Lepista problem during my visit to Europe than any other aspect of American mycology.

"C'était un grand pas," a Swiss mycologist sadly informed me, "Mais en arrière." (It was a big step, only backwards.) In fact, several of his colleagues felt the transfer to Clitocybe represented the greatest step backwards in mycology of this century. The Brits were no less amused. The name Lepista was one of the oldest mycological traditions they had. They tiptoed around the genus at Kew as if concerned at waking the dead.

The French reaction was different.

"Lepista! Lepista!" they howled at me during the great fall show at Oyonnax in the French Alps in 1989. "You Americans...why have you killed Lepista, enh?"

No easy answer, even for the professionals. In fact I suspect one Scandinavian mycologist was so incensed that he sunk several of Bigelow's Clitocybes in retaliation.

As amateurs, we don't know how Lepista and Clitocybe intergrade microscopically but we think we can tell them apart in the field. There is a certain pleasant aroma and firmness and stipe texture associated with Lepista. The lubricous caps are another typical trait. There are subtle differences, easier to learn than describe. There are some Clitocybes, notably **Clitocybe nebularis** and **Clitocybe fragilipes** (Favre) that look like typical Lepistas, and at least one Lepista, **L. flaccida** (now in Paralepista), that looks like a thin-fleshed Clitocybe.

Smith and Bigelow tried to clear this up for us. The hallmarks of Lepista have been pinkish or yellowish spore deposits, roughened spores, and the presence of clamp connections. We learn in this article that they were originally treated as a section of Paxillus, but were elevated to genus status by Worthington Smith in 1870. Then, Maire, in 1913, created Rhodopaxillus to accommodate species with ornamented pinkish spores and no cystidia, including **Rhodopaxillus nudus.** Vagaries existed because neither Fries nor Worthington Smith had designated a type species originally. Perhaps as a result, W.G. Smith and Fries did not list the same species under Lepista. Rolf Singer finally solidified the Lepista group in *Agaricales in Modern Taxonomy.*

Bigelow and Smith concluded that Lepista and Clitocybe intergraded because two species of Clitocybe, **Gerhardtia highlandensis** and **Clitocybe pseudoirina,** have slightly ornamented spores. There was more crossover when the white-spored **Lepista flaccida** was discovered to have the same spore ornamentation as the pink-spored **Lepista subconnexa**. They concluded that spore ornamentation could not be used in separating the two

Cortinarius alboviolaceus

Cortinarius camphoratus

Cortinarius cupreorufus

Cortinarius variicolor

Cortinarius iodeoides   *Photo by Richard Morrison*

Cortinarius olympianus

genera. Gill attachment could not be used either. There was complete gradation from decurrent to sinuate in both Lepista and Clitocybe. Finally, spore color became a non-issue. They discovered that **Clitocybe nebularis, C. robusta, C. odora, C. catervata**, and **C. phyllophila** all had colored spores.

I don't know what arguments the Europeans used to refute these conclusions. DNA profiling eventually solved the issue. Lepista was validated by using **Lepista irina** for the tests in one phylogeny chart emailed to me by Joe Ammirati.

Here in Washington, Blewits have a number of lookalikes within and without the genus. Here they are in no particular order:

Panus conchatus: Although the cap colors can mimic those of **Lepista nuda**, the white gills and habit of fruiting on logs clearly separate them.

Lepista tarda: A smaller, thinner version of the blewit, but equally edible, is found locally around compost heaps, edges of gardens, and moldy straw.

Lepista glaucocana: This beautiful and uncommon Lepista is entirely pale grayviolet and has a frosted look.

Lepista nuda var. tridentina: From Europe, this rare variety has dark brown caps with a white fringe at the margin. Index Fungorum now lists it as a synonym of **Lepista nuda**.

Lepista personata: Differs by its more fawn colored caps that contrast more with its purple stem. It has slightly more verrucose spores, and according to Jairul Rahaman, a flavor reminiscent of lavender and vanilla.

Cortinarius camphoratus: Differs by having innately fibrillose caps, rusty spores, and a strong odor of garbage.

Cortinarius traganus: According to Moser it is the **var. odoratus** which often has an odor of pears. It further differs from the Blewit by its ochre to brownish gills when young that soon turn rusty from the spores. Daniel Winkler contends that it smells like raclette.

Cortinarius cupreorufus: This collection, found on the Evergreen College campus by Jack Waytz, differs by its ochre-fawn colored caps with violet margins and clavate-bulbous stem bases.

Cortinarius iodeoides: Differs from the blewit by its rusty spores, bitter cap pellicle, and viscid velar material.

Cortinarius variicolor: Differs by having gills and cap turn rusty-brown in age. Although eaten in parts of Europe, I have no data on its edibility here.

Cortinarius alboviolaceus: The rusty spores, silky gray-violet caps and whitish velar material on young stems separate it from the Blewit. The sample here was found by Jairul Rahaman at Coronet Bay.

Cortinarius cyanites: Differs by its rusty spores, appressed fibrillose cap surface, and purple gills that bruise red-violet when scratched.

Cortinarius occidentalis: An all-purple Cort with all parts turning more purplish lilac when bruised. Differs also by the flaring marginate basal bulb that tends to disappear in age.

All Corts have rusty spore prints. **Lepista nuda** does not. There are dozens of other purplish species of Cortinarius, but

Cortinarius traganus

Cortinarius cyanites

Cortinarius occidentalis

Panus conchatus, top and bottom

these mentioned here are the most likely to be found in our area. As for edibility they are in the "edibility unknown" category or gastro-intestinal irritants at best.

As for flavor, most mushroom guides give the Blewit high grades despite the slippery texture. Arora writes, "it has the dubious distinction of being one of the few purple foods that actually tastes good." In *Wild Food*, Roger Phillips notes that the strong perfumy odor persists in the cooking. Perhaps to capitalize on that odor, Jack Czarnecki offers a recipe with Blewits, butter, cream, onions, and Pernod. It's expensive but worth every penny.

Fortunately, Blewits can hold their own without the Pernod. Out of the blue I once got a call from Kathryne Minge, a lady in her eighties who was a member of Northwest Mushroomers but never went to a foray or a meeting. She lived on the north end of Lake Whatcom and wanted to know if I could identify the mushrooms in her yard. There were plenty, she said. I arrived to discover a massive fruiting of **Tricholoma imbricatum** all around her driveway.

"You won't eat those," I told her.

Undaunted, she then led me to the east side of the house, and there before me was a spectacular ring of **Lepista nuda** completely encircling an ancient fir. The caps were 10–12 cm wide, almost all in pristine condition.

"You eat one first," she told me. We harvested three or four of them and headed for the kitchen. To my extreme consternation, the only thing we had to cook them with was a stick of margerine. Luckily there was a little salt nearby. My mood elevated as the Blewits cooked down. A fabulous aroma took over the kitchen. When the liquid disappeared and they turned a bit brown, we removed them from the pan. I had to eat one and a half before she took her first bite. At this point she must have been wondering if she would get to eat one at all. They were just so good I could barely stop to talk. At the end she still looked a little dubious.

"I have a family gathering coming up," she said, "I'm not sure I can get them to eat these or not."

"Their loss, your gain," I told her. Either way, she would have plenty to spare.

Lincoff and Mitchel caution us to never eat the Blewits raw. According to Sartory and Maire they contain a thermolabile hemolysin that attacks red blood cells and is responsible for some minor poisonings. The same hemolysin is found in **Tricholoma saponaceum** and **Tricholoma sulphureum**. Luckily, the toxin is destroyed by cooking.

Finally, there is a factor known as idiosyncratic sensitivity syndrome. There have been reports of this syndrome with **Lepista nuda**. It means that there are cases where folks who have eaten the species for years with impunity, suddenly develop a sensitivity to it, and are sickened by it. The only defense might be smaller portions as you get older.

Ironically, cooked Blewits also have health benefits. Peter McCoy notes that they are high in vitamin B-1, support the nervous system, regulate blood sugar and metabolism, open the third eye, and treat headaches and insomnia. He added that they are anti-viral, anti-bacterial, anti-microbial, and anti-cancer.

If you introduced them to a toxic dump site, they would accumulate arsenic and mercury. We could perhaps use them to help clean up the waterfront in Bellingham.

Even more to the point, take the spore print before eating **Lepista nuda**. A belly full of **Cortinarius traganus** would be no fun at all.

BIBLIOGRAPHY

Joe Ammmirati, Tuula Niskanen, Kare Liimatainen, I. Kytovuori, B. Dima, & Tobias Froslev, *The Largest Type Study of Agaricales to Date: Bringing Identification and Nomenclature of Phlegmacium into the DNA Era* in *Persoonia* 33 (98–140), 2014.

David Arora, *Mushrooms Demystified*, 1986. Ten Speed Press, Berkeley, Calif.

Howard Bigelow & A.H. Smith, *The Status of Lepista—A New Section of Clitocybe* in *Brittonia* 21 (144–177), 1969.

J.Breitenbach & F. Kranzlin, *Fungi of Switzerland, Vol. 3*, 1991. Edition Mykologie, Lucerne, Switzerland.

Jose Antonio Cadinanos, *Cortinarius Subgenus Pghlegmacium—Raros o Interesantes in Fungi Non Delineati XXIX*, 2004.

Jack Czarnecki, *Joe's Book of Mushroom Cookery*, 1986. Atheneum, New York, NY.

E.A. Ellis, *British Fungi: Book 1*, 1986. Jarrold Colour Publications, Norwich, England.

Bruce Fuhrer, *A Field Companion to Australian Fungi*, 1985. The Five Mile Press, Hawthorn, Victoria, Australia.

Gary Lincoff & D.H. Mitchel, *Toxic and Hallucinogenic Mushroom Poisoning*, 1977. Van Nostrand Reinhold, New York, NY.

Peter McCoy, *Radical Mycology*, 2016. Chthaeus Press, Portland, Ore.

Meinhard Moser, *Keys to Agarics and Boleti*, 1983. Translated and published by Roger Phillips, London.

David Pegler, *A Preliminary Agaric Flora of East Africa, 1977*. Her Majesty's Stationary Office, London.

Roger Phillips, *Wild Food*, 1983. Little, Brown & Co., Boston, Mass.

Jean-Marie Polese, *Le Guide des Champignons des Alpes*, 2003. Tandem Verlag, Chamalieres, France.

Robert Rogers, *The Fungal Pharmacy*, 2011. North Atlantic Books, Berkeley, Calif.

A.H. Smith, *Studies in the Genus Cortinarius I* in *Contributions from the University of Michigan Herbarium 2*, 1939.

Linus Zeitlmayr, *Wild Mushrooms—An Illustrated Handbook,* 1955. Th. Knaur Nachf. Verlag, Munich, Germany.

— Digerness

Leucoagaricus leucothites (Vittadini) Wasser

Photo by Richard Morrison

No matter what you call it, Woman on Motorcycle presents a dilemma.

Leucoagaricus leucothites, a.k.a. Woman on Motorcycle, is a rather unfamiliar name for a very familiar mushroom. One of the three or four most common, fleshy lawn mushrooms in the Pacific Northwest, it has long been known as **Lepiota naucina**. In this case the name change is not due to DNA profiling, but rather by the board of the International Code of Botanical Nomenclature. They decided to push the starting date of fungal nomenclature back from the era of Fries and Persoon to a much earlier time. In this case, the **Agaricus leucothites** of Vittadini in 1835 preceded the **Agaricus naucinus** of Fries in 1838. The earlier name takes the priority. The species was moved to **Lepiota naucina** by Kummer in 1871 and subsequently to **Leucoagaricus leucothites** by Wasser in 1977.

No matter what you call it, Woman on Motorcycle presents a dilemma. Since it has free gills, white spores, and a ring on the stem, the perennial problem has been confusion with the deadly white Amanitas. The two dangerous white Amanitas in our area are **Amanita smithiana** and **Amanita silvicola**. The former differs from **Leucoagaricus leucothites** by having a very shaggy appearance about the cap and stem. The latter has a stouter stem with obvious volval remnants at the stem base. This is lacking in **L. leucothites**.

Nonetheless, encounters with Woman on Motorcycle can be nerve wracking. I remember cooking up a batch from my cousin's lawn in Maryland when I was in my twenties. We care-fully checked for the presence of a volva at the stem base before embarking on the macho sautée. We found the flavor mediocre at best. This appraisal may have been affected by the psychology involved. All through the meal we wondered if we had inadvertently left a volva behind in the ground. The sautée became less attractive the more we dwelled on it, and I have to confess, I haven't eaten one since.

On the other side of the coin there are those who have partaken of it and swear it is one of the best edibles they ever had. You don't want to miss out on something like this, so you spend time putting it into your basket, then out of your basket until finally you are rescued by the finding of **Agaricus campestris** in another part of your lawn.

Here, then, is a sampling of opinions from various sources: **Ellen Naylor** (a former NMA club member who moved back to Michigan): "A wonderful edible. One of my personal favorites."

LOOK-ALIKES

Agaricus campestris from Vermont

Agaricus arvensis

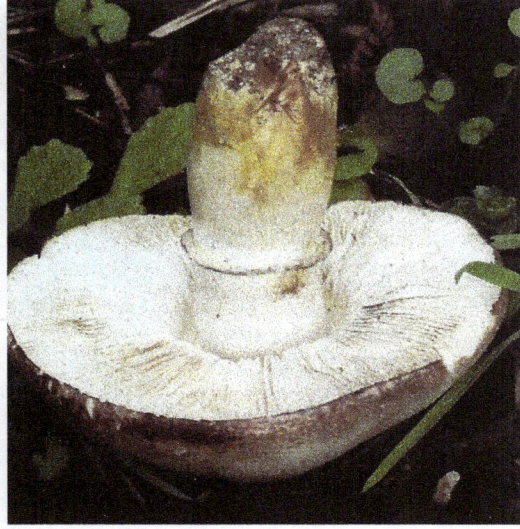

Lepiota leucothites sensu lato

Charles McIlvaine: "It was first reported as edible by Peck in 1875 under the name **Agaricus naucinus.** It rewards the favor by which it has been received as an esculent, being equal to the common mushroom (**Agaricus campestris**), and quite free from insects. Its cultivation as a marketable crop is possible and probable."

W.B. McDougall: "Just as good to eat as the store bought Agaricus. Its taste, even when uncooked, is mild and pleasant. The surface of the cap has a sort of kid leather quality which is unmistakable."

Ansel Stubbs: "A bushel of these fine mushrooms were gathered the first week of October on a golf course near Kansas City, and were enjoyed by several families."

Vincent Marteka: "The white Lepiota has caused mild to severe diarrhea in some people."

David Biek: "Edible and considered good by many. Sample a small amount at first because some people are sensitive to it."

Ammirati, Traquair, & Horgen: "Some people, who have eaten it for years, have been poisoned by it, which suggests more toxic strains exist."

Dr. Mike Beug, on his website entitled *Poisonous and Hallucinogenic Mushrooms* (http://academic.evergreen.edu/projects/mushrooms/), has a slightly different take on it. He notes that **Leucoagaricus leucothites** is often found along roads and in golf courses where pesticides have likely been sprayed. Since mushrooms tend to absorb and accumulate heavy metals and pesticides, gastrointestinal discomforts could arise from their ingestion.

Woman on Motorcycle is one of the first mushrooms to appear on your lawn with the autumn rains. It prefers grassy places along roads, golf courses and pastures, or even disturbed soils. The caps run from 4–15 cm wide and are nearly spherical at first, becoming convex to plane in age. They are usually white to cream color, sometimes tinged pinkish, straw color, or grayish at the disc. The texture is either smooth or with tiny, concolorous, bran-like scales. The gills are free, crowded, white at first, but soon becoming pinkish to grayish pink, and finally brown in age. The edges can be flocculose and often darker. Stems run up to 1 ½ cm thick and 5-15 cm long. They are pure white, glabrous, equal or with an enlarged clavate base. When handled they stain yellowish or brownish. They are reported to be stuffed at first, then hollow in age. The veil is a thick, membranous white ring on the stem, movable in age. Spores are white to very faintly pinkish. They are dextrinoid in Melzer's solution. Charles Horton Peck found the spores to measure 8–10 x 5–8 µm. European **L. naucina** had more globose spores, measuring

295

6–7 µm. Ammirati, Traquaire, & Horgen found spore sizes to be variable, but always thick-walled with an apical germ pore. Odor and taste are mild.

According to McIlvaine, one way to separate them from the deadly white Amanitas is to place a cap, gills facing down, on a hot frying pan. If it's an Amanita, the gills will remain white. If it's Woman on Motor-cycle, the gills will turn brown.

Leucoagaricus leuco-thites is a cosmopolitan spe-cies. Besides North America, it has been found all over Eu-rope, Australia, and even in the Usambara Mountains of Tan-zania.

The problem, of course, is how do we separate it from the deadly white Amanitas in the field? The main thing is to con-centrate on the stem base. The stem bases of **Leucoagaricus leucothites** are bald. Those of the Amanitas have some sort of volval material, either a sack-like cup or bands of velar tis-sue. It's rather important not to leave a separable volva behind in the lawn when you pick one. Here are the look-alikes, begin-ning with the species in Ama-nita:

Amanita ocreata: Probably the deadliest white Amanita on the West Coast, it associates with live oak in California, and extends up into Oregon. It dif-fers by having a large sac-like volva at the base of the stem.

Amanita smithiana: Differs by having a cottony to scaly cap surface, a more shaggy stipe, and a base that is often napiform and rooting below. It goes after the kidneys first.

Amanita silvicola: Differs by having cottony velar material

Amanita silvicola   *Photo by Richard Morrison*

Amanita mappa from Scotland   *Photo by Rod Tulloss*

around a marginate bulb at the stem base. Suspected of being poisonous.

Amanita bisporigera: A slender, deadly white Amanita from east of the Rockies, it differs by having 2-spored basidia and a rounded bulb at the base enveloped in a volval sac.

Amanita verna: A large white Amanita from the Northeast down

LOOK-ALIKES

Agaricus fissuratus

Agaricus micromegathus

Amanita bisporigera from Maryland

into West Virginia that differs by its larger spores and thick, saccate volva at the base of the stipe. Deadly.

Amanita virosa: Another large, deadly white Amanita headquartered in the southeast that has globose spores, a membranous sack at the stem base, and flesh that turns yellow in KOH.

Amanita muscaria var. alba: Differs by its bands of velar material at the stem base and pointy tan warts on the cap surface.

Amanita mappa: A slender species with white warts on the cap surface and a prominent basal bulb. Formerly known as **Amanita citrina var. alba** or just **Amanita citrina**.

Amanita vaginata var. alba: Differs by lacking a ring on the stem and having a volval sack that adheres to the stem base.

Amanita crenulata: A New England species of mixed coniferous woods that differs by its mealy to powdery volva at the stipe base. Cap discs are usually pale ochre.

Lepiota naucinoides s.l.: This large, fleshy version that has tan colored caps and stems that bruise brown when touched is found in flower pots. Sequencing showed it to be the same as 'normal' **L. leucothites.**

Leucoagaricus carneifolius: Differs by having gills that turn strongly rose colored in age.

Lepiota subvolvata: Differs by fruiting in sand dunes in Spain and by having a large marginate basal bulb along with a fugacious, delicate volva.

Lepiota schulzeri: A white Lepiota from the east coast with a basal bulb that is laterally bent. Probably not edible since it nailed Louis Krieger with gastrointestinal distress.

Tricholomella constricta: Formerly in the genus Calocybe, this European species differs by its adnexed gills and farinaceous odor.

Tricholoma albidum: An all white Tricholoma with roughly the same stature that differs by its sinuate gills with decurrent tooth.

Volvopluteus gloiocephalus: Differs by having pink spores, no ring, and a sack-like volva at the stem base. A photo of the white version can be seen as a look-alike of **Amanita phalloides**.

(Since several white-capped species of Agaricus can share the same lawns with Woman on Motorcycle, and also have free gills and velar material on their stems, I am adding a few here even though their gills will eventually turn chocolate from their spores.)

Agaricus micromegathus: A diminutive, thin-fleshed species that has an odor of anise or almonds and stains yellow when bruised. Edible but rarely collected.

Agaricus campestris: Often found socializing with Woman on Motorcycle, it can be separated right away by its pinkish gills that turn brown in age.

Agaricus arvensis: Differs by its often massive size, exquisite flavor, white caps with a propensity to stain yellow, and the skirt-like ring with a cogwheel pattern on the lower side.

Agaricus fissuratus: Also appears in lawns, but differs by its cogwheel pattern on the underside of the ring, the more straw colored caps in age, and

LOOK-ALIKES

Amanita vaginata var. alba

Amanita crenulata from Maine

Amanita mappa ss auct. southeast from Georgia

the white squamules on the stem below the ring.

Whether you opt for the breakfast sautée or not, it is always a treat to wake up after the first September rains and discover this lovely white mushroom all over your lawn. Miron Hard seems to have agreed. "It has the advantage over the meadow mushroom in that the gills retain their white color and do not pass from a pink to a repulsive black," he wrote.

Addendum - Sadly we have heard from Dr. Beug that one person who mistook Amanita bisporigera for Woman on Motorcycle has died.

Amanita smithiana

BIBLIOGRAPHY

Joe Ammirati, J.A. Traquair, & Paul Horgen, *Poisonous Mushrooms of the Northern United States and Canada*, 1985. University of Minnesota Press, Minneapolis, Minn.

David Arora, *Mushrooms Demystified*, 1986. Ten Speed Press, Berkeley, Calif.

Alan & Arleen Bessette, Bill Roody & Steve Trudell, *Tricholomas of North America*, 2013. University of Texas Press, Austin, Texas.

David Biek, *Mushrooms of Northern California*, 1984. Spore Prints, Redding, Calif.

Guillaume Eyssartier & Pierre Roux, *Le Guide des Champignons de France et Europe*, 2012. Editions Belin, Paris.

Nina Faubion, *Some Edible Mushrooms and How to Cook Them*, 1972. Binfords & Mort, Portland, Ore.

Miron Hard, *Mushrooms, Edible and Otherwise*, 1908. Dover Publications, New York, NY.

David L. Hawksworth, *Mycologist's Handbook*, 1974. Commonwealth Mycological Institute, Surrey, England.

Lexemuel Hesler, *Notes on Southern Appalachian Fungi—XI* in *Journal of the Tennessee Academy of Science* 29, No.3 (205–219), 1954.

David T. Jenkins, Amanita of North America, 1986. Mad River Press, Eureka, Calif.

Louis C.C. Krieger, *The Mushroom Handbook*, 1967. Dover Publications, New York, NY.

Vincent Marteka, *Mushrooms: Wild and Edible*, 1980. W.W. Norton & Co., New York, NY.

W.B. McDougall, *Mushrooms*, 1925. Houghton Mifflin Co., Boston, Mass.

Charles McIlvaine & Robert Macadam, *One Thousand American Fungi*, 1902. Dover Publications, New York, NY.

David N. Pegler, *A Preliminary Agaric Flora of East Africa*, 1977. Her Majesty's Stationary Office, London.

Helen V. Smith, *A Revision of the Michigan Species of Lepiota* in *Lloydia* 17 (307–328), 1954.

Ansel Stubbs, *Wild Mushrooms of the Central Midwest*, 1971. University Press of Kansas, Lawrence, Kansas.

Melanoleuca verrucipes (Fries) Singer

The odor itself is complex, outperforming even wines in subtlety.

It was June 1, 1998, and we had been invited to a barbecue in a new subdivision north of Lake Whatcom in Bellingham. When we arrived at the Stein residence, four-year-old Claire led me to the back of the house where flowers were pushing up out of new mulch along the base of the wall. The flowers were interspersed with medium sized white mushrooms with black scabers on their stems. They looked like slender Tricholomas with Leccinum type stipes. I had never seen anything like them. Children are lower to the ground and often see mushrooms before adults do. Here was the prime example! Another odd feature of these specimens was the sticky, gelatinous stem base. Each bulbous stem base had a gelatinized sheath. In the photo you can see the dirt clinging to it, showing that the lower part of the stem had been underground.

Stuff like this eats away at you. I drove around for weeks thinking about it. There was nothing like it in American literature. When my wife finally said, "Whom are you talking to now?," I knew it was time to move on.

The mystery was solved three years later with the arrival of the October 2001 issue of *Field Mycology*. This is a British publication I had just started subscribing to. There, in an article by Alick Henrici, was a photo of the very same species. I discovered that until recently, **Melanoleuca verrucipes** was considered a rare species of roadsides and meadows in remote mountains of central Europe. But it was now on the move and could be found at sea level in mulch beds in Germany, Holland, and now Kew Gardens in England. If you were a mushroom and wanted to be noticed, this would be a good choice of location. As Geoffrey Kibby informed me, "This is suddenly a highly successful mushroom." Since its first low altitude record in Germany in 1982, **Melanoleuca verrucipes** has been found by Hongo & Imazeki in Japan, and by Dr. Redhead in Olympia, Washington, in 1993. Brandon Matheny and Paul Kroeger have also found it in urban settings, where Paul calls it "an alien invader."

The caps of this collection were 3–10 cm wide, convex to plane with wavy, incurved margins. The surface was smooth, dry, and areolate due to dry weather. The context was fleshy, white. Gills were adnexed to sinuate, white. Edges entire and lamellulae plentiful. Stems were 1–2 ½ cm thick and 4–6 ½ cm long. They were tough, whitish, longitudinally ridged, and sparsely coated with dark brown to blackish scabers. They tapered at mid-stipe before expanding to incrassate at base. Stem bases were encased in a grayish to isabelline gelatinous sheath to which dirt clung to with such tenacity that even a faucet rinse could not dislodge it. Some of the stem bases had coarse tan mycelium. The odor was soapy and slightly fetid. The taste was sweetish but astringent. The spores were white and amyloid in Melzer's. They were found scattered in disturbed mulch in a flowerbed.

European descriptions describe the caps as obtusely umbonate and buff to pale grayish ochre with a pale brown center. The texture is dull silky to velvety. The gills can be adnate to short decurrent. The stems can range to 10 cm long and be subfibrillose rather than longitudinally ridged. Nowhere is there a mention of the gelatinized base, a strong character in my estimation.

Microscopically, spores were elliptical, finely verrucose, and measured 8.4–10 x 4.3–5.5 µm. The cheilocystidia appeared to be variable. Some were subcapitate and septate. Others were narrowly lanceolate with bald apices. And still others were urticoid with crystals at the apices, a rare type of cystidia known as the "stinging hair" variety because they resemble the stinging hairs of nettles. The pileipellis was a non-differentiated cutis of radially parallel hyphae. The stipitipellis was adorned with branched and knobby ventricose caulocystidia up to 21 µm in width. The scabers on the stem were brown in KOH, and subglobose to clavate. And finally the stem base consisted of entangled and branched hyphae 2.2–7.2 µm wide in a gelatinized zone. No clamps were seen.

So far, no one seems to have eaten it. The odor itself is complex, outperforming even wines in subtlety. Marcel Bon thought it to be fruity or mealy-earthy. Duhem & Courtecuisse likened it to coumarin or new mown hay. Moser thought it fruity like aniseed or cheese. Breitenbach & Kranzlin found it to be like anise or bitter almonds changing to fruity or like cheese rind in age. And Boekhout likened it to anise with an unpleasant component. With such a wide selection of odors it would be a challenge to find the right wines for it.

Melanoleuca verrucipes, the Warty Footed Melanoleuca, has appeared on soil, dung, wood chips, or compost heaps in gardens, parks, roadsides, and meadows. There doesn't seem to be any other species it can be confused with. After DNA sequencing, ITS double peaks produced this result: the collection here was a 100% match with European **Melanoleuca verrucipes**.

The bigger question may be how does an uncommon mushroom of central European mountains suddenly evolve into a global fungal weed in just two decades. The change in altitude and habitat is so stark that maybe we shouldn't be surprised that new features have sprouted as well.

BIBLIOGRAPHY

Teun Boekhout, *Melanoleuca in Flora Agaracina Neerlandica, Vol. 4,* 1999.

Marcel Bon, *The Mushrooms and Toadstools of Britain and Northwestern Europe,* 1987. Hodder & Stoughton, London.

J. Breitenbach & F. Kranzlin, *Fungi of Switzerland, Vol. 3,* 1991. Edition Mykologie, Lucerne, Switzerland.

Regis Courtecuisse & Bernard Duhem, *Mushrooms and Toadstools of Britain and Europe,* 1992. Harper-Collins, London.

Alick Henrici, *Notes and Records in Field Mycology 2 (4)*, October, 2001.

Rokuya Imazeki, Tsuguo Hongo, & Keisuke Tubaki, Coloured Illustrations of Fungi of Japan, 1957. Hoikusha Publishing Co., Osaka, Japan.

Walter Julich & Meinhard Moser, Colour Atlas of Basidiomycetes, 1995. Gustav Fischer Verlag, Stuttgart, Germany.

Calvin Kauffman, *The Genus Clitocybe in the United States* in *Papers of the Michigan Academy of Science, Arts, and Letters 8 (153–214)*, 1927.

Till Lohmeyer & Ute Kunkele, *Les Champignons*, 2006. Parragon, Bath, England.

Meinhard Moser, *Keys to Agarics and Boleti,* 1983. Translated and published by Roger Phillips, London.

Jean-Marie Polese, *The Pocket Guide to Mushrooms*, 2005. Tandem Verlag, Chamalieres, France.

Svengunnar Ryman & Ingmar Holmasen, *Svampar*, 1984. Interpublishing AB, Stockholm, Sweden.

Jan Vesterholt, *Melanoleuca in Funga Nordica*, 2008. Nordsvamp, Copenhagen.

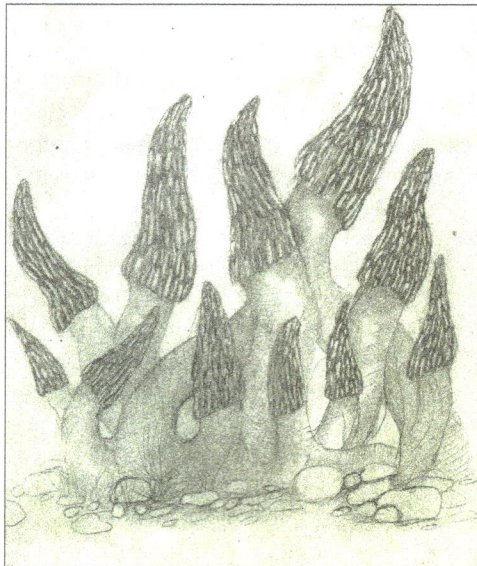

Morchella snyderi Kuo & Methven

The deeply ridged or lacunose stems are a strong indication for Morchella snyderi.

"Morels have long been so sought after and have such an affinity for burn areas that the practice of slashing and burning to produce a morel crop the next year was banned by royal decree in medieval Germany." This quote was posted by George Ellison online in the Smoky Mountain News. It tells you to what extremes people have gone to get their morels from probably time immemorial. Entire books have been written on how to find them, how to cook them, or how to preserve them. Until quite recently there were only a few Latin names to choose from, and each author could feel free to select any of them according to his personal bias. This was almost foolproof because it was generally thought they were all the same microscopically. But then came DNA.

Morel nomenclature is going through a tumultuous time. Both Michael Kuo from Illinois and Philippe Clowez from France produced independently new keys for a greatly expanded vision of the genus Morchella. DNA profiling has backed them up. Fortunately for the world of morel aficionados, they hadn't quite gone to press with their final versions. This allowed time for Kerry O'Donnell, Kuo's DNA expert, to get over to France to compare Kuo's findings with those of Clowez. At the time of this writing, we still don't know how it will play out. According to Clowez there is lots of fine tuning left, mainly to analyze significant collections from the past.

What we do know is that Kuo & Methven's **Morchella snyderi** did survive the amalgamation with Clowez's collections. It keys out in Kuo's *Revision of Morchella Taxonomy*, 2012, to **Morchella snyderi** because of its blackish ridges in age, the lacunose stems, and the fact that it was found in the eastern Cascade Mountains among mountain conifers in a non-burn site. The new Franco–American morel key, when it does arrive, will lean heavily on geographical location and substrate, including tree association. After that will probably come a dazzling array of ghost species, i.e., those species that share the same micro and macro morphologies but differ radically in DNA.

The collection pictured here in the main photo was found at Salmon Le Sac in eastern Washington in late May of 1985. We know that it is a true Morchella because the species is entirely hollow and the bottom of the cap attaches directly to the stem. Roger Phillips, Nicky Foy, and Dan Digerness were with me at the time. Some of the same specimens in this photo also appeared in Roger's *Mushrooms of North America*

Left to right: Dan Digerness, Buck McAdoo, and Roger Phillips near Cle Elum Ridge in 1985.   Photo by Nicky Foy

Morchella importuna from Bellingham

on page 301. Here, he presents them under the name **Morchella elata**, almost a generic term for the western black morel at the time. DNA sequencing has now shown that the original **Morchella elata** from Sweden has a different DNA from our Pacific West Coast version, which is mainly found in wood chip mulch and is now called **Morchella importuna**.

The largest morel in this cover photo of **M. snyderi** was 10 cm tall. The range for **Morchella snyderi** is 6–14 cm tall. Caps had deep, irregularly vertical pits of a paler brown color with dark brown to black ridges, a sign that these were mature specimens. The species is supposed to have 16–22 primary vertical ridges with much fewer sunken horizontal ridges. Stems were deeply furrowed and expanded at the bases, and the cap margins formed a small ridge before joining the stems. This "ridge" is now called a sinus. The sinus for **M. snyderi** is noted as 2–4 mm wide and 2–4 mm deep. The stems in this collection were granular to finely tomentose, and hollow with chambered bases in age. The deeply ridged or lacunose stems are a strong indication for **Morchella snyderi**. The spores of **M. snyderi** measure 25–37 x 15–23 μm, which are among the largest in the genus.

There may be several burn site look-alikes in the eastern Cascades. One of these is **Morchella eximia**, pictured here. Some appear darker than these depending on local conditions. They can have white stems or stems with a pinkish flush. One of the main issues with these burn site morels is whether to rinse off the carbon powder or brush it off prior to cooking. Opinions seem to run fifty-fifty on this procedure.

There have always been two basic groups of morels— the Elata group and the Esculenta group. The Elata group is composed of the dark morels while the Esculenta group holds the blonde morels. **Morchella snyderi** appears with the black morels in the Elata group.

According to Michael Kuo the taxonomic situation surrounding the black morels has traditionally centered around **Morchella elata**, **Morchella conica**, and **Morchella angusticeps**. **Morchella elata** was introduced by Elias Fries from Sweden in 1822. Beyond the problem of the lost type, the original description was so cursory that even finding a neotype would be problematic. The history of **Morchella conica** offers no relief. Kuo tells us that there is no type (that is, the original specimen representing the species concept), and the original 19th century description is so inadequate that it is not clear whether a black or blonde morel was the type. It is interesting to note that the *Index Fungorum* lists **Morchella conica** as synonym of **Morchella vulgaris**. This name emerges from **Morchella es-**

culenta var. vulgaris in 1801. It is indeed an earlier starting date than **Morchella conica** Persoon of 1818, but how can a blonde morel have a dark variety unless other factors were at play?

Phylogenetic studies conducted in 2014 finally highlighted **Morchella conica** as a *nomen dubium*, a loose canon used over centuries for both dark and blonde morels, including even **Morchella esculenta**. The authors concluded the name should be forever retired from use.

The third black morel name used often in North America is **Morchella angusticeps** Peck, introduced in 1879 from West Albany, New York. Unlike the first two names, there is an actual type to go by, and an authentic deposit in a herbarium. Perhaps because of this rare authenticity, this is the only black morel name that Dr. Nancy Weber recognizes for North America in her book, *A Morel Hunter's Companion*. Peck had separated it from **Morchella conica** and from **Morchella elata** by spore size and by shape of paraphyses. However, microscopic characters among morels were more variable than Peck supposed. Perhaps more damaging is that he failed to provide a cap color. A watercolor of it shows a morel with yellowish pits and pale ridges. This did nothing to deter Seaver, who re-described the species in 1928 with smoky brown pits and black ridges. Most popular guides describe **Morchella angusticeps** as having narrower caps than those of **M. conica** and **M. elata**, and a cap margin that

Morchella eximia

merges evenly with the stipe, not forming a ridge or sinus where they meet up.

At this point in time we don't know how many new names of morels there will be for North America. In his most recent key to the species, Kuo starts off by dividing them by color of ridges, the black ridged ones compared to those with rufescent or yellowish ridges. But then it turns out that each of these genetically distinct species can have a variable appearance according to age of specimens or what kind of soil it was found on. It just underlines how complicated the sorting of the morels remains.

One species not mentioned in anyone's key is **Morchella canaliculata**. It was described by the McKnights as a **Morchella angusticeps** look-alike that fruited in the same places. Even the *Index Fungorum* makes no mention of it.

We have probably not seen the end of new names. Cris Colburn, our former long-time club treasurer, once returned to our Morel Madness base camp with an all-black morel with a smooth stem. This was in April, 2010. It was diminutive and about to rot. My first thought was to get it to Dr. Nancy Weber before it rotted further. So I stuck it in the cooler for the 3-hour drive back to Bellingham. By the time I reached home, the ice had melted, and the specimen was floating in water. Later, Nancy reported that she had been hard pressed to find a spore.

Traditionally, the dark morels of Europe have been called either **Morchella elata** or **Morchella conica**. While most experts were content to describe the differences between them, one expert was so frustrated by their contradictions that he described ten new species, four new varieties, and six new forms in his book, *Les Morilles*, published in Lausanne in 1984. This was Emile Jacquetant.

LOOK-ALIKES

Morchella americana

Verpa bohemica

His book is now out of print. The *Index Fungorum* has no record of five of his new species and claims that the rest were invalidly published, citing Article 37.1 of the Code of International Botanical Nomenclature. This article states that names are invalid if types are not indicated. By omitting to name a type for each collection, Jacquetant prevented 20 new morel names from being admitted to the literature.

However, he has not been ignored. Philippe Clowez has resurrected some of his species after much DNA sequencing of his own. It reminds me of that classic phrase: the road to perfection is always under construction.

As for perfection, there are ways to bring forth the earthy, unique flavor of the morel. Jack Czarnecki, author of *Joe's Book of Mushroom Cookery*, suggests that a low heat method should

be used when sautéing morels. A typical recipe would commence with sautéing sliced onions in butter over medium heat for one minute. You would then add the morels and cook another minute. Then you would turn the heat down to low and cook uncovered until water begins to be released. At this point raise the heat to simmer and continue until all water has evaporated. Now you can add the final ingredients. The Czarneckis use salt, sugar, and soy sauce to maximize the morel flavor. Or they might add chopped green or red peppers or caraway seeds. These are flavors that support the morel flavor instead of dominating it.

There are things to watch out for. You don't want to pick specimens that have desiccated in the field even if they had been in their prime before the heat wave struck. They are worthless in the frying pan. Czarnecki further advises us to check our morels carefully when buying them commercially. Signs of moisture in a box could indicate the morels have begun to rot from the center of the box outward. Also, if you purchase dried morels, check for worm holes. "This means you will have large numbers of tiny bugs crawling out of them during reconstitution."

Probably no mushrooms reconstitute better from dried specimens than morels and boletes. You can also cook them after they have been frozen. There is a toxin in all morels that disappears upon cooking. According to Robert Dale Rogers, "morels contain small amounts of hemolysins, which destroy red blood cells;

however these are destroyed by cooking." He further reports that ripe black morels have large amounts of beta-alanine. "This is a compound found in hydrolized human hair." We know that some people are allergic to morels even after cooking. Others report stomach upsets if they mix alcohol with morels.

The greatest mass poisoning in mushroom history occurred when 77 out of 483 people became ill simultaneously from eating black morels. This took place in Vancouver, British Columbia, on June 8, 1991, at one of the best hotels in the city. The name of the hotel was not revealed in the original article for legal reasons. The victims had all convened to honor a retiring police chief. The first course consisted of morels and shiitakes marinated in soy sauce, sesame oil, sambal sauce, and oyster sauce before being mixed with egg fettucini. The morels were served raw. Within about ten minutes the guests were competing for the few public toilets that could be found. "Worshipping at the ceramic shrines" was the way Dr. Denis Benjamin described the scene.

The breakdown on the effects of the raw morels was interesting. Only 24 of the victims were rounded up for a survey. About half of them had reported consuming alcohol. Twenty of them reported nausea within 15–30 minutes. Sixteen of them reported diarrhea beginning 6 ½ hours later and lasting from 20 minutes to 13 hours. Twelve reported vomiting after half an hour had passed. The bouts of vomiting

LOOK-ALIKES

Gyromitra esculenta   *Photo by Richard Morrison*

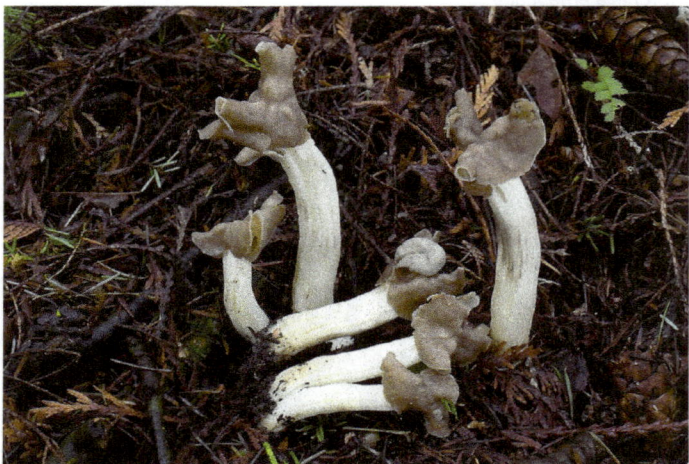

Helvella maculata   *Photo by Richard Morrison*

lasted from 20 minutes to one hour. Seven reported cramps. Four reported a rapid and severe sensation of bloating. Two reported a hives-like rash. The only person hospitalized was the man who ate his wife's portion also.

As for look-alikes, **Verpa bohemica** along with several Gyromitras and Helvellas have long been known as the False Morels.
Verpa bohemica: Differs from the true morels by having skirt-like caps with bases free from their stems. It is considered edible with caution. Trace toxins can accumulate the more you partake of the species and one day snare you with gastrointestinal problems.
Gyromitra esculenta: Differs by having lobed and irregularly folded caps, not the pits and ridges of the morels. It is reputed to contain monomethylhydrazine, an ingredient used in rocket fuel. Paul Kroeger notes that it is also carcinogenic, causing liver cancer. If cooked without parboiling, it raises toxic fumes over your

frying pan. Gyromitran poisoning can begin with bloating, nausea, vomiting, and diarrhea. It can end with jaundice, delirium, convulsions, coma, liver and kidney failure, and death. Charlie Volz, a former member of the Pacific Northwest Key Council, always parboiled it before eating it. He preferred the flavor to morels. He has since passed away, but not due to gyromitran poisoning. Since it has caused deaths in Europe, it cannot be recommended here.

Helvella maculata: Differs from morels by having longitudinally grooved stems and convoluted to saddle-shaped caps. Edibility unknown for this one, but its close relative, **Helvella vespertina**, is considered edible and bland.

The mycologist, S.M. Zeller, once found morels up to 28 cm tall along a fencerow in Corvallis, Oregon. He was so moved by this vision of what he called **Morchella elata** that he broke into myco lyrics, writing "ascoma are conical, hollow, of two distinct layers, covered by a deep, lacunose hymenial tissue with longitudinal ribs netted between, with very large lacunae having secondary labyrinthine folds extending to the cap tissue within."

Maybe we can ignore cap color. The only morel that reaches this size in Kuo and associates' new key is **Morchella esculentoides**, now called **Morchella americana.**

At breakfast recently with my cousin Rob Deford of Boordy Vineyards, I was expounding on the paradox of all the new possibilities from DNA studies with few types in Europe to compare them with.

"You shouldn't be worried," he said, "As long as you have the butter, the cream, and the wine."

BIBLIOGRAPHY

Joe Ammirati, J.A.Traquair, & Paul Horgen, *Poisonous Mushrooms of the Northern United States and Canada*, 1985. University of Minnesota Press, Minneapolis, Minn.

David Arora, *Mushrooms Demystified*, 1986. Ten Speed Press, Berkeley, Calif.

Denis Benjamin, *Mushrooms—Poisons and Panaceas*, 1985. W.H. Freeman, New York, NY.

Regis Courtecuisse & Bernard Duhem, *Mushrooms and Toadstools of Britain and Europe*, 1995. Harper-Collins, London.

Jack Czarnecki, *Joe's Book of Mushroom Cookery*, 1986. Atheneum, New York, NY.

Henry Dissing & Finn-Egil Eckblad, *Pezizales in Nordic Macromycetes, Vol. 1*, 2000. Nordsvamp, Copenhagen.

David L. Hawksworth, *Mycologist's Handbook*, 1974. Commonwealth Mycological Institute, Surrey, England.

Emile Jacquetant, *Les Morilles*, 1984. Editions Piantanida, Lausanne, Switzerland.

Paul Kirk (ed.), *Index Fungorum*, http://www.indexfungorum.org/names/Names.asp

Paul Kroeger, *"Yumm!" Said the Police Chief* in *Mushroom the Journal*, Issue 33, Vol. 9, No. 4, Fall, 1991.

Michael Kuo, *Morels*, 2005. University of Michigan Press, Ann Arbor, Mich.

Michael Kuo, Damon Dewsberry, Kerry O'Donnell, M. Carol Carter, Stephen Rehner, John David Moore, Jean-Marc Moncalvo, Stephen Canfield, Steven Stephenson, Andrew Methven, & Thomas Volk, *Revision of Morchella Taxonomy* in *Mycologia*, 2012.

Kent & Vera McKnight, *Peterson Field Guides—Mushrooms*, 1987. Houghton Mifflin Co., Boston.

Franck Richard, Jean-Michel Bellanger, Philippe Clowez, Regis Courtecuisse, Karen Hansen, Kerry O'Donnell, Mathieu Sauve, Alexander Urban, & Pierre-Arthur Moreau, *True Morels of Europe and North America: Evolutionary Relationships Inferred from Multilocus Data and a Unified Taxonomy* in *Mycologia* 106 (14–166), 2014.

Roger Phillips, *Mushrooms of North America*, 1991. Little, Brown & Co., Boston.

Nancy Weber, *A Morel Hunter's Companion*, 1988. Two Peninsula Press, Lansing, Mich.

Samuel L. Zeller, *Contributions to Our Knowledge of Oregon Fungi—II* in *Mycologia* 19 (130–143), 1927.

The Odd Couple: *Morchella sp. & Geopyxis carbonaria*

*Where does one end and
where does the other start?*

One of the advantages of writing a club oriented mushroom guide is that we can showcase unusual finds brought in by club members. Nothing we have seen yet seems more unusual than this merger of morel with Pyxie Cup. The specimens were brought in by Eric Swisher from the annual May Morel Madness foray in the Lake Wenatchee area of eastern Washington in 2002. This is not a doctored photo. As Eric speculated, "where does one end and where does the other start?" Is nature trying to graft a new genus, the Morchellyxis? Does the flavor of the morel affect the flavor of the Pyxie Cup (a Gary Lincoff term) in a positive way or vice versa?

One wonders if this is a saprophytic arrangement or a symbiotic one. The two species are still recognizable as distinct entities although both are smaller than typical, and the exterior cup surface of the Geopyxis is not normally all white. Since morels can form sclerotia, is it possible that they form a new substrate for the Geopyxis? I could find nothing in the literature about this phenomenon, but flail away I will.

One interesting question is since the Geopyxis is fruiting from the same stem as the Morchella, which mycelium is providing the nutrients? Are both species stunted by the competition? It appears that both are feeding off the soil and therefore not parasitizing each other. What we are seeing is most likely a random event where the mycelium of both species became entangled. Still, what are the odds that both species would fruit simultaneously?

Geopyxis carbonaria is a common burn site discomycete, goblet shaped with a slender stem. The interior hymenial surface can vary in color from yellowish cardboard to brick-brown. The exterior surface is usually the same color but paler. The margin of the cup is white, and crenulate or toothed. The stem, often buried in the substrate, is thin and white.

Microscopically the spores are housed in an ascus with a lid at the apex. These types of ascomycetes are called "operculates." The ascus carries eight spores, and when they are ready to be discharged, the ascus swells, causing the lid to open from the pressure, which allows the spores to escape. The spores of this Geopyxis were elliptical, smooth-walled, and eguttulate, meaning without an oil drop in the context. They measured 11.4–14.3 x 5.7–7.4 µm, a bit narrower than typical

for the species. The paraphyses, which are long, slender, sterile cells interspersed with the asci, were septate (had cross walls), and sported little knobs and protuberances at the apices, which was appropriate for the species.

At this point Dr. Fred Rhoades suggested I check out Dr. Tom Volk's website. As you may know, mushroom growers had been thwarted for centuries in their attempts to grow morels in cultivation. A researcher by the name of Ron Ower was finally able to achieve this. After intensive study of the morel life cycle, Tom Volk refined Ower's technique, and was able to produce them himself. This eventually led to a move by Domino's Pizza to take out a patent for morels on their pizzas. However, biology doesn't always cooperate with big business, and so far I have not seen a morel on one of their pizzas. But the Tom Volk web site was enlightening.

In brief, the life cycle starts with a mature morel. After a good rain, the asci swell and the spores are released. If they land on friendly soil, they begin to germinate tiny knobs, which gradually extend into a maze of interwoven hyphae called the primary mycelium. The mycelium then forms little knots of tissue known as a sclerotium composed of large cells with very thick walls. According to Tom, this enables the morel to survive a harsh winter. Dr. Nancy Weber verifies the sclerotium but believes the morel creates one only when adverse conditions warrant it. She also believes the sclerotium stores nutrients for the fruiting body. Once the sclerotium is formed it can either give birth to a fruiting body or produce another mass of hyphae called the secondary mycelium. One of the problems encountered in cultivation is that the second option is far more likely to occur than the first. Tom mentions that other complexities also hinder the creation of a morel.

Therefore the odds must be astounding for a Geopyxis to fruit simultaneously with a successful morel. Since Geopyxis doesn't have to produce a sclerotium to fruit, it may be easier to cultivate. Perhaps Domino's Pizza should revisit the possibilities. Bits of **Geopyxis carbonaria** with the morel flavor might be just as attractive.

Addendum: Since composing this article, Peter McCoy discovered that morels can produce edible sclerotia on grains, and that during cultivation they need a "cold period and a passage through a nutrient poor zone."

BIBLIOGRAPHY

J. Breitenbach & F. Kranzlin, *Fungi of Switzerland, Vol. 1*, 1984. Edition Mykologia, Lucerne, Switzerland.

Gary Lincoff, *The Audubon Society Field Guide to North American Mushrooms*, 1981. Alfred A. Knopf, New York, NY.

Peter McCoy, *Radical Mycology*, 2016. Chthaeus Press, Portland, Ore.

Fred Seaver, *North American Cup Fungi*, 1928. Self-published, New York, NY.

Edmund Tylutki, *Mushrooms of Idaho and the Pacific Northwest: Discomycetes*, 1979. University Press of Idaho, Moscow, Idaho.

Tom Volk, *http://botit.botany.wisc.edu/toms_fungi/morel.html*.

Nancy Weber, *A Morel Hunter's Companion*, 1988. Two Peninsula Press, Lansing, Mich.

Mycena galericulata (Scopoli) S.F. Gray

"No other species has been so frequently misidentified in North America as Mycena galericulata."

There is something about this particular taxon that grabs my attention whenever I see it. Despite the rather drab coloration of caps and stems, I can scarcely pass it by without shooting another photo of it. **Mycena galericulata** fruits throughout the spring and fall in the Pacific Northwest, and sometimes in the winter if the weather is mild. But no matter what the season I invariably get fooled into thinking I am seeing it for the first time. Called the Common Mycena by Gary Lincoff or the Cowl Mycena by Frederick Clements, it is only when I have returned to my lab that it dawns on me that I've captured yet another subtle variation of the same entity.

First off, it is much larger than a typical Mycena. Secondly, the caps have inrolled margins at first, which is more of a Collybioid trait than a Mycenoid one. Thirdly, the cap colors vary from gray to tan to pale brown to cinnamon-gray to just plane brown. And fourthly, the caps change shape from obtusely conic to plane with an umbo as the fruiting bodies mature.

It seems others have been fooled as well. Murrill once described it as **Collybia dentata**. Kauffman introduced it as **Collybia rugulosiceps.** And Peck described it under the name **Collybia ligniaria**. All of the above plus others prompted A.H. Smith to write, "no other species has been so frequently misidentified in North America as **Mycena galericulata**." R.A. Maas Geesteranus, the late, great Dutch Mycena expert, looking at a world view of the species, discovered that **M.**

Mycena maculata   *Photo by Fred Rhoades*

Mycena overholtsii

Mycena quinaultensis

314

LOOK-ALIKES

Mycena clavicularis

Mycena robusta

Mycena stipata

galericulata had 37 synonyms not beginning with the genus Agaricus.

The caps of **Mycena galericulata** measure 2–6 cm wide. They are roughly conical at first becoming flattened out to convex or plane with or without an obtuse umbo. They are radially rugulose (finely wrinkled) with barely striate margins, and so cartilaginous that they frequently split from margin to disc. The surface is smooth, lubricous, but not viscid. Cap colors vary in many shades of gray to brown, usually darker at the disc. Gills are adnexed, generally subdistant, and strongly intervenose. They are white to pallid gray often flushed with pale pink in age. Stems are 2–5 mm thick and 5–12 cm long. They are grayish white above becoming brownish towards the base. Hollow, cartilaginous, smooth to twisted striate, they become matted hairy at the base which often roots deeply into the rotten hardwoods they are found upon. Odor and taste are farinaceous to radish-like. Spores are white and amyloid in Melzer's. They are often found in compact clusters at the bases of rotten hardwood stumps, but have been found in lawns above buried wood.

Microscopically, the basidia can be 2 or 4-spored. The spores are ellipsoid and measure 8–10 x 5.5–7 μm. The sterigmata are stout, and the cheilocystidia are shaped like clubs with numerous finger-like projections.

Found all through the United States, Europe and Canada, Japan, Iceland, Kashmir, Sikkim, and even in the Murree

Hills of West Pakistan, the Cowl Mycena is truly cosmopolitan in range. The type, originally from a region called Krain between Austria and Yugoslavia, has been lost, so a neotype was selected from the same area.

Although most folks don't bother to collect Mycenas for the table, **M. galericulata** is large enough and often numerous enough to warrant attention. Both Ansel Stubbs and W.B. McDougall found it to be a good edible, Stubbs discarding the stems as too tough to eat. McIlvaine thought highly of it, writing "the caps and stems when young make as good a dish as one cares to eat. The substance is pleasant and the flavor delicate. They are best served in their own fluids, after washing, for ten minutes, and seasoned with salt, pepper, and butter."

After reading this endorsement I felt obliged to try it. I found a big break at Cowichan Lake, B.C., and took them back to my galley about three days later. I fried up about 12 caps in butter until crisp. They were an excellent bacon substitute for my medium boiled egg. There was just a twinge of an attractive flavor I haven't found anywhere else. And I had no ill effects from the dish.

Perhaps because of descriptions like McIlvaine's, mushroom authors ever since have felt the need to scribble admonitions. Typical of these is advice from the McKnights: "Edibility unknown but not recommended. The very numerous gray species of Mycena on wood have been frequently misidentified, even when microscopic characters were used."

And care should be taken. The purplish **Mycena pura** is a very poisonous mushroom with a bewildering variety of cap colors of its own. This is probably the biggest threat, but there are a number of similar species of unknown edibility that could be confused with it.

Among these could be:

Mycena maculata: This is a very close look-alike, differing mostly by having reddish blotches on the gills. However, this is a variable trait and does not occur in all collections. According to Roger Phillips, this species too is edible.

Mycena robusta: This is another large, local, lead colored species, but it fruits on conifer duff, not on rotten wood. It can handle cold weather, but again, no one even comments on the edibility.

Mycena stipata: Also lignicolous and locally common, it differs by its strong alkaline odor, slightly acrid taste, smaller stature, and lack of intervenose gills.

Mycena abramsii: Another local brown Mycena that fruits on leafy debris and further differs by its lack of an odor, white strigose stem base, and distinct subcylindrical spores.

Mycena amicta: The brown capped form can resemble M. galericulata, but differs by its separable pellicle, granular cap texture when young, and possible blue strand of mycelium at the stem base.

Mycena quinaultensis: Differs by its gelatinous caps and stems when young. The almost black-brown caps fade in age, but it fruits on needle duff, not wood.

Mycena clavicularis: Another gray-capped species that differs by fruiting on pine needle duff, a viscid stem, and clavate cystidia with short obtuse projections.

Mycena overholtsii: A high altitude Mycena found on rotten conifer wood near snowbanks in the spring. It also differs by having

LOOK-ALIKE

Mycena leptocephala

LOOK-ALIKES

Mycena amicta—brown capped form

Mycena abramsii   *Photo by Fred Rhoades*

strigose to tomentose stem bases often joined together in clusters.

Mycena leptocephala: Differs by its alkaline odor, fusoid cheilocystidia, and nearly translucent striate margins when aged.

There are enough look-alikes out there to make identification a bit dicey. If you think you have found **Mycena galericulata**, run it by Dr.

Fred Rhoades. He is our local expert on the Mycenas and has benefited from a long correspondence with Maas Geesteranus over identification issues with our Pacific Northwest Mycenas. He can tell you whether you identified it correctly or not. Whether it heads for the frying pan after that is up to you.

BIBLIOGRAPHY

David Arora, *Mushrooms Demystified*, 1986. Ten Speed Press, Berkeley, Calif.

Frederick Clements, *Minnesota Mushrooms*, 1910. University of Minnesota Press, Minneapolis, Minn.

Guillaume Eyssartier & Pierre Roux, *Le Guide des Champignons de France et Europe*, 2011. Editions Belin, Paris.

Jakob E. Lange, *Studies in the Agarics of Denmark, Part I*, Dansk Botanisk Arkiv 1, No. 5 (1–40), 1914.

David Largent, *Entolomoid Fungi of the Western United States and Alaska*, 1994. Mad River Press, Eureka, Calif.

Gary Lincoff, *The Audubon Society Field Guide to North American Mushrooms*, 1981. Alfred A. Knopf, New York, NY.

R.A. Maas Geesteranus, *Some Myceneae of the Himalayan Foothills* in Persoonia 15 (33–53), 1992.

R.A. Maas Geesteranus, *Conspectus of the Mycenas of the Northern Hemisphere—4. Section Mycena* in Proceedings of the Koninklijke Nederlandse Akademie van Wetenschappen 88 (339–369), 1985.

W.B. McDougall, *Mushrooms*, 1925. Houghton Mifflin Co., Boston.

Charles McIlvaine & Robert Macadam, *One Thousand American Fungi*, 1902. Dover Publications, New York, NY.

Kent & Vera McKnight, *Peterson Field Guides – Mushrooms*, 1987. Houghton Mifflin Co., Boston.

Roger Phillips, *Mushrooms and Other Fungi of Great Britain & Europe*, 1981. Pan Books, Ltd., London.

A.H. Smith, *North American Species of Mycena*, 1947. University of Michigan Press, Ann Arbor, Mich.

Ansel Stubbs, *Wild Mushrooms of the Central Midwest*, 1971. University Press of Kansas, Lawrence, Kansas.

Mycena haematopus (Persoon ex Fries) Kummer

Haematopus means "blood foot" in Latin, a reference to the color the stem bleeds when cut.

It is my pleasure to share with you one of the reasons why fiberglass boats are so much more expensive than wooden ones in the Pacific Northwest. They are easier to keep up. Yes, this fine colony of **Mycena haematopus** is fruiting out of my line locker in the cockpit of my 1939 Bristol Bay Double-Ender. In fact, it has fruited twice in the course of four years, and worse than that, a **Spinellus fusiger** that attacked the decaying Mycenas also settled on the lines. And so you see, it is no myth. I spent most of the summer of 1996 trying to save my cockpit from my avocation.

Heamatopus means "blood-foot" in Latin, the species so named because the stem oozes a dark red fluid when cut. This puts it in Section Lactipedes of the genus Mycena.

The caps are 1–4 cm wide, almost egg-shaped at first, expanding to broadly conic with an umbo in age. Margins are striate to occasionally sulcate with a recurved edge when mature. The lovely crenate "skirt," or sterile flaps in mycological lingo, began as sterile bands that connected cap margins to upper stems. As the caps expanded, this skirt remained on the cap margin rather than attach itself to the stem.

The caps are first covered with a dense pruinose coating, but soon become moist and polished, the margins becoming translucent striate in age. The discs are dark red brown to brick color fading to flesh tones or grayish vinaceous on the margins. The gills are adnate and ascending, crowded to subdistant, and whitish to grayish vinaceous. They stain a sordid reddish-brown in age, a trait that has led to confusion with **Mycena maculata**, another common Mycena of the Pacific Northwest.

The gill edges are white and floccose, hinting of the almost sure presence of cheilocystidia. The hollow stems measure 4–10 cm

LOOK-ALIKE

Mycena sanguinolenta

long and 1–2 mm thick. They are pallid at the apex becoming pinkish brown to dark vinaceous towards the base. The upper part is covered at first with a whitish to pale cinnamon pruina (powder) while the base can be heavily white strigose (covered with white hairs). Both caps and stem bases exude the dark red juice when cut. The odor is mild, the spore deposit is white, and the taste can be mild or bitterish.

We must thank Dr. Alexander Smith for the above description, lifted right out of his Mycena monograph. Smith thinks it is the easiest of all the Mycenas to recognize once you learn the characteristics. Clyde Christensen is not so sure. He claims that in dry weather the stem refuses to produce a latex, which in my mind would make it much more difficult to identify. It is certainly a widespread species, occurring all over Europe, North America, and Japan. Dr. Smith does add that although **Mycena haematopus** is easy to recognize, there are intergrading forms depending on climactic conditions, nutrients, and the substrate. The Blood-Foot Mycena grows singly to cespitose on decaying wood from spring through fall throughout the northern hemisphere.

The spores are ellipsoid, amyloid in Melzer's, and measure 7–12 x 4–7 µm. The cheilocystidia are abundant and fusiform in shape.

The species is often attacked by **Spinellus fusiger**, which envelops the fruiting bodies in spiky white threads. The Spinellus allows the Mycena the time to disperse its own spores, a strategy to its own advantage, before eventually reducing the caps to a "puddly soup" in the words of Mollen and L. Weber.

According to Amy Miller in her superb key on the Northwest's Mycenas, other local species that exude a blood-red juice are **Mycena haematopus var. marginata** and **Mycena sanguinolenta**. The former differs in having reddish gill edges and stems up to 15 cm long, while **Mycena sanguinolenta** fruits on moss and conifer duff and has dark red-brown gill edges. Other look-alikes are as follows:

Mycena atkinsoniana: An East Coast species which differs in having yellow gills with maroon edges, and fruits on the ground.

Mycena haematopus var. cuspidata: An alpine species which fruits in the aspen zone near Snowmass, Colorado. This variety has a sharply pointed umbo that either splits in half or folds over in age, a fruity odor, an intensely bitter taste, and vinaceous-brown hairs on the stem base. It grows on aspen.

Mycena erubescens: A species recorded from Michigan. It also bleeds wine red, has a bitter taste like quinine, and fruits around wood chips and stumps.

Mycena capillaripes: Differs by its brownish caps with vinaceous gray margins, pinkish gill edges, and nitrous odor. And the stems do not bleed when cut.

Mycena seynii: A European species with pale flesh-brown caps that fruits on pine cones.

LOOK-ALIKES

Mycena maculata

Mycena seynii from Spain

The stems do not bleed when broken.

As for reports on edibility, here are five quotes that give you the general idea:

David Biek: "Edibility unknown. Bitter taste is a deterrent."

Lincoff & Pacioni: "Can be eaten but quality bad."

McKnight & McKnight: "Edible but said to be tasteless and little used."

David Arora: "Too small to be of value."

Charles McIlvaine: "This pretty plant can often be gathered in considerable quantity, and well repays the collector."

In older guides, the names **Mycena haematopoda** (still preferred by Moser), and **Galactopus haematopus** are sometimes used.

According to Trudell & Ammirati, **Mycena haematopus** can fruit on conifers and hardwoods. Pacioni & Lincoff note that it has a preference for birch and oak. Bandoni & Szczawinski write that it likes alder. Kuo & Methven claim that it causes a white rot. So although I cannot detemine what kind of wood my marine plywood consisted of, I can at least predict what color my cockpit would have become over time.

BIBLIOGRAPHY

David Arora, *Mushrooms Demystified*, 1986. Ten Speed Press, Berkeley, Calif.

Robert Bandoni & Adam Szczawinski, *Guide to Common Mushrooms of British Columbia*, 1976. British Columbia Provincial Museum, Victoria, B.C., Canada.

David Biek, *The Mushrooms of Northerrn California*, 1984. Spore Prints, Redding, Calif.

J. Breitenbach & F. Kranzlin, *Fungi of Switzerland*, Vol. 3, 1991. Edition Mykologia, Lucerne, Switzerland.

Clyde Christensen, *Common Fleshy Fungi*, 1955. Burgess Publishing Co., Minneapolis, Minn.

Ernest Emmett, Arne Aronsen, Thomas Laessoe, & Steen Elborne, *Mycena in Funga Nordica*, 2012. Nordsvamp, Copenhagen.

Vera Evenson, *Mushrooms of Colorado*, 1997. Denver Botanic Gardens, Denver, Colo.

Guillaume Eyssartier & Pierre Roux, *Le Guide des Champignons de France et Europe,* 2011. Editions Belin, Paris.

Rokuya Imazeki, Tsuguo Hongo, & Keisuke Tubaki, *Common Fungi of Japan in Color*, 1970. Hoikusha Publishing Co., Osaka, Japan.

Michael Kuo & Andy Methven, *100 Cool Mushrooms*, 2010. University of Michigan Press, Ann Arbor, Mich.

Charles McIlvaine & Robert Macadam, *One Thousand American Fungi*, 1902. Dover Publishing, New York, NY.

Kent & Vera McKnight, *Peterson Field Guides—Mushrooms*, 1987. Houghton Mifflin Co., Boston.

Amy Miller, *Trial Key to the Mycenoid Species in the Pacific Northwest*, 1981. Pacific Northwest Key Council, Seattle, Wash.

Orson & Hope Miller, *North American Mushrooms*, 2006. Morris Book Publishing, Guilford, Conn.

Cora Mollen & Larry Weber, *Fascinating Fungi of the North Woods*, 2007. Kollath+Stensaas Publishing, Duluth, Minn.

Giovanni Pacioni & Gary Lincoff, *Simon & Schuster's Guide to Mushrooms*, 1981. Simon & Schuster Co., New York, NY.

Roger Phillips, *Mushrooms and Other Fungi of Great Britain & Europe*, 1981. Pan Books, Ltd., London.

A.H. Smith, *North American Species of Mycena*, 1947. University of Michigan Press, Ann Arbor, Mich.

A.H. Smith & D.H. Mitchel, *Notes on Colorado Fungi, III: New and Interesting Mushrooms from the Aspen Zone* in *Mycologia* 70 (1052), 1978.

Steve Trudell & Joe Ammirati, *Mushrooms of the Pacific Northwest*, 2009. Timber Press, Portland, Ore.

"If you go down in the woods today, you're sure of a big surprise." Art by Alex McAdoo

Mycena pura (Persoon ex Fries) Kummer

Photo by Richard Morrison

. . . twenty different forms and varieties have been described over two centuries.

Mycena pura, that cheerful little purple mushroom that brightens the dimmest of forest floors, is a bit more complicated than it appears. Although one of the fleshiest of the Mycenas, it comes in a bewildering array of colors, setting up an extravaganza for lumpers and splitters alike. It seems that 20 different forms and varieties have been described over two centuries, only two of which until recently have been elevated to species status in some guides. These would be the **var. rosea** = **Mycena rosea**, an all pink version of **Mycena pura**, and the **var. pseudopura**, elevated to **Poromycena pseudopura** by Singer in 1949. To approach the scope of the issue from another direction, the Index Fungorum lists 29 synonyms for **Mycena pura**.

According to David Arora, caps of **Mycena pura** have to have some purple or lilac in them, but other colors exist, such as white, pale ochre, brownish pink, pink, pale blue gray, pinkish chestnut, that some authorities believe intergrade to the extent that they can't be consistently separated. When not found in its most common violet coloration, you have to zone in on the ambiance of this fungus.

The caps range from 2–7 cm wide, and are broadly conical to bell shaped at first, becoming convex to plane with uplifted margins in age. They are subviscid when moist, smooth with translucent-striate margins. They are also hygrophanous, meaning they fade as they age. The gills are adnexed to adnate with decurrent tooth. They are usually intervenose with three tiers of lamellulae. They are whitish to pale violet to grayish with a white edge. The stems measure 3–7 cm long and 2–7 mm thick. They are colored like the cap or paler in most variations. They are terete to compressed, equal except for a slightly enlarged base, and hollow. A thin covering of whitish to yellowish fibrils is usually found at the base. The mushrooms smell strongly of radish. The spore deposit is white and amyloid in Melzer's. The flesh turns yellow in KOH.

Microscopically, Brian Perry found the spores to be narrowly elliptic and measure 7.6–9.6 x 3.2–4.8 μm. The cheilocystidia and the pleurocystidia are similar. Shapes vary considerably from saccate on a short pedicel to fusiform with elongated necks to utriform with small apical projections. The pileipellis is an ixocutis of filamentous hyphae in a gelatinous matrix. Caulocystidia are mucronate to clavate. The gill trama is of parallel, inflated

VARIATIONS

Mycena pura var. rosea

Mycena pura form purpurea

hyphae, and lactifers are commonly seen.

Dr. A.H. Smith must have spent time poring over all the cap color varieties. In his Mycena monograph he summed up this leisurely pursuit by stating "since there are numerous intergradations between colors, one soon gives up trying to distinguish any subdivisions of them. I have not been able to correlate any slight differences in spore size with shape and abundance of pleurocystidia, but it may be possible to recognize certain forms or varieties on this basis."

For lumpers, this is your "out" statement. For splitters, here is your list of color forms and varieties along with brief descriptions where possible:

Mycena pura form armeniaca: Rosy orange caps with striate margins and bright purple stems.

Mycena pura form citrina: Pale straw colored caps, white gills, and flesh to lilac colored stems.

Mycena pura form purpurea: Whitish caps and dark purple stems. Found near the South Pass Road in May.

Mycena pura form roseo-brunnescens: Pale flesh-brown caps, white gills and stems. In Uzbekistan with juniper.

Mycena pura var. alba: Entirely white. Fred Rhoades has found it up the Canyon Creek Road in July.

Mycena pura var. azurea: A Bouchet variety.

Mycena pura var. carnea: Has more fleshy and fibrillose stems.

Mycena pura var. gracilenta: A Hennings variety.

Mycena pura var. ianthina:

VARIATIONS

Mycena pura var. nov.? from Lopez Island

Mycena pura var. nov.? from Vendovi Island

Mycena pura var. alba

LOOK-ALIKES

Mycena pura var. nov.? from Tibet Photo by Alex McAdoo

Mycena rutilantiformis

Mycena pelianthina

Whitish caps with faint lavender hues, and white stems with lavender apices.

Mycena pura var. lilacina: Found in Chile.

Mycena pura var. lutea: Has ochre-yellow caps and violet stems.

Mycena pura var. luteorosea: A Marcel Bon variety.

Mycena pura var. marplatensis: Possibly found where the Rio Plata meets the sea. A Raithelhuber var.

Mycena pura var. mediterranea: Found under cistus bushes in Sardinia. Description in Agarica 17.

Mycena pura var. multicolor: Greenish gray-blue caps with yellow umbos and pinkish-violet stems.

Mycena pura var. pallida: A Raithelhuber variety.

Mycena pura var. pseudopura: Rosy caps becoming whitish, no odor, stems rosy-white drying brown.

Mycena pura var. raphanacea: Definitely not var. pseudopura.

Mycena pura var. rosea: A large pink version with umbonate caps.

Mycena pura var. roseoviolacea: A version close to this was found under Monterey cypress on the Hawaiian island of Moloka'i.

Mycena pura var. violacea: According to Maas Geesteranus, this has dark violet stems.

Mycena pura var. nov.?: A find from Lopez Island. It had grayish-tan caps with tawny discs and dark purple stems. Brian Luther identified it to species. (He didn't need to take it any further. He was a lumper at the time.)

Mycena pura var. nov.?: This

variety from Vendovi Island has a pale cinnamon disc crowning a pale gray cap with a faint bluish tinge. Very close to **var. multicolor**.

Mycena pura var. nov.?: A Tibetan variety with maroon discs fading to pallid brick color and then grayish lilac at margins.

There are, of course, other Mycenas that somewhat resemble. These are:

Mycena pearsoniana: A European species with decurrent white gills, inamyloid spores, brownish-pink caps, and a rooting stem base. Has been collected in Haida Gwaii, B.C.

Mycena sororia: A recently described species that looks like **Mycena rosea** but has a different DNA profile, and larger spores that measure 7.5–8.5 x 4.8–5.5 μm. Caps are a little more violet and stems rosy purplish. A European species.

Mycena diosma: A species with grayish-violet gills, pinkish-brown stems, and purple-brown caps. It has a strong odor of radish mixed with a box of cigars, and dacryoid spores. European.

Mycena kuehneriana: Hazel colored caps tinged with rose and lilac. Stems concolorous. Gills white with a rosy tinge, short decurrent. Found in Michigan and Manitoba.

Mycena subaquosa: In the Purae group, but all white with a translucent stem.

Mycena zephira: Has livid reddish to pinkish-white caps with brownish tinge at disc. Stems with white squamules when young, and no odor.

Mycena rutilantiformis: Perhaps the largest of all Mycenas, it has brickish-pink gill edges.

LOOK-ALIKES

Mycena purpureofusca from California

Cortinarius bibulus

Cortinarius iodes from Mass.

LOOK-ALIKES

Laccaria amethysteo-occidentalis   Photo by Richard Morrison

Inocybe pallidicremea, (formerly Inocybe lilacina)

Lepista tarda   Photo by Richard Morrison

Mycena pelianthina: Another purplish species that differs by its purple gill edges.

Other look-alikes not in Mycena are as follows:

Inocybe pallidicremea: A poisonous species which has pale gray-violet caps, fruits in the same locations, but has brown spores.

Laccaria amethysteo-occidentalis: Differs by its thick gills, intensely purple colors, and tough, fibrous stems.

Cortinarius bibulus: A small purple-brown Cort with rusty spores.

Lepista tarda: A pale violet species with pale pinkish spores that lacks the radish odor and fruits on edges of lawns and compost heaps.

Cortinarius iodes: An East Coast Cortinarius with random whitish spots on the purple caps, and again, the rusty spores.

Gymnopus iocephalus: Also has a purple cap, but differs by its lined-striated and lumpy cap surface plus an unattractive odor of garlic, gunpowder, and sauerkraut.

Pseudobaeospora deckeri: Another bright purple agaric with white spores that often fruits in clusters from coastal California and differs by having a strong green reaction when KOH is applied to the cap surface.

Pseudobaeospora pilodii: Differs by its silky cap surface with obtuse papillate umbo, dextrinoid spores and gill attachment so deeply notched as to appear free. The pileipelis is a hymenoderm palisade.

Mycena pura is cosmopolitan. It has been found in Japan, most of Asia, all of Europe, Hawaii, East Africa, Greenland, Patagonia, Uttar Pradesh, Venezuela, North Africa, the Antilles, all over North America, and north of the Arctic Circle. It fruits by itself or in small groups under Douglas fir, pine, oak, and beech. If you have conifers in your yard, you've probably seen it there. It likes humus, moss, detritus, rotting foliage and needle duff, always favoring damp situations. If you see your toddler crawling towards one, remove either as soon as possible.

The problem is that **Mycena pura** is now considered to be poisonous. The rumblings may have started at the turn of the century, but by 1922 enough was known for Carleton Rea to label it poisonous. William S. Thomas included a statement by Murrill in his 1928 field guide declaring "It has been condemned as dangerous to eat, but it needs more investigation." In 1977, Lincoff and Mitchel listed **Mycena pura** as being poisonous, the main suspect being muscarine. In 1976, C.H. Eugster identified the presence of epimuscarine. In 1979, Kubicka & Svrcek found it to be "weakly toxic in large amounts." Then in 1983, Belliardo & Massano reported on a couple that ate close to a pound of **Mycena pura var. rosea** in a consommé. About

Pseudobaeospora pilodii from Virginia

an hour and a half after the meal they began sweating and salivating, experiencing bradycardia, hypertension, colicky stomach pain, and diarrhea, perhaps not in that order. These are symptoms typical of muscarine poisoning. It's a toxin that affects the sympathetic nervous system. By 1985, Roger Heim reported it to be psychotropic and muscarinic. And finally in 2006, Orson Miller reported that it contains muscarine Type 2 toxins, and furthermore, the caps and gills are bioluminescent when fresh. This was backed up by Robert Rogers who affirmed that Pink Mycena (**M. pura var. rosea**) exhibited luminosity on cap, stem, gills, and mycelium.

Although Lincoff and Pacioni inform us that **Mycena pura** is edible in small amounts, perhaps the best advice is that of David Biek's. "I avoid radish tasting mushrooms as a matter of principle."

Addendum: *The Index Fungorum* now lists **Poromycena pseudopura** as a synonym of **Mycena pura**.

Addendum 2: A three-gene phylogeny has now shown that as many as eleven species could be lurking in the Mycena pura complex. One of these, the beautiful **Mycena pura var. lutea**, was raised to species status in the same article. It is now **Mycena luteovariegata**.

BIBLIOGRAPHY

Joe Ammirati & Gary Laursen, *Arctic and Alpine Mycology*, 1982. University of Washington Press, Seattle, Wash.

Joe Ammirati, J.A.Traquair, & Paul Horgen, *Poisonous Mushrooms of the Northern United States and Canada*, 1985. University of Minnesota Press, Minneapolis, Minn.

David Arora, *Mushrooms Demystified*, 1986. Ten Speed Press, Berkeley, Calif.

Flavio Belliardo & Graziella Massano, *Determination of a-Amanitin in Serum by HPLC* in *Journal of Liquid Chromatography* 6 (551–558), 1983.

Denis Benjamin, *Mushrooms — Poisons and Panaceas*, 1985. W.H. Freeman, New York, NY.

David Biek, *The Mushrooms of Northern California*, 1984. Spore Prints, Redding, Calif.

J. Breitenbach & F. Kranzlin, *Fungi of Switzerland*, Vol.3, 1991. Edition Mykologia, Lucerne, Switzerland.

Dennis Desjardin, Brian Perry, & Don Hemmes, *A Ruby Colored Pseudobaeospora Species Is Described as New from Material Collected on the Island of Hawaii* in *Mycologia* 106 (456–463), 2014.

Ernest Emmett, Arne Aronsen, Thomas Laessoe, & Steen Elborne, *Mycena in Funga Nordica*, 2008. Nordsvamp, Copenhagen.

Guillaume Eyssartier & Pierre Roux, *Le Guide des Champignons de France et Europe*, 2012. Editions Belin, Paris.

Roy Halling, *The Genus Collybia in the Northeastern United States and Adjacent Canada* in *Mycologia Memoirs* 8 (1–148), 1983.

Christoffer Harder, Thomas Laessoe, Tobias Froslev, Flemming Ekelund, Soren Rosendahl, & Rasmus Kjoller, *A Three-Gene Phylogeny of the Mycena pura Complex Reveals 11 Phylogenetic Species and Shows ITS to be Unreliable for Species Identification* in *Fungal Biology* 117 (764–775), 2013.

Don Hemmes & Dennis Desjardin, *Mushrooms of Hawaii*, 2002. Ten Speed Press, Berkeley, Calif.

Rokuya Imazeki, Tsuguo Hongo, & Keisuke Tubaki, *Coloured Illustrations of the Fungi of Japan*, 1957. Hoikusha Publishing Co., Osaka.

Walter Julich & Meinhard Moser, *Farbatlas der Basidiomyceten*. Gustav Fischer Verlag, Stuttgart, Germany.

Gary Lincoff & D.H. Mitchel, *Toxic and Hallucinogenic Mushroom Poisoning*, 1977. Van Nostrand Reinhold, New York, NY.

Margaret McKenny, Daniel Stuntz, & Joe Ammirati, *The New Savory Wild Mushroom*, 1987. University of Washington Press, Seattle, Wash.

Orson & Hope Miller, *North American Mushrooms*, 2006. Morris Book Publishing Co., Guilford, Conn.

Gabriel Moreno, Jose-Luis Manjon, & Alvaro Zugaza, *La Guia de Incafo de los Hongos de la Peninsula Iberica*, Tomo II, 1986. Incafo S.A., Madrid.

Meinhard Moser, *Keys to Agarics and Boleti*, 1983. Translated and published by Roger Phillips, London.

Giovanni Pacioni & Gary Lincoff, *Simon & Schuster's Guide to Mushrooms*, 1981. Simon & Schuster, New York, NY.

David Pegler, *A Preliminary Agaric Flora of East Africa*, 1977.

David Pegler, *Agaric Flora of the Lesser Antilles*, 1983. Her Majesty's Stationary Office, London.

Brian Perry, *Mycenas of California*, doctorate, 2002.

Miguel Angel Pérez-De-Gregorio, Joaquim Carbó, & Carles Roqué, *Algunos Hongos Interesantes de Girona* in *Fungi Non Delineato*, Pars XLIV, 2009.

Roger Phillips, *Mushrooms and Other Fungi of Britain and Europe*, 1981. Pan Books, Ltd., London.

Carleton Rea, *British Basidiomycetes*, 1922. Strauss & Cramer, Hirschberg, Germany.

Robert Rogers, *The Fungal Pharmacy*, 2011. North Atlantic Books, Berkeley, Calif.

Helene Schalkwijk-Barendsen, *Mushrooms of Western Canada*, 1991. Lone Pine Publishing, Edmonton, Alberta.

Christian Schwarz, *Pseudobaeospora deckeri Sp. Nov. — A New Agaric from Central California* in *Mycotaxon* 119 (483–485), 2012.

A.H. Smith, *North American Species of Mycena*, 1947. University of Michigan Press, Ann Arbor, Mich.

Mirko Svrcek, *The Hamlyn Book of Mushrooms and Fungi*, 1983. Artia, Prague.

Mirko Svrcek & Jiri Kubicka, *Champignons d'Europe*, 1979. Artia, Prague.

William S. Thomas, *Field Book of Common Mushrooms*, 1928. G.P. Putnam's Sons, New York, NY.

A Tale of Two Nolaneas: *Nolanea sp.* and *Nolanea clandestina*

. . . a hardy species, able to withstand cold winters in open pastures when other species have long since disappeared.

Sometimes the oddest of mushroom discoveries occurs right up the street from where you live. I was driving by a neighbor's lawn in the dead of winter in 2003 when I spotted a solitary black mushroom poking up through the grass. I made a mental note of this appearance and drove on. Overnight about an inch of snow fell. The next morning the little black mushroom was still there, a small black button in the snow. I parked the car to take a look. Brushing the snow from around the stem I perceived the telltale longitudinally striated stem of an Entolomoid fungus. There was only one specimen. My camera was way across town. So I made an arbitrary decision. I decided to let it be. End of story for 2003.

For the rest of the winter I castigated myself for not pursuing it further. Not many agarics can handle such cold conditions. Maybe it was a new species. You always wonder "what if... what if...?" in cases like this. A real professional would have collected it.

But fate eventually bailed me out. On December 24, 2004, I was driving by the same lawn when I spotted two of the little black mushrooms plus a few larger floppy brown ones next to them. It was time to bring out the camera and do them up.

As I approached the cluster, tripod in hand, I became confused. Was I looking at two different species here, or one species that altered its appearance as it matured? **Panus conchatus**, for instance, does just that. It can be bright violet at first but soon ages to a tan or pallid brick color. What were the odds of two separate Entolomoid species appearing in the winter right next to each other at the same time? Thinking this highly unlikely, I shot the photo as if they were all one species, taking care to place the two floppy brown ones on the right and the two diminutive black ones on the left (see feature photo, previous page). Then it was time to write them up.

The diminutive blackish ones had caps measuring 1 ½–3 cm wide. They were convex with inrolled margins. The color was umber black, not at all blue. The surface was smooth and matte, not at all scumy except at disc. The cap context was thin, tan. The gill attachment was emarginate, the edges entire and slightly wavy. The gills were tan with pallid edges. The stems were 2–4 mm thick and 2½–4½ cm long. They were dark brown with white tomentum at the base, longitudinally striate and hollow. The spores were pink. The taste was mild but the odor clearly

ANOTHER VIEW

Nolanea sericea

farinaceous. They were fruiting in a mossy lawn not far from a giant blue spruce.

Meanwhile the floppy brown specimens had caps measuring 4–5 cm wide. They were convex to plane with obtusely papillate centers. The cap margins were faintly striate, lobed, and irregularly wavy with upturned edges in age. The color was a silky dark brown fading hygrophanously from the disc first. The surface was smooth, matte. The context was thin and brown. The gills were adnexed, distant, dusty brown and subventricose. The stems measured 5–7 mm thick and 4 ½–6 ¼ cm long. They were dark brown becoming paler towards the base, hollow, equal, glabrous. The spores were pink. The odor and taste strongly farinaceous. They were found about a foot away from the little blackish specimens. At this point it began dawning on me that the differences in field characters were substantial.

In Europe the vast majority of mycologists consider all Entolomoid species to belong to the genus Entoloma. Nolanea, Leptonia, Claudopus, Alboleptonia, etc,. are all considered to be sections of Entoloma. But Dr. Dave Largent, author of the definitive key on West Coast Entolomoid species, has elevated all these sections to generic levels. Before embarking on the microscopic data needed to key out these specimens, I needed to consult his giant key to get an idea what to look out for. All Entolomoid spores are angular, usually 5–7 sided, but some are more elongated than others. Isodiametric spores are those that have nearly the same length as width. The quotient, or ratio of width to length, has to be from 1 to 1.20. If they are slightly more elongated, they are called subisodiametric. Another very tricky area is what happens at the disc or center of the cap. Very often you can see radially repent hyphae from the cap margin towards the disc, but once there, you discover branched and entangled hyphae with possible hyphal ends sticking out, suddenly appearing more like a derm than a cutis. Are these hyphal ends just that or are they pileocystidia? The combinations of micro characters are rendered more confusing by subtle changes as the carpophores mature. Beyond all this is the question of pigmentation. Some species have intracellular pigmentation which seems to vanish in a wash in KOH. Others have encrusted pigmentation, tiny black lumps on the hyphal walls of the pileipellis that don't wash out with KOH. All you can hope for is that you get a clear reading when ferreting out these variations. And variations to species there are! Very few genera have this many variations in a monograph. It's a monumental work that Dr. Largent has produced, but with so many variations lurking within, the keys can be frustrating to work with.

It was now time to confront the microscope. I usually do this by downing two cups of Songbird Coffee to get really pumped, put the specimen in a humidity chamber in preparation for sectioning, and put on the reggae. It's my own way of getting ready for war. When the focus level pushes the music to the background, I'm ready to go.

The little umber-black capped mushrooms were tackled first. They had angular 6-sided spores measuring 7.2–7.5 x 7.7–7.9 µm. The Q was 1.21, putting it right on the edge of isodiametric. The pileipellis consisted of radially repent hyphae with distinctly incrusted walls. Towards the disc the hyphae became branched and entangled, more of a derm. I didn't spot obvious pileocystidia. There were no cheilocystidia, no pleurocystidia. The basidia were 4-spored and clavate. No clamp connections. The caulocystidia consisted of clumps of clavate hyphal ends near the stem apex, some of them branched. The gill trama was of sinuous parallel hyphae without incrustations.

The above assemblage of characters led me to **Nolanea farinolens** (now **Entoloma ortonii** in *Index Fungorum*) in Section Cosmeoexonema. But there was a problem. Largent's photo looked nothing like our specimens. The caps were striate to the disc and more of a gray-brown color, not umber-black and matte. Fortunately, Largent has a paragraph on close relatives and lookalikes after each description. One of these was the common **Nolanea sericea**, which poisoned a dog on Whidbey Island in the fall of 2005. Largent described it as having pileocystidia. Those hyphal ends turned out to be more than just hyphal ends. It's all a question of how much experience one has in the genus. The other thing I had missed was the encrustations on the walls of the gill trama hyphae. I suppose you don't see them with every cross section of a gill, but you can't just throw in the towel. You have to give yourself at least five hours to find them, and only then can you say they aren't there. The result? The diminutive black mushroom was indeed **N. sericea**.

I now turned my attention to the floppy brown-capped specimens with the papillate umbos. The spores were 5–7 sided and also isodiametric with a Q of 1.17. Both the hyphae of the gill trama and the pileipellis were incrusted. The contextual hyphae were undifferentiated. There were no clamps, no pleuros, and no cheilos. Eventually the combination of brown gills, glabrous stems, and incrustations led to **Nolanea clandestina**, an exciting brown species not found in any North American popular guide. According to Largent's monograph, **Nolanea clandestina** has been found by Calvin Kauffman in Clallam County in 1925, Bill Isaacs in King County, and by Largent himself in San Juan County since then. This may be the first record from Whatcom County.

In Europe, **Nolanea clandestina** (as Entoloma, of course) is found in grasslands and open places in forests. Its most telling field characteristic appears to be the distant gills that are brown from the beginning. An excellent photo of it can be seen in Moser & Jülich's *Farbatlas der Basidiomyceten*.

So, in the end, I mailed a copy of this article to Dave Largent. He was happy to reply that I had nailed the unusual **Nolanea clandestina** but was perplexed why I had problems with the common **Nolanea sericea**. He informed me it was a hardy species, able to withstand cold winters in open pastures when other species had long disappeared from the landscape. I have featured another photo of it so you can visually compare the winter version with the early fall version seen in the lead photo. Look different? That's no surprise. It is now suspected that a complex of species comprises **Nolanea sericea**.

BIBLIOGRAPHY

Lexemuel Hesler, *Entoloma in Southeastern North America* in *Nova Hedwigia, Beihefte* 23, 1967.
Dave Largent, *Entolomoid Fungi of the Western United States and Alaska*, 1994. Mad River Press, Eureka, Calif.

Bob Ramsey, *Trial Field Key to the Species of Entolomaceae*, 1996. Pacific Northwest Key Council, Seattle, Wash.
Noah Siegel & Christian Schwarz, *Mushrooms of the Redwood Coast*, 2016. Ten Speed Press, Berkeley, Calif.

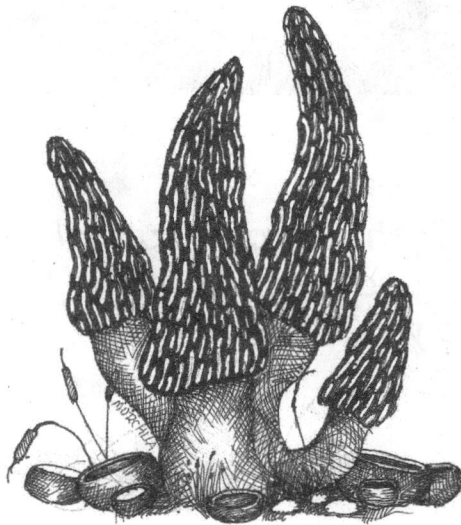

Nolanea pseudostrictia Largent

. . . tall stature, and shiny brown conical caps when young tend to arrest your attention and stop you in your tracks.

Our newsletter editor, Jack Waytz, was on one of his daily dog walks up Galbraith Mountain on March 15, 2007, when he spotted what looked like miniature Siamese rice paddy hats emerging from the mosses on the side of the trail. They were found under western red cedar and later transferred to my lily garden under spruce for the photo shoot due to heavy rain. The second photo, this page, shows the same species a year later at the original site. Here the caps have flattened out in age but retain the papillate umbo.

Nolanea pseudostrictia has hitherto been a rather rare species. It was first described by Largent from Redwood National Park in Humboldt County, California. It is now showing up more and more in forays when one of us bothers to look at the microscopic features. Despite having a wide range from British Columbia down to California and east to Wyoming, I had only found it once before. This was at Crystal Springs east of Seattle in late May of 1987. These were fruiting in leaf mulch under alder and vine maple. The caps in this collection were plane, with wavy, lobed margins and a sharp umbo. The fact that each collection appeared with very different trees implies that this is a saprophytic species.

In this collection, the caps measured 3 ½–5 ½ cm wide. They were so fragile that chunks broke off during the measuring process. They were smooth, appearing silky shiny from a distance. The incurved margins were so finely striate as to be barely discernable. Cap color was dark brown fading to pale brown when drying out. The context was brown, thin. Gills were adnexed, very crowded, pallid tan to dingy buff before the flesh colored spores took over. There were four tiers of lamellulae, and gill edges were entire. The stems were 1–1 ¼ cm thick and 8 ½–13 cm long. They were tan to pale brown, hollow, and strongly twisted striate, equal or expanding slightly towards the base. Some of the specimens had flattened bases, and all had white tomentum. Spores were pinkish and the odor and taste were mild (or slightly grassy according to Bob Ramsey).

Microscopically the spores were angular and 5–6 sided, usually with one large oil drop in the center. They measured 7.2–8.5 x 8.6–10 μm. The quotient was 1.16. The basidia were very long with short sterigmata. Clamps were present at the bases. There were no cystidia. The pileipellis was a cutis of repent hyphae 4-10 μm wide. Coarse, black incrustations appeared on the walls of these hyphae and also more rarely on the walls of the tramal hyphae. The presence of clamps and incrustations are diagnostic and separate the species from several look-alikes.

Dr. Largent introduced **Nolanea pseudostrictia** in his massive monograph on the West Coast Entolomoid species. Subsequently Bob Ramsey included a further description in his Pacific Northwest Key Council key. Since then it has received a mention in *Mushrooms of the Redwood Coast*.

In forays past we have probably misidentified this species as **Nolanea verna** because it is conical when young and appears in the spring. But **Nolanea verna** differs by its silky gray-brown cap surface, appressed-fibrillose brown stem, and caulocystidia at the stipe apex. Other look-alikes are as follows: **Nolanea strictior**—Differs by its darker brown cap disc and longitudinally striate, silky white stems that become brownish-orange in age. Otherwise the differences are microscopic in nature. It has no clamps and lacks the incrustations on the hyphal walls in the pileipellis. **Nolanea substrictior**—Differs by its brown gills and strong farinaceous odor. **Nolanea hirtipes**—This is another species with a long, stiff, striated stem. It differs by its

Second year fruiting of Nolanea pseudostrictia at Sudden Valley

yellow-brown caps, rancid farinaceous to iodine odor, and abundant mycelium at the stem base.

Nolanea hebes—Differs by having a farinaceous odor and much smaller caps up to 2 cm wide. Stems up to 6 cm long.

Nolanea strictior var. isabellina—A taxon from Tennessee that differs by its smoky olive-brown caps that fade to a pallid straw color in age, and lack of clamp connections. However, in Europe this would be known as **Entoloma strictius**.

Nolanea occidentalis—Another long-stemmed northwest Nolanea that differs by having a brown Mycenoid cap up to 3½ cm wide and very distant gills.

A species outside of the Entolomoid group that bears a superficial resemblance to the long stemmed Nolaneas is the common Deer Mushroom, **Pluteus exilis**. This differs by its more lubricous cap surface, lack of a papillate umbo, free gills, and habit of always fruiting on wood. True **P. cervinus** is now a rare species found on wood chips.

Dr. Largent once emailed me that some species in Nolanea would be impossible to identify unless you found a collection representing all its growth stages. In the case of **Nolanea pseudostrictia** you want to find young specimens with whitish gills before spores and age have darkened them. So many look-alikes have brownish gills when young.

Like almost all species in the Entolomaceae, **Nolanea pseudostrictia** should be considered poisonous. Stomach distress in all its forms and varieties would be the likely experience.

LOOK-ALIKES

Pluteus exilis (formerly Pluteus cervinus)

Nolanea strictior from Haida Gwaii, B.C.

Despite the culinary glitch, this is an attractive species to find in the woods. The tall stature, and shiny brown conical caps when young tend to arrest your attention and stop you in your tracks. And without Dr. Largent's monograph, we wouldn't have found a correct name for it in the first place.

BIBLIOGRAPHY

Guillaume Eyssartier & Pierre Roux, Le Guide des Champignons de France et Europe, 2012. Editions Belin, Paris.

Lexemuel Hesler, *Entoloma in Southeastern North America* in *Nova Hedwigia, Beihefte* 23, 1967.

Dave Largent, Entolomoid Fungi of the Western United States and Alaska, 1994. Mad River Press, Eureka, Calif.

Machiel Noordeloos, Entoloma in North America, 1988. Gustav Fischer Verlag, Stuttgart.

Bob Ramsey, Trial Field Key to the Species of Entolomaceae, 1996. Pacific Northwest Key Council, Seattle, Wash.

Noah Siegel & C. Schwarz, *Mushrooms of the Redwood Coast*, 2016. Ten Speed Press, Berkeley, Calif.

Ophiocordyceps myrmecophila (Cesalpino) G. Sung, J. Sung, Hywel-Jones & Spatafora

By Dr. Fred Rhoades

Photo by Fred Rhoades

*All Cordyceps are parasites, either
on subterranean fungi or on insects.*

The unsuspecting ant in the lead photo is the victim of one species from a most unusual genus of fungi. Although they look like small coral fungi, Cordyceps is a genus of ascomycetes related to the springtime morel, and even more closely related to the Lobster Mushroom that turns certain Russulas red in the fall. All Cordyceps are parasites, either on subterranean fungi or on insects. To find the host of a Cordyceps you must dig down under the fruiting body.

Ophiocordyceps myrmecophila is a small fungus, one of those prizes awarded to mushroom hunters who get down close to their prey. Generally, the exposed height of the fungus is about half an inch. Excavation of about that much below the fruiting body unearths the remains of the host ant. Each ant produces one fruiting body. The spores are produced in tiny chambers (perithecia) embedded in the spherical stroma (cap). You can imagine these perithecia under the slight lumps in the photo, and the chambers' exits are barely visible as darker orange splotches in the lighter orange stroma background. This particular species is defined by the type of host and the unusual, elongated shape of the perithecia.

One wonders about how such fungal species get around. The following description is pieced together from descriptions by other authors and by my experience in finding this species. It is not uncommon in western Washington. I have run across examples at least four times locally, usu-

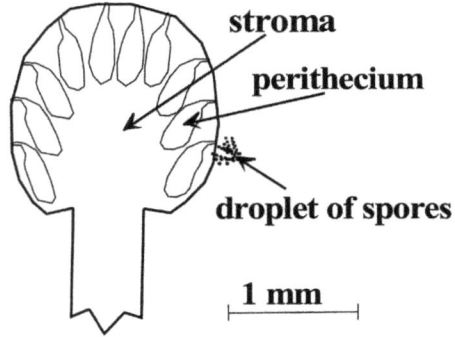

stroma

perithecium

droplet of spores

1 mm

ally while searching for my friends, the Mycenas.

Ophiocordyceps myrmecophila especially likes carpenter ants. At least that is where I've always found them. Like all ascomycetes, Cordyceps produce sexual spores in asci, elongate cells that in the case of morels are found lined up like cordwood all over the morel's sponge-like cap. **Ophiocordyceps myrmecophila** produces a few asci in each of up to 50 perithecia (see diagram). Each ascus produces eight spores, but each spore breaks up into as many as 50 parts, so the net effect is that **Ophiocordyceps myrmecophila** produces considerable, very tiny, reproductive parts. These spores ooze out of the hole from each perithecium, collecting in small droplets on the surface of the stroma. Most often they are picked up directly by passing prey or other animals that carry the spores to habitat for future prey. The innocent little ants may consume the spores unknowingly, or the spores germinate and grow directly into the ant between breaks in the exoskeleton. Eventually the fungal body (the mycelium, composed of the threads that grow from the spore) invades every corner of the ant's body. In the photo you can see the mycelium exuding between joints in the ant's exoskeleton.

Infected ants probably sense something is wrong long before their demise. They may get an urge to intern themselves at the right depth.

In all my futile scratching for truffles I have never seen a living carpenter ant half an inch underground. In every case of an ant infected by **Ophiocordyceps myrmecophila**, that's where I have found them. The ant eventually becomes immobile in its grave, and the fungus consumes the last bit of its host, producing the fruiting body up through the ground's surface. Although that occurs not quite as fast as the juvenile form of the parasite in the movie "Alien," there are some gruesome similarities to the growth of the stalked stroma out through the abdomen of the ant.

At some time in the life cycle, the fungus produces asexual spores, i.e., spores that will germinate to give rise to genetic clones of the parent fungus. This is a general characteristic of ascomycetes and is one reason why they are such successful parasites,

Cordyceps militaris   *Photo by Daniel Winkler*

unlike the mushroom producing basidiomycete groups, which have far weaker powers of asexual spore production. Although I have not observed these for **Ophiocordyceps myrmecophila**, this fungus likely reproduces asexually before producing fruiting bodies. In one unusual case several years ago, I found about ten separate fruiting bodies, each on a separate ant, buried within one or two square inches of surface area. This situation is hard to explain in any case, but suggests that the fungus was transmitted from host ant to host ant asexually, and that all were induced to be buried in the same area.

This story requires that I delve into the messy situation regarding sex and "asex" in fungi. This problem is similar to the dichotomy between larvae and adults of some insects, such as butterflies. They may be found at different times or in different places. Until someone makes the connection, the caterpillar and the butterfly may be regarded to be different animals with different scientific names, etc. Fungi growing in favorable environments, such as in Petri dishes in laboratory culture, often reproduce only asexually, forming what are commonly called molds. We commonly know these because they grow in human habitats, such as stale bread, overripe fruit, etc. It turns out that many of these molds (but not all, and that's another story) reproduce sexually as well, often producing ascomycete fruiting bodies; but they do so late in their lives, and often only in natural habitats, not in culture.

French naturalist, Louis Tulasne, and his draftsman brother, Charles, were some of the first to observe the connections between the asexual spore states of ascomycetes and their sexual fruiting bodies, and they were the first to illustrate these. Written in 1865, *Selecta Fungorum Carpologia* provides numerous illustrations of several species of Cordyceps along with comments on their natural history, especially in regards to their asexual spore states. Other species, such as **Cordyceps militaris**, the Trouping Cordyceps, which grows in our area on beetle pupae, produce asexual spores early in spring or summer, and sexual fruiting bodies in the fall. This is the typical ascomycete pattern. The asexual spores of **Cordyceps militaris** are assigned the name *verticillium* by modern mycologists. This is a genus of molds that is very commonly isolated from soil. It may well be that similar asexual spores from **Ophiocordyceps myrmecophila** are common enough in soil to infect numerous ants early in the season for this fungus.

I have found **Ophiocordyceps myrmecophila** throughout the years here. One of my collections was collected in March. I distinctly remember the second time I found the species. It was during a moss seminar with the Olympic Park Institute in June. Scrambling over a moss carpeted log, I noticed what I thought was a small orange **Mycena oregonensis**. On closer inspection, I saw there were no cap and gills, and I recognized my find. Calling the class over to the log, I bravely predicted that a surprise waited below the fungus. Digging carefully with a penknife revealed the tiny ant at the base. I wish I had asked for bets as to what we would find!

In any case, keep your eyes peeled for this oddity. If nothing else, you will find yourself in the minute realm of many fungi that we otherwise rarely observe during our pursuit of larger

LOOK-ALIKE

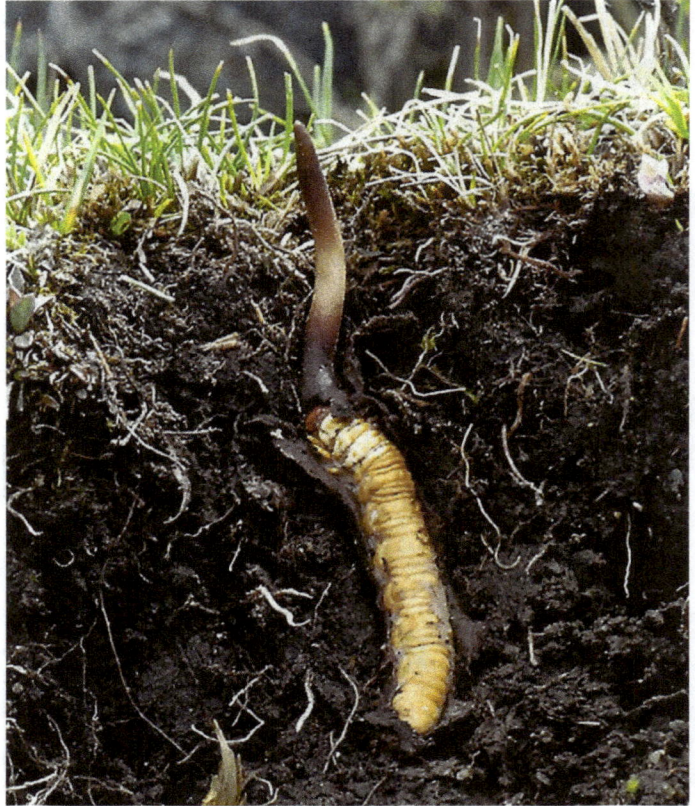

Ophiocordyceps sinensis from Tibet   Photo by Daniel Winkler

prey. Do not fear, however. I know of no species of Cordyceps that parasitizes humans!

One final piece of trivia—the easiest place to find an unusual species of Cordyceps is in the Chinese apothecary shops in Seattle and Vancouver. There you will find neat red-ribbon-wrapped packages of caterpillars infected with the species, **Ophiocordyceps sinensis**. The dried caterpillar mummies are ground up and instilled into tea, which is said to invigorate the lives of consumers, if you know what I mean. As far as I know, no one has tested the effects of **Ophiocordyceps myrmecophila**. Chocolate covered Ant Fungus, anyone?

BIBLIOGRAPHY

David Arora, *Mushrooms Demystified*, 1986. Ten Speed Press, Berkeley, Calif.
A.H. Smith, *Mushrooms in Their Natural Habitats*, 1949. Sawyer's, Lancaster, Penn.

Helen & A.H. Smith & Nancy Weber, *How to Know the Non-Gilled Mushrooms*, 1981. William C. Brown, Dubuque, Iowa.
Charles & Louis Rene Tulasne, *Selecta Fungorum Carpologia*, 1865.

Ossicaulis lignatilis (Persoon ex Fries) Redhead & Ginns

Dried stems are so hard that razor blades
have snapped in half during sectioning.

Found on October 26, 1990, at the Stimpson Family Nature Reserve just west of Lake Whatcom, this collection, according to Dr. Lorelei Norvell, represents the first recording of **Ossicaulis lignatilis** from the Pacific Northwest. In the earlier days, you walked down a path from the parking lot until you reached a giant log jam of fallen conifers about 60 yards in. That pile of logs has long since disintegrated, but at the time, for years it had harbored a treasure trove of unusual species. The "Bone Hard Wood Inhabiter" may have topped this list.

Common in England, occasional in Japan, but widespread in northern Europe, **Ossicaulis lignatilis** is considered a rare species that prefers to fruit on hardwoods such as elm, poplar, birch, oak, and beech. According to Steve Trudell, it is found less commonly on conifers, the situation we have here. (Kauffman reported it from Michigan on eastern hemlock, so this is not a first.) In the United States it is known mostly from Minnesota east to New England and further south. It particularly likes to fruit on the insides of hollow logs or stumps.

Taxonomically, the species has been rather nomadic, bouncing around for decades between Pleurotus and Clitocybe, with side excursions into Nothopanus and Pleurocybella. Hopefully Redhead and Ginns have laid the migrations to rest with their new genus Ossicaulis. **Ossicaulis lachnopus** and **O. lignatilis** may be the only species in it. It was separated from other genera

by the bone hard texture when dried and the structure of the pileipellis. Instead of the usual Clitocyboid cuticle of radially parallel hyphae, **Ossicaulis lignatilis** has a pileipellis composed of irregularly forked and branched anastomizing hyphae, some with gnarled outgrowths and coralloid ends. And in contrast to Clitocybe and Pleurotus, dried stems of **Ossicaulis lignatilis** are so hard that razor blades have snapped in half during sectioning.

Although capable of growing up to 12 cm wide in Europe, these caps measured up to 5 ½ cm wide. Broadly convex to plane with involute margins when young, the caps are sometimes found with radially lined surfaces, as seen here. Thin and tough, the margins become uplifted in age. The caps are creamy white but can develop gray-brown tones when moist or in their final stages. The surface is felty smooth often with a silky-shiny luster. The stems are central to mostly eccentric and can bruise pale ochre to pale orange when touched. They are usually curving off the log, longi-

LOOK-ALIKES

Pleurotus dryinus

Pleurotus populinus

LOOK-ALIKES

Pleurotus ostreatus from New Jersey

Pleurocybella porrigens

Hypsizygus tessulatus

tudinally fibrillose becoming powdery at the apex. They are equal or taper towards the base, and measure 2–8 cm long and up to 1 ½ cm thick. The flesh is pithy and white, tough and pliant, and the tomentose bases root deeply into the rotten wood. The gills are adnate to notched, sometimes subdecurrent. Narrow, shallow, crowded, and often forked, the edges are smooth at first becoming ragged in age. White at first, they turn pale yellowish to ochre buff when older. Taste and odor are strongly farinaceous (like flour), but the species also can have a fruity or fungal odor according to some authors. The spores are white, inamyloid, and vary in shape from ellipsoid to oval to subglobose depending on who looked at them. For instance, Roger Phillips reported oval spores measuring 4.5 x 2.5 µm. E.J.H. Corner found ellipsoid spores measuring 4–4.7 x 2.5–3 µm. Watling & Gregory found larger ellipsoid spores measuring 4–6 x 3–3.5 µm, while Breitenbach & Kranzlin reported subglobose spores measuring 4–6 x 4–5 µm. Watling & Gregory wrote that it can be separated from its look-alikes by its tough stem, white color, and strong rancid mealy smell.

And there are plenty of look-alikes:

Leucopaxillus piceinus: Differs by its bitter taste, pungent odor, and strongly forked gills that turn dark yellow in age.

Pleurotus dryinus: This is a large, fleshy, white, lignicolous species that turns yellowish in age and has a felty ring near the stem apex that leaves velar remnants on the cap margin.

Pleurotus ostreatus: Differs by having fleshy pale tan to dark gray-brown caps and by not turning rock hard when dried.

Hypsizygus elongatipes: Has soft, hollow stems up to 22 cm long and white caps with pinkish tinges that often have watery spots at disc.

Hypsizygus tessulatus: Usually has creamy to pale brown caps with a pinkish tinge and a marbled look, larger globose spores, and longer stems that enlarge at the base.

Panus conchatus: Often fruits in clusters on hardwoods, but has lilac colors when young with caps becoming more tan in age.

Pleurocybella porrigens: Angel Wings have larger spores, and a more delicate texture, even flabby according to some.

Pleurotus populinus: Has more cardboard-colored caps and fruits on cottonwoods.

Ossicaulis lachnopus: This is a Mediterranean species that fruits on beech and differs by having tiny spores and central stems.

The Bone Hard Wood Inhabiter has also had its share of synonyms, and these are important when considering reports on edibility. Under the name **Pleurotus circinatus**, Miron Hard noted that "it makes quite a delicious dish when well cooked." Under that same name, Charles McIlvaine commented "its flavor is pleasant, and texture when cooked, quite tender." On another page, under the name **Pleurotus lignatilis** he noted "this is a good species in every way." No one else seems to have commented on edibility except for Steve Trudell who suspects that the unpleasant odor and tough texture would make it not worth eating. Dr. Oz would probably consider it an excellent stool hardener, and just for the record, it causes a brown rot of hardwoods.

BIBLIOGRAPHY

J. Breitenbach & F. Kranzlin, *Fungi of Switzerland, Vol. 3,* 1991. Edition Mykologia, Lucerne, Switzerland.

Dorothy Brown, *Trial Field Key to the Pleurotoid Species in the Pacific Northwest,* 1981. Pacific Northwest Key Council, Seattle, Wash.

Stefan Buczacki, Chris Shields, & Denys Ovenden, *Collins Fungi Guide,* 2012. Harper-Collins, London.

E.J.H. Corner, *The Agaric Genera: Lentinus, Panus, and Pleurotus* in *Nova Hedwigia, Beihefte* 69, 1981.

Regis Courtecuisse & Bernard Duhem, *Mushrooms & Toadstools of Britain & Europe,* 1995. Harper-Collins, London.

Guillaume Eyssartier & Pierre Roux, *Le Guide des Champignons de France et Europe,* 2012. Editions Belin, Paris.

Miron Hard, *Mushrooms Edible and Otherwise,* 1908. Dover Publications, New York, NY.

Calvin Kauffman, *The Agaricaceae of Michigan,* 1922. Michigan Geological and Biological Survey, Lansing, Mich.

Thomas Kuyper, *Ossicaulis in Flora Agaricina Neerlandica 3 (132),* 1995. A.A. Balkema, Rotterdam, Holland.

Jakob Lange, *Flora Agaracina Danica, Vol. 2,* 1936. Society for the Advancement of Mycology, Copenhagen.

Charles McIlvaine & Robert Macadam, *One Thousand American Fungi,* 1902. Dover Publications, New York, NY.

Roger Phillips, *Mushrooms of North America,* 1991. Little, Brown & Co., Boston, Mass.

Scott Redhead & James Ginns, *A Reappraisal of Agaric Genera Associated with Brown Rots of Wood* in *Transactions of the Mycological Society of Japan* 26 (362–370), 1985.

Judy Roger, *Trial Field Key to Leucopaxillus Species in the Pacific Northwest,* 1981. Pacific Northwest Key Council, Seattle, Wash.

Steve Trudell & Joe Ammirati, *Mushrooms of the Pacific Northwest,* 2009. Timber Press, Portland, Ore.

Jan Vesterholt, *Ossicaulis in Funga Nordica,* 2008. Nordsvamp, Copenhagen.

Roy Watling & Norma Gregory, *Crepidotaceae, Pleurotaceae, and Other Pleurotoid Agarics* in *British Fungus Flora* 6, 1987. Royal Botanic Garden, Edinburgh.

Panaeolus papilionaceus (Bulliard) Quelet

The great variety of cap colors and textures has for centuries prompted experts to divide them into four separate species.

Since we've covered most other habitats in our "Mushroom of the Month" selections, it is time to direct our gaze to one that bears a special meaning in Whatcom County, that of field and dung. Perhaps our most common field and dung fungus locally is the cosmopolitan **Panaeolus papilionaceus**. Panaeolus in Greek means "all variegated." Papilionaceus derives from the Latin papilion for butterfly. "Moth" might be the more appropriate term. The drab colors, the often moth-like texture of the caps are helpful hints towards the identification of these ubiquitous pasture lovers. The "variegated" most likely refers to the gill faces, which soon acquire a mottled appearance as the spores mature at different times. This phenomenon is unique to Panaeolus and separates them in the field from Psathyrella. If you aren't convinced the salt and pepper look is there, you can move on to the chemical test. Spores of Panaeolus do not fade in concentrated sulphuric acid. They do fade with Psathyrella.

It turns out that caps aren't always satiny squamulose. They can look ratty and unappetizing or quite elegant with their delicate white appendiculate margins when fresh. Sometimes they can be shiny and smooth. At other times and on other substrates they can be obscurely wrinkled. The great variety of cap textures and colors has for centuries prompted experts to divide them into four separate species. In a classic case of DNA studies solving a difficult complex, Ewalt Gerhardt ascertained that **Pan-**aeolus campanulatus, **Panaeolus retirugus, Panaeolus papilionaceus**, and **Panaeolus sphinctrinus** were all the same species. Bulliard authored both **P. papilionaceus** in 1781 and **P. campanulatus** in 1792. The earlier name takes precedence. Two other synonyms reported from North America were **Panaeolus carbonarius** (Batsch) ex Saccardo and **Panaeolus semilanceatus** Peck non J.Lange.

When a major breakthrough like this one takes place, an amended species description is in order. To be technically correct it must absorb in this case all of the characters associated with the four formerly segregated species. If you google "Michael Kuo, **Panaeolus papilionaceus**" you will see that Kuo achieves this with a nice economy of words. If you are not near your computer, you will be treated with the following Gerhardt description.

Caps of the Variegated Butterfly are 1–4 cm wide, narrowly campanulate to broadly convex, sometimes with obtuse umbo. Surfaces vary from shiny glabrous to satiny-mothy or distinctly wrinkled. In age the caps can become rimosely cracked or mi-

LOOK-ALIKE

Psilocybe semilanceata

nutely squamulose or both. Colors vary from mouse gray to ivory with ochre discs, brownish gray with fawn discs (as seen in the lead photo), olive gray to olive black, tan, pale tawny, or even vinaceous buff. Despite this wide array of coloration, most experts felt it was easier to separate the complex using these features than microscopic ones, which always seemed to intergrade. Breitenbach & Kranzlin wrote "those forms can only be separated by macroscopic features which are greatly influenced by habitat, weather conditions, and amount of substrate." When you take into account that **Panaeolus papilionaceus** and all its synonyms have been recorded from North America, Europe, Japan, Chile, East Africa, Australia, the Antilles, and Mexico, you suspect a variation in substrates. But according to Hora, tropical specimens are restricted to horse dung. Others may disagree.

Young specimens are adorned at the cap margins with a white, tooth-like appendiculate veil, a character often used by researchers to separate it from other species of Panaeolus. Svrcek also noticed a secondary, cobwebby veil that connected margin to stipe that soon disappeared without a noticeable trace. It must be the most fleeting cortina in the world.

The gills are adnate to adnexed, sometimes ventricose, and usually grayish tan at first. They soon get that salt and pepper look as the black spores mature unevenly. At probably the same time, the gill edges become white to pallid, a sure sign the cheilocystidia have arrived. Stems are 1–4 mm thick and 6–15 cm long. They are hollow, brittle (breaking with a snapping sound, according to Svrcek), and smooth beneath a powdery white to grayish coating. Often striated at the apex, stems vary in color from whitish to ochre-brown to blackish, mimicking the caps in variations. Odor and taste are mild. Spores are black or dark purple brown in deposit. Habitats vary from directly on cow or horse dung, next to cow and horse dung, manure rich gardens and pastures, or rich areas in woods.

Georges Ola'h, who studied the group extensively, divided the "campanulatus-retirugis-sphinctrinus" group from other species of Panaeolus by their smooth spores, lack of pleurocystidia, and lack of a ring on their stems. He then separated the three by spore sizes, which typically intergraded, if you take the broad view.

Microscopically, the spores are smooth, thick walled, and lemon or almond shaped in profile due to a germ pore on one end. Taken as a composite measurement, they are 10.8–18.5 x 7–12.6 µm. Basidia are 4-spored without clamps at the bases. Cheilocystidia are cylindrical-flexuous or more rarely clavate to fusoid-ventricose with narrowed apices. The pileipellis is hymeniform, composed of clavate cells with a few cylindrical pileocystidia

LOOK-ALIKE

Panaeolus acuminatus

amongst them. Clamps are present and caulocystidia are present at the stem apex.

The closest relative is probably **Panaeolus papilionaceus var. parvisporus**, which differs by not having an obvious appendiculate veil. In his key on the Panaeoloideae, translated into English, Gerhardt first separates Panaeolus from Panaeolina by spore color. Panaeolus has a black spore print. Panaeolina has a dark brown spore print. If you then follow dry cap cuticle, cystidia of gill faces not consisting of thick-walled metuloids, and velar material present, you get to Panaeolus section Panaeolus. Then if you follow "ring absent" and sulphidia absent on the gill faces, you arrive at **Panaeolus papilionaceus**. The **var. parvisporus** has slightly shorter spores and cap margins indistinctly appendiculate.

I've seen them in Maine and I've seen them off the Kickerville Road in Washington state, and the one thing I can safely surmise is that plenty of **Panaeolus papilionaceus** have been eaten by seekers of the Liberty Cap. Immature specimens can ressemble **Psilocybe semilanceata** to the untrained eye. They share the same habitat, have dark spores and gills, small brownish bell-shaped caps, and slender stems. Closer scrutiny brings out the differences. The Liberty Cap will have purple-brown spores while **P. papilionaceus** has black spores. The cap cuticle of the Liberty Cap is sticky to viscid when moist while the wet caps of **P. papilionaceus** look merely water soaked. The caps of **Psilocybe**

LOOK-ALIKES

Panaeolus foenisecii

Tubaria furfuracea

semilanceata have an acute umbo. Those of **Panaeolus papilionaceus** do not. The stems of the Variegated Butterfly are stiff and brittle. Those of the Liberty Cap are pliant and have blue stains at the bases. Although Arora points out that **Psilocybe semilanceata** doesn't grow on dung or on lawns, there are some whom may disagree here in Whatcom County, especially if you accept a golf course as substituting for a lawn.

Other look-alikes are as follows:

Panaeolus acuminatus: Differs by the extremely hygrophanous caps that fade quickly from dark brown to pale grayish tan. It also lacks dentate velar material on the cap margins.

Panaeolus foenisecii: Shares the same habitats but has dark brown spores and grayish gills without mottled faces.

Psathyrella conissans from Minn.   Photo by Richard Morrison

Candolleomyces candolleana from B.C..

Panaeolus subbalteatus: Also fruits on dung but has a more cinnamon-brown cap with a dark brown marginal band and a thicker, more reddish stem beneath white tomentum.

Panaeolus cyanescens: Recorded from Florida and Louisiana, this differs by its smooth brown caps that fade hygrophanously to pale gray and the tendency of the stems to bruise blue when handled. **Panaeolus olivaceus**: Differs by its smooth grayish-olive caps, faintly roughened spores, and the habit of fruiting on soil not associated with dung.

Psathyrella conissans: Differs by fruiting in cespitose clusters

around tree stumps. It has pale watery brown to chestnut colored caps and vinaceous-red spores.

Candolleomyces candolleana: An extremely fragile species that is found around tree stumps and buried wood. It further differs by its ochre-brown caps that fade to buff and the dark brown spores.

My theory, then, at the onset of this article, was that **Panaeolus papilionaceus** must be harmless for the table. My only reservation about ingesting it myself had been the consideration of flavor, whether horse or cow, depending on the host substrate. As I read more and more comments on the culinary experiences I adjusted my priorities. Here, then, is a sampling of opinions:

Calvin Kauffman: "Its bad reputation goes back to 1816 and should not be taken seriously. A Minneapolis report says that two rather delicate ladies ate of it—two tablespoonfuls of stew. Drowsiness came on quickly, a sensation of intoxication, dizziness, trembling, staggering, numbness, contraction of the jaw, constriction of the throat, precordial distress, headache, and mild but irritant diarrhea. In one case, the heart was intermittent for a week." (Lincoff and Mitchel suspect a misidentification of the species.)

Charles McIlvaine: "I have seen it produce hilarity in a few instances, and other mild symptoms of intoxication, which were soon over, and with little reaction. Many personal testings have been without effect. Not dangerous, but should be eaten with caution."

Myron Hard: "Captain McIlvaine in his book speaks of this mushroom producing hilarity or a mild form of intoxication. I should advise against its use."

Paul Stamets: "I have not felt any effect, other than malaise, even when I ingested nearly 30 specimens. Hence, I consider **P. papilionaceus** to be inactive." (In his section on Panaeolus, the genus, he mentions that other species of Panaeolus are latent producers of psilocybin or psilocin. Most all of them produce urea, serotonin, and tryptophan.)

George Atkinson: "The plants have several times been eaten raw by me, and while they have a nutty flavor and odor, the taste is not entirely agreeable in this condition because of the accompanying slimy sensation." (This quote is in the field guide by William Sturgis Thomas, but attributed to Atkinson.)

David Biek: "Weakly hallucinogenic when eaten raw. 30–50 caps are said to be an average dose. It contains psilocybin, and according to one mycologist, pantherin, a toxin also found in **Amanita muscaria**."

Gary Menser: "The presence of psilocybin has been confirmed in species from Oregon and California. Chemical analysis consistently shows the presence of unidentified factors."

Wells & Mitchel: "Many cases of poisoning blamed on dung inhabiting Coprinus species are actually **Panaeolus campanulatus**."

Lincoff & Mitchel: "According to Miller, **Panaeolus campanulatus** contains pantherin and related toxins. They can produce sickness and hallucination but do not contain

LOOK-ALIKES

Formerly Panaeolus sphinctrinus from B.C.

Panaeolus cyanescens from Dominican Republic

Panaeolus olivaceus

psilocybin or psilocin. Ibotenic acid, muscimol, muscazone, and possibly other toxic metabolites including pantherin, tricholomic acid, and solitaric acid have been reported in **Panaeolus campanulatus**."

William Thomas: "Although pronounced edible by all authorities, being of nutty flavor and agreeable odor, it does not appeal to mycophagists. Dr. W.W. Ford recently investigated this species and found an extract of it fatal to guinea pigs."

This last culinary appraisal was attached to **Panaeolus retirugus**. But go figure. If you amalgamate all the characters in a new combination, you should amalgamate the edibility factors as well. Furthermore, Thomas had a point about those mycophagists. Eighty-one years later and the Variegated Butterfly still awaits a recipe.

Taking it a step further, if DNA sequencing has proved that four hitherto different species are now the same entity, wouldn't the toxins also be the same? Probably not so, according to Robert Rogers. **Paneolus retirugus** contains antibiotic diterpene with the mycelial culture containing pleuromutilin. **Panaeolus papilionaceus** is a "high producer of inulinase and invertase at an optimum pH of 6.5 and sixty degrees Celsius." **Panaeolus sphinctrinus** "produces laccase isoenzymes and manganese peroxide with activity at high pH levels." **Panaeolus campanulatus** contains psilocybin, baeocystin, and serotonin, and has been used as a hallucinogen. Known as "the laughing mushroom" in China, it is also active against E. coli. Who knows which one of these was fatal to guinea pigs?

BIBLIOGRAPHY

David Arora, *All That the Rain Promises and More*, 1991. Ten Speed Press, Berkeley, Calif.

David Biek, *Mushrooms of Northern California*, 1984. Spore Prints, Redding, Calif.

J. Breitenbach & F. Kranzlin, *Fungi of Switzerland*, Vol. 4, 1995. Edition Mykologia, Lucerne, Switzerland.

Ewalt Gerhardt, *Taxonomische Revision der Gattungen Panaeolus und Panaeolina* in *Bibliotheca Botanica*, Heft 147 (1–149), 1996.

Karen & Richard Haard, *Poisonous & Hallucinogenic Mushrooms*, 1977. Cloudburst Press, Seattle, Wash.

Miron Hard, *Mushrooms, Edible & Otherwise*, 1908. Dover Publications, New York, NY.

Rokuya Imazeki, Tsuguo Hongo, & Keisuke Tubaki, *Common Fungi of Japan in Color*, 1970. Hoikusha Publishing Co., Osaka.

Calvin Kauffman, *The Agaricaceae of Michigan*, 1918. Michigan Geological and Biological Survey, Lansing, Mich.

Michael Kuo, *Panaeolus papilionaceus*. MushroomExpert.com.

Gary Lincoff & D.H. Mitchel, *Toxic and Hallucinogenic Mushroom Poisoning*, 1977. Van Nostrand Reinhold Co., New York, NY.

Charlers McIlvaine & Robert Macadam, *One Thousand American Fungi*, 1902. Dover Publications, New York, NY.

Gary Menser, *Hallucinogenic and Poisonous Mushroom Field Guide*, 1978. Ronin Publishing, Berkeley, Calif.

Georges Ola'h, *Le Genre Panaeolus: Essai Taxonomique et Physiologique*, 1969. Herbier Louis Marie, Paris.

David Pegler, *Agaric Flora of the Lesser Antilles* in *Kew Bulletin Additional Series IX, 1983*. Her Majesty's Stationary Office, London.

Carleton Rea, *British Basidomycetaceae*, 1922. Strauss & Cramer, Hirschberg, Germany.

Robert Rogers, *The Fungal Pharmacy*, 2011. North Atlantic Books, Berkeley, Calif.

A.H. Smith, *The North American Species of Psathyrella*, 1972. New York Botanical Garden, Bronx, NY.

Helen & A.H. Smith & Nancy Weber, *How to Know the Gilled Mushrooms*, 1979. William C. Brown, Dubuque, Iowa.

Paul Stamets, *Psilocybin Mushrooms of the World, 1996*. Ten Speed Press, Berkeley, Calif.

Mirko Svrcek, *The Hamlyn Book of Mushrooms and Fungi*, 1983. Artia, Prague, Czechoslovakia.

William Sturgis Thomas, *Field Book of Common Mushrooms*, 1928. G.P. Putnam's Sons, New York, NY.

Roy Watling & Norma Gregory, *British Fungus Flora 5 / Strophariaceae & Coprinaceae*, 1987. Royal Botanic Garden, Edinburgh.

Mary Wells & D.H. Mitchel, *Mushrooms of Colorado and Adjacent Areas*, 1970. Denver Museum of Natural History, Denver, Colo.

Wikipedia.org, *Panaeolus papilionaceus var. pavisporus*.

Panaeolus semiovatus (Sowerby) Lundell & Nannfeldt

If picking for the table, it helps to offer the pasture owner the mushrooms stem first.

It was May 2nd, 2011, and despite heavy rains in April, no reports of new mushroom sightings were coming into my office. Therefore I was a bit taken off guard when Rich Kohr, one of the maintenance chiefs at the Herald Building, motioned me aside in the sixth floor corridor.

"By the way," he said, "Forgot to bring one in. My brother has a farm out on the Van Wyck Road. There, next to a barn right next to the road is a pile of horse manure. There are large, white mushrooms growing on that pile. Think they could be edible?"

"Large, white?" I repeated.

I was there. Small, white would have implied **Coprinopsis nivea.** Rich's description implied a fungus I hadn't seen before.

It was drizzling when I arrived at the pile. The mushrooms looked like a mini forest of eggs on sticks. Right away I could see they weren't in Coprinus because the gills weren't deliquescing. Older gills were pure black. Some of the caps were 8 cm wide and looked like bell-shaped World War I helmets rising out of the dung. The odd thing was the presence of velar remnants on most of the stems.

Back at the office, it didn't take long to key them out. It turned out that almost everyone else has seen this mushroom but me. It is cosmopolitan, found around the world from Hawaii to Europe to the Yukon wherever there is horse dung, or even sheep, cow, or donkey dung, according to Breitenbach & Kranzlin.

An iconic photo of a single specimen of **Panaeolus semiovatus** on a pyramid-shaped pile of horse dung can be found in *The Wild Mushroom* by George McCarthy. The shot transforms the mushroom into a monument.

There is no dearth of field descriptions. Caps can be 3–9 cm wide and are at first egg shaped, then hemispherical, and finely broadly bell shaped in age. Cap colors range from ivory to tan to grayish tan or pale brownish, all on the same pile. They are tacky when moist, shiny when dry, and usually finely wrinkled or rugulose. When dried in the sun, the caps become cracked or areolate. The cap margins can project beyond the gills. They are straight or incurved and occasionally flecked with veil remnants. According to A.H. Smith, the cap colors are affected by sunlight. They tend to be darker in the shade. The cap context is whitish, but yellowish just beneath the cuticle and at the base of the stem. It should also be mentioned that the fruiting bodies are fragile, which is a typical trait of species with cellular cap structures. The gills are sharply adnexed at first, then become adnate as the caps expand, and finally end up almost free. They are gray to pale brown when young, but soon become mottled gray and black as the spores mature. This salt and pepper look is due to the spores maturing at different times, a hallmark of Panaeolus. Gill edges soon become white fimbriate. When the gills are finally all black, the caps have begun to sag.

Stems can be 6–20 cm long and 3–15 mm thick. Kibby mentions that the great variability in sizes is due to the relative nutrients in the dung. An especially rich piece of horse dung can produce a 25-centimeter stem. The stems are stiff, brittle, hollow, cartilaginous, and terete (perfectly rounded) until expanding slightly at the base. The upper part is powdery and striated where the gills once adhered to it. The stems are white

P. semiovatus with a better view of the veil

above the ring and pale tan below. Bases are sometimes found with appressed white mycelium. The partial veil tears away from the cap margin as the cap expands and settles unevenly on the stem. This thin, membranous ring is usually torn and soon vanishes, leaving a ring zone marked by the black spores that had originally landed on the ring. Rings are usually fluted or striated with crenate margins. The second **P. semiovatus** photo shows the ring being torn as it transitions from cap margin to stem. The spores are black in deposit, the taste is mild, and the odor reported as mild, like straw, or slightly fungoid.

Panaeolus semiovatus appears in temperate climates around the globe in the northern hemisphere. Roberts & Evans have it shaded in for New Zealand while Poliwoda et al. claim it has turned up in Tierra del Fuego.

As for edibility, opinions in the literature tend to swing from one extreme spectrum to another. A few prime examples: **Lorentz Pearson**: "**Panaeolus separatus**, 'a synonym,' is definitely poisonous, causing hallucinations."

Vera & Kent McKnight: "Not recommended. Some Panaeolus are poisonous."

Bruno Cetto: "Senza interesse."

J. Walton Groves: "Species of Panaeolus should not be eaten and can cause a form of intoxication."

Pegler & Spooner: "Inedible, possibly poisonous."

Andreas Neuner: "Although not poisonous by any means, the environment it has chosen

LOOK-ALIKES

Panaeolus antillarum

Coprinopsis nivea

appears somewhat unappetizing and uninviting. Its value as an edible fungus has therefore not yet been established."

Soothill & Fairhurst: "Said to be poisonous."

David Arora: "Edible, according to most sources. There is one dubious report of psilocybin containing specimens from Colorado."

A.H. Smith: "Edible and good, but not recommended. The genus contains a number of species that cause Psilocybin type poisonings. Smaller specimens could be confused with these."

Helene Schalkwijk-Barendsen: "Sometimes it is hallucinogenic."

Dickinson & Lucas: "The fungus consumes a certain amount of the dung, and in so doing, some of the material consumed becomes a part of the fungus itself."

Charles McIlvaine: Under the former name of **Anellaria separata**,

MORE DUNG LOVERS

Psilocybe merdaria from England

Psilocybe cubensis from Calif.

Psilocybe merdicola from Spain

he noted "It is substantial in flesh, excellent in substance and flavor. Cook soon and not over 15 minutes."

There seemed to be no time to lose, so I gathered up the collection and headed for my boat galley with mixed emotions. After sautéing four caps in salted butter, I have to agree with Smith and McIlvaine. The flavor was very, very good. The caps absorbed the salted butter and brought out a rich, salty taste on a par with the Gypsy Mushroom.

A day later, Jack Waytz also took the culinary plunge. He pronounced them to be good, and thought they had a slight smoky flavor. Who knows? Maybe a little pre-spontaneous combustion was present. There was no tinge of horse nor dung, and no hallucinogenic experience either. The spirit of our cofounder, Dave Jansen, lived on.

Since only a few of our readers own horses, most sightings of this mushroom will be on other people's properties. It is always good etiquette to knock on the door and inquire about availability. If picking for the table it is helpful to offer the specimens to the pasture owner stems first. The reaction will be immediate. "By all means, take every last one of them!" will be the response.

Microscopically, there is plenty to look at. Spores are huge, dark brown in KOH, and thick-walled. Moreno, Manjon, & Zugaza report spore measurements of 16-22 x 9-14 µm. There is a clear and present hyaline germ pore either centrally located at the apex or obliquely off-center. It was once thought that specimens with obliquely lateral germ pores might represent a different species, but Breitenbach & Kranzlin found both kinds of germ pore locations in the same spore deposit. The spores are ellipsoid in profile and slightly pip shaped or obscurely angled in face view. The basidia are 4-spored and measure 23-30 x 10-12 µm. Clamps are present at the bases. The gill trama is of subparallel hyphae verging on interwoven. The hyphae in the center of the gill measure 11.5-18 µm wide. The pleurocystidia are saccate, clavate, or mucronate, and measure 32-34 x 12-14 µm. The refracted pale yellow contents allow them to be termed "chrysocystidia." The cheilocystidia are highly variable in shape, including all the shapes of the pleurocystidia plus fusoid-ventricose with flexuous walls. According to Orson Miller, these clavate-rostrate cheilocystidia are a distinctive feature of **Panaeolus semiovatus** and separate it from younger fruiting bodies of **Panaeolus antillarum**. The cap cuticle is a hymeniform palisade of clavate to pyriform cells several layers deep, and interspersed frequently with filiform, clavate, subcapitate, or lageniform pileocystidia. Beneath the cellular layers of the pileipellis, the context soon becomes gelatinous and outlines of the hyphae become hard to discern. A.H. Smith described the context as "floccose."

Panaeolus semiovatus, also known as the Sticky Mottlegill or the Dung Mottlegill depending on which author you follow, has been moved around nomenclaturally. Jakob Lange stuck it in Stropharia in 1923 due to the ring on its stem. It does look like a larger version of **Protostropharia semiglobata**, which ironically doesn't have a ring. In various guides, it can be found under its numerous synonyms, including **Panaeolus separatus**, **Anellaria separata**, **Anellaria semiovata,** or even **Anellaria fimiputris** in older British guides.

Some lookalikes and close relatives are as follows:

Panaeolus antillarum: Another whitish Panaeolus of a smaller stature with campanulate caps up to 5 cm wide. There is no velar material and the gill edges are white pruinose. Also found with horse dung. Although first found in the Antilles it has now been found in Poland and the Yukon.

Panaeolus phalenarum: According to Lincoff & Pacioni this has whitish caps tinged reddish, no ring, and an odor of burnt sugar. It differs further from **P. semiovatus** by its dentate cap margin. Poliwoda et al consider it a variety of **Panaeolus semiovatus**.

Coprinopsis nivea: Also found on herbivore dung, it has much smaller egg-shaped caps with white powdery granules, no ring on the stem, and a tendency for the cap to deliquesce in age.

Psilocybe merdaria: Also appears in pastures with horse dung, it differs by the small cinnamon-brown to dark ochre caps up to 4 cm wide, and yellowish gills that age dark brown.

Psilocybe cubensis: Found with both horse and cow dung, it differs by its persistent membranous ring and the tendency to bruise blue where touched. It is native to the Caribbean and the Southeastern US.

Psilocybe merdicola: Also fruits on herbivore dung, but differs by its ochre-brown caps and much smaller stature.

Considering the favored habitat, **Panaeolus semiovatus** is just one more reason to check out the Kentucky Derby. While everyone else is at the track, you can be quietly foraying the stalls and paddocks, and with any luck, find an esoteric complement for your evening bourbon mash.

BIBLIOGRAPHY

David Arora, *Mushrooms Demystified*, 1986. Ten Speed Press, Berkeley, Calif.

J. Breitenbach & F. Kranzlin, *Fungi of Switzerland, Vol.4*, 1995. Edition Mykologia, Lucerne.

Bruno Cetto, *I Funghi dal Vero, Vol. 2*, 1980. Arti Grafiche Saturnia, Trento, Italy

Colin Dickinson & John Lucas, *The Encyclopedia of Mushrooms*, 1979. Van Nostrand Reinhold Co., New York, NY.

Vera Evenson, *Mushrooms of Colorado*, 1997. Denver Botanic Gardens, Denver, Colo.

Ewald Gerhardt, *Panaeolus in Funga Nordica*, 2008. Nordsvamp, Copenhagen.

J. Walton Groves, *Edible and Poisonous Mushrooms of Canada*, 1979. Research Branch, Agriculture Canada, Ottawa.

Geoffrey Kibby, *Mushrooms and Toadstools*, 1979. Oxford University Press, London.

Geoffrey Kibby, *Colour Encyclopedia of Mushrooms and Toadstools*, 1979. Cathay Books, London.

Michael Kuo & Andy Methven, *100 Cool Mushrooms*, 2010. University of Michigan Press, Ann Arbor, Mich.

George Massee, *British Fungi and Lichens*, 1900. George Routledge & Sons, London.

George McCarthy, *The Wild Mushroom*, 1996. Fountain Press, Surrey, England.

Charles McIlvaine & Robert Macadam, *One Thousand American Fungi*, 1902. Dover Publications, New York, NY.

Vera & Kent McKnight, *Peterson Field Guides—Mushrooms*, 1987. Houghton Mifflin, Boston.

Orson Miller, *Interesting Fungi of the St. Elias Mountains, Yukon Territory, and Adjacent Canada* in *Mycologia* 60 (1190–1203), 1968.

Orson & Hope Miller, *North American Mushrooms*, 2006. Morris Book Publishing Co., Guilford, Conn.

Gabriel Moreno, Jose Luis Manjon, & Alvaro Zugaza, *La Guia de Incafo de los Hongos de la Peninsula Iberica, Tomo 2*, 1986. Incafo S.A., Madrid.

Andreas Neuner, *Chatto Nature Guides' Mushrooms and Fungi*, 1978. Chatto & Windus, London.

Giovanni Pacioni & Gary Lincoff, *Simon & Schuster's Guide to Mushrooms,* 1981. Simon & Schuster, New York, NY.

Lorentz Pearson, *The Mushroom Manual*, 1987. Naturegraph Publishers, Happy Camp, Calif.

David Pegler & Brian Spooner, *The Mushroom Identifier*, 1992. Smithmark Publishers, New York, NY.

Anna Poliwoda, Mark Halama, Danuta Witkowska, & Izabela Jasicka-misiak, *An Adentive Panaeolus antillarum in Poland with Notes on its Taxonomy, Geographical Distribution, and Ecology* in *Cryptogamie Mycologie* 35 (3–22), 2014.

John Ramsbottom, *Larger British Fungi*, 1965. Trustees of the British Museum, London.

Carleton Rea, *British Basidiomycetaceae*, 1922. Strauss & Cramer, Hirschberg, Germany.

Peter Roberts & Shelley Evans, *The Book of Fungi*, 2011. University of Chicago Press, Chicago.

Helene Schalkwijk-Barendsen, *Mushrooms of Western Canada*, 1991. Lone Pine Publishers, Edmonton, Alberta.

A.H. Smith, *Studies in the Dark-Spored Agarics* in *Mycologia* 40 (669–707), 1948.

A.H. Smith, *Mushrooms in Their Natural Habitats*, 1949. Sawyer's, Lancaster, Penn.

A.H. Smith & Nancy Weber, *The Mushroom Hunter's Field Guide*, 1980. University of Michigan Press, Ann Arbor, Mich.

Eric Soothill & Alan Fairhurst, *The New Field Guide to Fungi*, 1978. Michael Joseph, London.

Daniel Stuntz & Bill Isaacs, *Pacific Northwestern Fungi* in *Mycologia* 54 (272–298), 1962.

Elsie Wakefield & R.W.G. Dennis, *Common British Fungi*, 1981. Saiga Publishing, Surrey, England.

Roy Watling & Norma Gregory, *Strophariaceae and Coprinaceae in British Fungus Flora 5*, 1987. Royal Botanic Garden, Edinburgh.

DIGERNESS 1/18/15

Panus conchatus (Bulliard) Fries

The fruiting bodies stick around
for a long time, eventually drying
up instead of rotting.

It was most likely in September of 1988 when I heard a tentative knock on my door. In a moment, in walked Dan Digerness, beard and all, seemingly more jazzed than usual. He had a mushroom to show me. Now there is nothing that Dan enjoys more than to present me with a fungal puzzle I can't figure out in front of him. This did not disappoint. It was a small purple mushroom about 4 cm wide with beautiful lilac pubescence at the base of the stem. The gills were decurrent and the spores would turn out to be white. Only one specimen. He had found it on a log in a thin stretch of hardwoods between the railroad tracks and Wharf Street near the south end of Cornwall Avenue in Bellingham, proper.

It would not key out for me. Not in Arora, not in Moser, not in the Pacific Northwest Key Council keys. It was hard to fathom how any mushroom so outrageously purple could have avoided the notice of professionals from the beginning of time. Dan was cackling away to fit the band. After A.H. Smith & Singer I had to toss in the towel.

It took another three years to figure out why. This time it was former club member John Baker who gave me a call. He had found something unusual across from his home in the 100-Acre Woods. We strolled about 80 yards in and there they were.... A whole colony of what appeared to be flesh-tan Clitocybes marching down a wild cherry log. And right in the center was a cespitose clump of all-purple specimens, smaller than the rest. I was as ecstatic as I dared to be.

It turned out that **Panus conchatus** radically changes as it matures. The juvenile specimens are always some shade of violet. No key picks up on this. They all center on mature fruiting bodies that are mostly leather in color. As it grows, the tough, coriaceous carpophores lose their violet color with caps becoming flesh tan to dark ochre or chestnut ochre before fading to beige tan in age.

LOOK-ALIKE

Pleurotus pulmonarius

The fruiting bodies stick around for a long time, eventually drying up instead of rotting. All these phases have led to 39 synonyms in the *Index Fungorum*. It might be a record for fleshy agarics fruiting on wood.

The literature tells us that caps of **Panus conchatus** can range from 4–17 cm wide. They are smooth with inrolled margins at first. As they expand, they become irregularly fan-shaped to shallowly funnel shaped with lobed margins. The surface changes from smooth with finely appressed tomentum to innately fibrillose and then scaly at the disc in maturity. Sometimes these scales are in concentric zones. The context is white, flexuous, and leathery. The gills are decurrent and fork at the bases. They are shallow, violet at first, then whitish to cream tan in age. Giuseppe Pace claims they turn rusty when bruised. The gill edges are entire, not saw-toothed as in species of Lentinus. The stems are eccentric or laterally attached. They seem very short in relation to cap width. They measure 2–5 cm long and ½–3 cm thick. The surface is roughly fibrillose and tapers towards the base. They start out with a purple bloom becoming concolorous with the cap in age. The spores are white, inamyloid, and turn yellow in Melzer's solution. I found the taste to be slightly soapy and the odor pleasantly mild, reminiscent of **Lepista tarda**.

Oddly enough, recent phylogenetic analysis showed that despite the gills, **Panus conchatus** belongs with the Polyporaceae.

Panus conchatus means the "Conch-Like Tumor" in Latin. Conch-Like must derive from the clusters of imbricate, confluent caps it forms on logs. "Tumor" is a sad misnomer. According to Robert Rogers, the species has a 100% inhibition rate against sarcoma 180 and Ehrlich carcinoma. In China it is used to cure pain in the legs, numbness in the legs, lumbago, and discomfort in tendons and blood vessels. You can even purchase a Tendon-Easing Pill in China that is made from it.

In the Pacific Northwest it is found on alder, cottonwood, and wild cherry. In Europe and the Appalachians it prefers beech, birch, elm, or poplar. They are found worldwide in temperate zones, and perhaps due to their durable, tough fruiting bodies, also in the tropics. Hongo recorded them from Papua, New Guinea. Corner found them in Malaysia and Borneo. Guzman has them from Panama.

The Conch Panus produces a white rot in wood and is saprobic on logs, stumps, and buried roots. Fergus suspects it is also a parasite, having found it on living trees.

As for look-alikes, the species is just too tough and leathery to be a Clitocybe. A list of potential look-alikes follows here:

Panus neostrigosus: Perhaps the closest look-alike, it has a much more densely hairy cap.
Lentinus levis: A large whitish species with coarsely hairy caps.
Gomphus clavatus: Has the violet to tan coloring but has gills in the form of thick ridges.
Pleurotus pulmonarius: It has white gills from the very begin-

LOOK-ALIKES

Hypsizygus tessulatus

Gomphus clavatus

(Some name changes: Panus neostrigosus was Panus rudis, Lentinus levis was Panus strigosus, Panus strigellus was Lentinus strigellus, and Neolentinus cyathiformis was Neolentinus schaefferi.)

ning, lubricous tan colored caps, and often lacks a stem.
Neolentinus cyathiformis: Has velvety cream colored to pale brownish caps that run up to 20 cm wide and finely toothed gill edges.
Panus strigellus: A tropical species with violet tinges that has a much smaller stature.
Hypsizygus tessulatus: Differs by lacking purplish tones on cap and stem.

Microscopically, the species has smooth, ellipsoid spores measuring 5–7.5 x 2.5–3.5 µm. The cystidia are thick-walled, the basidia clamped at the bases, and the gill trama described as irregular. What seems most unusual for an agaric is the dimitic context. There are both generative and skeletal hyphae in the pileal trama. Corner found the skeletal hyphae to have densely oily contents and extend up to 1,500 µm in length.

Descriptions of **Panus conchatus** can be found in numerous guides under the names **Panus torulosus**, **Lentinus conchatus**, or **Pleurotus conchatus**. The *Index Fungorum* considers these names to be synonyms.

As for edibility the flesh is so tough that lengthy cooking is not even a subject. Dr. Orson Miller noted "edible when young," with no particular comment on the flavor. Fischer and Bessette mentioned a mediocre flavor. It can be surmised that older specimens must be chewed on for quite some time for this flavor to emerge. Pacioni thought it had a slight odor of aniseed and a faint earthy flavor. Pace, Rinaldi, & Tyndalo all thought it had a turnip flavor. And McIlvaine, out to make the most of a poor situation, wrote "the fungus is tough when old, but makes an excellent gravy." Most other authors consider it inedible.

If you ate one by mistake, the result is harmless. Although no time soon will **Panus conchatus** appear in a mycophagist's cookbook, there are other benefits. Anti-cancerous properties? In 2004, a team of researchers isolated a compound from **Panus conchatus** that they called panepoxydone. It proved to be an inhibitor of transcription factors that are favorable in the production of cancer. Too bad the Conch Panus is a somewhat rare species. Although, since it has been found in the wild sharing logs with Oyster mushrooms, it might be possible to cultivate it using the same methods.

BIBLIOGRAPHY

David Arora, *Mushrooms Demystified*, 1986. Ten Speed Press, Berkeley, Calif.

Cornelis Bas, Thomas Kuyper, Machiel Noordeloos, & Else Vellinga, *Pleurotaceae* in *Flora Agaracina Neerlandica 2 (27)*, 1990.

J. Breitenbach & F. Kranzlin, *Fungi of Switzerland, Vol. 3*, 1991. Edition Mykologia, Lucerne.

E.J.H. Corner, *The Agaric Genera: Lentinus, Panus, and Pleurotus* in *Nova Hedwigia, Beihefte 69*, 1981.

Regis Courtecuisse & Bernard Duhem, *Mushrooms and Toadstools of Britain and Europe*, 1995. Harper-Collins, London.

Charles Fergus, *Illustrated Genera of Wood Decay Fungi*, 1960. Burgess Publishuing Co., Minneapolis, Minn.

Alan & Arleen Bessette & David Fischer, *Mushrooms of Northeastern North America*, 1997. Syracuse University Press, Syracuse, NY.

Gaston Guzman & Meike Piepenbring, *Los Hongos de Panama*, 2011. Instituto de Ecologia, Xalapa, Veracruz, Mexico.

Miron Hard, *Mushrooms Edible and Otherwise*, 1908. Dover Publications, New York, NY.

Tsuguo Hongo, *Agarics from Papua—New Guinea: 2* in *Reports of the Tottori Mycological Institute 11*, (29–41), 1974.

Ying Jianzhe, Mao Xiaolan, Ma Qiming, Zong Yichen, & Wen Huaan, *Icons of Medicinal Fungi from China*, 1987. Science Press, Beijing.

Charles McIlvaine & Robert Macadam, *One Thousand American Fungi*, 1902. Dover Publications, New York, NY.

Orson & Hope Miller, *North American Mushrooms*, 2006. Morris Book Publishing Co., Guilford, Conn.

Orson Miller & Donald Manning, *Distribution of the Lignicolous Tricholomataceae in the Southern Appalachians* in *The Distributional History of the Biota of the Southern Appalachians 4 (307–344)*, 1976.

Guiseppe Pace, *Mushrooms of the World*, 1998. Firefly Books, Buffalo, NY.

Giovanni Pacioni & Gary Lincoff, *Simon & Schuster's Guide to Mushrooms*, 1981. Simon & Schuster, New York, NY.

Roumyana Petrova, Abraham Reznick, Solomon Wasser, Cvetomir Denchev, Eviatar Nevo, & Jamal Mahajna, *Fungal Metabolites Modulating NF-KB Activity: An Approach to Cancer Therapy and Chemoprevention* in *Oncology Report 19 (299–308)*, 2008.

John Ramsbottom, *A Handbook of the Larger British Fungi*, 1965. Trustees of the British Museum, London.

Augusto Rinaldi & Vassili Tyndalo, *The Complete Book of Mushrooms*, 1974. Crown Publishers, New York, NY.

Bill Roody, *Mushrooms of West Virginia and the Southern Appalachians*, 2003. University Press of Kentucky, Lexington, Kentucky.

Helen & A.H. Smith & Nancy Weber, *How to Know the Gilled Mushrooms*, 1979. William C. Brown, Dubuque, Iowa.

Eric Soothill & Alan Fairhurst, *The New Field Guide to Fungi*, 1978. Michael Joseph, London.

Roy Watling, *Identification of the Larger Fungi*, 1973. Hulton Educational Publications, Amersham, Bucks., England.

Wikipedia.org, *Panus conchatus*.

Ben-Zion Zaidman, Majed Yassin, Jamal Mahajna, & Solomon Wasser, *Medicinal Mushroom Modulators of Molecular Targets as Cancer Therapeutics* in *Applied Microbiology and Biotechnology* 67 (453–468), 2005.

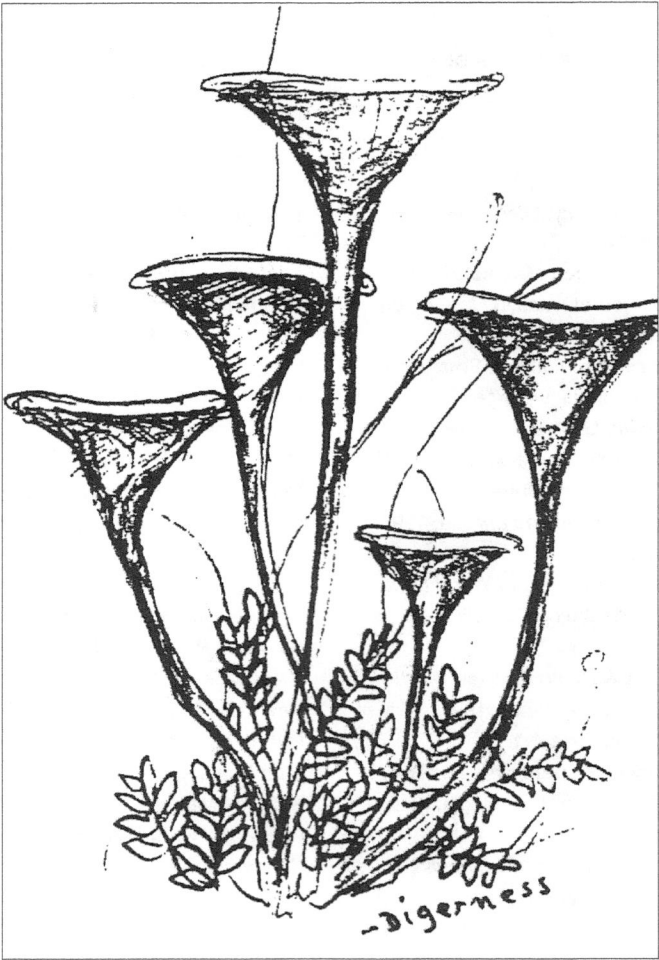

~Digerness

Peziza arvernensis Boudier

They looked like soggy pieces of leather,
draped over the decomposing log.

It all started when Bob Mooers, retired roofer extraordinaire, brought this odd ascomycete to our May meeting in 1993. The flattened brown fungus lay on the inspection table like a pizza left out in the rain. It was so trashed that members seemed to avoid it on instinct, as if it might give off an unpleasant odor when touched. But this did not daunt Bob. He picked it up, thrust it at me, and demanded to know what it was. When he laid it back on the table it cracked in five pieces.

It turned out to be the Peziza question of the century.

I told Bob it might be **Peziza vesiculosa**, but this specimen was too far gone to deal with. He would need to get back out to his secret morel patch and find more. As luck would have it, I would get another shot at it later.

On July 29th, 1993, I found the same Peziza (see lead photo) on rotten cedar at the Stimpson Family Nature Reserve near Lake Whatcom in Bellingham. They looked like soggy pieces of leather, draped over the decomposing log and also on the ground in front. So much for keying the Peziza by habitat. The carpophores were 12 cm wide and colored ochre chestnut inside and out. The margins were lacerate and irregularly wavy but not overtly fimbriate. There were no pustules on the exterior surface. They seemed to be over-mature specimens that had flattened in age.

Then, on October 23rd, a second fruiting occurred on the same cedar log. This time the fruiting bodies were younger (lower photo). They were cup-shaped and measured 4–6 ½ cm wide. Some had no stems. Others had stems up to 6 mm long, obscurely indented. The interior hymenium was smooth and not convoluted. The exterior surface was minutely furfuraceous with a hand lens. All the carpophores were more or less tawny, and the cup margins finely crenulate.

Under the microscope the tips of the asci turned blue in Melzer's, a strong sign we had a Peziza. The spores were ellipsoid, finely punctate, and measured 14.4–16.7 x 8.6–10 µm. There were eight per ascus, uniseriate, with no guttules in the contexts. The asci measured 214–246 x 11–14 µm. All these clues seemed to steer me in the direction of **Peziza silvestris** (now con-

Another view of Peziza arvernensis

Disciotis venosa from California

Peziza vesiculosa   Photo by Richard Morrison

Peziza badia

sidered a synonym of **Peziza arvernensis**). But the asci were thicker than the measurements given by Tylutki, and the tips of the paraphyses narrower. When I added in the facts that the typical convoluted hymenial surface was lacking and the species had fruited on conifer wood, I knew it was time to bring in Dr. Nancy Weber.

Besides being Dr. A.H. Smith's daughter, she is our resident Northwest expert on the discomycetes. She answered on the third ring. I immediately broke into a full description of the specimens. This monologue went on for quite some time.

"Well," she finally asked, "have you examined the paraphyses?"

Paraphyses are those slender and sterile filaments that occasionally appear between the asci like ghostly space fillers. I had informed her that so far I had only measured the widths of the tips. I hadn't measured lengths because I hadn't seen a whole one yet.

"Well, you see, that's a problem," she told me, "You need to see the bases of the paraphyses to determine whether they are branched or not."

"And if they are?"

"Then you have **Peziza micropus** or something in that group."

I tried for two days to see the paraphyses forked at their bases. Sometimes it took half an hour just to locate a paraphysis. Squash mount after squash mount went by. The tips of the asci seemed to be in pairs, but no matter what I did, I could not get a clear view of a base. I had to rest the case.

Then, in the spring of 1994, a most fortunate turn of events took place. Dr. Weber and the strange Peziza arrived in Ellensburg simultaneously. Nancy had been invited to deliver the lecture at the annual spring foray held by the Pacific Northwest Key Council. After the lecture I informed her of my difficulties in trying to view an entire paraphysis. She suggested I try separating the material with pins.

As if on cue, Judy Roger trotted over with a pair of probes. Judy is one of my mentors and an accomplished Oregonian amateur mycologist. She seemed happy to demonstrate the technique. Wielding the probes like chopsticks, she began piercing and pulling at a tiny scab of material from the hymenium. You could barely see the resulting shards with the naked eye. Some of these were then squashed on a slide. Sure enough, after about five minutes, we all had an unobstructed view of a forked base. I had the distinct impression Nancy had known they would be there.

The next dilemma was that **Peziza micropus** didn't really match up with my collection beyond the presence of a stem, the branched paraphyses, the chestnut colored hymenium, the spore size, and the fact it also fruits on rotten wood. But that wood is known to be beech, elm, alder, or willow, not coniferous wood. It differs from our collection in the pustulate exterior surface that turns whitish as it ages. It also varies in the smaller stature, never ex-

LOOK-ALIKES

Peziza repanda

Peziza petersii

Peziza praetervisa

LOOK-ALIKES

Discina ancilis

Gyromitra melaleucoides

Auricularia fuscosuccinea from Colombia

ceeding 6 cm in width. Above all, the ellipsoid spores are smooth, not finely ornamented. Both **Peziza arvernensis** and **Peziza micropus** are fragile. Both have a well-developed inner layer of interwoven hyphae, and both have spores without guttules.

Meanwhile, **Peziza arvernensis** is supposed to be without a stem or have a minuscule knob about 2 mm by 2 mm. The exterior surface is almost always distinctly paler than the inner surface. Yet the spores and the larger size of our specimens fit the concept well. Steve Trudell's photo o**f P. arvernensis** is the closest to our collection in the popular guides.

The implication is that other species of Peziza have been found with branched paraphyses. In Brian Spooner's key to Peziza and Plicaria, published in 2001, a branched paraphysis is not even a diagnostic character in the key. To further complicate the issue, Legon and Spooner showcased **Peziza micropus** in *The Mycologist* 4, 1990. The cup margins were described as distinctly crenate to dentate, but there was no mention of a split paraphyses. Fruiting bodies are only 2–4 cm wide, and it was suggested to be a possible synonym of **Peziza repanda**.

Nine of the most common look-alikes are as follows:

Peziza vesiculosa: Differs by fruiting on dung and having a scurfy, pallid exterior.

Disciotis venosa: Differs by its pallid, pustulate exterior and much larger spores at 19–25 x 12–15 µm. It is said to be poisonous if eaten raw. According

367

to Thompson it can also have paraphyses split at the bases.

Peziza repanda: Also fruits on wood, but has a scurfy, cream colored exterior.

Peziza badia: Differs by having a dark olive-brown interior surface and a finely granular ochre-brown exterior. It also differs by having reticulate spores.

Peziza petersii: Differs by fruiting at burn sites. Fruiting bodies are often compressed in packed clusters, and grow up to 4 cm wide.

Peziza praetervisa: Also fruits on burn sites. It has a dark brown to mauve-brown hymenial surface and a whitish exterior with a lavender tinge.

Gyromitra melaleucoides: Differs by its whitish exterior surface and stalk, and caps that are often downcurved when young.

Gyromitra olympiana: A much smaller species up to 5 cm wide with a brown interior hymenial surface and a pallid exterior. Mature spores will have flattened with rounded apiculi at one or both ends.

Discina ancilis: Formerly known as **Discina perlata,** it has a deep red-brown interior and a translucent buff to pale tan exterior. It is a good edible that we sauté for breakfast at Morel Madness when the morels don't show up.

Auricularia fuscosuccinea: Can also spread sheet-like over its substrate but differs by being a basidiomycete with a more rubbery texture.

As for edibility, no one seems to bother with **Peziza arvernensis** except Calonge, who wrote, "edible but mediocre." The best thing to do with it would be to grind it into powder and spread it all over your nearest woods to find out what substrate it will emerge from next. And as we all suspect, the more the substrates accumulate, the more likely it will appear in future keys.

BIBLIOGRAPHY

Sean Abbott & R.S. Currah, *The Larger Cup Fungi and Other Ascomycetes of Alberta*, 1989. University of Alberta Devonian Botanic Garden, Edmonton, Alberta.

David Arora, *Mushrooms Demystified*, 1986. Ten Speed Press, Berkeley, Calif.

F. De Diego Calonge, *Setas*, 1979. Ediciones Mundi-Prensa, Madrid.

Bruno Cetto, *I Funghi dal Vero, Vol. 5*, 1987. Arti Grafiche Saturnia, Trento, Italy.

R.W.G. Dennis, *British Ascomycetes*, 1978. J. Cramer, Hirschberg, Germany.

Guillaume Eyssartier & Pierre Roux, *Le Guide des Champignons de France et Europe*, 2012. Editions Belin, Paris.

Gaston Guzman & Meike Piepenbring, 2011. *Los Hongos de Panamá*, Instituto de Ecologia, Xalapa, Mexico.

Nick Legon & Brian Spooner, *Peziza Micropus* in *The Mycologist* 4, 1990.

Michael Jordan, *The Encyclopedia of Fungi of Britain and Europe*, 1995. David & Charles, Newton Abbot, England.

Helen & A.H. Smith & Nancy Weber, *How to Know the Non-Gilled Mushrooms*, 1981. William C. Brown, Dubuque, Iowa.

Brian Spooner, *The Larger Cup Fungi in Britain, Part 3: The Genera Peziza and Plicaria* in *Field Mycology* 2 (2), 2001.

Steve Trudell & Joe Ammirati, *Mushrooms of the Pacific Northwest*, 2009. Timber Press, Portland, Ore.

Edmund Tylutki, *Mushrooms of Idaho and the Pacific Northwest: Discomycetes*, 1979. University Press of Idaho, Moscow, Idaho.

Peziza sp.

They were found scattered over the matted feathers of a dead crow.

It wasn't even September yet and I was feeling the itch. I had heard through the underground express that rains in late August of 1997 might have already brought out the chanterelles around North Cascades National Park. So I drove out to my 'secret location' east of the town of Glacier and proceeded to look around. After two chanterelles in four hours, I was ready to pack it in. It was late in the afternoon of August 29th when I burst through some bracken fern to find a dead crow lying in a small depression. And scattered over the surface of the crow feathers was a colony of pale ochre cup fungi. Cup fungi are not supposed to appear on bones and feathers. This substrate is associated with the genus Onygena whose fruiting bodies resemble miniature puffballs on tiny stalks.

Once back in town I contacted Dr. Nancy Weber in Corvallis, Oregon. Specimens were subsequently sent to her, and at her suggestion, also to Dr. Donald Pfister, director of the Farlow Herbarium at Harvard University. Seems like I had found something of interest.

Eventually I heard back from Dr. Pfister. He initially thought the cup fungus to be **Peziza fimeti**, a species found on dung. But he noted the spore sizes to be far too small. My Peziza was likely to be either a new species or an obscure member of the **Peziza varia** group.

Peziza varia? I went to town on it. One source I looked up had about ten photos of this taxon, each one quite different from the next. The name is in-deed appropriate. According to European sources, **Peziza varia** sensu stricto had two outstanding microscopic features. It had moniliform paraphyses and a textura of five layers. Paraphyses are thin, cylindrical or string-like structures found mixed in with the asci in the hymenium. Moniliform would imply unevenly bloated sections between the septa, or a chain-like appearance. Textura is a term for the layers of a cross section of the fruiting body. **Peziza varia** sensu stricto is supposed to have five layers with the central layer consisting of longitudinal hyphae that look like dark lines at 100x.

Edmund Tylutki, an ascomycete expert from Idaho, found just three layers in his collection of **P. varia**, perhaps signifying the presence of a **P. varia** group. He found a middle layer of interwoven hyphae nearly parallel to the hymenium. On either side were large "globose to polyhedral cells and randomly oriented hyphae."

I found neither of these configurations on the Peziza featured here. The paraphyses are simply septate and the textura seemed uniformly honeycombed.

However I had made a mistake. I had taken microscopic measurements with KOH on reconstituted material. Dr. Mike Beug informed me that I should have used water on fresh material. The KOH tends to swell spore sizes and perhaps obliterate any ornamentation within. It can also eliminate the fine granular contents in the paraphyses.

Nonetheless here is my description of the Peziza on crow: The carpophores were shallowly cupular with even margins. The cups measured only 9–16 mm wide. They were pale ochre tan, appearing slightly water logged, and became finely white furfuraceous when dried. The interior hymenial surface was smooth and slightly darker than the exterior surface. There was no stem. They were found scattered over the matted feathers of a dead crow.

LOOK-ALIKE

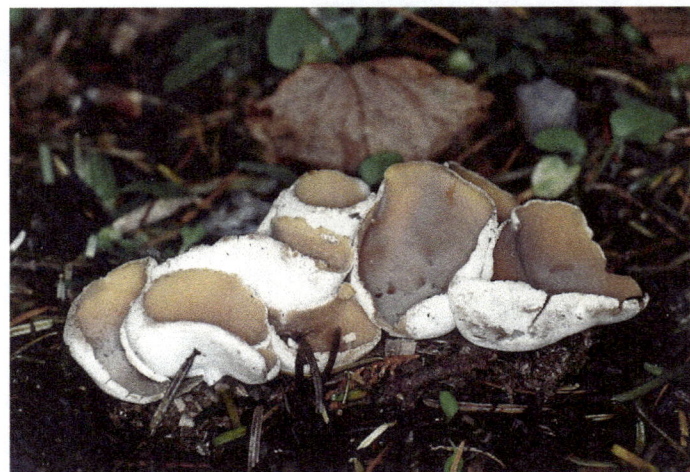

Peziza varia

Microscopically, the asci (tubular structures that house the spores) were operculate (had hinges at the apices from where the spores are discharged). The asci measured 193–210 x 9–9.7 µm, and the tips turned blue in Melzer's solution. The spores were elliptical and uniseriate. They measured 12.9–13.4 x 6.4–7.2 µm. The paraphyses were septate and measured 93–122 x 2.1–2.6 µm. The tips were usually curved and enlarged to 4–4.6 µm wide. The contents were finely granular. A cross section of the cup looked uniformly honeycombed and turned yellow in KOH.

Back in 1879, Emile Boudier was the first to discover that the tips of the asci in the genus Peziza turned blue in iodine. Spooner now adds the genera Plicaria and Plicariella to the list. The differences between them is that the latter two have globose spores while Peziza has elliptical spores. It was also noticed that the blue staining reaction was stronger in some species than in others. In 1978, Van Brummelen discovered that variations in the thickness of a mucilaginous substance in the periascus accounted for this variation.

According to Martin and Pamela Ellis, the only cup fungus ever recorded on feathers has been **Peziza linteicola**. The cups are dark brown with crenulate margins, quite different from what we see here.

One last observation might concern how the crow died. If it had been surprised and eaten by a fox it might have defecated in its death throes. This would change the substrate to feathers and dung. However, a second look at the dried material shows no sign of dung.

On behalf of our club we would like to thank Dr. Pfister for his observations. Due to the small size of the spores we suspect we have a new species, so if anyone out there stumbles into another collection on bird feathers, please gather the specimens and contact me or Dr. Mike Beug. We will make sure the collection gets to the proper authority.

Addendum: A specimen did reach Peziza expert Karen Hansen in Norway. Unfortunately the ITS sequencing failed.

BIBLIOGRAPHY

Michael Beug, *Overcoming Identification Challenges with Ascomycetes* in *Fungi,* Vol. 6, No. 4, 2013.

J. Breitenbach & F. Kranzlin, *Fungi of Switzerland,* Vol.1, 1984. Edition Mykologia, Lucerne, Switzerland.

R.W.G. Dennis, *British Ascomycetes,* 1978. J. Cramer, Hirschberg, Germany.

Martin & J. Pamela Ellis, *Microfungi on Miscellaneous Substrates,* 1988. Croom Helm, London.

Karen Hansen, Thomas Laessoe, & Donald Pfister, *Phylogenetics of the Pezizaceae with an Emphasis on Peziza* in *Mycologia* 93 (958–990), 2001.

Donald Pfister, *New Records of Cup Fungi from Iceland with Comments on Some Previously Reported Species* in *Nordic Journal of Botany* 25, No. 1-2 (104–112), 2007.

Donald Pfister, Gianfranco Medardi, Angela Lantieri, Katherine LoBuglio, & Gabriele Cacialli, *Clarification of Peziza fimeti with Notes on P. varia Collections on Dung* in *Mycotaxon* 121 (465–476), 2012.

Fred Jay Seaver, *North American Cup Fungi,* 1928. Self-published, New York, NY.

Brian Spooner, *The Larger Cup Fungi in Britain, Part 3: The Genera Peziza and Plicaria* in *Field Mycology,* Vol. 2, No. 2, 2001.

Edmund Tylutki, *Mushrooms of Idaho and the Pacific Northwest: Discomycetes,* 1979. University Press of Idaho, Moscow, Idaho.

Phaeolepiota aurea (Mattuschka ex Fries) Maire

In fact, it looks like a Cystoderma gone mad.

Phaeolepiota aurea, a.k.a. the Golden Bootleg, a.k.a. the Golden False Pholiota, is in that elite group of fungi that can knock your socks off from 50 yards out. It's definitely a class A brake slammer if you happen to be driving up a logging road in the Pacific Northwest in the fall, and you just hope no other vehicles are behind you when it happens. The richly colored golden-orange caps, massive size, great floppy ring, and uniquely granular surface texture for a mushroom this size immediately rivet your attention. The fact that the species prefers disturbed ground means that you will most likely spot it when driving, biking, or hiking along a dirt road. It is usually associated with alder, vine maple, old-growth Douglas fir, and nettles, fruiting up through thick weeds on roadsides where most fungi wouldn't find clearance.

The feature photo shows more mature specimens with the cap granules washed off by rain. The photo below depicts younger specimens near the button stage with caps loaded with granules.

In the United States and Canada, **P. aurea** are confined to the Pacific Coast from Alaska to California, being more plentiful in Alaska than anywhere else. They are found throughout Europe but considered extremely rare. Hongo reports them from Japan while Singer has recorded them from parts of subtropical Asia. Daniel Winkler has found them in Colombia. Here in Whatcom County, Jack Waytz finds them year after year in the same locations. One of these is about five miles up the Canyon Creek Road, off the Mount Baker Highway, on the right side heading northeast. The other is up the Galbraith Mountain Road that starts near Gate 9 at Sudden Valley. I have found them a couple of times along a horse trail behind Lake Padden, on the side of the Hannegan Trail, and up the Coal Creek Road from out of Glacier. The fact that I even bother to report these sites shows you how uncommon it is, even in our area.

Arora writes, "This beautiful mushroom is as distinctive as it is rare. No other large, brownish-spored mushroom [he more accurately lists the spore colors as yellow-brown to orange-buff] has golden brown to pale orange caps with a granulose coating on both cap and stem." In fact, it looks like a Cystoderma gone mad. Some authors suggest that if **Cystoderma amianthinum** could reach this size and turn a bit more orange in hue, it would look like **Phaeolepiota aurea**. Others think it resembles a fleshy, terrestrial Pholiota with a mealy veil.

Watling, Orton, & Gregory describe the caps as 7–25 cm wide, plane to convex with a blunt umbo. Cap margins remain incurved for a long time becoming wavy and lobed in age. The caps are saffron orange to yellow ochre and are at first covered with saffron colored granules, which eventually wear off. Margins are hung with white, appendiculate velar remnants where the veil tore free. The granular membranous ring covers the gills when young, then becomes an upward flaring ring on the stem before collapsing into a sort of torn skirt in age. The rings are smooth on their upper sides but granular beneath, the granules continuing down the stem from there. The gills are adnate to subdecurrent, whitish ageing to saffron and eventually rusty from spores. They are crowded and have even edges that become crisped in age. Stems are 5–28 cm long and 1–4 cm thick. They are equal or clavate-bulbous at the base. The apex is floccose to powdery white, then smooth above the ring. The ring extends from 2–4½ cm out from the stem. The lower part of the stem can

Young Phaeolepiota aurea

be ribbed or strongly striate down to the tomentose to strigose base. The stems are solid and firm, the context white at first but soon ageing yellowish and then reddish at the stem base. Although every author reports the taste as "mild," there are disagreements over the odor. The above authors reported the odor as of newly mown grass. Pacioni & Lincoff thought it was strongly aromatic. Kate Michell reports a pleasant floury smell, and a Wikipedia site thought it reminiscent of burnt almonds.

Microscopically, the spores are smooth to very slightly roughened, subfusoid in shape, and usually with an oil drop inside. According to Watling, they measure 10–13 x 4–6 µm and have a suprahilar depression but no germ pore. Orson Miller reports them as inamyloid. Overholts thought they tended to cohere in two's and four's in KOH and "at best were unfavorable objects for study." The basidia are 4-spored and cylindric. Clamps are present, but there are no cystidia. The pileipellis is of smooth, filamentous hyphae 3–10 µm wide. There are saccate to clavate to fusiform pileocystidia with finger-like projections and saffron colored walls. The floccose veil is composed of spherical cells.

There really aren't any look-alikes, but in olden days they were sometimes confused with the giant **Gymnopilus junonius** (formerly known as **G. spectabilis**), which differs by fruiting on wood and having rusty spores and a bitter taste. Another potential look-alike might be **Cortinarius caperatus** (for-

LOOK-ALIKE

Cortinarius caperatus

merly in Rozites). This taxon has a smooth cap (never granular) with a wrinkled margin, a smooth ring, and a rusty spore deposit.

Over the centuries it has not been a simple task for mycologists to figure out exactly where **Phaeolepiota aurea** belonged. It began life as **Agaricus aureus** in 1777. Mattuschka described it first. Then in 1803, Schumacher introduced an **Agaricus vahlii**, which turned out to be the same species. Along with **Lepiota pyreneae** Quelet, the more updated **Pholiota vahlii** is considered a synonym. In 1887 Saccardo placed it in Pholiota. The British mycologist W.G. Smith moved it to Togaria in 1908. René Maire then suggested in 1911 that the powdery veil and smooth spores warranted creating a new genus for it. In 1928 he got around to publishing the new genus Phaeolepiota, and to this day, **Phaeolepiota aurea** remains the only species in it. Not happy with that, Kuhner and Romagnesi placed it in Cystoderma in 1953. Despite the obvious resemblance, this combination didn't catch on.

Overholts mentions that it was first found in British Columbia in North America. Dr. A.H. Smith then found a fruiting at Crescent Lake in the Olympic Peninsula on October 9, 1935. Some caps measured up to 25 cm wide with stems 20 cm long and 7 cm thick! One R. Stace-Smith then found a collection on Mount Baker on October 9, 1961, that now resides in the University of British Columbia herbarium. I mention these collections because the species appears to be more common now than it was then.

If it is a thrill to find the False Golden Pholiota, it may be even more of an adventure to eat one. Opinions vary on the flavor. Here they are, in no particular order:

Kate Michell, senior editor (no author was cited) of Field Guide to Mushrooms and Other Fungi of Britain and Europe: "Edible and tasty, mainly in central Europe."

Schalkwijk-Barendsen: "Pleasant."

Cetto: "Mediocre."

Gymnopilus junonius from England

Rinaldi & Tyndalo: "The flavor is strong and disgusting."
Graham: "Edible, but the caution of eating a small portion the first time should be observed. I like the nutty flavor while my wife, with no ill effects, finds it not to her liking."

I tend to agree with Cetto. I found that it had little flavor when sautéed in butter. But I was intrigued by the aromatic odor, and sensed that there might be a better way to cook it, maybe with soy sauce and sherry in the oriental style. But something held me back. I had heard that about 15% of the people who tried it had an allergic reaction to it. The symptoms were always of a gastro-intestinal nature.

Then, in October of 1989 I had an opportunity to view this phenomenon first hand. I had decided to go to the Vancouver Mycological Society's annual Clarence Schmok Foray, which was held that year in Pemberton, about a 40-minute drive north of Whistler. It was a terrific foray with about 40 to 50 folks in attendance. On the last night the chefs decided to cook up a frying pan of **Phaeolepiota aurea**. There was only enough for a piece per person, but even so, about 15% of the participants experienced a bout of diarrhea. Just as Harriette Parker had warned, they were edible for some but poisonous for others.

Then in the fall of 1991, Dr. Brooks Naylor and his wife Ellen, charter members of our own Northwest Mushroomers, wrote up a detailed article for our newsletter on their own adventures with the Golden Bootleg. Back on October 3, 1981, the Naylors had run into a big cluster along Highway 1 on the Kenai Peninsula in Alaska. They were able to identify the species from Ben Guild's *The Alaska Mushroom Hunter's Guide*. The author had noted, "**Phaeolepiota aurea** has caused severe gastrointestinal upsets in some people; care should be exercised when eating it for the first time. This very large and easily recognized mushroom is very common in Alaska's south-central area and is readily collected. Pick only the large, young buttons, some as big as baseballs, and leave the older specimens. The stems are tough. Wipe off the powdery covering before cooking." The Naylors heeded the advice. They ate small amounts at first. When nothing bad happened, they ate larger amounts on three separate occasions.

On September 26, 1991, back in Whatcom County, they found **P. aurea** again while hiking on a logging road off of the Sexon Road above the fish hatchery on the south fork of the Nooksack River. They found three large specimens and fried them up in margarine for lunch. By 4 p.m. Ellen felt nauseous. By 8 p.m. she was undergoing violent stomach disturbances, both vomiting and diarrhea, which continued until 3 a.m. She lost about seven pounds and took two days to get back to normal. Brooks was not as sick, but had three or four bouts of diarrhea the next day. What they couldn't understand was why they were able to eat it in Alaska, but not in Washington. Brooks speculated that there might be genetically different strains that vary in the amount of toxin produced. According to Watling, Orton, & Gregory, the species is considered to be a good edible in Europe. It is only on our side of the Atlantic that poisonings are recorded.

Intrigued by all the hoopla and deeply attracted by both the attractive appearance and the aromatic odor of **Phaeolepiota aurea**, Jack Waytz, our intrepid editor, had to try it. Going all out, he cooked up two pounds of it in a stir-fry with bamboo shoots, water chestnuts, sprouts, and sesame oil. He found nothing wrong with the flavor and loved the firm, meaty texture. But later he was sick with vomiting and diarrhea for 20 hours.

What none of us knew at the time was that Belgian mycologist Paul Heinemann had discovered hydrocyanic acid in **Phaeolepiota aurea** back in 1942. According to Stijve, Andrey, and Goessler, it is a metabolite also found in **Marasmius oreades**, **Pleurotus eryngii**, and **Infundibulicybe geotropa**, all considered good edibles. But **Phaeolepiota aurea** has about twice as much hydrocyanic acid as **Marasmius oreades,** about 500 mg/kg in its raw state. After cooking it goes down to 200 mg/kg, but that is still a high enough content to produce a poisoning syndrome in some people. Besides the hydrocyanic acid, the species also takes up cadmium, a toxic heavy metal. The combination is not encouraging for the table.

Despite these apparent negatives, Dr. Mike Beug writes that "hydrocyanic acid is present in such small amounts that it is not a health hazard." The toxin that causes the distress is not yet known.

Just out of curiosity I googled "hydrocyanic acid" to learn more about it. I read that hydrogen cyanide mixed with water produces hydrocyanic acid. Cassava leaves, widely consumed in tropical countries, contain this acid. This is why they are always boiled first. The burnt almond odor that some people can detect in **Phaeolepiota aurea** is a giveaway that hydrocyanic acid is present. Would boiling the species first get rid of the acid? Or would the acid remain and the flavor disappear?

Jack Waytz with Phaeolepiota aurea (before the meal)

I read on that hydrogen cyanide is a volatile compound that has been used as an inhalation rodenticide. The cyanide ions interfere with iron containing respiratory enzymes, and the rats soon die. Another term for it is Prussic acid. This is because it was originally isolated from a Prussian blue dye. Prussic acid is powerful stuff. It has been traditionally used as the killing agent in whaling harpoons.

BIBLIOGRAPHY

Joe Ammirati, J.A. Traquair, & Paul Horgen, *Poisonous Mushrooms of the Northern United States and Canada,* 1985. University of Minnesota Press, Minneapolis, Minn.

David Arora, *All That the Rain Promises and More*, 1991. Ten Speed Press, Berkeley, Calif.

David Arora, *Mushrooms Demystified*, 1986. Ten Speed Press, Berkeley, Calif.

Michael W. Beug, *Poisonous and Hallucinogenic Mushrooms.* Evergreen State College, Olympia, Wash. http://academic.evergreen.edu/projects/mushrooms/phm/

Bruno Cetto, *I Funghi dal Vero, Vol.1*, 1983. Arti Grafiche Saturnia, Trento, Italy.

Michael Eppinger, *Field Guide to Mushrooms and Other Fungi of Britain and Europe,* 2006. Bloomsbury Publishers, London.

First-Nature.com, *Phaeolepiota aurea*. www.first-nature.com/fungi/phaeolepiota-aurea.php

Dick Graham, *The Meandering Mushroomer,* 1978. Hancock House Publishers, Seattle, Wash.

Helmut & Renate Grünert, *Field Guide to Mushrooms of Britain and Europe*, 1991. Crowood Press, Ltd., Wiltshire, England.

Ben Guild, *The Alaskan Mushroom Hinter's Guide*, 1979. Alaska Northwest Publishing Co., Anchorage, Alaska.

Rokuya Imazeki, Tsuguo Hongo, & Keisuke Tubaki, *Common Fungi of Japan in Color,* 1970. Hoikusha Publishing Co., Osaka.

Orson & Hope Miller, *North American Mushrooms*, 2006. Morris Book Publishers, Guilford, Conn.

Brooks & Ellen Naylor, *More About Phaeolepiota Aurea: Golden False Pholiota* in *MushRumors, Vol.4, Issue 7*, 1991 (newsletter of the Northwest Mushroomers Association, Bellingham, Wash).

Lee Overholts, *A Monograph of the Genus Pholiota* in *Annals of the Missouri Botanical Garden* 14 (87–210), 1927.

Harriette Parker, *Alaska's Mushrooms*, 1994. Alaska Northwest Books, Anchorage, Alaska.

A.A. Pearson, *Agarics, New Records and Observations –II* in *Transactions of the British Mycological Society* 26 (36–49), 1943.

Augusto Rinaldi & Vassili Tyndalo, *The Complete Book of Mushrooms*, 1974. Crown Publishers, New York, NY.

Helene Schalkwijk-Barendsen, *Mushrooms of Western Canada*, 1991. Lone Pine Publishers, Edmonton, Alberta.

Rolf Singer, *Agaricales in Modern Taxonomy* in *Lilloa* 22 (1–832), 1949.

A.H. Smith, *Notes on Agarics from the Western United States* in *Bulletin of the Torrey Botanical Club* 64 (477–486), 1937.

Tjakko Stijve, Daniel Andrey, & Walter Goessler, *Phaeolepiota Aurea: A Beautiful and Mysterious Mushroom* in *Mushroom the Journal*, Fall 2002.

Steve Trudell & Joe Ammirati, *Mushrooms of the Pacific Northwest*, 2009. Timber Press, Portland, Ore.

Roy Watling, *Observations on the Bolbitiaceae, II. A Conspectus of the Family* in *Notes from the Royal Botanic Garden, Edinburgh* 26 (289–323), 1965.

Roy Watling, Peter Orton, & Norma Gregory, *Cortinariaceae* in *British Fungus Flora 7*, 1993.

Wikipedia.org, *Hydrocyanic Acid.*

- Digerness -

Pleurocybella porrigens (Persoon ex Fries) Singer

*They are so smooth and white and
delicate they seem cast from porcelain.*

From darkest decay in a hemlock log
Tiny stirrings of molds in the fog
A raven squawked in a silent world
While far below, mycelium curled
A sliver of moon, a dead nematode
And out of that log the Angel Wings rode

"Hark the herald angels sang," and **Pleurocybella porrigens** (a.k.a. Pleurotus porrigens, Nothopanus porrigens, Pleurotellus porrigens, Calathinus porrigens, Phyllotus porrigens) burst forth from a hemlock log. No matter how many times our mycologists feel the need to move the species, there is no better word for it than Angel Wings.

Whatever you want to call them the legendary Angel Wings are a striking sight in the deep, dark coniferous forests of the Pacific Northwest. They are so smooth and white and delicate they seem cast from porcelain. It has been more than once late in a fall season that a last minute find of Angel Wings has turned a dreary, hopeless foray into a success. Even beginners can identify Angel Wings in our local mountains for there is very little they can be confused with.

Pleurocybella porrigens, a close cousin of the Oyster mushroom, can be found from September through November in shelving tiers of overlapping clusters on rotting conifer logs, especially hemlock. The pure white, petal shaped to turbinate caps at first erupt from the log like tiny shoe horns, eventually expanding to fan-shaped with wavy, irregular margins. They differ from other Pleurotoid species by starting out in a resupinate form, lying flat on the substrate and facing outward. They then turn into eccentric orbicular tongues, usually emerging from the log without stems. The surface is minutely tomentose at first, then smooth and shiny, retaining tomentum only at the point of attachment. The flesh is

LOOK-ALIKE

Crepidotus applanatus

thin and pliable. Caps can reach widths of 10 cm or even a little beyond. The gills are deeply decurrent, crowded, often forked, and are white becoming cream to yellowish in age. The taste is mild. The odor is finely herbaceous-flowery fragrant. It is an ephemeral odor that vanishes in cooking. The spores are white, inamyloid in Melzer's.

Microscopically, the spores are smooth-walled, subglobose, and measure 5-7 μm. There are no cystidia. Basidia are usually 4-spored. However, A.H. Smith reported 1, 2, 3, and 4-spored basidia from a collection found at Emerson, Michigan in 1933. He noted that there were no abnormal developments, the weather seemed fine with no sharp changes of temperature. Yet, it still happened! (The world of fungi is full of mysteries like this. It makes fungi at least as interesting as humans.) Clamps are plentiful. The pileipellis is composed of radially repent hyphae with a forest of exerted ends. The context consists of interwoven hyphae. There is no gelatinous layer in the pileipellis. And it is the subglobose, inamyloid spores that place the species in Pleurocybella.

Angel Wings can be found from Alaska south to northern California along the Pacific Coast. They occur in Michigan and New England down into the southern Appalachians on the East Coast. In the mountains of Tennessee and North Carolina they have been reported on hardwood logs, such as birch. Fergus reported that they also fruit on living trees, but he gave a spore size of 3–4 μm, so he might have been looking at something else. They are also found in Japan, the Scottish highlands, and throughout mountainous regions of Europe.

A list of potential look-alikes follows here:

Crepidotus mollis: It differs by having rusty fibrils on the cap surface, gray gills that soon turn brown, and a brown spore print.

Crepidotus applanatus: A diminutive species with cream colored caps that shelves on wood, but differs by its brown spores.

Crepidotus malachius: Differs from Angel Wings by its brown spore print as seen on cap surfaces, and by the cap color which starts out tan, but soon fades to white.

Cheimonophyllum candidissimum: Can look like Angel Wings, but they never exceed the size of your fingernail.

Ossicaulis lignatilis: Differs by having a stem, a farinaceous odor, a very tough texture, and the habit of fruiting on hardwoods.

Phyllotopsis nidulans: Pallid forms could be confused with it, but they have a pinkish-brown spore print, a pungent and disagreeable odor, and yellowish gills.

Arrhenia acerosa: A diminutive species with silky gray caps that don't exceed two centimeters in width.

Pleurotus albolanatus: This was a species established by Peck because it did have a gelatinous layer in the pileipellis. It is now listed as a synonym of Angel Wings in the Index Fungorum.

Hohenbuehelia abietina: A European species that differs

LOOK-ALIKES

Crepidotus mollis

Crepidotus malachius from Vermont

Cheimonophyllum candidissimum from California

Arrhenia acerosa

Pleurotus flabellatus from Belize

Phyllotopsis nidulans from Minn.   *Photo by Richard Morrison*

in a lateral, velutinous stipe, white mycelial cords, and a farinaceous odor and taste.

Pleurotus flabellatus: A grayish-white tropical species with a flaccid fruiting body that can appear on almost any decaying matter, even old coconut husks.

Pleurotus means "aside" or "ear" in Greek. *Porrigens* means "stretching out" in Latin. So if you prefer the literal translation, Ears Stretching Out can usually be found in enough quantity for a meal. There is no dearth of opinion on the flavor:

Bandoni & Szczawinski: "Mild flavored. They can be dried, salted, and eaten uncooked."

Bruno Cetto: "Non commestibile. Troppo tenace." (He must have eaten Ossicaulis lignatilis by mistake.)

Dick Graham: "A safe mushroom for the beginner to try, and usually plentiful. The tough base should be discarded before cooking."

Jack Czarnecki: "The Oyster mushroom group are unusual because they contain vitamin C as well as minerals and protein."

Harriette Parker: "Mediocre for eating. Bland tasting and fragile. Works better if it is sautéed briefly over low heat with butter or oil, then added to pasta sauce, gravy, or omelettes."

Vincent Marteka: "Some people think Angel Wings are better tasting than Oyster mushrooms."

Fischer & Bessette: "Very similar in taste to the Oyster mushroom, but Angel Wings can be more tender. They are also so thin that they get easily saturated by butter in the frying pan." (On page 214 of their book, Edible Wild Mushrooms of North America, these authors present an elaborate recipe for Angel Wings and Scallops Crepes. Although just a bit of a cholesterol hit, the dish does look intriguing.)

To avoid the aforementioned saturation in the frying pan, I like to coat Angel Wings in ice-cold tempura batter, deep fat fry them, and sprinkle them with lemon juice and a little salt. The Haards have a quicker solution. They suggest rolling them in egg and then cracker crumbs, then fry until crispy. Either way, don't forget the Marie Sharp Habanero Pepper Sauce. It can cover over any sin you might commit.

Addendum: I hate to ruin this party, but long after this article was first written, eleven people in northern Japan, in 2004, died from ingesting Angel Wings. All of the victims had some degree of renal dysfunction before ingesting the Angel Wings. Then in 2009 another group of 17 Japanese with acute renal ailments succumbed to a meal of Angel Wings. The cause of the deaths was determined to be acute encephalopathy, "a type of degenerative neurological condition characterized by lesions in the brain." It was the second time that a mycotoxin had been involved in encephalopathy. It took the victims from 13-29 days to die. The culprit is an aziridine amino acid, now dubbed pleurocybellaziridine. Dr. Kawagishi and Dr. Kan found that concentrations of the acid could vary greatly from collection to collection. Researchers in Japan discovered that pleurocybellazuridine could destroy myelin, the protective barrier that surrounds critical brain cells. It is now suspected that both aziridine and carboxylic acid are necessary for cytotoxicity. Dr. Mike Beug, who investigated the incident, noted that the autumn of 2004 had been especially wet in southern Japan, producing ideal conditions for Angel Wings. People reported that they were three or four times their normal size. Unusually large concentrations of the pleurocybellaziridine could have been present. Researchers Hirokazu Kawagishi and Toshiyuki Kan are still working on the mechanism that led to the poisoning and why it affected only those with kidney disease. To me, it sounds like a perfect storm. To date, no one in North America has been poisoned by Angel Wings, but to be on the safe side, anyone with kidney complaints should avoid it like the plague.

BIBLIOGRAPHY

David Arora, *Mushrooms Demystified*, 1986. Ten Speed Press, Berkeley, Calif.

Robert Bandoni & Adam Szczawinski, *Guide to Common Mushrooms of British Columbia*, 1964. British Columbia Provincial Museum, Victoria, B.C.

Michael Beug, *Pleurocybella porrigens Toxin Unmasked?* North American Mycological Association, www.namyco.org/pleurocybella_toxin.php.

J. Breitenbach & F. Kranzlin, *Fungi of Switzerland, Vol.3*, 1991. Edition Mykologia, Lucerne, Switzerland.

Bruno Cetto, *I Funghi dal Vero, Vol.3*, 1979. Arti Grafiche Saturnia, Trento, Italia.

Jack Czarnecki, *A Cook's Book of Mushrooms*, 1995. Artisan, New York, NY.

Charles Fergus, *Illustrated Genera of Wood Decay Fungi*, 1960. Burgess Publishing Co., Minneapolis, Minn.

David Fischer & Alan Bessette, *Edible Wild Mushrooms of North America*, 1992. University of Texas Press, Austin, Texas.

Dick Graham, *The Meandering Mushroomer*, 1978. Hancock House Publishers, Seattle, Wash.

J. Walton Groves, *Edible and Poisonous Mushrooms of Canada*, 1979. Research Branch, Agriculture Canada, Ottawa.

Karen & Richard Haard, *Foraging for Edible Wild Mushrooms*, 1974. Cloudburst Press, Seattle, Wash.

Lexemuel Hesler, *Notes on Southeastern Agaricales* in *Journal of the Tennessee Academy of Science* 32, No.3 (198–207), 1957.

Rokuya Imazeki, Tsuguo Honga, & Keisuke Tubaki, *Common Fungi of Japan in Color*, 1970. Hoikusha Publishing Co., Osaka.

Hirokazu Kawagishi, Toshiyuki Kan, et al., *The Angel's Wing Mystery* in *Science and Technology* 89, No.13 (38–39), 2011.

Vincent Marteka, *Mushrooms: Wild and Edible*, 1980. W.W. Norton & Co., New York, NY.

Kent & Vera McKnight, *Peterson Field Guides: Mushrooms*, 1987. Houghton Mifflin, Boston.

Orson Miller & Donald Manning, *Distribution of the Lignicolous Tricholomataceae in the Southern Appalachians* in *The Distributional History of the Biota of the Southern Appalachians* 4 (307–344), 1976.

M. Nishizawa, A. Arai, T. Kuwabara, & N. Honma, *Accute Encephalopathy After Ingestion of 'Sugihiratake' Mushroom* in *Rinsho Shinkeigaku* 45, Issue 11 (818–820), 2005.

Harriette Parker, *Alaska's Mushrooms*, 1994. Alaska Northwest Books, Anchorage, Alaska.

Carleton Rea, *British Basidiomycetaceae*, 1922. Strauss & Cramer, Hirschberg, Germany.

A.H. Smith, *Mushrooms in Their Natural Habitats*, 1949. Sawyer's, Lancaster, Penn.

A.H. Smith, *New and Unusual Agarics from Michigan. I.* in *Annales Mycologici* 32 (471–484), 1934.

Elsie Wakefield & R.W.G. Dennis, *Common British Fungi*, 1981. Saiga Publishing Co., Surrey, England.

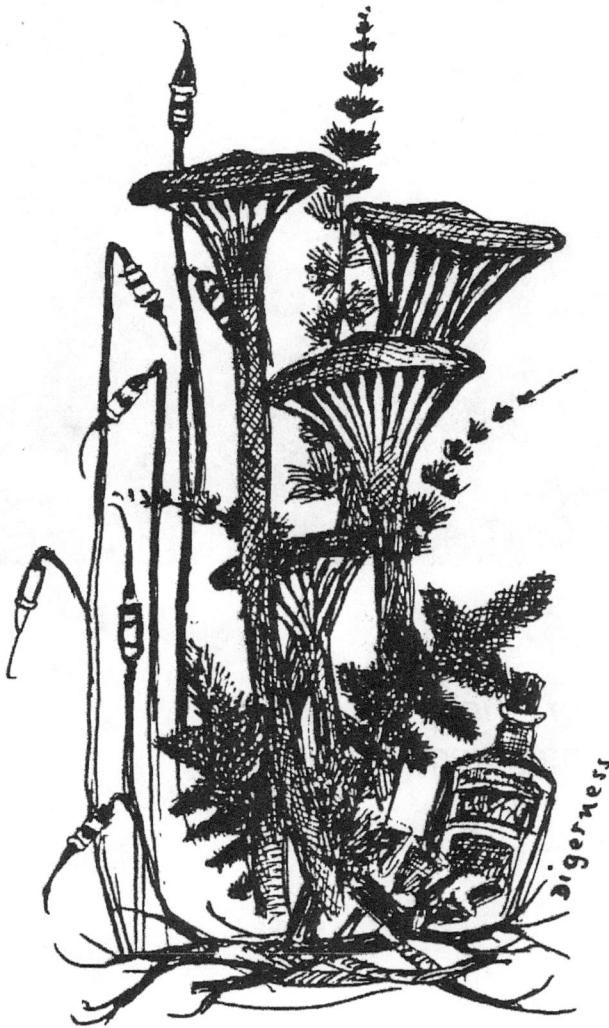

Panellus longinquus (Berkeley) Horak

*The migrations of P. longinquus
are even more intriguing than the
description.*

This lovely pinkish relative of the Oyster Mushroom had been misinterpreted by us for years. The specimens shown here were found by Paul Kroeger, Jeremy Ferrera, and myself at Cornwall Park in Bellingham on November 20, 1997. Prior to this find, we had been calling it **Panellus mitis** on our forays. The difference? Paul Kroeger. Since 1984 he had known what this was and we were lucky to have him with us.

Panellus longinquus, which sort of resembles pink Angel Wings, has caps that measure ½–4 cm in width. They are fan shaped to kidney shaped with inrolled margins, often irregularly lobed. Translucent when wet and often viscid, they become concentrically wrinkled when dry. Colors of young specimens are ivory to faint peach becoming a pinkish honey color in age. They are capable of being purple brown, a color variation I have not seen. The gills are short decurrent and cream colored, often with a tinge of peach. The stems are lateral, if present at all, ivory to pale yellowish and often with white tomentum at the base. The spore deposit is yellow-buff, and the spores are amyloid in Melzer's solution. The odor and taste are mild. Edibility still unknown.

Microscopically, the spores are oblong to sausage shaped and measure 6–11.5 x 3–5 μm. They are smooth-walled.

Panellus longinquus is almost always found on red alder logs, occasionally on maple in the Pacific Northwest. In Patagonia, where it also occurs, it fruits on Nothofagus, the ubiquitous beech of the area.

The migrations of **P. longinquus** are even more intriguing than the description. According to Petersen, Hughes, & Toyohara, the species originated somewhere around Tasmania, New Zealand, New Guinea, or southern Australia. From there, the authors speculate that ocean currents carried spores to Patagonia. The species has been found in both Chile and Argentina. From these locations, humans must have brought spores northward to the Pacific Northwest, maybe on the soles of shoes. DNA sequencing of specimens from all locations have proven compatibility between all groups!

In North America, **Panellus longinquus** ranges from the Oregon coast north to Haida Gwaii, British Columbia, Canada. Steve Trudell writes that it can be locally common in cool, wet autumns.

It was first described as **Panellus longinquus** by Reverend Berkeley. Dr. Scot Redhead then named our Northwest version **subspecies pacificus** because ours had whiter caps and a slight thickening of the walls of the caulocystidia. Dr. Petersen eventually eliminated the subspecies status. He discovered that pallid caps could also be found in Australia and Patagonia. Horak placed the species in Pleurotopsis in 1983.

The first published color photo of **Panellus longinquus** was probably the Roger Phillips' photo of **Clitopilus cretatus** in his *Mushrooms of North America* in 1991. That collection was found at Manzanilla, Oregon, on October 10, 1986.

It's not easy to find a name for a species that may have originated in Tasmania, migrated to Chile, and wasn't known from the Northwest until the research of Scot Redhead and Diane Libonati-Barnes placed it here in 1984. We are not sure how recently the species arrived here.

Panellus longinquus has long been mistaken for **Panellus mitis**, a species that differs in its smaller, whiter caps, ge-

More P. longinquus—a different view

latinized gill edges, and habit of fruiting on conifers. It also has much smaller spores, and is more likely to be found in the eastern Cascades.

So, thanks to the persistent efforts of Redhead and Libonati-Barnes, a regional fungal mystery that most of us were unaware of in the first place, has finally been solved.

As for edibility, there is an update. Both Jack Waytz and David Arora independently took the Pleurotopsis plunge. They both found it to have a fine flavor with a slightly slippery texture. Jack sautéed about five caps in butter, salt, and pepper. On a par with **Clitopilus prunulus** was his opinion.

BIBLIOGRAPHY

David Arora, *Mushrooms Demystified,* 1986. Ten Speed Press, Berkeley, Calif.

Dorothy Brown & Ian Gibson, *Trial Field to the Pleurotoid Species in the Pacific Northwest*, 2003. Pacific Northwest Key Council, Seattle, Wash.

Susan Libonati-Barnes & Scott Redhead, *Panellus Longinquus Subsp. Pacificus—A New West Coast North American Agaric Associated with Red Alder* in *Mycotaxon* 20 (205–212), 1984.

Ronald Petersen, Karen Hughes, & Takeshi Toyohara, *DNA Sequence and RFLP Analysis of Pleurotopsis Longinqua from Three Disjunct Populations* in *Mycologia* 90 (595–600), 1998.

Roger Phillips, *Mushrooms of North America*, 1991. Little, Brown & Co., Boston, Mass.

Steve Trudell & Joe Ammirati, *Mushrooms of the Pacific Northwest*, 2009. Timber Press, Portland, Ore.

Wikipedia.com, *Panellus longinquus*

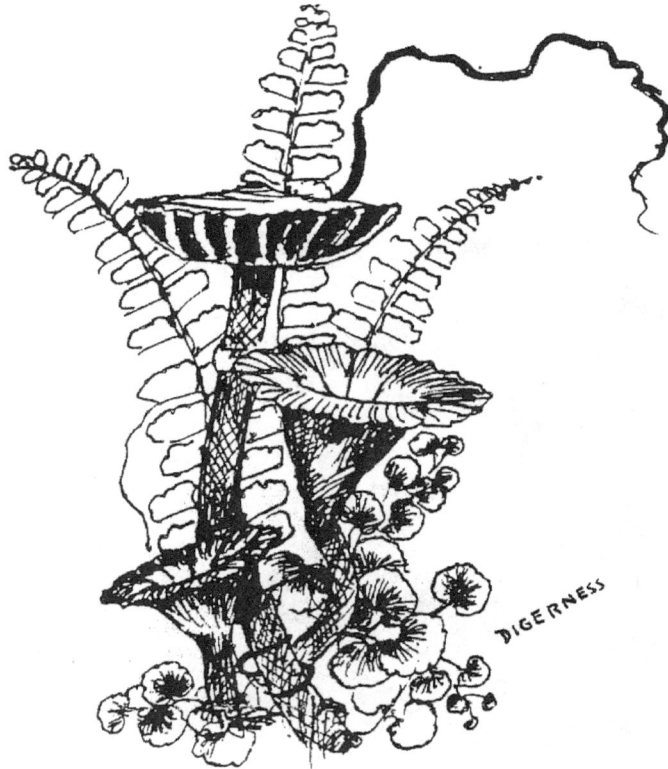

DIGERNESS

Pleurotus citrinopileatus Singer

The strong nutty flavor only comes with thorough cooking.

Whether it looks like a South Pacific coral clump or the finely fluted sculpture of a master ceramist, the Golden Oyster Mushroom must take its place as one of the world's most elegant species. The fact that in the U.S. they have only been grown from culture does nothing to detract from their beauty. Citrinopileatus means "lemon capped," an apt moniker for this exotic Chinese Pleurotus grown here in Bellingham by Sam Leathers. The specimens in the featured photo were grown by Sam using the same inoculation methods he demonstrated in his cultivation classes with the Oyster Mushroom.

The **Pleurotus citrinopileatus** spawn was available from Fungi Perfecti, an imaginative mushroom growing company run by Paul Stamets out of Olympia, Washington, that experiments with raising wild species in captivity. The Golden Oyster kits were very hard to obtain. Occasionally Cascadia Mushrooms of Bellingham, Washington, also has them for sale. If you were looking for food value, the more common kits of **Pleurotus eryngii** produced an even better flavor.

There is not much information on **Pleurotus citrinopileatus** in the popular guides. Duhem & Courtecuisse note that it is an edible and cultivated species related to **P. cornucopiae**. Ohira went one step further and created the combination **Pleurotus cornucopiae var. citrinopileatus** in 1987. He must have noticed that **P. cornucopiae** and **P. citrinopileatus** both exhibited multiple

caps arising from a single stem. Roberts & Evans mention that it was first described from the Russian far east. They now have it shaded in from North Korea all the way down through Indonesia.

Paul Stamets suggested I look up Rolf Singer's *Agaricales in Modern Taxonomy* to learn more. Here I discovered that **P. citrinopileatus** belonged to Section Pleurotus, the same section that **Pleurotus ostreatus** and **Pleurotus cornucopioides** belonged to. Although Singer didn't describe the Golden Oyster Mushroom in these pages, he did leave a reference to *Annales Mycologici* 41, (149), 1943, for further details.

It turned out that this German article housed the original Latin description for the species. **Pleurotus citrinopileatus** was touted as being one of the most valuable edible mushrooms of eastern Asia. Caps were described as vivid lemon yellow, up to 10 cm wide, and deeply funnel-shaped. They usually had an opening or a slit on one side. The gills were long decurrent, yellowish white, and narrow. Stems were white, eccentric, firm, usually branched from a single base. They measured 2–5 cm long and 2–8 mm thick. The flesh was white. The taste was mild, the odor aromatic. The spores were ellipsoid- cylindric, amyloid, and measured 7.5–9 x 3–3.5 μm. They fruited at the bases of elm trees from August through September.

In a more recent work, Zhishu, Guoyang, & Taihui describe the pileal epicutis as undifferentiated, the hyphal system as monomitic, the presence of clamps, the lack of all cystidia, the subparallel gill trama, and the clavate basidia measuring 27-34 x 4-8 μm. In the wild they claimed it was found on sugarcane residue in Asia and Africa. In the aftermath of the Dutch elm disease debacle, this is an unusual choice of substrates.

Along with the introductory description in the Singer article was a key in German. If you followed the leads for "thick walled

CLOSE RELATIVE

Pleurotus cornucopiae from Vermont

tramal hyphae," "no sclerotium," and then "glabrous bright yellow caps," you arrived at the species. This was vintage Rolf Singer. Always lead with your more obscure microscopic character and finish with a flourish in an obvious field character.

Several modern web sites offer more information. Shamanshop.net tells us that **P. citrinopileatus** needs plenty of air to develop normally. The Golden Oyster fruits easily on pasteurized straw, hardwood chips, sawdust, various grains, newspaper, and cardboard. According to the Fungi Perfecti brochure the caps will emerge within two weeks with a sustained temperature of 65–75 degrees. Shroomery.org tells us that the species thrives at high temperatures and won't even fruit below 65 degrees. After harvesting they quickly lose their bright yellow coloring. Stem bases are imbued with cottony white mycelium. Spores are pale pinkish buff, and long distance shipping is impractical because of the fragility of the caps. The flavor is bitter and spicy if only partially cooked. The strong nutty flavor only comes with thorough cooking.

But there is more to life than food. Following the lead of Lance Howell with his reishi mushrooms that resemble the contorted sculptures of Giacometti, one could grow the Golden Oyster as much for art as for culinary delights.

CLOSE RELATIVE

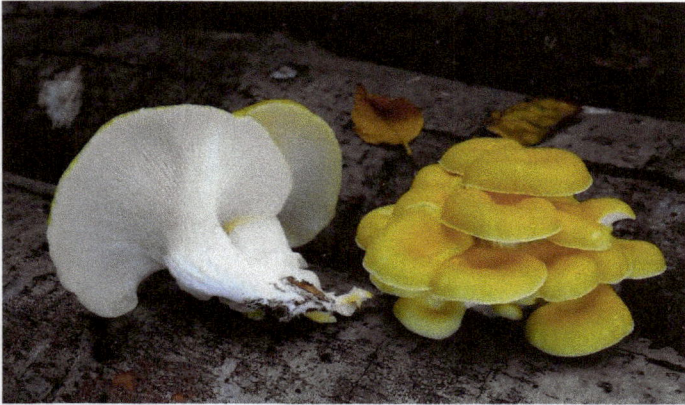

Pleurotus citrinopileatus   *Photo by Richard Morrison*

BIBLIOGRAPHY

Regis Courtecuisse & Bernard Duhem, Mushrooms & Toadstools of Britain & Europe, 1995. Harper-Collins, London.

Peter Roberts & Shelley Evans, *The Book of Fungi*, 2011. University of Chicago Press, Chicago & London.

Rolf Singer, *The Agaricales in Modern Taxonomy* in *Lilloa* 22 (1–832), 1949.

Rolf Singer, *Das System der Agaricales III* in *Annales Mycologici* 41 (149), 1943.

Bi Zhishu, Zheng Guoyang, & Li Taihui, The Macrofungi Flora of China's Guangdong Province, 1993.

Plicatura nivea (Sommerfeldt ex Fries) Karsten

Photo by Dan Crape

It is associated with white rot and always occurs above 40 degrees latitude.

Originally published as **Merulius niveus** Fries in 1828, and first noticed from Lapland, the Snowy Plic is both infrequent and inedible. Yet for those who live on the edge of all things obscure, they might appear intriguing or even inspiring. They must have appeared as such to our past editor, Dan Crape, who rounded up these in Arroyo Park, just south of Bellingham, back in November of 1993. Although **Plicatura nivea** circles the globe in northern latitudes, it is only now becoming more common locally. Luckily, Dan aimed his camera at it during his photography phase, thereby capturing a species yet to appear in color in any popular North American mushroom guide to date. Let's face it. There's room for improvement. But considering that Dan was shooting what looked like a white shag carpet on a dark surface (the rotten log) in the dim November light, it could have been worse.

Since I assumed it to be some sort of Polypore, I mailed it off to Dr. R.L. Gilbertson, the co-author of *North American Polypores*. Dr. Gilbertson, a strong advocate of tree associations, was able to identify it even though it doesn't appear in his monograph. It doesn't appear there because it is thought to be a member of the Corticiaceae, a group more resembling resupinate

scabs. The second photo here demonstrates the species in its younger, more scabby form. Fortunately, Dr. Jim Ginns, a world authority on these saprophytic scabs, wrote an article entitled *Taxonomy of Plicatura nivea* in 1970. He described the fruiting bodies as growing up to 10 cm by 3 cm by 5 mm thick with tan to whitish caps, matted tomentose and sometimes zonate. The caps start out white and become orange-brownish to yellowish in age. They are fully plastered to the wood or semi-pileate, the cap edges lifting partially off the log or stump they are on. The margins are mycelioid to granulose. The hymenial surface is neither poroid nor gill-like. Breitenbach & Kranzlin describe it as "tuberculate to plicate-venose." Dr. Ginns described it as "crust-like, often fissured, glabrous or slightly pruinose, even or rugose, the folds when present up to 1 mm wide and 0.5 mm deep, branched, interrupted, not forming pits." Murrill, in an earlier time, thought they were "plicate, unequal, narrow, interrupted, undulate, crisped, and white."Jan Vesterholt chips in with "pseudo gills folded, forked, dentate-merulioid, and white." At least everyone agrees on the color. No matter how you like it described, the surface is confusing enough to entice the folks at MycoBank on-line to suggest

Plicatura nivea just beginning to lift off the log

it might be a synonym of **Plicaturopsis crispa**, another species with a wildly original spore-bearing surface.

Microscopically, spores are narrowly cylindric and measure 4-5 x 0.7-1 μm. They are white in deposit, smooth, amyloid, and slightly curved. The basidia are 4-spored and very thin. The clamps are huge medallion clamps, and the hyphal system is monomitic.

Perhaps because of the confusing fertile surface, the Snowy Plic has been hard to place. Fries had it placed in Merulius, figuring it had a merulioid hymenium. Karsten later took it out of Merulius and put it in Plicatura because the type species of Merulius had a more cartilaginous texture and became hard and brittle when dried. Curtis G. Lloyd placed it in the genus Radulum as **Radulum cuneatum.** Charles Peck introduced a **Plicatura alni**, which turned out to be a different color phase of the same species. Undaunted, he moved it to the genus Trogia, perhaps hoping the dilemma would now disappear.

Plicatura nivea has had its share of synonyms. Besides Lloyd's **Radulum cuneatum** and Peck's **Plicatura alni,** Berkeley described it as **Merulius rimosus**. Fries described it twice, first as **Merulius niveus** in the Elenchus in 1828, then as **Merulius petropolitanus** in the Epicrisis. Dr. Ginns eventually corralled all the synonyms in his 1970 article on the species. He placed it in a group intermediate between those members of the Corticiaceae that have a negative or a positive oxidase reaction.

Byssomerulius corium

Tyromyces chioneus from Vermont

Immature Trametes pubescens

Antrodia carbonica

Postia placenta

Oxyporus cuneatus from Rockport State Park

He further noted that **Plicatura nivea** is saprophytic on green alder, occurring more rarely on birch, willow, linden, and cottonwood. It is associated with white rot and always occurs north of 40 degrees latitude. Collections have been made in Russia, Finland, Norway, eastern Siberia, Alaska, British Columbia, Washington, Manitoba, Newfoundland, and Michigan.

Good color photos of **Plicatura nivea** can be seen in *Svampar* by Svengunnar Ryman and in *Fungi of Switzerland,* Vol. 2. Electron microscope blow-ups of the 4-spored basidia, the sausage shaped spores, and an immature basidia can be seen in Jean Keller's *Atlas des Basidiomycetes.*

Since the species can be described as having an effused-reflexed growth pattern, it has its share of look-alikes. A number of these are shown here:

Antrodia carbonica: White, usually annual, widely effused scab that differs by never branching off the surface of the wood it fruits on. It further differs by having a trimitic hyphal system and cylindrical spores.

Byssomerulius corium: Also protrudes from the surface of the log it is on, but the buff to pale ochre pore surface has a contrasting white cottony edge.

Trametes hirsuta: Resupinate, immature fruiting bodies bear a resemblance, but soon differ by developing a hairy, zonate, grayish white surface with an ochre cap margin.

Trametes pubescens: A close look-alike that differs by having angular pores on the undersurface compared to the tuberculate, plicate-venose hymenial surface of **Plicatura nivea**.

Tyromyces immitis: Differs by its rancid odor, and rough, cheesy white to yellowish cap surface with tiny black dots.

Tyromyces chioneus: Another white species, but with a much thicker context, a dimitic hyphal system, and rounded to angular pores.

Postia placenta: Differs by its salmon-pink pore surface that ages cream color and its gloeoplerous hyphae in the trama.

Oxyporus cuneatus: Although closely resembling **P. nivea**, this differs by having a true poroid hymenial surface and a strong preference for fruiting on the bark of western red cedar.

There are other whitish taxa in Antrodia, Oligoporus, and Tyromyces, but none share both the allantoid, amyloid spores and giant medallion clamps seen in the Snowy Plic.

Plicatura nivea is now the only species left in its genus. The people at Wikipedia on-line figure that its broader relationships remain undefined. They contend it could be either in the Amylocorticiaceae or the Tricholomataceae. It is a species of "incertae sedis" or uncertain placement, no simple achievement in this era of DNA sequencing.

Thanks go out to Dan Crape for bringing this enigma to our attention, and to Jim Ginns for shining a flashlight on it. Since this time, the Snowy Plic has become common in old growth conifer stands along the coast.

BIBLIOGRAPHY

J. Breitenbach & F. Kranzlin, *Fungi of Switzerland*, Vol.2, 1986. Edition Mykologie, Lucerne, Switzerland.

Ian Gibson, *Key to the Veined Fungi of the Pacific Northwest*, 2007. Pacific Northwest Key Council, Seattle, Wash.

Robert Gilbertson & Leif Ryvarden, *North American Polypores*, Vol.1, 1986. Fungiflora A/S, Blindern, Norway.

Robert Gilbertson & Leif Ryvarden, *North American Polypores*, Vol.2, 1987. Fungiflora A/S, Blindern, Norway.

James Ginns, *Taxononmy of Plicatura nivea* in *Canadian Journal of Botany* 48 (1039–1043), 1970.

James Ginns, *Merulius S.S. & S.L.: Taxonomic Disposition and Identification of Species* in *Canadian Journal of Botany* 54 (137–139), 1976.

James Ginns, *Polypores of British Columbia*, 2017. Crown Publications, Victoria, B.C.

Verne Ovid Graham, *Mushrooms of the Great Lakes Region*, 1944. Dover Publications, New York, NY.

Calvin Kauffman, *The Agaricaceae of Michigan*, 1918. Michigan Geological and Biological Survey, Lansing, Mich.

Jean Keller, *Atlas des Basidiomycetes*, 1997. Union des Societes Suisses de Mycologie, Neuchatel, Switzerland.

William Murrill, *Agaricaceae in North American Flora 9*, 1910–1915.

MycoBank.com, *Plicatura nivea*.

Carleton Rea, *British Basidiomycetae*, 1922. Strauss & Cramer, Hirschberg, Germany.

Svengunnar Ryman & Ingmar Holmasen, *Svampar*, 1984. Interpublishing, Stockholm, Sweden.

Steve Trudell & Joe Ammirati, *Mushrooms of the Pacific Northwest*, 2009. Timber Press, Portland, Ore.

Edmund Tylutki, *Mushrooms of Idaho & the Pacific Northwest*, Vol. 2, 1987. University Press of Idaho, Moscow, Idaho.

Jan Vesterholt, *Plicatura and Chaetoporellacaea in Nordic Macromycetes*, Vol. 3, 1997. Nordsvamp, Copenhagen.

Jan Vesterholt, *Plicaturaceae in Funga Nordica*, 2008. Nordsvamp, Copenhagen.

Wikipedia.com, *Plicatura nivea*

Pluteus petasatus (Fries) Gillet

They have the agreeable odor of
black elderberry flowers.

This striking and rather locally uncommon Pluteus was found in May of 1997 at the Fairhaven Co-op garden by Vince Biciunas. Since Vince not only helped initiate the Co-op Garden, but is also one of two charter members left in Northwest Mushroomer Association, and has had for many years kept us all informed of every upcoming mushroom event, it is fitting that she was the one to find it. They were fruiting on a pile of wood chip mulch used for the paths between garden plots.

Vince's collection consisted of specimens with caps 3½–8 cm wide, with dry, convex caps that had rusty brown squamules at the centers becoming more fibrillose towards the margins. The ground color was white to buff, and the context was white and thickish. The gills were free from the stem, white at first, and finally pinkish from the spores. They were crowded, deep, rounded at the edges, and interspersed with five tiers of lamellulae, (the smaller gills that don't extend far from the cap margin.) The stems were 1–1¼ cm thick and up to 7½ cm long. They were solid, stiff, and white becoming brownish fibrillose towards a barely emarginated basal bulb. The spore deposit was dark pink and the odor the same as that of **Pluteus cervinus**, a sort of peculiar radish-turnip mix. So much for my description. If we flesh it out through the literature, we discover that **Pluteus petasatus**, along with **Pluteus magnus**, is the largest and meatiest of all species of Pluteus with caps ranging up to 20 cm in width! The caps are slightly sticky or viscid when fresh, and are often lined at the margin or "striate to the middle" as Kauffman wrote. The scales at the disc can range in color from pale ochre to dark rusty, and the odor is described as "slightly of radish" by most authors, but as the stale smell of elder blossoms by Marcel Bon of France. More optimistically, they have the agreeable odor of black elderberry flowers according to Moreno, Manjon, & Zugaza of Spain.

Pluteus petasatus is found throughout North America, South America, and Europe often in great clusters on sawdust piles, rotting wood mulch, or manured straw. It can also be found on soil under oak, maple, or sweetgum.

Microscopically, **P. petasatus** is something of a thrill. Examination of a gill face showed scintillating, hyaline metuloids shooting out from the hymenium like icicles with tiny horns at the ends. These are the famed horned pleurocystidia of Stirps Cervinus in the genus Pluteus. It is a strong character that separates **Pluteus cervinus**, **Pluteus petasatus**, **Pluteus salicinus**, **Pluteus pellitus**, and now many others from the rest of the species in Pluteus. The gill trama were found to be subparallel to convergent, and the pileipellis to be a cutis of filamentous hyphae without clamps. The spores were broadly elliptical with a solitary oil drop in the centers. They measured 5.6–6.9 x 3.7–4.6 µm. Although the species is supposed to have thin-walled cheilocystidia, we found none. Dr. Else Vellinga of the Netherlands emailed me that this is not unusual for **P. petasatus**. The cheilocystidia are scarce and hard to find because "it often looks like the whole lamellar edge dissolves and is prone to bacterial decay." These, I imagine, are the sorts of idiosyncrasies that can drive a mycologist mad.

Not too many authors discussed edibility, but they all deemed **Pluteus petasatus** to be edible. Here are a sampling of opinions: **Horn, Kay, & Abel**: "Fine but not the best. Like **Pluteus cervinus**, but larger and meatier."

Vince Biciunas at the mushroom show   Photo by Migo Biciunas

LOOK-ALIKES

Volvopluteus gloiocephalus

Entoloma rhodopolium

Lyophyllum decastes

Marcel Bon: "Edible but poor quality."

David Arora: "Edible and very good. The best of the genus for the table."

John David Moore: "Gather young, firm individuals, taking care to brush them clean without breaking the sometimes easily split caps. You may notice a faint radish odor. Nothing of the radish comes through in the cooked mushroom. This mushroom can pick up a lot of dirt and debris, especially under wet conditions. You may have to rinse it under running water to clean the gills. (For purists, this is the kiss of death.) If sautéed in butter for three minutes, it has a gelatinous texture and a flavor like unseasoned Styrofoam. If dried, it is not worth reconstituting."

My inclination is to disagree. If it tastes anything like **Pluteus cervinus**, it will have a fine parsnip-like flavor. The secret to cooking the Deer Mushroom is to hard fry it until it is almost crispy. I imagine the same method would work with **P. petasatus**.

And **Pluteus petasatus** has its share of look-alikes. In no particular order, here they come:

Volvopluteus gloiocephalus: Differs by having a cup-like volva at the base of the stem. If you make a mistake, you don't pay for it. It is also edible.

Entoloma rhodopolium: A mushroom that differs by having its gills reach the stem, fruits on the ground near hardwoods, and has a glabrous gray-brown cap without squamules at the cap disc. It is to be considered poisonous.

Lyophyllum decastes: The Fried Chicken Mushroom prefers to fruit on gravel on the sides of roads, but sometimes makes a mistake and shows up in wood chip mulch. It differs by its white spores, greasy-lubricous cap texture, and tendency to fruit in giant clumps. Also a decent edible.

Pluteus pseudoroberti: Differs by having black scales on the cap disc.

Neolentinus lepideus: Differs by its coarser cap scales, white spores, and serrated gill edges.

Pluteus lipidocystis: Differs by having an association with conifer wood, no cheilocystidia, and the presence of lipids in the hymenium.

Pluteus hongoi: Differs by its more slender stature, paler grayish caps with pale brown squamules at disc, raphanoid odor, and stipes without darker fibrils.

Agaricus arvensis: This shot represents that other European concept for the Horse Mushroom acknowledged by Dr. Kerrigan. Note the pale brown scales on the cap. This differs from Pluteus by its dark brown spores and gills in age.

Other names batted around in the past are **Pluteus curtisii** and **Pluteus patricius**. *Index Fungorum* now lists these as synonyms of **Pluteus petasatus** with the exception of Berkeley's original concept of **Pluteus curtisii** now becoming a synonym of **Pluteus cervinus**. **Pluteus petasatus** in the sense of Bresadola is simply something else, and if you were to read all of this prior to dining

Pluteus hongoi from Vermont

Agaricus arvensis from Scotland

on **P. petasatus,** remember that it took a lot of work to sort out all the vagaries and get the correct species on the table.

Addendum: DNA sequencing has now revealed that our former concept of **Pluteus cervinus** should now be called **Pluteus exilis**. **P. cervinus** still exists, but is a rare species found in wood chip mulch.

BIBLIOGRAPHY

David Arora, *Mushrooms Demystified*, 1986. Ten Speed Press, Berkeley, Calif.

Partha Banerjee & Walter Sundberg, *The Genus Pluteus Section Pluteus in the Mid-western United States* in *Mycotaxon* 53 (189–246), 1995.

Cornelis Bas, Thomas Kuyper, Machiel Noorde-loos, & Else Vellinga, *Flora Agaracina Neerlandica* 2, 1990. A.A. Balkema, Rotterdam, Holland.

Alan & Arleen Bessette, William Roody, & Dail Dunaway, *Mushrooms of the Southeastern United States*, 2007. Syracuse University Press, Syracuse, NY.

Alan & Arleen Bessette & Orson & Hope Miller, *Mushrooms of North America in Color*, 1995. Syracuse University Press, Syracuse, NY.

Marcel Bon, *Mushrooms and Toadstools of Britain and Northwestern Europe*, 1987. Hodder & Stoughton, London.

J. Breitenbach & F. Kranzlin, *Fungi of Switzerland*, Vol.4, 1995. Edition Mykologia, Lucerne.

Regis Courtecuisse & Bernard Duhem, *Mushrooms and Toadstools of Britain and Europe*, 1995. Harper-Collins, London.

Bruce Horn, Richard Kay, & Dean Abel, *A Guide to Kansas Mushrooms*, 1993. University Press of Kansas, Lawrence, Kansas.

A. Justo, E. Malysheva, T.Bulyonkova, E. Vellinga, G. Cobian, N. Nguyen, A. Minnis, & D. Hibbett, *Molecular Phylogeny and Phylogeography of Holarctic Species of Pluteus Section Pluteus* in *Phytotaxa* 180 (1–85), 2014.

Calvin Kauffman, *The Agaricaceae of Michigan*, 1918. Michigan Geological and Biological Survey, Lansing, Mich.

Michael Kuo, 100 Edible Mushrooms, 2007. University of Michigan Press, Ann Arbor, Mich.

Nick Legon & Alick Henrici, Checklist of the British and Irish Basidiomycota, 2005. Royal Botanic Gardens, Kew, Surrey, England.

Gabriel Moreno, Jose Luis Manjon, & Alvaro Zugaza, *La Guia de Incafo de los Hongos de la Peninsula Iberica*, Tomo II, 1986. Incafo S.A., Madrid.

Meinhard Moser, *Keys to Agarics and Boleti*, 1983. Translated and published by Roger Phillips, London.

Peter Orton, *British Fungus Flora IV—Pluteaceae: Pluteus and Volvariella*, 1986. Royal Botanic Garden, Edinburgh, Scotland.

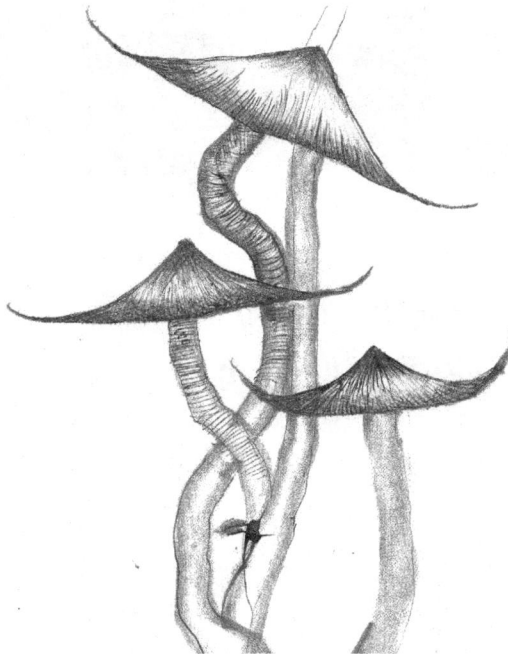

Polyporoletus sylvestris (Overholts ex Pouzar) Audet

When boiled in water, the water
turns the color of grape juice.

It was on October 19, 2018, and we were up on Easy Pass to collect mushrooms for our fall show. There were a lot of noteworthy LBM's around and Jack Waytz had gotten about 60 yards ahead of me on the trail. Then I heard this strangulated shout. In a few minutes down came Jack cradling a large polypore in both hands. He knew he had found something of interest. Lawn green smudges had sprung up wherever he had touched it. I immediately thought of the Greening Goat's Foot, a.k.a. **Albatrellus ellisii**, the only polypore I knew that behaved like this. I informed Jack that according to Arora in Mushrooms Demystified, this was an edible species. That was all it took. The entire polypore ended up in his kitchen. He contacted Arora for culinary tips. After hearing that it was best to soften the mushroom by boiling it first, Jack watched in awe as the water turned the color of Welch's grape juice in front of him. Perhaps becoming more inspired he proceeded to eat the whole thing.

No one knew it at the time, but Jack had just consumed a bit over a pound of **Polyporoletus sylvestris**, an exceedingly rare species belonging to a genus whose every member screamed 'edibility unknown'. How in blazes could this mistake have been made? I had actually worked with Polyporoletus before, just not with the one that also turned green when handled. Turns out I had not absorbed Dr. Jim Ginns' full description of this taxon in *Polypores of British Columbia* carefully enough. Let this be a lesson to others!

Polyporoletus sylvestris was first found at Cowichan Lake, B.C., on Vancouver Island in 1929. This was prior to the introduction of the genus Polyporoletus. Then in 1936 Walter Snell introduced **Polyporoletus sublividus** from the Great Smokies. He had a bit of a struggle deciding between Boletus and Polyporus, thus the name was a combination of both. The central diagnostic feature were the spores. They were double walled with partitioning and evenly distributed pock marks between them. Then in 1941, Overholts published **Polyporus sylvestris** and **Polyporus canaliculatus** from the Pacific Northwest. Both of these had the same unique spores. However he forgot to supply a Latin description for **Polyporus sylvestris**, so it didn't become a valid species until Pouzar authenticated it in 1972. Then he placed it in the genus Albatrellus. Even later, in 1987, Gilbertson and Ryvarden listed both of these polypores as synonyms of **Polyporoletus sublividus**. Perhaps naturally suspicious of all these chess moves, the French Canadian Serge Audet conducted DNA sequencing tests on all three in 2010. The result? All three were autonomous species.

According to Dr. Ginns, whose description we follow here, **Polyporoletus sylvestris** is usually found solitary on the ground in the company of conifers in the subalpine zone. The caps can run up to 18 cm wide and come in variegated colors of olive-gray, pale ochre, or fawn, often with yellow orange tinges. The texture is suede at first becoming more bald and rimose in age. The context is white to yellow orange becoming lilac gray when cut. After several hours the context changes to buff, primrose yellow, or greenish yellow. It bruises bright green where touched. The pores are decurrent, rounded to angular and then radially elongated in age. They are grayish to grayish-lilac, as seen in the featured photo. The stipe can be lateral or central and run up to 13 cm long. They are a dull olive-gray with weak lilac tints.

Microscopically, the spores are subglobose to broadly ellipsoid and measure 8–13 x 6.5–10 microns. The outer spore wall is finely wrinkled. The hyphal system is monomitic with frequent clamp connections, and no cystidia were seen.

Polyporoletus sylvestris has been recorded at least ten times in British Columbia from Vancouver north to Callahan Lake near Whistler. Paul Kroeger tells me he usually finds it at altitude near the tree line in the mountains. In the U.S. it has been recorded from Washington, Idaho, and Oregon.

But this is not the end of the story. There are at least two other species of Polyporoletus in the Pacific Northwest. One of these is **Polyporoletus bulbosus**, a taxon entirely black-brown in color. The former **Polyporoletus canaliculatus** is a synonym. The other is an intriguing possibility.

The Polyporoletus, pictured on the next page, arrived amongst us at a club meeting on September 18, 2000. It was brought to us by Jeremy Ferrera. He had found it during a hike at altitude above Marblemount. He seemed to remember hemlocks being nearby. He had tossed it into his backpack where it proceeded to pulverize the softer agarics already in there. Although we rinsed it off to observe its full glory, the damage had been done. DNA sequencing tests performed by Pablo Alvarado in 2018 were hopeless. The specimens were too contaminated. Nonetheless there were other characters worth noting. Its bald and rimose cap surface differed from that of **Polyporoletus sublividus**, whose caps are described as more tomentose-fibrillose. It also seemed to differ from **Polyporoletus sylvestris** in three different ways. It clearly had cheilocystidia, shown here. It also had a pure white cap context with purple spots at first. This was so dramatic it was Disneyesque. These spots eventually faded away to a dull ochre-gray to rusty gray color over all. And finally, no part of the fruiting body turned green on touch. More collections are needed to firm up a species concept.

As for look-alikes, the closest must be **Albatrellus ellisii**, the Greening Goat's Foot. This differs by its very coarsely hairy caps that darken dramatically with age. It also differs by its white pores that turn green in age. The half rotten specimen pictured here smelled so badly it had to be tossed from the car. Paradoxically, when fresh, the steamed context looks and tastes like white chicken with a hint of some herb not yet discovered by man.

LOOK-ALIKES

Albatrellus ellisii

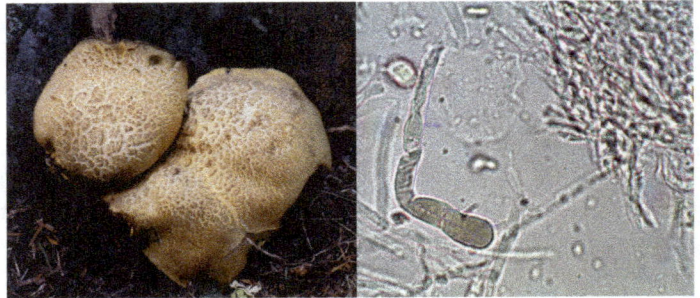

Polyporoletus from Marblemount and its cheilocystidia

And this brings us back to Jack's appraisal of the flavor of **Polyporoletus sylvestris**. I received a cell phone message that the flavor was complex, but he liked it. There was a richness to it and an undercurrent of citrus. He never experienced any ill effects and would certainly partake of it again.

That's a bit unlikely. He may have eaten the fifteenth one ever found in the world.

BIBLIOGRAPHY

Serge Audet, *Essai de Découpage Systematique du Genre Scutiger: Albatrellopsis, Albatrellus, Polyporoletus, Scutiger, et Description de Six Nouveaux Genresen* in *Mycotaxon* 111 (431–464), 2010.
Robert Gilbertson & Leif Ryvarden, *North American Polypores, Vol. 2*, 1987. Fungiflora A/S, Blindern, Norway.
Brian Luther, *New Genera of Albatrelloid Fungi with an Emphasis on Species from Washington State* in

Bulletin of the Puget Sound Mycological Society 468, 2011.
Lee Overholts, *The Polyporaceae of the United States, Alaska, and Canada*, 1953. University of Michigan Press, Ann Arbor, Mich.
Lee Overholts, *New Species of Polyporaceae* in *Mycologia* 33 (90–102),1941.
Walter Snell, *Notes on Boletes V.* in *Mycologia* 28 (463–475), 1936.

Polyporus tuberaster Jacquetant ex Fries

I do remember that it took an inordinately long time to pull the stems from the soil and couldn't figure out why.

This widespread but rather uncommon polypore prefers the drier climate of the eastern Cascades to conditions on our western side. Anybody going on a Morel Madness weekend should keep an eye out for it. These in the photo were found by Jack Waytz in early May of 2004 off of the Lake Creek Road outside of Winthrop. He found 20-30 of them in clumps near burned stumps. I had found a solitary specimen on May 9, 2003, on burnt ground at a campsite up Icicle Canyon outside of Leavenworth. Dr. Jim Ginns had identified it for me, and now thanks to Jack's Eldorado, we could now photograph it and taste it.

The somewhat odd thing is that both of us had missed the significant sclerotium that always accompanies the species when it fruits from the ground. These sclerotia are potato-like masses composed of earth, sand, and pebbles bound together by whitish hyphae and mycelial strands. They have a marbled appearance when cut, and can weigh up to 20 pounds. I suppose we missed them because they resembled the earth around them. I do remember that it took an inordinately long time to pull the stems from the soil and couldn't figure out why. But according to Arora the sclerotia themselves are valuable. He writes that they are sold in markets in southern Italy. People plant them in flowerpots, water them regularly, and harvest the polypores that erupt. Evidently you can score several years of **Polyporus tuberaster** with this method.

Long known as the Tuckahoe, the black sclerotium was once mistaken for fossilized pemmican. The context of young specimens is olive green and easily cut. The odor is cinnamon to floral-fruity. When old sclerotia are soaked in water, they absorb up to 50% of their weight. According to Robert Rogers, the Cree used to call it "ground medicine" and used it to cure rheumatism. One of the metabolites in the fruiting body is tuckalide, which inhibits cholesterol biosynthesis.

Also known as the Stone Fungus (due to the sclerotium), **Polyporus tuberaster** has caps up to 15 cm wide, a depressed to umbilicate cap center, and irregularly lobed margins. The caps are scaly becoming more fibrillose towards the thin and lacerate margins. The scales are ochre brown to tawny brown on a pallid ochre ground. The context is fleshy becoming rigid when dried. The stems are central when they fruit on the ground, but lateral to off-center when found on wood. They can measure up to 6 cm long and 1 ½ cm thick. The stipe color is white to pale ochre with a narrow black zone near the base. This zone is often obscured by white tomentum. The pore surface is white to pale tan. One specimen bruised brown when handled. The tubes measure up to 5 mm long and are decurrent on the stem. The tube mouths are quite large, polygonal in shape becoming more radially elongated or even dentate in age. The stems arise from a large brown or black sclerotium, which is rubbery when fresh, rock hard when dried. Even when fruiting on hardwood stumps such as aspen, there is often a connection through the wood to an underground sclerotium. The Stone Fungus causes a white rot in hardwoods.

The spores are white in deposit, cylindric in

LOOK-ALIKE

Polyporus radicatus from Vermont

LOOK-ALIKES

Onnia tomentosa

Polyporus tuberaster on oak from Spain

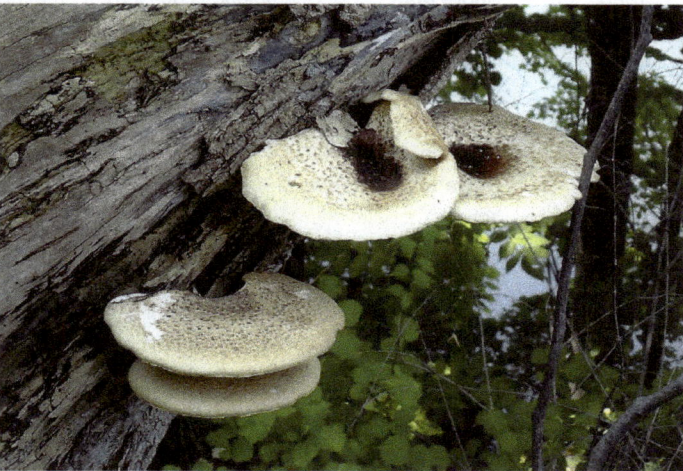

Cerioporus squamosus from Vt. (formerly in Polyporus)

shape to oblong-ellipsoid, and measure 10-16 x 4-7 μm. The hyphal system is dimitic, meaning they have two kinds of hyphae, in this case generative and skeletal. Both the generative hyphae and the bases of the basidia have clamps. In North America, **Polyporus tuberaster** ranges from British Columbia south to Arizona. It has also been reported from Germany, Holland, Italy, England, Sweden, Russia, and Japan. The larger specimens with sclerotia are more common in the Mediterranean regions. And this brings up a nomenclatural puzzle.

In the northern regions of Europe a smaller version of **P. tuberaster** fruits on oak and beech twigs, and even gorse stems. It is a collective group and includes the names **Polyporus lentus, Polyporus floccipes, Polyporus forquignoni,** and **Polyporus coronatus**. Since all of these are microscopically identical with **Polyporus tuberaster,** the lumpers have turned them all into synonyms.

Polyporus lentus has caps up to 5 cm wide, has no sclerotium, no black at the stem base, and an odor of aniseed. It fruits on the dead wood of oak and beech. **Polyporus coronatus, Polyporus floccipes,** and **Polyporus fagicola** are all synonyms. Dr. Herman Jahn, who studied this group, figured that **Polyporus forquignoni** was a dwarf form of **Polyporus lentus**. It has cap scales concolorous with the ground color, fringed margins, and white stems that become floccose at the base. Splitters, such as Moser, generally recognize these differences. They conclude that only **Polyporus tuberaster** sports the sclerotium. As Jahn points out, cultural studies need to be made to determine whether they are conspecific or not.

According to Marchand, the entire complex is related to **Cerioporus squamosus**, commonly found in almost any guide you pick up. **Polyporus squamosus** is lignicolous, has no sclerotium, a thicker and tougher context, and more flattened scales on the cap surface. Other look-alikes include **Polyporus radicatus** of the East Coast. Instead of a sclerotium, it has a long, black, rooting stem. Locally, **Polyporus tuberaster** could be confused with **Jahnoporus hirtus** (**Albatrellus hirtus**), which has a cinnamon brown, hairy cap, a very bitter taste, and no sclerotium. **Neofavolus alveolaris** differs by its diamond shaped pores and flattened rusty-orange triangular cap squamules.

LOOK-ALIKE

Jahnoporus hirtus   *Photo by Richard Morrison*

While a few authors claim that **Polyporus tuberaster** is inedible, most concur that it is edible but tough. Thanks to Jack's generosity, I was invited to partake of the specimens in the main introductory photo. After turning golden brown in the frying pan, I found them to be a crunchy version of **Boletus edulis**! No wonder they sell the sclerotia in Italy.

But in Australia, they do us one better. The giant and related **Laccocephalum mylittae** is not only edible, the sclerotium, which can weigh up to 40 pounds, is also edible.

BIBLIOGRAPHY

David Arora, *Mushrooms Demystified*, 1986. Ten Speed Press, Berkeley, Calif.

J. Breitenbach & F. Kranzlin, *Fungi of Switzerland, Vol. 2*, 1986. Edition Mykologia, Lucerne.

Regis Courtecuisse & Bernard Duhem, *Mushrooms and Toadstools of Great Britain and Europe*, 1994. Harper-Collins, London.

Robert Gilbertson & Leif Ryvarden, *North American Polypores*, 1986. Fungiflora, S.A. Blindern, Norway.

Gary Lincoff, *The Audubon Society Field Guide to North American Mushrooms*, 1981. Alfred A. Knopf, New York, NY.

André Marchand, *Champignons du Nord et du Midi, Vol. 3*, 1974. Societe Mycologique des Pyrenees Mediterraneennes, Perpignan, France.

Meinhard Moser, *Keys to Agarics and Boleti*, 1983. Translated and published by Roger Phillips, London.

Giovanni Pacioni & Gary Lincoff, *Simon & Schuster's Guide to Mushrooms*, 1981. Simon & Schuster, New York, NY.

Jens Petersen, *Polyporus in Nordic Macromycetes, Vol.2*, 1992. Nordsvamp, Copenhagen.

Elsie Wakefield & R.W.G. Dennis, *Common British Fungi*, 1981. Saiga Publishing, Surrey, England.

Psilocybe baeocystis A.H. Smith & Singer

Stamets has it tied for fourth in the world with psilocybin content.

This potent hallucinogenic Psilocybe was about the last species I expected to find in Bellingham. We were certainly within its range. But no one I knew had reported it locally. It was late October in 1994 when I checked out the silver birches for **Leccinum scabrum** on Port of Bellingham property. I had left the birches empty handed when I spotted this group in roadside bark chip mulch. As Paul Kroeger likes to point out, the more powerful the organization that owns the land, the more likely you are to find them. Perhaps the wood chip mulch is of a higher quality.

I thought the species was Collybioid at first. By the time I got them into the car, the stem bases had turned blue from my touch. I haven't seen the species since.

Wikipedia, the online giant, tells us it was first found in Eugene, Oregon in 1945. Dr. Smith and Dr. Singer then report a sighting by Dr. Frank Sipe in decaying peat moss next to a greenhouse in Eugene on November 12, 1958. In that same year, Smith and Singer published it in *Mycologia*. (I would like to surmise that the coastal Indians knew about it long before this, but owing to the preferred habitat of bark chips and peat moss, we can't dismiss the theory that the species has been brought here from somewhere else.)

Then in 1962, tragedy struck. A child died of cerebral edema in a hospital in Milwaukee, Oregon. The child had had a fever of 106 degrees for three days. It was thought that **Psilocybe baeocystis** was the mushroom responsible. Dr. Smith later determined that the real culprit was **Psilocybe cyanescens** with perhaps a Galerina or two thrown in. But it was too late. **Psilocybe baeocystis** has been known as that infamous child killer ever since.

According to Jochen Gartz, two groups working independently found psilocin and psilocybin in **Psilocybe baeocystis** in 1962. There was then speculation over whether these alkaloids caused the death of the child or whether they triggered an epilectic episode. In 1967, Leung & Paul found baeocystin in the "Little Blue Bell." And according to Jonathan Ott, norbaeocystin was isolated from it a year later.

Paul Stamets, in *Psilocybin Mushrooms of the World*, ranks **Psilocybe baeocystis** as tied for fourth with **Psilocybe cyanescens** in psilocybin content. It ranks second in the world in psilocin content.

LOOK-ALIKES

Psilocybe cyanescens   Photo by Richard Morrison

Psilocybe ovoideocystidiata from N.J.

Psilocybe stuntzii from Port Townsend, Wash.

Faded specimens of Psathyrella piluliformis from Calif.

Psilocybe azurescens from Ore.

If combined contents of psilocybin, psilocin, and baeocystin were measured, it would rank second in the world after **Psilocybe azurescens**, a species native to the northern Oregon coast.

According to Ammirati, Traquair, & Horgen, "the compounds found in Psilocybin mushrooms are indole alkaloids, specifically hydroxyltyptamine derivatives." There is a probability that the blue staining reaction is related to these compounds. Stamets notes that **Psilocybe baeocystis** contains 0.15% to 0.85% psilocybin, 0.59% psilocin, and up to 0.10% baeocystin, a nontoxic alkaloid not found in any other species. Ammirati et al. concluded that "psilocybin is the phosphate ester of psilocin. They are similar in many respects to one of the essential amino acids, tryptophan, found in cellular proteins. The psilocybin is rapidly hydrolyzed into psilocin, the true pharmacological agent, when the mushroom is ingested. Psilocybe resembles serotonin in its effect on nerve transmission, and it is this reaction to the nervous system that causes the alterations in perception." Thus the birth of the phrase "anyone up for a trypt?"

The possible illegality of possessing **P. baeocystis** has in no way prevented the spread of the Little Blue Bell, as Stevens & Gee call it. Wikipedia reports that it was found in Maine in 2007. The Bessettes and Fischer included it in their *Mushrooms of Northeastern North America*, which covers an area from Manitoba to North Carolina. To date, differences between collections from the West Coast and those from back east are confined to odor, none for West Coast specimens and farinaceous for those from the Bessette & Fischer domains.

Psilocybe baeocystis caps are 1 ½–5 ½ cm wide, broadly conic at first, then campanulate to convex with the hint of an umbo. They are dark olive brown to pale ochre brown, often with gray-blue tinges. They are also hygrophanous, drying to a beautiful oyster gray with a copper tinge at the disc. The margins are finely striate and incurved, becoming tightly lobed in age. So tightly that Paul Kroeger likens the appearance to bottle caps, and you can spot the beginning of this tendency on the uppermost specimen in this photo. Typical of many Psilocybes, the caps are covered with a viscid pellicle. Jeffrey Fine notes that in age they develop a greenish tinge on the margins. The gills are adnate to sinuate, grayish to dark cinnamon-brown with whitish edges before becoming purple brown from the spores. They are rather shallow and sometimes tinted purple. The stems are 5–7 cm long and only 2–3 mm thick, often irregularly bent or twisted. They are pale gray brown with an overlay of fine, whitish fibrils. The apex is white to pale yellow and the base usually bluish. There is a thin, cortinate veil that soon vanishes. Distinct rhizomorphs are present at the base. The spores are purple gray. The whole fruiting body bruises blue when handled. According to Stamets, it can be found on wood chips, decaying conifer

LOOK-ALIKES

Psilocybe pelliculosa

Macrocystidia cucumis   *Photo by Richard Morrison*

mulch, lawns with high lignin content, and even on old Douglas fir cones. According to Kroeger, it used to be quite common in Vancouver in bark chip mulch around major corporations, centers of higher learning, and the like. It may be a candidate for the endangered species list. Paul hasn't seen it for two to three decades.

Much of the above description was taken from Stamets, but others have added their observations. Gary Menser found the gill faces to be somewhat mottled, the stems cartilaginous and stuffed with loose fibrils, and the translucent cap pellicles to be sticky when moist. Jeffrey Fine discovered that the cap context was brownish. David Biek found the species in yellow pine forests in coniferous humus in northern California. Ammirati, Traquair, and Horgen found and measured the caulocystidia, and then examined the properties of the vanishing veil microscopically. Neither of these features were mentioned by Smith and Singer.

Microscopically, the spores are thick-walled, ellipsoidal with a suprahilar depression, and have a distinct germ pore. They are truncated at the other end, and sometimes compressed. Ammirati et al. measured them at 8.8–14.6 x 6.6–7.3 µm. The basidia are 4-spored. The cheilocystidia are fusoid to ampullaceous with long, thin necks and subacute apices. They measure 20–30 x 4.5–6 µm. There are no pleurocystidia.

Look-alikes abound:

Psilocybe cyanescens: Yet another Pacific Northwest species that enjoys the same habitats. In general it has brighter cap colors ranging from chestnut brown to caramel, and wavy cap margins in age. According to Arora, it has a less conical cap and a more copious veil than **Psilocybe baeocystis**.

Psilocybe strictipes: Differs by having a much longer stipe in relation to cap diameter, and caps that fade to straw color when drying.

Psilocybe caerulescens: Looks like a cross between **P. baeocystis** and **P. cyanescens**, but

LOOK-ALIKE

Psyathyrella umbonata (Calif.) Photo by Richard Morrison

has a range from Alabama to Brazil.

Psilocybe caerulipes: Has smaller spores, more rusty cinnamon colored gills, and caps that are more cinnamon brown. It is found throughout the Midwest and eastern states, and has even showed up in Mexico.

Psilocybe ovoideocystidiata: A recently described look-alike from the East Coast that has been found on the West coast. It differs by having two kinds of cheilocystidia and two kinds of pleurocystidia, and the fruiting bodies do not blue when touched.

Psilocybe pelliculosa: Differs by fruiting in dense clusters and having more the aspect of a Mycena with its bell-shaped caps with striate margins.

Psilocybe stuntzii: Differs from **Psilocybe baeocystis** by the membranous ring on the stem.

Psilocybe azurescens: One of the world's most potent Psilocybes, caps can reach 10 cm in widths. Differs by its obtusely umbonate cap discs and twisted, cartilaginous stems almost always with blue stains.

Parasola conopilea: Differs by its fragile fruiting bodies and the presence of setae (hairs) in the pileipellis.

Psathyrella piluliformis: Has dark red-brown caps that fade to ochre when drying. Also differs by fruiting on hardwood stumps and logs, usually in giant clusters.

Psathyrella umbonata: Also fruits on wood chip mulch, but differs by its hollow, long white stems with mealy apices.

Macrocystidia cucumis: Fruits in the same habitats but differs by its fishy to cucumber odor, pinkish-ochre spore deposit, and contrasting velvety black stems.

Galerina venenata: The most dangerous lookalike for Psilocybin hunters, it killed a teenage girl from Oak Harbor who mistook it for a Liberty Cap. It fruits on lawns and has the same toxins as **Galerina marginata**. Caps are cinnamon-brown fading quickly to yellowish-white. Gills are golden-tawny, adnate, and subdistant. Odor and taste are farinaceous, the taste becoming more bitter and disagreeable the more you chew on it. It has a thin ring pressed against the stem apex and usually cottony white mycelium at the base of the stem. A photo can be seen in A Field Guide to Western Mushrooms by A.H. Smith.

Different experts offer different advice on the consumption. Ammirati et al. caution against

Paul Kroeger and Pete Trenham, connoisseurs of the wood chip fungi

notes that **Psilocybe baeocystis** loses a lot of its potency after drying. In fresh condition, he feels that one or two caps should be sufficient for an experience. Our own local expert on these matters, Richard Haard, noted that **P. baeocystis** gives a strong visual adventure. To make sure you get there, Dr. Andrew Weil suggests as few as four fruiting bodies are needed for an adult dose.

Addendum: Anyone engaged in collecting Psilocybe mushrooms should be acutely aware of small ochre brown lookalikes with rusty spores and rings on their stems. These are likely to be deadly Galerinas or Conocybes.

eating them. They wrote that "dangerous symptoms such as severe dysphoria (the opposite of euphoria), vomiting, prostration, and occasional paralysis have been reported." Dr. Mike Beug also counsels against ingestion since both the mushrooms and the people can vary in intensity and reaction levels respectively. Stamets

BIBLIOGRAPHY

Joe Ammirati, J.A. Traquair, & Paul Horgen, *Poisonous Mushrooms of the Northern United States and Canada*, 1985. University of Minnesota Press, Minneapolis, Minn.

David Arora, *Mushrooms Demystified*, 1986. Ten Speed Press, Berkeley, Calif.

Alan & Arleen Bessette & David Fischer, *Mushrooms of Northeastern North America*. Syracuse University Press, Syracuse, NY.

David Biek, *Mushrooms of Northern California*, 1984. Spore Prints, Redding, Calif.

Jeffrey Fine, *The Stropharioidiae of Western Washington*, doctorate, 1972.

Jochen Gartz, *Magic Mushrooms Around the World*, 1996. Lis Publications, Los Angeles, Calif.

Gaston Guzman & Richard Gaines, *New Species of Hallucinogenic Psilocybe (Fr.) Kummer from the Eastern U.S.A.* in *International Journal of Medicinal Mushrooms* 9 (75–77), 2007.

Karen & Richard Haard, *Poisonous and Hallucinogenic Mushrooms*, 1977. Cloudburst Press, Seattle, Wash.

Paul Kroeger, *Keys to the Dark-Spored Strophariaceae of British Columbia*, 2008. Pacific Northwest Key Council, Seattle, Wash.

Gary Lincoff & D.H. Mitchel, *Toxic and Hallucinogenic Mushroom Poisoning*, 1977. Von Nostrand Reinhold, New York, NY.

Gary Menser, *Hallucinogenic and Poisonous Mushroom Field Guide*, 1977. Ronin Publishing Co., Berkeley, Calif.

Jonathan Ott & Jeremy Bigwood, *Teonanacatl, Hallucinogenic Mushrooms of North America*, 1978. Madrona Publishers, Seattle, Wash.

Rolf Singer & A.H. Smith, *A Taxonomic Monograph of Psilocybe, Section Caerulescentes* in *Mycologia* 50 (262–303), 1958.

Helen & A.H. Smith & Nancy Weber, *How to Know the Gilled Mushrooms*, 1979. William C. Brown, Dubuque, Iowa.

A.H. Smith, *The North American Species of Psathyrella*, 1972. New York Botanical Garden, Bronx, NY.

Paul Stamets, *Psilocybin Mushrooms of the World*, 1996. Ten Speed Press, Berkeley, Calif.

Jule Stevens & Richard Gee, *How to Identify and Grow Psilocybin Mushrooms*, 1978. Sun Magic Publishing, Seattle, Wash.

Ramaria sandaracina var. chondrobasis Marr & Stuntz

Another name for the Orange
Clump is the Red Dye Coral.

At every fall show we seem to get flooded with colorful coral fungi. The Orange Clump, as Kit Scates called it, is one of the more gorgeous Ramaria species that doesn't show up that often. To key it out, we used Kit's own Key Council key to the Ramarias. Kit Scates created the Pacific Northwest Key Council, so we were confidant we would arrive at a name eventually. The Orange Clump is found throughout the Pacific Northwest and northern California in conifer duff under western hemlock and Douglas fir. There is a great photo of it by Herb Saylor in California Fungi online.

The Orange Clump belongs to the **Ramaria sandaracina** complex. True **Ramaria sandaracina** has fruiting bodies 5–10 x 3–9 centimeters in size. Branches and tips are a moderate orange yellow with the tips bruising gray violet when handled. There is a yellow zone at the top of the stems before they become whitish below. It has an odor of green beans when fresh, a mild taste, and a gelatinized stem context mostly found at the base. The context is described as "fleshy-fibrous becoming brittle in age." The base is single or semi-divided. Microscopically, the basidia have clamps at their bases, and the spores are small for Ramaria, measuring 8.3 x 4 µm, and ornamented with papillate, cyanophilous warts. It is more slender than the other varieties.

Ramaria sandaracina var. euosma differs by having yellow tips on the branches, a more robust stature, a sweet, fragrant odor, rubbery context,

and fewer gloeoplerous hyphae (filled with granular contents).

Ramaria sandaracina var. chondrobasis, pictured here, has the same fused-mass stem base and stocky stature as the **var. euosma**, with fruiting bodies measuring up to 15 x 13 centimeters. It differs by having orange tips on the branches, the green bean odor, and a more gelatinous stem base. These gelatinous streaks are best seen when stems are cut lengthwise.

Under the microscope I discovered ellipsoid, warty spores with a size range of 7.8–10 x 3.5–4.3 µm. The contextual hyphae were monomitic (of one type), with clamps. They measured 2.9–5.7 µm in width. I found one slenderly clavate basidium with two long sterigmata, slightly curved. We learn from Tylutki that the basidia can be 1–4 sterigmate, and the spore deposit is a dark yellow orange. He included the **var. chondrobasis** in his key to vinescent (wine bruising) Ramarias. Some of the hyphae in the stipe context were gloeoplerous.

LOOK-ALIKES

Ramaria longispora

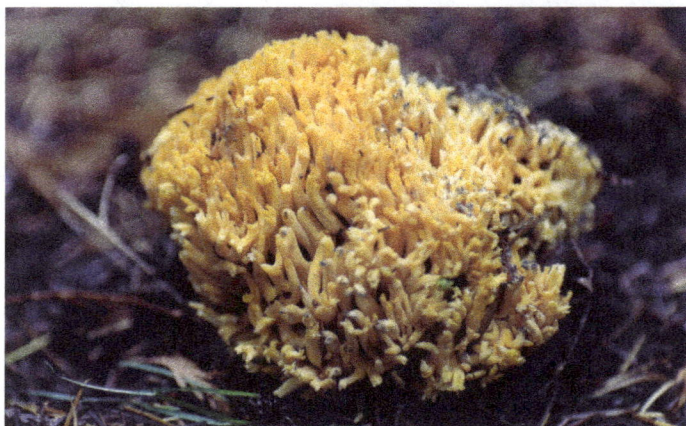

Ramaria flavigelatinosa var. megalospora

LOOK-ALIKES

Ramaria aurantiisiccescens

Ramaria leptoformosa

As with most Ramarias, there are a number of look-alikes:

Ramaria largentii: Found in the Pacific Northwest and in Europe, it differs by not having a gelatinous stem base, having much larger spores, and not having tips that bruise gray violet.

Ramaria gelatiniaurantia: Differs by lacking the odor of green beans, and doesn't have clamp connections. (The clamp connections are a big deal here.)

Ramaria conjunctipes var. tsugensis: Also lacks clamp connections and differs further by having a fasciculate growth pattern (many stems growing in a tight bundle).

Ramaria aurantiisiccescens: Differs by lacking both clamp connections and the green bean odor.

Ramaria raveneliana: Differs by its fasciculate growth pattern, more orange-flesh colored branches, and hollow interior.

Ramaria flavigelatinosa var. megalospora: Differs by having bright yellow branch tips that fade to pale yellow in age.

Ramaria longispora: Differs by its yellow branch tips and single to subcompound stem base. Relatively common in the Pacific Northwest.

Ramaria leptoformosa: Differs by lacking the yellow band on upper stipe and the less gelatinous consistency.

As for edibility, the word for **Ramaria sandaracina var. chondrobasis** is to proceed with caution. Species of Ramaria with gelatinized hyphae can cause gastrointestinal distress. Specifically, Ramarias with orange branches and yellow tips are to be avoided. This is the coloration of **Ramaria formosa**, a well-documented stomach upsetter. **Ramaria sandaracina var. euosma** with its yellow tips would fall into this group. If determined to try it, I would sautee a small portion at first. If the result is even slightly disturbing, save the rest for dyeing your t-shirts. Another name for the Orange Clump is the Red Dye Coral.

LOOK-ALIKES

Ramaria raveneliana

Ramaria formosa from Spain

BIBLIOGRAPHY

David Arora, *Mushrooms Demystified*, 1986. Ten Speed Press, Berkeley, Calif.

Michael Castellano, Jane Smith, Thomas Odell, Efren Cazares, & Susan Nugent, *Handbook to Strategy I Fungal Species in the Northwest Forest Plan*, 1999. U.S. Department of Agriculture, Forest Service, Portland, Ore.

Ron Exeter, *Summary of the Pacific Northwest Ramaria Subgenera Echinoramaria, Laeticolora. Lentoramaria and Ramaria*, 2003. Pacific Northwest Key Council, Seattle, Wash.

Ron Exeter, Lorelei Norvell & Efren Cazares, *Ramaria of the Pacific Northwestern United States*, 2006. United States Department of the Interior, Bureau of Land Management, Salem, Ore.

Daryl Grund & B.J. McAfee, *The Clavarioid Fungi of Nova Scotia* in *Proceedings of the Nova Scotian Institute of Science* 32 (1–73), 1981.

Currie Marr & Daniel Stuntz, *Ramaria of Western Washington* in *Bibliotheca Mycologica* 38, 1973.

Margaret McKenny, Daniel Stuntz, & Joe Ammirati, *The New Savory Wild Mushroom*, 1987. University of Washington Press, Seattle, Wash.

Kit Scates & Michael Beug, *Trial Field Key lo the Species of Ramaria in the Pacific Northwest*, 2009. Pacific Northwest Key Council, Seattle, Wash.

Edmund Tylutki, *The Mushrooms of Idaho and the Pacific Northwest, Vol. 2*, 1987. University Press of Idaho, Moscow, Idaho.

Russula 'brevipes' Peck

Be prepared to plunge into a jungle of close relatives, nasty look-alikes, and confused identities.

If you are one of those who occasionally hikes or bikes around Lake Padden in the fall, you may have noticed what David Arora calls "shrumps" on the side of the trail. These are nothing more than miniature upheavals in the forest duff, and if you look a little closer you will discover a dirty whitish mushroom causing the shrump. Since the caps can be broadly funnel-shaped, a good amount of soil, duff, and conifer debris often obscures the disc. You have most likely found **Russula brevipes,** the Short-Stemmed Russula. This ubiquitous species is found under conifers in the Northwest, pine in the Southwest, oak and pine elsewhere, and even reported from Fort de France, Martinique, by Pegler. It is also sold for food in the market in Ozumba, Mexico, and also reported from Pakistan in 2006. Whether you call it the Short Stalked White Russula (Lincoff) or the Stubby Brittlegill (McKnights), you will soon be calling it something else if you mistook it for a matsutake.

The third photo shows what these Russulas look like as you pass them in the woods. Local connoisseurs call them "Earth Movers," a phrase first coined by Bill Wright of Clark's Point.

Russula brevipes gets huge. The convex to funnel-shaped caps can get up to 20 cm wide. They are a dingy white to cream color, soon staining a sordid yellow-brown from handling or where the larvae have dug channels. The margins are inrolled, and the surface is matt, somewhat sticky when moist. The flesh is thick, firm, brittle, and white.

LOOK-ALIKES

Russula cascadensis

R. brevipes moving earth at South Lake Padden

The cap cuticle peels up to one-third of the distance from margin to disc. The odor is mild or a bit like decaying shellfish in age, and the taste is mild to slightly peppery. The gills are usually decurrent, and are white to ivory in age. They are crowded, narrow, intervenose, and occasionally forked near the stem. Mollen & L. Weber claim the gills are alternately long and short. The stems range from 2 ½ to 4 cm thick and 3–8 cm long, considerably shorter than the widths of the caps. They are white, chalk-like, equal or tapering downwards. All parts of the mushroom stain slowly brownish when handled.

The spores are white or cream in deposit. According to Hesler,

LOOK-ALIKES

Russula chloroides from Switzerland

Russula brevipes var. acrior   Photo by Richard Morrison

Russula acrifolia from France

they measure 9–11 x 8.5–10 µm with warts 1–1.7 µm high accompanied by a continuous or broken reticulum (the fine lines that connect warts). The ornamentation is amyloid in Melzer's. The cap cuticle is composed of repent hyphae.

Easy enough to recognize? For those who think they've got it, just skip to the last several paragraphs on edibility and general advice. For the rest of you, prepare to plunge into a nightmarish jungle of close relatives, nasty look-alikes, and confused identities.

Just for beginners, **Russula brevipes** was for years known as **Russula delica** in North America. Mistakenly. In older guides, such as Miron Hard's *Mushrooms Edible & Otherwise,* you will find a photo of **Russula brevipes** with the name **Russula delica** attached to it. Or else you will find mixed descriptions of the two species as an author struggles to make sense of the discrepancies. It didn't help that Rolf Singer considered **Russula brevipes** to be a synonym of **Russula delica**. However, **R. delica** is the European counterpart to **Russula brevipes**. It has much thicker and more distantly spaced gills. Although Peck reported it in 1880, several authors surmise it has yet to be found in North America.

It was Charles Peck who first described **Russula brevipes** from Quogue, New York, in 1890. In the 1900 issue of *Report of the New York State Botanist* he noted that "our species is closely related to **Russula delica**, but is separated from it by the unpolished cap surface, the dingy yellowish stains of the cap, the close gills and their tardily acrid taste, and the larger, warty spores." A few more differences could be added. Romagnesi described the spores of **Russula delica** to be adorned with flattened spines, not the long ones noted by Hesler. Knudsen, Vauras, & Ruotsalainen combine traits normally associated with another European Russula, **Russula chloroides,** with those of **Russula delica**. They write that both can have a narrow band of turquoise at the top of the stem, gill edges sometimes turquoise when dried, and a fruity odor that becomes herring-like in age. Classical North American **Russula brevipes** lacks the fruity odor, the turquoise gill edges, and the turquoise band at stem apex.

Both Russulas belong in Subsection Lactarioideae, which consists of those larger, thick-fleshed Russulas with whitish caps that may stain tan to brownish in age, and the presence of lamellulae.

Close relatives of **Russula brevipes** likely to be found in the Pacific Northwest are the following:

Russula brevipes var. acrior: According to Darryl Grund, who did his thesis on Washington State Russulas, the **var. acrior** is the correct name for the specimens with a pale greenish tint to the gills and a turquoise band at the stem apex. He described the odor and taste as mild at first, with no bitter component, and claimed they were common under conifers from Maine to Washington. He reported spore sizes as

LOOK-ALIKE

Russula albidula from Georgia

Russula 'raoultii'   *Photo by Richard Morrison*

Russula 'adusta'

LOOK-ALIKES

Russula cremoricolor

Lactarius deceptivus from Mass.

Lactarius controversus from Lake Stevens

10.2–11.6 x 8.9–9.5 µm. Trudell & Ammirati disagree with Grund's taste findings. They find the taste to be acrid, ergo the **var. acrior.** There is a suspicion on both sides of the Atlantic that European **Russula chloroides** and **Russula brevipes var. acrior** could be conspecific.

Russula brevipes var. megaspora: This Californian variety differs from **R. brevipes v. brevipes** by its larger spores measuring 9–14 x 8–12 µm. Dr. Bart Buyck questions whether spore size in this case is worthy of a separate variety.

Russula cascadensis: A smaller version of **Russula brevipes** with a nauseating odor and an intensely acrid taste. The initial taste is not bitter before the acridity kicks in. Caps only grow up to 12 cm wide and often appear as if covered with a fine fawn-brown "dust." The stems do not change color when bruised, and the spores are much smaller than those of **R. brevipes**, measuring 6.5–8.2 x 5.5–6.5 µm. They are also found with conifers. Grund found them to be most plentiful on Whidbey Island. And Bart Buyck found the odor to be indistinctive.

Russula vesicatoria: Another smaller version of **Russula brevipes** that does not have alternating short and long gills, and is bitter to astringent at first before becoming so intensely acrid it can blister your lips. Groves places this species in Florida and on the West Coast. Orson Miller notes that the gills frequently fork near the stipe, but places the species in Maryland and Virginia. The Florida collections appeared in sandy soils under two and three-needle pines. They have a maple syrup odor, distinctive pileocystidia, and spores with low ornamentation.

Other North American Russulas in Subsection Lactarioideae that could be confused with the Earth Movers are:

Russula inopina: A mild-tasting species that lacks mucronate pileocystidia, has sparsely reticulated spores, and filiform, flexuous terminal cells in the pileipellis. It has pale cream spores, numerous lamellulae, and is found with conifers in the Northeast.

Russula angustispora: A smaller species with caps up to 7 ½ cm wide and only found with Virginia pine. It has much narrower spores than any other Russula in the Subsection Lactarioideae.

Russula romagnesiana: A species concept created by Shaffer to replace **Russula chloroides var. parvispora** of Europe. It is mild tasting and has very small spores with prominent ornamentation. Buyck and Adamcik subsequently discovered that it differs from **R. chloroides var. parvispora** by the glutinous sheaths on its hyphal ends and the presence of bi-capitate pileocystidia at the cap discs. So it is valid enough to stand on its own. Known from Michigan and Mississippi.

Several North American Russulas not in Subsection Lactarioideae but still confused with Russula brevipes are:

Russula pallidospora: Differs by having a strong odor of green apples, and has pale ochre to yellow spores. Kibby and Fatto have found it in New

LOOK-ALIKES

Amanita silvicola

Lactifluus vellereus from Vermont

Jersey and New Hampshire.

Russula albidula: An acrid tasting, viscid capped species from the Deep South. With white spores.

Russula 'adusta': A pallid member of the Compactae group whose flesh turns reddish when bruised, and then smoky brown over time. Recent DNA sequencing has shown that our west coast **Russula adusta** is comprised of two new species, both closely related.

Russula cremoricolor: A smaller species with caps up to 10 cm wide, viscid when young, acrid tasting, and cream colored with pale yellowish discs. Common in the Pacific Northwest.

Russula raoultii: Differs by its viscid cream to straw-colored caps, and much smaller spores.

Other Northwest mushrooms not in Russula that could be confused with **Russula brevipes** are:

Tricholoma murrillianum: This differs by its firm caps that do not shatter when thrown against a tree, a large partial veil in the form of

Tricholoma acerbum from France

Hygrophorus subalpinus from Idaho

Cantharellus subalbidus

a disheveled ring on the stem, and a unique spicy odor that can't be mistaken for anything else. The white caps develop cinnamon colored stains and fibrils in age. And this is the Pacific Northwest's Matsutake.

Amanita silvicola: Differs by its cottony cap surface and cottony velar material just above the bulb at stem base. Most likely poisonous.

Hygrophorus subalpinus: This chunky high mountain species differs by its waxy gills, smooth spores, bulbous stem base, and the fleeting presence of a flaring ring just above that base.

Lactarius deceptivus: Usually found in the company of **R. brevipes**. According to Voitk, Peck was so fooled by its resemblance to the Earth Mover that he named it thus. It has white latex when the gills are scratched, and white cottony tissue on the cap margin.

Lactifluus vellereus: Differs by its wooly cap, white latex that stains the gills brown, and distant gills that do not fork.

Lactifluus piperatus: Differs by its extremely acrid taste, white latex, and much smaller spores. (All of these Lactarioid species exude a white latex when their gills are cut. The transparent beads of water sometimes found on the gill edges of **Russula brevipes** are not latex.) All of these species of Lactarius are intensely acrid, so it is unlikely you would eat one by mistake. But not impossible. The Russians are known to pickle acrid specimens of both Lactarius and Russula.

Lactarius resimus: Differs by its viscid yet tomentose caps that are white at first, but pale ochre in age. The white latex stains the gills pale greenish yellow.

Lactarius controversus: A strongly acrid species with white latex that does not change color in age, caps with pinkish to brownish stains, and flesh to salmon colored gills.

Cantharellus subalbidus: The white chanterelles are chunky enough to get confused with the Earth Mover, but the distant ridges that substitute for true gills easily distinguish them.

Russula brevipes should not be confused with large, white Amanitas because the latter have free gills and either rings on their stems or volval material at their bases.

And of course, Europe has its own menagerie of look-alikes. Here they are in brief:

Russula pseudodelica: A species with pronounced and isolated spines on its spores. According to Rinaldi & Tyndalo, it has an odor of herrings and a rosy to yellowish hue to the gills. Marchand claims it is just a synonym of **Russula pallidospora**.

Russula delica var. trachyspora: A species reported from Spain with thick, distant gills, an acrid taste, sharp, funnel-shaped caps with inrolled margins, and spores with long spines and very few reticulations. Knudsen, Vauras, & Ruotslainen turn this into **Russula chloroides var. trachyspora**, and note that the spines are over 1.5 µm in length. Some authors note that it sits halfway between **Russula delica** and **Russula chloroides**.

Russula delica var. puta: A variety authored by Romagnesi, it has thin, distant gills, satin white caps that become spotted red-brown, an almost sweet taste, rather small spores with strong reticulations, and bottle-shaped swellings in the sphaerocysts in the cap cuticle.

Russula chloroides: The possible counterpart to North American **R. brevipes var. acrior** if one can overlook the much smaller spores. Traditionally, this is a species with a blue-green band at the stem apex, bluish-green tints in the gills, and

TRANSFORMATION

Hypomyces lactifluorum parasitizing Russula brevipes

an acrid taste. Marchand described the stem as mild tasting but the gills as acrid. The gills are crowded, not distant as in **R. delica.** The odor of **R. chloroides** is described by Moser as "mouldy, even fishy to strongly fruity."

All of these Russulas are suspected to be part of a complex, and even if you thought you had succeeded in sorting them out, DNA sequencing will probably resort them all over again. To make matters more interesting, Czech authors Dermek, Kluzak, Svrcek, Kubicka, & Smotlacha have reported **Russula brevipes** from Eastern Europe. Their version of **R. brevipes** features the same spore size, a mild to slightly piquant taste, and a turquoise band at the top of the stem.

Russula acrifolia: A European Russula in Section Compactae with brown caps and white margins. The flesh reddens when bruised and the gills are sharp tasting.

Tricholoma acerbum: A European Trich that differs by its adnate gill attachment, acrid taste, and involute cap margins.

Meanwhile, back on our side of the Atlantic, no one agrees on the tastes involved. For **Russula brevipes var. acrior**, McKenny, Stuntz, & Ammirati describe a slight to strong peppery taste. Grund thinks it is mild. Glick thinks it is edible, while all others describe it as acrid. Both Orson Miller and Harry Thiers describe the taste of **Russula brevipes** as mildly or slightly acrid. It is clearly peppery and many may have spat it out before that acrid moment arrived.

If you are among the many who have escaped the nomenclatural jungle, reconnect here. We can now explore opinions of the flavors pertaining to **Russula brevipes**.

David Arora in 1986: "So large, so mediocre. Better kicked than picked."

McKenny, Stuntz, & Ammirati: "Edible but rather tasteless. It is best cooked with meat or in other sauces, whose flavor it then assumes."

Roger Phillips: "The flavor is unpleasant becoming slowly acrid" (which others dispute, claiming the acrid properties disappear in cooking).

Helene Schalkwijk-Barendsen: "Some people get upset stomachs from it" (a reaction that A.H. Smith attributes to **Russula cascadensis**.)

Charles McIlvaine and **Charles Peck**: "Excellent when fresh specimens are fried in butter."

Jack Czarnecki, author of *Joe's Book of Mushroom Cookery,* does not include **Russula brevipes** in his list of 16 favorite Russulas for the table. However, the closely related **Russula delica** is among them. Jack suggests high heat sautéing in butter as the best means of cooking Russulas in general. He also cautions us not to pile up our Russulas in our collecting baskets. The bottom layer will turn into crumbs. "The brittleness, though, will disappear in cooking."

David Arora in 2013: David actually cooked up a batch of **Russula brevipes** for Jack Waytz and I just after our fall wild mushroom show. He cut them into chunks and boiled them in water for about ten minutes. He then hard sautéed them in a little virgin olive oil and salt. They were bland but of a nice texture. All the peppery qualities had vanished. We could easily envision them going into an Irish stew.

But by far the best way to improve the flavor of **R. brevipes** was brought up by Lincoff. Just wait until it is attacked by the parasite, **Hypomyces lactifluorum**, and you will have a tasty Lobster Mushroom instead. As Steve Trudell puts it, "Only here does a dense mass of mummified material come to the rescue of a Russula."

Addendum: Recent DNA results have shown that true **R. brevipes** Peck is an east coast species. Our western **R. brevipes** consists of four different species. One is found under oak, one has larger spores and is **Russula brevipes v. megaspora**, and the other two remain undescribed.

BIBLIOGRAPHY

David Arora, *All That the Rain Promises and More*, 1991. Ten Speed Press, Berkeley, Calif.

David Arora, *Mushrooms Demystified*, 1986. Ten Speed Press, Berkeley, Calif.

Robert Bandoni & Adam Szczawinski, *Guide to Common Mushrooms of British Columbia*, 1976. British Columbia Provincial Museum, Victoria, B.C.

Anna Bazzicalupo, B. Buyck, I. Saar, J. Vauras, D. Carmean, & M. Berbee, *Troubles with Mycorrhizal Mushroom Identification where Morphological Differentiation Lags Behind Barcode Sequence Divergence* in *Taxon* 66 (791–810), 2017.

Alan Bessette & Walter Sundberg, *MacMillan Field Guide to Mushrooms*, 1987. MacMillan Publishing Co., New York, NY.

Bart Buyck & Slavomir Adamcik, *Type Studies in Russula Subsection Lactarioideae from North America and a Tentative Key to the North American Species* in *Cryptogamie Mycologie* 34 (259–279), 2013.

Jack Czarnecki, *Joe's Book of Mushroom Cookery*, 1986. Atheneum, New York, NY.

Ray Fatto & Geoffrey Kibby, *Keys to the Species of Russula in Northeastern North America*, 1990. Kibby-Fatto Enterprises, Somerville, N.J.

Phyllis Glick, *The Mushroom Trail Guide*, 1979. Holt, Rinehart, & Winston, New York, NY.

Darryl Grund, *A Survey of the Genus Russula Occurring in Washington State*, 1965. Doctoral dissertation.

David Hawksworth, *Trouble Over Cap Colors and Species Concepts in Russula* in *Fungus* 8 (61–62), 2017.

Lexemuel Hesler, *A Study of Russula Types* in *Memoirs of the Torrey Botanical Club* 21, No.2 (1–59), 1960.

Greg Hovander, *Russula Round-Up*, 2007. Pacific Northwest Key Council, Seattle, Wash.

Henning Knudsen, Juhani Ruotsalainen, & Jukka Vauras, *Russula in Funga Nordica*, 2008. Nordsvamp, Copenhagen.

Gary Lincoff, *The Audubon Society Field Guide to North American Mushrooms*, 1981. Alfred A. Knopf, New York, NY.

André Marchand, *Champignons du Nord et du Midi, Vol.5*, 1977. Societe Mycologique des Pyrenees Mediterraneennes, Perpignan, France.

Charles McIlvaine & Robert Macadam, *One Thousand American Fungi*, 1902. Dover Publications, New York, NY.

Margaret McKenny, Daniel Stuntz, & Joe Ammirati, *The New Savory Wild Mushroom*, 1987. University of Washington Press, Seattle, Wash.

Orson Miller, *Mushrooms of North America*, 1972. E.P. Dutton & Co., New York, NY.

Hope & Orson Miller, *North American Mushrooms*, 2006. Morris Books Publishing, Guilford, Conn.

Cora Mollen & Larry Weber, *Fascinating Fungi of the North Woods*, 2007. Kollath + Stensaas, Duluth, Minn.

Meinhard Moser, *Keys to Agarics and Boleti*, 1983. Translated and published by Roger Phillips, London.

Giovanni Pacioni & Gary Lincoff, *Simon & Schuster's Guide to Mushrooms*, 1981. Simon & Schuster, New York, NY.

Charkles Peck, *Report of the New York State Botanist*, 1900.

David Pegler, Agaric Flora of the Lesser Antilles in *Kew Bulletin Additional Series* IX (1–669), 1983. Her Majesty's Stationary Office, London.

Roger Phillips, *Mushrooms of North America*, 1991. Little, Brown & Co., Boston.

Henri Romagnesi, *Les Russules*, 1985. Strauss & Cramer, Hirschberg, Germany.

William C. Roody, *Mushrooms of West Virginia and the Central Appalachians*, 2003. University Press of Kentucky, Lexington, Ky.

Robert Shaffer, *The Subsection Lactarioideae of Russula* in *Mycologia* 56 (202–231), 1964.

Helene Schalkwijk-Barendsen, *Mushrooms of Western Canada*, 1991. Lone Pine Publishers, Edmonton, Alberta.

A.H. Smith & Nancy Weber, *The Mushroom Hunters' Field Guide*, 1980. University of Michigan Press, Ann Arbor, Mich.

A.H. Smith & Nancy Weber, *A Field Guide to Southern Mushrooms*, 1985. University of Michigan Press, Ann Arbor, Mich.

Jack States, *Mushrooms and Truffles of the Southwest*, 1990. University of Arizona Press, Tucson, Ariz.

Mirko Svrcek, *The Hamlyn Book of Mushrooms and Fungi*, 1983. Artia, Prague.

Mirko Svrcek & Jiri Kubicka, *Champignons d'Europe*, 1983. Artia, Prague.

Harry Thiers, *Russulaceae in Agaricales of California*, 1997. Mad River Press, Eureka, Calif.

Steve Trudell & Joe Ammirati, *Mushrooms of the Pacific Northwest*, 2009. Timber Press, Portland, Ore.

Andrus Voitk, *A Little Illustrated Book of Common Mushrooms of Newfoundland and Labrador,* 2007. Gros Morne Co-operating Association, Rocky Harbour, Newfoundland.

Russula igorii nom. prov. Hovander

Photo by Dan Digerness

He managed to record the most beautiful Russula I'd ever seen.

In the olden days Dr. A.H. Smith would often entitle a contribution to a scientific journal with "New or Unusual North American Agarics." The Russula pictured here is most likely new to the Pacific Northwest and possibly the most unusual find ever for Whatcom County. According to local Russula expert Greg Hovander it appears to be new to science.

There is quite the story behind it. In the summer of 1986 I went sailing with an old college buddy, Dr. Bruce Reiter, up to Desolation Sound. I had no idea how long we would be gone, so in a moment of weakness decided to loan my camera to local mushroom aficionado, Dan Digerness. Dan is the artist who sketched the mushroom drawings in this book. He's highly talented in this, but it had been some time since he had last held a camera. Nonetheless he was into it. He shot off like a rocket to all his special spots in the county.

It was sometime in July when he came upon this group of Russulas in Cornwall Park. They were in the center of a ring of old Douglas fir and western red cedar. Realizing instantly that here was an unusual species, he took the shot that you see on the lead page. He managed to record the most beautiful Russula I'd ever seen.

A bit further along in time, I discovered that Greg Hovander had sampled this Russula. He thought they had a firm and excellent texture with a mild flavor that acquiesced to other flavors around it.

But the mushroom gods

LOOK-ALIKE

Russula parazurea from England

were with us. After seeing this photograph and rushing back to Cornwall Park to try to find more (to no avail), I found a solitary specimen at Berthusen Park near Lynden. This was in September of 1986. It was also under cedar. The following description was made from that specimen.

The cap was 11 cm wide, broadly convex, and dry. The color was slate blue becoming pinkish ochre at the center. The margins were not striate and the cap cuticle peeled only one-quarter of the way to the disc. The context was lavender under the cuticle, but white below. The gills were adnate, crowded, equal, and yellow ochre from the spores. They were forked near the stipe and intervenose near the margin. The stem measured 3 cm thick and 9 ½ cm long. It was white flushed with pink and bruised slowly brown when rubbed. It was tapered slightly at the base. The odor and taste were mild. The spores were yellow ochre and amyloid in Melzer's. There was no flesh change with ammonia. Greg Hovander later noted that the gills were more flexible and rubbery than those of other Russulas. He also added more details in his *Russula Round-Up.* The spores were subglobose and measured 7.5–10.5 x 6.5–9.5 μm. The odor was faintly fruity. Caps could reach 20 cm in width. They were dry unless subviscid in very wet weather. They were olive green when young or in shade or bluish purple to blue when in partial sunlight. (Greg can be spotted at fall shows sitting around a table of Russulas while taking notes on cap color reactions to water applied from a paint brush.) They literally change color in front of your eyes. According to his appendix in *Russula Round-Up*, condensed tannins called proanthocyanidins "are capable of hydroxylating, dehydroxylating, and polymerizing under certain conditions to create reds, purples, blues, or no color at all. Conditions that influence color are the amount of molecules present, water and pH (acid base) status of tissues, and association with stabilizing molecules, air, heat, and light. When conditions favor the cationic form of proanthocyanidins, red is produced. Blue is produced when neutral to anionic forms occur." This is why so many Russulas start off greenish and end up reddish or purplish after much rain.

The gills stained slowly brown when bruised. Stems and cap context turned honey yellow to light tan in 15 minutes when scraped. Gill attachments varied from adnexed to subdecurrent. The application of $FeSO_4$ turned the stem orange brown in half a minute, then gray brown in 15 minutes. The fruiting bodies are firm, not fragile, and they were found about 14 miles north of Ocean Shores on the east side of Highway 109. They show up from July through October, associating with Douglas fir, hemlock, and cedar.

Dan wanted to know what it was. All I could tell him was where it wasn't. Not in Moser, not in Ben Woo's Key Council key, not even in Grund's thesis where dozens of nom. provs. are included. I allowed that it might be described in some obscure journal where not even Romagnesi could find it. In exasperation I turned to Ben Woo. I write "exasperation" because Ben was often inundated with Russula requests and replied scathingly if you sent him a common one. He has since passed away, but for half a century he was our beloved West Coast Russula authority. He might be our only chance at finding a name for this species.

I mailed him half the specimen and hoped for the best. Four and a half months later, he wrote back.

"Dear Buck, four and one half months is not too bad for me. Most folks are lucky to get a reply at all. The Russula you sent was an excellent collection and your notes were good. Yours is the first report of this Russula from our area, and for all that I can find, the first collection in North America."

He had decided that it was close to the European **Russula parazurea**. But there were two reservations, one from me and one from him. **Russula parazurea** has white spores and a complete reticulation between the warts on the spores. The specimen I sent to Ben had barely reticulate spores. Ben acknowledged this, but blamed it on a new scope he was just breaking in.

I then made a more thorough search into the European literature. After some time I unearthed a species called **Russula parazurea var. ochrospora**. Photos of it could be seen in *Bollettino del Gruppo Micologico G. Bresadola di Trento*, Anno 27, Vol. 3–4, 1984, and in Count Bruno Cetto's *I Funghi dal Vero*, Vol. 6. I thought we had hit the jackpot. Photos looked just like ours with one glaring exception. There was no rosy flush on the stems and no mention of the stems turning brownish when rubbed.

In 1985 in *Documents Mycologiques* 14, Livio Quadraccia upgraded the name to species status, now calling it **Russula ochrospora**. It was a rare species, found only in Ravenna and Emilia, Italy, in public gardens under oak. It was about this time that Greg Hovander felt enough was enough. Bellingham, Washington, is nowhere near the Italian Adriatic coast, and cedar is nowhere near oak. Something had to be done.

Now Greg has been for years one of the top identifiers for the sprawling Snohomish County Mycological Society centered in Everett. He is also a member of the Pacific Northwest Key Council and was at this time finishing up his work on *Russula Round-Up*, his contribution to the keys on genera. Subsequent DNA sequencing of Ben Woo's extensive Northwest collection of Russulas revealed a plethora of name changes. There is also Darryl Grund's work to consider. Back in 1965 he described 47 nom. provs. in his thesis. Although many are suspected of being repetitive, more new taxa could arrive from that source.

It turned out that our mysterious blue-gray Russula was already in Greg's key under the name **Russula igorii** nom. prov. Club member Walt Ketola had been finding it for years out near Ocean Shores in sandy soil under Douglas fir and spruce. Every couple of years Walt would bring specimens to their fall show in October.

So I got a letter from Greg detailing about 11 differences between our species and the Adriatic "counterpart." I agreed with about four of them, but the main one was the spore ornamentation. This is a major separation point in Russula, and the two couldn't have been further apart.

The Russula is named after Igor Malcevski, a great fungal enthusiast also in the Snohomish Club. Igor has served for years as the longest running newsletter editor in the Cenozoic era.

In a subsequent letter, Greg brought up the need for a team of Russula experts to work on the Pacific Northwest species. Back in 1965, Darryl Grund described 47 nom. provs. in his thesis. These were Russulas collected in a three-year period. As far as I know, only one, **Russula stuntzii**, was singled out from these and published as a new species. Many of the rest, I have heard, are either invalid or repetitive species. Nonetheless, the Pacific Northwest seems to be a fertile area for Russula exploration, and what better way to start than introduce the sensational **Russula igorii** nom. prov.?

BIBLIOGRAPHY

Bollettino del Gruppo Micologico G. Bresadola di Trento, *Anno 27 Vol. 3–4*, 1984.
Bruno Cetto, *I Funghi dal Vero, Vol.6*, 1969. Arti Grafiche Saturnia, Trento, Italy.
Darryl Grund, *A Survey of the Genus Russula Occuring in Washington State*, 1965. Doctoral dissertation.
Greg Hovander, *Russula Roundup*, 2010. Pacific Northwest Key Council, Seattle, Wash.

Russula stuntzii Grund

It's the only Russula in the state that
can fruit on rotten conifer logs.

When I first moved to the Northwest in the early 1980s I occasionally ran into an unusually beautiful Russula I couldn't key out anywhere. The caps were pale grayish buff with a lavender component as if a water colorist had painted a pale violet wash over the surface. It often had a marbled look, little islands of white emerging through the lavender haze. No other violet-capped Russula had the same feel to it, and it was relegated to my growing pile of unknowns. But I began to suspect that such a striking Russula must have been noticed by others, and these suspicions were born out later when I discovered Darryl Grund's 1965 doctorate entitled A Survey of the Genus Russula Occurring in Washington State. To my delight, the pale lavender-gray mystery keyed out easily to **Russula pallidolivida** nom. prov.

Ben Woo, our Russula expert on the Pacific Northwest Key Council, had steered me in that direction. Out of all the questionable nom. provs. in Grund's thesis, Ben thought that **Russula pallidolivida** was the most authentic and the best candidate to be published as a species. He neglected to tell me it already had been pub-lished. Grund himself published it as **Russula stuntzii** in *Mycotaxon* 9 in 1979. The name honors Dr. Daniel Stuntz, his professor at the time of his doctorate.

Grund described the caps as 3.5–8.3 cm wide, broadly convex to plane becoming depressed at the disc with uplifted margins in age. Margins were barely striate to tuberculate striate. The cuticle was separable from ¼ to ½ the way to the disc from the margin. The surface was glabrous, viscid when moist and polished when dry. They were grayish white with paler mottled patches and often with a lavender tinge. The gills were adnate to adnexed, white to buff, and very rarely forked or with lamellulae. The stems were 3–7½ cm long and 1–2¼ cm thick. They were white, equal to clavate or abruptly expanded at the apex, and smooth to longitudinally wrinkled. Spores were white to cream. Odor was mild and taste was acrid. They were found solitary with hemlock and fir.

Once it was published, Dr. Harry Thiers was able to track it down in California where he found it to be widely distributed in "coastal forests and

CLOSE RELATIVE

Russula cremoricolor from Calif.

Russula phoenicea

Russula grisea from Florida

Russula cf medullata from Maine

montane areas." He discovered it was the only Russula in the state that could fruit on rotten conifer logs. A lignicolous Russula! He found a specimen or more with caps up to 10 ½ cm wide and stems up to 3 cm thick. Otherwise, his description agrees with Grund's.

The lead photo derives from a collection found at Deception Pass Park in mid-November, 1990. My notes differ from Grund's type description in two ways. The gills bruised slowly pale brown when handled, and the specimens seemed to have the pungent odor associated with **Lepiota cristata**. Since no one else mentions this odor, either **L. cristata** had shared the collecting basket with it or the species has this odor only when young or at Deception Pass Park. I suspect the former.

Microscopically, Grund found globose spores measuring 7–7.5 x 8–9.5 µm. The warts measured 1.5 µm tall with partial reticulation between them. Pileocystidia, cheilocystidia, and pleurocystidia were all present. The flesh became deep violet with a-naphthol.

As might be expected, several experts noted look-alikes: **Russula cremoricolor**: Differs from **R. stuntzii** by its ivory-yellow cap with no hint of gray or lavender, and spores that have no reticulation between them. **Russula anomala**: Also lacks reticulation between spores. It's a thin-fleshed, white-capped species from Suffolk County, New York, that Peck introduced after finding it once. **Russula pantoleuca**: A species from Lake Wachusett, Massachusetts, that has a mild taste, more yellowish caps, a weak odor of apples, and an association with hardwoods.

Russula grisea: Differs by its yellow spores, preference for oak, and grayish caps tinged with lilac.

Russula cf medullata: Differs by its tan caps with sometimes olive to pinkish tinges, ochre spores, and gills that fork near the stem.

Russula phoenicea: Differs by its usually mild taste and dull purple-brown caps with olive tinges that become darker at discs.

Russula ionochlora: A European species with gray-green caps and purple margins that is found in temperate hardwood forests.

Russula vinosa: A large, fleshy Russula that comes in many colors from purple to reddish to olive green with lavender flushes. The stems stain fleetingly pink when scratched. Usually with Sitka spruce.

Grund recorded **Russula stuntzii** from Barlow Pass at 2,360 feet of altitude, and from the White River Valley near Auburn, Washington. I found it in

LOOK-ALIKES

Russula vinosa

1990 and again in 1992 at Deception Pass Park on the coast. Greg Hovander has it from Camp Cornet, which is also a part of the same park. Steve Trudell extends the range up into British Columbia. He has a photo of it showing pale tan caps with lobed margins. Dr. Thiers has a shot showing two caps, one with a dark olive disc and pale lavender margins, the other with an umber disc and pinkish margins. Both photos stray so far from the type description that either an editor made a mistake or these are examples of extreme proanthocyanidinism.

Grund wrote that "**Russula stuntzii** is a beautiful and striking Russula. It was collected only twice during the three years I examined the Washington flora, and there were no collections of it in the University of Washington herbarium. It is a rare mushroom."

BIBLIOGRAPHY

Anna Bazzicalupo, B. Buyck, I. Saar, J. Vauras, D. Carmean, & M. Berbee, *Troubles with Mycorrhizal Mushroom Identification where Morphological Differentiation Lags Behind Barcode Sequence Divergence* in *Taxon* 66 (791–810), 2017.

Darryl Grund, *A Survey of the Genus Russula Occurring in Washington State,* 1965. Doctoral dissertation.

Darryl Grund, *New and Interesting Taxa of Russula Occurring in Washington State in Mycotaxon 9, (93–113),* 1979.

David Hawksworth, *Trouble Over Cap Colors and Species Concepts in Russula* in *Fungus* 8 (61–62), 2017.

Greg Hovander, Russula Roundup, 2007. Pacific Northwest Key Council, Seattle, Wash.

Geoffrey Kibby, *The Genus Russula in Great Britain,* 2012, London. Self-published.

Noah Siegel & Christian Schwarz, *Mushrooms of the Redwood Coast,* 2016. Ten Speed Press, Berkeley, Calif.

Harry Thiers, *Agaricales of California 9: Russulaceae,* 1997. Mad River Press, Eureka, Calif.

Steve Trudell & Joe Ammirati, *Mushrooms of the Pacific Northwest,* 2009. Timber Press, Portland, Ore.

Russula versicolor J. Schaeffer

By Christine Roberts

*To find them, you'll need to be
there in front of the lawn mower.*

I was supposed to write about **Russula exalbicans** Secretan, which I got all excited about when I found it all over the lawns of our apartment complex shortly after moving to Bellingham from Vancouver Island, British Columbia. It was associated with the birches there, which I thought were European rather than native birch (note that there are no native birch on Vancouver Island).

This was a first record of **R. exalbicans** in the Pacific Northwest. Lest you think this is unusual, there are so many undocumented species of mushrooms out here to be found that getting something "new" in a season is a high probability event!

So why did I think it was **R. exalbicans**? Well, when I tasted it, it was initially mild with a distinctly peppery aftertaste, not really acrid, but definitely not completely mild either. It varied in colour from reddish purple to pale greenish white, some were dull green, some a bit more reddish, some brownish purple, and they faded dramatically. The cap surface, slightly viscid when wet, was often broken up into minute scales, a term called *chagrinate* in Romagnesi, which refers to shark skin—a leather popular in the 1920s for elegant furniture.

The stipe had yellowish bruising at the base, sometimes further up but not discolouring inside the stipe, occasionally this yellowing showed up on the cap surface of old fruitbodies. They had a fruity smell like stewed apples, and a deep cream spore print: number "IIIa" on Romagnesi's spore color scale. All these characters suggested to me something close to the Sardoninae group (like **R. queletii**), except with birch, thus the Exalbicantinae—a sister taxon—to which it keyed out easily in Romagnesi. I looked through my books in that section and bingo! **Russula exalbicans** had all those features. When I checked the spores, they matched the descriptions and drawings in Romagnesi and in Sarnari. The photos matched too. Even the pileocystidia had the sort of bubbled contents often seen in that section, though they did not stain as strongly in sulphovanillin as I would have expected, but then the staining reaction of this chemical seems to be related to the acrid taste: the more peppery, the darker in sulphovanillin. I thought I had it nailed, and for the next couple of years I confidently pronounced these mushrooms as being **R. exalbicans**!

But my original photos and descriptions of "**R. exalbicans**" were on a now-defunct computer. I nipped over to the field site and combed the lawns for more collections. Sparse pickings since the weather was very dry, but enough small ones showed up to star in a new photo and make a new collection.

I like to look things up from the beginning again when I collect something I haven't seen for a couple of years, just in case it got renamed in the meantime. That is when I turned up the description for **Russula versicolor** in Harry Thier's book *Agaricales of California: III: Russula*.

The description for this species also matched pretty well the characters of my mushroom, including an association with birch. It also keyed out (not so easily) to **R. versicolor** in Romagnesi, but it appears there are several forms varying in spore size. **R. versicolor** is placed in the Tenellae along with **R. puellaris** which

LOOK-ALIKE

Russula montana

Russula puellaris from France

normally has very different characters to those in the Exalbicantinae. Most other species in the Tenellae taste mild, have larger and often darker spores, and don't fade as dramatically as **Russula versicolor**. So what are the differences and how can they be told apart?

Firstly, Schaeffer originally described **R. versicolor** from North America, so it is an indigenous species whereas **R. exalbicans** is European and has not been reported from the Pacific Northwest. Periodically, European species turn up in places they never were before due to the introduction of host trees. Witness the appearance and spread of **Amanita phalloides** in this region, so we need to be careful of assuming something is or is not likely to be here.

Secondly, although the spores of the two species are very similar in shape, ornamentation and colour, those of **R. versicolor** range slightly smaller than those of **R. exalbicans** by around 1μm in each dimension. The clincher though, is in the cap cutis where specialized hyphae termed pileocystidia have rounded ends and more septa (1–3) in **R. versicolor** than those of **R. exalbicans** with 0–1 septa and occasional capitate ends. The latter also react more strongly with sulphovanillin. The difference is subtle and you need a microscope and some nasty chemicals to see this.

Besides the obvious resemblance to **Russula exalbicans**, four more follow here:

Russula abietina: Differs by its association with fir, its slightly darker yellow-ochre spore deposit, and its mild taste. In 1947 Singer considered it to be part of a complex that included **Russula versicolor**.

Russula montana: Differs by its more acrid taste, association with conifers, and having no parts that change color when bruised. Yet another Russula that varies greatly in cap color.

Russula puellaris: An extremely fragile species that differs by its mild taste, more tawny-vinaceous cap centers, and tendency for the entire fruiting body to turn yellowish in age.

Russula sapinea: A European Russula found with spruce in subalpine zones, it differs by its larger spores, mild taste, and ochre-yellow gills when mature.

Description of Fairhaven collections of **Russula versicolor**:

These Russulas appear in late summer through to the first really hard freeze, particularly where the grounds have been watered, and in some years can be quite abundant. The colours can vary from dark dull purple, light red, pale green, pink to pretty much white, and if they were not all found together you would think they were unrelated. They have a peppery taste, sometimes only slight, and the flesh stains a dingy yellow especially at the base of the stipe, but this yellowing is quite variable in intensity. The spores are unusually narrow for a species in this group of Russulas.

Macroscopic characters: Caps—3 to 8 cm, convex but soon cushion-shaped (depressed in centre, margins rounded), eventually plane (flat) but retaining a depression in the centre. Colours very variable, slightly brownish shades of cream, purple, pink, reddish, grey to dull green, fading almost to white with the surface breaking into minute concentric patches (chagrinate). Not very viscid even when wet and drying matte. Sometimes developing dull yellowish tints which make those with purple caps appear brownish.

Flesh—White, initially quite firm but brittle, becoming softer and more fragile in age, not changing to slightly yellowing at and under the cutis.

Gills—Deep cream with a slightly orange cast when viewed edge-on, rounded at cap margin, adnate at stipe, no forking or subgills, moderately spaced, broadest in outer third, pliable, not bruising.

Stipe—Short, about 1/3 to ½ the cap diameter and about 0.8 to 2.5 cm thick, broadest at base, white, rarely with a pinkish tinge, generally bruising strongly yellow-brown especially at the base and occasionally throughout. Not bruising as much inside. Stipe flesh initially solid, developing irregular cavities inside and eventually being hollowed out by larvae.

Spore print—Deep cream to pale yellow, IIIa on Romagnesi's scale.

Habitat—Around planted birch trees on grounds around Fairhaven Park Apartments. To find them you'll need to be there ahead of the lawn mower otherwise there are only decapitated stipes and tiny buttons. This fact may influence the ratio of stipe length to cap diameter, which may not be the same in woodland-grown **Russula versicolor**.

Microscopic characters:
Basidia—Mostly 4-spored, around 12.5 μm wide and around 37–40 μm long.

Spores—6.5–8.2 (9) x 5–6 μm, obovate to ellipsoidal, L:W ratio 1.3–1.5, warts blunt, to around 0.7μm high, joined by fine lines in a partial to almost complete reticulum, often in rows, sometimes zebroid in part, occasional small isolated warts in between the mesh, (Patterson/Woo types 2B-C).

Suprahilar patch—Amyloid, circa 2 μm diameter.

Pleurocystidia and cheilocystidia—Fusoid, normal, staining weakly purple in sulphovanillin.

Cutis—An ixodermis with a turf of epicutal hyphae circa 3 μm wide and narrowly clavate pileocystidia 5–13 μm wide by 50–80 μm long, ends mostly rounded rather than capitate, smaller ones aseptate, longer ones with 1–2 septa, end cells not or only slightly inflated but some with a slight cinched in appearance at

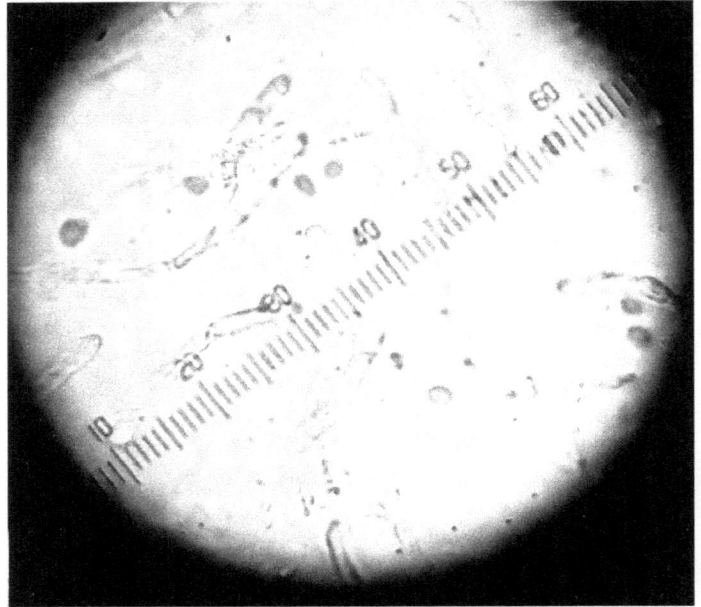

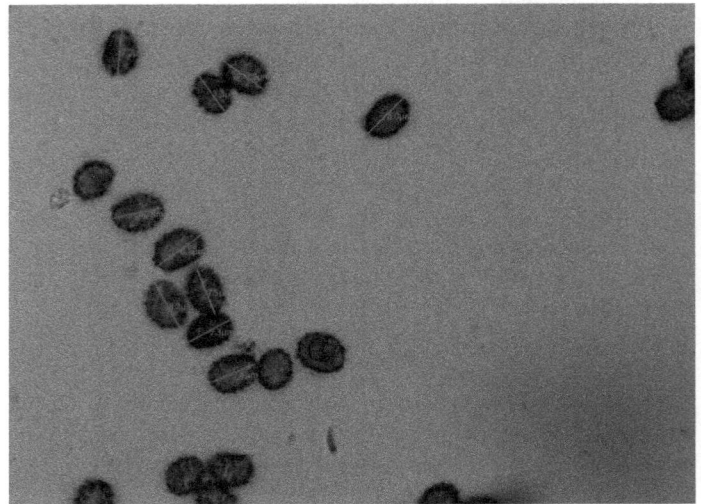

Pileocystidia in the cap (top) and spores (bottom) of Russula versicolor

the septa, not or barely staining in sulphovanillin. Contents
often with a banded or bubbled
appearance in sulphovanillin in
some sections of epicutis.

All in all a nice lesson in
foreign versus indigenous
names. Sometimes it is tempting to reach for a convenient
European name when a per-
fectly good local name already
exists. In either case, it is a nice
suburban Russula worthy of
some much needed literary
exposure.

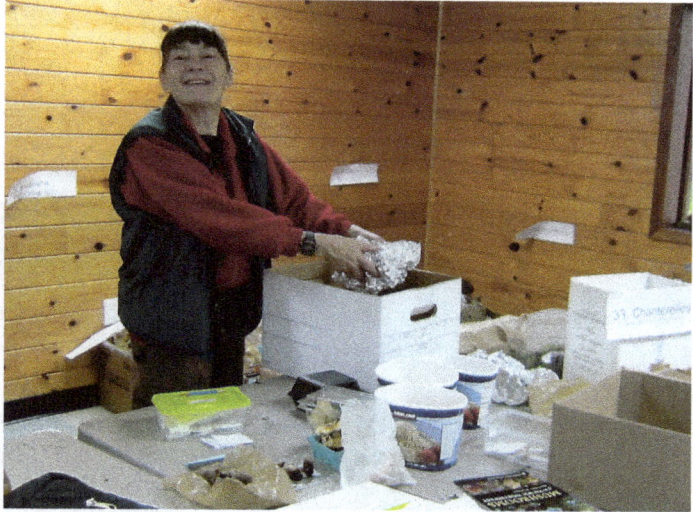

Christine Roberts identifying Russulas at the Wild Mushroom Show

BIBLIOGRAPHY

Anna Bazzicalupo, B. Buyck, I. Saar, J. Vauras, D. Carmean, & M. Berbee, *Troubles with Mycorrhizal Mushroom Identification where Morphological Differentiation Lags Behind Barcode Sequence Divergence* in *Taxon* 66 (791–810), 2017.
Vera Evenson, *Mushrooms of the Rocky Mountain Region*, 2015, Timber Press, Portland, Ore.**David Hawksworth,** *Trouble Over Cap Colors and Species Concepts in Russula* in *Fungus* 8 (61–62), 2017.

Henri Romagnesi, *Les Russules d'Europe et d'Afrique du Nord*, 1996 reprint. Strauss & J. Cramer, Hirschberg, Germany.
Mauro Sarnari, *Russula Nuovo o Interessanti dell' Italia Centrale e Mediterranea XXV* in *Bollettino Associazone Micologica ed Ecologica Romana* 33 (21), 1994.
Harry Thiers, *The Agaricales of California: 9 Russulaceae I. Russula*, 1997. Mad River Press, Eureka, Calif.

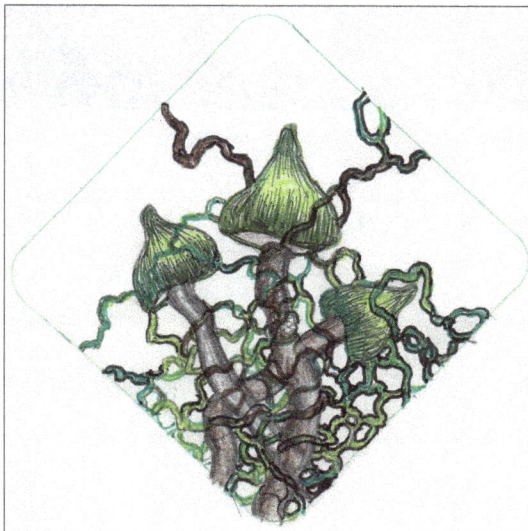

Russula xerampelina (Schaeffer ex Secretan) Fries

By Buck McAdoo and Christine Roberts

The caps can come in many colors.

Russula xerampelina, or the Shellfish Brittle-Gill, if you prefer the Kent McKnight name, is probably the best-known edible Russula found in the Pacific Northwest. It extends, according to Arora, all the way to the Arctic Circle. **R. xerampelina** is a well-known European species extending all the way east to Ula on the Mediterranean coast of Turkey, and has even appeared rarely in Greenland. And according to McCoy it has made it south to Costa Rica. In our area it is found mostly with Douglas fir in the fall. It can also associate with alder, beech, oak, hemlock, and pine. The caps are usually red violet or the deep purple you see here.

The main problem with separating it from other Russulas is that the caps can come in many colors. As Ronald Rayner puts it, "Very varied in color; livid purple, livid red, blood, vinaceous, dark vinaceous, brown vinaceous, brick, fawn, cinnamon, honey, buff, or straw, and combinations thereof."

Czech mycologists Pilat & Usak, perhaps wondering what caused such a variation in cap colors, broke it down to habitat. Caps are

LOOK-ALIKES

Russula atropurpurea from Mass.

Russula brunneoviolacea var. roseolipes nom. prov. Grund

wine to purple to brilliant carmine in conifer woods. Under aspen or birch, caps are olivaceous to greenish yellow. In beech woods on calcareous soils, caps are pale olive to brown red or a vivid pink to flesh pink. At least 14 varieties have been described in the literature, most of them according to cap color. In his masters thesis on Pacific Northwest Russula, Darryl Grund produced a special key just for the forms and varieties. A few, such as **Russula elaeodes**, have been elevated to species status.

Caps can run up to 30 cm wide, are convex to shallowly depressed at disc and viscid when moist. The gills are adnate to adnexed, white at first, but soon yellowish from the spores. The stems are thick, generally clavate at the base, and have a spongy context. They are cream to white, and if the caps are in the pinkish to purple range, often flushed with pink.

One sure method of identifying the Shellfish Brittlegill is to scratch the base of the stem with your fingernail. It will soon turn pale yellow unless the specimen is too far gone to react. In a little while the rest of the stem will turn brownish where you handled it. The gills also turn brown when bruised, and a dirty gray when dried. For the Russula addicts who routinely walk around with such things, the application of ferrous sulphate on any part of the fruiting body will turn the flesh green. This is the only Russula besides **Russula graveolens** that will offer this reaction outside of the Compactae group.

The spores are pale yellowish, subglobose, and have amyloid warts with extremely thin anastomizing reticulations barely visible with the microscope. The taste is mild and the odor pleasant when young. In age it smells like crab, lobster, cooked shrimp or even herring. The seafood odor is from trimethylamine. Coker didn't like it. "Odor strong and disagreeable on drying," he noted, "and remaining noticeable on the hands for a long time after touching."

Russula atropurpurea in the sense of Peck is a synonym of **Russula xerampelina**. Using the Peck name for it in *One Thousand American Fungi*, Charles McIlvaine wrote, "many were eaten and enjoyed. Only fresh plants are acceptable, and they should be cooked as soon as gathered. Even in wilting they become unpleasant."

Those are just the negatives. Most folks enjoy the nutty flavor of **Russula xerampelina**. I remember one meal in particular. Back in mid-November of 1987, we had a break in the weather on Bellingham Bay. Actual sun was forecast for the weekend. My friend Chuck Herbert came down from Vancouver, B.C., and we decided to sail to Orcas Island to try the legendary breakfast at the Olga Café. A fine northwester propelled us across Rosario Strait. By mid-afternoon we were motoring up Obstruction Pass with rocks, giant conifers, and homesteads on either shore. We anchored that night in Buck Bay, played a bit of backgammon, and turned in. Real stars were vis-

LOOK-ALIKES

Russula vinosa (formerly our Northwest R. occidentalis)

Russula elaeodes

ible from the deck. In the morning we rowed to the wharf. The water was so clear at the end of the wharf that we could see the Dungeness crabs groping in and out of the seaweed. The Olga Café wouldn't open for another twenty minutes, so with nothing better to do, we decided to amble around the property. Chuck is a tree topper by trade, and so no stranger to the world of fungi. We had barely gotten into the slight rise behind the restaurant when he began whooping. There beneath the Douglas fir, the conifer duff was pocked with purple. **Russula xerampelina** was everywhere. It was "Bye Bye French Toast Evangeline" and "Hello Shellfish Brittlegill Sauté." We loaded our jackets with prime specimens and headed back to the wharf.

Back on board the Anhinga, we simply sautéed them in butter. They were so bland that we wondered what the fuss was about. Then Chuck did an amazing thing. He sprinkled a little salt. Suddenly the rich flavors of cashew nuts with a nice bacon contingent assaulted our taste buds. It was one of the finest breakfasts we

Russula mendocinensis from Calif.

Russula murrillii

ever had on the water.

The world of Russula is rather complex. There are copper colored Russulas that look nothing like the typical purple **Russula xerampelina** yet key out to it in Romagnesi's key. And there are quite a few **Russula xerampelina** look-alikes not even in the lengthy list of varieties. Here they are in no particular order:

Russula graveolens: This species, according to Roger Phillips, has the same seafood odor, has stems that turn yellow-brown when scratched, pale ochre spores, mild taste, and caps that are reddish-brown to ochre with violet tinges at the margins. The only real difference, according to Moser's key, seems to be that it grows with deciduous trees and has partly reticulate spores.

Russula purpurata: A species with dark purple caps occurring on the east coast and in Europe. It can also be carmine in color according to Kibby and Fatto. It has the same kind of spores with isolated warts, the same shellfish odor, the same sort of stem flushed with pink that stains ochre-brown in age. It differs by

having slightly smaller spores, differently shaped hairs in the pileipellis, and an association with beech and oak instead of conifers.

Russula vinosa: Cap colors vary from shades of red to purple. It differs by its white stems that stain grayish when bruised, a mealy texture when cooked and unappetizing flavor.

Russula zelleri: A purple-brown species with brown discs known from Oregon. Spores are pale ochre, ovoid, and have isolated warts. The stems do not bruise when scratched.

Russula vinosobrunnea: A European species also found in the Pacific Northwest, according to Roger Phillips. Caps are dark purple-brown, gills pale yellow-ochre and strongly intervenose. Stems are white and flushed pinkish, but don't change color when scratched.

Russula atropurpurea: A species with red-violet caps that become purple-black at the centers. Spores are white, and stems are white becoming grayish in age. Odor sometimes fruity, like apples.

Russula brunneoviolacea: Has vinaceous-brown to olive-brown caps and pale yellow-orange spores. Gills are sub-distant and buff. The white stems stain yellow-brown at the base when bruised.

Russula brunneoviolacea var. roseolipes nom. prov.: A Grund variety with pinkish stems.

Russula cessans: Has purplish red caps and deep ochre spores that are partially reticulate. Gills ochre and stem white. (This is the Pearson description. Moser allows for pale violet caps with brownish centers, also).

Russula elaeodes: Long considered a variety of **R. xerampelina**, it has dark brown to black to dark olive caps.

Russula mendocinensis: Differs by its strongly acrid taste, no particular odor, and a white stem that bruises pale orange when handled.

Russula olivacea: Can also have purplish to greenish to brownish caps and a pinkish stem, which does not go yellow when scratched. Also, ferrous sulfate applied to the stem turns the surface pinkish-brown, not blue-green.

Russula amoenipes: A smaller, more fragile version of **Russula xerampelina** found with Scotch pine in Europe. The stems are entirely pale pink slowly bruising honey-brown when touched.

Russula favrei: Another purple-brown species with a strong shellfish odor, the stem bruises ochre-brown when scratched, not pale yellow. Found with mountain spruces in Europe.

Russula murrilli: Differs by its mild odor, pruinose cap when young, and white stem that does not bruise yellowish when scratched.

Russula cyanoxantha: Also appears on the West Coast but lacks the shellfish odor, has white spores, and variegated cap colors ranging from mottled purples to mottled greens. Our North American **R. cyanoxantha** differs from the European one, and will need a new name.

Finally, there is another character that seems to be an aid to identification only with

Russula 'cyanoxantha' from Mass.

Russulas and Amanitas. This is the distance the cap cuticle can peel from margin to disc. Take a centimeter ruler and measure half the cap diameter. Then take a probe and etch the surface at the ¼, 1/3, ½, 2/3, and ¾ distances from margin inwards. Then, using your fingernails, pull back the cap cuticle towards the center as far as it will go. **Russula xerampelina** will peel back ¼ to ½ of the way from the margin. **Russula vinosa**, on the other hand, peels only at the margin or halfway to disc. You need a lot of these to override the overlapping. With a cup of black tea and a roaring fire, what better way could there be to spend a rainy November afternoon in the Pacific Northwest? Every genus has its idiosyncracies. With Russula, you need all the help you can get.

As Buck has mentioned, the Pacific Northwest seems to be rich in varieties and species in the **Russula xerampelina** group. Some are separate species, some represent points on a continuum of variation, and some we are trying to figure out. Since cap colors can vary widely within a species, other dependable characters are useful. Common to all specimens in the **R. xerampelina** group is a bruising reaction on the stem to a dull, pale yellow that soon turns brown, a fishy or crab-like odor especially when old, and a blue-green staining reaction to ferrous sulfate rubbed on the stem.

Most other Russulas stain a pinkish-brown or at most grayish with this reagent. (A 4-lb. bag of ferrous sulfate is available from garden centers for about $8 and should last an entire mushroom club for years since you need only one crystal at a time. Choose brands with light blue translucent crystals, avoiding the sandy or brownish colored ones. Lab suppliers sell purer versions for more money.)

Notice I wrote that this was an almost surefire method of identification. In Grund's 1965 thesis on the Russulas of Washington State, he described a **Russula isabelliniceps** nom. prov. that seems to be a cross between **Russula olivacea** and **Russula occidentalis**. When the stem is rubbed with ferrous sulfate it turns grayish-green and then black overnight. This is a different reaction than the blue-green of the **R. xerampelina** group, but one can be fooled. This species is found with spruce on the coast and in the mountains. It has the typical yellow to brown bruising reaction on the stem but is slow to develop the fishy odor. Its cap is a mixture of pinks, light brown, and light olive-green often covered with a pale brown pruina that makes it look like suntanned Caucasian skin. I think it may be a valid new species, but that is yet to be confirmed.

All varieties of **Russula xerampelina** seem to be edible and good. But if you have allergies to seafood, beware. You may get the same reaction from eating shrimp-smelling Russulas as to shrimp!

On the other hand, it can't be that bad for you. It is known to lower cholesterol, helps with rheumatoid arthritis, and is an anti-oxidant, anti-inflammatory, anti-cancer, and anti-microbial.

BIBLIOGRAPHY

Joe Ammirati & Gary Laursen, *Arctic and Alpine Mycology*, 1982. University of Washington Press, Seattle, Wash.

David Arora, *Mushrooms Demystified*, 1986. Ten Speed Press, Berkeley, Calif.

A. Bazzicalupo, B. Buyck, I. Saar, J. Vauras, D. Carmean, & M. Berbee, *Troubles with Mycorrhizal Mushroom Identification where Morphological Differentiation Lags Behind Barcode Sequence Divergence* in *Taxon* 66 (791–810), 2017.

D. Desjardin, M.Wood, & F. Stevens, *California Mushrooms*, 2016. Timber Press, Portland, Ore.

Darryl Grund, *A Survey of the Genus Russula Occurring in Washington State*, 1965. Doctoral dissertation.

David Hawksworth, *Trouble Over Cap Colors and Species Concepts in Russula* in *Fungus* 8 (61–62), 2017.

Greg Hovander, *Russula Roundup*, 2008. Pacific Northwest Key Council, Seattle, Wash.

Mustafa Isiloglu & Roy Watlin, *Macromycetes of Mediterranean Turkey in Edinburgh Journal of Botany* 49, 1992.

Geoffrey Kibby & Ray Fatto, *Keys to the Species of Russula in Northeastern North America*, 1990. Kibby-Fatto Enterprises, Somerville, N.J.

Charles McIlvaine & Robert Macadam, *One Thousand American Fungi*, 1902. Dover Publications, New York, NY.

Peter McCoy, *Radical Mycology*, 2016. Chthaeus Press, Portland, Ore.

Kent & Vera McKnight, *Peterson Field Guides – Mushrooms*, 1987. Houghton Mifflin, Boston.

Meinhard Moser, *Agarics and Boleti*, 1983. Translated and published by Roger Phillips, London.

A.A. Pearson, *Agarics, New Records and Observations in Transactions of the British Mycological Society* 22, 1938.

Roger Phillips, *Mushrooms of North America*, 1991. Little, Brown & Co., Boston.

Albert Pilat & Otto Usak, *Mushrooms*, 1954. Artia, Prague.

Ronald Rayner, *Keys to the British Species of Russula*, 1985. British Mycological Society, Surrey, England.

Noah Siegel & Christian Schwarz, *Mushrooms of the Redwood Coast*, 2016. Ten Speed Press, Berkeley, Calif.

Sarcomyxa serotina (Persoon) Karsten

Photo by Richard Morrison

*Extended cooking eliminates
all the bitterness.*

If you happen to be out in the woods in our soggy weather from late October through January you might encounter this odd Pleurotoid fungus with an olive greenish cap and ochre-orange gills. It will always be fruiting on wood, most likely red alder or wild cherry in our area. If you take it home and try keying it out you will land on **Panellus serotinus** or **Pleurotus serotinus** depending on which guide you use. This has now changed. DNA sequencing has now placed this species in a second group of the Hygrophoroid clade along with Phyllotopsis and Xeromphalina. Another genus had to be found for it. Enter Sarcomyxa. The Finnish mycologist Karsten had come up with this name in 1891, so it was resurrected for the occasion. The genus Sarcomyxa encompasses Pleurotoid species with white, allantoid spores that turn dark blue in Melzer's solution. They always fruit on wood and have olive to brownish caps with inrolled margins and lateral stems with punctate surfaces. As far as I know, **Sarcomyxa serotina** and **Sarcomyxa edulis** from China are the only species in it.

For those who tend to be dismayed or even disgusted with Latin name changes you are invited to use a number of popular names such as the Late Oyster Mushroom, Olive Oysterling, Greenbacks, or even the Green Oyster. For purists, it should be the Late Small Torch because that's what the etymology is for **Panellus serotinus**.

Sarcomyxa serotina is a cold weather mushroom. It seems to be brought out by the first heavy frost, curtains for most other species. It occurs all over North America, northern Asia and Europe down into Spain. It fruits on birch, beech, oak, maple, willow, alder, and more rarely coniferous wood. It is generally considered an easily recognizable mushroom.

The caps range from 3–15 cm in diameter and are mussel shaped to kidney shaped to fan shaped with inrolled margins at first. The surface is viscid becoming sticky when dry, and covered at first with a fine brown tomentum that soon wears off. The cap colors are olive green to dark green with gradations of gray, brown,

or even purple in some findings. Under the microscope the cap cuticle is gelatinized. This is perhaps a feature that prevents the mushroom from decomposing before it has a chance to release its spores. (So speculates Susan Libonati-Barnes, who has done a lot of work on this group). The ochre-orange gills are adnate to short decurrent. They are crowded, forked, and narrow. The stems, if present, are laterally attached, up to 2½ cm long, and yellow ochre covered with brown squamules or glandular dots. The flesh is white and thickish but greenish under the cap cuticle. Giuseppe Pace described it as "tenacious and mucilaginous." Odor and taste are considered mild by most. Some have detected a bitter component, and down in Spain a trio of authors thought the taste astringent and the odor unpleasant. The spore print is pale yellow and the spores themselves sausage shaped and amyloid. They measure 4–7 x 1–2 μm, and often have droplets in the context. In the Pacific Northwest, specimens are often found sterile…beautiful fruiting bodies with no spores at all.

There are a number of species that could in a pinch be considered as look-alikes: **Pleurotus ostreatus**: The true Oyster Mushroom differs by its white gills, buff to dark brown caps, and rudimentary stem compared with the lateral, squamulose, yellow-ochre stem of **Sarcomyxa serotina**. **Pleurotus columbinus**: Also can have olive colored caps, but the white spores and white gills easily show the difference.

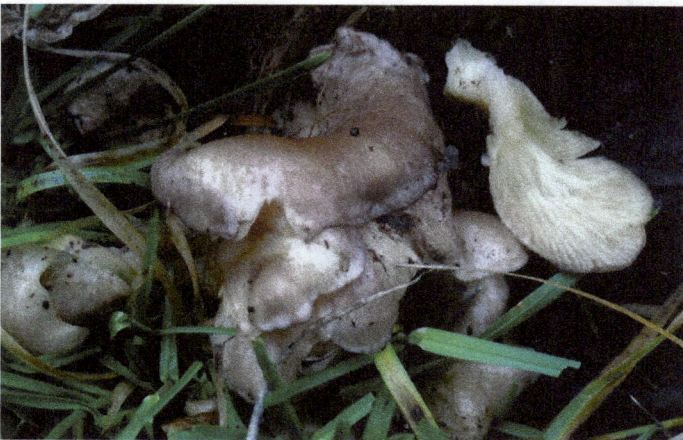

Sarcomyxa serotina with pinkish-brick caps from Lake Stevens, Wash.

Tapinella panuoides: Differs by its dingy ochre to brownish spore print, lack of a stem, and yellowish gills that can be peeled from the cap flesh by your fingernail.

Phyllotopsis nidulans: Differs by its pink spores and a coarsely hairy orange cap. David Arora writes that it has an odor of rotten eggs or sewer gas, so it is unlikely to be eaten by mistake.

Hohenbuehelia petaloides: Differs by fruiting in clusters in wood chip mulch, the white gills, lubricous brown caps, and the presence of setiform metuloids. (The collection pictured was found by Dave Jansen at the Pink Chateau.)

Hohenbuehelia thornii: Differs by its tomentose cap surface when young and its finely verruculose spores. This collection was found in a potted plant.

Crepidotus crocophyllus: This much smaller mushroom differs by its rusty to brown caps with cinnamon fibrils. There is no olive in it.

Crepidotus aureifolius: This is an East Coast species that has orange gills at first, but the brown spores and pale yellow caps with orange squamules separate it.

Most European authors consider **Sarcomyxa serotina** inedible or not worth picking. They site a chewy texture and a slightly bitter flavor.

Opinions from other mycophagists are as follows:

Alan Bessette & David Fischer: "This may be one of the most underrated of edible gilled mushrooms. The stalk is too tough to eat, but the caps are a worthwhile harvest.

Sarcomyxa serotina with purplish caps   Photo by Richard Morrison

Extended, slow cooking eliminates the bitterness. They can be used in most any recipe. They can simply be sautéed after simmering, and are good in casseroles, soups, and gravies. They are by no means mediocre."

Dave Jansen, cofounder of Northwest Mushroomers: "For the record you can get rid of the bitterness by dousing them with soy sauce. It's good mixed with rice. I eat it whenever I see it."

Jairul Rahaman, past president of the Snohomish Mushroom Club: "I have tried it twice. On both occasions I have found it bland."

Charles McIlvaine: "Its flavor is not marked, but being a late species, it satisfies the longing of the mycophagist for his accustomed food." (Indeed, it might be the only edible out there when you are going through 'mushroom withdrawal' at season's end. Another

LOOK-ALIKE

Pleurotus ostreatus from Maryland

448

LOOK-ALIKES

Crepidotus crocophyllus from Calif.

Hohenbuehelia thornii   Photo by Richard Morrison

Hohenbuehelia petaloides

benefit is the total absence of larvae. The cold weather takes care of that midsummer problem.)

Chuck Nafziger, former president of Northwest Mushroomers: "My method of cooking it is to dry fry the mushroom for some time to get rid of the extra moisture. I press them down with a spatula until they no longer sizzle. When they start to darken, add the butter and the chopped onions until the onions caramelize. You can also experiment with red peppers and garlic. It needs to be cooked for some time to bring out an attractive flavor."

Margot Evers, a French lady in our club with a lot of panache, who has since passed away, thought she had been poisoned by it. She had partaken of three different species in a stew. The other two had no negative culinary histories, so the gastrointestinal issues had to be attributed to **Sarcomyxa serotina**. She was really out of sorts, having read that it was edible. But what could we do? She either had an allergy to any of the three mushrooms or the mushrooms reacted to being cooked together.

Harriette Parker, writing about reports of ingestion from south-central Alaska, suggested that prolonged exposure to repeated thawing and freezing could produce toxins. This could simply be a case of consuming frozen specimens that may have partially rotted before they froze. As is the case with any new wild mushroom you sample, eat a small amount at first, just in case. She also noted that the species is a weak parasite capable of attacking living trees already weakened by disease or injury. It is a saprophyte that causes delignifying white rot of mostly hardwood logs.

In China and Japan it is sold in markets. The Japanese call it mukitake. Besides the culinary value, biochemical studies have revealed the presence of ergosterin and vitamins B1, B2, and C. The yellow context of the caps is thought to be due to high concentrations of methyl-riboflavin. Cultivation trials have already begun.

There is also a chance that it might have medicinal value for humans. A team of eight Japanese researchers has discovered that "fractional extracts from **Sarcomyxa serotina** have had a curative effect on non-alcoholic, fatty liver disease in obese, diabetic mice." It alleviates the disease "through suppression of monocyte chemoattractant protein 1 production in such mice." No mention of what effect it had on the more slender rats.

And indeed, what's not to like? Even if you didn't cook it long enough to overcome the bitter tinge, your pet mice, at least the obese and diabetic ones, will never thank you enough.

Addendum: It is interesting to note that each species, besides its lifetime goal to produce spores in a suitable environment, has its own history through taxonomic discoveries. In this case, **Sarcomyxa serotina** started out as **Agaricus serotinus** Persoon in 1793. In 1871, the German priest Kummer moved it to Pleurotus.

Although Karsten moved it to Sarcomyxa twenty years

LOOK-ALIKES

Tapinella panuoides from Rockport, Wash.

Phyllotopsis nidulans from Colorado.

Crepidotus aureifolius from Vermont

later, most experts preferred the use of Pleurotus. Here it remained until 1949 when Singer placed it in Hohenbuehelia. Just a year later the French mycologist Kuhner moved it to Panellus, where it has by and large remained until modern DNA sequencing called for the resurrection of Sarcomyxa.

It has now been taken out of the Tricholomataceae and belongs in the Typhulaceae. Go figure.

BIBLIOGRAPHY

Duur Aanen, Catherine Aime, Joseph Ammirati, Timothy Baroni, Neale Bougher, Judd Curtis, Graciela Daniele, Mathew DeNitis, Dennis Desjardin, Zai-Wei Ge, David Hibbett, Valerie Hofstetter, Karen Hughes, Richard Kerrigan, Bradley Kropp, Jean Lodge, Brandon Matheny, Jean-Marc Moncalvo, Lorelei Norvell, Andrew Parker, Michelle Seidl, Jason Slot, Else Vellinga, Rytas Vilgalys, & Zhu-Liang Yang, *Major Clades of Agaricales: A Multilocus Phylogenetic Overview* in Mycologia 98 (982–995), 2006.

Arora, David, *Mushrooms Demystified*, 1986. Ten Speed Press, Berkeley, Calif.

Alan Bessette & David Fischer, *Edible Wild Mushrooms of North America*, 1992. University of Texas Press, Austin, Texas.

Koji Nagao, Nao Inoue, Masashi Inafuku, Bungo Shirouchi, Takanori Morooka, Saori Nomura, Naoki Nagamori, & Teruyoshi Yanagita, *Mukitake Mushroom Alleviates Nonalcoholic Fatty Liver Disease Through Suppression of Monocyte Chemoattractant Protein 1 Production in db/db Mice* in *Journal of Nutritional Biochemistry* 21, Issue 5 (418–423), 2010.

Peter Jordan, *Encyclopedia of Fungi of Britain and Europe*, 2004. David & Charles, Newton Abbot, England.

Calvin Kauffman, *The Agaricaceae of Michigan*, 1918. Michigan Geological and Biological Survey, Lansing, Mich.

Geoffrey Kibby, Mushrooms and Toadstools: A Field Guide, 1979. Oxford University Press, London

Paul Kirk (ed.), *Index Fungorum*, http://www.indexfungorum.org/names/Names.asp

Susan Libonati-Barnes, *Systematics of Tectella, Panellus, Hohenbuehelia, and Resupinatus in the Pacific Northwest*, doctorate, 1981.

Charles McIlvaine & Robert Macadam, *One Thousand American Mushrooms*, 1902. Dover Publications, New York, NY.

Kent & Vera McKnight, *Peterson Field Guides— Mushrooms*, 1987. Houghton Mifflin, Boston.

Orson Miller & Donald Manning, *Distribution of the Lignicolous Tricholomataceae in the Southern Appalachians* in *The Distributional History of the Biota of the Southern Appalachians* 4 (307–344), 1976.

Gabriel Moreno, Jose-Luis Manjon, & Alvaro Zugaza, *La Guia de Incafo de los Hongos de la Peninsula Iberica, Tomo II*, 1986. Incafo, S.A., Madrid.

Mycokey.org, *The Genus Sarcomyxa*.

Guiseppe Pace, *Mushrooms of the World*, 1998. Firefly Books, Willowdale, Ontario.

Harriette Parker, *Alaska's Mushrooms*, 1994. Alaska Northwest Books, Anchorage, Alaska.

Roger Phillips, *Mushrooms of North America*, 1991. Little, Brown & Co., Boston.

Jean-Marie Poles, *The Pocket Guide to Mushrooms*, 2005. Tandem Verlag, Chamalieres, France.

Peter Roberts & Shelley Evans, *The Book of Fungi*, 2011. University of Chicago Press, Chicago.

Duane Sept, *Common Mushrooms of the Northwest*, 2006. Calypso Publishing, Sechelt, British Columbia.

David Spahr, *Edible and Medicinal Mushrooms of New England and Eastern Canada*, 2009. North Atlantic Books, Berkeley, Calif.

Paul Starosta & Christian Epinat, *Fungi*, 1999. Benedikt Taschen Verlag, Cologne, Germany.

Sarcosphaera coronaria (Jacquin ex Cooke) Boudier

In Europe it is on the
endangered species list in
over a dozen countries.

Sarcosphaera coronaria is not likely to be confused with any other species. When you first approach it in the woods, it looks like an old tennis ball badly chewed by a large dog. You are about to pass it up, tired by being fooled all day by random bits of trash, when you approach closer and discover the interior is a lovely purplish color, and realize no tennis ball manufacturer in the world is going to go to these lengths when designing the product. What comes to mind are those gorgeous amethyst crystals hidden in coarse rock that you see at rock shows.

Known as the Crown Fungus in Arora's guide, **Sarcosphaera coronaria** is the only member of its genus. It is closely related to Peziza because of the cupular shape of the fruiting body and because, like Peziza, the tips of its asci turn blue in Melzer's solution. But it differs from Peziza by beginning life below ground. It begins as a hollow, bladder-shaped form, gradually becoming more spherical. Sometimes this chamber can have 2–4 infolded walls. As it breaks through the soil it opens at the apex to form an irregular hole through which the spores will escape. This hole

LOOK-ALIKES

Peziza moseri

Peziza praetervisa

continues to expand, eventually splitting into 7–10 petal-like rays, which become reflexed in age. Sometimes these star-shaped rays barely break the surface, and you are left staring at a purple hole in the ground. So if you are looking for that weird mushroom experience out in the woods, this would not be too shabby.

Completely open, the fruiting body can measure up to 20 cm wide. The outer surface (peridium) is grayish white and furfuraceous (minutely roughened, slightly waxy). Sand and dirt are often found clinging to it, testimony to its passage from below. The interior hymenial surface is whitish at first, but soon turns lavender above ground before ageing to a brownish lavender at full maturity. The context is white, thick, and brittle. The species is usually stalkless, but James Trappe has a black and white photo of one with a thick, short stem. The straw colored base is sometimes accompanied with white mycelium or a root-like appendage. The odor is reported as imperceptible, the taste mild to barely sweet. The spore deposit is pale yellow. It fruits solitary or in packed clusters in sandy or calcareous soils in the spring, but can be found in the summer at higher elevations. Fruiting bodies that are packed together often coalesce. And according to Breitenbach & Kranzlin, it fruits year after year in the same place.

Microscopically, this is an ascomycete. Eight spores to an ascus (a sort of hollow tube with a lid at one end that houses the spores.) At maturity, the lid opens to allow the spores to be discharged. As Kent McKnight describes it, "a breath of air incites discharge of a huge cloud of spores." The spores are ellipsoid with blunt ends and verruculose in oil immersion. They each have two guttules (oil drops), and measure 13.5–18 x 7–8.5 µm. The paraphyses (sterile filaments interspersed with the asci) are often branched near the apices, septate, and speckled with purple-brown granules, which are thought to produce the violet hues of the hymenial surface.

Sarcosphaera coronaria has been found under spruce, fir, pine, beech, and oak, but is considered a saprobic species. Dr. A.H. Smith determined it was a generally rare species, but locally abundant in a few select areas such as south of the Salmon River in central Idaho or in the eastern Cascades where the Northwest Mushroomers' Morel Madness takes place. In Europe it is on the endangered species list in over a dozen countries, and has been proposed for protection under the Bern Convention. Nonetheless it is a widespread species, having been reported from the most northernmost regions of Canada, eastern Europe, North Africa, and the Arabian peninsula.

Nomenclaturally, **Sarcosphaera coronaria** has too many synonyms to list on one page. The most common by far is **Sarcosphaera crassa**, which is used about 50% of the time in popular guides. The *Index Fungorum* is prefering **S. coronaria.** A few of the other synonyms are **Sarcosphaera eximia**, **S. macrocalyx, S.**

LOOK-ALIKES

Scleroderma cepa   *Photo by Dan Digerness*

Scleroderma polyrhizum from Spain

dargelasii, and **Pustularia coronaria**. At least one early authority thought it was a truffle and created a new genus for it... Caulocarpa!

Sarcosphaera means "fleshy sphere" in Greek. *Coronaria* means "crown" in Latin. So if you do encounter it during a foray, be sure to shout, "I just found the round, fleshy crown!" The rest of us will know exactly what you mean.

As for look-alikes and close relatives, there are very few.

Sarcosphaera coronaria var. nivea: Differs by having a white interior hymenial surface that stays white through the end of its stay on earth.

Peziza ammophila: Another large cup fungus found half immersed in sand, but the interior is brown, and a root-like stem extends underground.

Scleroderma polyrhizum: Splits into star-like rays when aged. However, this is an earthball with a solid black interior that turns into a mass of spore powder when mature. Earth stars have rays by definition. They clearly differ by having spore sacs in the center of the rays.

Scleroderma cepa: A locally common earth ball that ruptures irregularly to reveal the blackish gleba in the interior.

Peziza moseri: Differs by its smaller cups at 3 cm wide and its occurence on burnt ground only.

Peziza praetervisa: Another burn site Peziza with more of a violet-brown color in the hymenium and two oil drops in the spores.

Opinions on edibility vary widely, but lean towards the pessimistic. A.H. Smith never tried it. He shied away from it due to the cartilaginous nature of the peridium. Calonge considered it poisonous when raw. It causes violent gastrointestinal distress only relieved by vomiting. Everyone seems to agree with that assessment. But after parboiling it is generally considered to be edible. Here are a few illuminating comments:

Count Bruno Cetto: "Not very appetizing due to the elastic consistency."

David Biek: "Poisonous."

Lorentz Pearson: "Species that have been tested have been declared edible and good by some mycophagists and poisonous by others."

Lucius Von Frieden: "Poisonous when raw or slightly cooked or spoiled. Edible when perfectly cooked."

Roberts & Evans: "The Violet Crown Cup contains gyromitrin, a potentially lethal poison common in Gyromitra."

Jack States: "Reported to be a good edible. Must be cooked first."

David Arora: "Not recommended. It concentrates a significant amount of arsenic from the soil. And according to one source, it tastes like a rubber eraser softened by time."

Orson Miller: "It has a delicate flavor. I have eaten this and like it, but it requires much cleaning."

André Marchand: "Poisonous when raw. Effects similar to Gyromitra poisonings. It is edible after parboiling. It can then be fried with garlic and parsley. It also makes a nice potage when puréed."

Ammirati, Traquaire, & Horgen: "**Sarcosphaera crassa** is on the list of gastrointestinal irritants and is also suspected of monomethylhydrazine poisoning."

Rinaldi & Tyndalo: "Poisonous when raw. Edible only if unripe, parboiled, and well cooked. Retains a rather elastic texture."

Orr & Orr: "The Gyromitrin toxin has been reported in Sarcosphaera. Consider it poisonous."

Elsie Coulter: "I have sampled it creamed and pickled and find it to be completely tasteless both ways."

Lincoff & Mitchel: "Pilat mentions a fatality for a person who ate **Sarcosphaera crassa** raw."

So there you have it. The gamut runs from life to death. As tempting as it may look, **Sarcosphaera coronaria** would probably make a better brooch than a parboiled appetizer filled with paté foie gras.

BIBLIOGRAPHY

Joe Ammirati, J.A. Traquair, & Paul Horgen, *Poisonous Mushrooms of the Northern United States and Canada*, 1985. University of Minnesota Press, Minneapolis, Minn.

David Arora, *All That the Rain Promises and More*, 1991. Ten Speed Press, Berkeley, Calif.

David Arora, *Mushrooms Demystified,* 1986. Ten Speed Press, Berkeley, Calif.

David Biek, *Mushrooms of Northern California*, 1984. Spore Prints, Redding, Calif.

J. Breitenbach & F. Kranzlin, *Fungi of Switzerland, Vol. 1*, 1984. Edition Mykologia, Lucerne, Switzerland.

Francisco de Diego Calonge, *Setas*, 1979. Ediciones Mundi-Prensa, Madrid.

Bruno Cetto, *I Funghi dal Vero, Vol.1*, 1970. Arti Grafiche Saturnia, Trento, Italy.

Elsie Coulter, *Trial Key to the Pezizaceae of the Pacific Northwest*, 1988. Pacific Northwest Key Council, Seattle, Wash.

Henry Dissing, *Pezizales in Nordic Macromycetes, Vol.1*, 2000. Nordsvamp, Copenhagen.

Pamela & Martin Ellis, *Microfungi on Miscellaneous Substrates*, 1988. Croom Helm, London.

Vera Evenson, *Mushrooms of Colorado*, 1997. Westcliffe Publishers, Denver.

Michael Kuo & Andy Methven, *100 Cool Mushrooms*, 2010. University of Michigan Press, Ann Arbor, Mich.

Gary Lincoff & D.H. Mitchel, *Toxic and Hallucinogenic Mushroom Poisoning*, 1977. Van Nostrand Reinhold, New York, NY.

André Marchand, *Champignons du Nord et du Midi, Vol.2*, 1973. Societe Mycologique des Pyrenees Mediterraneennes, Perpignan, France.

Margaret McKenny & Daniel Stuntz, *The Savory Wild Mushroom*, 1962. University of Washington Press, Seattle, Wash.

Kent & Vera McKnight , *Peterson Field Guides: Mushrooms*, 1987. Houghton Mifflin, Boston.

Orson Miller, *Mushrooms of North America*, 1972. E.P. Dutton & Co., New York, NY.

Robert & Dorothy Orr, *Mushrooms of Western North America*, 1979. University of California Press, Berkeley, Calif.

Lorentz Pearson, *The Mushroom Manual*, 1987. Naturegraph Publishers, Happy Camp, Calif.

Augusto Rinaldi & Vassili Tyndalo, *The Complete Book of Mushrooms*, 1972. Crown Publishers, New York, NY.

Peter Roberts & Shelley Evans, *The Book of Fungi*, 2011. University of Chicago Press, Chicago.

Helene Schalkwijk-Barendsen, *Mushrooms of Western Canada*, 1991. Lone Pine Publishers, Edmonton, Alberta.

Fred Jay Seaver, *North American Cup Fungi (Operculates)*, 1928. Self-published, New York, NY.

A.H. Smith, *The Mushroom Hunter's Field Guide*, 1977. University of Michigan Press, Ann Arbor, Mich.

Jack States, *Mushrooms and Truffles of the Southwest*, 1990. University of Arizona Press, Tucson, Ariz.

Mirko Svrcek, *The Hamlyn Book of Mushrooms and Toadstools*, 1983. Artia, Prague.

James Trappe, Michael Castellano, Zane & Chris Maser, *Key to Spores of the Genera of Hypogeous Fungi of North Temperate Forests*, 1989. Mad River Press, Eureka, Calif.

Edmund Tylutki, *Mushrooms of Idaho and the Pacific Northwest: Discomycetes*, 1979. University Press of Idaho, Moscow, Idaho.

Lucius Von Frieden, *Mushrooms of the World*, 1969. Bobbs-Merrill, Indianapolis, Indiana.

Squamanita pearsonii Bas

Species of Squamanita fruit on other mushrooms, transforming them into galls at their stem bases.

Helen Bassler, up from Sedro Wooley, had just arrived with her basket of fungi for the 1997 fall show. She had had a really good day collecting at the Rockport State Park. Her basket was overflowing with Ramarias and Russulas and all the colors of fall. Nestled among them, however, was one little cespitose cluster of a species that made my jaw drop. It had recurved purple scales on cap and stem, and a yellow stem base. I had never seen anything like it. As Helen later related to Margaret Dilly, "He removed that mushroom from circulation as if it were the Hope Diamond."

The caps of these specimens were 1½–2 cm wide, broadly conical and slightly umbonate. They were squamose from disc to margin, the scales becoming sparser and smaller towards the margin. The purple-black scales were upturned at the disc, then flattened out on a pallid grayish-tan ground towards the margin. The gills were adnexed to emarginated, whitish, subdistant, and subventricose. One specimen was intervenose. Gill edges were entire, wavy, and there were two tiers of lamellulae. Stems were 5–5 ½ cm long and 5–5 ½ mm thick. They were more or less napiform, narrowing at base and apex. Flattened purple-black scales at mid-stipe contrasted with a grayish-mauve ground color that became dingy ochre yellow at base. The apex above the scaly zone was smooth and slightly punctate. The odor was powerful and unpleasant, like passed gas. The spores were white and turned dextrinoid in Melzer's solution.

Microscopically, the spores were ellipsoid, smooth, and measured 7.4–9.3 x 3.9–4.4 µm. The basidia were 4-spored, slenderly clavate, and clamped at the bases. There were no cystidia. The pileipellis was a cutis of smooth-walled hyphae, smoky brown in KOH. There were numerous large clamps at the septa. Species of Squamanita also have asexual spores called chlamydospores. These were found at the stem bases. They were hyaline, double-walled, subglobose to obovoid, and covered with embedded warts. I measured several at 11.4 x 10.5 µm. Then I found others considerably larger at 17.2–19.9 x 17–17.2 µm. These larger chlamydospores plus the slightly thinner regular spores were the only characters that didn't match perfectly with typical **Squamanita pearsonii**.

All species of Squamanita are rare. What defines the genus is the ability to parasitize other mushrooms, the presence of asexual chlamydospores in the former host fungus at the stem base, and the presence of both hyaline and colored spores in the same fruiting body. The first Squamanita ever recorded was called **Lepiota odorata** in 1918. In 1965, Cornelis Bas introduced **Squamanita pearsonii** from Inverness, Scotland. The collection had been found in moss under Scotch pine. Since then, other collections have been made in Strathy and in Wales. It has also been recorded from Mount Fuji in Japan, where it was found fruiting next to **Cystoderma amianthinum**. Dr. Bas found another collection in Holland. Breitenbach & Kranzlin found it in Switzerland. There is another report of a finding in the Spey Valley in Britain in a remnant Caledonian forest. And Dr. Daniel Stuntz found it at Tunnel Creek, Washington, in 1975. According to Gareth Griffith et al., only ten collections have been made worldwide.

Species of Squamanita fruit on other mushrooms, transforming them into galls at their stem bases. This gall was not collected

THE PREFERRED VICTIM

Cystoderma amianthinum

by Helen, probably because it had already decomposed. **Squamanita pearsonii,** named after London mycologist A.A. Pearson, is thought to parasitize **Cystoderma amianthinum.** The chlamydospores belong to the former Cystoderma, not the Squamanita.

The genus Squamanita is also unique because it harbors species that have amyloid spores, inamyloid spores, and dextrinoid spores. Dr. Watling termed the spores of **Squamanita** **pearsonii** to be pseudo-amyloid, thereby adding yet another reaction. The combination of white gills, dextrinoid spores, and strongly contrasting purple-black scales separates **Squamanita pearsonii** from other members of the genus.

Thanks go out to Dr. Scott Redhead for mailing me the breakthrough monograph on Squamanita. Without this key I wouldn't have identified the species.

BIBLIOGRAPHY

Joe Ammirati, Scott Redhead, Lorelei Norvell, G.R. Walker, & M.B. Puccio, *Squamanita Contortipes, the Rosetta Stone of a Mycoparasitic Agaric Genus* in *Canadian Journal of Botany* 72 (1812–1824), 1994.

Cornelis Bas, *The Genus Squamanita* in *Persoonia* 3 (331–359), 1965.

J. Breitenbach & F. Kranzlin, *Fungi of Switzerland, Vol.4*, 1995. Edition Mykologia, Lucerne.

Ian Gibson, *Squamanita in the Pacific Northwest*, 2007. Pacific Northwest Key Council, Seattle, Wash.

Gareth Griffith, Krzysztof Gajda, Andrew Detheridge, Bryn Dentinger, William McAdoo, Brian Douglass, John Bingham, Victoria Bowmaker, **Alex Turner, & Debbie Evans**, *Strangler Unmasked: Parasitism of Cystoderma amianthinum by Squamanita paradoxa and S. pearsonii* in *Fungal Ecology*, 2019.

Thomas Laessøe, *Squamanita in Funga Nordica*, 2008. Nordsvamp, Copenhagen.

Meinhard Moser, *Keys to Agarics and Boleti*, 1983. Translated and published by Roger Phillips, London.

Roy Watling, *Notes on Some British Agarics, IV* in *Notes from the Royal Botanic Garden, Edinburgh* 33 (325–331), 1974.

Roy Watling & Evelyn Turnbull *Agarics and Boleti* in *British Fungus Flora* 8, 1998. Royal Botanic Garden, Edinburgh.

Stropharia albivelata (Murrill) Norvell & Redhead

*It's downright unfair, but some fungi
don't always conform to our rules.*

Perhaps one of the most attractive mushrooms ever introduced to me by Dr. Fred Rhoades is **Stropharia albivelata**, a rather rare species found only in coastal forests of the Pacific Northwest. Fred found it year after year at the same site down a logging road a few miles southwest of Lake Sammish. The site has been clearcut for some years now, and **Stropharia albivelata** hasn't appeared there since.

The specimens shown here had shown up at our 2017 fall mushroom show. The caps ran up to 5 ½ cm wide and were convex to plane with a slight umbo. The margins were shallowly incurved. The pellicle was slimy viscid and dried to a varnished appearance. The texture was smooth and the colors were vinaceous-brown at the disc fading to pinkish gray at the margins. Gills were adnate and whitish at first, before becoming cinnamon brown from the spores. The stems ran up to 8 ½ cm long and 8 mm thick. They were white and silky smooth above a flaring white ring that came off through handling. The stem was cottony scaly below the ring, turning yellowish where handled near the base over time. They were hollow and of equal thickness throughout. The large, white, membranous ring was down-curved, striate on top and floccose underneath. Stout, cord-like rhizomorphs emanated from the stem bases. The odor and taste were mild, and the spore deposit was a cinnamon brown.

Dr. A.H. Smith reported that although not exceedingly rare, only two or three specimens are ever found at a time. As for edibility, he wrote, "Not recommended. I have no data on it, and since some of the Pholiota species have turned out to be poisonous, caution is the word." No other author even brings up the subject.

Dr. Smith's mention of Pholiota highlights the idiosyncrasy. Due to its rusty spore print it had for years remained in Pholiota where Murrill first placed it. The type was found in the fall of 1911 in woods near Seattle by Murrill, and published in 1912. Its closest relative appears to be **Pholiota sipei**, a species discovered by Dr. Frank Sipe in douglas fir duff near Willamette, Oregon in 1947. It differs from **Stropharia albivelata** by its larger spores, a more floccose and yellowish ring, and by having both leptocystidia and chrysocystidia. The large leptocystidia of **Pholiota sipei** are absent in **S. albivelata**. Caps of **Pholiota sipei** are described as viscid, smooth, and pale to dark vinaceous brown.

Another possible look-alike is **Hebeloma incarnatulum**. It can also have a pinkish-brown cap disc, but differs by its brown spores, radish odor, and expanded stem base.

In Whatcom County, **Stropharia albivelata** has been recorded from Hannegan Pass and Silver Fir Campground. The *Handbook to Strategy 1 Fungal Species in the Northwest Forest Plan* states that it

LOOK-ALIKES

Stropharia hornemannii

Hebeloma incarnatulum

is only known from 38 sites in the Pacific Northwest where the spotted owl lives.

To flesh out a fuller description from the literature, we learn that gill edges can be white emarginated, the gills arcuate, the caps thin and subumbonate, and stems often pruinose above the ring, but floccose below.

Microscopically, the spores are smooth and ellipsoid with a tiny germ pore. They measure 7–9 x 4–5.5 µm. The pleurocystidia are clavate to mucronate with the yellow refractive contents that allow them to be called chrysocystidia. The pileipellis is an ixocutis (radially oriented hyphae in a gelatinous matrix). And finally there are acanthocytes on the mycelial hyphae. Acanthocytes are clusters of crystalline or stellate cells possibly unique to Stropharia. They can be found on the thick mycelial cords.

In the year 2000, Redhead & Norvell had seen enough. They transferred **Pholiota albivelata** to Stropharia. It was a fine way to celebrate the millennium. The evidence was overwhelming. The presence of chrysocystidia, acanthocytes, large and membranous ring, and viscid caps are all hallmarks of Stropharia. Only the rusty to dark yellow-brown spore print had kept it in Pholiota. Overholts, Smith, Murrill, and Stuntz & Isaacs had all assigned more weight to the color of the spore print than to the other characteristics.

Mycologists are always wrestling with these issues. Dr. Smith was fully aware of the problem. He wrote of **Pholiota sipei**, a close relative, "Sipe's notes clearly indicate the spores as cinnamon, and the gills as becoming cinnamon from the spores, otherwise one would immediately place the species in Stropharia." (**Pholiota sipei** is a very rare mushroom. It has only been found twice and is suspected to be a hybrid between **Stropharia albivelata** and **S. hornemannii**. It needs to be found again before it can be properly placed.)

DNA sequencing cinched the argument for **Stropharia albivelata**. It was found to belong in Stropharia where its closest look-alike is now **Stropharia hornemannii**. An excellent photo of **Pholiota albivelata** can be seen in Smith's *A Field Guide to Western Mushrooms*.

The transfer does produce a keying dilemma. In all keys to genera there is a choice between dark brown to purple-brown spores verse rusty to cinnamon brown spores. Despite now being a Stropharia, the species would either have to be keyed out in Pholiota as before, or a parenthesis created for it, something along the lines of (excepting **Stropharia albivelata** which goes with the purple-brown spores).

It's downright unfair, but some fungi don't always conform to our rules.

BIBLIOGRAPHY

David Arora, *Mushrooms Demystified*, 1986. Ten Speed Press, Berkeley, Calif.

Michael Castellano, Jane Smith, Thomas Odell, Efren Cazares, & Susan Nugent, *Handbook to Strategy 1 Fungal Species in the Northwest Forest Plan*, 1999. U.S. Department of Agriculture, Forest Service, Portland, Ore.

Lexemuel Hesler & A.H. Smith, *North American Species of Pholiota*, 1968. Lubrecht & Cramer, Monticello, NY.

Paul Kroeger, *Keys to the Dark-Spored Strophariaceae of British Columbia*, 2008. Pacific Northwest Key Council, Seattle, Wash.

William Murrill, *The Agaricaceae of the Pacific Coast II* in *Mycologia* 4 (294–308), 1912.

Lee Overholts, *Pholiota* in *North American Flora* 10, Part 4 (261–276), 1924.

Lee Overholts, *A Monograph of the Genus Pholiota* in *Annals of the Missouri Botanical Garden* 14 (87–210), 1927.

Scott Redhead & Lorelei Norvell *Stropharia Albivelata and its Basionym Pholiota Albivelata* in *Mycotaxon* 76 (315–320), 2000.

Kit Scates & Tina Gospodnetich, *Trial Field Key to the Species of Pholiota in the Pacific Northwest*, 1981. Pacific Northwest Key Council, Seattle, Wash.

A.H. Smith, *A Field Guide to Western Mushrooms*, 1975. University of Michigan Press, Ann Arbor, Mich.

Helen & A.H. Smith & Nancy Weber, *How to Know the Gilled Mushrooms*, 1979. William C. Brown, Dubuque, Iowa.

Daniel Stuntz & Bill Isaacs, *Pacific Northwestern Fungi* in *Mycologia* 54 (290–292), 1962.

Jan Vesterholt, *Hebeloma* in *Funga Nordica*, Nordsvamp, Copenhagen, 2012.

Stropharia caerulea Kreisel

By Buck McAdoo and Richard Morrison

*It's a saprobe, feeding on and
breaking down non-living matter.*

It isn't every season that a mushroom club is in the midst of its annual fall show when a member saunters into the big room with a gem like **Stropharia caerulea**. Perhaps feeling a little claustrophobic among the event crowds, WWU mycology student Caleb Brown decided to roam around Bloedel-Donovan Park for a little fresh air. Lo and behold a little time passes and he finds a cluster of **S. caerulea** on old wood chip mulch. The date? October 18, 2015. A small posse of us went back out there to find more and the lead photo shows the result from that occasion.

When you spot a mushroom this beautiful you wonder how the term "toadstool" ever came into use. It happens to have a European origin so the description you are about to read comes from both Kreisel, who rescued the taxonomic concept from confusion, and Watling & Gregory, who find it often in the British Isles.

Stropharia caerulea starts out with viscid blue-green caps that have a separable epidermal pellicle. The caps measure 3-12 cm wide and are convex to plane, often with a slight umbo. Very shortly the blue-green color starts to fade to yellowish-green to ochre in large patches, then pallid straw color in age. At the same time the sparse white scales on the caps begin to disappear. Meanwhile the veil is also trying to vanish. It starts out as a white cover over the gills, advances to the appendiculate stage by hanging briefly off the cap margin, then pauses at mid-stipe as a ring reduced to a few white shards before leaving the carpophore except for some impressive white scales below the ring zone.

The caps are so hygrophanous that even the context fades from bluish to straw color. The gills are adnate to emarginate with a tooth. They are pale flesh color for some time, then fawn color before the spores turn them dark brown in age. Gill edges are entire and the same color as the gill faces. The stems are 4-10 cm long and up to 1.2 cm thick. They are pale blue-green at first but soon fade to buff with an olive-buff tinge at base. The apex remains white pruinose with striated white silky fibrils below. The indistinct ring zone gives way to isolated white scales just above the equal to clavate stem base. Dense white mycelial strands often penetrate the substrate. The spore deposit is umber brown, without purple tones. The taste is mild to pleasant while the odor is "mushroomy" to faintly acid-pungent.

Besides wood chip mulch, it can be found in waste places near nettles, margins of woods, abandoned gardens, under hedgerows, and in sand dunes. Paul Stamets has found it on litter enriched by manure. It can be found from September on into November.

As for microscopic characters, the spores are ellipsoid to ellipsoid-ovate, smooth walled, light brown, and measure 7-11 x 4.4-5 µm. The basidia are 4-spored, clavate. The pileipellis is a

Older Stropharia caerulea showing areolate caps

Stropharia pseudocyanea

Stropharia aeruginosa from Switzerland

cuticle of narrow, filamentous hyphae less than 5 µm wide in a gelatinized matrix. Clamps are present. The gill trama consists of inflated, interwoven hyphae with clamps. Both the cheilocystidia and the pleurocystidia have chrysocystidia among them. These are cystidia with yellow refractive contents. Of all the bluish capped Stropharias, **S. caerulea** is the only one that has both. The cheilocystidia are fusiform to slightly long-necked and measure 28-55 x 10-16 µm. Claviform cells can sometimes be found. The pleurocystidia are similar or more fusiform (tapered at both ends) in shape. The hyphae on the stem are vertically parallel and measure 8-12.5 µm wide. A few caulocystidia are found at the stem apex only.

The second photo here shows a collection Buck found on the embankment behind the Herald Building parking lot in downtown Bellingham in the fall of 2013. The caps were Disneyesque, with what looked like turquoise scales on a straw colored ground. He jammed on the brakes and made the collection. Back in the lab-office, the microscope revealed a different story. If these had been scales the pileipellis would have been bristling with extended hyphal ends or pileocystidia. Instead he saw a gelatinous matrix 350 µm thick with broken hyphal shards scattered throughout it. The "scales" were nothing more than areolate patches caused by the process of drying up.

Known popularly as the Blue-Green Slime Head or the Blue Roundhead, **Stropharia caerulea** is found in Spain, France, Germany, the British Isles, Scandinavia, Newfoundland, and the Pacific Northwest. It's a saprobe, feeding on and breaking down non-living organic matter. It has had a number of look-alikes that have since been absorbed as synonyms, and a few that remain in the Northwest. In no particular order, these are:

Stropharia aeruginosa: Differs by retaining its blue-green color longer, by having a cap margin with copious veil remnants hanging off it, by having vinaceous-brown gills with whitish gill edges, and by a more persistent and showy ring. Microscopically it differs by having capitate cheilocystidia with no chrysocystidia among them.

Stropharia pseudocyanea: A smaller, thinner Stropharia that is found in tall grasses near the edges of swamps. The glutinous blue-green caps are only

465

3 cm wide and fade quickly to straw color in age. The gill edges are dentate. The thin stem is covered with white fibrils and squamules, and there is white mycelium at the base. Peter Orton reports that the stem is so soft that it is hard to keep it from getting squished when picked. It also has a strong odor of black pepper, giving rise to its common name, the Peppery Roundhead.

Pholiota subcaerulea: First described by A.H. Smith & Hesler from Portland, Oregon in 1968, the viscid gray-green caps run up to 4 cm wide but soon fade to cinnamon-buff in blotches. The gills are pale brown aging to dull cinnamon-brown. The spore deposit is rusty instead of dark brown. The habitat is grassy areas or with debris under conifers in the fall. The photo here depicts a solitary specimen found at Sandy Point in 1983. It is an extremely rare species. Neither of us have seen it since.

(Perhaps worthy of note, the 2003 Key Council key to Northwest Pholiota lists this as a synonym of **Stropharia pseudocyanea**, but the authoritative website *Index Fungorum* now accepts **Pholiota subcaerulea** as the correct name.)

The taxonomic history of **S. caerulea** wends along a convoluted and sometimes befuddling trail. The species was initially named **Agaricus politus** in 1788 by the English mycologist and illustrator James Bolton from specimens found near Halifax, England. Then, in 1791 Bolton named another bluish British mushroom of uncertain provenance **Agaricus**

Pholiota subcaerulea

cyaneus. In 1953 the Finnish mycologist Tuomikoski redescribed Bolton's **Agaricus cyaneus** and transferred it to the genus Stropharia as **S. cyanea**. This was accepted by several eminent mycologists at this time. However, in a 1980 paper the German mycologist Hanns Kreisel concluded that Tuomikoski wrongly applied the name **Stropharia cyanea** to what was actually **Stropharia aeruginosa** after reviewing illustrations by Bolton in an 1820 publication. He then erected **Stropharia caerulea** as a new species, listing **Agaricus politus** Bolton and Tuomikoski's **Stropharia cyanea** as synonyms. As a side note, the **Agaricus cyaneus** of Bolton in 1791 was rendered an illegitimate name because previously in 1784 Buller had used this same name for another species. By international botanical nomenclatural rules, two different taxa can't have the same name, and the earliest name has precedence.

Although **Stropharia caerulea** is the accepted current name and **S. cyanea** a synonym, some mushroom resources still have this in reverse. Noordeloos created another wrinkle in 1995 when he transferred all bluish Stropharias to the genus Psilocybe. The mycological community did not accept this transfer. They remained in Stropharia, but a new synonym was created.

As for the edibility of the Blue-Green Slime Head, there are few comments. Kreisel described the taste as pleasant but did not comment on edibility. Pegler & Spooner claim that **Stropharia aeruginosa**, **Stropharia caerulea**, and **Stropharia albocyanea** are all poisonous. No one comments on the flavor. O'Reilly mentions that others consider **Stropharia caerulea** to be possibly poisonous.

Because of the blue color some authorities have suspected the presence of psychoactive alkaloids in **S. caerulea** and its relatives. Buczacki and Shields mention it has both psilocin and psilocybin. Stamets, in discussing it as **Psilocybe caerulea**, noted it might be mildly psychoactive. Watling & Gregory note that traces of psilocybin have been found in collections from Scotland. However, the magic mushroom website shroomery.org informs us that "there are no psychoactive species of Stropharia, blue or otherwise." Borovicka et al., when studying psychoactive indoles in mushrooms, have even used **Stropharia caerulea** as a non-active control. With better options available, taking a trip with blue-green Stropharias may not produce the desired result.

And finally, in *Mushrooms of the Pacific Northwest* Trudell & Ammirati noted that collections of both **S. aeruginosa** and **S. caerulea** seemed to intergrade in our area. They wondered if these two species might represent a single variable species or possibly a third undescribed species. It seems that in the current world of fungal taxonomy, change is the rule, so best to stay tuned.

BIBLIOGRAPHY

James Bolton, *An History of Fungusses Growing About Halifax* 1:30 tab 30, 1788.

James Bolton, *An History of Fungusses Growing About Halifax*, App. 3:143, t. 143, 1791.

James Bolton, *Beschreibung der um Halifax waschenden Pilze*. Bd. IV, Berlin, 1820.

James Bolton, *Phylogenetic and Chemical Studies in the Potential Psychotropic Species Complex Psilocybe atrobrunnea with Taxonomic and Nomenclatural Notes* in Persoonia 34 (1–9), 2015.

Stefan Buczacki, Chris Shields, & Denys Ovenden, *Collins Fungi Guide*, Harper-Collins, London, 2012.

Paul Kirk (ed.), *Index Fungorum*, http://www.indexfungorum.org/names/Names.asp

Hanns Kreisel, *On the Taxonomy of Stropharia aeruginosa Sensu Lato* in *Beihefte Sydowia* 8, (228–232), 1980.

Michael Kuo, *Stropharia caerulea*. www.mushroomexpert.com

Thomas Laessøe, *Mushrooms*, 2013. DK publishing, London.

N.W. Legon & Alick Henrici, *Checklist of British and Irish Basidiomycota at Royal Botanic Garden, Kew, England*, 2015. basidiochecklist.info/index.htm

Shroomery.org, *Magic Mushrooms Demystified*, 2015.

Mycobank.org, *Stropharia cyanea*.

Machiel Noordeloos, *Notulae ad Floram Agaricinum Neerlandicum—XXIII. Psilocybe and Pholiota* in Persoonia 16 (127–130), 1995.

Pat O'Reilly, *Fascinated by Fungi*, 2011. First Nature.

Peter D. Orton, *Notes on British Agarics.VI* in *Notes from the Royal Botanic Garden, Edinburgh* 35 (147–154), 1976.

David Pegler & Brian Spooner, *The Mushroom Identifier*, 1992. Smithmark, New York, NY.

Svengunnar Ryman, *Stropharia (Fr.) Quel.* in *Funga Nordica* (965–970), 2012. Nordsvamp, Copenhagen.

Kit Scates & Tina Gospodnotich, *Trial Key to the Species of Pholiota in the Pacific Northwest*, 2003. Pacific Northwest Key Council, Seattle, Wash. svims.ca/council/Pholio.htm.

A.H. Smith & Lexemuel Hesler, *The North American Species of Pholiota*. Hafner Publishing Co., New York, NY., 1968.

Paul Stamets, *Psilocybin Mushrooms of the World*, 1996. Ten Speed Press, Berkeley, Calif.

Steve Trudell & Joe Ammirati, *Mushrooms of the Pacific Northwest*, 2009. Timber Press, Portland, Ore.

Risto Tuomikoski, *Notes on Finnish Agaricales* in *Karstenia* 2 (26-32), 1953.

Roy Watling & Norma Gregory, *Strophariaceae & Coprinaceae p.p.* in *British Fungus Flora* 5, 1987. Royal Botanic Garden, Edinburgh, 1987.

Stropharia rugosoannulata Farlow ex Murrill

By Buck McAdoo and Sam Leathers

Its natural habitat appears to be uncertain.

Diminutive specimens of S. rugosoannulata on wood chips from N.J.

Every now and then, whether in lean seasons or those of plenty, there appears a great mushroom. For me, that mushroom this year was **Stropharia rugosoannulata**, a species rarely found in the wild. The fact that the Wine Cap Stropharia was grown right in Bellingham by Sam Leathers, and perhaps others in his cultivation group, does nothing to diminish the glory of this species. This is one of the few species I know of whose flavor matches its stunning appearance. So after a brief description, I'll turn this article over to Sam Leathers, a pioneer member of Northwest Mushroomers, and the first to initiate a cultivation branch.

Although listed in most guides as growing to 15 cm in width, some of us have seen enormous specimens produced by Sam that were almost twice that size. The cap color is at first a striking burgundy to ruddy brown that can become grayish vinaceous to even pale ochre in age. According to Kibby and Roody, cap colors can also change from exposure to light. Those in direct sunlight turn ochre a lot faster. From start to finish, the caps have the incurved margins of the classic Frisbee, but often become wavy in age. The flesh is thick, soft, and white. Remnants of the partial veil can sometimes cling to the cap margin. The gills are white at first, then gray to dark purple gray as the spores mature. They are adnate to adnexed, but tend to secede in age, leading to possible confusion with species of Agaricus. The stems are 10–15 cm long and 1–3 cm thick. They are equal or taper towards the apex from a bulbous base. They are dry, smooth, and white, often staining yellowish when older. Thick, white rhizomorphs are usually found at the base. The spores are purple black. The taste is mild and the odor is mildly of radish or freshly cut grass. The large, flaring, double ring is found on the upper part of the stem. The white upper surface is deeply, radially grooved. The lower part is felt-like and split into claw-like points that extend beyond the upper part. *Rugosoannulata* means "wrinkled ring" in Latin. Thus, the taxon is named more for the unique appearance of this ring than it is for its prodigious size or wine-red cap color. Other common names enjoyed by this mushroom are King Stropharia, Garden Giant, and Godzilla Mushroom. Upon making itself known to Jack Czarnecki, he wrote, "it indeed looks as though Godzilla is wreaking havoc upon earth when these benign creatures appear, sometimes growing to five or more pounds apiece."

A lot of credit must go to Paul Stamets, from whose Fungi Perfecti kit Sam Leathers grew these monsters. Besides Fungi Perfecti, kits of **Stropharia rugosoannulata** can be ordered from Cascadia Mushrooms in Whatcom County. Only Duhem and Courtecuisse in Europe mention caps attaining 30 cm in width. **Stropharia rugosoannulata** has been found in New Zealand, Australia, South America, all across Asia, North America, and Europe, but almost always with wood chips or on cultivated ground. The type was found by Farlow near Newton, Massachusetts, on cultivated ground. A second collection was found in a corn field near Waban, Mass., on September 13, 1905.

They fruit on bark mulch, rotting straw, wood chips, and compost around gardens, only rarely occurring in the wild. This sets up an interesting question. As A.H. Smith wrote, "its natural habitat appears to be uncertain."

Authors who mention specimens in the wild only state they were found in woods and sizes were nowhere near those of the cultivated versions. The second photo shown here bears this out (previous page). These diminutive specimens were found on wood chips on a path in the Whittemore Preserve near Oldwick, N.J., on May 24, 2012. They were so badly devoured by slugs that you couldn't see any velar material left. After I shot the photo, the stems fell off when picked. There appears to be no strict recording of these "finds in the wild."

As a result, the Wine Cap Stropharia is regarded as a non-native species wherever it shows up. If cave men hadn't

Hypholoma lateritium from Vermont

progressed from hunting and gathering, this gift from the gods may never have come to exist. Perhaps in hopes of discovering an origin, Smith concluded, "large fruitings have been found around rhododendrons."

The Wine Cap Stropharia also appears to be a strong candidate for mycoremediation. According to Robert Rogers, "preparations of extra-cellular manganese peroxidase from the species have been found to rapidly convert and breakdown the explosive amino nitro-toluenes. It is also an efficient degrader of benzopyrene, polycyclic aromatic hydrocarbons and other toxins, especially in the presence of manganese."

Taxonomically, **Stropharia rugosoannulata** has a slightly muddled history. European specimens were first called **Stropharia ferrii**. This is now a synonym. Forms with yellow caps were called **Stropharia ferrii var. flavida**. In Japan, Hongo authored a **form lutea** for the yellow-ochre specimens. This is also considered a synonym by the *Index Fungorum*. There is also a **Stropharia imaiana** Benedix, described from Japan in 1961, which *Index Fungorum* now lists as another synonym. Benedix also described a **Stropharia eximia** from East Germany in 1960. This is a large species with pearly white caps that develop grayish scales in age. The caps sometimes have violet tinges. The gills are serrate, gray at first, then violet brown in maturity. There is a fragile ring on the upper stem. According to Moser, its relationship to **Stropharia rugosoannulata** had yet to be clarified. This statement was made in 1978. In 1981, Kreisel moved it to **Stropharia rugosoannulata form eximia**.

The Wine Cap Stropharia can also find wood chips in the wilds. I found a nice colony in the summer of 2012 on wood chip mulch next to a bathroom at a rest stop in New England.

As for look-alikes, there are precious few:

Hypholoma lateritium: Can resemble it, but never comes with the large, membranous ring on the stem.

Stropharia hornemannii: Could be confused with old ochre specimens of the Wine Cap Stropharia, but differs by the white scales below the ring on the stipe.

Stropharia hardii: Differs by its viscid ochre-brown caps and gray-brown gills.

Species of Agaricus have chocolate brown spores and free gills. All considered, there are not many mushrooms out there to confuse it with.

Microscopically, the spores are elliptic, thick-walled with a germ pore, and measure 9.4–13 x 7–9 µm. The pileipellis is a cutis of radially parallel hyphae with clamps. Cheilocystidia are clavate, ventricose, vesicular, or lageniform with an apical protrusion. Some are chrysocystidia when the contents turn yellow in KOH. Pleurocystidia are fusiform ventricose. The mycelial hyphae are strongly elongated, often with medallion clamps.

Stropharia rugosoannulata is also very, very edible. It made my top five in the third or fourth bite. It seemed to have the perfect texture when sautéed in butter along with a rich macadamia flavor that put it on a par with **Boletus edulis**. Most authors rate it "edible and choice." Centuries before the type was described from Newton, Massachusetts, Schalkwijk-Barendsen writes that it came west from Russia with Napoleon's army. (Now that's insider knowledge). When people migrate, the Wine Cap Stropharia migrates right along with them. Arora writes that it is the best in the genus for the table. (The competition is not stiff.) Jack Czarnecki, author of *Joe's Book of Mushroom Cookery*, adds his opinion: "When young it is meaty and firm. As it matures, the ratio of gills to flesh becomes quite high, resulting in a flabby, soft, overall texture. But the flavor is very good, and the stock it produces from blanching is very much like chicken stock, but darker, which makes it very attractive for sauces." He suggests that it is not a good mushroom for preserving. In *A Cook's Book of Mushrooms*, he has a recipe for Grilled Rockfish with Stropharia. He also writes "they are great grilled after painting with Oyster sauce or chipotlé purée. Or they can be treated the same as Portobellos."

Nonetheless, Robert Dale Rogers issues a warning that they should not be consumed for more than 2–3 days in a row. Some people have experienced nausea and indigestion. They may have eaten undercooked specimens or simply hogged out. Or it may be because the Wine Cap Stropharia contains the human blood type A hemagglutinate.

Although Wine Cap Stropharias can be easily grown at home if directions are carefully adhered to, one should be aware of pesticides or fertilizers if poaching in unfamiliar gardens. Thanks to Sam's success, we now have proof that the Wine Cap Stropharia grows just fine in Whatcom County. Here, then, is the story behind the propagation.

Since you have read this far, perhaps, just perhaps, your taste buds and curiosity are titillated to the point that you might want to try growing **Stropharia rugosoannulata** in your own back yard. Besides producing a choice edible, you will impress your neighbors and add ornamental beauty to the landscape. Follow a few simple steps and you can be harvesting this choice mushroom from early summer until the fall frost. Spring is an ideal time to get started.

But first, let me (Sam Leathers) give thanks to Dave Jansen for introducing me to the Garden Giant some five years ago. With a batch of starter spawn and a wheelbarrow load of hardwood chips, you have the basic essentials to get started.

The fact that this mushroom, according to Stamets, can tolerate a temperature range of –5 degrees to 90 degrees Fahrenheit, and in addition, has an aggressive appetite for alder or maple sawdust or woodchips, makes it easy to cultivate in the Pacific Northwest.

What's needed? We have mentioned spawn and chips. Spawn comes in a one-gallon sized bag, which contains **Stropharia rugosoannulata** mycelium growing on sawdust or straw. It costs about $25. A gallon of spawn will inoculate a bed of sawdust or chips that is 4 feet wide, 8 feet long, and 4–6 inches deep. The sawdust and wood chips mixture should be clean, damp, and recently cut.

The location of the bed is an important consideration. Best results occur when you select a site that has shade, good drainage, a fair amount of humidity in the soil, and is protected from the wind. However, if your spot doesn't meet all these conditions, don't worry. (Except for good drainage since **Stropharia rugosoannulata** doesn't like wet feet.) Areas under fruit trees, shrubs, tall vegetables and the like can be desirable spots.

Once the bed is established with the sawdust/chips mixture at a depth of at least 4 inches, it is ready for inoculation. To do this, take a golf ball sized chunk of spawn and bury it about 2 inches deep in the substrate. Repeat this step over the entire bed, spacing the steps about 12 inches apart.

The hardest work is now done. From here on it is only necessary to do a couple of things. First, be sure to keep the bed moist, but not saturated, like your flowerbed or garden. After about four weeks, take a peek at the mycelium to see how it is doing. It should be clearly evident that the mycelium is spreading from the spawn to the adjacent substrate material. In another month or so the mycelium should begin to reach the surface. At this point a casing layer of clean topsoil, free of lime additives, should be spread 1–2 inches deep over the bed. According to Stamets, certain microorganisms in the soil interact with the mycelium to stimulate fruiting. Avoid using sterilized potting soil.

Keep the bed moist and you should have mushrooms appearing in another 2–4 weeks. Spotting the first mush-

Stropharia hornemannii

room is incredibly exciting—like being a brand new parent.

Harvest your mushrooms in the button stage for best flavor.

Flushes of mushrooms, with prudent watering, will occur in waves every three or four weeks until cold fall weather arrives.

Finally, from experience I have found that it is best to leave the weeds in the bed. Although unsightly, they seem to provide a humid environment near the bed surface. However, I find it best to quickly remove all mushrooms, including the stems that are past their prime. This reduces the activity of mushroom flies that lay eggs on or near the mushrooms, which in turn produce the larvae which in turn causes the cook to yell "Worms!"

I can recommend the following material sources. Spawn can be ordered from Fungi Perfecti, P.O. Box 7634, Olympia, Washington, 98507 or from Cascadia Mushrooms, info@cascadiamushrooms.com. They are now located a bit north of Bellingham. Sawdust and chips can be obtained by phoning your local arborist or tree service outfit and reserving the material in advance.

Avoid cedar like the plague.

Addendum: In Hungary it is grown in rows of baled wheat straw simply wetted down and inoculated. And about four million pounds of **Stropharia rugosoanulata** are produced annually in France.

BIBLIOGRAPHY

David Arora, *Mushrooms Demystified*, 1986. Ten Speed Press, Berkeley, Calif.

Alan Bessette, *Mushrooms of the Adirondacks*, 1988. North Country Books, Utica, NY.

Marcel Bon, *The Mushrooms and Toadstools of Britain and Northwestern Europe*, 1987. Hodder & Stoughton, London.

J. Breitenbach & F. Kranzlin, *Fungi of Switzerland, Vol.4*, 1995. Edition Mykologia, Lucerne.

Regis Courtecuisse & Bernard Duhem, *Mushrooms & Toadstools of Britain & Europe*, 1995. Harper-Collins, London.

Jack Czarnecki, *Joe's Book of Mushroom Cookery*, 1986. Atheneum, New York, NY.

Jack Czarnecki, *A Cook's Book of Mushrooms*, 1995. Artisan, New York, NY.

William Farlow, *Illustrations of the Larger Fungi*, 1929. Farlow Herbarium, Harvard University, Cambridge, Mass.

Jeffrey Fine, *The Stropharioidae of Western Washington,* 1972. Doctorate.

David Fischer & Alan Bessette, *Edible Wild Mushrooms of North America*, 1992. University of Texas Press, Austin, Texas.

Louis Imler & Jan Rammeloo, *Icones Mycologicae 93–110*, 1985. Jardin Botanique National de Belgique, Meise, Belgium.

Bill Isaacs & Daniel Stuntz, *Pacific Northwestern Fungi* in *Mycologia* 54 (272–298), 1962.

Geoffrey Kibby, *An Illustrated Guide to Mushrooms and Other Fungi of North America*, 1993. Dragon's World, London.

Kent & Vera McKnight, *Peterson Field Guides— Mushrooms*, 1987. Houghton Mifflin, Boston.

Edmund Michael, Bruno Hennig, & Hanns Kreisel, *Handbuch fur Pilzfreunde 4*, 1984. Gustav Fischer Verlag, Stuttgart, Germany.

Meinhard Moser, *Keys to Agarics and Boleti*, 1983. Translated and published by Roger Phillips, London.

William Murrill, *Dark-Spored Agarics—II. Gomphidius and Stropharia in Mycologia* 14 (121–142), 1922.

Umberto Nonis, *Guides des Champignons Gastronomiques*, 1984. Hippocrene Books, New York, NY.

Giovanni Pacioni & Gary Lincoff, *Simon & Schuster's Guide to Mushrooms*, 1981. Simon & Schuster, New York, NY.

Peter Roberts & Shelley Evans, *The Book of Fungi*, 2011. University of Chicago Press, Chicago.

William Roody, *Mushrooms of West Virginia and the Central Appalachians*, 2003. University Press of Kentucky, Lexington, Ky.

Helene Schalkwijk-Barendsen, *Mushrooms of Western Canada*, 1991. Lone Pine Publishing, Edmonton, Alberta.

Helen & A.H. Smith & Nancy Weber, *How to Know the Gilled Mushrooms*, 1979. William C. Brown, Dubuque, Iowa.

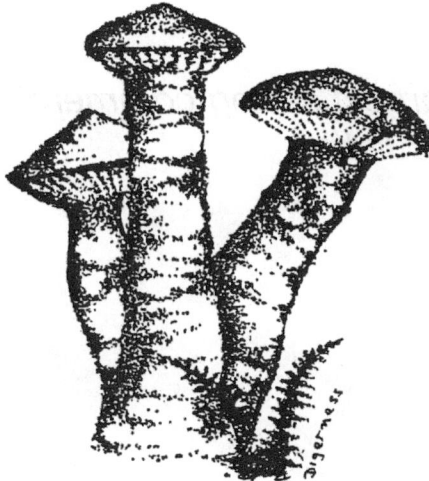

Suillus luteus (Linnaeus) Roussel

It could be the largest selling commercial mushroom in circulation.

Faded caps of older Suillus luteus

Suillus luteus, the original Slippery Jack, is the only two-star Suillus in Michigan. Compared to the assortment of insipid Suillae we have in the Pacific Northwest, it could be a three-star in Whatcom County. The term "Slippery Jack" needs a bit of clarification. When I lived in San Francisco, the local **Suillus pungens** was called Slippery Jack. It turns out that all species of Suillus can be called Slippery Jacks. But **Suillus luteus** is the type species for the genus and was called Slippery Jack specifically. If you can't live with this, then the strict Latin meaning, the "Golden Yellow Little Pig," might suit you more.

The species was first described by Linnaeus as **Boletus luteus** in 1753. Roussel then moved it to Suillus in 1796. Fries sanctioned the name in 1821. It has essentially remained in Suillus except for a brief sojourn in Ixocomus where you can find it under that genus in guides by Maublanc or Usak & Pilat. For a time, the type specimen for **Suillus luteus** was lost. But somehow, miracle of miracles, time was found to find a neotype at the same original location in Sweden. The concept received its anchor again.

The caps of **Suillus luteus** range from 5–12 cm wide, are rounded at first becoming plane to convex in age. The surface is viscid to glutinous in wet weather, sticky in dry. Anything through which it grows adheres to the cap. It is usually streaked beneath the slime. The color is at first a dark rusty brown or reddish brown (see lead photo). Older specimens are a more yellow-brown to ochre (see photo this page). According to Dr. Thiers, the partial veil, which includes the slime layer on the cap, can change color depending on the amount of moisture in the air. The cap flesh is white becoming pale yellow towards the tubes. The tubes are 3–7 mm deep, adnate to short decurrent, and whitish to pale yellow becoming olive yellow in age. There is no color change when bruised. The pore mouths become spotted with brown as the clusters of cheilocystidia mature. The stems are 4–8 cm long and 1–2 ½ cm thick. They are glandular dotted above and below the ring, white to pale yellow at first, then dingy yellow to even brownish towards the base in age. The ring is white and flaring at first, which may be why the French call it "La Nonette Voilée." The underside of this ring soon becomes a purplish gray or purplish brown, a character unique among all species of Suillus. This purplish zone can become chocolate in dry conditions and get plastered to the stem. The spores are brown to dull cinnamon. They are smooth-walled, narrowly inequilateral in profile, and measure 7–9 x 2.5–3.5 μm. The cheilocystidia are narrowly clavate to lageniform but so encrusted with brown pigmentation as to often obscure the outlines.

Odor and taste are mild. The cap cuticle turns dark gray with KOH while the context turns pinkish and then pale blue gray in stages.

The Slippery Jack fruits in our area from September into early November. Its favorite host is pine followed by spruce. It is a truly cosmopolitan species found with Scots pine, red pine, mountain pine, white pine, black pine, or jack pine depending where in the globe these are found. The best places to find it locally are in suburban yards or city parks where non-native pines have been planted. It prefers pines that are ten years old or more. Charles Horton Peck was the first to suspect that it wasn't native to North America. Since then, it has been reported from New Zealand with Pinus radiatus, from Kenya with Pinus patula, from the slopes of Mount Kilimanjaro, from China, from northern Siberia and the Kola Peninsula, from the Cotopaxi National Park in Ecuador, and from Chile where much gets exported abroad as "pine bolete."

We are glad it is here, providing many an urban meal when time is too tight to foray elsewhere.

The closest look-alike to the Slippery Jack is the Slippery Jill. This is **Suillus subluteus**, smaller in size with a more slender stem. Instead of a macho purple brown ring it has a feminine baggy ring with no purple in it. Caps are pale ochre at first, then are streaked with smoky brown filaments before ending up with a sooty appearance. They sometimes fruit right along with the Slippery Jacks.

LOOK-ALIKES

Suillus caerulescens from California

Suillus subolivaceus

Suillus grevillei var. badius from Scotland

Suillus ampliporus

Suillus clintonianus

Other look-alikes follow here:

Suillus acerbus: Differs by fruiting in cespitose clusters only with Monterrey pine, does not stain blue when handled, and has a strong acidic taste. The Bessettes and Roody claim it is a synonym of **Suillus fuscotomentosus**.

Suillus caerulescens: By far our most common local Suillus, it differs by having a white fibrillose ring on the stem and a stem base that slowly turns turquoise blue when nicked. Velar material on the cap margin is also white.

Suillus ponderosus: Mimics **Suillus caerulescens**, differing mainly in the yellow velar material hanging from the cap margins and adorning the stipe when young.

Suillus pungens: Young specimens differ by having milky droplets on their pore surfaces. It further differs by not having a ring on the stem. **Suillus subolivaceus**— Also has a large gelatinous ring on the stem, but it's a whitish ring with an olive-brown underside. The dingy ochre-gray caps and almost black glandular dots on the stipe help distinguish it from the Slippery Jack.

Suillus umbonatus: Differs by its gelatinous brownish ring and much thinner stature.

Suillus clintonianus: Differs by forming a cottony white ring on the stipe and by associating only with larch.

Suillus grevellei var. badius: Differs from the above by having darker brick colored caps without a yellow ground color.

Suillus ampliporus: Differs by its hollow stem and white cottony ring.

There are mixed opinions on flavor and edibility of **Suillus ampliporus**. Everyone agrees that the viscid cap pellicle must be peeled off before cooking. It turns into pure slime in the frying pan. Some people have a gastrointestinal reaction to **Suillus luteus**, which some attribute to ingestion of the slimy cap pellicle. Many species of Suillus contain thiaminase, according to Robert Rogers, which can trigger swift movement of the bowels. The dried version must not share this trait because Chile exports significant amounts of it yearly to Europe.

I have always peeled off the tubes also. Others dry the tubes and grind them into powder. They can then be used as a spice for omelettes and stews.

Here now are some culinary opinions from the experts: **Aurel Dermek**: "This species is full of flavor and easily digested when used in soups,

477

sauces, and meat dishes. It can be pickled with other species of mushrooms but contains too much water to be dried successfully."

Charles McIlvaine: "Once carefully cleaned, it is of choice consistency and good flavor."

Jack Czarnecki: "It has a strong and distinctive flavor all its own and is not much less tasty than the cèpe (Boletus edulis). The character can be described as very musty."

Wikipedia: "Edible but causes allergic reactions with some people. Gastrointestinal symptoms could be due to high levels of arabitol."

Andre Marchand: "Good to eat. Even better than **Suillus granulatus**."

Jianzhe, Xiaolan, Qiming, Yichen, & Huaan: "It is used for treating Kashin-Beck disease and is one of the main ingredients in Pine Mushroom Elixir." (Kashin-Beck disease is thought to be partially due to low levels of selenium. It causes swollen joints and is prevalent in China, North Korea, Tibet, and Siberia.)

Andreas Neuner: "The flesh is very soft with a pleasant, slightly sour taste. It decays rapidly and must be eaten right away."

Lucius Von Frieden: "Mature fruiting bodies are inferior in flavor. Discard cap margins in older specimens and also stems from the ring down."

I personally prefer **Suillus luteus** pickled and have had good results with Dr. Orson Miller's pickling recipe on the back pages of his *Mushrooms of North America*. Once pickled it has a texture of olives and an earthy, zesty flavor. I had no

LOOK-ALIKES

Suillus ponderosus

Suillus pungens from Calif.

Suillus umbonatus from Oregon

problems floating one in a martini.

Although generally considered the poor man's **Boletus edulis** by most connoisseurs, Jack Czarnecki calculates that **Suillus luteus** could be the largest selling commercial mushroom in circulation…as a diluter for **Boletus edulis.** He also offers a good recipe for Slippery Jack Soup. He makes his own stock with vegetables and beef bones. **Suillus luteus** and onions are sautéed in butter and sprinkled with flour. The stock is then added and simmered for ten minutes. Sour cream or crème fraîche is added at the end along with chopped dill.

Perhaps inspired by such recipes during the early, heady days of our club, a few of us would occasionally indulge in lawn raids throughout Bellingham. **Suillus luteus** was one of several targets. Armed with burlap sacks we would take turns leaping out of our van to poach mushrooms.

Once, when it was my turn to pick, the colony of Slippery Jacks was so huge that I didn't notice a door swing open in the home. An elderly man had walked out cradling a shotgun in his arm. The guys in the van were probably too shocked for speech. The shadow of the barrel fell across the mushrooms. There was nothing for me to do but look up. To this day I have never witnessed a more puzzled expression.

"Feller," the man drawled, "I spend a lot of money every year on fungicides… and you want these things?"

That was the last lawn raid for us. While the owner permitted us to cart off the Slippery Jacks, none of us wanted to cook them up. Potentially years of fungicides is a powerful deterrent. Guns and roses have at least some sort of romantic connotation. Guns and fungicides? Not so good.

BIBLIOGRAPHY

Alan & Arleen Bessette & William Roody, *North American Boletes*, 2000. Syracuse University Press, Syracuse, NY.

Jack Czarnecki, *Joe's Book of Mushroom Cookery*, 1986. Atheneum, New York, NY.

Jack Czarnecki, *A Cook's Book of Mushrooms*, 1995. Artisan, New York, NY.

Aurel Dermek, *The Spotter's Guide to Mushrooms and Other Fungi*, 1984. Slovart Publishers, Bratislava, Slovakia.

Dennis Desjardin, Michael Wood, & Fred Stevens, *California Mushrooms*, 2015. Timber Press, Portland, Ore.

David Fischer & Alan Bessett, *Edible Wild Mushrooms of North America*, 1992. University of Texas Press, Austin, Texas.

Ying Jianzhe, Mao Xiaolan, Ma Qiming, Zong Yichen, & Wen Huaan, *Icons of Medicinal Fungi from China*, 1989. Science Press, Beijing.

Andre Marchand, *Champignons du Nord et du Midi*, Vol. 2, 1973. Societe Mycologique des Pyrenees Mediterraneennes, Perpignan, France.

Teresa Marrone & Drew Parker, *Mushrooms of the Northwest*, 2019. Adventure Publications, Cambridge, Minn.

Charles McIlvaine & Robert Macadam, *One Thousand American Fungi*, 1902. Dover Publications, New York, NY.

R.F.R. McNabb, *The Boletaceae of New Zealand* in *New Zealand Journal of Botany* 6 (137–176), 1968.

Orson Miller, *Mushrooms of North America*. E.P. Dutton & Co., New York, NY.

Andreas Neuner, *Chatto Nature Guides' Mushrooms and Fungi*, 1978. Chatto & Windus, London.

Mary Palm & Elwin Stewart, *Typification and Nomenclature of Selected Suillus Species* in *Mycologia* 78 (325–333), 1986.

David Pegler, *A Preliminary Agaric Flora of East Africa*, 1977. Her Majesty's Stationary Office, London.

A.H. Smith & Harry Thiers, *The Boletes of Michigan*, 1971. University of Michigan Press, Ann Arbor, Mich.

Mirko Svrcek, *The Hamlyn Book of Mushrooms and Fungi*, 1983. Artia, Prague.

Harry Thiers, *California Mushrooms: A Field Guide to the Boletes*, 1975. Hafner Press, New York, NY.

Lucius Von Frieden, *Mushrooms of the World*, 1969. Bobbs-Merrill, Indianapolis, Ind.

Wikipedia.org, *Suillus luteus*.

Suillus tomentosus (Kauffman) Singer

*It is possible the edibility varies
with the variety eaten.*

It's been a number of years now since club member Harold Mead first found an odd collection of **Suillus tomentosus** under shore pine near Heart Lake just south of Anacortes. The odd part, of course, is the specimen on the far left of the featured photo. It has a totally different pore color. Harold had no problem keying it out. But Harold is a colorist, as you would expect an expert photographer to be. Orange is orange and dingy ochre is dingy ochre. So why would a collection of this rather unexciting Suillus suddenly show up with carrot orange pores? I agreed with Harold. I found it perplexing.

Suillus tomentosus, a.k.a. the Poor Man's Slippery Jack, was first described by Calvin Kauffman from Tolland, Colorado, in 1921. It is known to be a variable species. There are variations in cap colors (see photo below of a specimen from southeastern Oregon), cap fibrils, pore mouths, and even the glandular dots on the stipe. But there is nowhere in the literature a reference to pure orange pores. The internet shed no light. If you google "orange-pored boletes" you get **Boletus subvelutipes** and relatives, whose normal pore colors are orange.

I had two theories. The orange pores would represent a genetic event similar to an albino specimen. Or there were carotenes in the soil that were picked up by the mycelium. There was

also a possibility that Harold had found a new species. I didn't know where to go with this. Then, in the winter of 2014, I received my copy of *Field Mycology*. There, on page 15 of the January issue was a photo of **Suillellus satanas** from Spain. Three of the carpophores had the normal blood-red pores. A fourth had bright orange pores. It appeared to be the same syndrome, only now in the genus Suillellus.

An email to the editor revealed that he had seen this same orange-pored syndrome before in **Boletus erythropus**, **Rubroboletus legaliae**, and **Leccinellum crocipodium**. This meant five different genera within the Boletaceae shared this trait. In some cases the orange pored specimen was so close to the nearest specimen with normal pore color that their caps were touching. It would be hard to think of them as two separate organisms.

The next course of action was to examine both pore colors microscopically. We used one of Harold's orange-pored specimens from the Anacortes area and an ochre-spored specimen found with lodgepole pine at Easy Pass by Jack Waytz. The results are in the table, next page.

There was more variation than I had expected. I then suspected that the orange pored anomalies had led to some misidentifications. If you fasten on the differences in spore and cys-

Suillus tomentosus from southeast Oregon

tidia sizes, you might see why.

With no new information forthcoming, let's get into normal **Suillus tomentosus**. Most authors list caps at 5–12 cm wide, convex to plane with inrolled margins at first. However, Bandoni & Szczawinski reported monsters up to 20 cm wide with stems 15 cm long in British Columbia. They are subviscid under a coating of dense fibrils that become more separated as the cap expands. The grayish-olive fibrils also change color in age in the Rockies. They become so reddish in higher elevations that one thinks the entire cap is red. Coastal specimens keep their grayish-olive fibrils, which cover a generally straw colored ground color. Inland from the Pacific Coast, cap colors are canary yellow to yellow orange. Stems are reportred as 4–11 cm long and 1–3 cm thick. They are equal or slightly expanded at the bases, yellow brown and covered with glandular dots. These dots are gray brown at first, then become deep violet to black in age. If smeared from handling, the whole stem turns brown. According to Kauffman's original description the tubes are yellow ochre at first, then tawny olive in age. From the Colorado Rockies, Evenson reports cinnamon colored pores that stain brown to bluish brown when bruised. Most authors report a strong bluing reaction from the pore surface, but a weaker reaction in all other parts. There is no velar material. The tubes are adnate or depressed when reaching the stem. The basal mycelium is whitish at first becoming pale vinaceous to red-

	Orange-Pored	Ochre-Pored
Spore sizes	8.9–12 x 3–4.5µm	7.7–9.4 x 2.8–3.4µm
Caulocystidia	30–47 x 5–7µm	45–70 x 7.5–10µm
Cheilocystidia	27–49 x 5–7.2µm	26–48.5 x 5–7µm
Pleurocystidia	52.5–64 x 13.8–16.8µm	35–57 x 6–8µm

LOOK-ALIKES

Suillus variegatus from Scotland

Suillus bellinii from Spain

dish at maturity. And the spores are dark olive brown.

According to McKenny & Stuntz, no other Northwestern bolete has both the bluing reaction and the brownish color of very young pores.

The Poor Man's Slippery Jack is always found with pine, especially two-needle pine. It prefers shore pine on the Pacific coast, jack pine in Michigan, New Brunswick, and Quebec, and lodgepole

LOOK-ALIKE

Xerocomus subtomentosus

Suillus tomentosus, sequenced - another view.

pine in the Sierras, the Rockies, and the eastern Cascades. Besides these locations, it has been found by Kroeger in sand dunes on Haida Gwaii, B.C., reported from North Carolina by Ernst Both, noticed by Grund and Harrison on Cape Breton Island, and seen by Yoshikazu Murata on Hokkaido, Japan, in 1976.

A number of close relatives and look-alikes follows here:

Suillus discolor: Differs by having dark brown to olive-brown tube mouths at first, reddish tones at the base of the stem, a cap context that turns pinkish and then lilaceous with KOH, and basal mycelium that is ochre to salmon buff. This variety is particularly common at Priest Lake, Idaho.

Xerocomus subtomentosus: Differs by its dry, velvety brown cap surface that often becomes areolate in age. It has no glandular dots on the stem, and can be found with both oak and pine.

Suillus variegatus: A very similar European species that differs by lacking glandular dots on the stem, by having bronze colored spores, and by having flesh that turns gray when cooked. Found with Scotch pine in Scotland.

Suillus subvariegatus: Lacks the glandular dots on the stem, has spores 9–14 μm long, and pale yellow to pale orange tubes.

Suillus fuscotomentosus: Differs by having areolate olive-brown caps with fibrils that do not turn blue when bruised, and yellow pores.

Suillus americanus: Differs by its appendiculate velar remnants on the cap margins, brighter yellow viscid caps, and failure to turn blue when bruised.

Suillus punctipes: A species from eastern North America that has an almond odor and does not stain blue.

Suillus subaureus: Another eastern species that differs by its brown spores and a cap context that stains reddish when bruised.

Suillus hirtellus: Differs by its dull cinnamon spores and a pore surface that turns vinaceous-brown when bruised.

Suillus californicus: A questionable species with a dry, subtomentose cap, black glandular dots on a yellow stem, and yellow pores that exude drops that blacken in age. The flesh does not bruise blue.

Boletinus punctatipes: Differs by its smooth pale orange caps, brownish pores, and larger cystidia.

483

Suillus reticulatus: Differs by its viscid red-brown caps and yellow stems with yellow reticulation on the upper half.

Suillus bellinii: A Mediterranean species found with two-needle pines, it differs by its whitish, viscid caps with pale mauve to chestnut discolorations in age.

Microscopically, Dr. Thiers gives the most thorough report. Spores were described as sub-fusiform, narrowing slightly at both ends, thin walled, and measuring 7–11 x 3.5–4.5 μm. The tube trama was gelatinous in KOH and divergent. The pileus cuticle was a tangled ixotrichodermium with scattered fascicles of hyphae representing the scales on the cap surface. Caulocystidia, cheilocystidia, and pleurocystidia were all clavate to cylindrical. No clamps were seen. The only thing I can add to this description is the presence of a few mucronate cystidia (a nipple on the apex) among the caulocystidia of both ochre-pored and orange-pored specimens.

At about this time, Dr. Fred Rhoades came over to supervise the set-up for taking photos of microscopic features. This is a tremendous step forward, including the calibration of the images on the monitor, and here you see our first effort....the candelabra cheilocystidia of ochre-pored **S. tomentosus**.

As you might expect from a Suillus that can evidently reach 20 cm in width, a number of experts have tried dining on it. Here is a smattering of their opinions:

Harold Mead with partner Maggie Sullivan at NMA's Wild Mushroom Show

Geoffrey Kibby: "When cut, it has an acid, fruity odor."

Grund & Harrison: "It apparently has an acid taste even after cooking."

Smith & Thiers: "The taste starts off mild, but by the time the squamules turn reddish, the taste is often rather acid. Sometimes the reverse is true."

Vera Evenson: "It has a reputation as a second class edible and is best when very young."

Bandoni & Szczawinski: "Edible and good."

David Biek: "Edible and good. One of the better species."

David Arora: "Insipid. In a group noted for its blandness, it ranks near the bottom."

Harry Thiers: "Edible but of poor quality."

Hope & Orson Miller in 1980: "The flavor is not outstanding, but the great numbers make it a desirable choice. We have fed 30 people at a time in the Canadian Rockies, and most have enjoyed the taste."

Hope & Orson Miller in 2006: "**Suillus tomentosus** has caused gastric upset, including diarrhea and vomiting. Edible with caution."

Smith: "Since there are a number of variations of this species, it is possible that the edible qualities vary with the variety eaten."

Dr. Smith might be onto something. If you ate a plateful of the orange-pored variety you might discover a brand new flavor or maybe a new way of getting sick.

BIBLIOGRAPHY

David Arora, *All That the Rain Promises and More*, 1991. Ten Speed Press, Berkeley, Caif.

David Arora, *Mushrooms Demystified*, 1986. Ten Speed Press, Berkeley, Calif.

Robert Bandoni & Adam Szczawinski, *Guide to Common Mushrooms of British Columbia*, 1964. British Columbia Provincial Museum, Victoria, B.C.

Alan & Arleen Bessette & William Roody, *North American Boletes*, 2000. Syracuse University Press, Syracuse, NY.

Ernst Both, *The Boletes of North America*, 1993. Buffalo Museum of Science, Buffalo, NY.

Guillaume Essartier & Pierre Roux, 2011. *Le Guide des Champignons, France et Europe*, Editions Belin, Paris.

Vera Evenson, *Mushrooms of Colorado*, 1997. Denver Botanic Gardens, Denver.

Darryl Grund & Kenneth Harrison, *Nova Scotian Boletes* in *Bibliotheca Mycologica* 37 (1–283), 1976.Calvin Kauffman, *The Mycological Flora of the Higher Rockies of Colorado* in *Papers of the Michigan Academy of Science, Arts, and Letters* 1 (101–150), 1921.

Geoffrey Kibby, *An Illustrated Guide to Mushrooms and Other Fungi of North America*, 1993. Dragon's World, London.

Paul Kroeger, Bryce Kendrick, Oluna Ceska, & Christine Roberts, *The Outer Spores: Mushrooms of Haida Gwaii*, 2012. Mycologue Publications, Sidney-by-the-Sea, B.C.

Hope & Orson Miller, *Mushrooms in Color*, 1980. E.P. Dutton, New York, NY.

Hope & Orson Miller, *North American Mushrooms*, 2006. Morris Book Publishing, Guilford, Conn.

Yosikazu Murata, *The Boletes of Hokkaido 1. Suillus micheli ex S.F. Gray emend Snell* in *Transactions of the Mycological Society of Japan* 17 (149–158), 1976.

Giovanni Pacioni & Gary Lincoff, *Simon & Schuster's Guide to Mushrooms*, 1981. Simon & Schuster's, New York, NY.

Rolf Singer, Walter Snell, & Esther Dick, *Notes on Boletes, XI* in *Mycologia* 51 (564–577), 1959.

A.H. Smith & Harry Thiers, *A Contribution Toward a Monograph of North American Species of Suillus*, 1964. University of Michigan Press, Ann Arbor, Mich.

A.H. Smith, Harry Thiers, & Orson Miller, *The Species of Suillus and Fuscoboletinus of the Priest River Experimental Forest and Vicinity* in *Lloydia* 28 (120–138), 1965.

A.H. Smith & Nancy Weber, *The Mushroom Hunters' Field Guide*, 1958. University of Michigan Press, Ann Arbor, Mich.

Walter Snell & Esther Dick, *The Boleti of Northeastern North America*, 1970. J. Cramer, Lehre, Germany.

Eric Soothill & Alan Fairhurst, *The New Field Guide to Fungi*, 1978. Michael Joseph, London.

Harry Thiers, *California Boletes III. The Genus Suillus* in *Madrono* 19 (148–160), 1967.

Harry Thiers, *California Mushrooms: A Field Guide to the Boletes*, 1975. Hafner Press, New York, NY.

Harry Thiers, *The Genus Suillus in the Western United States* in *Mycotaxon* 9 (285–296), 1979.

Harry Thiers, *The Status of the Genus Suillus in the United States* in *Nova Hedwigia, Beihefte* 51 (247–278), 1975.

Tremella encephala Willdenow

The consistency is dependent on the amount of host material it engulfs.

At first glance, these two photos of **Tremella encephala** appear to represent different species. One is flesh colored and so shiny as to appear opalescent. The other looks like a rubbery, pale orange cerebrum dusted with white powder. There is perhaps no jelly fungus as varied in appearance as **Tremella encephala**, happily called "Conifer Brain" by Roberts & Evans.

The introductory photo represents the more typical flesh colored form. It was found at Birch Bay on April 18, 1986, on a dead Douglas fir branch. **Tremella encephala** parasitizes **Stereum sanguinolentum**, and you can see these scab-like fruiting bodies in the photo. This specimen was subglobose to cerebriform with irregularly lobed margins, somewhere between rubbery and gelatinous in texture, and of a pale flesh color. It was fruiting alongside the Stereum, not on it.

The photo below represents a find by the late Dave Wenzler on Chuckanut Mountain on May 26, 1991. The consistency was tough and rubbery, not gelatinous. The brain-like blob measured 3 ½ by 4 ½ cm. The colors varied from pale orange to yellow orange dusted with a layer of white powder. When cut in half vertically, the interior was duplex. It had an inner hard, white core surrounded by the rubbery orange exterior, roughly 1 mm thick. Dave had found a colony of these on coniferous wood in a clear cut.

I didn't even know the genus. Dr. Scott Redhead took a look at it during his sabbatical at the University of Washington. He immediately pointed out the huge sterigmata on the basidia that looked like tuning forks. The longest measured 140 mm in length. (The average sterigma might measure 2–5 mm in length.) The basidia were almost spherical, measuring 16–17 x 13–15 µm. They were clamped at the bases, and when looked at in cross-section, looked like sections of a grapefruit. The spores were ovate and measured 8.6–10 x 7–8.9 µm. Scott informed me we were looking at a Tremella. He seemed surprised I hadn't examined one microscopically before.

No matter. Everything to time. Now that I knew the genus, it was time for Dr. Robert Bandoni, the jelly fungus expert who lived just across the border in Delta, British Columbia. By now it was 1994. Dr. Bandoni kindly agreed to take it on. He wrote back that it was indeed **Tremella encephala**, noting that "basidiocarp form and color are both extremely variable. The white fuzzy appearance is caused by heavy sporulation, the bloom consisting of spores, epibasidia, yeast cells, etc., and is common in Tremellas only under ideal conditions for sporulation. There were abundant clamps and chlamydospore-like cells in the context. The hyphae of the host (the Stereum) make up the bulk of the fruiting body, and also determine its size and consistency. The actual Tremella consists only of the thin, gelatinous layer on the surface. The context of this outer layer is monomitic, meaning it has only

Tremella encephala with heavy sporulation

T. encephala's obliging host, Stereum sanguinolentum, from B.C.

generative hyphae, in this case without clamps. The inner core has clamped hyphae. There are a dozen or so species in this group. The consistency in each case is dependent upon the amount of host material it engulfs."

This parasitic transformation so influenced Fries that he created another genus for it in 1818, the genus Naematelia. It never really caught on. Bandoni resurrected it in 1966 and then subsequently sank it. He argued that these were true Tremellas simply encompassing parasitized Stereums, not a new genus in itself. According to Rockett & Kramer, the immature basidia are called probasidia. According to Martin, as the basidia grow they turn into metabasidia and feature four cruciate-septate sections. **Tremella encephala** also has smaller secondary spores called chlamydospores. These measure 6–8 x 5–6 µm and are derived from the parasitized Stereum.

Although first recorded from Europe, the Conifer Brain is a worldwide species with collections recorded from Argentina, Australia, Japan, North America, and Asia. It has several look-alikes:

Tremella aurantia: A.k.a. Witches Butter differs by its more convoluted, gelatinous texture and its bright yellow-orange color that fades in age. It parasitizes **Stereum hirsutum** on numerous hardwoods, including the alder seen in the photo.

Myxarium nucleatum: A whitish jelly fungus that turns pale brick color to pinkish-brown in age, but also differs by having

Tremella aurantia from Sudden Valley, Wash.

Tremella fuciformis from Dominican Republic

Phaeotremella foliacea from California

LOOK-ALIKE

Ductifera pululahuana

hard, cream colored granules within the gelatinous lobes.

Exidia thuretiana: Tough, gelatinous, white fruiting bodies up to 1 cm wide, but often fused in masses on hardwood logs. It can become pinkish in age, but differs by drying out into a yellow crust.

Tremella fuciformis: Differs by having more translucent fruiting bodies consisting of upright branches and lobes that sag when hydrated. A pan tropical species.

Phaeotremella foliacea: Differs by its pale brown to dark brown ruffled folds and slightly larger subglobose spores at 7–9 x 6.5–8.5 μm. This brown gelatinous mass can reach 15 cm in width.

Ductifera pululahuana: A white to ivory jelly fungus on debarked hardwood logs that gets tinged brown or purplish in age. It also differs by its allantoid spores.

The few guides that cover **Tremella encephala** claim it is a rare species. The taste and odor are reported as fungoid. The dried up fruiting bodies look like cinnamon-brown lumps on a log. And there is not much news on edibility. According to Francisco de Diego Calonge, it appears in northern Spain "where it could generate some interest as an edible because the brain-like appearance, the hard interior, and the habit on pine make it easy to identify." On the other hand, Stefan Buczacki, termed the species "inedible." Bruno Cetto went one step further and commented on the edibility with just one word, "wertlos."

BIBLIOGRAPHY

Robert Bandoni, *The Genus Naematelia* in *American Midland Naturalist* 66 (319–328), 1961.

Stefan Buczacki, *Fungi of Britain and Europe*, 1989. University of Texas Press, Austin, Texas.

Francisco de Diego Calonge, *Setas—Guia Ilustrada*, 1979. Ediciones Mundi-Prensa, Madrid.

Bruno Cetto, *Enzyklopadie der Pilze, Band 1*, 1987. Arti Grafiche Saturnia, Trento, Italy.

Dennis Desjardin, Michael Wood, & Fred Stevens, *California Mushrooms*, 2015. Timber Press, Portland, Ore.

Pamela & Martin Ellis, *Fungi Without Gills*, 1990. Chapman & Hall, London.

Ian Gibson, *Trial Field Guide to Pileate Jelly Fungi in the Pacific Northwest*, 2008. Pacific Northwest Key Council, Seattle, Wash.

Walter Julich, *Parasitic Heterobasidiomycetes on Other Fungi* in *International Journal of Mycology and Lichenology* 1 (189–203), 1983.

George W. Martin, *Revision of the North Central Tremellales* in *State University of Iowa Studies* in *Natural History* 19, No.3, 1952.

Gabriel Moreno, Jose Luis Manjon, & Alvaro Zugaza, *La Guia de Incafo de los Hongos de la Peninsula Iberica, Tomo I*, 1986. Incafo, S.A., Madrid.

Peter Roberts & Shelley Evans, *The Book of Fungi*, 2011. University of Chicago Press, Chicago.

Timothy Rockett & C.L. Kramer, *The Tremellales of Kansas* in *Transactions of the Kansas Academy of Science* 76 (107–137), 1973.

Anna-Elise Torkelsen, *Tremellaceae in Nordic Macromycetes, Vol. 3*, 1997. Nordsvamp, Copenhagen.

Anna-Elise Torkelsen, *The Genus Tremella in Norway* in *Nytt Magasin for Botanikk* 15 (225–239), 1968.

Roy Watling, *Identification of the Larger Fungi*, 1973. Hulton Educational Publications, Amersham, England.

Tricholoma 'apium' J. Schaeffer

*The odor is a combination of fennel,
smoked chicory, and a floor detergent.*

Tricholoma apium demonstrating occasional blue stem base

As do most of these myco-adventures, it all started off with a hike along a trail. It turns out that almost every day of the year, Jack Waytz, our newsletter editor, walks his dogs up a dirt road on Galbraith Mountain just west of Sudden Valley. Occasionally I join him on a dog walk for the fungi that abound on the sides of the road. It was on October 14, 2004, a rather grim light sort of day, and after about an hour we left the road to foray above an embankment. Jack was a little ahead and after a few minutes urged me to look at an interesting Cortinarius he had found. But I was thrashing around in thick, uneven conifer duff battling with a tangle of downed Doug fir branches. While trying to extricate myself I almost stepped on a cluster of brown capped mushrooms. Turning one over, I discovered copious mycelium.

"Hold it a sec!" I shouted back, "I've got to deal with this odd Leucopaxillus first."

And so the saga began.

The specimens had dull brown areolate (cracked) caps, stems that tapered towards the base, and a powerful odor I couldn't identify. Back at the lab the following day I discovered the spores remained inamyloid in Melzer's solution. This was no Leucopaxillus. A key to genera soon landed me on Tricholoma.

I then turned to the Tricholoma section of *Fungi of Switzerland*, Vol. 3 to look at drawings of microscopic features I should look out for. At the very second page of Tricholomas, I froze in my tracks. There, right in front of me, was a photo of the specimens we found off the trail.

The microscopic data soon affirmed the connection. We had stumbled across (literally) **Tricholoma apium**, a species apparently so rare that it has been on the endangered species list in Europe. Even today it is on the red list of threatened species in Norway. This was the Tricholoma Paul Kroeger had advised me to be on the lookout for. He had found it numerous times in the Mount Elphinstone forest in British Columbia, and due to its rarity, its presence in Elphinstone had spared portions of that forest from being clearcut.

Two photos are needed to do it justice. In the lead photo, you can see the mycelium at the stem base. Below the mycelium you can see the ashy gray substance of the soil. Northwestern collections of **T. apium** tend to fruit from the ashy-gray A-E layer of podzolic soils. Leached minerals from the upper layer of humus tend to accumulate here. This phenomenon is not mentioned for European specimens. In the above photo you can see the fissured caps, a hallmark of the species. The specimen on the left shows a blue-gray discoloration at the stem base. This trait is also missing from European descriptions.

Caps range from 4–15 cm wide. They are irregularly convex with low, broad umbos and strongly inrolled margins. The surface is dry, mat, and tomentose at first becoming cracked and squamulose in age. The squamules are brown on a paler brown to ochre brown ground. The margins are lobed and sometimes faintly striate. Several Dutch authors believe the caps are white at first, but turn brownish in sunlight.

There are two cap color versions in both Europe and North America. One is the brown to ochre brown seen here. They can even become rusty brown in age. The other is an olive to yellow-green version I have not yet seen. The gill attachment is notched to emarginate or almost free. They are very crowded, white at first, then with a yellowish buff tinge in age. In our specimens a few were forked halfway to the stem. And Pilat discovered that very rarely the gills will turn black when bruised. The stems measure from 1–2 ½ cm thick and 4–15 cm long. They are white floccose at the apex becoming minutely squamulose below. The lower half darkens to sordid ochre or gray in age (or even gray blue). Moser described the stems as turning yellowish when bruised. The spores were buff in deposit, inamyloid. The odor was very peculiar. It was sort of a combination of fennel, toasted chicory, and a commercial floor detergent. European authors

Tricholoma sulphurescens

Tricholoma subsejunctum from Georgia

often describe the odor to be like celery or fenugreek.

Microscopically, I found smooth-walled, subglobose spores with prominent apiculi. Most contained oil drops. The spores measured 4–4.5 x 2.9–3.9 µm. The quotient was 1.33. (The Tricholoma expert, Alfredo Riva, found the spores to be more globose with a quotient of 1.14.) The basidia were 2–4 spored, clavate, and rather slender. They measured 23–27.2 x 5.1–5.7 µm. The gill trama were of parallel hyphae 3.3–14.9 µm in width. No cystidia were seen. Nor any clamps. The pileipellis consisted of roughly parallel but intertwining hyphae 2.9–12.9 µm wide, with some exerted ends.

As for reagents, the cap context supposedly turns gray green in ferrous sulphate while the gills stain yellow in NH3.

Just as authorities tend to disagree on the odor of **Tricholoma**

Tricholoma caligatum var. nardosmium from Georgia

apium, there are also varying opinions on taste. Here are a few samples:

Bas, Kuyper, Noordeloos, Vellinga: "Taste mild to somewhat spicy or subfarinaceous."

Alfredo Riva: "Taste sweetish, aromatic."

Umberto Nonis: "Taste agreeable."

André Marchand: "Taste sweet, weakly in sync with the odor."

I found the taste to be mild but peculiar. Umberto Nonis found it to be edible and of a good flavor. Marchand found it to be edible in reduced quantities and mixed with other mushrooms. Bruno Cetto wrote, "consumed in massive quantities it renders the pasta inedible due to the bitter taste." After carefully considering these opinions, I took a specimen down to the boat for a quick sauté. For comparison purposes I also took along a chanterelle and one **Russula vinosa**. The chanterelle got an "A." The **Russula vinosa** got a D (poor flavor and mealy texture.) And the **Tricholoma apium** got a C+. It had a firm texture and acceptable flavor with no negative after effects.

In the Pacific Northwest, **T. apium** seems to prefer old-growth Douglas fir. In Europe it is found under pine and spruce in poor, sandy soils in northern Italy and throughout central Europe.

Its closest look-alikes include:

Tricholoma sulphurescens: Which differs by having flesh that turns yellow when cut.

Tricholoma luridum: Which differs by its farinaceous odor and larger ellipsoidal spores.

Tricholoma columbetta: Which has larger spores, a bitter taste, and an odor faintly of radish.

Tricholoma psammopus: Differs by having a slightly bitter taste and a dense covering of rusty-brown squamules on the stem.

Tricholoma subsejunctum: A species from the Deep South that can have the same gray-brown cap color but has a more virgate texture of innate fibrils radiating from disc to margin.

Tricholoma caligatum var. glaucescens: Another southern species that can have some blue on the upper stipe, but the caps are more radially scaly than those of **T. apium**. It also has a disagreeable taste.

Tricholoma murrillianum: Differs by its often massive size, huge cottony ring on the stem, and potent aroma of cinnamon and other spices.

Tricholoma caligatum var. nardosmium: Yet another southern variety that differs by its radially brown scaly caps and odor of spikenard, which derives from an aromatic plant in the valerian family in India.

Julius Schaeffer first described the olive-capped version of **Tricholoma apium** from Germany in 1925. (This competent mycologist remains to this day the only professional to have died from mushroom poisoning. He ate **Paxillus involutus**, far more toxic in Europe than in the Pacific Northwest.) Then in 1946 Pilat & Svrcek introduced the brown-capped version as **Tricholoma helviodor** from Czechoslovakia. They named it helviodor because it smelled like **Lactarius helvus**. These authors maintained that up until 1959 **Tricholoma helviodor** had not been found outside of Czechoslovakia. Eventually Moser discovered that the two species were conspecific microscopically and created the combination **Tricholoma apium var. helviodor**. It is this brown capped version that I had found. However, if you are try-

Tricholoma caligatum var. glaucescens from Georgia

ing to use an endangered fungus to save a forest, trying to explain **var. helviodor** to a room full of timber barons might not get you very far. Eventually the lumpers prevailed and the **var. helviodor** is now a synonym of **Tricholoma apium**.

In brief, **Tricholoma apium** can be told apart from all other Tricholomas by its olive to brownish cracked caps, the powerful but confused odor, the very small spores, and the tendency of the stems to taper towards their bases. Collections from the Pacific Northwest can sometimes have a gray-blue tinge at their stipe bases and copious white mycelium. Since none of these characteristics have been noted for European collections, I have put apostrophes around 'apium' at the heading. DNA sequencing can give us an answer down the road.

It turns out that **Tricholoma apium** has a history in the Pacific Northwest. Dr. Stuntz used to call it "that cracked mud-capped Tricholoma." He found it in 1963 at Silver Springs near the White River, and also near Poulsbo. Dr. A.H. Smith found it at the Longmire Campground. Ben Woo also logged a collection at Greenwater River. Presumably all these finds were from Washington State. And according to Dr. Redhead,

Dr. Clark Ovrebo claims to have found it in Michigan. Meanwhile, up in British Columbia, Paul Kroeger has found it so often in the Pacific Northwest, he wonders if it might it not have originated here. He has found the brown-capped version at Buntzen Lake on the lower mainland and in the Cowitchan Valley on Vancouver Island. He has found the olive-capped version at Whistler and on Bowen Island, all these finds from British Columbia. Oluna Ceska has found the **Tricholoma apium** twice on Vancouver Island, once at Point No Point near Sooke, and once at Wickinninnish Beach near Tofino. And let's not forget Fortunato Armellini who found a collection near Hope, B.C.

This article ends with an intriguing theory of Kroeger's. Since the only spot on earth where **Tricholoma apium** seems almost common is the Elphinstone Forest, might it not have originated there? In the early days of colonization, exploring biologists often sent back plant and tree samples to their motherlands. Spores might have been transported in this manner to Germany, Italy, Czechoslovakia, France, Switzerland, and Norway, all the countries, according to Riva, where it has been found.

BIBLIOGRAPHY

Cornelis Bas, Machiel Noordeloos, & Else Vellinga, *Strophariaceae, Tricholomataceae in Flora Agaracina Neerlandica 4, (107–148)*, 1999.

Alan & Arleen Bessette, William Roody & Steve Trudell, *Tricholomas of North America*, 2013. University of Texas Press, Austin, Texas.

J. Breitenbach & F. Kranzlin, *Fungi of Switzerland, Vol. 3*, 1991. Edition Mykologia, Lucerne.

Bruno Cetto, *I Funghi dal Vero, Vol.2*, 1976. Arti Grafiche Saturnia, Trento.

Regis Courtecuisse & Bernard Duhem, *Mushrooms and Toadstools of Britain and Europe*, 1994. Harper-Collins, London.

Final Report, *Forest Practices Board—Complaint 950036*, 1996.

Gro Gulden, *Tricholoma in Nordic Macromycetes, Vol.2*, 1992. Nordsvamp, Copenhagen.

André Marchand, *Champignons du Nord et du Midi, Vol. 9*, 1986. Societe Mycologique des Pyrenees Mediterraneennes, Perpignan, France.

Edmund Michael, Bruno Hennig, & Hanns Kreisel, *Handbuch für Pilzfreunde, Vol. 3*, 1987. Gustav Fischer Verlag, Stuttgart.

Meinhard Moser, *Keys to Agarics and Boleti*, 1983. Translated and published by Roger Phillips, London.

Umberto Nonis, *Guide des Champignons Gastronomiques*, 1984. Hippocrene Books, New York, NY.

Albert Pilat & Otto Usak, *Mushrooms and Other Fungi*, 1961. Peter Nevill, London.

Alfredo Riva, *Tricholoma (Fr.) Staude in Fungi Non Delineati V*, 1998.

Alfredo Riva, *Tricholoma (Fr.) Staude in Fungi Europaei*, 1988. Edizioni Candusso, Alassio, Italy.

Steve Trudell & Joe Ammirati, *Mushrooms of the Pacific Northwest*, 2009. Timber Press, Portland, Ore.

DIGERHEGS

Tricholoma populinum J. Lange

By Dr. Tillman Moore

*Almost all stems were hollow,
even in the button stage.*

I think you may agree that most of our mushroom marauders stalk the wily "shrooms" by using our visual apparatus. Certainly, we "look" for mushrooms on our forays. But I have heard a few gnarly aficionados claim they could smell the caps while on a favorable jaunt in the woods. It might even be true, although I doubt it, because a fair spread of the fruiting bodies does release a few trillion spores on a given day, and they could tickle the olfactory bulbs. Pigs do sniff out truffles, after all. I suppose someone will claim they can "hear" mushrooms as they pop through the turf or as their spores hit the ground. That will be the day!

Whatever the case, with the Poplar Tricholoma, I found still another way, namely by feeling them with my feet, or more accurately with my boots. I sensed these sometimes invisible mushrooms by stepping on them and realizing that old terra firma was not as firma as it should be. I was wearing hiking boots because it was in mid-November after an average wet fall. The sensation was a rubbery squish as I walked between several large cottonwood trees. Beneath the grass and dirt were dozens upon dozens of brownish mushrooms in the grassy carpet within 50–60 feet of a lake. A week later, many I had missed the first time around had erupted through the cover to form traditional caps, but I did discover them first by the sensation of "feel," or more accurately, proprioception.

What I had found were hundreds of little humps (Arora calls them "mushrumps") in the grass in no discernable pattern. Under them were clusters of 3 to up to 6 mushrooms with brownish, rounded caps. Dirt was stuck to the sticky 2–7 cm wide caps. These were darker in the center, changing somewhat abruptly to a pale buff about a centimeter in from the margins. The only unpleasant experience was sore fingers pricked by runners of berry canes, almost always in proximity to the mushrooms which were

LOOK-ALIKE

Tricholoma pessundatum from California

within 10–20 feet from the cottonwoods. The gills were white, more adnate than notched, and close, browning when old or bruised, and tending to be brittle, but not as much as in Russula. A careful spore print was definitely white.

The caps and stems were obviously attractive to slugs externally, as well as two types of fly larvae internally, even in some young specimens. These critters work their way to the caps as both the mushroom and the maggots mature. The buttons arose directly from the bases of mature stems and had brown caps even at 3–4 mm in size. No veil was ever observed. On breaking the cap, a strong farinaceous or branny odor was obvious, and the thick flesh was rubbery, firm, and white. It did not discolor when cut or bruised. Bunches of mushrooms were supported by often curved stems 1–4 cm thick which were sometimes expanded at the bases, beneath which the stems tapered and appeared to originate from a single point. No basal mycelial mass, volva, or ring was observed.

The dull white stems were often twisted grotesquely and were always rusty brownish at their extreme tapered bases, and central and confluent with the abundant flesh of the caps. The stems were tough, certainly more rubbery than chalky or fibrous, and did not break easily. Most of the stems were hollow or cavernous, even in the button stage, and in many of the more mature specimens, the central hollow contained 3–5 white, string-like strands 1–2 mm thick lying free in the

Tricholoma imbricatum

cavity. None were pithy or stuffed at any stage, as I understand these terms.

Now the above original description very well fits the genus Tricholoma and the species populinum. However, hollow stems are a characteristic of some unfriendly Tricholomas, and all the books I had looked at had described the stems of **Tricholoma populinum** as solid. My curiosity was quickly aroused to seek help! I brought some specimens to the 1995 Wild Mushroom Show for the experts to key out, and wrote a single-spaced full-page letter to David Arora, from whom I have still not heard. Buck McAdoo correctly identified the mushroom. He also made his exotic and occasionally slightly dusty collection of reference books available for further research, thereby helping with the following admittedly incomplete description. Thanks for both! But any error in this brief synopsis is solely my responsibility.

The genus Tricholoma belongs to the Order Agaricales and the Class Hymenomycete in the Subdivision of Basidiomycetes. They constitute a large division of terrestrial mushrooms with a central fleshy stalk, volva and veil generally absent, white to pale cream spore print, mycorrhizal in general, and peaking in September through January. Its species are perplexing even to the professional. It is stated that there are 91 described species of 26 genera in the Tricholo-

mataceae, and this is still only a modest portion of the group prefaced with *Trich*, meaning hair or fringe. Careful authors, ascribing original definitive descriptions, credit Jakob Lange, a 19th century Danish mycologist, for identifying this specific mushroom. **Tricholoma populinum** is extensively described in Arora's book, *Mushrooms Demystified*.

Germane to the nature of the stem, Arora lists it as solid without reservation, as do at least two other authors. Interestingly, most descriptions of the hollow or solid issue regarding the stems of **Tricholoma populinum** are either omitted or non-committal. *The New Savory Wild Mushroom* was also non-committal but showed, in a photo, a sectioned **T. populinum** with a hollow stem and a pair of possible string-like fibers. Indeed, in *Champignons du Nord et du Midi*, Tome 9, by André Marchand, it states that the stem can be "parfois caverneux" meaning occasionally hollow. This trait he attributed to **Tricholoma populinum form campestre**. My understanding of "form" is that it is associated with a non-heritable variable, as opposed to "variety," which represents a heritable variable. Marchand also states that the flesh beneath the cuticle is pink, but I did not know to have looked for this characteristic and therefore didn't peel, just washed hard. Relating to this characteristic, the experts disagree whether the flesh stains reddish or not.

Most British authors either totally fail to mention this species or say it is rare.

All authors state the Sandy or Poplar Tricholoma to be edible, but differ in their enthusiasm. At first, Buck and I were cautious because of the inexact descriptions. I tried a slice or two fried in butter on a steak without ill effects. Then we progressively tested the dried mushrooms I had collected in the winter of 1995. There were essentially no fruitings of **T. populinum** in the same area in 1996, due to an early spell of bitter cold weather. The reconstituted specimens tasted good to me, (robust, smoky, meaty, musky) after rehydration, and neither of us suffered ill effects. Many of our members ate this mushroom in quiche at our annual Survivors Banquet in 1997. It is known that native Americans have harvested and consumed this mushroom for centuries. Arora states that **Tricholoma equestre**, **T. portentosum**, and possibly **T. imbricatum** are also edible, but advises avoidance of all other Tricholoma species because of possible confusion with the poisonous **Tricholoma pardinum** and **Tricholoma pessundatum**. Helene Schalkwijk-Barendsen describes the Tricholoma family as "confining mushrooms of which a few are choice, several less than choice, and some mildly poisonous, but none are fatal." The careful mycophagist will be certain that a brown, sticky, wavy margined cap, close gilled, white-sporing, thick stalked mushroom that is definitely growing under cottonwoods is the only one even considered for consumption. It will be cespitose (attached at the bases in clumps), and strongly farinaceous or branny in odor, which dissipates on drying. The stems can be hollow and may contain white, stringy structures in the cavity. It will be a rewarding and delicious experience if you can beat the vermin to this good, even excellent mushroom.

Addendum: Since Dr. Moore wrote this article, I (Buck) discovered that **Tricholoma pessundatum**, **Tricholoma imbricatum,** and **Tricholoma ustale** are all considered look-alikes. **T. ustale** differs by having a bitter taste and associates with oak and beech. **T. pessundatum** by its dark chestnut colored caps and associations with conifers and oak. And **T. imbricatum** by its flattened cap fibrils on a dull brick-brown ground, and its association with pine and spruce.

More importantly, two species of Tricholoma, both long considered edible, have since caused deaths in Europe. These are **Tricholoma equestre** and **Tricholoma auratum**. The latter is a stockier, larger version of the former with a more sulphur yellow stem. The *Index Fungorum* now considers it a synonym of **Tricholoma equestre**.

LOOK-ALIKE

Tricholoma ustale from Oak Harbor, Wash.

BIBLIOGRAPHY

David Arora, *Mushrooms Demystified*, 1986. Ten Speed Press, Berkeley, Calif.

Didier Borgarino & Christian Hurtado, *Le Guide des Champignons*, 2011. Edisud, Aix-en-Provence, France.

J. Breitenbach & F. Kranzlin, *Fungi of Switzerland*, *Vol.3*, 1991. Edition Mykologia, Lucerne.

Guillaume Eyssartier & Pierre Roux, *Le Guide des Champignons de France et Europe*, 2012. Editions Belin, Paris.

Phyllis Glick, *The Mushroom Trail Guide*, 1979. Holt, Rinehart, & Winston, New York, NY.

Gro Gulden, *Tricholoma in Nordic Macromycetes*, *Vol. 2*, 1992. Nordsvamp, Copenhagen.

Morten Lange & F. Bayard Hora, *A Guide to Mushrooms and Toadstools*, 1963. E.P. Dutton, New York, NY.

David Largent & Harry Thiers, *How to Identify Mushrooms to Genus, II: Field Identification of Genera, André Marchand, Champignons du Nord et du Midi, Tome 9*, 1986. Mad River Press, Eureka, Calif.

Margaret Mckenny, Daniel Stuntz, & Joe Ammirati, *The New Savory Wild Mushroom*, 1987. University of Washington Press, Seattle, Wash.

Fred Rhoades, *Fungus Notes*.

A.H. Smith & Nancy Weber, *The Mushroom Hunters' Field Guide*, 1980. University of Michigan Press, Ann Arbor, Mich.

Nancy Turner, Harriet Kuhnlein, & Keith Egger, *Plant Taxonomic Systems and Ethnobiology of Three Contemporary Indian Groups of the Northwest, Part I* in *Canadian Journal of Botany* 65, No.5 (921–927), 1987.

Tricholomopsis decora (Fries) Singer

The vast majority wrote, "edibility unknown."

In 1939 Rolf Singer created the genus Tricholomopsis to represent those species with yellow gills, stems, and basic ground color of the cap, white, smooth, inamyloid spores, large cheilocystidia, and the habit of growing on wood. **Tricholomoposis decora** (the species epithet meaning "beautiful" in Latin) is an important member of this genus. It appears every fall on our club forays but never in great quantity. It is one of those species that Margaret Dilly is referring to when she says, "Let's label all the easy ones first just to get names on the table. We can circle back later for the tough ones." It is the only species in Tricholomopsis that has dark grayish-olive to blackish squamules on the yellow cap surface. Up until now we just got it out on the table and forgot about it. But after reading about a severe poisoning case in the summer 2008 issue of Mushroom the Journal, **T. decora** deserves a little more thought.

Known as the Queen's Coat by Schalkwijk-Barendsen, the Black Tufted Wood Tricholoma by McKenny & Stuntz, the Decorated Mop by Gary Lincoff, and the Yellow Rider by the McKnights, **Tricholomopsis decora** is found throughout northern Europe and North America on conifer wood, being especially fond of hemlock and spruce. In Europe it is mostly found in the mountains.

If you are a little put out by the plethora of common names, consider its nomenclatural Latin history. Fries introduced the species as **Agaricus decorus** in 1821. Gillet moved it to Clitocybe in 1874. Karsten

Floccularia albolanaripes

moved it to Cortinellus in 1879. Quelet moved it to Tricholoma in 1882 and to Gyrophila in 1886. Saccardo moved it to Pleurotus in 1887. Kuntze moved it to Dendrosarcus in 1898. Maire declared it a variety of **Tricholoma rutilans** in 1916.... All this before Singer moved it to Tricholomopsis in 1939.

Moser describes the caps as measuring 5–10 cm wide, but Roger Phillips lists them up to 17 cm wide with stems up to 18 cm long! They are generally smaller than Moser's measurements in our area. Convex to domed at first, with incurved margins, the caps become depressed to umbilicate in age. The ground color is golden yellow, adorned with the olive-brown to dark grayish concentrically arranged scales, always more crowded at disc. The gills are a brighter yellow with entire edges that can become crenulate or pruinose in age. They are adnate, often with decurrent tooth, and readily secede from the stem. Stems run from 5–8 cm long and up to 1½ cm thick. They are solid at first, then hollow in age, sometimes centrally attached and sometimes eccentric. They are yellow with faintly pruinose apices and grayish fibrils or scales on a yellow ground near base. The odor is mild and the taste mild to slightly bitter. The spores are white, inamyloid, smooth-walled, and elliptical. A.H. Smith gives the measurements as 6–7.5 x 4.5–5 µm. In California, Arora reports them on rotting redwood. They seem to prefer downed hemlock branches and logs further north, causing a white rot of coniferous wood. Most authors report them as widespread but rather rare, never found in quantity.

This is a taxon that probably would not have been a candidate for a Mushroom of the Month profile if not for one event. A lady named Kathy Richmond, an articulate nurse from Idaho, got extremely poisoned by it. Since **Tricholomopsis decora** is more common here than where she found it in the wilds of Idaho, I thought it worthwhile encapsulating her story. She was foraying in a remote wilderness area late in the afternoon when she thought she found **Floccularia albolanaripes**. This was a species she

LOOK-ALIKES

Tricholomopsis decora - another look.

Tricholomopsis sp.   *Photo by Richard Morrison*

hadn't seen in years but always wanted to try. She picked three or four specimens as darkness fell and looked forward to a gourmet breakfast. Her husband Dave is a physician. He didn't think the mushrooms looked right for **Armillaria albolanaripes**. There was no ring on the stem and no appendiculate velar material on the cap margin. Kathy reckoned that snow could have destroyed the ring. She cooked them up anyway.

About half an hour later she noticed a hot flash coming on. This was no normal hot flash. Her skin became beet red and she began salivating excessively. She couldn't swallow it fast enough. Then she began sweating so heavily that she had to change clothes every five minutes three different times. When she started seeing double she knew the mushrooms were the cause. She and her husband, who had declined the meal, soon realized she was experiencing parasympathetic nervous system toxicity. She induced vomiting to flush out any undigested pieces, but it was already

too late. Her blood pressure dropped to 60 over 40 and her pulse was at 50. She was on the verge of no return. Luckily, Dave had some atropine on hand. He started an IV right on the kitchen table. Soon the pulse and blood pressure normalized. The hot flashes were replaced by chills so bad that she couldn't get warm under four wool blankets. After an hour of the shakes, she gradually returned to normal.

They had no idea what Kathy had eaten. Luckily, Dr. Orson Miller had retired to Idaho, and two days later he identified the culprit as **Tricholomopsis decora**. There is no way that such an experienced mycologist could get this wrong. What happened here is rather unsettling and another example of the mysterious ways of mushrooms.

If Dr. Miller hadn't seen the specimens personally, I would have surmised she had partaken of the look-alike Tricholomopsis pictured here. This is a possible new species that looks like a diminutive **Tricholomopsis decora** with rusty orange fibrils at the cap centers becoming squamulose towards the margins. It has subglobose spores measuring 7–7.7 x 6–7.2 µm, and forests of random versiform cheilocystidia measuring 56–69 x 2.1–4 µm. In a poor light, one could easily mistake it for **Tricholomopsis decora**.

But first there are lessons to be learned from their identification process. First of all, it's never a good idea to try to identify mushrooms in a failing light. Secondly, if there is an important feature missing, such as the ring, pay attention to that. And thirdly, tone down the anticipation factor. The fact that Kathy wanted to dine on that species so badly might have affected her judgment. It goes without saying that we are grateful she decided to publish her misadventure with **Tricholomopsis decora**. We wouldn't want this happening to anyone else.

Now comes the rather mysterious part. I looked up 48 sources on **Tricholomopsis decora** and not one used the term poisonous. The vast majority made no comment on the edibility or wrote "edibility unknown." The most damning report came from Pegler & Spooner, the British authors of *The Mushroom Identifier*. They noted "inedible and unpleasant." Eight other sources deemed **Tricholomopsis decora** to be inedible or of no culinary value. Three thought it was edible but not very good. But Bruno Cetto, Phyllis Glick, A.H. Smith, and Rinaldi & Tyndalo all listed it as edible. I then remembered that during David Arora's identification session this past fall at Silver Lake, a fellow in our club came up to David with **T. decora** in hand and informed him that he had eaten it without problems. I then turned to Orson Miller's *Mushrooms of North America* for possible help in the matter. This was the first mushroom guide I owned. There in the margin next to **Tricholomopsis decora** I had penned "good flavor." I must have sampled it when I lived in California in the early 1980s, but I do not recall the experience.

Would I eat it again? Maybe

LOOK-ALIKES

Tricholomopsis rutilans

Phaeolepiota aurea, Whatcom County, Wash.   Photo by Erin Moore

one at a time. I am no allergist, but the reaction inflicted on Kathy Richmond seemed worse than any allergy by itself could bring on.

Only the **Armillaria mellea** syndrome comes to mind. There have been reports of people in the Pacific Northwest who have dined in the Honey Mushroom group for years without ill effects. Then one day they will become violently sick from it. Since the first reports came in, **Armillaria mellea** has been broken up into five or six different species, so it is hard to say if just one of these "new" species is responsible or not. The substrate itself has been suspect. The **Armillaria mellea** group can parasitize conifers and hardwoods. Maybe certain trees are capable of striking back under certain conditions and inflict a toxin on the ingester. The irony is that the invading fungus isn't hurt in any way . . . only the people who eat it are.

Besides **Floccularia albolanaripes** and **Tricholomopsis sp.** (the look-alike still in search of a name), there are three other look-alikes that could be considered:

Phaeolepiota aurea: Some folks might confuse this with the Decorated Mop, but the large floppy ring and habit of fruiting on the ground are clearly different.

Tricholomopsis rutilans: Happily known as Custard and Plums, **T. rutilans** is a much larger species with beautiful wine colored scales on a yellowish ground.

Tricholomopsis sp.: Throughout the Northwest there is occasionally found a species with yellow cap, gills, and stem that differs by having orange scales on its cap. It has unusually long and narrow basidia, vermiform cheilocystidia, and nearly globose spores. If not for Dr. Orson Miller's assessment, I would have suspected Kathy of having dined on this.

Then again, **Tricholomopsis decora** is not a parasite. There really is no simple explanation here. Susan Goldhor points out in *Mushroom the Journal* that "one shouldn't minimize idiosyncratic responses to wild foods. Mushrooms are full of fascinating chemicals which give them unique colors, flavors, curative properties, and some properties that are not so friendly.'"And then if you add people to the mix with all of our different chemical make-ups leading to different types of allergies, furthermore affected by any prescription drugs in the mix, the combination with a marginal mushroom just might have led to Kathy's nightmarish experience.

BIBLIOGRAPHY

David Arora, *Mushrooms Demystified*, 1986. Ten Speed Press, Berkeley, Calif.

J. Breitenbach & F. Kranzlin, *Fungi of Switzerland, Vol.3*, 1991. Edition Mykologia, Lucerne.

Bruno Cetto, *I Funghi dal Vero, Vol.3*, 1983. Arti Grafiche Saturnia, Trento.

Robert Gilbertson & K.J. Martin, *Synopsis of Wood Rotting Fungi on Spruce in North America, Part III* in *Mycotaxon* 10 (479–501), 1980.

Phyllis Glick, *The Mushroom Trail Guide*, 1979. Holt, Rinehart, & Winston, New York, NY.

Susan Goldhor, *Caught in the Fungal Web (Envy, Crime, & Poisonings)* in *Mushroom the Journal*, Fall 2008.

J. Walton Groves, *Edible and Poisonous Mushrooms of Canada*, 1979. Research Branch, Agriculture Canada, Ottawa, Ontario.

Calvin Kauffman, *The Genus Clitocybe in the United States* in *Papers of the Michigan Academy of Science, Arts, & Letters* 8, (153–214), 1927.

Paul Kirk (ed.), *Index Fungorum*, http://www.indexfungorum.org/names/Names.asp

Gary Lincoff, *The Audubon Society Field Guide to North American Mushrooms*, 1981. Alfred A. Knopf, New York, NY.

André Marchand, *Champignons du Nord et du Midi, Tome 9*, 1986. Societe Mycologique des Pyrenees Mediterraneennes, Perpignan, France.

Margaret McKenny & Daniel Stuntz, *The Savory Wild Mushroom*, 1981. University of Washington Press, Seattle.

Vera & Kent McKnight, *The Peterson Field Guides: Mushrooms*, 1987. Houghton Mifflin, Boston.

Meinhard Moser, *Keys to Agarics and Boleti*, 1983. Translated and published by Roger Phillips, London.

David Pegler & Brian Spooner, *The Mushroom Identifier*, 1992. Smithmark Publishers, New York, NY.

Roger Phillips, *Mushrooms and Other Fungi of Great Britain & Europe*, 1981. Pan Books, London.

Kathy Richmond, *An Almost Deadly Mistake* in *Mushroom the Journal of Wild Mushrooming*, Summer 2008.

Augusto Rinaldi & Vassili Tyndalo, *The Complete Book of Mushrooms*, 1974.

Helene Schalkwijk-Barendsen, *Mushrooms of Western Canada*, 1991. Lone Pine Publishing, Edmonton, Alberta.

A.H. Smith, *Mushrooms in Their Natural Habitats*, 1949. Sawyer's, Lancaster, Penn.

A.H. Smith, *Tricholomopsis in the Western Hemisphere* in *Brittonia* 12 (41–70), 1960.

A.H. Smith, *A Field Guide to Western Mushrooms*, 1975. University of Michigan Press, Ann Arbor, Mich.

Mirko Svrcek & Jiri Kubicka, *Champignons d'Europe*, 1980. Artia, Prague.

Vascellum pratense (Persoon) Kreisel

*Old worn specimens look like
discarded cigar butts.*

Some time during the sordid September of 1996 I received my first ever phone call to come identify a fungus a toddler had chewed on. The call was from a Catholic Community Center near Sehome High School in Bellingham. The toddler had found it on a lawn. The child was doing just fine. The parents were worried about latent effects. They had heard that some toxins took several days to bring up symptoms.

The mushroom turned out to be **Vascellum pratense**, our most common lawn-dwelling puffball. Although attractively white and edible in its pristine white stage, the specimen dangled for my inspection was cracked and damaged, displaying a rather lurid shade of yellow-green from the spore mass (gleba) inside. There was an outline where teeth had chomped on the endoperidium (wall encompassing the gleba). It looked capable of poisoning Babar the elephant.

"It probably didn't taste very good," I informed the director of the center, which was not the news he wanted to hear. He was relieved to find out it wasn't a poisonous species in itself. I pointed out the obvious… a rotten one could cause stomach distress, and an uncooked rotten one even worse. After all, some folks in Colorado had recently been hospitalized after smoking puffballs, but this didn't seem to rivet the director.

The Pasture Puffball started out in the genus Lycoperdon even before the time of Linnaeus. Taxonomy was conducted in a different way back then, and anything with a semi-spherical fruiting body, including slime molds, was placed in Lycoperdon. Smarda created the genus Vascellum in 1958. According to Bob Ramsey, who wrote the trial key to the Lycoperdales for the Pacific Northwest Key Council, species in the genus Vascellum differ from Lycoperdons by having the "exoperidium and the endoperidium decompose simultaneously across the top to form a very large opening, longer than wide, often to the full diameter of the top, and a distinct separation between sterile base and gleba."

A brief explanation of terms might help. The exoperidium consists of the outer layer of soft spines that are often found on puffballs. The endoperidium is the enveloping wall of the puffball. The opening at the top of the gasterocarp is where the spores are released and subsequently dispersed by the wind. Gleba is a technical word for spore mass, and the sterile base is the area below the gleba and separated from it by a parchment-like membrane.

Vascellum pratense is a ubiquitous puffball found around the world with the exception of lowland tropics. The fruiting bodies (gasterocarps) run from 2–5 cm wide, and according to Schalkwijk-Barendsen, can reach 8 cm tall. They are pear-shaped to globose to turbinate with an outer covering of soft white spines and granules, which soon wear off. The interior is at first white and not especially firm, even in its freshest state. As the puffball matures the interior becomes yellow-green and then a sort of olive brown before ending up as a mass of powdery dark olive brown spores. The sterile base is slightly furrowed and clearly separated from the spore mass by a diaphragm. According to Arora, the sterile base becomes brownish or purplish in age. The endoperidium, or outer wall, also changes as it ages. It starts out white, then turns dingy ochre to a sort

LOOK-ALIKE

Vascellum lloydianum   *Photo by Dan Digerness*

Lycoperdon curtisii from Vermont, which differs from V. pratense by the pyramidal white spines on its white peridium

of shiny metallic brown before rupturing across the top to form a large, jagged pore that widens and crumbles until only the "bowl" of a sterile base is left. As Pegler & Spooner put it, "the old worn fruiting bodies resemble discarded cigar butts." Larger ones have been described as indented garbage cans. The visual aspect plus the mediocre flavor has induced Arora to write "better neglected than collected."

Microscopically, the spores are globose, thick-walled, and finely spiny. They measure 3.5–4 x 3.5–4.5 µm. The basidia are short and clavate, 1–4-spored, and measure 8–18 x 5–7 µm. The sterigma can run up to 5 µm in length. Below the membrane lies a zone called the sub-gleba. It consists of a mass of cellular pseudot-issue. The gleba itself consists of spores and abundant tubular hyphae called paracapillitium. These are thin-walled, branched, hyaline hyphae, 3–5 µm wide, with septa and amorphous incrustations. There are also much scarcer hyphae 2–4 µm wide, also septate, branched, and thin-walled, but dark brown in KOH. These are the capillitium. The membrane between the gleba and the sterile base consists of an inseparable layer of flattened lacunae. Vascellum has a more powdery type of gleba than Lycoperdon, whose gleba is more cottony.

The Pasture Puffball is nitrophilous (loves nitrogen), meaning it thrives in well-manured lawns, golf courses, pastures, and parks. It is often found with another puffball, **Bovista plumbea**. It is probably more common on the Pacific Coast than anywhere else in the world.

A.H. Smith introduced a close look-alike to **V. pratense**, this one also from the West Coast, which he called **Vascellum lloydianum**.

This differed from typical **V. pratense** by having a less distinct membrane between sterile base and gleba, and by opening at the top in one raggedy tear instead of stellate tears. (The featured photo is clearly **Vascellum pratense**, but the second photo includes a fruiting body with a single ragged tear across the top which suggests **Vascellum lloydianum**.) Spores often were endowed with a short stub of a pedicile. Dr. Smith suspected that it might be conspecific with **Vascellum subpratense**, a species introduced by Lloyd in 1905 as **Lycoperdon subpratense**, and since sunk by Demoulin in 1971. The *Index Fungorum* now lists it as a synonym of **Lycoperdon pratense**.

Indeed, there may be some confusion in the nomenclature. In *Index Fungorum*, **Vascellum pratense** is now listed as a synonym of **Lycoperdon pratense**. This transfer derives from DNA sequence data obtained from north European species and published in *Mycological Research* 112 by Larsson & Jepsson. They noted that "the Lycoperdon clade includes species from Lycoperdon, Vascellum, Bovistella, Morganella, Handkea, and Calvatia. The structure within the Lycoperdon clade is unresolved and several clades are more or less unsupported." **Vascellum pratense** is listed within the Lycoperdon 1 clade under Subgenus Vascellum. However, Scott T. Bates, in a thesis published in Arizona, wrote that DNA sequencing proved that Vascellum is a strong monophyletic genus, and he included **Vascellum pratense** and **Vascellum intermedium** in his clades of Arizona Lycoperdaceae. The contrasting view is best expressed by Stephanie Jarvis in her thesis on California Lycoperdaceae. She noted that "ITS sequence data suggests that both *Lycoperdon pratense* and *L. lloydianum* are two separate species with strong bootstrap and PP support within the Vascellum clade of Lycoperdon." Furthermore, *Vascellum depressum* was the type for the genus Vascellum. Since it has long been accepted as a synonym for *Lycoperdon pratense*, this now transfers the genus Vascellum to Lycoperdon.

Michael Kuo took advantage of his description of **Vascellum pratense** by using it as a launching pad for his five rules of puffball consumption. These are: 1) Do not eat puffballs near car exhaust, 2) Eat only when interior is white, 3) Do not eat puffballs that show embryonic outlines of a cap and stem when cut in half lengthwise. These are likely to be Amanita buttons, 4) Be aware that puffballs can have a laxative effect on some people, so just eat a small amount at first, and 5) Do not eat puffballs with hard, black interiors. These are likely to be poisonous Sclerodermas.

On the other hand, there is a use for the Pasture Puffballs other than placing them in unhappy places on a golf course to confuse the competition. John David Moore, in Kuo's *One Hundred Edible Mushrooms*, claims you can toss them into soups as a sort of fungal dumpling. Although mild in flavor, they become rich when sautéed in butter. He even has a recipe where sautéed slices are laid on top of creamed asparagus. You can get that greenish look without mature gasterocarps after all.

Addendum: Recently published European guides and *Index Fungorum* are using **Lycoperdon pratense.**

BIBLIOGRAPHY

David Arora, *Mushrooms Demystified,* 1986. Ten Speed Press, Berkeley, Calif.

Scott T. Bates, *Arizona Members of the Geastraceae and Lycoperdaceae,* 2004. Thesis at Arizona State University.

J. Breitenbach & F. Kranzlin, *Fungi of Switzerland, Vol. 2,* 1986. Edition Mykologia, Lucerne.

Vincent Demoulin, *Lycoperdon Subpratense C.G. Lloyd Nomen Rejiciendum* in *Mycologia* 63 (1226–1230), 1971.

Stephanie Jarvis, *The Lycoperdaceae of California*, doctorate, 2014.

Michael Jordan, *The Encyclopedia of Fungi of Britain and Europe*, 1995. David & Charles, Newton Abbot, England.

Michael Kuo & Andy Methven, *One Hundred Edible Mushrooms*, 2007. University of Michigan Press, Ann Arbor, Mich.

Thomas Laessoe, Gary Lincoff, & Anna Del Conte, *The Mushroom Book*, 1996. DK Publishing, New York, NY.

Ellen Larsson & Mikael Jepsson, *Phylogenetic Relationships Among Species and Genera of Lycoperdaceae Based on ITS and LSU Sequence Data from North European Taxa* in *Mycological Research* 112, Issue 1 (4–22), 2008.

Kent & Vera McKnight, *Peterson Field Guides— Mushrooms*, 1987. Houghton Mifflin, Boston.

David Pegler & Brian Spooner, *The Mushroom Identifier*, 1992. Smithmark Publishers, New York, NY.

Patricio Ponce de Leon, *Revision of the Genus Vascellum* in *Fieldiana Botany* 32 (109–125), 1970.

Bob Ramsey, *Trial Field Key to the Geastraceae and Lycoperdaceae in the Pacific Northwest*, 1978. Pacific Northwest Key Council, Seattle, Wash.

A.H. Smith, *The Genus Vascellum in the United States* in *Travaux Mycologiques, Numero Special du Bulletin de la Société Linéene de Lyons* 43 (407–419), 1974.

A.H. Smith, *A Field Guide to Western Mushrooms*, 1975. University of Michigan Press, Ann Arbor, Mich.

Verpa bohemica (Krombholz) Schroeter

It's never a good idea to undercook your Verpas.

More commonly known as the Early Morel, **Verpa bohemica** is the first of the morels to appear in the spring, well before the local hardwoods have fully leafed out.

Caps of **V. bohemica** run from 1–5 cm wide and 2–5 cm long. They are ochre to ochre-brown in color and are folded into longitudinal, almost anastomosing ribs with rounded edges. The margins hang free from the stem like a skirt. The undersides of the caps are smooth and whitish to brownish. Thin, fragile, and mostly bell shaped, the caps are often flattened at the top, in which case Peck called them **Verpa bohemica var. truncata**, a name that has since been sunk.

The stems run up to 15 cm long and 3 cm thick. They are finely granular, whitish to buff becoming tan to pale orange-straw color in age. The interior is white cottony at first but soon chambered with hollow partitions. Odor and taste are mild except for old specimens, which can have a chlorine odor according to Helene Schalkwijk-Barendsen. The spore deposit is yellow ochre. Along the West Coast they are found in wet, swampy areas rich in decaying foliage and humus. They are especially associated with cottonwoods. Elsewhere they have an affinity for aspen, willows, rowans, and even vine maple.

Dr. A.H. Smith noted that there was also a giant form of this species, but since there were also intermediate sizes, he decided against creating a special form or variety out of it.

Microscopically, **Verpa bohemica** can be distinguished from all other species in the Morchellaceae by having asci with only two spores. All others have eight-spored asci. These spores are elongated-elliptical, smooth-walled, and huge. They measure 54–80 x 15–18 µm. No other discomycete comes close to this size.

The search for **Verpa bohemica** is a rite of spring in Whatcom County. I sally forth every three or four years to look for it when the nettles are 8–12 inches high. That's the indicator. In late March of 2004 I drove out to an undisclosed location in the vast Nooksack River delta, hid my car off-road, and entered my favorite cottonwood swamp. It was so early on a Sunday morning that wisps of fog were still hanging around the bases of the trees. The only sound was that of my boots gurgling in the muck while passing last year's devils clubs rearing here and there like ghoulish sculptures from hell. I finally topped a rise to the collecting zone, and there before me were scattered cans of Pabst Blue Ribbon beer and decapitated stems as far as I could see. The Good Ole Boys had been here the day before. Bandoni & Szczawinski have written that only the caps can be used, and the Good Ole Boys have taken this to heart.

No matter. First things first. I ambled around to see whether they might have dropped a full Pabst by mistake. Then I went to work. In half an hour I had an entire shopping bag full of stems. Same flavor as the caps. Just more of a spaghetti look in the pot. Pretty hoity-toity behavior for a bunch of Pabst drinkers.

Obviously, I really like the flavor of the Early Morel. It has a very subtle, swampy aftertaste that you can't get with any other mushroom. I always cook it with chicken. I fry up the chicken pieces in virgin olive oil. About ten minutes before the end I add a clump of chopped scallions, freshly ground black pepper, and the Verpas, stems or caps with stems. Just before the grand finale I add some salt

LOOK-ALIKE

Verpa conica

to taste and a fistful of cilantro leaves. Simple and scrumptious. But not to be repeated year after year. The toxins in **Verpa bohemica** tend to accumulate in the body. Everyone is different. There is no telling when you are going to cross that line.

There are others who can't stand the flavor of **Verpa bohemica**. They either don't like the swampy aftertaste or they have approached it the wrong way. They've either rehydrated dried specimens or they have put them in the freezer for later. The freezer eliminates all of the flavor and turns the Verpas into a soggy mass in the frying pan. The dried specimens smell like garbage and taste the same when reconstituted. **Verpa bohemica** is one species that must be eaten right away.

But once again, not too often. The Early Morel has a checkered history of edibility issues. Phyllis Kempton and Virginia Wells, two well-known mycologists operating out of Alaska, have the following experience to relate. They and a third friend had been eating **Verpa bohemica** from the same location year after year without any ill effects. Then in 1965, the fifth consecutive year, all three became sick from ingesting it. They had added them to an omelet for dinner. About four hours later 'A' felt bloated in the stomach and soon had diarrhea. 'B' felt a bit bloated and had diarrhea the next morning. 'C' had no problems. A week later the Verpas were eaten again. 'A' noticed bloating in three hours and vomited and had diarrhea throughout the night. 'B' com-plained of a severe bloated feeling and some stomach upset. 'C' had no problems overnight but felt bloated with stomach distress the next day.

Although each participant had a slightly different reaction, they all were affected. The implication is that trace toxins in **Verpa bohemica** probably accumulate in our systems. Kempton, Wells, and friend had just hit their saturation points. Parboiling eliminates this risk but might also eliminate the delicate flavor.

In another infamous encounter, Dr. A.H. Smith and his wife Helen also took a direct hit. According to their daughter, Nancy, they once had a quart of **Verpa bohemica** for lunch. Four hours later, Helen walked into a wall instead of the doorway she was aiming for. There were no swirling colors or feelings of euphoria. She then had great difficulty putting the cap back onto the vinegar bottle. Dr. Smith experienced difficulty in typing. He then lost a handball match to a person he usually beat. Neither of them suffered from stomach pains. The conclusion was that the quantity consumed was responsible for the temporary loss of muscular coordination.

These two classic cases have colored our feelings about **Verpa bohemica** ever since. Lincoff and Mitchel suspect that low levels of gyromitrin are present in **Verpa bohemica**. Arora notes that even today we don't know the compounds responsible for the malaise. Whatever the case it's never a good idea to undercook your Verpas.

The Early Morel can be separated from the true morels by its cap attachment. **Verpa bohemica** is only attached to the cap apex with margins hanging free from the stipes. The cap bases are fully attached to the stems in true morels. The one exception is **Morchella semilibera**, which is attached to the stem halfway between cap apex and cap margin.

The two other Verpas in North America that might be confused with **V. bohemica** are **Verpa conica** and **Verpa digitaliformis**. **Verpa conica** differs by having a smooth, brownish cap and asci with eight spores. **Verpa digitaliformis** has been reported from southern California by the McKnights and from Ohio by Miron Hard. The McKnights reported "soft reddish-orange scales on the stipe." Hard described the caps as olive umber in color, the stems up to 7 cm long, white with reddish tinge. There were reddish radicels at the stem bases. The asci harbored eight spores, and they could be found in spring and summer in moist ravines.

Abbott and Currah listed **Verpa digitaliformis** as a synonym of **Verpa conica**, but the *Species Fungorum* so far hasn't bought into it.

Verpa bohemica enjoys a wide geographical range in Europe and North America. Svrcek supplied us with a distributional map for Europe. The taxon is by far the most plentiful in eastern Europe. It has also been found in Austria, Switzerland, northern Italy, the Pyrenees, Macedonia, Corsica, Sweden, and Finland. In North America it can be found all over Canada on down to the Great Lakes states into West Virginia and the northeast corner of Iowa.

It is found along the Pacific Coast from northern California to Alaska. There are also reports from the western mountains and from the New England states.

The name **Verpa bohemica** means "Bohemian rod" in Latin. Krombholz first described it as **Morchella bohemica** from the forests around Prague in 1828. Boudier moved it to **Ptychoverpa bohemica** in 1907. This name is still in use today by mycologists who believe that **Verpa bohemica** should be separated generically from other Verpas. For instance, **Verpa conica** has eight spores per ascus instead of two, never smells like chlorine when old, and never leads to stomach upsets when eaten. Nonetheless, Schroeter moved the species to Verpa in 1908.

Other synonyms listed for **Verpa bohemica** by Seaver are **Morchella bispora** Sorokin, **Morchella gigaspora** Cooke, **Morilla bohemica** Quelet, and **Phalloboletus gigasporus** Kuntze. Whatever Latin name you prefer to attach to it, realize that you also have a choice among common names. Besides Early Morel, it has been called Bell Morel, Early Bell Morel, Thimble Morel, and Wrinkled Thimble Cap. The earliest name used has the priority.

LOOK-ALIKE

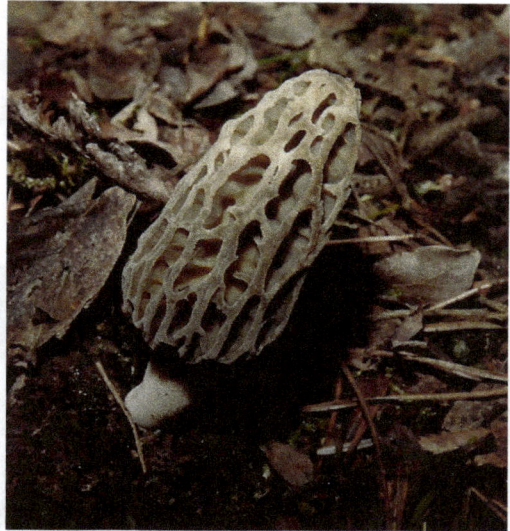

On **Morchella tridentina**, a true morel, the bottom of the cap attaches fully to the stem. On **V. bohemica** the bottom of the cap hangs skirtlike about the stem.

BIBLIOGRAPHY

Sean Abbott & R.S. Currah, The Larger Cup Fungi and Other Ascomycetes of Alberta, 1989. University of Alberta Devonian Botanic Garden, Edmonton, Alberta.

David Arora, All That the Rain Promises and More, 1991. Ten Speed Press, Berkeley, Calif.

David Arora, Mushrooms Demystified, 1986. Ten Speed Press, Berkeley, Calif.

Robert Bandoni & Adam Szczawinski, Guide to Common Mushrooms of British Columbia, 1976. British Columbia Provincial Museum, Victoria, B.C.

Miron Hard, Mushrooms, Edible & Otherwise, 1908. Dover Publications, New York, NY.

Donald Huffman, Lois Tiffany, & George Knaphus, Mushrooms & Other Fungi of the Midcontinental United States, 1989. Iowa State University Press, Ames, Iowa.

Phyllis Kempton & Virginia Wells, Studies on the Fleshy Fungi of Alaska. I. in Lloydia 30 (258–268), 1967.

Gary Lincoff & D.H. Mitchel, Toxic and Hallucinogenic Mushroom Poisoning, 1977. Van Nostrand Reinhold, New York, NY.

Charles McIlvaine & Robert Macadam, One Thousand American Fungi, 1902. Dover Publications, New York, NY.

Kent & Vera McKnight, Peterson Field Guides: Mushrooms, 1987. Houghton Mifflin, Boston.

Helene Schalkwijk-Barendsen, Mushrooms of Western Canada, 1991. Lone Pine Publishing, Edmonton, Alberta.

Fred Seaver, The North American Cup Fungi (Operculates), 1928. Self-published, New York, NY.

A.H. Smith, The Mushroom Hunter's Field Guide (revised), 1977. University of Michigan Press, Ann Arbor, Mich.

Leon Snyder, The Operculate Discomycetes of Western Washington, doctorate, 1938.

Mirko Svrcek, The Hamlyn Book of Mushrooms and Fungi, 1983. Artia, Prague.

Nancy Weber, A Morel Hunter's Companion, 1988. Two Peninsula Press, Lansing, Mich.

Xerocomellus zelleri (Murrill) Klofac

Photo by Richard Morrison

Despite the plethora of natural predators . . . Xerocomellus zelleri is a highly successful bolete.

Occasionally referred to as the poor man's **Aureoboletus mirabilis**, the edible **Xerocomellus zelleri** gives forth just a vestige of the lemony flavor and has been accused of having a mushier texture. Although it receives a lukewarm reception in our kitchens, it is avidly devoured by slugs and maggots. Whether these predators help or hinder the spread of the species, it can be found in abundance locally. Beyond Whatcom County it ranges from British Columbia down into Honduras and east to the Sierras and the Rockies. And just for the record, Roberts and Evans have shaded it down into Panama.

It adapts to mixed woods in the Pacific Northwest, equally at home with alder and fir. David Biek has found them in Redding, California, associated with live oak. Arora has reported them on rotten redwood stumps, bringing up the possibility that beyond having mycorrhizal relationships, they might be saprobic or even lignicolous. And further south in Honduras one can only imagine what they have glommed onto there.

Arora calls **Xerocomellus zelleri** our most colorful bolete. It is hard to argue against the colorful combination of purple-black

LOOK-ALIKES

Xerocomellus amylosporus

Aureoboletus mirabilis

to violet-gray caps, lemon yellow pores, and carmine stipes. Caps are 5-11 cm wide, convex and covered with a white powdery bloom at first. They soon become nodulose or rugulose (lumpy or wrinkled), and then smoother in age. If the weather dries up, they can develop red cracks in the cap surface. Cap colors range from blackish-brown, dark plum, dark chestnut brown to grayish-purple becoming pale gray-brown in age. There is often a pallid grayish band at the margin. The context is whiter to pale yellow, usually unchanging when bruised. The pore surface is pale yellow to greenish-yellow becoming more olive-yellow in age. The tubes can be 1 ½ cm long and usually bruise a dull slate blue. The stems are 5-8 cm long and 1-3 cm thick. They are equal or enlarged at the base where whitish to yellow mycelium can be found. They are either all red, granulose to punctuate, or often pale yellow at the apex (Roberts & Evans) or yellow at the base (Orson Miller). The spore print is olive-brown. The odor is mild while the taste is mild to slightly acidic.

William A. Murrill first discovered **Xerocomellus zelleri** in the Seattle area and named it after Sanford M. Zeller, another pioneer taxonomist at large in the West. He first published it under the name **Ceriomyces zelleri** in 1912, but simultaneously transferred it to Boletus in the same publication in case the international community wouldn't accept his new genus Ceriomyces, which, it turned out, they didn't. Then, in 1944, Snell transferred it to Xerocomus due to its large pores and relatively slender, non-reticulate stems. Klofac transferred it to Xerocomellus in 2011.

As for look-alikes, the closest by far is **Xerocomellus atropurpureus** of Siegel, Schwarz, & Frank. Recent DNA sequencing results have revealed a second species that is almost a twin. Other look-alikes follow:

Xerocomellus atropurpureus: Seems to almost intergrade with **X. zelleri** in the field. The caps differ by not having a velvety surface or a whitish powdery bloom when young. Neither do they have a pallid gray band at the margin.

Xerocomellus redeuilhii: Differs by its dark brown felty caps with maroon tinges and tapering to napiform stem bases. This is the new name for the European equivalent of **Xerocomellus dryophilus**.

Xerocomellus diffractus: Thought to be our most common northwest version of **X. chrysenteron**. Caps develop pale yellow cracks at first that soon turn pinkish or reddish. Pores are rounded and yellow at first, soon becoming angular and dingy yellow-olive. The deposit is dull olive-brown. Odor and taste are mild, the flavor quickly forgettable.

Xerocomellus amylosporus: A darker brown capped member of the same group with reddish-brown spores and pores that bruise blue-black.

Aureoboletus mirabilis: A much larger species with a hard, velvety, nodulose cap surface that is a uniform maroon-brown color. Always found on or next to hemlock logs and stumps. A good com-

LOOK-ALIKES

Xerocomellus atropurpureus

Xerocomellus diffractus

Xerocomellus redeuilhii from Greece   *Photo by Heidi Gustafson*

parison can be seen on page 164 of All That the Rain Promises and More.

Xerocomellus truncatus: Differs by its truncated spores. It has mustard yellow pores that instantly bruise ink-blue and pale brown caps with buff colored cracks.

Xerocomellus porosporus: A Midwestern species with smaller gray-brown to dingy yellow-brown caps without cracks. Stems are reddish-brown with upper part covered in minute dull brown scabers.

Xerocomellus mendocinensis: Looks like **X. diffractus**, differing mainly in its punctate red stipe with a brighter red band near the apex.

Boletus smithii: Differs by having red-brown to pinkish-brown caps and yellow stems with a red band at apex. Some feel this red band can migrate. Locally common in some years.

For those who may be tempted to eat **X. zelleri**, the reviews are somewhat mixed. Here are a few examples:

Roberts & Evans: "Some esteem it highly. It is commercially harvested in western Canada."

Michael Kuo: "Mediocre. Has a mushy texture and hardly any flavor. Prime specimens are firm with a lemony flavor. Darvin DeShazer uses them to add bulk to a dish."

Edmund Tylutki: "Edible and delicious."

Giovanni Pacioni: "Edible but not choice."

David Arora: "In my opinion it cooks up slimy and tasteless."

A.H. Smith: "Edible and choice. In recent years it has become a favorite in the Pacific Northwest."

Dick Graham: "Drying enhances the flavor."

Lori O'Dell: "Of poor flavor if sautéed fresh, but good and rich like other boletes if dried first and reconstituted later. It also makes a fantastic broth." To avoid a slimy texture she peels off the spongy pore layer before drying. The pores can be dried separately and then ground up later to be used as a spice.

Former club member Sonja Max finds the flavor to be subtle and complicated. When dry sautéed in a frying pan she found the flavor to be nutty. When sautéed in butter the texture became slippery and the flavor was like acorns with a hint of lemon at the end. Most of us haven't had acorns. It's a piece of work to boil away the bitter tannins to make them edible. But only by doing so will you come close to experiencing the enigmatic flavor of **Xerocomellus zelleri**.

BIBLIOGRAPHY

David Arora, *All That the Rain Promises and More*, 1991. Ten Speed Press, Berkeley, Calif.

David Arora, *Mushrooms Demystified*, 1986. Ten Speed Press, Berkeley, Calif.

David Biek, *The Mushrooms of Northern California*, 1986. Spore Prints, Redding, Calif.

Ernst Both, *The Boletes of North America*, 1984. Buffalo Museum of Science, Buffalo, NY.

D. Desjardin, M. Wood, & F. Stevens, *California Mushrooms*, 2016. Timber Press, Portland, Ore.

Dick Graham, *The Meandering Mushroomer*, 1978. Hancock House Publishers, Seattle.

Michael Kuo & Andy Methven, *100 Edible Mushrooms*, 2007. University of Michigan Press, Ann Arbor, Mich.

Hope & Orson Miller, *North American Mushrooms*, 2006. Morris Book Publishing, Guilford, Conn.

Giovanni Pacioni & Gary Lincoff, *Simon and Schuster's Guide to Mushrooms*, 1981. Simon & Schuster's, New York, NY.

Peter Roberts & Shelley Evans, *The Book of Fungi*, 2011.

Noah Siegel & Christian Schwarz, *Mushrooms of the Redwood Coast*, 2016. Ten Speed Press, Berkeley, California.

A.H. Smith, *Mushrooms in Their Natural Habitats*, 1949. Sawyer's, Lancaster, Penn.

Helen & A.H. Smith & Nancy Weber, *The Mushroom Hunter's Field Guide*, 1980. University of Michigan Press, Ann Arbor, Mich.

A.F.S. Taylor, U. Eberhardt, G. Simonini, M. Gelardi, & A. Vizzini, *Xerocomellus redeuilhii* in *Rivista di Micologica* 59 (2): 125, 2016.

Harry Thiers, *California Mushrooms: A Field Guide to the Boletes*, 1975. Hafner Press, New York, NY.

Edmund Tylutki, *Mushrooms of Idaho and the Pacific Northwest, Vol. 2*, 1987. University Press of Idaho, Moscow, Idaho.

Xylaria curta Fries

The conidiophores are sparingly branched, and form a compact layer on white stromatal tips.

This Northwest relative of Dead Man's Fingers was found by John Baker on the Lummi Indian Reservation in late March of 1993. Our club had been invited to foray there by Ernestine Ballew. The habitat was mixed woods with alder, maple, and cottonwood predominating. The specimens looked like diminutive versions of the cosmopolitan **Xylaria polymorpha**, but with a whitish bloom on the surface.

Fortunately for us, the genus Xylaria has long interested Fred Rhoades. He has examined numerous local collections under the microscope and discovered that all the **Xylaria polymorpha** look-alikes had significantly shorter spores. A provisional key to North American Xylaria by Jack Rogers showed that only **Xylaria curta** had spores this short. In another article, Rogers and Callan noted that there had been one recording of **Xylaria polymorpha** on apple in the Pacific Northwest, but that was it.

LOOK-ALIKES

Xylaria polymorpha from Maine

Xylaria Spec. Nov.

Xylarias always begin life in the conidial stage. Under the microscope the conidia are hyaline, elliptical, and smooth. They are easily blown away or rubbed away, leaving the charred and warted surface that can persist for years. The conidia are born on hyphal threads known as conidiophores. The coniophores of **Xylaria curta** are sparingly branched and form a compact layer on white stromatal tips. The fruiting bodies of Xylarias are called stromata. Many Xylarias start out with a ghostly white appearance from these conidiophores, but **Xylaria curta** retains these whitish squamules longer than most. The upper part of a fruiting body is likely to be white because that is where the growth occurs. The first mycologist to describe this conidial stage was Fernand Guéguen in 1909.

Eventually the sexual stage takes over. One way to think of a Xylaria is a fruiting body within a fruiting body. The fungus that you find in the woods is called the stroma. The interior consists of a solid white context with a palisade of what looks like black, oblong grains about ¾ to 7/8ths of a millimeter thick on the inner wall. These are tiny flasks called perithecia. Each perithecium contains myriads of asci, which in turn contain the spores. (A good electron scanning microscope photo of a perithecium can be found in *The Encyclopedia of Mushrooms* by Dickinson & Lucas.) Each ascus contains eight spores in a uniseriate arrangement. Interspersed with the asci are the paraphyses. These are thinner, string-like forms with no spores in them. The spores of **Xylaria curta** measure 9–10 x 4.5–6 µm compared to 20–31 x 5–10 µm for **Xylaria polymorpha**. Immature spores are hyaline with cellular appendages that disappear as they mature into a brown color. Many of these spores have an oil drop and all have a straight germ slit oriented lengthwise through their centers. The asci are long stipitate and measure 115–130 x 6–7 µm. The apical rings turn blue in Melzer's solution. When the spores are mature, they are forcibly ejected from the perithecia through openings called ostioles. These ostioles are papillate in shape and puncture the walls of the stroma, thereby giving the larger Xylarias their pimpled and rugose look. (See featured photo.) Each ostiolar canal has sterile filaments radiating from it. These are called paraphyses.

Each ascus has a ring or flap at the apex, resembling an inverted hat. This is a character unique for Xylaria. An excellent reference to most Xylaria idiosyncracies can be seen online at Tom Volk's Fungus of the Month for April, 2000. For instance, he mentions how **X. polymorpha** can discharge its spores over several years, which gives the spores a better shot at germination through the seasons.

The fruiting bodies of **Xylaria curta** are up to 5 cm long and 1 ½ cm wide. They have a roughened to rugose surface and obtuse apices. The interior is hard and white. The spore print is black. The whitish surface conidia can wear off completely in age, but usually remain in the pitted areas. The

Elaphocordyceps ophioglossoides from Georgia

shapes are clavate to broadly clavate or irregularly flattened, fruiting solitary or several arising from a common, raggedy base. According to Ramsbottom, "the base of the previous year's fruiting body acts as a sclerotium out of which a new fruiting body develops." In this sense it is a perennial. The growing stroma is also heliotropic (grows towards the sun), a reaction vital to the formation of the conidia.

Xylaria polymorpha is a generally larger species with no white left on it in age. Other look-alikes include **Xylaria castorea** from New Zealand, which has the small spores of **X. curta**, but has fruiting bodies in the shape of flattened beaver tails. **Xylaria longipes** is a more slender version of it that only reaches 1 cm in width, and is generally confined to sycamore. **Xylaria bulbosa** differs by having a yellow interior and an abruptly acute apex in most specimens. And **Xylaria scruposa**, known from Hawaii and Puerto Rico, has the clavate shape of **Xylaria curta**, but has larger spores midway between it and those of **X. polymorpha**.

A new species found in the Pacific Northwest, here seen in the photo entitled Spec. Nov., has a more slender fruiting body than **Xylaria curta**, even smaller spores, no white powder on the surface, and a tendency to stain the wood it grows on black.(It cannot be named here because it hasn't yet been officially published. However, if you absolutely must know this name, you can find it on page 348 of Dr. Mike Beug's *Ascomycete Fungi of North America*.)

The Xylaria anamorph pictured on the next page was found in the Stimpson Preserve in early November of 2011. To me, it looked like a relic from the Pleistocene. Fred Rhoades deserves full credit for tracing it to Xylaria. We aren't sure what species it belongs to, but if you section this beast you will see generative hyphae

A Xylaria anamorph

and masses of dacryoid conidia. Anamorphs are considered to be asexual forms of a species. If you aren't prepared for one you can have a devil of a time just getting it to genus.

As for look-alikes outside of Xylaria, **Elaphocordyceps ophioglossoides** comes to mind. It has a black, glossy surface, and also differs by fruiting on the underground truffle, **Elaphomyces asperulus**.

Mycologists researching the genus Xylaria had a tough time. As Jack Rogers noted, "Stromata of any given species often vary greatly in color, size, and sometimes in general shape. These variations are associated with stages of development, locality, and probably inherent variability." Add to this the early international confusion resulting from the cosmopolitan ranges of many of them. **Xylaria curta**, for example, was first described by Fries from Oahu. Elias Fries first discovered **X. curta** on a trunk in Hawaii in 1851. How spores of this species arrived from Hawaii to the Pacific Northwest is anyone's guess.

BIBLIOGRAPHY

J. Breitenbach & F. Kranzlin, *Fungi of Switzerland, Vol.1*, 1984. Edition Mykologia, Lucerne.

R.W.G. Dennis, *Some Xylarias of Tropical America* in *Kew Bulletin* 11 (401–444), 1956.

Colin Dickinson & John Lucas, *The Encyclopedia of Mushrooms*, 1979. Crescent Books, New York, NY.

Fernand Guéguen, *L'État Conidien du Xylaria Polymorpha* in *Bulletin de la Societé Mycologique de France* 25 (85–97), 1909.

John Ramsbottom, *Larger British Fungi*, 1965. Trustees of the British Museum, London.

Rogers & Callan, *Xylaria Polymorpha and its Allies in the Continental United States* in *Mycologia* 78 (391–400), 1986.

Jack D. Rogers & Brenda Callan, *Xylaria bulbosa, Xylaria curta, and Xylaria longipes in Continental United States* in *Mycologia* 75 (457–467), 1983.

Jack D. Rogers, *Provisional Keys to Xylaria Species in Continental United States* in *Mycotaxon* 26 (85–97), 1986.

Tom Volk, *Fungus of the Month, April 2000*. http://botit.botany.wisc.edu/toms_fungi/fotm.html

And the beat goes on. . . .   *Photo by Caitilin Brondino*

The Fungi Less Known

These are fungi that I have encountered over the years that may or may not be species new to science. They are here in case someone happens to recognize them and would like to follow them further. I could fill about 25 pages of these, as could others who have been collecting a similar length of time, but that would alter the main point of the book, namely to help the club members and beyond with identifying fungi that are already known. (There are a few fungi presented here that are well enough known but their photos showcase abnormal views.)

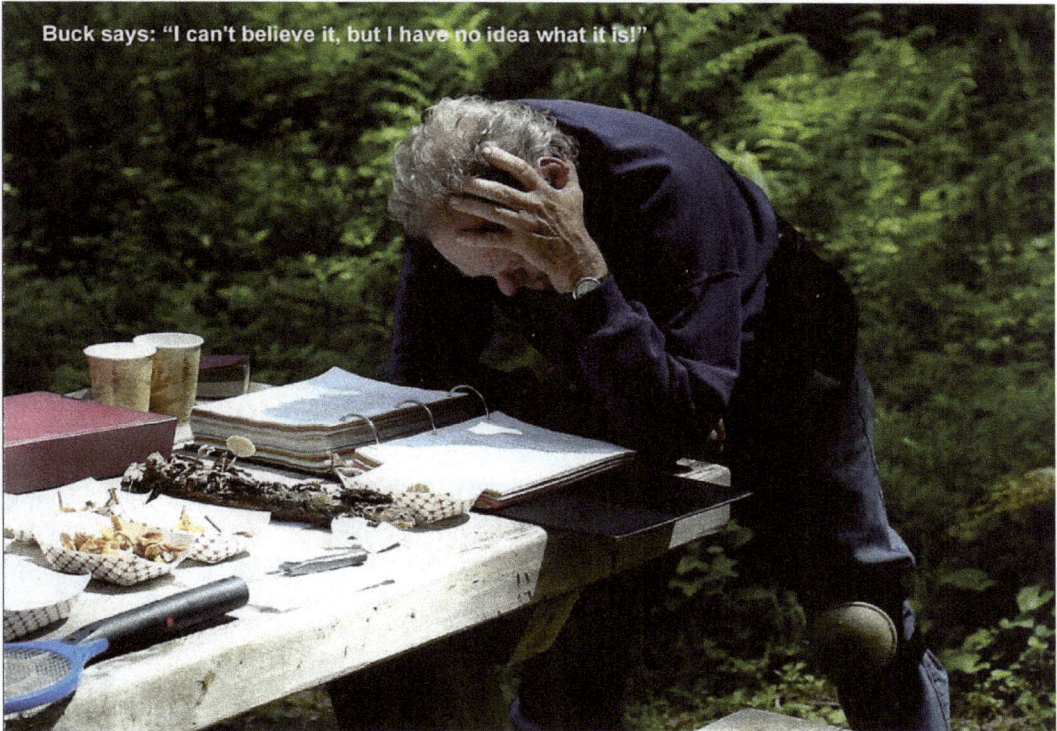

Buck says: "I can't believe it, but I have no idea what it is!"

Photo by Richard Morrison

The Cardboard-Colored Amanita

Always appearing at the exact same spot under conifers year after year, the two-toned cardboard colored caps seemed distinct. Club member Jack Waytz had found it four times in the Stimpson Family Nature Reserve just east of Bellingham, Wash. This collection was found on October 21, 2004. Caps ran up to 9½ cm wide and the stems 13–18 cm long. The crumbling gray volva at the stem base adhered to the base except for the upper margin. Caps could have pale gray velar patches. The stems were hollow, with one cottony partition near the base. Spores were globose, measuring 10–11.3 x 10.2–11.4 µm.

Well, after several years of speculation back and forth between Amanita expert Rod Tulloss and ourselves, Rod's DNA man and the Northwest Key Council's Matt Gordon of Oregon both concluded this was none other than **Amanita constricta**. Just a paler form of it.

That Puzzling Pest from the Kickerville Road

This one had plagued me for years. Found on the edge of a pasture among juncus grasses, specimens had been sent to Dr. O.K. Miller, Dr. Roy Halling, and Dr. Gaston Guzman for opinions. This is a bit of an imposition unless you check with the recipient first. Nonetheless, Dr. Guzman was able to eliminate Psilocybe as a candidate. The species had pale yellow gills, viscid caps, and thick-walled spores with germ pores. The spores measured 7.2–8.6 x 4.3–5.2 µm. Strong odor of green corn. Both pleurocystidia and cheilocystidia, but no clamps. The basidioles were polymorphic. I had never seen this before. Too many different

shapes to try to describe.

Finally, down to our last specimen, DNA results came in. ITS1 revealed 97% uncultured Hypholoma. An attempt at a species name failed. LSU was contaminated as were the basidio-primers. PCR also failed. All that is left of the collection is half a cap attached to one stem. The proposed name: **Hypholoma juncicola**, will have to wait.

The *Mycena speirea* That Is Anything But

Right from the get-go I want to thank Dr. Jim Johnson of Central Washington University for putting this oddball taxon through DNA testing. Whether I used A.H. Smith, Mas Geesteranus, or Moser, it always keyed out to **Mycena speirea**. Then when I went to compare them, there was nothing similar about them.

They were found on June 3, 2011, on the road to Lost Lake near the old Crystal Springs campground off Highway 90 in Washington state fruiting on a rather recently felled silver fir log.

Caps were pale brown to gray-brown fading hygrophanously to pale ochre-gray from margins first. Gills were short decurrent and distant, buff to grayish-tan. Stems were 2–3 cm long, white at the apex, then pale orange below. The pileipellis was of radially repent hyphae 3–4 hyphae deep with intracellular incrustation. This was totally different from the digitalized pileipellis of **Mycena speirea**. Dr. Johnson emailed me that it could represent a new genus. There are only two dried specimens of the fruiting bodies left. Could that explain why the brotherhood isn't rushing to our doors to compete for publishing honors? Ironically, **Mycena speirea** has found a new genus. It is now **Phloeomana speirea**.

Tricholoma saponaceum Gone Wild?

Or something else? This solitary specimen was found by Roger Phillips and Nicky Foy at the Bulis Pet Cemetery outside of Port Townsend on October 30, 2004.

It had white, inamyloid, subglobose spores measuring 4.9-6 x 3.9-5 µm, clamps in all tissues, mimicking **Tricholoma saponaceum** in most ways except for stature and cap color. The cap was only 3 ¼ cm wide but the stem was 17 ½ cm long and radicating in the moss. Could be a case of extreme variation due to depth of

moss. Found at the base of an old-growth Doug fir. I went back several years later and couldn't even find the tree. An ITS sequence analysis in 2018 revealed that this was 99% **Tricholoma saponaceum**.

The Gymnopilus with the Lubricous Cap

This oddity was brought to the 2017 Fall Show on wood chip mulch. Taste was bitter. Odor mildly pleasant.

Spores were rusty, dextrinoid, measuring 6.9–7.2 x 4.1–4.6 μm. Finely verrucose, ovoid to ellipsoid. Veil represented by a flattened scarlet band at stipe apex. Cap was 12 cm wide with a peelable cuticle. Cap context was watery buff and 1 ½ cm thick at disc. Stipe was tough, fibrous, buff with vinaceous-brown fibrils. Context of stem was yellow. Caulocystidia were clusters of clavate hyphae with clamped bases. The gill trama contained some dark gray hyphae with encrusted walls and rounded ends.

ITS sequencing has now shown that this taxon belongs in a complex including **G. aeruginosus**, **G. luteofolius**, and **G. suberis**, the latter being a rare European species found mainly on cork oak. Subsequent LSU sequencing then showed that **Gymnopilus suberis** was the most likely candidate of the three. It is a taxon endowed with cap scales, and looks nothing like the Gymnopilus pictured here.

The Blue Ganoderma of Silver Lake

Found on September 30, 2002, on an old conifer log, the cap of this mushroom was slate blue becoming dingy ochre towards the margin. It smelled like rotten radishes. The pore surface was dingy ochre-brown and did not change color when bruised. Tubes were 1 ½ cm long and dark mauve in color. Spores measured 11.2-13.4 x 6.9-7.2 μm. There was a maroon knob at the point of attachment, suggestive of **Ganoderma**

oregonense being attacked by a parasite. This is not the first blue Ganoderma to be found here.

The Albino Gyromitra from Salmon-Le-Sac

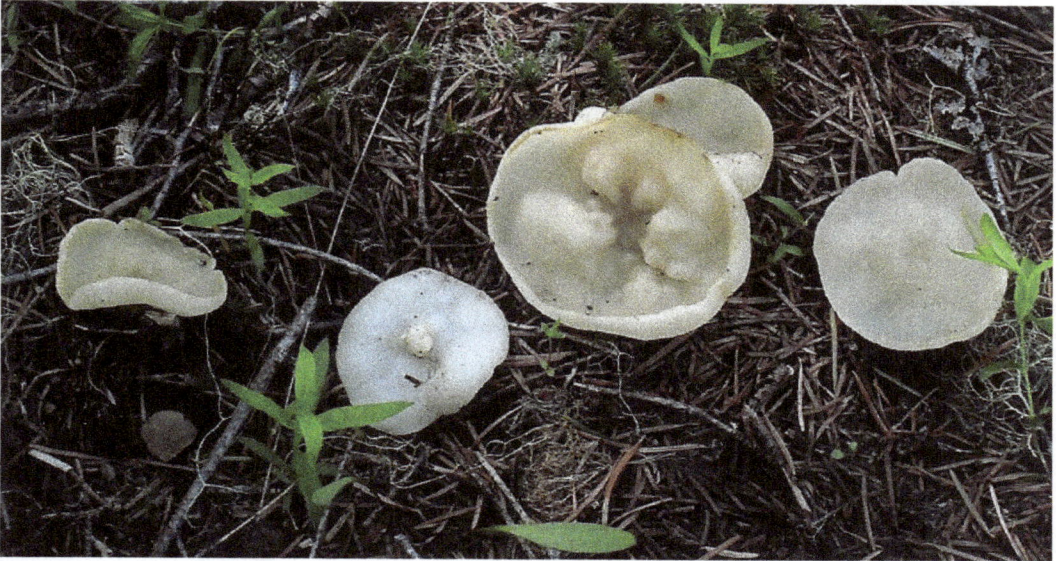

Who would have thought it possible? It had been 17 years since I had last visited Salmon-Le-Sac in the eastern Cascades. At that time I had found a white Discina in needle duff near the southwestern corner of the campground. Couldn't key it out anywhere. Returning to the scene 17 years later with the Dillys and Larry Baxter, there they were, right at the same spot! Dr. Mike Beug got excited. He'd been studying Discina for over a decade. A white one was new to him. He had probably heard about them, but having one in his hand was something else again. Back at Camp Koinonia samples were handed off to Dr. Jim Johnson for DNA testing. At about this time, Danny Miller emerged from his microscope. He had something to say. He had just keyed out the white discomycete to **Gyromitra melaleucoides**! It was a portent of things to come. We had no idea at the time that within three years, all Discinas would become Gyromitras for awhile.

ITS sequencing in 2018 revealed this to be 99% **Gyromitra melaleucoides**. The whitening of the carpophores probably derived from soil influences.

That Blood Red Mycena from Vendovi Island

Yet another mystery from Section Calodontes, this collection was found on the first mycological excursion to Vendovi Island in the San Juans. Found in hemlock duff, the sanguine caps and reddish gills with dark brown marginate edges seemed distinctive. Both the hollow stems and the caps had a yellowish context. Odor and taste strongly raphanoid. Spores were buff and amyloid. ITS sequencing pointed towards **Mycena pura** and **M. rosella** initially. LSU sequencing indicated a 99% match with **Mycena rutilantiformis** and **Mycena seminau**. It is neither of these. But at least we know the group.

Yellow Tinged Lepiota with the Odor of Fish

This looks like the ant that came to the picnic. The first collection found by Dr. Richard Morrison at Sudden Valley in 2013 under western red cedar had the yellowish hues one associates with **Lepiota magnispora**.

However, that species is named for its giant hump-backed spores up to 22 µm long. These spores were navicular and the perfect size for **Lepiota clypeolaria**. When Richard found subsequent collections at the same site in 2014 without any yellowing, we felt better about **L. clypeolaria**. But not all that better.

An ITS sequencing analysis in 2018 verified this as 99%

Photo by Richard Morrison

Lepiota clypeolaria. Does this mean the odor of fresh fish and the often yellow velar material on the stipe are inconsequential? Would an emended species description be called for?

That Enigma from Icicle Canyon

Can't blame anyone for not going here. The thick, furcate, distant, intervenose gills, white, amyloid spores, and tawny mycelium at the stem base are hard to replicate. The "granules" on the cap surface are actually cottonwood pollen. Basidia were only 22–27 μm long, too short for Hygrocybe. The combination of the substrate of buried wood, the colored rhizomorphs at stem base, and the conspicuous caulocystidia all pointed towards Xeromphalina. Club member Cris Colburn had found it in a mountain canyon in eastern Washington. Then in 2018, rpb2 sequence results led to a 100% match with **Xeromphalina enigmatica**, a relatively new species.

The Snowy Stropharia from Haines, Alaska

A beautiful white capped Stropharia up to 8 cm wide in conifer duff and birch debris in Haines, Alaska, in late August, 1982. It has strongly lobed margins and viscid caps. Stipes up to 9 cm long, smooth above ring, tomentose-squamose below. Spores were dark purple-brown. According to Dr. Gary Laursen, it is in the **Stropharia hornemannii** group. To search for this again in the same locale, you will need to carry a bell to alert the bears to your presence.Addendum: The entire collection has been donated to the Univ. of Washington herbarium.

The Massive Amanita with Bicolorous Stem

This monster in section Vaginatae was found solitary in the roadside muck at Silver Fir Campground in the Mt. Baker–Snoqualmie National Forest in October, 2013. The cap was 14 cm wide, the stem 3 cm thick and 17½ cm long. The thick white volval sack was mostly free from the stipe. The pale cinnamon-brown chevron pattern of flattened scales abruptly ended about halfway down the stem. The gills had dark brown edges, the lamellulae truncate endings.

In the fall of 2013 Rod Tulloss, our North American Amanita expert, was sent a portion of the fruiting body. I never heard what it might be, so in 2018 I sent a piece to Spain for DNA analysis. ITS sequencing showed it had a strong connection with Rod's 'OR01'. This represented a collection found near Brookings, Oregon, by Ron Pastorino on October 4, 2007. Rod then asserted that the photo shown here bore no resemblance to his 'OR01'. An expanded LSU sequence was then launched. The result was a 782/783 match with 'OR01'.

This is the elephant in the room. DNA studies are far more complicated than originally perceived. Sometimes the results can be far from what the researcher imagined.

Pholiota with the Pumpkin Pie Spice Odor

This impressively large and chunky Pholiota is always found on wild cherry. So far. I can't imagine that others haven't found it. The odor is every bit as distinct as that of the matsutake. But different. The caps run up to 14 cm wide, the stems up to 2 ½ cm thick, often eccentric coming off the log. They are pale yellow-ochre with vinaceous brown stains and velar shards. Tiny black hairs adorn the base. Gills are dingy olive-ochre with dark vinaceous edges. Caps are adorned with pointy flattened scales becoming rusty at disc. A few of the pleurocystidia are leptocystidia, meaning they become ochre in KOH. I fully expect someone to call me out on this. It simply has too many strong characters to have been ignored thus far. ITS sequencing in 2018 showed this to be 100% Pholiota. However it is not close to any other Pholiota logged into GenBank to date.

Vendovi Island Mystery with Unusual Collarium

This odd little Clitocyboid taxon with the arcuate, decurrent gills was found in moss on the embankment as you exit the tiny dock. The caps were hygrophanous, fading from ochre to straw-buff with a brown spot at disc. The pileipellis consisted of very thin, radially oriented hyphae with black encrusted walls. But the cat's meow were the caulocystidia. These were nests of vermiform cystidia at the stem apices with fusiform to utriform heads. ITS sequencing in 2018 showed this to be **Clitocybe subditopoda**. If you read the fine print in Bigelow's Clitocybe monograph you discover it can appear with or without the collarium.

The Cookie Flavored Flammulina

This odd-ball Flammulina showed up in a collecting basket that Margaret Dilly had leant to an unknown club member at a November Deception Pass Park foray. All we could surmise about it was that it was lignicolous due to the curved stipe. I took a tentative bite and discovered it was sweet just like a sugar cookie. Chuck Nafziger, Northwest Mushroomers Association president at the time, took a bite in turn, and seemed so pleased with the result that I had to ask him to save some for science.

And thanks to Dr. Ron Petersen and Dr. Karen Hughes, science was served. They put it through DNA sequencing. It ended up near **Flammulina velutipes**, but with an Asian footprint. Some of the microscopic features include clamps everywhere, ellipsoid spores with a Q of 2.17, and beautiful fusiform to utriform cheilocystidia with long tapering bases.

The flavor is so sweet you could bake it in the oven and have it with whipped cream. This solitary specimen now resides at the University of Tennessee herbarium in Knoxville.

Tawny-Ochre Russula with the Odor of Shellfish

Yes, the blue-green reaction with ferrous-sulphate puts it in the **Russula xerampelina** group. The pleurocystidia went red in sulpho-vanillin. But the encrusted walls of the primordial hyphae and the fact that the stem did not turn pale yellow when scratched all lead one away from **R. xerampelina** sensu stricto. It appeared at Razor Hone Road right after a downpour signaling the end of the worst summer drought Washington had endured in fifty years. The spores were pale straw colored in deposit. Under the microscope they had isolated warts up to 1.5 μm high.

In 2018, an ITS sequencing showed this to be a perfect match with a Russula collected by Anna Bazzicalupa in B.C. on October 26, 2013. The collection was slated to be part of an article on Northwest Russulas in Subsection Xerampelinae at that time.

The Black Lactarius with Lilac Stained Gills

Found in a lawn under an imported birch near Lake Padden on November 10, 2009. This black Lactarius with olive tones can reach 15 cm wide. It has white, unchanging latex and an acrid taste. The drying latex stains the gills lilac, not the dull green one would expect. The context turns instantly red-purple in KOH. Gills are a pale yellow-straw color spotted with dark brown stains in age. Edges are entire, emarginate with dark mauve-brown. In 2018, ITS sequencing revealed this to be 99% **Lactarius necator**. Since when has this well-known taxon shown violet stains on its gills that were not induced by KOH?

The Chestnut Amanita from Solduc Hotsprings

Another treasure from the Olympic Peninsula, this collection was found next to elk droppings in the Solduc Campground. The longest stipe was 29½ cm long. Caps were 7–10 cm wide and a dark chestnut color, darker at the disc, with grooved striations at the margins. Stems had orange-brown squamules in a chevron pattern on the upper half and were smooth and buff on the lower half.

ITS sequencing revealed a 98% match with one **Amanita aff. lignitincta** from Yunnan,

China. This is in the nom. prov. stage and has a smaller stature with caps up to 6 cm wide.

One Hundred Year Bolete from Mora Park

A diminutive but outstanding bolete found in Mora Park near La Push in late August, 1982. Caps up to 3 cm wide. Surface velvety and dark brown. Pores a brilliant salmon-orange instantly bruising ink blue. Stems up to 7 mm thick and just over 1 cm long. They are pale yellow and smooth, no sign of any reticulation. They become brown when dried. Found under old-growth hemlock. Not seen since.

(Dr. Thiers received a couple of specimens from this collection. He wrote back that he believed it was a new species. Since I had dried it in the oven with the oven door open, he could not be sure I had skew-

ered the tissue sizes. But if I found it again and dried it in a dehydrator, he would name it after me. He has now passed away and I haven't found anyone else who has seen it since.)

Addendum: The entire collection has been gifted to the herbarium at the University of Washington, Seattle.

April Fool Mushrooms

For a number of years our newsletter would feature a fake mushroom on April First. The only stipulation was the arrival of the newsletter on that exact date. Nonetheless, at least one person was fooled by one of these false profiles and spent weeks trying to research the name. For this reason, I have kept them apart from the main body of this work. It was tempting to sprinkle them among the true fungi, but it didn't happen. Why pollute a good thing?

The first two were created by Chas Gilmore, long since departed for the Kaw Valley Mushroom Club in Lawrence, Kansas. The rest were fabricated by myself. So without more ado, here they are, presented chronologically in the order they were first published.

April Fool   *Photo by Roy Kerr*

Pisolithellus conglomeratus (Pouquette) Le Brun

By Chas Gilmore

Seasoned truffle dogs and pigs have been known to run from their overpowering stench.

Pisolithellus conglomeratus

A more unlikely mushroom than **Pisolithellus conglomeratus** could hardly be imagined. But once found, even its name is seldom forgotten. April is a good month to look for it. Its preferred season in the Pacific Northwest is March through May. These specimens were fruiting from an embankment in the Chuckanut Mountains in late March of 1988.

P. **conglomeratus** shares with species of Astraeus, Battaraea, Podaxis, Geastrum, and Scleroderma the dubious distinction of preferring to fruit in harsh habitats such as sandy soil. These were fruiting directly from shale. Almost invisible, I doubt if I would have seen and photographed them if not for the scarcity of other fungi.

Conglomeratus refers to the mushroom's similarity to conglomerate rock. This similarity is most noticeable on the marbled pore surface. Looking like dull ends of shoehorns, **P. conglomeratus**' closest relative is **Pisolithus tinctorius**, the famed Dead Man's Foot or Cement Foot, commonly found in California or northern Oregon, but rarely seen in Washington. The caps of **Pisolithus tinctorius** can be enormous, attaining widths of 30 cm across, while those of P. conglomeratus rarely exceed 8–10 cm.

But what it lacks in size, **P. conglomeratus** makes up for in numbers. Spectacular finds of hundreds of fruiting bodies have been reported. Another difference is that **P. tinctorius** has a stalk, an unusually thick one covered with hard, hairy nodules that are more reminiscent of a science fiction creature's leg than a mushroom. **P. conglomeratus** has a lateral stalk or none at all, superficially linking it to Polyporus and other shelf or bracket fungi.

Pisolithus tinctorius is called the Bohemian Truffle in Europe while the less esteemed **P. conglomeratus** is dubbed Bohemian Tongue, sometimes even derogatorily. This is undoubtedly due to the fact that caught at the right stage, **P. tinctorius** has a delicious ginger odor and is easily cleaned for eating while **Pisolithellus conglomeratus**, with a similar aroma, is more difficult to clean. **P. tinctorius** also makes excellent brown and gold textile dyes whereas **P. conglomeratus** has only been known to stain teeth off-green.

In the world of mushrooming, timing is crucial, and praise can quickly turn to scorn. Fresh specimens are one thing, but few other fungi are so denounced as old specimens of **P. tinctorius** and **P. conglomeratus**. Seasoned truffle dogs and pigs have been known to run from their overpowering stench, rendering the noses of these valuable animals worthless for weeks. But everything said and done, the mushroom connoisseur knows that fresh specimens of **Pisolithellus conglomeratus** can be carefully cleaned for the table, an effort amply rewarded. Despite its unsavory appearance, the flesh of **P. conglomeratus** is as succulent as a chanterelle and more flavorful than **Tuber gibbosum**.

The spicy, exotic aroma perfectly compliments Glasgow casserole and other classic seafood dishes. So while you are out looking for morels this spring, keep an eye and a nose out for that rarest of delicacies, **Pisolithellus conglomeratus**. Happy hunting and bon appetit!

Cantharellus striatus Defridge

By Chas Gilmore

Large and fleshy, often growing in sessile groups of 8 to 20.

Cantharellus striatus

Common names for **Cantharellus striatus** are Early Chanterelle, Late Chanterelle, and King's Bane. First described by Henry Defridge, later studied extensively by S. P. Lingblumssen and M. Rasman, **Cantharellus striatus** is one of the most striking mushrooms of early spring. Large and fleshy, often growing in sessile groups of eight to twenty, this member of the Cantharellaceae is hard to miss. In clear weather its golden chestnut-brown stands out clearly in sylvan setting or the green and buff of lawn and field habitats.

Many has been the time after a long and fruitless hike through sedge and over sedge, under riparia or overdaria (over derry) that I have feasted my sore eyes on the plump and cheery caps of the Early Chanterelle...er Late Chanterelle, depending on how you look at it, or how you are feeling that day, or can even remember. It's a bit like being a splitter or a lumper in mushroom taxalingua, but that's another story.

The Early/Late Chanterelle has also been called the King's Bane, a decidedly unfeudal nomen whose origin must lie in **Cantharellus striatus'** delicatessen potpourri of flavor. Needless to say, all is not rosy with **Cantharellus striatus**, nor could this be expected with so unusual a fungus.

There was in fact a controversy: The King's Bane Controversy, it was called. It all started when Maynard Rasman brashly challenged Storndt Lingblumssen during a Northwest Mycological Society meeting in 1942. Storndt had always referred to **Cantharellus striatus** as the Early Chanterelle, but Rasman objected, not so much because he thought the nickname a misnomer, but simply as a matter of scientific principle. "I beg the attention of my august and distinguished colleague," Dr. Rasman had begun, in a historic speech that fortunately had been recorded for posterity by an auditor of the meeting who subsequently sent both Rasman and Lingblumssen a transcript of the proceedings. "But

537

because **Cantharellus striatus** can be found as early as early March and as late as late April, and early March is exactly four months behind early November, the end of the traditional bolete season, and late April is approximately four months before late August when the heart of the bolete season traditionally begins, the Early Chanterelle is as late as it is early. Therefore, ergo logicum sum, it might just as well be called the Late Chanterelle." These few words precipitated a tremendous row among the Society's normally reserved and even taciturn devotees. Lingblumssen was incensed at being so summarily confronted and obviously dispatched. "What sort of upstart rapscallion gibberdygosh are ye talkin, Doctoor Rasmoon," he retorted with a snorted, wheezing, stertorous accent. "Are ye tiltin' port or starboard?" (Storndt was famous for this last line; nobody seemed to know what it meant, but it didn't seem to matter. It intimidated some.) Whatever the case, he was far too upset over this fine point in common name etymology, but there was nobody there to tell him this, except Dr. Rasman, of course, who was pleasantly amused by the stir his simple statement had caused.

"Yes, **Cantharellus striatus** has always been called the Early Chanterelle," objected Ms. Ernestine Ogsdahl, one of Storndt Lingblumssen's greatest admirers (a Norwegian connection, no doubt).

"You just included her comment as a female token," someone accused the auditor.

"Don't get smart. There isn't time for that," snapped someone else.

I digress, though. Who cares what our forerunner mycologists did or said? And yet, a little history never hurt anybody as long as it's not overdone. No chance of that with me. Let's move on from what might be educational and inspirational to something more inane and a lot less boring: the rest of the description of Cantharellus striatus.

Habitat: Fields and lawns, along fencerows and at the edges of woods, usually in mossy soil, and always in association with fir. Found in California, Oregon, Washington, and British Columbia. Caps: 6-10 cm wide, sometimes larger. Similar to **Cantharellus formosus**, but different. The caps of Cantharellus striatus are golden chestnut while those of **Cantharellus formosus**

have an orange color and are a lot slimmer with indentations and crustaceans, normally dry except when wet....becoming spongy and soggy in age, but not enduring as in many Cantharellaceae. Margins with prominent overhang and often with pronounced lateral excursion.

Gills: None, you fool...Chanterelles have ridges, intermittent and random with no verifiable pattern.

Stalks: Lightly attached to earth, usually lighter than cap color and thicker than **Cantharellus subalbidus**, in fact, the thickest in all the Cantharellaceae. Unique among all chanterelles, the decurrent gill structure, runs the whole length of the stalk. This peculiar structure is what gives **Cantharellus striatus** its name. Neither gills nor pores, their exact purpose is unknown. Defridge thought they were residual tooth striations left by shrews and other rodents, an unconfirmed theory no longer taken seriously by anyone. Lingblumssen saw some connection with **Dacrymyces palmatus** parasitism, though exactly what and how he never satisfactorily explained. Rasman remained silent on this point. Wisely so, no doubt. The most seriously considered idea was that the structures were run-off conduits, crucial to **Cantharellus striatus** since excessive moisture turns them to mush.

Another peculiar characteristic of the stalk is that it peels, much in the manner of **Cantharellus cibarius**.

Odor: Farinaceous when soggy, otherwise pleasant, sometimes deliriously so, with an odor of carob, cinnamon, allspice, and honey.

Spore Print: Tawny. Lingblumssen claimed to have found small nodules resembling raisins in spore prints of **Cantharellus striatus**. Much of his pioneering work is now suspect.

Other: Flesh of cap turns blue when bruised, orange when boiled, purple when beaten, and green, red, or yellow when thrown against a tree. Melzer's reagent adds nothing to the flavor or appearance of the spores.

Edibility: A chef's choice. **Cantharellus formosus** places a distant second in my opinion. **Cantharellus striatus var. hiatus**, a variant found locally, has a distinct taste of blueberries, sometimes having a nutty, sweet flavor. This fungus can be safely eaten raw.

Pseudomorchella arenicola
(Czysk) Bullhaven

There have been only four recorded sightings in history.

Pseudomorchella arenicola

The Sand Loving Pseudo Morel, as the name means in Latin, has got to be one of Whatcom County's more curious shoreline species. Although many gilled fungi can fruit in sandy soils, it is rare to find an ascomycete so at home in sand and shell. It is almost safe to say that if the broken shells weren't there, **Pseudomorchella arenicola** wouldn't be there either. I say "almost" because it is such a rare species that not much is known about it. There have only been four recorded sightings in history, but all four shared an affinity for the calcareous substances found in crushed seashells.

First discovered on the shores of the Black Sea in 1943 by the brilliant Czech mycologist, Anton Czysk, it was later transferred out of the genus Morchella by Bullhaven to its correct position in Pseudomorchella. It was later discovered that Czysk was suffering from sunstroke when he tried to describe it. Bullhaven cleverly surmised this condition. Noting that the hymenial surface resembled more a conglomeration of pressed coffee beans than the chambered surface of a morel, he lifted it out of near certain oblivion in that overcrowded genus.

The stipe, also, was rather unusual for a Morchella. After repeated observations at the edge of the sea Bullhaven discovered the function of the tough, punctate-indented stem surface and the flattened suction cups at the base. It turned out that **Pseudomorchella arenicola** fruited at low tide just below the high water mark. The tough ornamented stem surface with the basal suction cups were needed to grip the sand as the high tide wavelets beat them to and fro.

Fruiting bodies of **P. arenicola** run from 6–9 cm tall and vary in color from ochre to brown to cinnamon brown. The stem is tawny until you get to the extreme base where it turns ochre again and subviscid at the flattened suction cups used for further gripping. Spore dispersal is another odd feature. When fully mature, the ovulatae or "coffee beans" split down the middle, emitting great puffs of olive powder. Winds then waft the spores down the beach, attracting shore birds, which then carry the spores in their webbed feet to distant migration sites.

Unfortunately, very little of the Sand Loving Pseudo Morel is edible. You have to get to them between tides before the spores mature. The hard, corky exterior hides a creamy interior core that is edible if beaten with a stone. Connoisseurs liken the experience to that of extracting meat from a sea slug. It is said that the ensuing flavor is so subtle that you will miss it if the accompanying food is anything other than rice.

Besides the Black Sea, collections of **Pseudomorchella arenicola** have been reported from Scotland, Massachusetts, and now....our own Birch Bay. The time to look for it is late March.

Otherwise the spring tides increase and litter the beaches with strands of kelp, a major nuisance when trying to spot this rare but cosmopolitan species.

Ganoderma immotum
Wannamaker et al.

This meant the new species was lurking in the freezer.

Ganoderma immotum

Although new names in Ganoderma seem to appear in the literature every decade or so, none is so refreshingly novel as **Ganoderma immotum**, a rare polypore that prefers maple to conifers in the Pacific Northwest. When Ivan Norelsky, a semi-obscure authority in the Lectiaceae, first spotted it outside his home near Mount Index, he'd sensed he'd found something unique. As he observed the fungus from his bathroom window he noticed that squirrels kept carrying off pieces of it into the upper boughs. It wasn't that the squirrels were carting them off that impressed him. It was the ease with which they tore off the chunks of the polypore from the host tree.

Norelsky had rushed to the base of the maple. Here he discovered bits of the shredded fungus littering the forest floor. He picked one up. It was very soft and somewhat spongy with a warm, farinaceous odor most unusual for a polypore. He wasted no time. Within an hour and a half he had it fully described under the name **Spongipellis farinaceous Norelsky**. Then he stuck it in his freezer for safe-keeping. There seemed to be no rush to publish. Since the squirrels had eaten all the other material in the area, there was no threat that some visiting polyporist would show up and describe it ahead of him. He went over and started a fire in his hearth. Then he uncorked a bottle of Buzzard's Breath Ale to celebrate. Norelsky was a bachelor and conservative by nature. Drinking beer with exotic labels was the only wild thing he did.

The importance of his discovery grew in his mind daily. He would remove the specimen from the freezer every third day and check it for any new characters. He had noted originally that the specimen measured 17 centimeters in width. It had a cinnamon colored, crustose cap. It was sessile, annual, and had a thick, cream colored band around the margin, reminiscent of Fomitopsis. The pore surface was more yellowish buff. The pores were round and widely separated without any particular pattern. Norelsky was intrigued by two characters in particular. One was that some of the pores could be found on the cap surface. Could this mean that Spongipellis was evolutionizing? The other was that the entire fruiting body was waxing paler over time. Can species of Spongipellis be hygrophanous? He dutifully jotted it down, not realizing for quite some time that a layer of ice had slowly encompassed the specimen.

Eventually, word of his find leaked out. It was probably when he tried to publish it in *Mushroom, the Journal*. There had been a brief series of board meetings when the publishers and editors had convened to discuss expansion in this direction, a flurry of activity that went nowhere except for one significant side effect. It attracted the attention of Pengus Wannamaker, the vulture of modern taxonomy. Pengus was the one personage you did not want sniffing around your genus. Although he was an accredited mycologist, he couldn't bear to describe anything new. He lived instead to alter those species names described by others. He was a tinkerer who planned raids on the genera of other mycologists with the same grim determination that one corporation would use in the attempted takeover of another. For this purpose he always had around him a string of graduate students. There were fifteen to twenty of these amateur investigators at any one time who could be dispatched around the globe… looking for mistakes. When the corrected names were published, Pengus Wannamaker always included his assistants in the authorship as *et al.* If they hungered for a little more recognition, Pengus would wag a finger to remind them. They hadn't got that degree yet, had they?

So, of course, it wasn't Dr. Wannamaker's vehicle that broke down in Ivan Norelsky's driveway one frosty December afternoon. It belonged to an et al. And a clever one, to boot. She had already discovered that Norelsky never sent dried herbarium specimens by regular mail to a university. He only sent freeze-dried material by express mail. This meant the new species was lurking in the freezer. She hoped the freezer would be somewhere near an exit door.

She arrived at the front door coughing badly and pointing to her Mazda where a smoke bomb had just been set off under the hood. Norelsky had barely time to register that the young lady was attractive. He took one look at the growing, sulphurous cloud, and suggested a jump. He told her he just happened to have cables in his root cellar.

"Now, it might not be the battery," he informed his visitor, "but there's no harm in trying."

He groped his way to the root cellar. His visitor didn't remain mystified for long. She scampered around until she found the kitchen. It was a miracle. The new Spongipellis was right in the front in the freezer compartment. She was out of the door and re-submerged in the cloud of smoke before Ivan returned with the cables.

The specimen was still rock hard when it reached Dr. Wannamaker's Mobile Mycology Lab a half hour later. Pengus was impressed with his grad student. "You are unflappable," he cooed, "Even imperturbable, and since it hasn't been published yet, we can dispense with the 'ex Norelsky'."

He changed the genus to Ganoderma because of the hardness of the pileus. He then fished out his pocket English-Latin dictionary from his glove compartment.

"Hmmm," he sighed. He noted that *immotus* was the name for "imperturbable," and thus the species was named.

Climacodon edificialis
Smaug & Hebnow

Buildings just weren't the same back in the day.

Climacodon edificialis

Anyone heading from a hardware store with a 2x4 cannot help but notice the soaring price of lumber nowadays. Despite the well publicized efforts of environmental agencies, the vast amount of clear cutting throughout the Northwest during the past decade combined with the equally voluminous exporting of timber to foreign nations has created a serious shortage in wood. As more builders have moved to particle-board and vinyl siding in response to the shortfall, it was only a matter of time before the polypores reacted. They too, like builders, have had to adapt to new substrates.

None, however, has been more successful locally than that ubiquitous polypore, **Climacodon edificialis**.

Like its closest relative, **Climacodon septentrionalis**, it fruits on wood, its massive clusters arising from a point of attachment only 2–4 cm in width at the base. But unlike **C. septentrionalis**, which fruits high up on living trees, the adaptable **Climacodon edificialis** is just as happy on vinyl siding, black top roofing, particle-board, and all grades of treated plywood, often engulfing two or more substrates in one fruiting.

Smaug and Hebnow, two graduate students in mycology out of Enumclaw, were the first to spot it. They were shocked one afternoon in late October of 1996 to find a giant, cinnamon colored polypore sprouting from the roof of their local IGA food store. Smaug borrowed a ladder and went up. From the ground it had looked like some kind of aborted Sparassis, but on closer inspection, the lanky, saurian-looking student began to realize that no amount of wine could save this one. It was nothing but a tough, inedible polypore whose shelving fruiting bodies had fused in age to form a corky, amorphous blob.

Hebnow had scrambled up behind him. A small, excitable sort of person, he circled the specimen several times, his head bobbing like a dachshund's.

"What genus! What genus is this?" he barked so stridently that Smaug broke out of his private funk at not finding a meal on the roof, and presently offered Climacodon. After all, they had had to climb a ladder to observe it. Not to be outdone by the competitive Smaug, Hebnow pointed out the edifice it was fruiting on, and a name for the species was born.

Since then, **Climacodon edificialis** has been the bane of builders and contractors throughout the Northwest. Here, in this photo taken by Lee Whitford in Nooksack, you can see the polypore fruiting from vinyl siding while it prepares to consume the plywood housing of the home owner's power meter.

Lee had interviewed the deeply disturbed owner.

"I went with vinyl to keep out the rain," he had muttered, "No one warned me about the toadstools."

"Maybe it was attracted by the power meter," Lee had offered in a helpful vein.

"Naaah! It's just nasty stuff," spat the home owner, who preferred to remain anonymous, "I'm contemplating a class action suit, but the who the hell do you sue? The electric company? The vinyl people? I can't even remember where I got that plywood. This creepy fungus eats everything."

Lee shook her head in commiseration. She considered inviting the man to join Northwest Mushroomers, but then realized the timing might not be right. She left him muttering about setting up a hotline on the internet and then drove home to develop her photos.

Climacodon edificialis is a bit strange, even for a polypore. The fruiting bodies are massive from the start, erupting overnight into compact, rounded clusters. The pileal surface is crustose to tomentose, dark chestnut to cinnamon in color, but often paling where the margins meet wood, vinyl, or soil. The context is dry, spongy-fibrous, brittle, and white. The hymenial or pore surface (not seen here) is buff to cream with minute pores, 11–12 per mm. While the taste is infinitely forgettable, the odor is not. The species smells like whatever substrate it is fruiting on, whether tar with black top, pulp mill with plywood, polyurethane with vinyl, and so on.

As I pored over the microscopic details in Smaug and Hebnow's publication, I wondered how such a monstrosity was created. How come there were no recordings of this species from the 19th century? Why could it not be found in any North American or European mushroom guides? How had it come into being? Under "Observations," Hebnow suggested that buildings just weren't the same back in the day.

It took a little time, but the answer, when it came, did not derive from the monographs on polypores. It came from the lumberyard at Sash & Door. I had been browsing around in search of pier blocks when I ran into a discarded pile of plywood. The layers were beginning to separate. I was wondering if humidity alone could have caused this problem when I noticed the mycelium. Stringy, pale orange rivulets of mycelium were permeating the plywood in all directions.

"Sorry. That's not for sale," a yard hand had hurried up to explain. Perhaps he had misinterpreted the intensity of my interest.

"Terrible experiment," he went on, "This company, and I just can't be more specific without facing a libel charge, had invented a new glue for the ply. I'm sure you've heard how glue manufacturers have studied how limpets adhere to rocks in ocean storms to formulate their glues. Well, some genius thought…why not do this with shelf mushrooms? Some of those bracket fungi are stuck so hard to tree trunks you have to saw them off."

He then winced and gestured towards the plywood stack. I followed the sweep of his arm. And there, at the very end of the stack, was a 3-foot diameter fruiting of **Climacodon edificialis**.

Ramaria bulbo-digitalis
Arambucco

Apparently there had been a scuffle under the table.

Ramaria bulbo-digitalis

Believe us, it was late in the day out at La Push on the Olympic Peninsula when Vancouver mycologist Paul Kroeger and I, exhausted from hours of tracking down Phaeocollybias under the Sitka spruce, ran into this curious coral fungus under salmonberry. In no mood for anything that might tax our intellects, I took a hurried photo and bagged the thing for later scrutiny. It was soon agreed on the way to the car that we would slice the Ramaria in half lengthwise so we could pursue an identification from both sides of the border.

It was only days later in the seclusion of my lab that I began to realize this was no ordinary Ramaria. It had been found solitary fruiting on ragged debris where beach ended and forest began. But aside from these comforting facts, the rest of the Ramaria departed abruptly from the realm of the mundane. Instead of slender branches arising from a common base of 6 cm or more, we had a great bulbous base with a last-minute eruption of crowns at the apex. It was as if someone had blown up a balloon to the pressure point until at the last moment the air had burst into fingers at the extremity. Perhaps the hyphae had become confused. Perhaps they had waited too long before realizing that branches were a part of it, too. It was just an odd combination. The gross morphological characters of this Ramaria now resembled a blow-up of the short rod-like projections on the pileipellis of a Mycena.

The field characteristics were easy enough to record. The fruiting body was 7 cm tall to the base of the apical fingers and 4 ½ cm wide. The color of the base was an attractive chestnut-ochre, the context white. The texture was a bit off for Ramaria, a little on the nodulose side, but maybe just the beginning of a Hypomyces attack. The "fingers" were lilac-flesh in color, the apices truncate or acute. In short, a qualified member of Section Wretchinomaria, but after that the trail went dead. There was no similar Ramaria in Arora or in Ramaria of the Pacific northwestern United States. Perhaps Paul was having better luck with the other half of the specimen in Vancouver, but the silence from that quarter equaled my own.

It began to look like a world key would be called for. With global warming coming on, the species could have arrived from South America, Australia, or even the Far East. It was Kroeger who came up with the idea of tracking down the most recent invaders and their origins. The most obvious of these was **Gymnopus peronatus**, up from Argentina. The taxon was everywhere you looked. Named after the heroic, iconic Eva Peron, it was smothering everything in its path. If Collybioid spores could make this journey, why not a Ramaria spore to boot? Boot, considered Paul. The spores must have arrived via boot treads.

By plane or boat was the question. A phone call to jeweler Poesh Binner on North Pender Island resolved the issue. Poesh lives in a cabin on a rocky crag that juts into the Haro Strait and has a fine view of the shipping traffic going by.

"All kinds of freighters from South America these days," he informed, "They're bringing up boatloads of Nothofagus from Chile so we Canadians can make more exotic furniture."

Ahh! The Trillium Company! Why hadn't I thought of that fungal moving company before? It was now more likely the Ramaria had Latino origins.

Meanwhile Kroeger had struck gold in Vancouver. Following his instinct that Ramarias were also known as "coral" mushrooms, he had located that obscure monograph, *Los Corales de la Costa Chileña by Quiñones y Tavares*. These were authors hitherto unknown to us. The keys started off innocently enough. But Paul soon discovered that Quiñones followed Singer while Tavares clung to A.H. Smith. Just prior to a new section in the key there would be an exchange of words. Something like:

"A la gran puta! Porque no mirastes esos incrustaciones?"

"No son alli, pendejo!"

"Estas tacaño. No quieras comprar un microscopio con contraste de fase. Es tu problema!"

"No importa. Mis estudiantes son de acuerdo. No existan incrustaciones!"

It was a tortuous trek through the keys, often accompanied by language unfamiliar to this native of Penticton. But finally, on page 297, the species sprang from the page! It was **Ramaria bulbo-digitalis**, the Fat Fingered Ramaria, and its history was as cryptic as its appearance.

It was first discovered by Jorge Arambucco in 1896, spotted again by Honrubia in 1939, and then cooked and eaten by the late Juan Pineda in 1964.

"El sabor era del mar," Juan had written, "Pero la textura era del otro mundo." Briefly translated: "The flavor was of the sea, but the texture was from another world." A sort of sinking feeling came over me as I realized I had rehydrated mine in spirits. But I gamely read on. Juan had served it to four friends along with a rather fruity Chilean wine. None of the five blamed the wine for what happened next. Apparently there had been a scuffle under the table. Different friends went off at different times, depending on the rapidity of their digestive tracts. After that, the print went blank. And the authors, Quiñones y Tavares, had chosen to leave it blank. Censorship may have been strong in Chile in that era, and Juan may have had to abandon that table in a hurry. Quiñones y Tavares clearly did not want to be associated any longer.

Temporarily the mystery remains. The chemistry department at University of British Columbia is considering an investigation. Whatever properties lurk within **Ramaria bulbo-digitalis** might be useful in a time of war. Testosterone boosters to be sure.

Meanwhile Kroeger would like to clear up one inaccuracy from the field notes.

"If you remove the 'berry' from the 'salmonberry'," he informed me by email, "You will have a better idea of the habitat."

Clathropsis rubropetaloides (Brumph) Isakuchi

At this stage there is some argument over edibility.

Clathropsis rubropetaloides

Imagine arriving in late June at a long deserted burn site some 47 miles northeast of Twisp and spotting these red curiosities. Phil Smyth had never seen anything like them. He had only found seven morels all day. Not enough to pay for the gas expense. But if these were edible, there might be some hope left. He would take a few back to the regular meeting with Northwest Mushroomers Association the very next evening.

They created quite a buzz on the specimen table. Dr. Pritchard thought they might be edible when very young. All he could tell us for certain was that it was an evolutionary species, part ascomycete and part basidiomycete in its microscopic features, the first crossover species in the world of fungi. After his usual modest beginning, Pritchard geared up and elaborated further.

Known as the Red Petal Shedder, it first appears on a burn site as a glistening pink egg. At this stage there is some question over edibility. (The Japanese, who have a broader palate than our own, are said to adore the musky, feral flavor. Most other cultures simply gag.) Then, like any other puffball worth its salt, the taxon forms exterior petals while simultaneously growing an interior sac filled with a gelatinous matrix. It is within this matrix that the ten-spored asci will start to appear. Eventually this matrix will start to decay, producing an odor of mink gland. It is at this point that petals will start to unfold into rays (see specimen in background of photo). This is the signal for certain burn site beetles. They soon arrive in droves to cart away the rays. The rotting matrix is then revealed. This in turn attracts swarms of flies. They settle on the rotting egg and fly off with asci and spores in their feet. The life cycle is thus assured.

Another common feature, explained Doc Pritchard, was the presence of cheilocystidia. These were relatively huge microscopically, giant bottle-shaped forms with feather dusters at their apices. They could be seen with the naked eye as the floccose white fringes of the red petals.

"I don't like the name," spoke up Phil, "Hard as hell to pronounce."

"There's quite the story behind it," nodded Pritchard, "Both confusing and strange. I will look into it and report at the next meeting. Meeting adjourned."

There was a stampede towards the table. Phil was alarmed. He had no idea others had been eyeing his Clathropsis.

"Order in the room!" thundered Pritchard, "Whoever brought

them in has first dibs on taking them out."

Dr. Hugh Pritchard was no stranger to the classic battles of mycologists racing to the finish line to publish their names of new species first. He recalled Karsten and Lange in 1894, Berkeley and Schweinitz in 1801, Gulliven and Twang in 1731, but nothing had prepared him for Brumph and Isakuchi in 1959. He further discovered, that although rare, the Red Petal Shedder was a widespread species. As luck would have it, the Clathropsis appeared in both Japan and Chile in 1958. Whoever published it first would have their name immortalized.

Colonel Alfredo Brumph, a retired member of General Pinochet's Department of the Interior, liked his mycology straight up. He realized early on that the presence of cheilocystidia made the species unique. But he went a step further. He zoned in on the feather duster appearance of the apices and named it **Clathrus pluma-peniculus**. No longer would the myco world laugh at his occasionally clumsy efforts with the microscope.

On the other side of the world, Dr. Kano Isakuchi was in shock. He was only days behind the Brumph publication and he wondered publicly how people wildly successful in the Pinochet regime were allowed into mycology in the first place. If Brumph was allowed in, why not Goebbels? He could also be kicking around down there, frothing at the genera.

Isakuchi found the Brumph name insufficient and therefore repugnant. He felt the gorgeous red exterior traits deserved to be showcased over the interior ones. He soon filed a formal complaint with the Board of the Code of International Nomenclature. This did not escape the notice of the Colonel. He would have none of it. He informed the General Committee that he would come out of retirement, if need be, and use his considerable military skills to stop the Isakuchi name transfer.

Isakuchi wandered in the streets of Osaka. Why hadn't the Code checked out his resumé? He was then informed that if he initiated a screening clause, it would be obvious whom he was directing it towards, and the consequences . . .

But Isakuchi couldn't let it go. The striking exterior of the species demanded to be acknowledged. He called it **Clathrus rubropetaloides** only to be informed that name was already taken. Unperturbed, he simply switched the genus name to Clathropsis. This was not a good move. It angered both Brumph and the stalwart nomenclaturalists. Isakuchi didn't want both parties against him. In an act of unparalleled generosity he had the Brumph name reinstalled in front of his. By the time the furor died down, he had moved his family to the Hunter Island group off the northwest corner of Tasmania.

Brumph had never seen anything like it. He didn't know whether to laugh or cry. Isakuchi, meanwhile, had found a deserted cabin to move into. There was a cave nearby in case that proved inadequate. He was comforted by the fact there was no vehicular ferry traffic to the island. Brumph could not arrive with machine guns and a tank. But just in case, he made an agreement with the local ferry boat captains to report any suspicious looking characters on board. They were to phone him before they left the dock. After 21 such calls in the first month, the frazzled Isakuchi spent his days in the cave.

He was reportedly still there twelve years after Brumph passed away.

"And so," Dr. Pritchard commenced at the next meeting of Northwest Mushroomers, "If any of you spot the Red Petal Shedder at the next Morel Madness foray, remember that man in the cave. Association, association, association."

Naucoria ungocola LeGras

Initially the valet ran into problems.

A few years back, when I discovered the bacterial fungus **Pseudomonas aeruginosus** fruiting in the diesel in the fuel tank in my boat, I thought I had found the Northwest's most eccentric fungus. Now, several years later and many dollars poorer, I've run into Naucoria ungocola, a brown-spored agaric that fruits on left-over grease in frying pans, woks, grills, and stove tops. This near human taste in food makes it homo sapiens' closest relative among the higher basidiomycetes.

It is a rare species. Those few who have been fortunate enough to sample **Naucoria ungocola** claim the flavor has an uncanny resemblance to its substrate, sometimes rich and buttery, sometimes just plain rancid. While the flavor is often in doubt, mycophagists do agree on one enduring aspect of the species. The invisible mycelial hyphae always leave a dull grayish-brown stain on the cookware long after the mushroom has disappeared. In older literature, this color was referred to as "drab." It takes

Naucoria ungocola   Photo by Brandy Cravens

a lot of elbow grease before this drab can be removed.

The rest of its history is every bit as uncanny. Francois LeGras, the intrepid French mycologist who published the species in 1904, first noted that the gills became evanescent in heat. Transfixed by this discovery, he was unable to move from his chair until gradually the stem, too, became evanescent in front of his eyes. At this point he had decided to eat the cap. There had been no point in watching an entire meal dissolve before his eyes. When a colleague asked him how the description was going, LeGras waited awhile before replying. Finally, here were his words: "It is like the four seasons. How can I say? It is constantly changing. For example, half an hour ago, the cap was two centimeters wide and ochre in color. Ten minutes ago it was 1 ½ cm wide and more of an ochre brown. And now it has vanished. It is quite the most evolutionary mushroom I have ever seen."

The colleague was reassured. Francois would never attempt to describe a new species that metamorphosed while you watched it. Sensing that French mycology was safe until the next sighting, perhaps a decade into the future, the colleague left the lab with LeGras still in it.

This turned out to be a mistake. Making every move with planned deliberation, LeGras opened the door to his fridge and removed a second tray with another fruiting body on it. He labored throughout the night on his official Latin description.

The cap was described as diminutive, lugubrious, becoming

evanescent in heat from the margins first. The gills were described as very few, very distant, becoming remote in age. Attached to unattached. The stem was mahogany umber, glistening with corpulent caulocystidia, terete becoming enlarged at base and apex. Both cap and stipe were glabrous to gelatinous.

Then LeGras turned to his microscopic examination. Having heard that some dark-spored species can have dextrinoid reactions, he applied a drop of Melzer's solution to a gill surface. The drop rolled off. He tried again. The drop again was repelled. As he began to sweat, a warm cloud of humidity enveloped his head and immediate surroundings. Thinking he needed a smaller surface, he tried sectioning a gill only to see it melt on the slide.

"Tant pis." he shrugged. He turned to his notes and wrote "spores variable, repelled by Melzer's." And he was done.

It was subsequently published in *Le Journal Mycologique du Midi*. The ensuing uproar crossed the British Channel. Lord Carnival, who had been closing in on Naucoria for years, insisted on observing the holotype. The French were mortified. They soon realized that firing the editor would do nothing to mollify the Lord. For nearly six months no Frenchman would tell him which herbarium the specimen had been sent to. Lord Carnival had to resort to searching through the literature to search for possible enemies of LeGras. Surely there must have been a battle over placement or nomenclature somewhere. But LeGras was that great rarity among mycologists… a man who had never crossed swords with anyone because he had always worked in genera no one else wanted!

Beside himself with frustration, Lord Carnival dressed his valet in the garb of an American artist of the Ash Can School and sent him across the channel to explore "every blasted herbarium in France."

Looking back on it all, one suspects Lord Carnival of wanting to sink **Naucoria ungocola**. Probably he wanted to send it to Leptoglossum, a genus with very few gills and white spores. Perhaps he felt that the similarity in gills would trump the difference in spore color. Besides, there was an intriguing rumor circulating in France… namely that no spores had ever been detected for **Naucoria ungocola**. He would have carte blanche, place the damn thing anywhere he wanted.

Initially the valet ran into problems. The French curators couldn't understand why an American artist with a Welsh accent would want to haunt their herbariums. He had to explain over and over again that while there were many paintings of fungi in their fresh state, no one as yet had thought to paint them in their herbarium state. Desiccation was a big part of the Ash Can School. This sort of logic made just enough sense to the curators to allow him a day or two in a herbarium. The period of grace would inevitably end at the first sighting of one of the awful sketches by a mycologist.

Being escorted out of one herbarium after another soon became a way of life. Lord Carnival was beside himself. Even a real American could have done better. But then, one afternoon, there was a turnaround. The valet had gotten into the prestigious herbarium at the Université de Lyons. He was about to abandon his daily search when his fingers glided over an envelope a bit darker than the rest. Taped to the top flap was a tiny note: **Naucoria ungocola** LeGras. The valet peered over his shoulder to the left and to the right. All was quiet in the gloom. His pulse quickened as he realized he was closing in on his goal. At the same time an imperceptible sadness descended over his temples. Duping the curators had been a bit of a lark. He'd seen some fine country, sampled wines unheard of in Britain, and eaten quite well. Now it was about to end.

The valet opened the flap of the envelope. He tapped it upside down over a white blotter pad. Nothing came out. He tapped it again. Still nothing. He took a deep breath and peered into the confines of the envelope. There was no doubt about it. Reverse evolution had finally arrived. **Naucoria ungocola** had transmogrified into the substrate it had fruited from.

Cordyceps chaotica Dzu

He had never seen such a luxurious tomentum.

Cordyceps chaotica

Weintraub Krull wasn't sure about what she was seeing. She was on her weekly patrol of her backyard garden on the lookout for more whiskey bottles possibly buried there by Harvard Krull, her husband. At this point it is hard to decide what comes next, either Harvard Krull and his fixation with the German mycologist Kummer or the giant Cordyceps (for that is what it turned out to be) fruiting from a beetle in her wood chip mulch. She noted that the beetle had stopped moving. She re-emerged from her kitchen with a tiny porcelain saucer and moved the 'ménage à deux' to Harvard's study.

Although a long-time member of Northwest Mushroomers Association, Harvard is not well known by many in the club. He shows up every three or four years at the Survivor's Banquet. He's the 40-year-oldish sort of guy with the Harris Tweed jacket and the faded jeans. He will be the only person in the room drinking directly out of a wine bottle. If you are in the act of having a conversation with Harvard, you don't want to stand too close. You might get conked in the jaw on an upward swing.

The problem is that Harvard is on a personal mission. Just the thought of the mycologist Paul Kummer, a former priest from the city of Zerbst in the eastern part of Germany, will bring a mist to Harvard's eyes, another swing of the bottle. In the history of mycology Harvard realized that no one else had come close to the brilliance of Kummer. This modest man of the cloth seemed never to have authored a new species. Yet his name was attached to thousands. This was a sign of genius, concluded Harvard. While other mycologists battled disease and mosquitoes in the tropics, back pain and leg cramps in remote mountain ranges, Kummer needed only to sit at his desk and wait for the new descriptions to trickle in. White, decurrent gills? This becomes a Clitocybe. Rusty spores and bitter taste? Now that's a Gymnopilus. The name of Kummer accompanied every transfer.

More than a century has passed, but finally another nomenclatural bonanza was at hand. DNA sequencing methods were creating new species at a rate not seen since the 1870's. There was opportunity here. If he could somehow capitalize, have his name attached as Kummer once did, the name of Krull would resound through the ages. He plotted night and day. It had finally driven him to drink.

Weintraub knew the precise moment Harvard had spotted the Cordyceps by the roar that came from the study. Harvard was aghast. He had never seen a Cordyceps like it. He measured the fruiting body. It was 1 cm thick and 5 ½ cm tall. Only **Cordyceps capitata** exceeded these dimensions, but it had a different appearance and never fruited on beetles. Besides this, the perithecia were totally random while the stroma seemed to be undifferentiated from the stalk. And that cottony tomentum at the base.... He had never seen such a luxurious tomentum.

He spent the next three weeks chasing it down in North American literature. He got nowhere. The more often he struck out among the native monographs, the more excitable he became. This one could be his alone!

But Harvard had never heard of Taiwan mycologist Ling Chee Dzu.

To his fellow mycologists in the Far East, Dr. Dzu was often an enigma about to happen. When sober he was acknowledged as the greatest technician of his time. But Ling Chee was known to inhabit opium dens. His judgments were sometimes of the whimsical sort. His vocation compelled him to author new species whether on opium or not. He needed to be watched like a hawk.

During the afternoon of September 9, 1993, according to his notes, he had managed to elude the mycologist appointed to follow him around. Taking this as his cue, he had returned from his den, located the Cordyceps he had found the week before, and taken a bite. The result had been almost catastrophic. He had named the taxon on the spot to reflect his subsequent movements.

Meanwhile, back in Washington state, Harvard was growing desperate. He had heard of the infamous **Cordyceps syniensis**, that beloved aphrodisiac from Tibet. Perhaps this was the species Weintraub had found. He searched online for '**Cordyceps syniensis**'. Nothing ever came up.

"Why don't you just eat it?" teased Wientraub, "It is eating you up, bit by bit. You need to turn this around, no?"

Weintraub was literally from Zerbst. She had been captured during Harvard's one pilgrimage to the former Kummer Rectory. She had even shown Harvard the bronze scissors that Kummer had used to make his separations.

"And what about you?" Harvard had asked. "Am I supposed to take it, too?"

Harvard didn't think so. There was nothing he could find on women ingesting **Cordyceps syniensis**.

"You should stand by, though," he advised, "And be prepared for whatever is coming."

She gave a funny little laugh. This whole avocation was becoming absurd.

"Well, here goes," shrugged Harvard. He bit off the top two-thirds of the carpophore.

"Just in case," he leered at her, "That black negligee from Berlin."

Harvard could not remember what words came next. What he did remember was a dizzy feeling as he approached his computer. He had managed to sit down in front of it and get online. The salty flavor of the Cordyceps had now been replaced by a numbing sensation. The roof of his mouth had begun to pulse. A low humming sound emanated from the ceiling. In some alarm, Harvard had stabbed at the keyboard. Lightheadedness had engulfed him in waves. His junk mail came on. Sound of trumpets from out on the street. Sound of car crashes. Harvard rolled his eyes, clutched his chair for support. The words 'Sexually Explicit' flashed across the monitor. Harvard stabbed again. The entire monitor began to convulse in waves. Bands of naked women began flying about, various body parts expanding and contracting at will. Notes of Chinese punk rock sliced the air like cliff swallows. The humming sound was now a drone from the center of the earth. Harvard sagged forward in his chair. The sound of his forehead banging against the keyboard brought Weintraub in from the kitchen.

"You should have keyed it better," she said. She switched off the computer. And all the porn went away.

Collybia arachnoidea La Virage nom. prov.

All these to be washed down with Red Bull, Fat Tire, Amp, Black Hook, or Moose Drool.

There was no tactful way of putting it. Just a godawful photo of the mushrooms. Both were out of focus. The only thing clear about it was the spider web resting on the caps.

Celeste took a sip of her Nicaraguan coffee.

There was clearly something of great importance about the photo. One of her eyebrows raised inquiringly. I began to wonder if I was being timed.

We were now in the Bellingham Food Co-op Café. The tables were packed with street people, college students, eco-women, gardeners, and other pro-organics. They had all looked up when Celeste strode in. The tall stature, the auburn hair in a loose bun, the theatrical gait, the dark eyes that took everything in.

And now those eyes were trained on me, perhaps singled out as a springboard for one of her plans.

"You still not see it," she grieved, "But right now you are looking at history, l'histoire de la future. Thees photo shows evolution about to happen."

"It shows a mushroom trying to look like a stone."

Collybia arachnoidea

"The mushroom ees not important. The spider ees the thing."

She was convinced the mushroom had acted symbiotically. It wanted the spider to be there. She said there had been even more webs under the gills than could be seen on the cap. The spider had spun a web because it could feel the vibrations of the larvae within. When those larvae hatched the web would be waiting for the emerging flies.

"But how can this benefit the mushroom?" I asked, "By the time the flies have hatched, the mushroom has started to rot."

"They are working on it, both spider and mushroom," she smiled.

She mentioned the obvious, that the aim of the mushroom was to reproduce its kind. Therefore the longer the gills were able to dispense spores, the better the future of the mushroom. The larvae were a problem. They destroyed the mushroom before all the spores matured. If the spiders could now pick off the flies there would come a time when the spiders would advance even more. They would leave their webs to drill into the context. Then they would feast on the larvae within.

"And thees ees the dream of the mushroom," she concluded.

She paused to glance around the café. Then she moved her fingers up to her bun and began pulling out strands of hair from the sides. I figured she must be trying to fit in. Then she glanced around again. After a few minutes, almost imperceptibly, other girls all over the café began fidgeting with their hair. It seemed like she had started a fad. Celeste smiled expansively.

She thought the presence of the spider was enough to warrant a new species. But she had to have the blessing of Dr. Lamelleaux. Without that she couldn't proceed.

Dr. Maurice Lamelleaux, the Hebeloma King from northern France. He was perhaps the most austere, the most exacting mycologist of his generation. I wondered how she had gotten mixed up with this eminence.

"You veel need more coffee. Que barbare! Not even a croissant to eat."

Dr. Lamelleaux was known, on both sides of the Atlantic, as the first to get hysterical about the types. The vanishing types. The type, it may be said, was the one specimen in an acknowledged herbarium that represented an entire species. Hundreds were already missing, mostly from overuse or decay. And hundreds more were about to go. With DNA sequencing coming on, the pressure to find types to conduct the sequencing was already overwhelming. It was only going to get worse. Dr. Lamelleaux had taken drastic action. He announced that for every student who sought a degree in mycology, the final exam and dissertation could be replaced by the finding of a neotype. This would be a replacement specimen from the exact same location where the first one was found.

The news spread like wildfire. It was the lottery of all time. Students from all over France and her former colonies were intrigued. They could be sent anywhere in the world, and if they found their type, no dissertation at the end. Celeste remembered the big day. Hundreds of students had engulfed the hallways around Lamelleaux's lab. A large hat had been passed around. Each student had extracted a piece of paper with a mushroom name on it. Celeste had drawn **Collybia bakerensis**, a rather obscure species from a place called Anderson Creek near a town called Glacier in the state of Washington, U.S.A. Her boyfriend, Marcel, drew **Entoloma subtropicum** from a small town in northern Sri Lanka. Squeals of delight or howls of dismay filled the corridors.

But Dr. Lamelleaux had created some work for himself. About 240 students needed to be housed and fed. It was, he said, like inventing a mycological Peace Corps.

Celeste had to wait two months for her predestination with Dr. Maurice. She had grown up in Reims, a semi-industrial town about an hour north of Paris. There had been weekend piqueniques in the countryside, a pass for the club swimming pool, horse riding at Epernay, endless get-togethers with her circle of friends. At lunch breaks from her lycee, they would sip the great champagnes of the region and nibble on the crispy "gateaux de Reims," a sort of pink sugar cookie that was the perfect accompaniment to champagne.

Dr. Maurice had ushered her into his office.

"You will live here," he pointed out. He had brought up Google Earth, and now Celeste hovered in front of the monitor while the aerial view of Glacier unfolded. He had found a burned out spot just to the east of the town. Behind the burned area were three shacks on the edge of a field. They were lined up along a curved dirt road. They looked just big enough for a hobbit. The middle one had been available for rent.

"And now, we turn to your food," said Lamelleaux, "I have made certain connections."

Indeed he had. A mycologist in Seattle had dispatched a grad student to drive to Glacier with orders to photograph any food he saw. Now these photos were about to be revealed. Celeste, peering intently, noticed jars of El Sabroso Pork Rinds, bags of Cheetos, Ruffles, Golden Grahams just on one shelf. Below this were Red Hot Blues, Western Family Hotdog Relish, Oberto Beef Jerky. All this to be washed down with Red Bull, Amp, Fat Tire, Black Hook, or Moose Drool.

"These are exotic flavors," explained Lamelleaux, "But as a French person you will have to get used to them."

Her training site had been in the Pyrenees. French altitude and Graham convenience store food. Her village had been the same size as Glacier. Only the issues were different.

When I met her at the Bellingham Co-op she had already done five months in Glacier. She had logged days out near Anderson Creek in vain. She desperately needed to find **Collybia bakerensis**. Only then would Dr. Lamelleaux support her new **Collybia arachnoidea**, the only species in the world that attracted spiders.

"You'll need a crowbar," I told her, "It likes to hide inside of conifer bark."

"Zee spiders?"

"No. The mushroom."

She would have to stand in line at Hardware Sales, like everyone else.

The irony is that Celeste has become at home in Glacier.

"Moose Drool, better than Kronenburg," she nodded, "And zee woods, they are full of mushrooms!"

She said she was pressuring Dr. Lamelleaux to purchase the burnt spot. He could build a lab there and have French students come every year.

Boletus aguacatus Ovorp nom. prov.

A new member of Section Mirabiles may arrive once in a century.

Boletus aguacatus

It is not very often that one finds a new bolete in Section Mirabiles. While the nodulose cap surface and the smooth stipe without reticulations indicate that this is where **Boletus aguacatus** belongs, we may never know for sure. In this case the story of the discovery of this hauntingly familiar Boletus may be stranger than the Boletus itself.

The whole episode started when I heard a sharp rap on the door of my study on the sixth floor of the Herald Building. It was late on a Wednesday afternoon in late November when not even a journalist would be wandering down the corridor.

The door opened before I could reach it, and a questioning face peered in.

"Buck McAdoo? Have I got the right place?" I was asked.

A most peculiar sort of fellow edged in. Large and a bit fleshy, he had short brown hair so sharply cropped at the temples that it looked sculpted in stone. The hair came to a point at the forehead with two lesser points above the ears. Sort of a Batman style only broken up by an absurd earring that looked at first like a mother-of-pearl paper clip dangling from the left lobe.

"Tangent Ovorp," he announced, "I'm a taxonomist."

We shook hands. The faint but pungent odor of tea tree oil wafted up from his lower extremities.

"How did you find me?" I asked.

Turned out that he had found a copy of an old NAMA membership list. For the Bellingham area, only Fred Rhoades and I were listed as people to consult in case of a mushroom poisoning. Figuring that we must be the local mushroom gurus, he had flipped a coin and come here. I was beginning to wonder what the result might have been if the coin toss had gone the other way when a yelp interrupted the reverie.

"Aha!" he seized, "You have the British Check List, I see."

Indeed I did. I had it open on my desk to check out the latest synonym list for **Mycena galericulata**, a taxon that had fooled me in the field that very morning. Misery loves company. It always brought me up to see that others had missed it, too. The Check List was an important work listing all the species found in Britain with lists of synonyms and misapplied names in italics below each accepted mushroom name. It was even helpful in the Pacific Northwest.

My new visitor now marched over to the volume, flipped a few pages, nodding appreciatively.

"I follow Ricken," he said.

"Adalbert Ricken, the German priest?" I asked.

"Very prolific. Man of the cloth," he verified. "He must have had the greatest herbarium of his time. Just look in these pages. You find him everywhere."

Indeed one did, I surmised. The sensu Rickens were hard to miss. I was suddenly at a loss for words.

"To be sure, he was only human," droned on my guest, "Made a mistake here and there, but towards the end he was hitting on all cylinders."

Well, that did it for me. I decided right then to ask him what he wanted.

"I'm up here to look for rooftop Galerinas and late season Pholiotas," he grinned.

He explained that moss covered roofs and leaf-clogged gutters were good places for Galerinas. Since most folks didn't clean their gutters in November, it was a great substrate for potential new ones. As for Pholiotas, the places to look for those were nurseries that were shut down for the season. Both habitats would require some ingenuity. Yours truly, of course, was expected to lead him to both.

"Peck, Murrill, Singer, Smith…. all the great ones," he was droning on, "They all collected in the Pacific Northwest but none remained in November when the weather turned bad. The result? Most of the late season stuff has never been named. Enter Tangent Ovorp." And he gave a little bow.

I stared up at him with an eye half cocked.

"Have you checked in with Don?" I wondered.

Don, of course, was our world class mycologist down in Seattle. Whenever a taxonomist was visiting the area, the protocol was to inform Don first. Everyone gained. Don would learn that the visitor would not be sniffing around his genus, and the visitor would be taken care of. Maybe a lunch. Most likely a foray with a top amateur leading him on it. Tangent Ovorp had jumped the protocol.

"Oh, Don?" yawned Tangent, "Not this time. He wouldn't go to my lecture on Tephrocybe of the North Central Tetons five years ago in Tacoma."

"Well, maybe Don doesn't believe in Tephrocybe. Some don't, you know," I shrugged. "Just think about it. Would you drive for 45 minutes through some of the worst traffic in the Northwest to see a genus you didn't acknowledge existed?"

I was expecting some sort of witty response. Instead, my visitor turned rigid. He stared icily into the distance, a vein beginning to throb at the sculpted hairline of his right temple. I realized I had to move on…quickly.

"Maybe he just got stuck in the traffic," I suggested.

"I got the point," Tangent recovered, "No further excursions in that direction."

We agreed to meet at nine the next day, at the Koy Café on the corner. Tangent made an about face and trudged down the corridor. Tangent Ovorp. The name was somehow familiar, but I just couldn't pull it up.

On the ride out the next day to the first of several deserted nurseries I learned a little more about Tangent.

He had grown up in Brigham City, Utah. This was not exactly a world heritage site for the fungi. He had first encountered mushrooms on a family picnic to Antelope Island when he was just 14. It's an island about nine miles offshore in the Great Salt Lake. It's a place where the antelope still play and the buffalo still roam, and if you go to a place called Mushroom Springs, you can still find the giant **Agaricus osecanus** fruiting near the buffalo dung. Later, he told me, he found more fungi in a park in Brigham City when the lawns were sprinkled there.

"I was only 22 when they took my eldership away," he grimaced, "It was the beginning of a downward spiral for me."

It turned out that he had been spotted by a

temple leader dashing between the sprinklers to pick the mushrooms. "Prancing Among the Fairy Rings" had been the headline in the local paper. Followers of the Latter Day Saints do not indulge in that kind of behavior, and Tangent had been made an example of.

His wife left him shortly after.

"She just couldn't take it anymore. I just couldn't stop looking for mushrooms and folks were crossing the street to avoid her. But before she left, she gave me this parting gift."

Tangent then pointed to his earring, a subject I had been trying to avoid all along. A closer glance revealed a whitish rectangular shape with a concave interior. On the top was a little golden knob, roughly fusoid-ventricose, if you know what I mean. The rest was white porcelain with a mother-of-pearl glaze.

"It's a urinal," muttered Tangent, "The classical kind, like they have in Grand Central Station."

"Are there two of them?" I inquired. I had no idea what to say.

"Nope. Just the one," he nodded, "My ex said that whoever guessed what it was on the first guess would get to be my next wife."

"Any luck with that?" I offered.

"Been twelve years and no girl has ever come close."

"But many have tried," I suggested.

"That is correct. Mormon women don't want to stay single for long. Been very frustrating for some of them."

He had been told that the only way he could get his eldership back would be to volunteer for a number of missionary expeditions. He had volunteered for many such missions and had picked up the language each time. It turned out that he was a natural linguist. Even if he was not on a mission, he could pick up jobs as an interpreter wherever he forayed.

"I've authored new species in eleven languages," he smiled at me.

He figured it was the greatest advantage he had over other mycologists.

By now we had pulled into the parking lot of the second nursery on our list. The first had been locked solid. Ovorp spotted a pair of **Pholiota spumosa** even before the car had braked. He was on hands and knees in front of them, poking at the earth around them with a pocket knife, even before I arrived.

"**Pholiota spumosa**," I announced, "Probably our most common November Pholiota."

"Not so," disagreed Ovorp, "That species fruits on wood according to Smith and Hesler, or if on soil, it has to be coniferous soil."

The specimens were about ten feet out on a lawn, no wood or conifers nearby.

"Could be buried wood," I suggested, "Could be coming off a dead tree root a foot down or more."

"Do you see wood? Do you see a neighboring conifer?" he chided, "This is a new variety, and if the micro characters don't match **Pholiota spumosa**, it's likely a new species."

He carefully prodded up a stem base. There was no wood chip at the end of it.

"See," he grinned in triumph, "Meet the **var. graminicola,** if all goes well in the lab."

I was too taken aback for speech. Here was a fungus I thought I had known like the back of my hand.

We edged beyond an unlocked fence gate and were soon near the center of the nursery. Here stood a large wooden box overflowing with compost. Tangent was not more than five feet away from it when he let loose a startled cry.

"Oh, my God!" he shouted, "Take a look at this here bolete!"

There at our feet sat a pair of glistening maroon caps emerging through the spruce duff.

"Forget the Galerinas! Forget the Pholiotas!" bellowed Tangent, "A new member of Section Mirabiles may arrive once in a century."

And suddenly I remembered who this was. Tangent Ovorp. There had been mutterings at Key Council meetings. I remembered one professional saying that he couldn't be trusted. "If the fungus blushes, it's a new one." Another mycologist at the table had called him a "shotgun mycologist."

"If he names everything he sees, he's bound to get a few new ones," he had sighed.

By now Tangent was digging up the specimens and easing them onto tin foil. All he could say was "Oh, man. Oh, man," as he lurched to the car with his prize. I could see that collecting was done for the day.

Back at my office I was treated to a rare privilege…the witnessing of a type description composed right on my desk. "Caps 5-6 ½ cm wide," I was reading, "subnodulose to uniformly pitted. Obtusely campanulate, tough, coriaceous, dark maroon with mottled dark green tinges near the margins. Margins naked, not incurved. Context thick, pale yellow becoming more green at margins. Pores distant, about one mm in width. Dissepiments casual. No immediate change of color upon bruising."

Here, Ovorp paused in mid-sentence.

"We'll have to observe what happens over time," he cautioned me.

"Stipe smooth, napiform," he continued writing, "Velar material represented by random pale yellow patches near apex. Stem dark tawny brown with pallid zone at base. One thick, grayish mycelial strand extending from base (magnifying glass). Odor none. Taste mild, even pleasant. Spore deposit...."

"We'll have to wait on that, too," he solemnly intoned.

Tangent duly jotted down the habitat and told me he had to get moving to get this under wraps. Who knows? Some other mycologist may be racing him to publication.

"But what about the microscopic details?" I asked.

"That'll come later, my good man. I only work with dried material."

He carefully shunted the specimens back onto the tin foil.

"Do you think it's mycorrhizal with spruce," I ventured.

"Could be," he quipped, "You saw the rhizomorph as well as I did."

Suddenly, he was almost out the door. I realized I might not see Ovorp again for awhile.

"So, what's next?" I shouted at the departing figure.

"University of Samarkand. The herbarium there. They house everything I bring them."

A year passed. I heard nothing more from Tangent Ovorp, and nothing about the proposed **Boletus aguacatus** in the literature. Just on a whim, I decided to email Dr. John Horribull. He was the only expert who had ever dared publish with Ovorp. He was bound to know something, one way or another.

"That odd bolete with the chartreuse pore surface?" he emailed back. "I don't really know what happened. Some awful accident in the dehydrator. Totally unforeseen. He says he's going to try for another one, but not until he gets a better dehydrator."

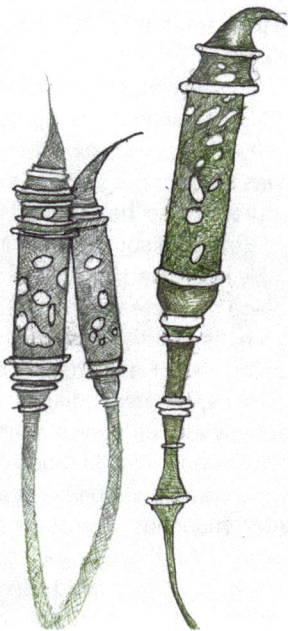

Weraroa cucumagna Gunston & Haggard

Invitations to international conferences were sure to follow.

Weraroa cucumagna

Ferdinand Gunston realized it was delivery time on the microscope. He knew he was confronted with an enigma. He just didn't know how far it might go. He was self-taught on the microscope, and now he was monumentally frustrated.

All during the morning he had peered into his lenses while the spores swam slowly in and out of view. He had used a pair of probes to put a tiny clump of spores on a slide, applied a drop of KOH, and then the slip cover... just as it said in the book. After the KOH, the spores were all over the glass. He followed one spore cluster tumbling slowly from left to right. When it seemed to stop, he would quickly move his micron measurement bar, but always too late. There was a lot at stake here. The measurements had to be perfect. He'd been at it for an hour and still no measurement. The spores had then approached the edge of the slip cover. Here had been hope. But instead of fetching up at the edge, they had rotated back out, having caught some micro eddy, and then had traveled all the way back across his lenses.

Only one thing left to do. Ferdinand removed the slide from the platform and took off the slip cover. This in itself was a gamble. He then scratched at his head until dandruff snowed down on the spores.

"If I see you do zat one time more, I deevorce I go file!"

Nguwar was the daughter of a Myanmar general. She spoke in a harsh metallic voice that took no prisoners. Ambushed again. It was hard for her to understand about the spores. Again, for the hundredth time, he had tried to explain the reason for the dandruff.

"Eet ees disgusting! No Myanmar man mek dandruff."

He had found her in one of those catalogues of Asian women looking for mates in the U.S.A. Although he had come to mycology in his middle years, he had found it a solitary and time-consuming affair. He felt he had no extra time to be going to bars and churches, the usual places where you found them. By marrying her he would be banishing the dreadful loneliness inherent in his vocation and simultaneously increase his stature within the academic community he so needed to reach. He had seen them at NAMA meetings. They seemed to him to be taciturn, meticulous men with that peculiar gate associated with botany. Nguwar could be enticing. She would represent something exotic, something slightly mysterious. Invitations to international conferences were sure to follow.

"Een my country, no dandruff. All men hair clean!"

But something had gone terribly wrong.

His gaze returned to the dried specimens in the cellophane bag. He had emailed the photo a week earlier to Dr. Jonah Haggard, a retired botanist who lived on the outskirts of town. Dr. Haggard had emailed him back immediately. He had found something highly unusual and secotioid, but it would take awhile for Dr. Haggard to be able to come over to observe microscopic features.

Secotioid. He had no idea what that meant. All he could write was that the bases of the caps were sealed tight against the apices of the stems. He had sought spores in vain in that area. The caps appeared to be thimble shaped. Neither had he found spores on the cap surfaces.

"Where are the friggin' spores! He had shouted.

"All mushroom disgusteen," she had retorted, "Why you want spores? Only mek teengs worse."

By the fourth day he realized he was face to face with a peridium. The spores would be locked up inside, not on the capitate white hairs sprouting on the surfaces of mature specimens. These he had mistaken for external asci.

"I deed'n leave my fodder house for dees!" wailed Nguwar. She had stared out at him with unfeigned incredulity.

But they hadn't been asci either. Just hairs. Another word for hairs was setae. Important to remember in case he found himself at a conference. Under the microscope they had been thick-walled, sort of like skeletal hyphae in a polypore. He had no idea what the function might be.

"Odder men mek money. You only mek dandruff," she accused.

He had decided it was a good time to take field measurements. This always seemed to calm her down...temporarily. The act of laying down cap and stem against the millimeter bar, the subsequent jotting down of the measurements, all this gave her a sense of propriety she couldn't get from the dandruff operation. He had measured the setae first only to discover they were so long that they extended far beyond the micrometer. Another hurdle to get across. The hairs on the lower part of the peridium were coated with an orange-brown powder. He jotted down "cinnamon pruinose." Those peridia without

setae had roughened surfaces. These were tiny concolorous scales just waiting to evolve into setae. All of this, of course, he had had to surmise.

Nguwar was still staring out at him from the kitchen doorway. He had hoped at one point to train her as an assistant. But then he realized that he, too, was untrained. He had spurned the Krebs Cycle as a younger man. Now he was feeling the heat.

Nguwar returned to the kitchen. The sound of rattling, clanging pots and pans. A scene of furious thoughts. He could expect another ambush any minute now.

"Stems up to 6 ½ cm long," he had written down, "And 4-7 mm thick." Why bother with all this, he had pondered. What herbarium would even care? They wanted established taxa for DNA sequencing, not something he couldn't get to genus. So far, this was an absolute nightmare. No spores and setae so long they couldn't be measured.

Ferdinand, on the fifth day, had sliced up a peridium vertically from base to apex. Inside were structures so foreign that he was momentarily staggered. Then he recalled that Dr. Haggard had used the term *secotioid* in his email message. He looked up the term in the Snell & Dick Glossary. It wasn't there. Mycology on the hoof. There were little cul-de-sacs everywhere. He looked in the glossary in *One Thousand American Fungi*. Not there either.

"Gleba not good name for daughter!" shouted Nguwar. She had snuck back from the kitchen. That metallic voice again. She had discovered just last week she was pregnant. 'Gomphus' for boy, 'Gleba' for girl, he had told her. Both went great with Gunston. But she had done some research, discovered that neither were in the hundredth most popular names for Americans.

"Not to worry," he had told her, "Thanks to you, they will all think it's a Myanmar name. Very normal over there."

"You liard!" she had shrieked, "Not Myanmar name, not good Burma name. No name at all!"

Ferdinand was now reaching for Kauffman's *Agaricaceae of Michigan*. Here was a mycologist he liked.

Surely 'secotioid' would be in there. It wasn't.

"You no eat here until name change," she announced.

Nguwar was his nine-to-five job. Other people had real jobs. He had Nguwar.

"Okay, okay," he threw up his hands, "Find something to do. I study mushrooms. You study something, a book maybe."

"Mushrooms ees sheet! I hate mushrooms!" she wailed, "Next week no mushrooms allowed in house."

He would have to deal with this later. For now, he would have to find the meaning of secotioid if he wanted to describe for publication. It would be too embarrassing to ask Dr. Haggard. He might check out a more modern glossary. Probably 'secotioid' hadn't been invented in the time of Kauffman.

On the other hand, he couldn't ignore her completely. Not that there was any threat of silence. Her doctor had advised him not to over excite his spouse. He had found her to be unusually emotional, and anything that set her off would also disturb the fetus. He had told Ferdinand that it was time to step up to the plate.

Ferdinand crumpled to the floor as if hit by an invisible dart. This was all for her benefit. She would realize she had made a direct hit. He took a quick glance in her direction. She was actually smiling. It was the greatest smile in the world. It just never seemed to come at the right moment.

There were piles of books all over the floor. Ferdinand began rummaging around. He finally picked up a volume entitled *The Gasteromycetes of the Eastern United States and Canada* by Coker and Couch. And here on page 53, someone named Otto Kunze actually described a secotium.

"Peridium above ground with a long or short stalk, which extends entirely through the sporiferous portion as a stout columella which is continuous above with the peridium. Gleba spongy, cellular; tramal plates arising from the peridium wall and also connected with the top or greater part of the columella, and filling the space between them, somewhat lamellate, very sinuous with a more or less horizontal direction suggesting an unopened agaric with sinuous gills; capillitium not present. Dehiscence basal and longitudinal, the peridium usually separating slightly from the stem below and in some cases expanding more or less, after the manner of a young agaric. Basidia clavate with 2-4 apical, stipitate, smooth or rough spores."

"No mushroom in house," she repeated, "Ver bad for baby. Bad for wife. Next week army man come, tek mushrooms away."

This was likely to be the Myanmar solution. There probably has been no mycologist over there for one hundred years.

"Think beyond the box," he pleaded, "Our son or daughter, whichever way it goes, might take mushroom study back to Myanmar."

The face of Nguwar had suddenly crumpled. Her whole body began to shake. And then the sobbing began. It was uncontrolled sobbing. He might as well have announced the end of the earth. He tried to console her, sling an arm around her shoulder, but she pushed him away, slammed a door and went back to the kitchen.

Ferdinand went back to the microscope. He now had real information. He found the tramal plates. The purple-brown gleba was halfway between spongy and powdery. The powdery would most likely represent the mature spores.

The dandruff had done the job! Individual spores and even clumps of spores had fetched up against these murky clouds like flotsam and jetsam. The spores were smooth and egg shaped. He could now proceed with measurements.

It was at this point that Dr. Jonah Haggard had arrived at the front door. While not a mycologist sensu stricto, he could be enticed over if something unusual was underfoot. He had taken a couple of mycology courses en route to his doctorate. When he had seen the photo Ferdinand had emailed him, he had not rushed over. He had wanted to get a little feedback from colleagues who agreed to look at the photo.

"Where's that Weraroa of yours?" he now boomed.

"Weraroa?" asked Ferdinand.

"Why...my lad. You don't know Weraroa?"

Dr. Haggard was a big man, and in his own words, a big fan of all things secotioid.

"Weraroa", he went on to explain, "Was the only genus in history to be named after a remote atoll in the South Pacific. It was a Maori name. A Maori found the first one out there, and not giving a damn about Greek or Latin, named it for the place he found it."

Jonah Haggard seemed to find this highly rewarding. For a moment he beamed down at Ferdinand. Then a tiny crease appeared in his brow. He began to look a little concerned.

"But you know," he almost whispered, "They are not supposed to occur in the Pacific Northwest."

He slid into the chair next to Ferdinand's.

"See that plant in your photo?" he went on, "The one in the lower right foreground? Looks a bit like the beginning of a May apple, but a little bit off. Where did you find this collection?"

"Where beach meets sea," Ferdinand replied. He was now tired, emotionally drained from his encounter with Nguwar.

"That could be anywhere," prompted Doc Haggard.

Ferdinand decided to tell him. Why risk an illegitimate publication.

"You know that small cove on Bellingham Bay, the one just north of Clark's Point," he said, "Well, it was beyond the high tide mark fruiting from some herbaceous debris up against a drift log."

"Not May apple," muttered the doctor.

"Spores must have floated in with the tide," suggested Ferdinand.

"The nearest known Weraroa would be **Weraroa cucullata**," mused Dr. Haggard. He pointed out that it was a species that preferred mountains, and that it was much smaller and paler than the one they were looking at here.

"Global warming," mumbled Ferdinand, "Currents can carry spores anywhere in the world."

Dr. Jonah Haggard nodded a weary assent. He had Ferdinand switch chairs with him. It was time to look in the microscope.

"The spores are ovate," he confided, "But what's all the cloudy material around them?"

Ferdinand froze in his chair. He suddenly realized he had forgotten to remove the dandruff-laden slide from the platform.

"Not sure," he muttered, "Could be exterior encrustations, maybe even gelatinization. You're the doc. You tell me."

"I'll be damned. The stuff is actually in islands."

"Encrusted gelatinization," offered Ferdinand.

Dr. Haggard had to admit he hadn't heard of that, nor had he seen setae on the outer surface of a peridium before.

"Calls for a new section in Weraroa?" inquired Ferdinand.

"And then some," winced Haggard. This was going to be more work than he had surmised.

Dr. Jonah went to work on the literature search. After a year and a half he was satisfied no other Weraroa like this had been published. They decided to call it **Weraroa cucumagna**, the Big Cucu Weraroa, because it was larger than the Late Cucu Weraroa, and didn't appear as late in the seasons. It finally appeared in the Argentine journal *Lilloa* in the spring of 2007.

A lot has happened in the time since publication. Nguwar had quietly one evening made a bonfire of Ferdinand's herbarium. He had gone to a movie and forgotten to lock the cellar door. Twenty-five years of collections up in smoke. She moved back to Myanmar shortly after and sued the Asian matchmaker organization that had put her in the catalogue in the first place. She was suing on the grounds of inadequate disclosure.

As for Ferdinand Gunston, he never published again. The rest of his life was spent trying to extract his daughter Victoria from Myanmar. Even the genus Weraroa took a hit. Thanks to DNA sequencing, all have been moved to Leratiomyces, and another great name in nomenclature was sent packing to the mists of time.

Hericium niveopendulum Qvisto

They were pure white, glabrous, brittle, enticingly translucent.

Hericium niveopendulum   Photo by Beth Woods

It was sometime in February that I got the call from Dean Kiler. He phoned me from Glacier to say he'd found what looked like a relative of the Lion's Mane that wasn't in any of his mushroom books. His wife Janice couldn't figure it out either. That was not a good sign. Would I come out and look at it? We would meet in the usual place.

That would be Frosty's in Maple Falls. This was the place where Dean felt most at home in the county. The steaks were always on Dean. He knew it was a fifty mile round-trip for me. There had to be an enticement.

"Hericium, man!" Dean beseeched me, "There aren't any bad ones in it. At least according to the wife."

Dean was the ultimate edibility nut. His dad had been in the Air Force all his life. Dean had grown up all over. Once, during a stint in Germany, Dean had been introduced to Steinpilze. After one bite of the King Bolete, he was hooked. When he got married and moved to Waco, Texas, he discovered

the place had a serious flaw...very few mushrooms. Those that did show up looked like experiments in cardboard origami.

So he did the natural thing. He sent Janice on a bus trip around the country. Her instructions were to look out the window and phone him whenever she saw mushrooms. It was two weeks before he got that call.

"Dean," she had said, "I see big white mushrooms on a lawn."

"Any idea where you're at?"

"Right next to the lawn it says Bellingham Public Library."

"You done good, girl. You can get off that bus right now and start lookin' for real estate in that county."

It didn't take them long to dig in. Within the first week they discovered the closer to Glacier the more mushrooms there were. Dean got a job with a logging outfit. Janice discovered Northwest Mushroomers Association. Few of us probably remember Dean and Janice. They used to attend forays at Doug Fir and Silver Fir Campgrounds back in the mid-1990s. Dean would wear a T-shirt that read "Anything Goes." Janice would try explaining to everyone why they didn't go to other forays. It entailed lots of driving and since that's what Dean did every day it was too much like work. But... back to the present situation.

"Okay, Dean," I caved, "Lunch at Frosty's."

The weather was cold and clear, probably around 15 degrees. I had to wonder. What kind of mushroom could fruit in such conditions? There were snowmelt mushrooms. I realized this. Maybe Dean's find would emerge from their ranks.

I arrived to find Dean already in the parking lot peering over his truck bed. Janice was inside, he said, securing a table. The log you see in this photo had not been allowed to enter Frosty's, so Dean had remained outside to keep it from being ripped off. What I saw was astounding. An alder log covered with a palisade of curvaceous white spines mostly cylindrical in shape. A few of the spines had broken off and lay scattered on the pickup bed. I climbed aboard with my made in China plastic centimeter ruler. The spines measured 4–9 cm long and were up to 3 mm thick. They were pure white, brittle, glabrous, enticingly translucent. They emerged directly from the ancient alder log. But instead of hanging in a compact cluster like the Lion's Mane, the spines often curved in graceful arcs across the face of the log. This was no normal species of Hericium.

"I'll have to do a literature search," I told him.

"Come in and have a beer!" He thumped me on the back.

Dean always got a big kick out of seeing me stumped. The only thing better was when I identified a new edible for him. Maybe in time he'd get both.

We found Janice pouting at the table.

"Dean has banned all Latin names from the house," she announced.

"What's with that, Dean?"

"It's all because of **Cantharellus formosus**," Janice cut in, "It used to be **Cantharellus cibarius**. Since that's his favorite food, it's like changing a name in a supermarket."

"That's right!" thundered Dean, "We don't need the Vatican telling us how to call our mushrooms. They are chanterelles pure and simple."

Janice sighed and pawed at her steak. Life with Dean wasn't easy. After a few years he had become a Slope Assessor. This was due to his background as a surveyor. Wherever he went he was sure to upset someone. If he assessed a slope as being too steep for logging, he'd anger his outfit. If it got logged anyway, he would infuriate the environmentalists. It never helped that he always wore the "Anything Goes" T-shirt on such occasions.

"I don't know, Dean," I told him, "There may not be a Latin name for your Hericium yet."

Back in Bellingham I went to my computer and checked out the *Index Fungorum* for all temperate species of Hericium. Nothing unusual came up. Not until I found Petrak's Lists,

published in 1920, did a *nomen novum* emerge. This was **Hericium niveopendulum** Qvisto. I googled the name. The species had been published in *Nytt Magasin für Botanik* 2, 1911. It took less than a day for our reference librarian to track down the issue and get her Scandinavian counterpart to scan the article to me. All articles would be in Norwegian. It would cost me $15 and maybe more for an interpreter.

"The thing to do," she told me, "Is hang out around Norway Hall until an old-timer shows up."

This I proceeded to do. I had heard there was a translation site on the internet but had no idea how to access it. It took five hours before a Norwegian speaker showed up. I'd had to circle the building several times to appear not to be loitering.

The interpreter explained he was pressed for time, but the article seemed short enough. Indeed, I thought. There were only six sentences under a dim black and white photo of a white mushroom on a log. It even made Peck look wordy.

The author, one Thor Qvisto, had measured spines and base. He had noted morning colors and afternoon colors. At the bottom of the description was a sad note. The editors had written that Thor would be publishing no more. He had sailed into an iceberg at the age of 33. His country was listed as Lapland.

I phoned up Dean and told him we'd found a reference.

"There is a problem," I went on, "There doesn't seem to be any microscopic info at all. I've never seen anything like it."

"Who cares about that," enthused Dean, "How does he say to cook it?"

"Amazing," I said, "Thor does make a comment here. He wrote that it is best with Aquavit just before dinner."

"Forget the Latin!" snapped Dean, "No dead lingo in our home."

In the background I could here him order Janice to drive down to Graham's for butter and garlic before they closed.

"Bon appetit," I responded, "And let me know how it tasted."

Sadly enough it has been fourteen years now and I haven't heard from the Kilers since.

Vascellum purpureoglebum Pranks, Emmert, Finkelstein, Blurtt, Talbott, Malheureux, Tonk, Goggenblitzmayr, Smith, Church, & Ziggot

No spores. . . . no new species. Simple as that.

Vascellum purpureoglebum

Henry Baines was not sure what he was seeing. The sun had finally come out and he was still in the pasture, trespassing. This was not a good thing. If he stood out here much longer he could expect to hear sirens. But an inner voice told him "not so fast." This might be important. He fished out his Nikon from his backpack and took the shot. Then he carefully removed the puffballs and put them in his other ziplock bag. He took out a small writing pad and jotted down "substrate — grasses." Then he reviewed his photo. He noted there were two kinds of grasses in it. So he plucked up both kinds and slipped them in the bag with the puffballs. Just in case.

It hadn't always been this way. He had originally entered the pastures for the Liberty Caps. Then, unaccountably his mind had taken more in. He began to notice the other fungi, all kinds of shapes and sizes, not just in the pastures, but right in the roadside ditch-

es. He could even find them in the short, critical time between "sun is up" and "got to make it back to the car."

The brotherhood was of the furtive sort. They would drift in at different times to the Old Town Café for breakfast. They would nod silent greetings, then take stock in their numbers. If someone was missing he could have been rounded up out in the fields. Probably busted. Grim looks were passed around the tables. One of them would have to tell the girlfriend. Henry never wanted to be that person. He defended against this possibility by sitting at the communal table and spreading out his mushroom finds. They wouldn't dare ask him if strangers were all around him, commenting on his mushrooms.

But Henry wasn't all that popular at the Old Town Café. The proprietor noted that not everyone wanted to be surrounded by Mycenas and Galerinas that time of day. And it made his friends nervous. Some of these mushrooms resembled the Liberty Caps, and no one needed the extra attention.

Today turned out to be different. Henry had spread out his puffballs on newspaper. While an old timer had tried to read the box scores between fruiting bodies, a waitress offered to cook them for him. Henry was pondering this when a voice cut in behind him.

"I see you have a Vascellum," the lady said. She was a middle-aged woman with a pencil thin smile. She spoke with smug authority.

"Oh my God! It's got purple gleba!" she shrilled.

Henry began to feel nonplussed. Here were two terms he hadn't heard before. Introductions were exchanged. All around the dining room folks were wondering what 'purple gleba' could mean.

Her name was Sarah Gray. She explained that she was a regional botanist who dabbled in mycology. It wasn't the mushrooms themselves that got her excited, but the taxonomy game that went with them. Each published mushroom had a set of characters that went with it. But if a subsequent researcher could prove that mistakes had been made that could send it to a different genus, then that researcher would have his name with the mushroom, too. It was like bridge, she said. Large egos were bruised all the time. She had succeeded in this just once. After a two-year stretch of relative fame, her name had been axed via DNA sequencing. She was itching to get back. Henry's Vascellum looked like the winning ticket alright.

"See the fragile peridium? See the great cracks in the sides where the spores escaped? It can't be any other genus."

They would go together that very evening to a Northwest Mushroomers' meeting, find out if others had seen his Vascellum.

"You should get it published," the president had subsequently advised, "I've seen nothing like it in popular guides."

"The problem, Henry," she explained, "We aren't well enough known."

Henry concurred. He was only known from the communal table at the Old Town Café.

"We will have to get an expert to join us."

The membership began to mill. People strained to recall who had worked in Vascellum before. Who would the lucky doc be? They agreed to report their findings at the next meeting, a month away.

Sarah didn't have to wait that long. She discovered that a Dr. John Pranks had put out a key to Calvatia in the 1970s. Another genus of puffball. He should slide right in.

"Whoa! Who did you say this was?" the voice had boomed over the phone, "Henry and Sarah who? I'm sorry. I'm just not familiar with those names."

After much cajoling and myco-banter Dr. Pranks had yielded up his email address. He would wait to see a photo before committing. Sarah scanned it and sent it within five minutes.

Dr. Pranks had stared it down for a long time (personal communication). He was more transfixed by what he didn't see than by what he saw. He groaned audibly. Then he phoned them back.

"I see no gleba," he informed Sarah, "No gleba, no spores. No spores, no new species. Simple as that."

"We'll get some for you," Sarah entreated, "We'll scrape the peridiums. Whatever it takes!"

She was so close to fame it made her neck crawl. Dr. Pranks allowed that he would await the gleba in the mail, but he wasn't optimistic. He had never seen a gleba with such a bright hue. But things could have happened. He had been away from the Lycoperdaceae for over forty years.

Henry went right to work. He took his only scalpel to the knife sharpener's place behind Hardware Sales. His next move was to meticulously shave the purple zones inside the peridiums. He shaved and shaved until the powder turned white.

"That will do," announced Sarah. The sound of the scraping seemed a little over the top.

Together they mailed a packet of the scrapings along with an entire fruiting body to Dr. Pranks.

"Got it," he had emailed back. But then no news at all. Weeks went by, then months. He was absent from all networks.

"These things take time," asserted Sarah, "the literature search has to be exhaustive. The worst scenario is to duplicate an existing. Dr. Pranks is aware of that."

Then out of the blue they got a phone call. It was the scientific adviser for the club. He had spotted a new Vascellum published in the latest *Mycotaxon*. They rushed to the library to find it online.

"This is weird," frowned Sarah, "Neither of our names are here."

"But I'm the one who found it!" shouted Henry. They swooned against each other for support.

Dr. Pranks had been expecting their call.

"In modern taxonomy," he told them, "a lot more researchers are involved. Of course, I'm in it. I wrote it up. Emmert is my pseudonym. He's in it in case my enemies go after Pranks. Finkelstein, Blurrt, and Talbott. Three of my top grad students. We have to encourage them or they might defect. Leave mycology entirely. Malheureux and Tonk, both are trilingual. They did the heavy lifting, traveling to remote herbariums around the world to check on similar species. Goggenblitzmayr captained the DNA team. Smith purified the chip. Church sterilized the chamber. Ziggot locked up the facility at the end of each day. Without Ziggot all the priceless equipment could have walked. Now I think you couldn't help but agree. Just having the beginner's luck to find the specimens is the least of all these."

Xylaria &*$!x^#

He had no inkling of the path that lay ahead.

Dr. Anchises Schecter had always wanted to visit the Muir Woods. The legendary lure of the giant coast redwoods interspersed with bay laurel, big leaf maple, and tanoak all bathed daily by the relentless Pacific fogs was almost too much to bear. It would be a mycorrhizal paradise for conifer and deciduous aficionados alike. He wanted to get there as badly as any Arab ever wanted to reach Mecca.

Administrative duties at the University of the Skagit had held him back. For almost 50 years.

If a crisis arrived while he was not there, he wouldn't be able to forgive himself. But now he was retired. His wife Myrtle had told him it was time to cut loose.

Xylaria !$&x^#*

Dr. Schecter was unprepossessing in appearance. He had the stooped shoulders and downcast head of some of the local homeless. Mothers passing by on the sidewalk would tell their kids not to end up like this.

This assessment couldn't be further from the truth. This humble looking personage had put the University of the Skagit on the map. Once he had acquainted himself with DNA sequencing, he had single handedly thrown the slime molds out of the kingdom of fungi. For this unprecedented act, he had at first been besieged by reporters. They wanted to know if the slime molds would get their own kingdom, and if so, what it would be called.

"I've done enough, fellows," he had replied, "We should leave the labeling to the next generation."

"My Anchises is modest to a fault," chimed in Myrtle, "Of course he knows what the new name will be. He just wants to see what young scholar will get there first."

Finally the great day arrived. They climbed into their RV and headed for the Muir Woods, just twelve miles north of the Golden Gate Bridge.

Muir Woods National Monument read the sign at the entrance. Dr. Anchises Schecter maneuvered the RV into a special parking lot for such beasts, and took a deep breath. A pileated woodpecker landed on a trunk nearby. It was a special moment. These towering redwoods were 800 years old. Even the silence seemed Pleistocene.

He and Myrtle stuffed their sandwiches into brown paper bags. These were then loaded into backpacks. Anchises strapped a camera to his waist. Myrtle indicated a loop trail straight ahead, and off they went. A few Psathyrellas hid behind a stump, then a spectacular break of the Sulphur Tuft. It was on!

They continued in silent awe for another 400 yards.

"Whoa! What have we here!" exclaimed Anchises. He had stopped so abruptly he had nearly been crashed into by Myrtle.

For there, just to the left of the trail, was about the strangest fungus he had ever seen. Multibranched and pocked with tiny holes, it looked like something in the Xylariaceae. It was fruiting in moss from the base of a deciduous stump.

"Better hurry," urged Myrtle, "Looks like that slug is into it."

Dr. Schecter pulled out his camera and took the shot. Always a pleasure to capture other life forms along with the fungi. He was so happy he was almost purring. He edged right up to the fungus and took a closer look. Interesting. The entire fruiting body was pocked with holes the size of pin heads. Anchises knew that ostioles expelled the spores in the genus Xylaria. But never like this. Not right through the peridium and then the stroma like cannonballs going through a fort. He squinted in concentration. Somewhere way back in the periphery of memory he had heard of this group. They were definitely not native to the Pacific Northwest. There had been something disturbing, something not quite right about them. Eastern European entities with a murky history.

Myrtle plucked the specimen off the stump and stuck it in a lunch bag just before the slug would have reached it. They continued on the loop trail and found only half-devoured Russulas often with the banana slugs still on them.

At about 3 p.m. they re-emerged onto the parking lot.

"Excuse me, sir, may we have a look into your lunch bags?"

Two park rangers had sidled up to them. One had short cropped red hair and the other was a woman with steel rimmed glasses.

"Picnicking is not allowed in the park," she explained.

The red haired ranger relieved Anchises of his lunch bag. His lips were pursed in disapproval even before he had a look inside.

"Oldest trick in the book," sighed the woman ranger. She hauled out her camera to take the incriminating shot.

The red headed ranger now held the Xylaria by two fingers. The woman took the shot and put away her camera.

"Evidence," she stated, "No fungi are allowed to leave the park. This is a $3,000 fine. Your license, sir?"

"You can't be serious!" cried Myrtle, "You have no idea who he is. This is Dr. Schecter himself. The man who kicked the slime molds out of the kingdom of fungi. Without the knowledge of people like my husband, you wouldn't know the names of the fungi you have."

"I don't care who he is, ma'am," replied the redhead, "It's a blanket law. No nature products can leave the park."

"Can you imagine," added the ranger, "If everyone took a mushroom out of the park, it would deprive others from seeing them."

Myrtle was so nonplussed she couldn't speak.

"You can come to our office and pay the fine now by credit card or fill out a card for a court appearance. But I must forewarn you, we haven't lost a case in 23 years."

She grabbed the specimen from her cohort. As she did so, one of the branches broke off. It fell back into the lunch bag held by her fellow ranger. He passed it back to Anchises, pointing to a garbage can where he could dispose of it.

No one could have suspected it at the time, but that broken branch would carry Dr. Anchises Schecter all the way to the California State Supreme Court.

The court date was set for three months away. Plenty of time, thought Anchises, to come up with a name for the fungus. He had talked it over with Myrtle and came up with a line of defense.

He would prove to them that this was a non-native species. As such it was a danger to the native fungi in the park. If it proliferated, it could overwhelm some native mushrooms. His other point would involve the slug. It was clear that in a matter of hours the fungus would be toast. He wasn't sure what sort of strength this argument would have.

Dr. Schecter knew his way around the sources of mycological research. Before they drove back to Washington, he and Myrtle downloaded all the info they could find on Xylaria at Berkeley and at San Francisco State.

Once back on the home front, research began in earnest. An original find of a fungus resembling his was from the Sudetenland, dating back to 1807. Maximillian De Houri had found a collection at the base of a stump. He had published it as **Xylaria fuscoatra** and deposited the dried specimens at a herbarium in Budapest. Noting the prodigious pockmarks created by the exploding ostioles, he had created the Subgenus Ostiolatus, Section Ostiolatus, Subsection Enigmaticus, the latter term referring to his feelings when he first encountered it.

Not much different than mine, mused Anchises. So far, so good. A rather straightforward publication. But the species was evidently extremely rare. The next find wasn't until 1891. It was found by the brilliant Austrian Xylariacist Hammelbein in the subalpine area of Austria. It was a single carpophore. Hammelbein had taken it to Budapest for a comparison.

"Oh, no! Anything but this," groaned Anchises.

Myrtle hurried in from the sitting room. She found Anchises slumped over his desk, his head lying on the keyboard.

"That idiot, De Houri! Hammelbein discovered a mixed type. Two different spore sizes, two different kinds of paraphyses."

"You can't blame De Houri, dear. Something this strange, you would never suspect there were two of them."

Anchises forced a thin smile. Myrtle always had a way of reframing a problem.

But it was time to move on. He could envision Hammelbein hunched over the various branches and shards. If De Houri had selected one specimen to be the holotype, which one was it?

"Dammit," muttered Anchises, speaking for Hammelbein as well.

According to his careful notes, Hammelbein had proceeded to separate the one entire specimen from the ones in pieces. This made good sense. The micro-characters would have derived from the shards.

"Noooooooooo!" boomed Anchises. The sound could be heard clear across College Way.

"It can't be. It just can't be."

Myrtle scurried back in. After all, $3,000 was at stake here.

"That idiot, De Houri," repeated Anchises, "He designated all three specimens as types. We now have a number of paratypes. No wonder Hammelbein stopped writing."

Indeed he had. He must have been beside himself. At the bottom of a page, he had scribbled in some desperate notes. Some of the microscopic features in his Austrian specimen did indeed match up with some of the features found in the shards. He then took the pieces he had examined back with him to his herbarium in Vienna, thereby creating a syntype.

And it wasn't until 1954 that another member of Subgenus Ostiolatus, Section Ostiolatus, Subsection Enigmaticus was found again. The location was now Latvia. A young German by the name of Krauser had found it. He had just received his doctorate in mycology and was eager to publish it as a new species.

Little did he know of the path ahead.

Exhausting research eventually brought up the presence of the pieces brought to Vienna by Hammelbein. He had no inkling that they might represent a mixed type. Nothing daunted, he proceeded to jot down micro-characters that fit well with his own specimen. If they didn't fit, they were just passed over. He had committed a further obfuscation, the dreaded *pro parte*. So instead of creating **Xylaria atrofusca spec. nov.**, Krauser had launched **Xylaria fuscoatra** in the sense of Krauser.

Anchises slumped in his chair. It seemed the end of the road. Krauser had examined an isotype, the term for a piece of an original holotype that had found its way to a different herbarium. But what about that entire specimen left behind in Budapest? Krauser said nothing about it.

Myrtle bustled in with coffee and croissants from the Mount Vernon Co-op. They were the best in the Northwest. Anchises should start to pick up.

"So, how about a neotype?" she brightened, "All you have to do is find another one from the original location."

"That won't work," whispered Anchises, "The original forest is now corn fields as far as the eye can see. The ethanol craze. It even affects mycology."

"Oh, Anchises, you are so smart," she smiled.

"Google Earth, dear. A child can do it."

"Isn't there another kind of type, one you can resort to when the original type is ambiguous?"

"Yes, the epitype. The Muir Woods specimen could be used as an alternative interpretive type, but who would buy it? We're an ocean away from all other finds."

After another week of pondering, Anchises realized his branch from the Muir Woods Xylaria could not be named. All the relatives were mired in chaos. There seemed no way out. It was at about this time that Myrtle came waltzing back in.

"But Anchises," she laughed, "If it can't be named, it just doesn't exist."

"Doesn't exist?"

"And if it doesn't exist taxonomically, how can you be fined for taking it out of a park?"

The trial opened in Sacramento with quite a bit of press. Mushroom picking in the parks had been an issue for quite some time, but now the great Dr. Schecter himself was playing a part. Representatives from county, state, and national parks all over California were in attendance. The Sierra Club sent over Greta Harrison, their legal adviser, a septuagenarian with dozens of victories under her garters.

"Let the trial begin!" thundered the judge.

The Muir Woods rangers were the first to take the stand. They came fully prepared with their Xylaria specimen and the photo that came with it.

"The specimen is exhibit A, sir," explained the ranger with the steel rimmed glasses.

"And the photo is exhibit B, your honor," chimed in her cohort, "Consider it the lectotype."

"You are using lectotype in the wrong sense," interjected Anchises.

"I meant paratype," shrugged the ranger.

"Even worse!" shouted Anchises.

Greta Harrison winced as if she were in pain.

"Order in the court!" bellowed the judge.

"Lectoparatype," suggested a member of the audience.

"Paralectotype," offered another.

"Will someone explain to me the difference between the two?" asked the judge.

"It's complicated, your honor. If you are from a university lab in a First World country like France, you can use 'lectoparatype'. But if you are from a lab in an emerging Second World country such as South Africa, 'paralectotype' is more appropriate."

There was a serious pause. Only a few in the room could recognize this was no definition at all.

Dr. Schecter was then invited to take the stand. The opposition was grinning in their seats. They already figured what Dr. Schecter's defense would be. The issue of native verse non-native species, and they were fully prepared.

"Your honor, I would like to propose that the specimen I took from the park does not technically exist. It cannot be named via the rules from the International Code of Botanical Nomenclature. Therefore it cannot exist taxonomically and perhaps legally becomes a non-entity."

He then proceeded to detail his research into the origins of the Xylaria. His last hope had been the presence of that entire specimen left behind in the herbarium at Budapest. That had ended with a kleptotype.

"Kleptotype? inquired the judge.

"That is when a specimen is sent from one herbarium to another, but never arrives at its destination."

The jurors began to wake up. They had no idea that crimes were committed in herbariums.

"And so," proceeded Anchises, "The herbarium of origin no longer harbors the specimen. No longer can any comparison be made. The fungus we removed thence becomes no more important than the grass from the park that is stuck to our boot treads."

"But this is absurd," interrupted the red headed ranger, "The doc took a specimen of nature from the park. That's all you have to know. Kazam!"

Arguments flared back and forth across the isle. Then the judge requested that the jury retire to a chamber to conclude with a verdict. It seemed like they deliberated forever.

The jury foreman led his fellow jurors back in.

"Our jury is hung, your honor. Nine of us favor the arguments put forth by Dr. Schecter. Two of us could not discern the difference between 'duplicate' and 'isotype'. And a third got too bothered by the kleptotype to render any opinion at all."

"The result," he continued, "is that we don't recommend a fine for Dr. Schecter at this time."

Myrtle wiped a tear from her eye.

Greta Harrison, legal counsel for the Sierra Club, had heard enough. She stomped out of the back of the courtroom, wattles shaking in indignation. A reporter soon caught up with her out on the sidewalk.

"I will tell you just one true thing," she snapped, "You will never have to sit through a farce like this again."

In succeeding weeks she persuaded the Sierra Club to offer scholarships to college graduates interested in taxonomy. There would initially be five of them strategically placed around the country. Never again would rangers and lawyers have to stand by helplessly while being bombarded by types and kinds of types. These taxonomists would be ready at any time to march forth from their labs to prosecute the larceny decimating the parks.

Meanwhile, Dr. Anchises had departed Sacramento with a feeling of vindication.

"You know, dear, that Xylaria still has no name," teased Myrtle.

"And so, it ceases to exist," he grinned. And then he maneuvered their RV out of the parking lot.

"Anyone seen my morels?" Art by Alex McAdoo

Glossary

acanthocytes prickly or spiny structures

acicular needle shaped

acidulous a harsh, sour taste

adnate gills attached to a stem at right angles

adnexed gills attached narrowly, tapering towards stem

allantoid sausage shaped with rounded ends

ampullaceous swollen at base

amyloid a dark blue reagent reaction with Melzer's solution

anastomizing forming a network of secondary gills or ridges

apical pertaining to the apex or top

apical crystals – tiny crystals that resemble glass shards at the tops of cystidia

apiculate – having an apiculus

apiculus a rounded or sharp point at the base of a spore

appendiculate the presence of veil remnants that hang from a cap margin

arcuate gills that arc inwardly, following the curve of the cap

areolate the presence of cracks appearing in a cap, usually due to dry weather

asci long, thin sac-like cells in which spores are produced

ascomycetes fungi that produce their spores inside an ascus

ascus singular of asci

astringent a sharp taste that causes the mouth to pucker or 'draw together'

attenuate gradually narrowing.

bacilliform rod-shaped

basidium a usually clavate structure with 'hooked horns' at the apices from where the spores emerge

basidia plural of basidium

bilateral hyphae hyphae that diverge from the mediostratum in gill trama that may become more parallel with it in age

binding hyphae thick-walled, much branched hyphae without septa in the hyphal system of polypores

campanulate bell-shaped

canescent covered with a whitish, hoary down

capitate having a knob at the apex

carpophores fruiting bodies

catenate in chains

catenulate in little chains

caulocystidia rod-shaped to clavate or bottle-shaped structures found on the surface of stems

cespitose fungi fruiting with stems attached at their bases

cheilocystidia cystidial structures that protrude from the gill edges

chlamydospores thick-walled secondary spores almost always found with parasitic fungi

chrysocystidia cystidia emerging from below the basidia that often have golden yellow contents or refringent corpuscles in age.

clamps a swelling or bump that can appear at cross-walls (septa) in hyphae

clavate a thickening, either at the base of the stem or the apex of basidia

clavate-rostrate having a

beak at the apex, above a clavate base

columella a persistent, axial, non-spore-bearing zone in a fruiting body

conidia thin-walled, secondary spores borne terminally on specialized hyphae

context the fleshy interior zone of caps

convergent hyphae that are seen in the cross-section of a gill that turn inward towards the mediostratum

cortical hairs hairs protruding from the outer rind of a fruiting body

cortina a cobwebby inner veil that attaches the cap margin to the stem

cortinate possessing a cortina

crenate scalloped or notched, often pertaining to gill edges

crenulate very finely notched

cruciate having the form of a cross

crystalline exudates exuded crystals

crystallized apices the tops of cystidia covered with shards

cutis a type of pileipellis that resembles a stack of parallel pipes

cyanophilous readily absorbing a gentian-blue dye

cylindric of the same diameter throughout the length

dacryoid tear-shaped, spores that are narrowed at one end

deciduous broad-leafed

decurrent gills that run down the stem

decurrent tooth adnate gills

that have separated ends that run down the stem

dextrinoid tissues that turn red in Melzer's solution.

dimidiate semi-circular, half-round in shape

dimitic having two different types of hyphae in a pileal context

discomycete cup-shaped or disc-shaped ascomycetes that have an exposed spore bearing surface at maturity

distant widely separated gills

divergent hyphae in the gill trama that branch away from the mediostratum

eccentric not centered, such as an off-center stem attachment

eguttate without oil drops

eguttulate without little oil drops

ellipsoid in the shape of an ellipse or almost of an oval

emarginate gill attachments that are notched at the stem or referring also to a margin at the top of a bulb at the stem base

endosporium a thin, innermost membrane of a spore wall

evanescent soon disappearing

exosporial verruculae minute spines that have penetrated the outer wall of a spore

exosporium the outer membrane of a spore wall

farinaceous having an odor of flour

fasciculate crowded in bundles, often referring to stems or scales

fibrillose hairy filaments that are thread-like and parallel to each other

filamentous having such filaments

filiform slender as a thread

fimbriate minutely fringed gill edges or minutely torn cap margins

floccose loosely cottony, fluffy

free gill attachments that don't reach the stem

fugacious quickly vanishing, like very minimal velar material on a stem

funiculi 'ropes'

furcate forked

furfuraceous scurfy, covered with bran-like particles

fuscous a smoky gray-black color

fusiform tapered at both ends

fusoid somewhat fusiform

fusoid-ventricose often refers to a cystidia or spore that is bellied out in the center and tapers at the ends

generative hyphae thin-walled, smooth, basic hyphae in polypores

geotropism gravity oriented movement, for instance when a polypore on a felled tree trunk then grows at a right angle from the log so the spore bearing surface will face the ground

germ pores a thinned spot in a spore wall

gill trama the hyphae in the center of a cross-section of a gill

glabrous smooth

gleba the spore mass inside a puffball

gloeocystidia cystidia with horny or gelatinous consistencies filled with granular or oily contents

gloeopleurous hyphae with strongly refractive contents that tend to stain brightly with Melzer's solution

granulose covered with granules

gregarious fruiting in company, many over a small area

guttules oil drops inside a spore

haplotype a single type chosen from many

hilar appendix a short spine emanating from the basal end of a spore

holotype the one specimen chosen to represent a species in a herbarium

hyaline transparent

hygrophanous fading to a paler color when drying

hymeniform erect cystidia usually in a palisade on a pileipellis

hymenium spore bearing surface

hymenophoral pertaining to the fertile surface and area next to it in a fungus

hyphae the basic filaments or tubular structures within a fruiting body

hypogeous fruiting underground

inamyloid not staining a different color when Melzer's solution is applied

incrassate thickened

intervenose having cross-veins in the spaces between gills

interwoven intermingled hyphae in the gill trama

involute incurved cap margins

isabelline the color of Queen Isabella's undergarments after years of use

isodiametric 5-6 sided

ixotrichoderm interlaced and erect hyphal ends in a gelatinized matrix of the pileipellis

lacrymoid tear shaped

lactifer a hypha bearing a

milk-like fluid

lacunose pitted surfaces in the stems of morels

lageniform long-necked

lamellar gilled surfaces

lamellulae the shorter gills that don't stretch from cap margin to stem

lanceolate lance-shaped

lecythiform ninepin shaped with a knob at the apex

leptocystidia large, thin-walled cystidia that don't originate in the trama

lubricous greasy, slippery to the touch

lumper a person who has a broad concept of a species, genus, or variety

medallion clamps exceptionally large clamps with septa

mediostratum the center part of the gill trama

membranous ring a thick-ish, doughnut shaped ring

merulioid with irregular pitted depressions and shallow tubes

metabasidia degenerating or modified basidia

metuloids thick-walled cystidia usually encrusted with crystals at the apices

monomitic only one type of hyphae in the pileal context

mucilaginous slimy

mucronate sharp pointed

mycelium the root-like filaments attached to a stem base

nodulose lumpy

nomenclature the naming of species and genera

obovoid reversely ovoid

palisade a type of pileipellis that consists of a tight mass of perpendicular cystidia

paraphyses slender, cylindric, and sterile structures interspersed with asci in an

ascomycete

partial veil an inner veil formed from filaments stretching from the stem to the cap margin

pedicel a slender stalk, usually on a cystidium or a spore

periascus an ascus with a covering

periclinal hyphae hyphae that are curved in the same direction as the surface of a pileipellis

peridial hyphae hyphae pertaining to the peridium

peridium the outer wall or 'coat' of a fruiting body

perithecia a rounded or oval structure with a slit within which asci are borne

pileal pertaining to the cap

pileipellis the cuticle layer on top of a cap surface

pileocystidia cystidia that are found on the pileipellis

pleurocystidia cystidia emerging from the face of a gill

pleuropodal having a lateral stem

plicate in fan-like folds

plicate-venose folds with veins

polymorphic of many shapes

probasidia basidia that have been transformed by thick-walled cysts that give rise to thin-walled extensions

pruinose powdery

pseudoparenchyma when the hyphae have adhered to each other in groups and are more or less isodiametric

pubescent covered with soft, downy hairs

punctate dotted

pyriform pear-shaped

quotient the ratio of length to width in a spore, often referred to as Q

radially repent hyphae hyphae in the pileipellis and/or cap context that run parallel with the cap surface

radicels rooting parts

ramose branched

raphanoid odor of radishes

reagent a substance used to detect a color change due to a chemical reaction

reflexed a term to describe a cap margin bending backwards

reticulate pertaining to a net-like pattern on the stem apices of some boletes

rhizomorphs cords of compacted mycelia at the bases of stems

rimose cracked

rugose coarsely wrinkled

rugulose finely wrinkled

saccate saclike

saprophyte fungi that fruit on debris, decomposing litter, etc.

scabrous with rough scabers

sclerotium a hardened mass of hyphae which form a lump of material

sensu lato in the broad sense

sensu stricto in the narrow sense

septa the cross-walls of hyphae

septate when hyphae have these cross-walls

seriate arranged in a connected series

serrate saw-toothed

serrulate minutely saw-toothed

silicious a silicate or limestone type of soil

sinuate a concave indentation of the gill edge at the stem connection

sinus the lower edge of the cap on a morel that tucks

under to meet the stem

skeletal hyphae thick-walled, non-septate hyphae

spathulate spoon shaped

sphaerocysts bloated, globular cells found in the Russulaceae

splitter a person who embraces a narrow concept of a species, a genus, or a variety

spores the 'seeds' of mushrooms

squamose covered with scales

squamules small scales

squamulose covered with small scales

sterigmata the horns at the apices of basidia from which spores are borne

stipe stem

stipitipellis the parallel hyphae found in the stem

striate having radiating lines on the cap margins or vertical lines on the stem

strigose having coarse, stiff hairs

stroma a cushion-like mass of fungal cells from which fruiting bodies can grow

subcapitate minimally capitate

subcoriaceous partially leathery

subdistant partly distant

subfusiform minimally spindle-shaped

subfusoid partly expanded at the middle.

subglobose not quite globose

subhymenium the zone just beneath the hymenium in the cross-section of a gill

sublubricous sort of greasy to the touch.

subpellis the layer just beneath the pileipellis

subtomentose sort of wooly

subumbonate with a minimal umbo

subvelutinous lightly velvety

subventricose minimally bellied out

sulcate grooved

sulphidia sulphur yellow projections on spore surfaces. Sometimes found in Panaeolus species

superior ring a ring located near the apex of the stem

suprahilar depression a round, smooth area just above the hilar appendage on a spore surface

synonym an alternative, discarded name for a species

taxon a taxonomic unit, another term for 'species'

terete evenly rounded like a broom handle

tomentose matted, entangled hairy filaments

tomentum the hairy filaments

trichodermial pertaining to the fibrillose covering of a cap or stem

trimitic when there are three kinds of hyphae in a pileal context

truncate a chopped off end of a spore or cystidia

tuberculate with wart-like or knob-like excrescences

tuberculose having tubercles

turbinate top-shaped

turf filamentous hyphal tips arising from a pileipellis

type an authentic deposit in a herbarium that represents the species concept

umbilicate having a small, sharp depression on the cap surface

umbo a rounded knob on the cap center

umbonate having an umbo

uncinate a narrow, decurrent extension of the gill edge at the stem apex

undulate wavy

unicellular hairs outgrowths of single epidermal cell cystidia sometimes found in poroid fungi

uniseriate a single row, such as spores in an ascus

universal veil the enveloping veil which stretches to leave patches on a cap surface or a volva at the stembase

urticoid resembling a hair from a stinging nettle

utriform bladder shaped

velutinous velvety

ventricose swollen in the middle

verrucose covered with small warts

verruculose covered with tiny warts

vesiculose bladder-like cystidia with an abruptly narrowed base

vinaceous pinkish wine colored

vinescent wine-red

virgate streaked with different colored fibrils

viscid slimy or slippery moist

volva the remains of the veil at the base of the stem

About the Author

The mushroom bug. It hits people in all walks of life. Once you are fairly well down that road with no hope of getting off it, you might take the time to look back and try to identify the markers that led you there. In my case it was not an academic trail. I exist today as a sort of bridge between the mycology docs and the general society of our local mushroom club, and that is where I belong.

I grew up on a sheep farm about an hour west of Baltimore. I must have missed the fungi on our spread, but only ten miles away my uncle Bobby Deford had access to cattle pastures. Every couple years or so we would get the call: the field mushrooms were up. We would drive over, load up our baskets, and indulge in culinary heaven. I had no idea at that time there was a world beyond cow pasture mushrooms.

During the same era, my parents would spend their summers chartering sailboats in Maine. Uncle Bobby would often join us. He loved the fishing adventures. He also brought along a book entitled *One Thousand American Fungi*. This was Charles McIlvaine's mushroom guide, published in 1902. Whenever we anchored up, my uncle would soon be ashore collecting every mushroom he could find. If he couldn't find the right name in McIlvaine he would meticulously sketch the fungus complete with tiny arrows indicating colors for stem, gills, and cap. It was both frustrating and fascinating. He had no idea Dr. Richard Homola, the renowned mycologist at the University of Maine, was just a few hours west at Orono.

Flash forward to 1969. I had just finished up with a two and a half year stretch as a Peace Corps volunteer in the West African sahel, and was enrolled in journalism at the graduate school of the University of Wisconsin. After two semesters I was told that I had been awarded a full scholarship but would have to wait a year for that to kick in. I'm an impulsive person with ADS. Waiting is not in my picture. I decided I would load up my life belongings in Ghost Host, my decrepit station wagon, and drive south of the border. I got as far as Puerto Barrios in Guatemala before all the tires gave out. A local ferry took me out to Livingston, a colorful town situated at the mouth of the glorious Rio Dulce. I dug in and

Art by Alex McAdoo

made friends. Soon it was suggested that I could make it down here by commercial shark fishing. I got my permit in Guatemala City, had a small boat built, and purchased a gill net from Abularach, a Turkish merchant from the interior. I rounded up my crew, Tono Casco and Fito Rodriguez, and headed off to Punta Mannabique for the shark fishing season that always precedes Lent, when all Catholics need to eat fish. Sharks are sold as "deep sea fish" to the Mayans of the interior. It soon became clear that a 17-foot hammerhead would not fit in a 14-boat with an 18 horse Johnson. We would need a bigger rig.

So what does this have to do with fungi? You will soon find out. I discovered that if I wanted a working boat ready to go I should go to Belize City and inquire on the waterfront. This I proceeded to do. I was directed to one Collet Mejia, a big burly guy who ran a gaming club in town. He had a boat, known in local waterfront lingo as a lighter, for sale. It was a flat-bottomed gaff rigged sloop with no cabin or engine. It was just a shell. It had a mast made from santa maria hardwood that was greased with beef fat, telephone cables for shrouds, and a bamboo boom. Just right for sharks. Collet was using it to haul sand from the Sibun River bar back to Belize City for a concrete outfit. He suggested I go on a sand run, see if it suited my needs. We took off with the land breeze at 4 a.m. Coffee was brewed on a truck tire rim in the stern. Reggae boomed from a radio.

While they were shoveling sand into the hull, I had nothing much to do. I waded ashore and headed into the mangroves. After a short time I spied something brilliant in the leaf muck. It was scarlet with blood red pores. A mangrove bolete! Solitary, with a cap about 7 cm wide. Every part of it bruised instantly blue-black. It was the last place I expected to find a mushroom. Mangrove tannin is strong stuff. It was fruiting about 30 feet in from the high tide mark. It was an omen I have come back to time and time again.

I bought the rig for $2,000 and lived on her for ten years. In the fall of 1979 I sold her to a Christmas tree farmer from Idaho. It was time to return to the states, and write up the whole adventure. I chose San Francisco. I lived in a walk-up above the Broadway tunnel. I had a hard time with the writing. I would smoke pack after pack trying to break through writer's block. Eventually I would just throw up my hands and drive out to the Presidio to hunt mushrooms. On one Sunday I found myself surrounded with a bevy of folks performing the same ritual. They were led by Larry Stickney, an imposing individual, who was delighted to find a new convert. He was understandably edgy. He had heard through the grapevine that both the Presidio and Golden Gate Park might soon be closed to mushroom foraging. This was his passion. To have this taken away was unthinkable.

It soon became evident that Larry was into the culinary aspects. If I wanted to know mushroom names I should look up Fred Stevens. I will always be grateful to Fred. No mushroom was too mundane. He lived in south San Francisco in a stucco home with a big gate. Inside the gate lurked two ferocious Dobermans, or maybe pit bull–Doberman cross breeds. They would go berserk at the sight of me. Fred had to take care of them before I could proceed further. With them around, getting Fred riled up over a mushroom identification was never an option. By this time David Arora's *Mushrooms Demystified* had come out. An entire world of fungi had opened up to me.

By 1982 I was through with San Francisco. Too many parking tickets. Too many speeding tickets. It was getting claustrophobic. A friend who had sailed with me in Guatemala suggested Bellingham, Washington.

"I live across the Canadian border in White Rock," he told me, "But Bellingham is more boring. It rains all the time and there won't be any diversions for your writing."

Rain and mushrooms. They go together like bacon and eggs. Within six months I was renting an A-frame out at Sandy Point. I found *Pholiota subcaerulea* right outside the front door. I had no idea it was supposed to be rare.

At around this time a girl I had known back in Livingston, Guatemala, had lost her husband in Mexico. She had two kids, ages three and nine. I had always liked Lidia. I suggested she come up and take a look around. She came up. She looked around. She enrolled at Western. Her kids found friends, got along in the local schools. I moved from Sandy Point to Garden Street in Bellingham. She moved from Fresno to Alabama Street and then High Street. I was suddenly involved.

It didn't take long for her to discover my mushroom mania. This was competition. I needed to consult with a mushroom authority to see if I had any future in it. We drove to Seattle,

That wild mushroom bouillabaisse . . . not highly recommended. If one of your guests is allergic to one of them, you'll never know which species nailed him.

presented ourselves to Dr. Joe Ammirati. This was not your everyday intrusion. Lidia was hanging on every nuance to every word. The mushrooms might prevent her kids from going to college. Joe acknowledged I had the mushroom bug. It was too soon to make a determination. Generally my type fizzled out, became like his brother Gene. Some knowledge but no real fungal drive. All he could do right now is recommend me for the Pacific Northwest Key Council. This was a group made up of professional mycologists and keen amateurs from Oregon, Washington, Idaho, Montana, and British Columbia.

I will be forever grateful he took the time to do so. They meet twice a year to foray together within these states and provinces. They also write up keys for different genera. It's an honor to be a part of this group.

It was a rough start. The first foray took place in Joe Ammirati's lab at the University of Washington in Seattle. We were all to huddle over the teeth fungi, paying especial attention to nuances of color. We were each assigned a chair with a microscope facing it. I'd never looked in one before. With a B.A. in art history you never needed one. My science college courses were in psychology and marine biology. I couldn't locate the light switch. To ask someone was beyond the beyond. I decided to go the bathroom and not stop until I reached Bellingham.

The next foray went a lot better. Joe eventually assigned me to the genus Collybia. This was way before it split up into Gymnopus and Rhodocollybia. The lady who had handled it was on the verge of retiring from the Key Council. The key was overdue for an upgrade. Keys are never really finished and final. New species and species new to an area are emerging continuously. My Collybioid key is already overdue for an upgrade. Every genus has its own special species complex within it. My bête noire is the *Gymnopus fuscopurpureus* complex. To treat it properly one would need to orchestrate DNA sequencing on the group, plus use phase contrast microscopy to see subtleties in hyphal ornamentation. I didn't get that degree. I would have had to gone back and gotten the B.S. at age 40 with a new family to take care of. And with the kind of ADS I have, I may well have showed up on the wrong day for the finals.

At about this time I received a tremendous gift from Roger Phillips. It was his hand-me-down Vickers microscope, made in Britain circa 1938. With lots of help from Dr. Fred Rhoades, who calibrated it, I gradually learned sectioning techniques to see different tissues in dried mushroom specimens. I also logged time in various botanical libraries jotting down where genera and species could be found in scientific monographs.

From these notes I constructed a massive index, without which I would not have been able to ferret out the more esoteric information in this guide.

After all is said and done, you know you have the mushroom bug when you sail by a tiny island, consisting of a rock with a patch of moss and a scraggly stunted conifer, and all you can think of is maybe there is a little brown mushroom over there indigenous to that rock alone.

Index of the People

Could someone remind me how I got here?

Buck McAdoo

580

Polypore collage

Andre Brondino

Index of the Fungi

Butyriboletus
abieticola - 28,120-122
appendiculatus - 122
fechtneri - 28,210-211
primiregius - 28,210-211
regius - 28,123-124,210-211

Byssomerulius
corium - 30,392-393

Callistosporium
luteo-olivaceum - 18,240-241

Caloboletus
calopus - 118
conifericola - 28, 118,122-123
frustosus - 28,117-118,123
radicans - 28,122-123
rubripes - 28,118-119,121,123

Calocybe
carnea - 19,241
gambosa - 162
naucoria - 19,240-241
onychina - 19,241

Caloscypha
fulgens - 31,50-51,125-128
incarnata - 127

Candolleomyces
candolleana - 26,349

Cantharellula
umbonata - 15,162-163

Cantharellus
alborufescens - 131
amethysteus - 225
cibarius - 131-132,538,563
formosus - 13,130,143,538,563
infundibuliformis - 192-193
lewisii - 193-294
pallens - 131
pallidus - 132
subalbidus - 13,129-132,423-424,538
subpruinosus - 143

Ceriomyces
zelleri - 515

Cerioporus
squamosus - 29,405-406

Cheimonophyllum
candidissimum - 15,380

Chlorencoelia
versiformis - 31,227-228

Chlorophyllum
brunneum - 17,135,138
esculentum - 135
molybdites - 26,134-136,138-140
molybdites var. marginata - 138
olivieri - 17
rhacodes - 18,37,135-136,138

Chroogomphus
leptocystis - 25,143
ochraceus - 143
tomentosus - 25,141-143,182,184

Chrysomphalina
chrysophylla - 193-194

Ciboria
batschiana - 146
rufofusca - 31,145-147

Clavaria
elveloides - 222

Clavariadelphus
caespitosus - 27,148,150
occidentalis - 27,149
pistillaris - 149-150
subfastigiatus - 27,149
truncatus - 27,150

Clitocella
popinalis - 164

Clitocybe
albirhiza - 15,96,151-154
atroviridis - 15,102-103
carnosior - 95
clavipes - 15,94,99
comitialis - 95,99
dealbata - 15,98,154-156,161-162
dilatata - 15,160,162-164
fragilipes - 288

Phaeolepiota
aurea - 20,177-178,232,372-376,504-505

Phaeomarasmius
distans - 182

Phaeotremella
foliacea - 30,488-489

Phalloboletus
gigasporus - 513

Phialea
merulina - 228

Phloeomana
speirea - 525

Pholiota
albivelata - 462
caperata - 179
curvipes - 205-206
dura var. xanthophylla - 46
flammans - 24,206
malicola - 262,264
sipei - 22,461-462
squarroso-adiposa - 172
subcaerulea - 23,466,576
subsquarrosa - 173
subvelutipes - 173
tuberculosa - 22
vahlii - 374

Phyllotopsis
nidulans - 380-381,448,450

Pleurocybella
porrigens - 14,343-344,378-379

Pleurotus
albolanatus - 380
citrinopileatus - 387-389
circinatus - 344
columbinus - 447
conchatus - 361
cornucopiae - 388
cornucopiae var. citrinopileatus - 388
cornucopioides - 388
dryinus - 14,342-343
eryngii - 376,388
flabellatus - 381

lignatilis - 344
ostreatus - 15,343-344,388,447-448
populinus - 15,342,344
pulmonarius - 15,359-360
serotinus - 447

Plicatura
alni - 392
nivea - 30,390-394

Plicaturopsis
crispa - 392

Pluteus
cervinus - 9,21,336,396-398
curtisii - 398
exilis - 9,21,336,398
hongoi - 398
lipidocystis - 398
magnus - 21
patricius - 398
pellitus - 21,396
petasatus - 21,395-398
pseudorobertii - 398
salicinus - 21,396

Polyozellus
marymargaretae - 13,224-225
multiplex - 102,225

Polyporoletus
bulbosus - 29,401
canaliculatus - 401
sublividus - 401-402
sylvestris - 29,400-402

Polyporus
canaliculatus - 401
coronatus - 405
fagicola - 405
floccipes - 405
forquignoni - 405
lentus - 405
radicatus - 29,404,406
sylvestris - 401
tuberaster - 29,403-406

Poromycena
pseudopura - 323,328

Postia
fragilis - 29,219
placenta - 393-394

Protostropharia
semiglobata - 25,45,47,356

Psathyrella
annulata - 26,178-179
conissans - 349
gracilis - 26
hydrophila - 264
lithocarpi - 26
piluliformis - 26,262,264,409,411
rugocephala - 178
umbonata - 411

Pseudoaleuria
quinaultiana - 31,51

Pseudoclitocybe
cyathiformis - 16,96

Pseudocraterellus
pseudoclavatus - 224

Psilocybe
azurescens - 26,409,411
baeocystis - 26,407-412
caerulea - 467
caerulescens - 411
caerulipes - 411
cubensis - 355-356
cyanescens - 26,408,411
merdaria - 355-356
merdicola - 355-356
ovoideocystidiata - 26,408,411
pelliculosa - 26,410-411
semilanceata - 26,346,348
strictipes - 26,411
stuntzii - 9,25,409,411

Ptychoverpa
bohemica - 513

Pulveroboletus
ravenelii - 211

Radulum
cuneatum - 392

Ramaria
aurantiisiccescens - 27,415
conjunctipes var. tsugensis - 415
flavigelatinosa var. megalospora - 414-415
formosa - 27,415-416
gelatiniaurantia - 27,415
largentii - 27,415
leptoformosa - 27,415
longispora - 27,414-415
raveneliana - 27,415-416
sandaracina - 27,414
sandaracina var. chondrobasis - 27,413-415
sandaracina var. euosma - 27,414-415

Rhizopogon
alexsmithii - 30,54
diplophloeus - 53

Rhodocollybia
butyracea var. asema - 21,96,98
oregonensis - 22,250-251
prolixa - 169

Rhodocybe
caelata - 22,162,164

Rhodopaxillus
nudus - 288

Rhodophana
nitellina - 21,241

Rozites
caperata - 179
colombiana - 179
emodensis - 179

Rubroboletus
legaliae - 481

Russula
abietina - 20,437
acrifolia - 419,425
adusta - 18,422
aeruginea - 20,79
albidula - 420,422
amoenipes - 444
angustispora - 422
anomala - 433
atropurpurea - 18,441-443
brevipes - 14,29,77,131,418-425
brevipes var. acrior - 14,419-421,425

www.ingramcontent.com/pod-product-compliance
Lightning Source LLC
Chambersburg PA
CBHW052129020426
42334CB00023B/2647